THE PILOT'S REFERENCE TO
ATC
PROCEDURES AND PHRASEOLOGY

By
Thomas S. Mills
CFII and ATP

THIRD EDITION

REAVCO Publishing
Van Nuys, California

© 1989 Thomas S. Mills
All rights reserved

Certain portions of this book have been compiled and edited from government publications and are not subject to copyright rules. Portions created by the author are copyrighted and may not be reproduced without permission from the author and publisher.

Comments and suggestions regarding this book should be directed to:
Editor
c/o REAVCO Publishing
P.O. Box 7902
Van Nuys, California 91409

Library of Congress Cataloguing-in-Publication Data.
Mills, Thomas S.-
The pilot's reference to ATC procedures and phraseology /
by Thomas S. Mills. — 3rd ed.
   p.   cm.
ISBN 0-935695-10-9

  1. Air traffic control—United States—Handbooks, manuals, etc. I. Title.

TL725.3.T7M55   1989   629.136'6—dc20   89-10550
                                                       CIP

Cover Design by Ronald Miller.
Typography by Irene Ing.

Printed in the United States of America by Delta Lithograph Co., Valencia, California 91355

NOTICE

The material in this book is derived from government publications. No liability is assumed for the use of this book or for any resulting damages. The author and publisher make no express or implied warranties of merchantability or fitness for its specific use. *Readers are advised to conform with all current governmental standards and regulations governing the safe operation of aircraft.*

ABOUT THIS EDITION

The Pilot's Reference to ATC Procedures and Phraseology was created to help fulfill the great need for pilots to understand today's U.S. Civilian Air Traffic Control System. In the fall of 1988, *A Call to Action: Joint FAA/Industry Partnership to Improve Pilot/Controller Communications* was "an appeal to each and every member of the aviation community to respond to the need for improved communications as a means of enhancing both system safety and system performance." This edition can help you answer that call.

Effective communication starts with the knowledge and respect of ATC (air traffic control) procedures, best learned from the air traffic controller's point of view. Therefore, this edition remains structured after the Controller's Handbook, the manual that prescribes air traffic control procedures and phraseology for use by personnel providing air traffic control services, so you may have access to their procedures.

Throughout the years, government rules and recommendations relating to pilot/controller interaction have been disseminated to the pilot community primarily via the *Federal Aviation Regulations* and the *Airman's Information Manual*. With this edition, you will find selected portions of these manuals conveniently arranged with the information from the Controller's Handbook. This enhances the descriptions of the procedures and can make your understanding of ATC even better.

To heighten your awareness of ATC phraseology, we added many more "hear-what-you-read" examples of pilot/controller dialogue. These exemplify the related procedures and illustrate how phraseology and number usage works. Many of these examples are "real-life" and were heard in various areas of the United States.

The result of this Third Edition is the creation of a universal air traffic control information manual useful to every level of experience. Used as an all-in-one reference in conjunction with the source material, this book provides the most complete resource to ATC information, information that can help you use the system more safely and effectively.

ACKNOWLEDGMENTS

The arranging and editing of information in this edition was a complicated endeavor made much easier by the support and contributions of the following individuals: Professor Jan Archibald, former student of mine and now flight instructor, worked beyond the call of duty in the various stages in this project. Her biggest contribution was the editing of the rearranged material in a plain language, easy-to-read format. The increased legibility and more attractive typestyles in this edition can be attributed to the suggestions of typographer Irene Ing. She and her staff also showed incredible patience and understanding when it came to the many changes and rearranging of material that was required. Thanks to Randy, Kelly, Carol, and Jeff, who helped arrange my vacation time to allow me to cover important phases of this project. Thanks again to all of you for answering my "call to action." Together we answered a much greater "Call to Action."

Thomas S. Mills

ATC PHRASEOLOGY REFERENCE
(References are to Paragraph Numbers)

Associated with many ATC procedures are carefully constructed phrases (ATC phraseology). These phrases help implement ATC procedures with minimal verbiage. All controllers are required to use these phrases when appropriate and pilots should be aware of their procedural as well as literal meanings.

The following list of words and phrases are used by ATC in communications with pilots. To gain a better understanding of the meaning behind the words and phrases used by ATC, refer to the paragraph(s) referenced with each word or phrase. Where a glossary reference is included, a definition of the term may be found in the Appendix, *Pilot/Controller Glossary*.

ABEAM (Glossary)
ACKNOWLEDGE 2-43, 2-44 (Glossary)
ADVISE INTENTIONS (Glossary)
AFFIRMATIVE 2-44, (Glossary)
AFTER COMPLETING LOW APPROACH/TOUCH-AND-GO, CLIMB AND MAINTAIN 4-174
AIR EVAC 2-68
AIR TAXI 3-172, 3-174, (Glossary)
ALL AIRCRAFT ON THIS FREQUENCY SQUAWK 5-36
ALTITUDE INDICATES 2-84
ALTITUDE RESTRICTIONS ARE CANCELLED (Glossary)
ALTITUDE UNKNOWN 2-84
ANTICIPATE ADDITIONAL . . . DELAY 4-100
AS FILED 4-35
ATC ADVISES . . . . (Glossary)
ATC CLEARS . . . . 4-32, (Glossary)
ATC REQUESTS . . . . (Glossary)
BEACON INTEROGATOR INOPERATIVE/MALFUNCTIONING 5-41
BOUNDARY WIND 3-33, 3-34
BRAKING ACTION ADVISORIES ARE IN EFFECT 3-40
BRAKING ACTION . . . . 3-39, (Glossary)
CANCEL TAKEOFF CLEARANCE 3-140
CAUTION WAKE TURBULENCE 2-80
CENTER WEATHER ADVISORY 2-120

CENTERFIELD WIND 3-34
CHAFF AREA BETWEEN 2-130
CHANGE TO ADVISORY FREQUENCY APPROVED 4-129, 6-47
CHANGE TO DEPARTURE 3-142
CHANGE TO MY FREQUENCY 2-45
CHANGE . . . TO READ 4-37
CHECK DENSITY ALTITUDE 3-103
CIRCLE THE AIRPORT 3-120
CIRCLE TO RUNWAY . . . . 4-130, (Glossary)
CLEARANCE VOID IF NOT OFF BY . . . . 4-42, (Glossary)
CLEARED AS FILED 4-35, (Glossary)
CLEARED FOR APPROACH 4-120, (Glossary)
CLEARED FOR CONTACT APPROACH 4-151
CLEARED FOR LOW APPROACH 3-120
CLEARED FOR STOP-AND-GO 3-120
CLEARED FOR STRAIGHT-IN . . . APPROACH 4-120
CLEARED FOR TAKEOFF 3-120, 3-139, (Glossary)
CLEARED FOR TAKEOFF FROM 3-176
CLEARED FOR THE OPTION 3-120, 3-124, (Glossary)
CLEARED FOR TOUCH-AND-GO 3-120
CLEARED FOR VISUAL APPROACH 4-141, 4-142, 4-143
CLEARED FOR . . . APPROACH 4-120, (Glossary)
CLEARED THROUGH . . . . (Glossary)
CLEARED TO FLY 4-65
CLEARED TO LAND 3-120, (Glossary)

v

(References are to Paragraph Numbers)

CLEARED TO ... AIRPORT 4-20
CLEARED TO ... CONTROL ZONE 6-71
CLIMB AND MAINTAIN 4-85
CLIMB AT PILOT'S DISCRETION 4-89
CLIMB THROUGH TCA APPROVED 6-51
CLIMB TO AND REPORT REACHING VFR-ON-TOP 4-163
CLIMB TO VFR WITHIN THE CONTROL ZONE 6-76
CLIMB VFR 4-164
CLOSED TRAFFIC APPROVED 3-125
CONTACT .... 2-45, (Glossary)
CONTACT FINAL CONTROLLER ON 5-144
CONTACT GROUND 3-161
CONTINUE 3-151
CONTINUE TAXIING 3-104
CONVECTIVE SIGMET 2-120, 2-121
CORRECTION .... (Glossary)
CROSS VICTOR 4-65
CROSS ... AT AND MAINTAIN ... AT KNOTS ... 5-91
CROSS ... AT OR ABOVE .... (Glossary)
CROSS ... AT OR BELOW .... (Glossary)
CROSS ... AT OR LATER THAN 7-30
CROSS ... AT .... (Glossary)
CROSS ... WITHOUT DELAY 3-104
CRUISE .... 4-85, (Glossary)
DELAY INDEFINITE .... 4-100, (Glossary)
DEPART ... HEADING 5-72
DEPARTURE FREQUENCY WILL BE 4-24
DEPARTURE FROM ... WILL BE AT YOUR OWN RISK ... TRAFFIC 3-176
DERELICT BALLOON REPORTED IN THE VICINITY OF 8-22
DESCEND AND MAINTAIN ... THEN REDUCE SPEED TO 5-91
DESCEND AND MAINTAIN 4-85, 4-88
DESCEND AT PILOT'S DISCRETION 4-89
DESCEND TO YOUR MINIMUM DESCENT ALTITUDE 5-143
DESCEND VFR 4-164
DEVIATION APPROVED, ADVISE WHEN ABLE TO 2-130
DIRECT 4-65, 4-69, (Glossary)
DIRECT TO THE FIX 4-65

DO NOT ACKNOWLEDGE FURTHER TRANSMISSIONS 5-146
DO NOT EXCEED ... KNOTS/MACH 5-91
ENTER LEFT/RIGHT BASE 3-150, 3-151
EXCEPT CHANGE ROUTE TO READ 4-35
EXECUTE MISSED APPROACH 5-152, (Glossary)
EXIT ... WITHOUT DELAY 3-104
EXPECT CLIMB/DESCENT CLEARANCE 4-87
EXPECT ENGINE STARTUP 4-45
EXPECT FURTHER CLEARANCE .... 4-22, 4-100, (Glossary)
EXPECT TO RESUME 5-73
EXPECT VECTOR ACROSS 5-77
EXPECT VECTOR ACROSS FINAL APPROACH COURSE FOR 5-113
EXPEDITE 2-65, (Glossary)
EXTEND DOWNWIND 3-120
FLIGHT CHECK 2-28, 2-68
FLY HEADING .... 5-72, (Glossary)
FLY HEADING ... WHEN ABLE PROCEED DIRECT 5-77
FLY PRESENT HEADING 5-72
FLY RUNWAY HEADING 5-100
FOLLOW ... TRAFFIC IS ... LANDING RUNWAY 3-120
FOR ENGINE START TIME 4-45
FOR VECTOR TO FINAL APPROACH COURSE 5-73
FOR VECTOR TO INTERCEPT 5-73
FOR VECTOR TO ... FINAL APPROACH COURSE 5-73
FUEL DUMPING BY ... TERMINATED 8-10
FUEL DUMPING IN PROGRESS OVER 8-10
GATE-HOLD PROCEDURES ARE IN EFFECT 4-45
GATE-HOLD PROCEDURES NO LONGER IN EFFECT 4-45
GLIDE SLOPE SIGNAL NOT PROTECTED 3-107
GLIDE SLOPE UNUSABLE 4-120
GO AHEAD (Glossary)
GO AROUND 3-120, (Glossary)
HAS YOU IN SIGHT AND WILL MAINTAIN VISUAL SEPARATION 2-87
HEAVY 2-20, 2-81, 3-126, (Glossary)
HOLD AS PUBLISHED 4-100
HOLD AT ... UNTIL 4-106, 6-29

ATC PHRASEOLOGY REFERENCE

(References are to Paragraph Numbers)

HOLD FOR RELEASE 4-42, (Glossary)
HOLD FOR WAKE TURBULENCE 3-128, 3-135, 3-137
HOLD FOR 3-104
HOLD IN POSITION 3-132
HOLD POSITION 3-104
HOLD SHORT OF RUNWAY 3-132
HOLD SHORT OF 3-104
HOLD SHORT 3-105
HOLD . . . OF . . . ON 4-103
HOVER TAXI 3-172, 3-174
HOW DO YOU HEAR ME? 5-145, (Glossary)
I SAY AGAIN . . . . (Glossary)
IDENT 5-34, 5-54, (Glossary)
IF FEASIBLE, REDUCE SPEED TO . . . . (Glossary)
IF FEASIBLE, SQUAWK 5-38
IF NO TRANSMISSION RECEIVED FOR . . . . (Glossary)
IF NOT OFF BY, ADVISE . . . OF INTENTIONS 4-42
IF NOT ON TOP AT . . . ADVISE 4-163
IF PRACTICAL, REDUCE SPEED TO 5-91
IMMEDIATELY 2-44, 2-65, (Glossary)
INCREASE SPEED TO . . . . 5-91, (Glossary)
INTERSECTION DEPARTURE 3-136
JOIN VICTOR 4-65
LEAVING THE TCA/TRSA 6-57
LEFT TRAFFIC 3-150
LIFEGUARD 2-25, 2-68
LOCAL SPECIAL VFR IN IMMEDIATE VICINITY OF . . . AIRPORT ARE AUTHORIZED UNTIL 6-75
LOCALIZER FREQUENCY IS 5-117
LOCALIZER SIGNAL NOT PROTECTED 3-107
LOW ALTITUDE ALERT, CHECK YOUR ALTITUDE IMMEDIATELY 2-88, (Glossary)
LOW LEVEL WIND SHEAR ADVISORIES IN EFFECT 3-34
MAINTAIN AT LEAST ONE ZERO MINUTES/TWO ZERO MILES SEPARATION FROM 7-33
MAINTAIN AT LEAST ONE/TWO THOUSAND FEET ABOVE/BELOW 7-53
MAINTAIN PRESENT SPEED 5-91
MAINTAIN SPECIAL VFR CONDITIONS WHILE IN CONTROL ZONE 6-71
MAINTAIN SPECIAL VFR CONDITIONS AT OR BELOW 6-74
MAINTAIN SPECIAL VFR CONDITIONS 6-75
MAINTAIN VFR CONDITIONS 4-160, 4-165

MAINTAIN VFR-ON-TOP 4-160, 4-161
MAINTAIN VISUAL SEPARATION FROM THAT TRAFFIC 2-87
MAINTAIN . . . . 4-23, 4-85, (Glossary)
MAINTAIN . . . THROUGH 4-85
MAINTAIN . . . UNTIL ESTABLISHED 5-114, 5-117
MAKE HALF-STANDARD RATE TURNS 5-136
MAKE LEFT/RIGHT THREE SIXTY/TWO SEVENTY 3-120
MAKE LEFT/RIGHT BASE 3-150
MAKE RIGHT TRAFFIC 3-151
MAKE SHORT APPROACH 3-120, 3-123
MAKE STRAIGHT-IN 3-150, 3-151
MAYDAY 9-2, (Glossary)
MED EVAC 2-25, 2-68
MISSED APPROACH COURSE IS 5-135
MISSED APPROACH PROCEDURE IS 5-149
MLS CHANNEL IS 5-117
NEGATIVE (Glossary)
NEGATIVE CONTACT 2-85, (Glossary)
NO DELAY EXPECTED 4-100
NO TRANSMISSIONS ARE RECEIVED FOR . . . ATTEMPT CONTACT ON . . . AND 5-137
NOT IN SIGHT, CLEARED TO LAND 3-157
NOVEMBER 2-20
NUMEROUS TARGETS VICINITY . . . . 2-84, (Glossary)
OTHER OPTION APPROVED 3-120
OVER 2-40, 2-41, (Glossary)
PAN-PAN 9-2, (Glossary)
PREPARE TO DESCEND IN 5-142
PREVIOUSLY ISSUED TRAFFIC NO LONGER A FACTOR 2-84
PRIMARY RADAR OUT OF SERVICE 5-76
PROCEDURE TURN INBOUND (Glossary)
PROCEED DIRECT 5-75
PROCEED TO 6-29
PROCEED 3-102, 3-104
PUBLISHED DECISION HEIGHT 2-11
PUBLISHED MINIMUM DESCENT ALTITUDE 2-11, 5-142
RADAR CONTACT 5-51, 7-4, (Glossary)
RADAR CONTACT LOST . . . . 7-4, (Glossary)
RADAR SERVICE TERMINATED . . . . 2-90, 5-36, 7-4, (Glossary)

ATC PHRASEOLOGY REFERENCE

(References are to Paragraph Numbers)

RECOMMENDED ALTITUDES WILL BE PROVIDED FOR EACH MILE ON FINAL TO MINIMUM DESCENT ALTITUDE/CIRCLING MINIMUM DESCENT ALTITUDE 5-140

REDUCE SPEED TO . . . THEN DESCEND AND MAINTAIN 5-91

REDUCE SPEED TO . . . . (Glossary)

RELEASED FOR DEPARTURE 4-42

REMAIN OUTSIDE THE ARSA AND STAND BY 6-43

REMAIN OUTSIDE THE TCA 6-51

REMAIN THIS FREQUENCY 2-45

REPLY NOT RECEIVED, IF YOU HEAR ME 9-44

REPORT LEAVING 7-50

REPORT REACHING 7-50

REPORT THE AIRPORT IN SIGHT 4-141

REPORT WHEN ABLE TO PROCEED VISUALLY TO AIRPORT/HELIPORT 5-141

REQUEST FLIGHT CONDITIONS 2-122

RESET TRANSPONDER, SQUAWK 5-40

REST OF ROUTE UNCHANGED 4-37

RESUME APPROPRIATE VFR ALTITUDE 6-44, 6-56

RESUME NORMAL SPEED 5-96

RESUME OWN NAVIGATION 5-77, (Glossary)

RIGHT TRAFFIC APPROVED 3-151

RIGHT TRAFFIC 3-150, 3-151

ROGER 2-44, (Glossary)

RUNWAY HEADING 4-50

RUNWAY . . . CLOSED/UNSAFE 3-37

RUNWAY . . . R-V-R/R-V-V 2-152

SAY AGAIN (Glossary)

SAY AIRSPEED 5-91

SAY ALTITUDE 5-30, (Glossary)

SAY HEADING (Glossary)

SAY MACH NUMBER 5-91

SIDE-STEP RUNWAY 4-132

SLIGHTLY LEFT/RIGHT OF COURSE 5-147

SPEAK SLOWER (Glossary)

SQUAWK 5-29

SQUAWK ALTITUDE 5-32

SQUAWK MAYDAY ON SEVEN SEVEN ZERO ZERO 5-38

SQUAWK ONE TWO ZERO ZERO 5-35

SQUAWK STANDBY, . . . SQUAWK 5-54

SQUAWK STANDBY/LOW/NORMAL 5-39

SQUAWK 4-25

SQUAWK . . . AND ALTITUDE 4-54

STAND BY (Glossary)

START ENGINES, ADVISE WHEN READY TO TAXI 4-45

STOP ALTITUDE SQUAWK, ALTITUDE DIFFERS BY 5-30

STOP ALTITUDE SQUAWK 5-32, (Glossary)

STOP SQUAWK 5-42, (Glossary)

STOP TURN 5-72, 5-136

STRAIGHT-IN APPROVED 3-151

STRAIGHT-IN 3-151

SUGGEST HEADING 3-73

TAXI INTO POSITION AND HOLD . . . . 3-133, (Glossary)

TAXI TO RUNWAY 3-104

TAXI VIA 3-104

TAXI WITHOUT DELAY 3-104

TAXI 3-104

THAT IS CORRECT (Glossary)

THEN, AS FILED 4-35

THIS WILL BE A NO-GYRO VECTOR 5-72

THIS WILL BE A NO-GYRO SURVEILLANCE APPROACH 5-136

THIS WILL BE A SURVEILLANCE APPROACH TO 5-135

TOWER CLEARANCE CANCELLED/NOT RECEIVED 5-15

TRAFFIC ADVISORIES AVAILABLE ON TRANSPONDER AIRCRAFT ONLY 5-6

TRAFFIC ALERT. ADVISE YOU . . . . 2-88, (Glossary)

TRAFFIC HOLDING AT 6-29

TRAFFIC NO LONGER A FACTOR 2-84, (Glossary)

TRAFFIC NUMEROUS TARGETS VICINITY 2-84

TRAFFIC . . . . (Glossary)

TRAFFIC . . . O'CLOCK . . . MILES . . . -BOUND 2-84

TRAFFIC . . . OPPOSITE DIRECTION ON PARALLEL RUNWAY/LANDING STRIP 3-128

TURN LEFT/RIGHT HEADING 5-72

TURN LEFT/RIGHT HEADING . . . FOR DF GUIDANCE 9-65

TURN . . . AND RETURN TO LOCALIZE/AZIMUTH COURSE 5-117

TURN . . . DEGREES LEFT/RIGHT 5-72

UNABLE (Glossary)

UNABLE CLOSED TRAFFIC 3-125

UNABLE DEVIATION 2-130

ATC PHRASEOLOGY REFERENCE

(References are to Paragraph Numbers)

UNABLE OPTION MAKE 3-120
UNABLE TO ISSUE . . . CLEARANCE 3-37
USE DME DISTANCES 7-34
VECTOR FOR SPACING 5-73
VERIFY ALTITUDE AND ALTIMETER SETTING 5-30
VERIFY ASSIGNED ALTITUDE 5-31, 7-7
VERIFY SQUAWKING SEVEN FIVE ZERO ZERO 9-21
VERIFY YOU HAVE INFORMATION 3-3
VERIFY . . . . (Glossary)
VFR DEPARTURE AUTHORIZED 4-40
VFR NOT RECOMMENDED (Glossary)
VFR-ON-TOP 4-160
VIA LAST ROUTING CLEARED 4-101

WEATHER AREA BETWEEN 2-130
WELL LEFT/RIGHT OF COURSE 5-147
WHAT IS YOUR HEADING AND ALTITUDE? 9-65
WHEN ABLE . . . . (Glossary)
WILCO 2-44, (Glossary)
WIND CALM 2-131, 3-93
WIND SHEAR ALERT 3-34
WIND SHEAR REPORTED 2-125
WORDS TWICE (Glossary)
YOU HAVE CROSSED THE FINAL APPROACH COURSE. TURN . . . IMMEDIATELY AND RETURN TO LOCALIZER/AZIMUTH COURSE 5-117
YOUR TRANSPONDER APPEARS INOPERATIVE/MALFUNCTIONING, RESET, SQUAWK 5-40

COMPENDIUM

	Page
About This Edition	iii
Acknowledgments	iv
ATC Phraseology Reference	v

Chapter 1. INTRODUCTION

Table of Contents	1-i

Chapter 2. GENERAL ATC PROCEDURES

	Table of Contents	2-i
Section 1.	Facilities	2-1
Section 2.	Phonetics and Numbers Usage	2-3
Section 3.	Aircraft Identification	2-6
Section 4.	Route and Navaid Description	2-9
Section 5.	ATC Communications Format	2-10
Section 6.	ATC Clearances and Service Priorities	2-13
Section 7.	Advisories	2-15
Section 8.	User Reports and Pilot Advisories	2-20
Section 9.	Weather Information	2-23
Section 10.	Altimeter Settings	2-28
Section 11.	Runway Visibility Reporting	2-30
Section 12.	General Flight Plan Information	2-32

Chapter 3. AIRPORT PROCEDURES

	Table of Contents	3-i
Section 1.	Automatic Terminal Information Service Procedures	3-1
Section 2.	Airport Traffic Areas	3-3
Section 3.	Communications Failure	3-4
Section 4.	Traffic Information and Airport Advisories	3-6
Section 5.	Airport Lighting	3-9
Section 6.	Tower Radar	3-13
Section 7.	Airport Surface Detection Procedures	3-14
Section 8.	Runway Selection	3-15
Section 9.	Taxi and Ground Movement Procedures	3-16
Section 10.	Aircraft Spacing	3-20
Section 11.	Takeoff	3-23
Section 12.	Landing	3-28
Section 13.	Helicopter Operations	3-33
Section 14.	Sea Lane Operations	3-37

Chapter 4. BASIC IFR PROCEDURES

	Table of Contents	4-i
Section 1.	IFR Flight Planning	4-1
Section 2.	Basic Clearance Items	4-5
Section 3.	Clearance Delivery	4-7
Section 4.	IFR Release Procedures	4-10
Section 5.	Departure Procedures	4-12
Section 6.	IFR Routes and NAVAID Limits	4-14
Section 7.	Altitude Assignments	4-18
Section 8.	Aircraft Holding	4-22
Section 9.	Arrival	4-25
Section 10.	Approach Clearance Procedures	4-27
Section 11.	Visual Approaches	4-31
Section 12.	Contact Approaches	4-34
Section 13.	VFR Clearances for IFR Operations	4-35
Section 14.	Practice Instrument Approaches	4-37

COMPENDIUM (Continued)

Chapter 5. BASIC RADAR PROCEDURES

	Table of Contents	5-i
Section 1.	General	5-1
Section 2.	Transponder Operation	5-3
Section 3.	Radar Identification and Service Termination	5-8
Section 4.	Separation	5-10
Section 5.	Vectors	5-12
Section 6.	Speed Adjustment	5-15
Section 7.	Departures	5-17
Section 8.	Approach Procedures	5-21
Section 9.	Radar Approaches	5-27

Chapter 6. TERMINAL AIRSPACE PROCEDURES

	Table of Contents	6-i
Section 1.	Terminal Airspace Descriptions and Basic Regulations	6-1
Section 2.	Terminal Radar Programs and Flight Procedures	6-3
Section 3.	Airport Radar Service Area Procedures - ATC	6-7
Section 4.	Stage III Procedures - ATC	6-9
Section 5.	Stage II Procedures - ATC	6-11
Section 6.	Special VFR	6-12

Chapter 7. NON-RADAR PROCEDURES

	Table of Contents	7-i
Section 1.	Position Reports	7-1
Section 2.	Initial Separation of Successive Departing Aircraft	7-3
Section 3.	Initial Separation of Departing and Arriving Aircraft	7-5
Section 4.	Longitudinal Separation	7-7
Section 5.	Lateral Separation	7-11
Section 6.	Vertical Separation	7-14
Section 7.	Timed Approaches	7-15

Chapter 8. SPECIAL FLIGHTS

	Table of Contents	8-i
Section 1.	Special Use and ATC Assigned Airspace	8-1
Section 2.	Fuel Dumping	8-4
Section 3.	Unmanned Balloons	8-5
Section 4.	Parachute Jumping	8-7

Chapter 9. EMERGENCIES

	Table of Contents	9-i
Section 1.	General	9-1
Section 2.	Hijackings and Bomb Threats	9-5
Section 3.	Emergency Radar Assistance	9-7
Section 4.	IFR Communications Failure	9-9
Section 5.	Direction Finding Service	9-12

APPENDIX/INDEX

Appendix	Pilot/Controller Glossary	A-1
Index		I-1

INTRODUCTION

Chapter 1
TABLE OF CONTENTS

		Page
1-1	Purpose and Intent	1-1
1-2	Source Material	1-1
1-3	References	1-1
1-4	Editorial Process	1-1
1-5	Word Meanings	1-1
1-6	ATC Phraseology	1-1
1-7	Pilot-Controller Dialogue	1-2
1-8	Notes	1-2
1-9	Annotations	1-2
1-10	Asterisks	1-2
1-11	Abbreviations	1-2

Chapter 1. INTRODUCTION

1-1 PURPOSE AND INTENT

a. The purpose of this book is to provide an easy to follow, easy to read reference on Air Traffic Control so that pilots may communicate more effectively through a practical understanding of procedures and phraseology.

b. The intent of this reference book is to provide pilots with more knowledge of ATC through the re-presentation and integration of the procedures and phraseology found in the *Air Traffic Control Handbook*, the explanations and recommendations found in the *Airman's Information Manual*, and the rules relating to air traffic control found in the *Federal Aviation Regulations*.

1-2 SOURCE MATERIAL

Information from the following publications is presented in this edition:*

a. *Air Traffic Control*, Order 7110.65E, including change 7, effective June 1, 1989.

b. *Airman's Information Manual*, June 1, 1989 issue.

c. *Federal Aviation Regulations*, up to and including change 83, effective February 1, 1989.

1-2 Note. — These government publications are available from the Superintendent of Documents on a subscription basis. The ordering information and status of these publications is published in Advisory Circular *AC 00-2, Advisory Circular Checklist (and Status of Other FAA Publications)*. AC 00-2 is issued every four months and can be obtained free-of-charge from: U.S. Department of Transportation, Distribution Requirements Section M494.1, Washington, DC 20590.

1-3 REFERENCES

a. References at the end of each paragraph (Chapters 2 through 9) cite the primary source material as follows:

(1) ATCH denotes the *Air Traffic Control Handbook*.

(2) AIM denotes the *Airman's Information Manual*.

(3) FAR denotes the *Federal Aviation Regulations*.

b. ATCH and AIM information are referenced by paragraph numbers. FAR references are to section numbers.*

1-3b Note. — Each manual has its own unique numbering system. ATCH references are to chapter and paragraph number, i.e., 2-131 means Chapter 2, paragraph 131. AIM references are to paragraph number, i.e., 155 means paragraph 155. FAR references are to Part and Section number, i.e., 91.3 means Part 91, Section 3.

1-4 EDITORIAL PROCESS

a. Where necessary, information from the *Air Traffic Control Handbook* is adapted to read from a pilot's point of view.

b. Related areas of the information from the *FAR's* and the *AIM* have been edited to fit into the structure of this reference book which has been styled after the *Air Traffic Control Handbook*.

c. Portions of the source material have been rewritten or omitted for readability and ease of understanding.

1-4 Note. — *THIS REFERENCE BOOK IS DESCRIPTIVE IN NATURE AND HAS NO REGULATORY AUTHORITY. PILOTS MUST CONFORM TO ALL CURRENT FEDERAL AVIATION REGULATIONS REGARDLESS OF ANY PROCEDURE, MINIMA, OR RULE DESCRIBED IN THIS BOOK.*

1-5 WORD MEANINGS

As used in this manual:

a. *Aircraft* means the airframe, crew members, or both.

b. *Approved separation* means separation in accordance with the applicable minima in the *Air Traffic Control Handbook*, Order 7110.65.

c. *Altitude* means altitude mean sea level, flight level, or both.

d. *Miles* means nautical miles unless otherwise specified, and means statute miles in conjunction with visibility.

e. *Course, Bearing, Azimuth, Heading, and Wind Direction* information will always be magnetic unless specifically stated otherwise.

f. *Time* when used in the context of a clock reading is the hour in Coordinated Universal Time (UTC) or the local equivalent, as appropriate, and the minutes. Change to the next minute is made at the minute plus 30 seconds, except time checks are given to the nearest quarter minute.

g. *Runway* means the runway used by aircraft (See Pilot/Controller Glossary) and in discussions of separation standards, is applicable to helipads with accompanying takeoff/landing courses.

h. The pronoun *he/his/him* is used in the generic sense.

1-6 ATC PHRASEOLOGY

a. The Air Traffic Control Handbook prescribes the exact phraseology controllers are to use in communications with pilots. The procedures associated with the phraseology are adapted to read from a pilot's point of view. The phraseology is presented in the wording from the Controller's Handbook.

1-6a Example. —

Controllers will issue a landing clearance and restate the landing runway number whenever there is a possibility of a conflict with another aircraft which is using or planning to use another runway, or when an instrument approach is being conducted to a runway that is closed.

ATC Phraseology:

Cleared to land, *or*

Cleared to land, Runway (runway number).

b. The use of a slant (/) between words means one word or the other is used in the phrase. Words in parentheses indicate the variable item used in the clearance, instruction, or advisory.

1-6b Example. —

Climb/Descend and maintain (altitude).

1-7 PILOT-CONTROLLER DIALOGUE

a. Examples of pilot-controller dialogue are presented to exemplify the procedure/s outlined in a particular paragraph.

b. Careful attention has been paid to the examples of ATC dialogue (phraseology) for exact wording and numbers usage. Examples of pilot dialogue are considered descriptions of appropriate acknowledgment and readback but may vary in style.

c. Controller dialogue is presented in ***bold italics***. Pilot dialogue is presented in *light italics*. Examples which could be either pilot or controller have normal type face with quotes.

1-7c Example. —

Glendale Tower, Cessna Seven Three Six Tango X-ray, ready for takeoff.

Cessna Seven Three Six Tango X-ray, Glendale Tower, cleared for takeoff.

d. A rule _____ is used to separate distinct examples.

1-8 NOTES

Explanatory statements which are related to the source material are set forth as notes.

1-9 ANNOTATIONS

Annotations are marked as follows:

a. Paragraphs/sections annotated with EN ROUTE or TERMINAL are only applied by the designated type facility. When they are not so designated, the paragraphs/sections may apply to both type (en route and terminal) facilities.

b. WAKE TURBULENCE APPLICATION inserted within a paragraph means that the remaining information in the paragraph requires the application of wake turbulence procedures by ATC.

1-10 ASTERISKS

As used in this manual, an asterisk (*) at the end of a paragraph, phraseology, illustration title, or table heading directs attention to a note associated with that item.

1-11 ABBREVIATIONS

As used in this manual, the following abbreviations have the meanings indicated.

Abbreviation	*Meaning*
ACDO	Air Carrier District Office
AGL	Above Ground Level
AIM	Airman's Information Manual
AIRMET	Airman's Meteorological Information
ALNOT	Alert Notice
ALS	Approach Light System
ALTRV	Altitude Reservation
ARINC	Aeronautical Radio Incorporated
ARSA	Airport Radar Service Area
ARSR	Air Route Surveillance Radar
ARTCC	Air Route Traffic Control Center
ASDE	Airport Surface Detection Equipment
ASR	Airport Surveillance Radar
ATC	Air Traffic Control
ATCH	Air Traffic Control Handbook
ATCAA	ATC Assigned Airspace
ATIS	Automatic Terminal Information Service
AT	Air Traffic
AWW	Severe Weather Forecasts Alerts
BRITE	Bright Radar Indicator Tower Equipment
CDT	Controlled Departure Time
CVFP	Charted Visual Flight Procedures
CWA	Center Weather Advisory
DARC	Direct Access Radar Channel
DF	Direction Finder
DH	Decision Height
DME	Distance Measuring Equipment
DVA	Diverse Vector Area
DVFR	Defense Visual Flight Rules
EARTS	En Route Automated Radar Tracking System
EDCT	Expected Departure Clearance Time
EFC	Expect Further Clearance
ELT	Emergency Locator Transmitter
E-MSAW	En Route Minimum Safe Altitude Warning
EOVM	Emergency Obstruction Video Map
ETA	Estimated Time of Arrival

Abbreviation	Meaning	Abbreviation	Meaning
FAA	Federal Aviation Administration	PAR	Precision Approach Radar
FAF	Final Approach Fix	PCA	Positive Control Area
FAR	Federal Aviation Regulations	PIREP	Pilot Weather Report
FL	Flight Level	PT	Procedure Turn
FSDO	Flight Standards District Office	RAIL	Runway Alignment Indicator Lights
FSS	Flight Service Station	RCC	Rescue Coordination Center
FW/SVFR	Fixed-Wing Special Visual Flight Rules	RCLS	Runway Centerline Light System
GADO	General Aviation District Office	RCR	Runway Condition Reading
GCA	Ground Controlled Approach	REIL	Runway End Identifier Lights
HIRL	High Intensity Runway Lights	RNAV	Area Navigation
IAP	Instrument Approach Procedure	RVR	Runway Visual Range
IAS	Indicated Airspeed	RVV	Runway Visibility Value
ICAO	International Civil Aviation Organization	SAFI	Semi-Automatic Flight Inspection
IDENT	Aircraft Identification	SAR	Search and Rescue
IFR	Instrument Flight Rules	SFL	Sequenced Flashing Lights
ILS	Instrument Landing System	SHF	Super High Frequency
IMC	Instrument Meteorological Conditions	SIAP	Special Instrument Approach Procedure
INREQ	Information Request	SID	Standard Instrument Departure
IR	IFR Military Training Route	SIGMET	Significant Meteorological Information
LAAS	Low Altitude Alert System	SSALR	Simplified Short Runway Approach Lighting Systems
L/MF	Low/Medium Frequency		
LLWAS	Low Level Wind Shear Alert System	STAR	Standard Terminal Arrival
LOM	Locater Outer Marker	STOL	Short Takeoff and Landing
MALS	Medium Intensity Approach Light System	SVFR	Special Visual Flight Rules
MALSR	Medium Approach Light System With Runway Alignment Indicator Lights	TACAN	TACAN UHF Navigational Aid (omnidirectional course and distance information)
MAP	Missed Approach Point		
MCA	Minimum Crossing Altitude	TCA	Terminal Control Area
MDA	Minimum Descent Altitude	TCDD	Tower Cab Digital Display
MEA	Minimum En Route (IFR) Altitude	TDZL	Touchdown Zone Light System
MIA	Minimum IFR Altitude	TEC	Tower En Route Control
MIRL	Medium Intensity Runway Lights	TERPS	U.S. Terminal Instrument Procedures
MLS	Microwave Landing System	TRACON	Terminal Radar Approach Control
MM	Middle Marker	TRSA	Terminal Radar Service Area
MOA	Military Operations Area	UHF	Ultra High Frequency
MOCA	Minimum Obstruction Clearance Altitude	USAF	United States Air Force
MRA	Minimum Reception Altitude	USCG	United States Coast Guard
MSAW	Minimum Safe Altitude Warning	UTC	Coordinated Universal Time
MSL	Mean Sea Level	VASI	Visual Approach Slope Indicator
MTR	Military Training Route	VFR	Visual Flight Rules
MVA	Minimum Vectoring Altitude	VHF	Very High Frequency
NAS	National Airspace System	VMC	Visual Meteorological Conditions
NASA	National Aeronautics and Space Administration	VOR	VHF Navigational Aid (omnidirectional course information)
NDB	Nondirectional Radio Beacon	VOR-DME	Collocated VOR and DME navigational aids (VHF and UHF course and UHF distance information)
NOAA	National Oceanic and Atmospheric Administration		
NOS	National Ocean Service	VORTAC	Collocated VOR and TACAN navigational aids (VHF and UHF course and UHF distance information)
NOTAM	Notice To Airmen		
NWS	National Weather Service		
NTZ	No Transgression Zone	VTOL	Vertical Takeoff and Landing
ODALS	Omnidirectional Approach Lighting System	VR	VFR Military Training Route

GENERAL ATC PROCEDURES

Chapter 2
TABLE OF CONTENTS

Section 1. FACILITIES

		Page
2-1	Control Tower	2-1
2-2	Approach Control	2-1
2-3	Departure Control	2-1
2-4	Air Route Traffic Control Center	2-1
2-5	Flight Service Station	2-1
2-6	Pilot Visits to Air Traffic Facilities	2-2
2-7—2-9	Reserved	2-2

Section 2. PHONETICS AND NUMBERS USAGE

2-10	Phonetic Alphabet	2-3
2-11	Numbers Usage	2-3
2-12	ATC Facility Identification	2-5
2-13—2-19	Reserved	2-5

Section 3. AIRCRAFT IDENTIFICATION

2-20	Aircraft Identification/Call Signs	2-6
2-21	Precautions In the Use of Call Signs	2-6
2-22	Description of Aircraft Types	2-7
2-23	Type Suffixes	2-7
2-24	Student Pilot Identification	2-7
2-25	Air Ambulance Flights	2-7
2-26	Description of Interchange or Leased Aircraft	2-8
2-27	Nonstandard Identification	2-8
2-28	Flight Inspection/'Flight Check' Aircraft In Terminal Areas	2-8
2-29	Reserved	2-8

Section 4. ROUTE AND NAVAID DESCRIPTION

2-30	Airways and Routes	2-9
2-31	NAVAID Terms	2-9
2-32	NAVAID Fixes	2-9
2-33—2-39	Reserved	2-9

Section 5. ATC COMMUNICATIONS FORMAT

2-40	Initial Call-Up	2-10
2-41	Subsequent Contacts	2-10
2-42	Similar Sounding Identifications	2-10
2-43	Acknowledgment of ATC Instructions	2-10
2-44	Acknowledgment of Immediate Action Clearances	2-11
2-45	Controller Initiated Frequency Changes	2-11
2-46	Acknowledgment of Frequency Changes	2-12
2-47	Compliance With Frequency Changes	2-12
2-48	Temporary Frequency Changes	2-12
2-49	Authorized ATC Transmissions	2-12
2-50	Frequency Use	2-12
2-51	Authorized Relays	2-12
2-52—2-59	Reserved	2-12

TABLE OF CONTENTS (Continued)

Section 6. ATC CLEARANCES AND SERVICE PRIORITIES

		Page
2-60	ATC Service Procedures	2-13
2-61	Clearance	2-13
2-62	Compliance With ATC Clearances and Instructions	2-13
2-63	Pilot Responsibilities	2-13
2-64	Amended Clearances	2-13
2-65	Expeditious Instructions	2-13
2-66	Service Priorities	2-14
2-67	Additional Services	2-14
2-68	Air Traffic Priority	2-14
2-69	Landing Priority	2-14
2-70—2-79	Reserved	2-14

Section 7. ADVISORIES

2-80	Wake Turbulence Cautionary Advisories	2-15
2-81	Wake Turbulence Procedures	2-15
2-82	Pilot Responsibility - Wake Turbulence	2-15
2-83	VFR In Congested Areas	2-15
2-84	Traffic Advisories	2-15
2-85	Acknowledgment of Traffic Advisories	2-16
2-86	Wind Effect	2-16
2-87	Visual Separation	2-17
2-88	Safety Alert	2-18
2-89	Merging Traffic (Target) Procedures	2-19
2-90	Termination of Traffic Advisories	2-19
2-91—2-99	Reserved	2-19

Section 8. USER REPORTS AND PILOT ADVISORIES

2-100	Safety of Flight Information	2-20
2-101	User Reports on NAVAID Performance	2-20
2-102	NAVAID Malfunction Reports	2-20
2-103	Aircraft Equipment Malfunction Reports	2-20
2-104	Aircraft Equipment Malfunctions - ATC Action	2-21
2-105	Minimum Fuel Advisory	2-21
2-106	Pilot Advisories on Bird and Other Wildlife Hazards	2-21
2-107	Reporting Bird and Other Wildlife Activities	2-21
2-108	Unmanned Balloons	2-21
2-109	Near Midair Collision Reporting	2-21
2-110	Aviation Safety Reporting Program	2-22
2-111—2-119	Reserved	2-22

GENERAL ATC PROCEDURES

TABLE OF CONTENTS (Continued)

Section 9. WEATHER INFORMATION

		Page
2-120	SIGMET or CWA Alert	2-23
2-121	Hazardous In-Flight Weather Advisory Service	2-23
2-122	PIREP Information	2-23
2-123	PIREP's Relating to Turbulence	2-24
2-124	PIREP's Relating to Airframe Icing	2-24
2-125	Wind Shear Reports	2-24
2-126	Clear Air Turbulence PIREP's	2-25
2-127	Radar Service for VFR Aircraft in Difficulty	2-25
2-128	ATC Radar Weather Display	2-25
2-129	Weather Avoidance Assistance	2-25
2-130	Weather and Chaff Deviation	2-26
2-131	Calm Wind Description	2-27
2-132	Prevailing Visibility Reports	2-27
2-133	Dissemination of General Weather Information	2-27
2-134—2-139	Reserved	2-27

Section 10. ALTIMETER SETTINGS

2-140	Altimeter Settings	2-28
2-141	Current Settings	2-28
2-142	Altimeter Issuance	2-28
2-143—2-149	Reserved	2-29

Section 11. RUNWAY VISIBILITY REPORTING

2-150	Runway Visual Range	2-30
2-151	Arrival/Departure Runway Visibility	2-30
2-152	RVR/RVV Reporting Terminology	2-30
2-153—2-159	Reserved	2-31

Section 12. GENERAL FLIGHT PLAN INFORMATION

2-160	Flight Plan - Information Required	2-32
2-161	IFR Flight Plans - General	2-32
2-162	Composite Flight Plan (VFR/IFR Flights)	2-32
2-163	Cancelling Flight Plan - IFR	2-32
2-164	Closing Flight Plan - VFR/DVFR	2-32

Chapter 2. GENERAL ATC PROCEDURES

Section 1. FACILITIES

2-1 CONTROL TOWER

a. An *Airport Traffic Control Tower* (ATCT) is a terminal facility that uses radio communications, visual signaling, and other equipment to provide ATC services to aircraft operating in the vicinity of an airport or on the movement area. A control tower authorizes aircraft to land or takeoff at the airport controlled by the tower or to transit the airport traffic area regardless of flight plan or weather conditions (IFR or VFR). A tower may also provide approach control services (radar or nonradar).

b. A *Nonapproach Control Tower* authorizes aircraft to land or takeoff at the airport controlled by the tower or to transit the airport traffic area. The primary function of a nonapproach control tower is the sequencing of aircraft in the traffic pattern and on the landing area. Nonapproach control towers also separate aircraft operating under instrument flight rules clearances from approach controls and centers. They provide ground control services to aircraft, vehicles, personnel, and equipment on the airport movement area.

2-1 References. — ATCH & AIM Glossary.

2-2 APPROACH CONTROL

An approach control facility is a terminal ATC facility that uses radar and/or nonradar procedures to provide approach control services to aircraft arriving, departing, or transiting airspace controlled by the facility. It provides radar ATC services to IFR and VFR aircraft operating in the vicinity of one or more civil and/or military airports in a terminal area and provides services to aircraft within or near a TCA (Terminal Control Area), ARSA (Airport Radar Service Area), or TRSA (Terminal Radar Service Area). A radar approach control facility may be operated by the FAA, USAF, US Army, USN, USMC, or jointly by FAA and a military service. Specific facility nomenclatures are used for administrative purposes only and are related to the physical location of the facility and the operating service generally as follows:

a. Terminal Radar Approach Control/TRACON (FAA).

b. Tower/Airport Traffic Control Tower/ATCT (FAA). (Only those towers delegated approach control authority.)

c. Radar Approach Control/RAPCON (Air Force/FAA).

d. Radar Air Traffic Control Facility/RATCF (Navy/FAA).

e. Army Radar Approach Control/ARAC (Army).

2-2 References. — ATCH & AIM Glossary.

2-3 DEPARTURE CONTROL

Departure control is a function of an approach control facility providing air traffic control service for departing IFR and, under certain conditions, VFR aircraft, i.e., an aircraft departing an airport within an ARSA.

2-3 References. — ATCH & AIM Glossary.

2-4 AIR ROUTE TRAFFIC CONTROL CENTER

a. An ARTCC (Air Route Traffic Control Center) is a facility established to provide air traffic control service to aircraft operating on IFR flight plans within controlled airspace and principally during the en route phase of flight. When equipment capabilities and controller workload permit, certain advisory/assistance services may be provided to VFR aircraft.

b. An ARTCC is divided into sectors. Each sector is handled by one or a team of controllers and has its own sector discrete frequency. As a flight progresses from one sector to another, the pilot is requested to change to the appropriate sector discrete frequency.

c. Prior to arriving at the destination, instructions may be received from ARTCC to contact approach control on a specified frequency.

2-4 References. — ATCH & AIM Glossary.

2-5 FLIGHT SERVICE STATION

FSS's (Flight Service Stations) are air traffic facilities which provide pilot weather briefings, en route communications, and VFR search and rescue services, assist lost aircraft and aircraft in emergency situations, relay ATC clearances, originate NOTAM's (Notices to Airmen), receive and process VFR and IFR flight plans, and monitor NAVAID's. In addition, at selected locations, FSS's provide En Route Flight Advisory Service (Flight Watch), take weather observations, issue airport advisories, and advise Customs and Immigration of transborder flights.

2-5 Reference. — AIM 152.

2-6 PILOT VISITS TO AIR TRAFFIC FACILITIES

a. Pilots are encouraged to visit air traffic facilities (Towers, Centers, and FSS's). It is requested that pilots contact the facility (telephone numbers are listed under U.S. Government, Department of Transportation) prior to the visit and advise of the number of persons in the group, the time and date of the proposed visit, and the primary interest of the group. With this information available, the facility can prepare an itinerary and have someone available to guide the group through the facility. On rare occasions, facilities may not be able to approve a visit due to facility workload or other reasons.

b. Pilots are invited to participate in "Operation Raincheck." Operation Raincheck is a program designed to familiarize pilots with the ATC system. One of the highlights of the program is the opportunity for pilots to observe controllers at work, view traffic on radar, and listen to radio and interphone communications.

2-6 Reference. — AIM 155.

2-7 thru 2-9 RESERVED

Section 2. PHONETICS AND NUMBERS USAGE

2-10 PHONETIC ALPHABET

Pilots and controllers use the ICAO pronunciation of numbers and, as necessary to clarify individual letters, the ICAO radio-telephony alphabet.

2-10 Table. — ICAO Phonetics and Pronunciation of Numbers

Character	Word	Pronunciation
0	Zero	ZE–RO
1	One	WUN
2	Two	TOO
3	Three	TREE
4	Four	FOW–ER
5	Five	FIFE
6	Six	SIX
7	Seven	SEV–EN
8	Eight	AIT
9	Nine	NIN–ER
A	Alpha	**AL** FAH
B	Bravo	**BRAH** VOH
C	Charlie	**CHAR** LEE
D	Delta	**DELL** TAH
E	Echo	**ECK** OH
F	Foxtrot	**FOKS** TROT
G	Golf	GOLF
H	Hotel	HOH **TELL**
I	India	**IN** DEE AH
J	Juliett	**JEW** LEE ETT
K	Kilo	**KEY** LOH
L	Lima	**LEE** MAH
M	Mike	MIKE
N	November	NO **VEM** BER
O	Oscar	**OSS** CAR
P	Papa	PAH **PAH**
Q	Quebec	KEH **BECK**
R	Romeo	**ROW** ME OH
S	Sierra	SEE **AIR** AH
T	Tango	**TANG** GO
U	Uniform	**YOU** NEE FORM
V	Victor	**VIK** TAR
W	Whiskey	**WISS** KEY
X	X-ray	**ECKS** RAY
Y	Yankee	**YANG** KEY
Z	Zulu	**ZOO** LOO

Note: Syllables emphasized in pronunciation are in bold face.

2-10 References. — ATCH 2-84; AIM 196.

2-11 NUMBERS USAGE

For air traffic control purposes numbers will be stated as follows:

a. Serial numbers — The separate digits.

2-11a Examples. —

Number	Statement
11,495	"One one four niner five."
20,069	"Two zero zero six niner."

b. Altitudes or flight levels:

(1) Altitudes — Each digit in the number of hundreds or thousands followed by the word "hundred" or "thousand" as appropriate.

2-11b(1) Example. —

Altitude	Statement
17,900	"One seven thousand niner hundred."

(2) Flight levels — The words "flight level" followed by the separate digits of the flight level.

2-11b(2) Examples. —

Flight Level	Statement
180	"Flight level one eight zero."
275	"Flight level two seven five."

(3) MDA/DH Altitudes — The separate digits of the MDA/DH altitude.

2-11b(3) Examples. —

MDA/DH Altitude	Statement
1,320	"Published minimum descent altitude, one three two zero."
486	"Published decision height, four eight six."

c. Time:

(1) General time information — The 4 separate digits of the hour and minutes based on the 24-hour clock in terms of Coordinated Universal Time (UTC).

2-11c(1) Examples. —

Time (12 hr.)	Time (24 hr.)	Statement
1:15 a.m.	0115	"Zero one one five."
1:15 p.m.	1315	"One three one five."

(2) When requested — The 4 separate digits of the hours and minutes in terms of UTC, by stating "Zulu," followed by the local standard time equivalents.

2-11c(2) Example. —

Time	Statement
1430 PST (2230 UTC)	"Two two three zero Zulu, one four three zero Pacific."

(3) Time check — The word "time" followed by the 4 separate digits of the hour and minutes, and nearest quarter minute.

2-11c(3) Example. —

Time	Statement
1415 ¾	"Time, one four one five and three-quarters."

(4) Abbreviated time – The separate digits of the minutes only.

2-11c(4) Examples. –

Time	Statement
1415	"One five."
1420	"Two zero."

d. Field elevation – The words "field elevation" followed by the separate digits of the elevation.

2-11d Examples. –

Elevation	Statement
17 feet	"Field elevation, one seven."
817 feet	"Field elevation, eight one seven."
2,817 feet	"Field elevation, two eight one seven."

e. The number "0," as "zero," except where it is used in approved "group form" for authorized aircraft call signs, and in stating altitudes.

2-11e Examples. –

"One zero thousand five hundred."
"Field elevation one six zero."
"Heading three zero zero."
"American Five Thirty."
"Eagle Flight Four Hundred."
"Cessna Four Zero Zero."

f. Altimeter setting – The word "altimeter" followed by the separate digits of the altimeter setting.

2-11f Example. –

Setting	Statement
30.01	"Altimeter, three zero zero one."

g. Surface wind – The word "wind" followed by the separate digits of the indicated wind direction to the nearest 10-degree multiple, the word "at," and the separate digits of the indicated velocity in knots.

2-11g Examples. –

"Wind zero three zero at two five."
"Wind two seven zero at one five gusts three five."

h. Heading – The word "heading" followed by the 3 separate digits of the number of degrees, omitting the word "degrees." Heading 360 degrees is used to indicate a north heading.

2-11h Examples. –

Heading	Statement
5 degrees	"Heading zero zero five."
30 degrees	"Heading zero three zero."
360 degrees	"Heading three six zero."

i. Radar beacon codes – The separate digits of the 4-digit code.

2-11i Examples. –

Code	Statement
1200	"One two zero zero."
0325	"Zero three two five."

j. Runways – The word "runway" followed by the separate digits of the runway designation. For a parallel runway, the word "left," "right," or "center" if the letter "L," "R," or "C" is included in the designation.

2-11j Examples. –

Designation	Statement
3	"Runway Three."
8L	"Runway Eight Left."
27R	"Runway Two Seven Right."

k. Frequencies – The separate digits of the frequency, inserting the word "point" where the decimal point occurs. Digits after the second digit to the right of the decimal point are omitted. When the frequency is in the L/MF band, the word "kiloHertz" is included.

2-11k Examples. –

Frequency	Statement
126.55	MHz "One two six point five five."
369.0	MHz "Three six niner point zero."
121.5	MHz "One two one point five."
135.275	MHz "One three five point two seven five."
302	kHz "Three zero two kiloHertz."

l. Speeds –

(1) The separate digits of the speed followed by "knots," except as required by speed adjustment methods.

2-11l(1) Examples. –

Speed	Statement
250	"Two five zero knots."
190	"One niner zero knots."

(2) The separate digits of the mach number preceded by "mach."

2-11l(2) Examples. –

Mach Number	Statement
1.5	"Mach one point five."
0.64	"Mach point six four."
0.7	"Mach point seven."

m. Miles – The separate digits of mileage followed by the word "mile."

2-11m Examples. –

"Three zero mile arc east of Nottingham."
"Traffic, one o'clock, two five miles, northbound, D-C-Eight, flight level two seven zero."

2-11 Reference. – ATCH 2-85.

2-12 ATC FACILITY IDENTIFICATION

Facilities will be identified as follows:

a. Airport traffic control towers — The name of the facility is stated followed by the word "tower." Where military and civil airports are located in the same general area and have similar names, the name of the military service is stated followed by the name of the military facility and the word "tower."

2-12a Examples. —

"Columbus Tower."

"Barksdale Tower."

"Navy Jacksonville Tower."

b. Air route traffic control centers — The name of the facility is stated followed by the word "center."

c. Approach control facilities — The name of the facility is stated followed by the word "approach." Where military and civil facilities are located in the same general area and have similar names, the name of the military service is stated followed by the name of the military facility and the word "approach."

2-12c Examples. —

"Denver Approach."

"Griffiss Approach."

"Navy Jacksonville Approach."

d. Functions within a terminal facility — The name of the facility is stated followed by the name of the function.

2-12d Examples. —

"Boston Departure."

"La Guardia Clearance Delivery."

"O'Hare Ground."

e. FAA flight service stations — The name of the station is stated followed by the word "radio."

2-12e Example. —

"Pittsburgh Radio."

2-12 Reference. — ATCH 2-86.

2-13 thru 2-19 RESERVED

Section 3. AIRCRAFT IDENTIFICATION

2-20 AIRCRAFT IDENTIFICATION/CALL SIGNS

Aircraft are identified as follows:

a. The aircraft type, the model, the manufacturer's name, or the prefix "November" will be stated, followed by the numbers/letters of the aircraft registration.*

2-20a Examples. —

"Jet Commander One Four Two Four."

"Douglas Three Zero Five Romeo."

"Bonanza One Two Three Four Tango."

"November One Two Three Four Golf."

(1) Air carrier and other civil aircraft having FAA authorized call signs — The call sign is stated followed by the flight number in group form followed by the word "heavy" if appropriate.*

2-20a(1) Examples. —

"American Twelve Twenty-two."

"Delta One Hundred."

"Eagle Flight Three Ten."

"United One Zero One."

"Cactus Fifty Heavy."

(2) When aircraft identification becomes a problem and procedures specified in (1) are used, the call sign will be restated after the flight number of the aircraft involved.

2-20a(2) Examples. —

"American Five Twenty-one American."

"Delta Five Twenty-one Delta."

(3) Air taxi and commercial operators not having FAA authorized call signs — The prefix "TANGO" is stated on initial contact, if used by the pilot, followed by the registration number. The prefix may be dropped in subsequent communications.

2-20a(3) Examples. —

"Tango Mooney Five Five Five Two Quebec."

"Tango One Two Three Four."

b. Foreign registry — One of the following is stated:

(1) Civil — The letters or digits of the aircraft registration or call sign.

2-20b(1) Example. —

"Canadian Foxtrot Lima Romeo Bravo."

(2) Air carrier — The abbreviated name of the operating company, followed by:

(a) The letters or digits of the registration or call sign.

2-20b(2)(a) Example. —

"Air France Foxtrot Lima Romeo Lima Golf."

(b) The flight number in group form.

2-20b(2)(b) Example. —

"Scandinavian Sixty-eight."

c. A pilot's name will be used in identification of an aircraft only in special or emergency situations.

2-20a Note. — The prefix "November" denotes a U.S. aircraft registry and should not be used when the aircraft manufacturer's name or type model is stated.

2-20a(1) Note 1. — "Group form" is the pronunciation of a series of numbers as the whole number, or pairs of numbers they represent rather than pronouncing each separate digit. The use of group form may, however, be negated by four digit identifiers or the placement of zeros in the identifier.

2-20a(1) Note 2. — "Heavy" denotes an aircraft capable of takeoff weights of 300,000 pounds or more. Most airlines will use the word "Heavy" following the company prefix and trip number when establishing communications or when changing frequencies within a terminal facility's area.

2-20 References. — ATCH 2-82, 2-87; AIM 193.

2-21 PRECAUTIONS IN THE USE OF CALL SIGNS

a. Improper use of call signs can result in pilots executing a clearance intended for another aircraft. *CALL SIGNS SHOULD NEVER BE ABBREVIATED ON AN INITIAL CONTACT OR AT ANY TIME WHEN OTHER AIRCRAFT CALL SIGNS HAVE SIMILAR NUMBERS/SOUNDS OR IDENTICAL LETTERS/NUMBERS* (e.g., Cessna Six One Three Two Foxtrot, Cessna One Six Two Two Foxtrot, Baron One Two Three Foxtrot, Cherokee Seven Seven Three Two Foxtrot, etc.).

b. Pilots must be certain that aircraft identification is complete and clearly identified before taking action on an ATC clearance. ATC will not abbreviate call signs of air carriers or other civil aircraft having authorized call signs. ATC may initiate abbreviated call signs of other aircraft by using the *prefix and the last three digits/letters* of the aircraft identification after communications are established. The pilot may use the abbreviated call sign in subsequent contacts with ATC. When aware of similar/identical call signs, ATC will take action to minimize errors by emphasizing certain numbers/letters, by repeating the entire call sign, repeating the prefix, or by asking pilots to use a different call sign temporarily. Pilots should use the phrase *"VERIFY CLEARANCE FOR* (complete call sign)*"* if doubt exists concerning proper identity.

2-21 Reference. — AIM 193.

2-22 DESCRIPTION OF AIRCRAFT TYPES

Except as provided in 2-22 **d,** controllers will describe aircraft as follows when issuing traffic information.

a. Military:

(1) Military designator, with numbers spoken in group form, or

2-22a(1) Examples. —

"F-Fourteen."

"B-Fifty-two."

"Fighter."

"Bomber."

(2) Service and type, or

(3) Type only if no confusion or misidentification is likely.

b. Air Carrier:

(1) Manufacturer's name or model.

(2) The company name or other identifying features are added when confusion or misidentification is likely.

2-22b Examples. —

"Lockheed Ten-eleven."

"American M-D Eighty."

"United Seven Thirty-seven."

"Southwest Seven Thirty-seven painted as Shamu."

c. General Aviation and Air Taxi:

(1) Manufacturer's model, name, or designator.

(2) Aircraft color is added when considered advantageous.

2-22c Examples. —

"Tri-Pacer."

"P-A Twenty-two."

"Cessna Three Ten."

"Green Apache."

d. When issuing traffic information to aircraft following a heavy jet, the word "heavy" will be specified before the manufacturer's name and model.

2-22d Examples. —

"Heavy Lockheed Ten-eleven."

"Heavy Boeing Seven Sixty-seven."

2-22 Reference. — ATCH 2-88.

2-23 TYPE SUFFIXES

The following suffixes should be used by pilots in identification of aircraft type when it is necessary to inform controllers of transponder and navigation equipment capability. The word "slant" is stated followed by the appropriate suffix pronounced phonetically.

/X — no transponder.

/T — transponder with no altitude encoding capability.

/U — transponder with altitude encoding capability.

/D — DME, but no transponder.

/B — DME and transponder, but no altitude encoding capability.

/A — DME and transponder with altitude encoding capability.

/M — TACAN only, but no transponder.

/N — TACAN only and transponder, but with no altitude encoding capability.

/P — TACAN only and transponder with altitude encoding capability.

/C — RNAV and transponder, but with no altitude encoding capability.

/R — RNAV and transponder with altitude encoding capability.

/W — RNAV, but no transponder.

2-23 Examples. —

"Cessna One Seventy-two, Slant Uniform."

"L-R Three Five, Slant Romeo."

2-23 References. — ATCH 2-57; AIM 298.

2-24 STUDENT PILOT IDENTIFICATION

a. The FAA desires to help the student pilot in acquiring sufficient practical experience in the environment in which he will be required to operate. To receive additional assistance while operating in areas of concentrated air traffic, a student pilot may identify himself as a student pilot during his initial call to an ATC facility.

2-24a Example. —

Bakersfield Approach, Cherokee Two Niner Four Five Uniform, student pilot, over.

Cherokee Two Niner Four Five Uniform, Bakersfield Approach.

b. This special identification will alert ATC personnel and enable them to provide the student pilot with such extra assistance and consideration he may need. This procedure is not mandatory.

2-24 Reference. — AIM 193.

2-25 AIR AMBULANCE FLIGHTS

a. Because of the priority afforded air ambulance flights in the ATC system, extreme discretion is necessary when using the term "LIFEGUARD." It is only intended for those missions of an urgent medical nature and to be utilized only for that portion of the flight requiring expeditious handling. When requested by the pilot, necessary notification to expedite ground handling of patients, etc., is provided by ATC; however, when possible, this information should be passed in advance through nonATC communications systems.

b. Civilian air ambulance flights responding to medical emergencies (first call to an accident scene, carrying patients, organ donors, organs, or other urgently needed lifesaving medical material) will be expedited by ATC when necessary. When expeditious handling is necessary, pilots shall add the word "LIFEGUARD" in the remarks section of the flight plan. In radio communications, pilots shall use the call sign "LIFEGUARD" followed by the aircraft type and registration letters/numbers.

2-25b Example. —

"LIFEGUARD Cessna Two Six Four Six."

c. Similar provisions have been made for the use of "AIR EVAC" and "MED EVAC" by military air ambulance flights, except that these military flights will receive priority handling only when specifically requested.

d. Air carrier and air taxi flights responding to medical emergencies will also be expedited by ATC when necessary. The nature of these medical emergency flights usually concerns the transportation of urgently needed lifesaving medical materials or vital organs. *IT IS IMPERATIVE THAT THE COMPANY/PILOT DETERMINE, BY THE NATURE/ URGENCY OF THE SPECIFIC MEDICAL CARGO, IF PRIORITY ATC ASSISTANCE IS REQUIRED.* Pilots shall ensure that the word "LIFEGUARD" is included in the remarks section of the flight plan and use the call sign "LIFEGUARD" followed by the company name and flight number, for all transmissions when expeditious handling is required. It is important for ATC to be aware of "LIFEGUARD" status, and it is the pilot's responsibility to ensure that this information is provided to ATC.

2-25d Example. —

"LIFEGUARD Delta Fifty-one."

2-25 References. — ATCH 2-87; AIM 193.

2-26 DESCRIPTION OF INTERCHANGE OR LEASED AIRCRAFT

a. Controllers issue traffic information based on familiarity with airline equipment and color/markings. When an air carrier dispatches a flight using another company's equipment and the pilot does not advise the terminal ATC facility, the possible confusion in aircraft identification can compromise safety.

b. Pilots flying an "interchange" or "leased" aircraft not bearing the colors/markings of the company operating the aircraft should inform the terminal ATC facility on initial contact the name of the operating company and trip number, followed by the company name as displayed on the aircraft, and aircraft type.

2-26 Reference. — AIM 194.

2-27 NONSTANDARD IDENTIFICATION

The same identification used by the pilot in his initial call-up may be used initially by ATC. After communication has been established the correct identification will be used.

2-27 Reference. — ATCH 2-87.

2-28 FLIGHT INSPECTION/'FLIGHT CHECK' AIRCRAFT IN TERMINAL AREAS

a. *"FLIGHT CHECK"* is a call sign used to alert pilots and air traffic controllers when an FAA aircraft is engaged in flight inspection/certification of NAVAID's and flight procedures. Flight Check aircraft fly preplanned high/low altitude flight patterns such as grids, orbits, DME arcs, and tracks, including low passes along the full length of the runway to verify NAVAID performance. In most instances, these flight checks are being automatically recorded and/or flown in an automated mode.

b. Pilots should be especially watchful and avoid the flight paths of any aircraft using the call sign *"Flight Check"* or *"Flight Check recorded."* The latter call sign, e.g., *"Flight Check Four Seven recorded,"* indicates that automated flight inspections are in progress in terminal areas. These flights will normally receive special handling from ATC. Pilot patience and cooperation in allowing uninterrupted recording can significantly help expedite flight inspections, minimize costly, repetitive runs, and reduce the burden on the U.S. taxpayer.

2-28 Reference. — AIM 247.

2-29 RESERVED

Section 4. ROUTE AND NAVAID DESCRIPTION

2-30 AIRWAYS AND ROUTES

Airways, routes, or jet routes will be described as follows:

a. VOR/VORTAC/TACAN airways or jet routes — The word "Victor" or the letter "J" is stated followed by the number of airway or route in group form. For RNAV routes the word "Romeo."

2-30a Examples. —

"Victor Twelve."

"J-Five Thirty-three."

"Victor Seven Ten Romeo."

"J-Eight Thirty Romeo."

"Offset one zero miles right of J-Eight Thirty Romeo."

b. VOR/VORTAC alternate airways — The word "Victor" is stated followed by the number of the airway in group form and the alternate direction.

2-30b Example. —

"Victor Twelve South."

c. L/MF airways — The color of the airway is stated followed by the number in group form.

2-30c Example. —

"Blue Eighty-one."

d. North American Route — The words "North American Route" are stated followed by the number of the route in group form.

2-30d Example. —

"North American Route Fifty."

e. MTR's — The letters are stated followed by the number of the route in group form.

2-30e Example. —

"I-R Five Thirty-one."

2-30 Reference. — ATCH 2-40.

2-31 NAVAID TERMS

Radials, arcs, courses, bearings, and quadrants of NAVAID's will be described as follows:

a. VOR/VORTAC/MLS NAVAID's — The name of the NAVAID is stated followed by the separate digits of the radial/azimuth (the word "degrees" is omitted) and the word "radial/azimuth."

2-31a Example. —

"Appleton zero five zero radial."

"Lindburg Runway Two Seven M-L-S, two six zero azimuth."

b. Arcs about VOR-DME/VORTAC/MLS NAVAID's — The distance in miles from the NAVAID is stated followed by the words "mile arc," the direction from the NAVAID in terms of the 8 principal points of the compass, the word "of," and the name of the NAVAID.

2-31b Example. —

"One five mile arc southwest of Grantsville."

c. Quadrant within a radius of NAVAID — Direction from NAVAID is stated in terms of the quadrant; e.g., NE, SE, SW, NW, followed by the distance in miles from the NAVAID.

2-31c Example. —

"Cleared to fly northeast quadrant of Phillipsburg VORTAC within four zero mile radius."

d. Nondirectional beacons — The course to or the bearing from the radio beacon, omitting the word "degree," is stated followed by the words "course to" or "bearing from," the name of the radio beacon, and the words "radio beacon."

2-31d Example. —

"Three four zero bearing from Randolph Radio Beacon."

2-31 Reference. — ATCH 2-41.

2-32 NAVAID FIXES

Fixes determined by reference to a radial/localizer and distance from a VOR-DME/VORTAC/ILS-DME or MLS will be described as follows:

a. When a fix is not named — The name of the NAVAID is stated followed by a specified radial/localizer/azimuth and the distance is stated in miles followed by the phrase "mile fix."

2-32a Examples. —

"Appleton zero five zero radial three seven mile fix."

"Reno localizer back course four mile fix."

"Hobby Runway One Two M-L-S, zero niner zero azimuth one two mile fix."

b. When a fix is named — The name of the fix is stated followed by the phrase "D-M-E fix" or "Waypoint" as appropriate.

2-32b Examples. —

"Shaum D-M-E fix."

"Shaum Waypoint."

c. Specific terms are used to describe a fix. Controllers will not use expressions such as "passing Victor Twelve" or "passing J-Eleven."

2-32 Reference. — ATCH 2-42.

2-33 thru 2-39 RESERVED

Section 5. ATC COMMUNICATIONS FORMAT

2-40 INITIAL CALL-UP

Pilots should use the following format:*

a. Name of facility being called,

b. Full aircraft identification,

c. Type of message to follow, or request if it is short, and

d. The word "over" if required.

2-40 Examples. —

Norwood Ground, Cessna Niner Four Five Zero Echo at Bluehill ready to taxi with DELTA.

Los Angeles Clearance, American Nine Eighty, Gate Forty-four, to Nashville with CHARLIE.

Albuquerque Center, Twin Cessna Five One Zero Five Bravo level one five thousand direct Santa Fe.

2-40 Note. — The term initial contact or initial call-up means the first radio call you make to a given facility, or the first call to a different controller within a facility.

2-40 References. — ATCH 2-76; AIM 192.

2-41 SUBSEQUENT CONTACTS

The following format is used in subsequent communications:

a. The facility name may be omitted.

b. The aircraft identification may be abbreviated by stating the type aircraft and last 3 digits or letters of the identification. ATC will not abbreviate similar sounding aircraft identifications or the identification of an air carrier or other civil aircraft having an FAA authorized call sign.

c. Messages and requests should be stated in the same transmission as long as they are short and to the point.

d. The word "over" may be omitted if the message requires an obvious reply.

2-41 Examples. —

Cessna Eight Eight Five request direct Richmond.

Skipper One Zero One downwind abeam for touch-and-go.

2-41 References. — ATCH 2-76, 2-77; AIM 192, 193.

2-42 SIMILAR SOUNDING IDENTIFICATIONS

Appropriate digits, letters, or similar sounding words are emphasized to aid in distinguishing between similar souding aircraft identifications. Additionally, ATC will notify each pilot concerned when communicating with aircraft having similar sounding identifications.

2-42 Example. —

United Thirty-one United, Miami Center, American Thirty-one is also on this frequency, acknowledge.

United Thirty-one United, roger.

American Thirty-one American, Miami Center, United Thirty-one is also on this frequency, acknowledge.

American Thirty-one American, roger.

2-42 Reference. — ATCH 2-83.

2-43 ACKNOWLEDGMENT OF ATC INSTRUCTIONS

a. *Pilots should acknowledge all call-ups or clearances* unless the controller advises otherwise.

b. When issuing information, clearances, or instructions, the controller must ensure acknowledgment by the pilot.

c. Pilots should read back *those parts* of ATC clearances and instructions containing altitude assignments or vectors, as a means of mutual verification. The readback of the "numbers" serves as a double check between pilots and controllers and reduces the kinds of communications errors that occur when a number is either "misheard" or is incorrect.

d. Pilots append or precede readbacks and acknowledgments with their aircraft identification. This aids controllers in determining that the correct aircraft received the clearance or instruction. The requirement to include aircraft identification in all readbacks and acknowledgments becomes more important as frequency congestion increases and when aircraft with similar call signs are on the same frequency.

e. Pilots should read back altitudes, altitude restrictions, and vectors in the same sequence as they are given in the clearance or instruction.

2-43e Examples. —

Cessna Zero Five Bravo, turn left heading zero one zero, climb and maintain eight thousand.

Left heading zero one zero, maintain eight thousand, Cessna Zero Five Bravo.

Mooney Three Five Mike, climb and maintain five thousand, contact Los Angeles Departure one two four point two.

Climb and maintain five thousand, one two four point two, Mooney Three Five Mike.

f. If altitude, heading, or other items are read back by the pilot, the controller must ensure the readback is correct. If received incorrectly, distorted, or incomplete, the controller will make corrections as appropriate.

2-43 References. — ATCH 2-72; AIM 192, 265.

2-44 ACKNOWLEDGMENT OF IMMEDIATE ACTION CLEARANCES

a. There are some occasions when the controller must issue time-critical instructions to other aircraft and he may be in a position to observe the response, either visually or on radar.

2-44a Examples. —
Cessna One One Charlie, turn left immediately heading two seven zero, break, Piper Six Seven Foxtrot, maintain five thousand, over.

Maintain five thousand, Piper Six Seven Foxtrot.

Cessna Two Three Bravo, go around.

b. If the situation demands a response, pilots should take appropriate action or immediately advise the facility of any problem. Pilots should acknowledge with their aircraft identification and one of the words "Wilco, Roger, Affirmative, Negative," or other appropriate remarks.

2-44b Examples. —
Cessna Two Five Mike, cancel takeoff clearance, hold in position.
Cessna Two Five Mike, roger.

Tomahawk One Four Lima, if able, start your right turn now, traffic to depart Runway Three One.
Tomahawk One Four Lima, wilco.

2-44 Reference. — AIM 192.

2-45 CONTROLLER INITIATED FREQUENCY CHANGES

a. Radio communications will be transferred before an aircraft enters the receiving controller's area of jurisdiction unless otherwise coordinated.

b. Radio communications will be transferred by specifying the following:

(1) The facility name or location name and terminal function to be contacted. TERMINAL: The location name is omitted when a controller transfers communications to another controller within his facility except as required.

(2) Frequency to use—except the following may be omitted:

(a) FSS frequency.

(b) Departure frequency if previously given or published on a SID (standard instrument departure) chart for the procedure issued.

(i) Ground or local control frequency if in the controller's opinion the pilot knows which frequency is in use.

(ii) The numbers preceding the decimal point if the ground control frequency is in the 121 MHz bandwidth.

2-45b Examples. —
Contact tower.

Contact ground.

Contact ground point seven.

Contact ground, one two zero point eight.

Contact Huntington Radio.

Contact departure.

Contact Los Angeles Center, one two three point four.

(3) Time, fix, altitude, or specifically when to contact a facility. The controller may omit this when compliance is expected upon receipt.

ATC Phraseology:

Contact (facility name or location name and terminal function), (frequency).

If required,

at (time, fix, or altitude).

2-45b(3) Example. —
Delta Four Thirty, contact tower one one eight point eight at the outer marker.

c. In situations where a control sector has multiple frequencies or when control sectors are combined using multiple frequencies, and aircraft will remain under the same controller's jurisdiction, radio communications will be transferred by the controller specifying the following:

ATC Phraseology:

(Identification) **change to my frequency** (frequency).

d. ATC will avoid issuing a frequency change to helicopters known to be single piloted during air-taxiing, hovering, or low-level flight.*

e. In situations where the controller does not want the pilot to change frequency, but the pilot is expecting or may want a frequency change, the following phraseology is used:

ATC Phraseology:

Remain this frequency.

2-45e Example. —
Cessna One Zero Five, remain this frequency, taxi to the ramp.

2-45d Note. — Helicopter pilots are expected to advise ATC of their single pilot status if unable to comply with a frequency change.

2-45 References. — ATCH 2-17; AIM 192.

2-46 ACKNOWLEDGMENT OF FREQUENCY CHANGES

a. When advised by ATC to change frequencies, acknowledge the instruction.

2-46a Example. —
American Nine Sixty-one, contact Fort Worth Center one three four point four seven.
One three four point four seven, American Nine Sixty-one, good day.

b. Initial call-up phraseology may be abbreviated when a pilot is instructed to *"change to my frequency."*

2-46b Example. —
United Two Twenty-two, change to my frequency one two zero point four.
One two zero point four, United Two Twenty-two.
United Two Twenty-two on one two zero point four.
United Two Twenty-two, roger.

2-46 Reference. — AIM 192.

2-47 COMPLIANCE WITH FREQUENCY CHANGES

When instructed by ATC to change frequencies, pilots should select the new frequency as soon as possible unless instructed to make the change at a specific time, fix, or altitude. If instructed to make the frequency change at a specific time, fix, or altitude, pilots should continue to monitor the frequency until reaching the specified time, fix, or altitude unless instructed otherwise by ATC.*

2-47 Note. — This paragraph should not be interpreted to mean that it is necessary to transmit immediately after selecting a new frequency. After selecting a new frequency, pilots should listen for the amount of activity, pace of the controller's instructions, and listen for an opportunity to fit into the flow of communications.

2-47 Reference. — AIM 192.

2-48 TEMPORARY FREQUENCY CHANGES

As necessary, ATC will authorize a pilot to temporarily change frequencies/interrupt his communications guard.

2-48 Example. —
Trinidad Eight Eight Five requests frequency change for two minutes.
Trinidad Eight Eight Five, roger. Approved as requested. Report back on frequency.

2-48 Reference. — ATCH 2-73.

2-49 AUTHORIZED ATC TRANSMISSIONS

Controllers are authorized to transmit only those messages necessary for air traffic control or otherwise contributing to air safety.

2-49 Reference. — ATCH 2-74.

2-50 FREQUENCY USE

Radio frequencies will be used for the special purposes for which they are intended. A single frequency may be used for more than one function except as follows:

TERMINAL: When combining positions in the tower, ATC will not use ground control frequency for airborne communications.

2-50 Reference. — ATCH 2-70.

2-51 AUTHORIZED RELAYS

Operational information will be relayed to aircraft or aircraft operators as necessary. ATC will not agree to handle such messages on a regular basis. The controller will give the source of any such message it relays.

2-51 Reference. — ATCH 2-75.

2-52 thru 2-59 RESERVED

Section 6. ATC CLEARANCES AND SERVICE PRIORITIES

2-60 ATC SERVICE PROCEDURES

Air traffic control service is provided in accordance with the procedures and minima in the *Air Traffic Control Handbook, Order 7110.65* except when:

a. Deviation is necessary to conform with ICAO Documents, National Rules of the Air, or special agreements where the United States provides air traffic control service in airspace outside the United States and its possessions.*

b. Other procedures/minima are prescribed in a letter of agreement, an FAA, or a military document.

2-60a Note. — Pilots are required to abide by FAR's or other applicable regulations regardless of the description of any procedure or minima in this reference book.

2-60 Reference. — ATCH 2-1.

2-61 CLEARANCE

A clearance issued by ATC is predicated on known traffic and known physical airport conditions. An ATC clearance means an authorization by ATC, for the purpose of preventing collision between known aircraft, for an aircraft to proceed under specified conditions within controlled airspace. *IT IS NOT AUTHORIZATION FOR A PILOT TO DEVIATE FROM ANY RULE, REGULATION, OR MINIMUM ALTITUDE, NOR TO CONDUCT UNSAFE OPERATION OF HIS AIRCRAFT.*

2-61 Reference. — AIM 260.

2-62 COMPLIANCE WITH ATC CLEARANCES AND INSTRUCTIONS

a. When an air traffic clearance has been obtained under either visual or instrument flight rules no pilot in command may deviate from that ATC clearance except in an emergency or unless he has obtained an amended clearance. If a pilot is uncertain of the meaning of an ATC clearance, he must immediately request clarification from ATC.

b. Except in an emergency, no person may, in an area in which air traffic control is exercised, operate an aircraft contrary to an ATC instruction.

c. Each pilot in command who deviates, in an emergency, from an ATC clearance or instruction, must notify ATC of that deviation as soon as possible.

d. Each pilot in command who (though not deviating from a rule of an FAR) is given priority by ATC in an emergency, shall, if requested by ATC, submit a detailed report of that emergency within 48 hours to the manager of that ATC facility.

2-62 References. — FAR 91.75; ATCH 2-18.

2-63 PILOT RESPONSIBILITIES

a. FAR 91.3(a) states: "The pilot in command of an aircraft is directly responsible for, and is the final authority as to, the operation of that aircraft." If ATC issues a clearance that would cause a pilot to deviate from a rule or regulation, or in the pilot's opinion, would place the aircraft in jeopardy, *IT IS THE PILOT'S RESPONSIBILITY TO NOTIFY ATC AND REQUEST AN AMENDED CLEARANCE.*

b. Similarly, if a pilot prefers to follow a different course of action, such as make a 360 degree turn for spacing to follow traffic when established in a landing or approach sequence, land on a different runway, takeoff from a different intersection, takeoff from the threshold instead of an intersection or delay his operation, *HE IS EXPECTED TO INFORM ATC ACCORDINGLY.*

c. When the pilot requests a different course of action, he is expected to cooperate so as to preclude disruption of traffic flow or creation of conflicting patterns. The pilot is also expected to use the appropriate aircraft call sign to acknowledge all ATC clearances, frequency changes, or advisory information.

2-63 Reference. — AIM 260.

2-64 AMENDED CLEARANCES

a. A pilot has the privilege of requesting a different clearance from that which has been issued by ATC if he feels that he has information which would make another course of action more practicable or if aircraft equipment limitations or company procedures forbid compliance with the clearance issued.

b. Pilots may also request clarification or amendment, as appropriate, any time a clearance is not fully understood, or considered unacceptable from a safety standpoint. In such instances, controllers should, to the extent of operational practicality and safety, honor the pilot's request.

c. Amendments to the initial clearance will be issued at any time an air traffic controller deems such action necessary to avoid possible separation conflict between aircraft. Clearances may require that a flight change altitude, turn, or "hold" prior to reaching the point where standard separation from other traffic would no longer exist.

2-64 References. — ATCH 2-18; AIM 263.

2-65 EXPEDITIOUS INSTRUCTIONS

a. The word *"immediately"* is used by ATC only when expeditious compliance is required to avoid an imminent situation.

b. The word *"expedite"* is used by ATC only when prompt compliance is required to avoid the development of an imminent situation.

c. In either case and if time permits, the controller will include the reason for this action.

2-65 Examples. —

Cessna Four Two Golf, turn left, immediately.

United Six Fifty-three, expedite across Runway Three One, traffic on a one and one half mile final.

2-65 Reference. — ATCH 2-5.

2-66 SERVICE PRIORITIES

First priority is given to separating aircraft and issuing safety alerts as required in the *Air Traffic Control Handbook, Order 7110.65*. Good judgment is exercised by ATC in prioritizing all other provisions of the handbook based on the requirements of the situation at hand.*

2-66 Note. — Because there are many variables involved, it is virtually impossible to develop a standard list of service priorities that would apply uniformly to every conceivable situation. Each set of circumstances will be evaluated on its own merit and when more than one action is required, the controller will exercise his or her best judgment based on the facts and circumstances known. That action which is most critical from a safety standpoint will be performed first.

2-66 Reference. — ATCH 2-2.

2-67 ADDITIONAL SERVICES

The primary purpose of the ATC system is to prevent a collision between aircraft operating in the system and to organize and expedite the flow of traffic. In addition to its primary function, the ATC system has the capability to provide (with certain limitations) additional services. The ability to provide additional services is limited by many factors, such as the volume of traffic, frequency congestion, quality of radar, controller workload, higher priority duties, and the pure physical inability to scan and detect those situations that fall in this category. It is recognized that these services cannot be provided in cases in which the provision of services is precluded by the above factors. Consistent with the aforementioned conditions, controllers will provide additional service procedures to the extent permitted by higher priority duties and other circumstances. The provision of additional services is not optional on the part of the controller, but rather is required when the work situation permits.

2-67 Reference. — ATCH 2-2.

2-68 AIR TRAFFIC PRIORITY

Air traffic control service is provided to aircraft on a "first come, first served" basis as circumstances permit, except the following:*

a. Priority is provided to civilian air ambulance flights, (LIFEGUARD), to military air evacuation flights (AIR EVAC, MED EVAC), and scheduled air carrier/air taxi "LIFEGUARD" flights. Pilots of air ambulance/evacuation aircraft will be assisted by ATC to avoid areas of significant weather and turbulent conditions. When requested by a pilot, ATC will provide notifications to expedite ground handling of patients, vital organs, or urgently needed medical materials.

b. Maximum assistance is provided to SAR (search and rescue) aircraft performing a SAR mission.

c. Special handling is provided as required to expedite Flight Check and SAFI (semi-automated flight inspection) aircraft.*

d. The movement of Presidential aircraft and entourage and any rescue support aircraft will be expedited.*

e. IFR aircraft will have priority over SVFR aircraft.

2-68 Note. — Air Carrier/Air Taxi usage of "LIFEGUARD" callsign indicates that operational priority is requested.

2-68c Note. — It is recognized that unexpected wind conditions, weather, or heavy traffic flows may affect controller's ability to provide priority or special handling at the specific time requested.

2-68d Note. — As used herein the terms Presidential aircraft and entourage include aircraft and entourage of the President, Vice President, or other public figures when designated by the White House.

2-68 References. — FAR 91.67; ATCH 2-4.

2-69 LANDING PRIORITY

A clearance for a specific type of instrument approach (ILS, MLS, ADF, VOR, etc.) to an aircraft operating on an IFR flight plan does not mean that landing priority will be given over other traffic. ATCT's handle all aircraft, regardless of the type of flight plan, on a "first-come, first-served" basis. Therefore, because of local traffic or runway use, it may be necessary for the controller, in the interest of safety, to provide a different landing sequence. In any case, a landing sequence will be issued to each aircraft as soon as possible to enable the pilot to properly adjust his approach.

2-69 Reference. — AIM 386.

2-70 thru 2-79 RESERVED

Section 7. ADVISORIES

2-80 WAKE TURBULENCE CAUTIONARY ADVISORIES

a. Wake turbulence cautionary advisories and the position, altitude if known, and direction of flight of the heavy jets are issued to:

(1) TERMINAL: VFR aircraft not being radar vectored, but are behind heavy jets.

Arriving Aircraft

2-80a(1) Illustration

(2) IFR aircraft that accept a visual approach or visual separation.

(3) TERMINAL: VFR arriving aircraft that have previously been radar vectored and the vectoring has been discontinued.

b. Cautionary information is issued to any aircraft if in the controller's opinion wake turbulence may have an adverse effect on it. When traffic is known to be a heavy aircraft, the controller will include the word "heavy" in the description.*

ATC Phraseology:

Caution wake turbulence (traffic information).

2-80 Example. —

Twin Cessna Four Five Mike, Runway Two Seven Left cleared for takeoff. Caution wake turbulence departing heavy Boeing Seven Sixty-seven Runway Two Seven Right.

2-80b Note. — Wake turbulence may be encountered by aircraft in flight as well as when operating on the airport movement area. Because wake turbulence is unpredictable, the controller is not responsible for anticipating its existence or effect.

2-80 Reference. — ATCH 2-20.

2-81 WAKE TURBULENCE PROCEDURES

a. Wake turbulence procedures are applied to aircraft operating behind heavy jets and, where indicated, to small aircraft behind large aircraft.*

b. The separation minima will continue to touchdown for all IFR aircraft not making a visual approach or maintaining visual separation.

2-81a Note. — For the purposes of Wake Turbulence Separation Minima, ATC classifies aircraft as Heavy, Large, and Small as follows:

a. Heavy—Aircraft capable of takeoff weights of 300,000 pounds or more whether or not they are operating at this weight during a particular phase of flight.

b. Large—Aircraft of more than 12,500 pounds, maximum certificated takeoff weight, up to 300,000 pounds.

c. Small—Aircraft of 12,500 pounds or less maximum certificated takeoff weight.

2-81 Reference. — ATCH 2-19; ATCH & AIM Glossary.

2-82 PILOT RESPONSIBILITY — WAKE TURBULENCE

Pilots are reminded that acceptance of instructions from ATC in the following situations is an acknowledgment that the pilot will ensure safe takeoff and landing intervals and accepts the responsibility of providing his own wake turbulence separation.

a. Traffic information,

b. Instructions to follow an aircraft, and

c. The acceptance of a visual approach clearance.

2-82 Reference. — AIM 551.

2-83 VFR IN CONGESTED AREAS

A high percentage of near midair collisions occur below 8,000 feet AGL and within 30 miles of an airport. When operating VFR in these highly congested areas, whether landing at an airport within the area or transiting the area, it is recommended that extra vigilance be maintained and that pilots monitor an appropriate frequency.

2-83 Reference. — AIM 571.

2-84 TRAFFIC ADVISORIES

Pilots receiving radar service by ATC facilities are advised of any targets observed on the radar display when in the controller's judgment their proximity may diminish to less than the applicable separation minima, unless an aircraft is operating within the Positive Controlled Airspace or omission is requested. Where no separation minima applies, such as for VFR aircraft outside an ARSA, TRSA, or TCA, controllers will issue traffic advisories to those aircraft. *THIS SERVICE IS NOT INTENDED TO RELIEVE THE PILOT OF HIS RESPONSIBILITY FOR CONTINUED VIGILANCE TO SEE AND AVOID OTHER AIRCRAFT.* This service is provided as follows:

a. To radar identified aircraft:

(1) *Azimuth* from aircraft in terms of the 12-hour clock.

(2) *Distance* from aircraft in miles.

(3) *Direction* in which traffic is proceeding and/or relative movement of traffic.*

(4) If known, *type* of aircraft and *altitude*.

ATC Phraseology:

Traffic, (number) **o'clock** *or, when appropriate,* (direction), (number) **miles,** (direction)-**bound** *and/or* (relative movement), *and if known,* (type of aircraft and altitude).

If altitude is unknown,

Altitude unknown.

2-84a Examples. —

Traffic, eleven o'clock, one zero miles, southbound, converging, D-C-Eight, one seven thousand.

Traffic, twelve o'clock, one five miles, opposite direction, altitude unknown.

(5) For aircraft displaying Mode C, not radar identified, controllers will issue "indicated" altitude.

2-84a(5) Example. —

Traffic, one o'clock, six miles, eastbound, altitude indicates six thousand five hundred.

(6) When requested by the pilot, radar vectors will be issued to assist in avoiding the traffic, provided the aircraft to be vectored is within the controller's area of jurisdiction or coordination has been effected with the sector/facility in whose area the aircraft is operating. If unable to provide vectoring service, the controller will inform the pilot.

(7) When rapidly maneuvering civil test or military aircraft prevent accurate issuance of traffic as in (1) above, the direction is specified from an aircraft's position in terms of the eight cardinal compass points (N, NE, E, SE, S, SW, W, and NW). This method may be terminated at the pilot's request.

(8) If the pilot informs the controller he does not see the traffic issued, the controller will inform him when the traffic is no longer a factor.

ATC Phraseology:

Traffic no longer a factor, *or*

(number) **o'clock traffic no longer a factor,** *or*

(direction) **traffic no longer a factor.**

2-84a(8) Examples. —

Previously issued traffic no longer a factor.

Two o'clock traffic no longer a factor.

Northbound traffic no longer a factor.

b. To aircraft that are not radar identified:

(1) Distance and direction from fix.

(2) Direction in which traffic is proceeding.

(3) If known, type of aircraft and altitude.

(4) ETA over the fix the aircraft is approaching, if appropriate.

ATC Phraseology:

Traffic, (number) **miles/minutes** (direction) **of** (airport or fix), (direction)-**bound,** *and if known,* (type of aircraft and altitude), **estimated** (fix) (time), *or*

Traffic numerous targets vicinity (location).

If altitude is unknown,

Altitude unknown.

2-84b Examples. —

Traffic, numerous targets, vicinity of Van Nuys Airport.

Traffic, one zero miles east of Forsythe V-O-R, southbound, D-C-Eight, descending to one six thousand.

Traffic, reported one zero miles west of Downey V-O-R, northbound, Apache, altitude unknown, estimated Joliet V-O-R one three one five.

Traffic, eight minutes west of Chicago Heights V-O-R, westbound, Mooney, eight thousand, estimated Joliet V-O-R, two zero three five.

2-84a(3) Note. — Relative movement includes "closing," "converging," "parallel same direction," "opposite direction," "diverging," "overtaking," "crossing left to right," "crossing right to left."

2-84 Reference. — ATCH 2-21.

2-85 ACKNOWLEDGMENT OF TRAFFIC ADVISORIES

Pilots acknowledge traffic advisories with statements such as "looking," "in-sight," "traffic in-sight," "negative contact," etc.

2-85 Reference. — ATCH & AIM Glossary; AIM 409.

2-86 WIND EFFECT

The examples depicted in the following illustrations point out the possible error in the position of this traffic when it is necessary for a pilot to apply drift correction to maintain this track. This error could also occur in the event a change in course is made at the time radar traffic information is issued.

a. In this illustration traffic information would be issued to the pilot of aircraft "A" as 12 o'clock. The actual position of the traffic as seen by the pilot of aircraft "A" would be 2 o'clock. Traffic information issued to aircraft "B" would also be given as 12 o'clock, but in this case, the pilot of "B" would see his traffic at 10 o'clock.

2-86a Illustration

b. In this illustration traffic information would be issued to the pilot of aircraft "C" as 2 o'clock. The actual position of the traffic as seen by the pilot of aircraft "C" would be 3 o'clock. Traffic information issued to aircraft "D" would be at an 11 o'clock position. Since it is not necessary for the pilot of aircraft "D" to apply wind correction (crab) to make good his track, the actual position of the traffic issued would be correct. Since the radar controller can only observe aircraft track (course) on his radar display, he must give due consideration to this fact when looking for reported traffic.

2-86b Illustration

2-86 Reference. — AIM 163.

2-87 VISUAL SEPARATION

a. Pilots in a terminal area, receiving traffic advisories and/or other ATC services, may be asked to maintain visual separation from another aircraft under the facility's control provided the pilot sees the traffic and the controller instructs him to maintain visual separation from it. This is accomplished as follows:

(1) Controllers will tell the pilot about the traffic, including position, direction of flight, and, unless it is obvious, the other aircraft's intention.

(2) Controllers must then obtain acknowledgment from the pilot that the traffic is in sight.

(3) Controllers will then instruct the pilot to maintain visual separation from that traffic.

2-87a (1) thru (3) Example. —

Falcon Zero Delta Alpha, traffic two o'clock, two miles southbound descending out of two thousand three hundred, a Cherokee on final for Runway One Eight Right.

Falcon Zero Delta Alpha, traffic in sight.

Falcon Zero Delta Alpha, roger. Maintain visual separation with that traffic, descend and maintain two thousand.

Falcon Zero Delta Alpha, roger, maintain two thousand.

(4) If the aircraft are on converging courses, controllers will inform the other aircraft of the traffic and that visual separation is being applied.

ATC Phraseology:

Traffic (clock position and distance), (direction)-**bound**, (type of aircraft), (intentions and other relevant information).

If applicable,

On converging course. Do you have it in sight?

If the answer is in the affirmative,

Maintain visual separation from that traffic.

If aircraft are on converging courses, controllers will advise the other aircraft:

Traffic (clock position and distance), (direction)-**bound**, (type of aircraft). **Has you in sight and will maintain visual separation.**

2-87a(4) Example. —

Cactus Four Twelve, traffic twelve o'clock four miles southbound, a Southwest Seven Thirty-seven on base for Runway Eight Left, on converging course. Do you have it in sight?

Cactus Four Twelve, affirmative.

Cactus Four Twelve, maintain visual separation from that traffic.

Cactus Four Twelve, wilco.

Southwest Six Zero Four, traffic twelve o'clock, three miles, a Boeing Seven Thirty-seven has you in sight and will maintain visual separation.

Southwest Six Zero Four, roger.

b. Visual separation is a means employed by ATC to separate aircraft only in terminal areas. (Center controllers may use visual separation only in conjunction with visual approach procedures.) There are two methods employed to effect this separation:

(1) The tower controller sees the aircraft involved and issues instructions, as necessary, to ensure that the aircraft avoid each other.

(2) A pilot sees the other aircraft involved and, upon instructions from the controller, provides his own separation by maneuvering his aircraft to avoid it. This may involve following in-trail behind another aircraft or keeping it in sight until it is no longer a factor or other separation exists.

c. Other approved separation, i.e., vertical, radar, must be assured before and after the application of visual separation by ATC. Weather conditions must allow the aircraft to remain within sight until other separation exists.

d. A pilot's acceptance of instructions to follow another aircraft or provide visual separation from it is an acknowledgment that the pilot will maneuver his aircraft as necessary to avoid the other aircraft or to maintain in-trail separation. In operations conducted behind heavy jet aircraft, it is also an acknowledgment that the pilot accepts the responsibility for wake turbulence separation.

e. WHEN A PILOT HAS BEEN TOLD TO FOLLOW ANOTHER AIRCRAFT OR TO PROVIDE VISUAL SEPARATION FROM IT, HE SHOULD PROMPTLY NOTIFY THE CONTROLLER IF VISUAL CONTACT WITH THE OTHER AIRCRAFT IS LOST OR CANNOT BE MAINTAINED OR IF THE PILOT CANNOT ACCEPT THE RESPONSIBILITY FOR THE SEPARATION FOR ANY REASON.

f. Pilots have a regulatory responsibility (FAR 91.67(a)) to see and avoid other aircraft when weather conditions permit.

2-87 References. — ATCH 7-10; AIM 274.

2-88 SAFETY ALERT

A safety alert will be issued to an aircraft if the controller is aware the aircraft is at an altitude which, in his judgment, places it in unsafe proximity to terrain, obstructions, or other aircraft. Once the pilot informs the controller that action is being taken to resolve the situation, the controller may discontinue the issuance of further alerts.*

a. Terrain/Obstruction Alert—A controller will immediately issue/initiate an alert to an aircraft if he is aware the aircraft is at an altitude which, in his judgment, places it in unsafe proximity to terrain/obstructions. The alert will be issued as follows:

ATC Phraseology:

(Identification) **low altitude alert, check your altitude immediately. The** *as appropriate,* **MEA/MVA/MOCA/MIA in your area is** (altitude),

or if past the final approach fix (nonprecision approach) *or the outer marker or the fix used in lieu of the outer marker* (precision approach),

The, *as appropriate,* **MDA/DH** (if known) **is** (altitude).

2-88a Examples. —

Cessna Eight Six Tango low altitude alert, check your altitude immediately, the M-V-A in your area is three thousand one hundred.

Baron Five Eight Bravo low altitude alert, check your altitude immediately, the M-D-A is six hundred eighty.

b. Aircraft Conflict Alert—A controller will immediately issue/initiate an alert to an aircraft if he is aware of another aircraft at an altitude which he believes places the aircraft in unsafe proximity. If feasible, the controller will offer the pilot an alternate course of action.

ATC Phraseology:

(Identification) **traffic alert** (position of traffic if time permits), **advise you turn left/right** (specific headings, if appropriate),

and/or

climb/descend (specific altitude, if appropriate) **immediately.**

2-88b Example. —

Cessna One Zero Five, traffic alert, advise you turn left immediately!

2-88 Note 1. — The issuance of a safety alert is a first priority (see paragraph 2-66) once the controller observes and recognizes a situation of unsafe aircraft proximity to terrain, obstacles, or other aircraft. Conditions such as workload, traffic volume, the quality/limitations of the radar sysem, and the available lead time to react are factors in determining whether it is reasonable for the controller to observe and recognize such situations. While a controller cannot see immediately the development of every situation where a safety alert must be issued, the controller must remain vigilant for such situations and issue a safety alert when the situation is recognized.

2-88 Note 2. — Recognition of situations of unsafe proximity may result from MSAW/E-MSAW/LAAS, automatic altitude readouts, Conflict Alert, or pilot reports.

2-88 Note 3. — Once the alert is issued, it is solely the pilot's prerogative to determine what course of action, if any, he will take.

2-88 Note 4. — The issuance of a safety alert cannot be mandated, but it can be expected on a reasonable, though intermittent basis. Once the alert is issued, it is solely the pilot's prerogative to determine what course of action, if any, he will take. This procedure is intended for use in time-critical situations where aircraft safety is in question. Noncritical situations will be handled via the normal traffic advisory procedures.

2-88 References. — ATCH 2-6; AIM 163, 406.

2-89 MERGING TRAFFIC (TARGET) PROCEDURES

a. Except while they are established in a holding pattern, ATC will apply merging target procedures to all radar identified:

(1) Aircraft at 10,000 feet and above.

(2) Turbojet aircraft, regardless of altitude.

(3) Presidential aircraft, regardless of altitude.

b. Traffic information will be issued to those aircraft listed in **a** whose targets appear likely to merge unless the aircraft are separated by more than the appropriate vertical separation minima.

c. If the pilot requests, controllers will vector aircraft to avoid merging targets of previously issued traffic.*

d. If unable to provide vector service, the controller will inform the pilot.

2-89c Note. — Aircraft closure rates are so rapid that when applying merging target procedures, controller issuance of traffic must be commenced in ample time for the pilot to decide if a vector is necessary.

2-89 Reference. — ATCH 5-8.

2-90 TERMINATION OF TRAFFIC ADVISORIES

a. When advisory service is no longer desired, pilots should advise the controller before changing frequencies and then change their transponder code to 1200, if applicable.

2-90a Example. —

Cessna Seven Seven Eight is clear of the area, request frequency change.

Cessna Seven Seven Eight, roger. Radar service terminated, squawk one two zero zero, frequency change approved.

b. When a controller desires to terminate radar services to a VFR aircraft due to airspace limitations, workload, etc., he will inform the pilot and advise him to squawk the VFR code.

2-90b Example. —

Cessna Eight Eight Four, leaving my airspace. Radar service terminated, squawk one two zero zero, frequency change approved.

2-90 References. — ATCH 5-13, 5-29; AIM 163.

2-91 thru 2-99 RESERVED

Section 8. USER REPORTS AND PILOT ADVISORIES

2-100 SAFETY OF FLIGHT INFORMATION

a. The pilot in command of each aircraft operated under IFR in controlled airspace shall have a continuous watch maintained on the appropriate frequency and shall report the following safety information by radio as soon as possible:

(1) Any unforecast weather conditions encountered; and

(2) Any other information relating to the safety of flight.

b. ATC must report as soon as possible to the appropriate FSS, airport manager's office, ARTCC, approach control facility, operations office, or military operations office any information concerning components of the NAS or any flight conditions which may have an adverse effect on air safety.*

2-100b Note. — FSS's are responsible for classifying and disseminating Notices to Airmen.

2-100 References. — FAR 91.125; ATCH 2-9; AIM 342.

2-101 USER REPORTS ON NAVAID PERFORMANCE

a. Users of the National Airspace System (NAS) can render valuable assistance in the early correction of NAVAID malfunctions by reporting their observations of undesirable NAVAID performance. Although NAVAID's are monitored by electronic detectors, adverse effects of electronic interference, new obstructions, or changes in terrain near the NAVAID can exist without detection by the ground monitors. Some of the characteristics of malfunction or deteriorating performance which should be reported include: erratic course or bearing indications; intermittent, or full, flag alarm; garbled, missing, or obviously improper coded identification; poor quality communications reception; or, in the case of frequency interference, an audible hum or tone accompanying radio communications or NAVAID identification.

b. Pilot reports should identify the NAVAID, location of the aircraft at the time of the observation, type of aircraft, and describe the condition observed. Reports can be made in any of the following ways:

(1) Immediate report by direct radio communication to the controlling Air Route Traffic Control Center (ARTCC), Control Tower, or FSS. This method provides the quickest result.

(2) By telephone to the nearest FAA facility.

(3) By FAA Form 8000-7, Safety Improvement Report. This is a self-addressed, postage-paid card designed for this purpose. These cards may be obtained at FSS's, Flight Standards and General Aviation District Offices, and General Aviation Fixed Base Operations.

c. In aircraft that have more than one transceiver, there are many combinations of possible interference between units. This can cause either erroneous navigation indications, or complete or partial blanking out of communications. Pilots should be familiar enough with the radio installation of the particular airplanes they fly to recognize this type of interference.

2-101 Reference. — AIM 19.

2-102 NAVAID MALFUNCTION REPORTS

When an aircraft reports a NAVAID malfunction, the controller will take the following actions:

a. Request a report from a second aircraft.

b. If the second aircraft reports normal operations, continue use, and inform the first aircraft.

c. If the second aircraft confirms the malfunction or in the absence of a second aircraft report, the controller will activate the standby equipment.

2-102 Reference. — ATCH 2-10.

2-103 AIRCRAFT EQUIPMENT MALFUNCTION REPORTS

a. The pilot in command of each aircraft operated in controlled airspace under IFR, shall report immediately to ATC any of the following malfunctions of equipment ocurring in flight:

(1) Loss of VOR, TACAN, ADF, or low frequency navigation receiver capability.

(2) Complete or partial loss of ILS receiver capability.

(3) Impairment of communications capability.

b. In each report required by paragraph **a**, the pilot in command must include:*

(1) Aircraft identification,

(2) Equipment affected,

(3) Degree to which the capability of the pilot to operate under IFR in the ATC system is impaired, and

(4) Nature and extent of assistance he desires from ATC.

2-103b Note. — Other equipment installed in an aircraft may effectively impair safety and/or the ability to operate under IFR. If such equipment, e.g., airborne weather radar, malfunctions and in the pilot's judgment either safety or IFR capabilities are affected, reports should be made as above.

2-103 References. — FAR 91.129; AIM 342.

2-104 AIRCRAFT EQUIPMENT MALFUNCTIONS — ATC ACTION

When a pilot reports an in-flight equipment malfunction, the controller will:

a. Determine the nature and extent of any special handling desired.

b. Provide the maximum assistance possible consistent with equipment, workload, and any special handling requested.

c. Relay to other controllers or facilities who will subsequently handle the aircraft all pertinent details concerning the aircraft and any special handling required or being provided.

2-104 Reference. — ATCH 2-7.

2-105 MINIMUM FUEL ADVISORY

If an aircraft declares a state of "minimum fuel," the controller must inform any facility to whom control jurisdiction is transferred of the minimum fuel problem and be alert for any occurrence which might delay the aircraft en route.*

2-105 Note. — Use of the term "minimum fuel" indicates recognition by a pilot that his fuel supply has reached a state where, upon reaching destination, he cannot accept any undue delay. This is not an emergency situation but merely an advisory that indicates an emergency situation is possible should any undue delay occur. A minimum fuel advisory does not imply a need for traffic priority. Common sense and good judgment will determine the extent of assistance to be given in minimum fuel situations. If, at any time, the remaining usable fuel supply suggests the need for traffic priority to ensure a safe landing, the pilot should declare an emergency and report fuel remaining in minutes.

2-105 Reference. — ATCH 2-8.

2-106 PILOT ADVISORIES ON BIRD AND OTHER WILDLIFE HAZARDS

Many airports advise pilots of other wildlife hazards caused by large animals on the runway through the Airport/Facility Directory and the NOTAM system. Collisions of landing and departing aircraft and animals on the runway are increasing and are not limited to rural airports. These accidents have also occurred at several major airports. Pilots should exercise extreme caution when warned of the presence of wildlife on and in the vicinity of airports.

2-106 Reference. — AIM 564.

2-107 REPORTING BIRD AND OTHER WILDLIFE ACTIVITIES

If a pilot observes birds or other animals on or near the runway, he should request airport management to disperse the wildlife before taking off. He should also contact the nearest ARTCC, FSS, or tower regarding large flocks of birds and report the—

(1) Geographic location,

(2) Bird type (geese, ducks, gulls, etc.),

(3) Approximate numbers,

(4) Altitude, and

(5) Direction of bird flight path.

2-107 Reference. — AIM 563.

2-108 UNMANNED BALLOONS

Pilots are urged to report any unmanned free balloons sighted to the nearest ATC facility with which communication is established. Such information will assist ATC facilities to identify and flight follow unmanned free balloons operating in the airspace.

2-108 Reference. — AIM 573.

2-109 NEAR MIDAIR COLLISION REPORTING

a. The primary purpose of the Near Midair Collision (NMAC) Reporting Program is to provide information for use in enhancing the safety and efficiency of the National Airspace System. Data obtained from NMAC reports are used by the FAA to improve the quality of FAA services to users and to develop programs, policies, and procedures aimed at the reduction of NMAC occurrences. All NMAC reports are thoroughly investigated by Flight Standards Facilities in coordination with Air Traffic Facilities. Data from these investigations are transmitted to FAA headquarters in Washington, D.C. where they are compiled and analyzed, and where safety programs and recommendations are developed.

b. A near midair collison is defined as an incident associated with the operation of an aircraft in which a possibility of collision occurs as a result of proximity of less than 500 feet to another aircraft, or a report is received from a pilot or a flight crew member stating that a collision hazard existed between two or more aircraft.

c. It is the responsibility of the pilot and/or flight crew to determine whether a near midair collision did actually occur and, if so, to initiate a NMAC report. Be specific, as ATC will not interpret a casual remark to mean that a NMAC is being reported.

d. Pilots and/or flight crew members involved in NMAC occurrences are urged to report each incident immediately:

(1) By radio or telephone to the nearest FAA ATC facility or FSS.

(2) In writing, in lieu of the above, to the nearest Air Carrier District Office (ACDO), General Aviation District Office (GADO), or Flight Standards District Office (FSDO).

e. Items to be reported:

(1) Date and Time (UTC) of incident.

(2) Location of incident and altitude.

(3) Identification and type of reporting aircraft, aircrew destination, name and home base of pilot.

(4) Identification and type of other aircraft, aircrew destination, name and home base of pilot.

(5) Type of flight plans; station altimeter setting used.

(6) Detailed weather conditions at altitude or flight level.

(7) Approximate courses of both aircraft; indicate if one or both aircraft were climbing or descending.

(8) Reported separation in distance at first sighting, proximity at closest point horizontally and vertically, length of time in sight prior to evasive action.

(9) Degree of evasive action taken, if any (from both aircraft, if possible).

(10) Injuries, if any.

f. An investigation will be conducted and will focus on existing radar, communication, and weather data. When possible, all cockpit crew members will be interviewed regarding factors involving the NMAC incident. Air traffic controllers will be interviewed in cases where one or more of the involved aircraft was provided ATC service. Both flight and ATC procedures will be evaluated. When the investigation reveals a violation of an FAA regulation, enforcement action will be pursued.

g. The district office responsible for the investigation and reporting of NMAC's will be:

(1) The Air Carrier or Flight Standards District Office in whose area the incident occurred when an air carrier aircraft is involved.

(2) The Flight Standards or General Aviation District Office in whose area the incident occurred in all other cases.

2-109 Reference. — AIM 582.

2-110 AVIATION SAFETY REPORTING PROGRAM

a. The FAA has established a voluntary Aviation Safety Reporting Program designed to stimulate the free and unrestricted flow of information concerning deficiencies and discrepancies in the aviation system. This is a positive program intended to ensure the safest possible system by identifying and correcting unsafe conditions before they lead to accidents. The primary objective of the program is to obtain information to evaluate and enhance the safety and efficiency of the present system.

b. This program applies primarily to that part of the system involving the safety of aircraft operations, including departure, en route, approach and landing operations and procedures, ATC procedures, pilot/controller communications, the aircraft movement area of the airport, and near midair collisions. Pilots, air traffic controllers, and all other members of the aviation community and the general public are asked to file written reports of any discrepancy or deficiency noted in these areas.

c. The report should give the date, time, location, persons and aircraft involved (if applicable), nature of the event, and all pertinent details.

d. To ensure receipt of this information, the program provides for the waiver of certain disciplinary actions against persons, including pilots and air traffic controllers, who file timely written reports concerning potentially unsafe incidents. To be considered timely, reports must be delivered or postmarked within 10 days of the incident, unless that period is extended for good cause. Reporting forms are available at FAA facilities.

e. The FAA utilizes the National Aeronautics and Space Administration (NASA) to act as an independent third party to receive and analyze reports submitted under the program. This program is described in ADVISORY CIRCULAR–00-46.

2-110 Reference. — AIM 580.

2-111 thru 2-119 RESERVED

Section 9. WEATHER INFORMATION

2-120 SIGMET OR CWA ALERT

a. A SIGMET (significant meteorological information) or CWA (center weather advisory) alert is broadcast once on all frequencies, except emergency, when any part of the area described is within 150 miles of the airspace under the controller's jurisdiction. The broadcast is not required if aircraft on the controller's frequency/s will not be affected.

b. Terminal facilities have the option to limit the SIGMET or CWA broadcast as follows: Tower cab and approach control positions may opt to broadcast SIGMET or CWA alerts only when any part of the area described is within 50 miles of the airspace under their jurisdiction.

c. The following information is included in SIGMET and CWA broadcasts:

(1) SIGMET or CWA ident.

(2) The term "convective" when applicable.

(3) General description of the area affected.

(4) Brief description of the type of weather.*

ATC Phraseology:

Attention all aircraft, SIGMET/Convective SIGMET/Center Weather Advisory (ident). (Brief description of area affected and type of weather.)

2-120 Examples. —

Attention all aircraft, SIGMET Delta Three. From Myton to Tuba City to Milford. Severe turbulence and severe clear icing below one zero thousand. Expected to continue beyond zero three zero zero Zulu.

Attention all aircraft, Convective SIGMET Two Seven Eastern. From the vicinity of Elmira to Phillipsburg. Scattered embedded thunderstorms moving east at one zero knots. A few intense level five cells, maximum tops flight level four five zero.

Attention all aircraft, Kansas City Center Weather Advisory Zero Three. Numerous reports of moderate to severe icing eight thousand through niner thousand, three zero mile radius of St. Louis. Light or negative icing reported four thousand through one two thousand remainder of Kansas City Center area.

2-120c(4) Note. — The description will be brief but contain enough information to alert pilots to significant weather conditions along their route of flight and to enable them to decide whether they should contact an FSS for more detailed information.

2-120 References. — ATCH 2-101; AIM 504, 508.

2-121 HAZARDOUS IN-FLIGHT WEATHER ADVISORY SERVICE

a. HIWAS (hazardous in-flight weather advisory service) is a continuous broadcast of in-flight weather advisories including summarized AWW (severe weather forecasts alerts), SIGMET's, Convective SIGMET's, CWA's, AIRMET's (airman's meteorological information) and urgent PIREP's (pilot reports). In those areas where HIWAS is commissioned, ARTCC, Terminal ATC, and FSS facilities have discontinued the broadcast of in-flight advisories. HIWAS is an additional source of hazardous weather information which makes these data available on a continuous basis. It is not, however, a replacement for preflight or in-flight briefings or real-time weather updates from Flight Watch (EFAS). As HIWAS is implemented in individual ARTCC areas, the commissioning will be advertised in the Notices to Airmen (Class II) Publication.

b. Where HIWAS has been implemented — A HIWAS alert will be broadcast on all except emergency frequencies once upon receipt by ARTCC and terminal facilities which will include an alert announcement, frequency instruction, number, and type of advisory updated, e.g., AWW, SIGMET, Convective SIGMET, or CWA.

2-121b Example. —

Attention all aircraft, monitor HIWAS or contact a flight service station on frequency one two two point zero or one two two point two for new convective SIGMET information.

2-121 Reference. — AIM 508.

2-122 PIREP INFORMATION

Significant PIREP information includes reports of strong frontal activity, squall lines, thunderstorms, light to severe icing, wind shear and turbulence (including clear air turbulence) of moderate or greater intensity, or other conditions pertinent to flight safety.

a. Controllers will solicit PIREP's when requested or when one of the following conditions exists or is forecast for their area of jurisdiction:

(1) Ceilings at or below 5,000 feet. These PIREP's will include cloud base/top reports when feasible. TERMINAL: Controllers will ensure that at least one descent/climbout PIREP, including cloud base/s, top/s, and other related phenomena, is obtained each hour when there is a ceiling at or below 5,000 feet.

(2) Visibility (surface or aloft) at or less than 5 miles.

(3) Thunderstorms and related phenomena.

(4) Turbulence of moderate degree or greater.

(5) Icing of light degree or greater.

(6) Wind shear.

(7) TERMINAL: Braking Action Advisories in effect.

b. Recorded with the PIREP's are:

(1) Time.

(2) Aircraft position.

(3) Type aircraft.

(4) Altitude.

c. PIREP's are obtained directly from the pilot, or if the PIREP has been requested by another facility, the controller may instruct the pilot to deliver it directly to that facility.

ATC Phraseology:

Request flight conditions: at present position, *or*

over (fix), *or*

along present route, *or*

between (fix) *and* (fix).

d. Some of the uses made of the reports are:

(1) The ATCT uses the reports to expedite the flow of air traffic in the vicinity of the field and for hazardous weather avoidance procedures.

(2) The FSS uses the reports to brief other pilots, to provide in-flight advisories, and weather avoidance information to en route aircraft.

(3) The ARTCC uses the reports to expedite the flow of en route traffic, to determine most favorable altitudes, and to issue hazardous weather information within the Center's area.

(4) The NWS (National Weather Service) uses the reports to verify or amend conditions contained in aviation forecast and advisories. In some cases, pilot reports of hazardous conditions are the triggering mechanism for the issuance of advisories. They also use the reports for pilot weather briefings.

(5) The NWS, other government organizations, the military, and private industry groups use PIREP's for research activities in the study of meteorological phenomena.

(6) All air traffic facilities and the NWS forward the reports received from pilots into the weather distribution system to assure the information is made available to all pilots and other interested parties.

e. Pilots should not be overly concerned with strict PIREP format or phraseology. The important thing is that the information is relayed so other pilots may benefit from the observation. If a portion of the report needs clarification, the controller will request the information.

2-122 References. — ATCH 2-102; AIM 520.

2-123 PIREP'S RELATING TO TURBULENCE

When encountering turbulence, pilots are urgently requested to report such conditions to ATC as soon as practicable. PIREP's relating to turbulence should state:

a. Aircraft location.

b. Time of occurrence in UTC.

c. Turbulence intensity.

d. Whether the turbulence occurred in or near clouds.

e. Aircraft altitude, or flight level.

f. Type of aircraft.

g. Duration of turbulence.

2-123 Reference. — AIM 522.

2-124 PIREP'S RELATING TO AIRFRAME ICING

Pilots should report icing to ATC, and if operating IFR, request new routing or altitude if icing will be a hazard. Pilots should be sure to give type of aircraft to ATC when reporting icing.

2-124 Reference. — AIM 521.

2-125 WIND SHEAR REPORTS

a. Because unexpected changes in wind speed and direction can be hazardous to aircraft operations at low altitudes on approach to and departing from airports, pilots are urged to promptly volunteer reports to controllers of wind shear conditions they encounter. An advance warning of this information will assist other pilots in avoiding or coping with a wind shear on approach or departure.

b. When describing conditions, use of the terms "negative" or "positive" wind shear should be avoided. PIREP's of *"negative* wind shear on final," intended to describe loss of airspeed and lift, have been interpreted to mean that *no* wind shear was encountered. The recommended method for wind shear reporting is to state the loss or gain of airspeed and the altitudes at which it was encountered.

2-125b Examples. —

Cessna One Two Three Four encountered wind shear, loss of two zero knots at four hundred feet.

American Seven Twenty-one encountered wind shear on final. Gained two five knots between six hundred and four hundred feet followed by loss of four zero knots between four hundred feet and the surface.

(1) Pilots who are not able to report wind shear in these specific terms are encouraged to make reports in terms of the effect upon their aircraft.

2-125b(1) Example. —

Gulfstream Four Zero Three Charlie encountered an abrupt wind shear at eight hundred feet on final, max thrust required.

(2) Pilots using Inertial Navigation Systems (INS) should report the wind and altitude both above and below the shear level.

2-125 Reference. — AIM 523.

2-126 CLEAR AIR TURBULENCE PIREP'S

CAT (clear air turbulence) has become a very serious operational factor to flight operations at all levels and especially to jet traffic flying in excess of 15,000 feet. The best available information on this phenomenon must come from pilots via the PIREP reporting procedures. All pilots encountering CAT conditions are urgently requested to report *time, location,* and *intensity* (light, moderate, severe, or extreme) of the element to the facility with which they are maintaining radio contact. If time and conditions permit, elements should be reported according to the standards for other PIREP's and position reports.

2-126 Reference. — AIM 524.

2-127 RADAR SERVICE FOR VFR AIRCRAFT IN DIFFICULTY

a. Radar equipped ATC facilities can provide radar assistance and navigation service (vectors) to VFR aircraft in difficulty when the pilot can talk with the controller and the aircraft is within radar coverage. Pilots should clearly understand that authorization to proceed in accordance with such radar navigational assistance does not constitute authorization for the pilot to violate FAR's. In effect, assistance is provided on the basis that navigational guidance information is advisory in nature, and the responsibility for flying the aircraft safely remains with the pilot.

b. Experience has shown that many pilots who are not qualified for instrument flight cannot maintain control of their aircraft when they encounter clouds or other reduced visibility conditions. In many cases, the controller will not know whether flight into instrument conditions will result from his instructions. To avoid possible hazards resulting from being vectored into IFR conditions, a pilot in difficulty should keep the controller advised of the weather conditions in which he is operating and the weather along the course ahead and observe the following:

(1) If a course of action is available which will permit flight and a safe landing in VFR weather conditions, non-instrument rated pilots should choose the VFR condition rather than requesting a vector or approach that will take them into IFR weather conditions; or

(2) If continued flight in VFR conditions is not possible, the noninstrument rated pilot should so advise the controller and indicate the lack of an instrument rating, declare a *distress* condition, or

(3) If the pilot is instrument rated and current, and the aircraft is instrument equipped, the pilot should so indicate by requesting an IFR flight clearance. Assistance will then be provided on the basis that the aircraft can operate safely in IFR weather conditions.

2-127 Reference. — AIM 450.

2-128 ATC RADAR WEATHER DISPLAY

a. Areas of radar weather clutter result from rain or moisture. ATC radars cannot detect turbulence. The determination of the intensity of the weather displayed is based on its precipitation density. Generally, the turbulence associated with a very heavy rate of rainfall will normally be more severe than any associated with a very light rainfall rate.

b. ARTCC's Narrowband Radar provides the controller with two distinct levels of weather intensity by assigning radar display symbols for specific precipitation densities measured by the narrowband system.

2-128 Reference. — AIM 511.

2-129 WEATHER AVOIDANCE ASSISTANCE

a. To the extent possible, controllers will issue pertinent information on weather or chaff areas and assist pilots in avoiding such areas when requested. Pilots should respond to a weather advisory by either acknowledging the advisory or by acknowledging the advisory and requesting an alternative course of action as follows:

(1) Request to deviate off course by stating the number of miles and the direction of the requested deviation. In this case, when the requested deviation is approved, the pilot is expected to provide his own navigation, maintain the altitude assigned by ATC, and to remain within the specified mileage of his original course.

(2) Request a new route to avoid the affected area.

(3) Request a change of altitude.

(4) Request radar vectors around the affected areas.

b. For obvious reasons of safety, an IFR pilot must not deviate from the course, or altitude, or flight level without a proper ATC clearance. When weather conditions encountered are so severe that an immediate deviation is determined to be necessary and time will not permit approval by ATC, the pilot's emergency authority may be exercised.

c. When the pilot requests clearance for a route deviation or for an ATC radar vector, the controller must evaluate the air traffic picture in the affected area and coordinate with other controllers (if ATC jurisdictional boundaries may be crossed) before replying to the request.

d. It should be remembered that the controller's primary function is to provide safe separation between aircraft. Any additional service, such as weather avoidance assistance, can only be provided to the extent that it does not derogate the primary function. It is also worth noting that the separation workload is generally greater than normal when weather disrupts the usual flow of traffic. ATC radar limitations and frequency congestion may also be a factor in limiting the controller's capability to provide additional service.

e. It is very important, therefore, that the request for deviation or radar vector be made as far in advance as possible. Delays may preclude ATC approval or require that additional restrictions be placed on the clearance.

f. To a large degree, the assistance that might be rendered by ATC will depend upon the weather information available to controllers. Due to the extremely transitory nature of severe weather situations, the controller's weather information may be of only limited value if based on weather observed on radar only. Frequent updates by pilots giving specific information as to the area affected, altitudes, intensity, and nature of the severe weather can be of considerable value. Such reports are relayed by radio or telephone to other pilots and controllers and also receive widespread computer dissemination.

g. Obtaining an IFR clearance or an ATC radar vector to circumnavigate severe weather can often be accommodated more readily in the en route areas away from terminals because there is usually less congestion and, therefore, offer greater freedom of action. In terminal areas, the problem is more acute because of traffic density, ATC coordination requirements, complex departure and arrival routes, adjacent airports, etc. As a consequence, controllers are less likely to be able to accommodate all requests for weather detours in a terminal area or be in a position to volunteer such routing to the pilot. Nevertheless, pilots should not hesitate to advise controllers of any observed severe weather and should specifically advise controllers if they desire circumnavigation of observed weather.

2-129 Reference. — AIM 511.

2-130 WEATHER AND CHAFF DEVIATION

a. Radar navigational guidance and/or deviation will be provided around weather or chaff areas when requested by the pilot. The word "turbulence" is not used in describing radar-derived weather.

ATC Phraseology:

Deviation approved (restrictions if necessary), **advise when able to:**

return to course,

or

resume normal navigation,

or

fly heading (heading),

or

proceed direct to (name of NAVAID).

2-130a Example. —

United Four Twenty-six, request twenty degrees right to avoid a build-up.

United Four Twenty-six, deviation approved. Advise when able to proceed direct Miami.

(1) Weather and chaff information is issued by defining the area of coverage in terms of azimuth (by referring to the 12-hour clock) and distance from the aircraft, or by indicating the general width of the area and the area of coverage in terms of fixes or distance and direction from fixes.

ATC Phraseology:

Weather/Chaff area between (number) **o'clock and** (number) **o'clock** (number) **miles,**

or

(number) **mile band of weather/chaff from** (fix or number of miles and direction from fix) **to** (fix or number of miles and direction from fix),

or

(level number and intensity adjective) **weather echo between** (number) **o'clock and** (number) **o'clock,** (number) **miles. Moving** (direction) **at** (number) **knots, tops** (altitude).

2-130a(1) Example. —

Level five intense weather echo between eleven o'clock and one o'clock, one zero miles. Moving east at two zero knots, tops flight level three niner zero.

(2) When a deviation cannot be approved as requested and the situation permits, an alternative course of action may be suggested.

ATC Phraseology:

Unable deviation (possible alternate courses of action).

b. In areas of significant weather, controllers will plan ahead and be prepared to suggest, upon pilot request, the use of alternative routes/altitudes.*

2-130b Note 1. — Weather significant to the safety of aircraft includes such conditions as tornadoes, lines of thunderstorms, embedded thunderstorms, large hail, wind shear, moderate to extreme turbulence (including CAT), and light to severe icing.

2-130b Note 2. — Phraseology using level number and intensity adjective is only applicable when the radar weather echo intensity information is determined by NWS radar equipment.

2-130 Reference. — ATCH 2-103.

2-131 CALM WIND DESCRIPTION

TERMINAL

The wind will be described as calm when the wind velocity is less than three knots.

2-131 Reference. — ATCH 2-104.

2-132 PREVAILING VISIBILITY REPORTS

When the prevailing visibility at the usual point of observation or at the tower level is less than 4 miles, tower personnel will take prevailing visibility observations and apply the observations as follows:

The lower of the two observations (tower or surface) is used for aircraft operations.

2-132 Reference. — ATCH 2-105.

2-133 DISSEMINATION OF GENERAL WEATHER INFORMATION

General weather information, such as "large breaks in the overcast," "visibility lowering to the south," or similar statements which do not include specific values, and any elements derived directly from instruments, pilots, or radar, may be transmitted to pilots or other ATC facilities without controllers consulting the weather reporting station.

2-133 Reference. — ATCH 2-106.

2-134 thru 2-139 RESERVED

Section 10. ALTIMETER SETTINGS

2-140 ALTIMETER SETTINGS

a. Each person operating an aircraft shall maintain the cruising altitude or flight level of that aircraft, as the case may be, by reference to an altimeter that is set, when operating—

(1) Below 18,000 feet MSL, to—

(i) The current reported altimeter setting of a station along the route and within 100 nautical miles of the aircraft;

(ii) If there is no station within the area prescribed in subdivision (i) of this subparagraph, the current reported altimeter setting of an appropriate available station; or

(iii) In the case of an aircraft not equipped with a radio, the elevation of the departure airport or an appropriate altimeter setting available before departure; or

(2) At or above 18,000 feet MSL, to 29.92" Hg.

b. The lowest usable flight level is determined by the atmospheric pressure in the area of operation, as shown in the following table:

Current Altimeter Setting	Lowest Usable Flight Level
29.92 (or higher)	180
29.91 thru 29.42	185
29.41 thru 28.92	190
28.91 thru 28.42	195
28.41 thru 27.92	200
27.91 thru 27.42	205
27.41 thru 26.92	210

c. To convert minimum altitude prescribed under FAR's 91.79 and 91.119 to the minimum flight level, the pilot shall take the flight-level equivalent of the minimum altitude in feet and add the appropriate number of feet specified below, according to the current reported altimeter setting:

Current Altimeter Setting	Adjustment Factor (feet)
29.92 or (higher)	None
29.91 thru 29.42	500
29.41 thru 28.92	1000
28.91 thru 28.42	1500
28.41 thru 27.92	2000
27.91 thru 27.42	2500
27.41 thru 26.92	3000

2-140 Reference. — FAR 91.81.

2-141 CURRENT SETTINGS

a. Current altimeter settings will be obtained from direct-reading instruments or directly from weather reporting stations.*

b. If a pilot requests the altimeter setting in millibars, controllers will request from the nearest weather reporting station the equivalent millibar setting.

2-141a Note. — The term "current" does not apply to altimeter settings reported or received as "estimated."

2-141 Reference. — ATCH 2-110.

2-142 ALTIMETER ISSUANCE

a. TERMINAL: The source of an altimeter setting will be identified when issued for a location other than the aircraft's departure or destination airport.

b. EN ROUTE: The source of all altimeter settings will be identified when issued.

ATC Phraseology:

The (facility name) (time of report if more than one hour old) **altimeter** (setting).

c. The altimeter setting will be issued:

(1) To en route aircraft at least one time while operating in the controller's area of jurisdiction. The setting for the nearest reporting station along the aircraft's route of flight will be issued.*

(2) TERMINAL: To all departures. Unless specifically requested by the pilot, the altimeter setting need not be issued to local aircraft operators who have requested this omission in writing or to scheduled air carriers.

(3) TERMINAL: To arriving aircraft on initial contact or as soon as possible thereafter. The tower may omit the altimeter if the aircraft is sequenced or vectored to the airport by the approach control having jurisdiction at that facility.

(4) EN ROUTE: For the destination airport to arriving aircraft approximately 50 miles from the destination if an approach control facility does not serve the airport.

d. If the altimeter setting must be obtained by the pilot of an arriving aircraft from another source, controllers will instruct the pilot to obtain the altimeter setting from that source.*

e. When issuing clearance to descend below the lowest usable flight level, controllers will advise the pilot of the altimeter setting of the weather reporting station nearest the point the aircraft will descend below that flight level.

f. When the barometric pressure is greater than 31.00" Hg., controllers will issue an altimeter setting of 31.00. The controller will issue actual barometric pressure if the pilot requests it, then restate the altimeter setting of 31.00.

2-142c(1) Note. — FAR 91.81(1) requires that the pilot set his altimeter to the setting of a station along his route of flight within 100 miles of the aircraft if one is available. However, issuance of the setting of an adjacent station during periods that a steep gradient exists serves to inform the pilot of the difference between the setting he is using and the pressure in the local area and better enable him to choose a more advantageous setting within the limitations of FAR 91.81.

2-142d Note 1. — The destination altimeter setting, whether from a local or remote source, is the setting upon which the instrument approach is predicated.

2-142d Note 2. — Approach charts for many locations specify the source of altimeter settings at nonFAA facilities, such as UNICOM's.

2-142 Reference. — ATCH 2-111.

2-143 thru 2-149 RESERVED

Section 11. RUNWAY VISIBILITY REPORTING

2-150 RUNWAY VISUAL RANGE

a. RVR (runway visual range) visibility values are measured by transmissometers mounted on towers along the runway. A full RVR system consists of:

(1) Transmissometer projector and related items.

(2) Transmissometer receiver (detector) and related items.

(3) Analogue recorder.

(4) Signal data converter and related items.

(5) Remote digital or remote display programmer.

b. The transmissometer projector and receiver are mounted on towers either 250 or 500 feet apart. A known intensity of light is emitted from the projector and is measured by the receiver. Any obscuring matter such as rain, snow, dust, fog, haze, or smoke reduces the light intensity arriving at the receiver. The resultant intensity measurement is then converted to an RVR value by the signal data converter. These values are displayed by readout equipment in the associated air traffic facility and updated approximately once every minute for controller issuance to pilots.

c. The signal data converter receives information on the high intensity runway edge light setting in use (step 3, 4, or 5); transmission values from the transmissometer, and the sensing of day or night conditions. From the three data sources, the system will compute appropriate RVR values. Due to variable conditions, the reported RVR values may deviate somewhat from the true observed visual range due to the slant range consideration, brief time delays between the observed RVR conditions and the time they are transmitted to the pilot, and rapidly changing visibility conditions.

d. An RVR transmissometer established on a 500 foot baseline provides digital readouts to a minimum of 1,000 feet. A system established on a 250 foot baseline provides digital readouts to a minimum of 600 feet, which are displayed in 200 foot increments to 3,000 feet and in 500 foot increments from 3,000 feet to a maximum value of 6,000 feet.

e. Ten minute maximum and minimum RVR values for the designated RVR runway are reported in the remarks section of the aviation weather report when the prevailing visibility is less than one mile and/or the RVR is 6,000 feet or less. ATCT's report RVR when the prevailing visibility is 1 mile or less and/or the RVR is 6,000 feet or less.

f. Details on the requirements for the operational use of RVR are contained in *FAA ADVISORY CIRCULAR–97-1, "RUNWAY VISUAL RANGE."* Pilots are responsible for compliance with minimums prescribed for their class of operations in appropriate FAR's and/or operations specifications.

2-150 Reference. — AIM 512.

2-151 ARRIVAL/DEPARTURE RUNWAY VISIBILITY

a. Current touchdown RVR/RVV (runway visibility value) is issued for the runway/s in use:

(1) When prevailing visibility is 1 mile or less, regardless of the value indicated.

(2) When RVR/RVV indicates a reportable value, regardless of the prevailing visibility.*

(3) When the observer has reliable reports, or has otherwise determined that the instrument values are not representative of the associated runway, the data will not be used.*

b. Mid/rollout RVR is issued when the value of either is less than 2,000 feet and less than touchdown value.

2-151a(2) Note. — Reporting values are: RVR 6,000 feet or less; RVV 1½ miles or less.

2-151a(3) Note. — A reliable source is considered to be a certified weather observer, air traffic controller, flight service specialist, or pilot.

2-151 Reference. — ATCH 2-121.

2-152 RVR/RVV REPORTING TERMINOLOGY

a. RVR/RVV information is provided by controllers stating the runway, the abbreviation RVR/RVV, and the indicated value. When issued along with other weather elements, controllers will transmit these values in the normal sequence used for weather reporting.

2-152a Examples. —

Runway One Four R-V-R two thousand four hundred.

Runway Three Two R-V-V three quarters.

b. When two or more RVR systems serve the runway in use, the indicated values for the different systems are reported in terms of touchdown, mid, and rollout as appropriate.

2-152b Examples. —

Runway Two Two Left R-V-R two thousand, rollout one thousand eight hundred.

Runway Two Seven Right R-V-R one thousand, mid eight hundred, rollout six hundred.

c. When there is a requirement to issue an RVR or RVV value and a visibility condition greater or less than the reportable values of the equipment is indicated, the condition is stated as *"MORE THAN"* or *"LESS THAN"* the appropriate minimum or maximum readable value.

2-152c Examples. —

Runway Three Six R-V-R more than six thousand.

Runway Niner R-V-R one thousand, rollout less than six hundred.

d. When a readout indicates a rapidly varying visibility condition (1,000 feet or more for RVR; one or more reportable values for RVV), the current value is reported followed by the range of visibility variance.

2-152d Examples. —

Runway Two Four R-V-R two thousand, variable one thousand six hundred to three thousand.

Runway Three One R-V-V three-quarters, variable one-quarter to one.

2-152 Reference. — ATCH 2-122.

2-153 thru 2-159 RESERVED

Section 12. GENERAL FLIGHT PLAN INFORMATION

2-160 FLIGHT PLAN — INFORMATION REQUIRED

Unless otherwise authorized by ATC, each person filing an IFR or VFR flight plan shall include in it the following information:

a. The aircraft identification number and, if necessary, its radio call sign.

b. The type of aircraft or, in the case of a formation flight, the type of each aircraft and the number of aircraft, in the formation.

c. The full name and address of the pilot in command or, in the case of a formation flight, the formation commander.

d. The point and proposed time of departure.

e. The proposed route, cruising altitude (or flight level), and true airspeed at that altitude.

f. The point of first intended landing and the estimated elapsed time until over that point.

g. The radio frequencies to be used.

h. The amount of fuel on board (in hours).

i. In the case of an IFR flight plan, an alternate airport, except as provided in FAR 91.83(b).

j. The number of persons in the aircraft, except where that information is otherwise readily available to the FAA.

k. Any other information the pilot in command or ATC believes is necessary for ATC purposes.

2-160 Reference. — FAR 91.83.

2-161 IFR FLIGHT PLANS — GENERAL

If weather conditions are below VFR minimums, a pilot must submit a complete flight plan and receive an air traffic clearance prior to departure from within, or prior to entering controlled airspace. Instrument flight plans may be submitted to the nearest FSS or ATCT either in person or by telephone (or by radio if no other means are available).

2-161 Reference. — AIM 298.

2-162 COMPOSITE FLIGHT PLAN (VFR/IFR FLIGHTS)

a. Flight plans which specify VFR operation for one portion of a flight, and IFR for another portion, will be accepted by the FSS at the point of departure. If VFR flight is conducted for the first portion of the flight, the pilot should report his departure time to the FSS with which he filed his VFR/IFR flight plan; and, subsequently, close the VFR portion and request ATC clearance from the FSS nearest the point at which change from VFR to IFR is proposed. The pilot must remain in VFR weather conditions until operating in accordance with the IFR clearance.

b. When a flight plan indicates IFR for the first portion of flight and VFR for the latter portion, the pilot will normally be cleared to the point at which the change is proposed. Once the pilot has reported over the clearance limit and does not desire further IFR clearance, he should advise ATC to cancel the IFR portion of his flight plan. Then, he should contact the nearest FSS to activate the VFR portion of his flight plan. If the pilot desires to continue his IFR flight plan beyond the clearance limit, he should contact ATC at least 5 minutes prior to the clearance limit and request further IFR clearance. If the requested clearance is not received prior to reaching the clearance limit fix, the pilot will be expected to establish himself in a standard holding pattern on the radial or course to the fix unless a holding pattern for the clearance limit fix is depicted on a U.S. Government or commercially produced (meeting FAA requirements) Low or High Altitude En Route, Area or STAR Chart. In this case the pilot will hold according to the depicted pattern.

2-162 Reference. — AIM 297.

2-163 CANCELLING FLIGHT PLAN — IFR

a. FAR 91.83 includes the statement "When a flight plan has been filed, the pilot in command, upon cancelling or completing the flight under the flight plan, shall notify the nearest FSS or ATC facility."

b. An IFR flight plan may be cancelled at any time the flight is operating in VFR conditions outside positive controlled airspace by the pilot stating *"CANCEL MY IFR FLIGHT PLAN"* to the controller or station with which he is communicating.

c. If operating an IFR flight plan to an airport with a functioning control tower, the flight plan is automatically closed upon landing.

2-163 Reference. — AIM 304.

2-164 CLOSING FLIGHT PLAN — VFR/DVFR

A pilot is responsible for ensuring that his VFR or DVFR flight plan is cancelled (FAR 91.83). A pilot should close his flight plan with the nearest FSS, or if one is not available, he may request any ATC facility to relay his cancellation to the FSS. *Control towers do not automatically close VFR or DVFR flight plans* since they do not know if a particular VFR aircraft is on a flight plan. If a pilot fails to report or cancel his flight plan within ½ hour after his ETA, search and rescue procedures are started.

2-164 Reference. — AIM 303.

Chapter 3
TABLE OF CONTENTS

Section 1. AUTOMATIC TERMINAL INFORMATION SERVICE PROCEDURES

		Page
3-1	General	3-1
3-2	ATIS Content	3-1
3-3	Information Changes	3-1
3-4	Pilot Actions	3-2
3-5—3-9	Reserved	3-2

Section 2. AIRPORT TRAFFIC AREAS

3-10	Definition	3-3
3-11	Operating On or In the Vicinity of an Airport Traffic Area	3-3
3-12	Clearances Required	3-3
3-13	Communications With Control Towers	3-3
3-14	Coordinated Airport Traffic Area Transit Authorization	3-3
3-15	Speed and Unusual Maneuvers	3-3
3-16—3-19	Reserved	3-3

Section 3. COMMUNICATIONS FAILURE

3-20	Application	3-4
3-21	ATC Light Signals	3-4
3-22	Receiver Inoperative	3-4
3-23	Receiver Only	3-4
3-24	Receiver-Only Acknowledgment	3-4
3-25	Transmitter and Receiver Inoperative	3-5
3-26	Departures	3-5
3-27	Warning Signal	3-5
3-28—3-29	Reserved	3-5

Section 4. TRAFFIC INFORMATION AND AIRPORT ADVISORIES

3-30	General	3-6
3-31	Vehicles/Equipment/Personnel On Active Runways	3-6
3-32	Vehicle/Equipment/Personnel and Traffic Description	3-6
3-33	Low Level Wind Shear Alert System	3-6
3-34	Low Level Wind Shear Advisories	3-6
3-35	Observed Abnormalities	3-7
3-36	Landing Area Condition	3-7
3-37	Closed/Unsafe Runway Information	3-7
3-38	Timely Airport Information	3-8
3-39	Braking Action Reports	3-8
3-40	Braking Action Advisories	3-8
3-41—3-49	Reserved	3-8

TABLE OF CONTENTS (Continued)

Section 5. AIRPORT LIGHTING

		Page
3-50	Emergency Lighting	3-9
3-51	Runway End Identifier Lights	3-9
3-52	Visual Approach Slope Indicators	3-9
3-53	Approach Lights	3-9
3-54	ALS Intensity Settings	3-9
3-55	Sequenced Flashing Lights	3-10
3-56	MALSR/ODALS	3-10
3-57	ALSF-2/SSALR	3-10
3-58	Runway Edge Lights	3-10
3-59	High Intensity Runway, Runway Centerline, and Touchdown Zone Lights	3-11
3-60	HIRL Associated MALSR	3-11
3-61	Medium Intensity Runway Lights	3-11
3-62	Simultaneous Approach and Runway Edge Light Operation	3-12
3-63	High Speed Turnoff Lights	3-12
3-64	Taxiway Lights	3-12
3-65	Obstruction Lights	3-12
3-66	Rotating Beacon	3-12
3-67—3-69	Reserved	3-12

Section 6. TOWER RADAR

3-70	General	3-13
3-71	Location Determination	3-13
3-72	Traffic Advisories	3-13
3-73	Suggested Headings/Directions	3-13
3-74	Limitations	3-13
3-75—3-79	Reserved	3-13

Section 7. Airport Surface Detection Procedures

3-80	Equipment Usage	3-14
3-81	Information Usage	3-14
3-82—3-89	Reserved	3-14

Section 8. RUNWAY SELECTION

3-90	Runway Identification	3-15
3-91	Runway Use	3-15
3-92	STOL Runways	3-15
3-93	Tailwind Advisory	3-15
3-94—3-99	Reserved	3-15

TABLE OF CONTENTS (Continued)

Section 9. TAXI AND GROUND MOVEMENT PROCEDURES

		Page
3-100	General	3-16
3-101	Ground Communications	3-16
3-102	Ground Traffic Movement	3-16
3-103	Airport Information	3-16
3-104	Taxi Information	3-17
3-105	Holding Near Runways	3-18
3-106	Taxiway Marking	3-18
3-107	Precision Approach Critical Area	3-18
3-108	Ground Operations Near Possible Wake Turbulence	3-19
3-109	Taxi During Low Visibility	3-19
3-110—3-119	Reserved	3-19

Section 10. AIRCRAFT SPACING

3-120	Sequence/Spacing Procedures	3-20
3-121	Maneuvering Turns	3-20
3-122	Low Approach	3-20
3-123	Short Approach	3-20
3-124	The Option	3-20
3-125	Request for Closed Traffic	3-21
3-126	Aircraft Categories/Classes	3-21
3-127	Simultaneous Same Direction Runway Operations	3-21
3-128	Simultaneous Opposite Direction Runway Operations	3-21
3-129	Reserved	3-22

Section 11. TAKEOFF

3-130	Position Determination	3-23
3-131	VFR Direction of Flight	3-23
3-132	Amended Clearances	3-23
3-133	Takeoff Position and Hold	3-23
3-134	Anticipated Takeoff Separation	3-23
3-135	Same Runway Takeoff Separation	3-23
3-136	Intersection Takeoffs	3-24
3-137	Intersection Takeoff Interval	3-25
3-138	Intersecting Runway Separation	3-25
3-139	Takeoff Clearance Phraseology	3-27
3-140	Cancellation of Takeoff Clearance	3-27
3-141	Takeoff Actions	3-27
3-142	Departure Control Instructions	3-27
3-143—3-149	Reserved	3-27

TABLE OF CONTENTS (Continued)

Section 12. LANDING

		Page
3-150	Pattern Terminology	3-28
3-151	Arrival Information	3-28
3-152	Same Runway Landing Separation	3-29
3-153	Intersecting Runway Separation	3-30
3-154	Pilot Responsibility-Runway Use	3-32
3-155	Landing Clearance Phraseology	3-32
3-156	Anticipated Landing Separation	3-32
3-157	Landing Clearance Without Visual Observation	3-32
3-158	Withholding Landing Clearance	3-32
3-159	Exiting The Runway After Landing	3-32
3-160	Runway Exiting Instructions	3-32
3-161	Change To Ground	3-32
3-162—3-169	Reserved	3-32

Section 13. HELICOPTER OPERATIONS

3-170	General	3-33
3-171	Ground Service	3-33
3-172	Taxiing	3-33
3-173	Takeoff and Landing Procedures-General	3-33
3-174	Helicopter Surface Operations	3-34
3-175	Frequency Changes	3-34
3-176	Helicopter Takeoff Clearances	3-34
3-177	Helicopter Departure Separation	3-35
3-178	Helicopter Arrival Separation	3-35
3-179	Simultaneous Helicopter Landings or Takeoffs	3-36
3-180	Helicopter Landing Clearances	3-36
3-181—3-189	Reserved	3-36

Section 14. SEA LANE OPERATIONS

3-190	Application	3-37
3-191	Departure Separation	3-37
3-192	Arrival Separation	3-37

Chapter 3. AIRPORT PROCEDURES

Section 1. AUTOMATIC TERMINAL INFORMATION SERVICE PROCEDURES

3-1 GENERAL

a. ATIS (Automated Terminal Information Service) is the continuous broadcast of recorded noncontrol information in selected terminal areas. Its purpose is to improve controller effectiveness and to relieve frequency congestion by automating the repetitive transmission of essential but routine information.

b. Airport information is identified by a phonetic letter code word at both the beginning and the end of the message except where omissions are required because of special programs or equipment. Each alphabet letter phonetic word will be used sequentially beginning with *ALPHA*, ending with *ZULU*, and repeated without regard to the beginning of a new day. In the event of a broadcast interruption of more than 12 hours, controllers will identify the first resumed broadcast message with *ALPHA*.

c. When arrival and departure information is broadcasted separately, each broadcast need only contain information appropriate for that operation.

3-1 References. — ATCH 2-125; AIM 161.

3-2 ATIS CONTENT

The following are included in an ATIS broadcast, as appropriate:

a. Time of weather sequence (UTC).

b. Weather information consisting of:*

(1) Ceiling.

(2) Visibility.

(3) Obstruction to vision (when applicable).

(4) Temperature.

(5) Dew point.

(6) Wind direction (magnetic) and velocity.

(7) Altimeter, and

(8) Other pertinent remarks included in the official weather observation; remarks of lightning, cumulonimbus, and towering cumulus must be included.

c. Instrument and/or visual approach/s in use.

d. The landing runway/s is specified unless the runway is that to which the instrument approach is made.

e. Departure runway/s (is given only if different from landing runway/s or in the instance of a "departure information" ATIS).

f. NOTAM's and notification of PIREP's/SIGMET's/Convective SIGMET's/CWA's pertinent to operations in the terminal area.

g. Runway braking action reports.

h. When low level wind shear (LLWS) is reported by pilots or is detected on a low level wind shear alert system (LLWAS).

i. Other optional information as local conditions dictate in coordination with ATC. This may include such items as an advisory to *"check density altitude,"* VFR arrival frequencies, runway friction measurement readings/values, temporary airport conditions, or other perishable items that may appear only for a matter of hours or a few days on the ATIS message.

j. Instructions for the pilot to acknowledge receipt of the ATIS message by so informing the appropriate controller on initial contact.

3-2 Example. —
Evansville Airport information GOLF. One seven four niner Zulu weather. Measured ceiling three thousand overcast. Visibility three, haze. Temperature seven two. Dew point five eight. Wind one eight zero at five. Altimeter two niner niner five. I-L-S Runway Two Two Approach in use. Landing and departing Runways Two Two and One Eight. Notice to airmen, Runways Niner/Two Seven closed. All Evansville departures contact clearance delivery one two six point six prior to taxi. V-F-R departures advise clearance delivery of initial heading in degrees and proposed altitude. Advise on initial contact you have information GOLF.

3-2b Note. — If the weather is above a ceiling/sky condition of 5,000 feet and the visibility is 5 miles or more, inclusion of the ceiling/sky condition, visibility, and obstruction to vision in the ATIS broadcast is optional.

3-2 Reference. — ATCH 2-127.

3-3 INFORMATION CHANGES

a. A new recording will be made when any of the following occur:

(1) Upon receipt of any new official weather, regardless of whether there is or is not a change in values.

(2) When runway braking action reports are received that indicate runway braking is worse than that which is included in the current ATIS broadcast.

(3) When there is a change in any other pertinent data, such as runway change, instrument approach in use, new or canceled NOTAM's/SIGMET's/CWA's/PIREP's, etc.

b. When a pilot acknowledges that he has received the ATIS broadcast, controllers may omit items contained in the broadcasts if they are current. Rapidly changing conditions will be issued by ATC.

3-3b Example. —
Latest R-V-R will be issued by the tower.

c. Controllers will broadcast on all appropriate frequencies to advise aircraft of a change in the ATIS code/message.

3-3c Examples. —
Attention all aircraft. White Plains information HOTEL is now current.

Attention all aircraft. Stockton information CHARLIE is now current, altimeter two niner eight five.

3-3 Reference. — ATCH 2-126.

3-4 PILOT ACTIONS

a. Pilots should notify the ATC facility on initial contact that they have received the ATIS broadcast by repeating the phonetic letter code word appended to the broadcast.

3-4a Example. —
Stockton Tower, Cessna Two Five Alpha Zulu, one five miles southwest, with information CHARLIE.

b. Controllers will ensure pilots receive all pertinent information contained in the ATIS broadcast. If a pilot does not state receipt of the current ATIS, controllers will ask the pilot to confirm receipt of the appropriate ATIS information.*

3-4b Example. —
Verify you have information CHARLIE.

c. While it is a good operating practice for pilots to make use of the ATIS broadcast where it is available, some pilots use the phrase "Have Numbers" in communications with ATC. Use of this phrase means that the pilot has received wind, runway, and altimeter information *only* and the controller does not have to repeat this information. It does not indicate receipt of the ATIS broadcast and should never be used for this purpose.

3-4b Note. — Controllers are advised to issue current ATIS information unless the pilot volunteers to obtain it.

3-4 References. — ATCH 2-126; AIM 161.

3-5 thru 3-9 RESERVED

Section 2. AIRPORT TRAFFIC AREAS

3-10 DEFINITION

Unless otherwise specifically designated, airport traffic areas consist of the airspace within a horizontal radius of 5 statute miles from the geographical center of any airport at which a control tower is operating, extending from the surface up to, but not including, an altitude of 3,000 feet above the elevation of the airport.

3-10 Reference. — AIM 130.

3-11 OPERATING ON OR IN THE VICINITY OF AN AIRPORT TRAFFIC AREA

Unless otherwise authorized or required by ATC, no person may operate an aircraft within an airport traffic area except for the purpose of landing at, or taking off from, an airport within that area. ATC authorizations may be given as individual approval of specific operations or may be contained in written agreements between airport users and the tower concerned.

3-11 Reference. — FAR 91.85.

3-12 CLEARANCES REQUIRED

A pilot may, at an airport with an operating control tower, operate an aircraft on a runway or taxiway, or takeoff or land an aircraft, if an appropriate clearance is received from ATC.

3-12 Reference. — FAR 91.85.

3-13 COMMUNICATIONS WITH CONTROL TOWERS

a. A pilot may, within an airport traffic area, operate an aircraft to, from, or on an airport having a control tower operated by the United States if two-way radio communications are maintained between that aircraft and the control tower.*

b. If the aircraft radio fails in flight, the pilot may operate that aircraft and land if weather conditions are at or above basic VFR weather minimums, he maintains visual contact with the tower, and he receives a clearance, by visual light signal, to land. If the aircraft radio fails while in flight under IFR, the pilot must comply with FAR 91.127.

c. At those airports where the U.S. Government operates the control tower and ATC has authorized noncompliance with the requirement for two-way radio communications while operating within the airport traffic area, or at those airports where the U.S. Government does not operate the control tower and radio communications cannot be established, pilots shall obtain a clearance by visual light signal prior to taxiing on a runway and prior to takeoff and landing.

3-13a Note. — It is a good operating practice for pilots to remain on the tower frequency for the purpose of receiving traffic information unless there is a good reason to leave the tower frequency before exiting the airport traffic area. In the interest of reducing tower frequency congestion, pilots are reminded that it is not necessary to request to leave the tower frequency once outside of the airport traffic area.

3-13 References. — FAR 91.87; AIM 221.

3-14 COORDINATED AIRPORT TRAFFIC AREA TRANSIT AUTHORIZATION

Controllers will coordinate with the appropriate control tower for transit authorization when they are providing radar traffic advisory service to an aircraft that will enter another facility's airport traffic area.*

3-14 Note. — The pilot is not expected to obtain his own authorization through each area when in contact with a radar facility.

3-14 Reference. — ATCH 2-16.

3-15 SPEED AND UNUSUAL MANEUVERS

a. Unless otherwise authorized or required by ATC, no person may operate an aircraft within an airport traffic area at an indicated airspeed of more than—

(1) In the case of a reciprocating engine aircraft, 156 knots (180 mph); or

(2) In the case of a turbine-powered aircraft, 200 knots (230 mph).

b. If traffic conditions permit, a pilot's request to cross an airport traffic area or exceed the airport traffic area speed limit will be approved. Approval of a speed in excess of 250 knots (288 mph) will not be made unless the pilot informs the controller a higher minimum speed is required.*

c. Controllers will not approve a pilot's request or ask a pilot to conduct unusual maneuvers within an airport traffic area if such maneuvers are not essential to the performance of the flight.*

3-15b Note. — FAR 91.70 permits speeds in excess of 250 knots (288 mph) when so required or recommended in the airplane flight manual or required by normal military operating procedures.

3-15c Note. — These unusual maneuvers include unnecessary low passes, unscheduled flybys, practice instrument approaches to altitudes below specified minima (unless a landing or touch-and-go is to be made), or any so-called "buzz jobs" wherein a flight is conducted at a low altitude and/or a high rate of speed for thrill purposes. Such maneuvers increase hazards to persons and property and contribute to noise complaints.

3-15 References. — FAR 91.70; ATCH 3-11.

3-16 thru 3-19 RESERVED

Section 3. COMMUNICATIONS FAILURE

3-20 APPLICATION

The following procedures are used by air traffic control towers in the control of aircraft, ground vehicles, equipment, and personnel not equipped with radio. These same procedures will be used to control aircraft, ground vehicles, equipment, and personnel equipped with radio if radio contact cannot be established. ATC personnel use a directive traffic control signal which emits an intense narrow light beam of a selected color (either red, white, or green) when controlling traffic by light signals.

3-20 Reference. — AIM 233.

3-21 ATC LIGHT SIGNALS

Air traffic control signals from the Table are used to control aircraft and the movement of vehicles, equipment, and personnel on the movement area when radio communications cannot be employed.

3-21 Table. — ATC Light Signals

Color and type of signal	Aircraft on the ground	Aircraft in flight	Movement of vehicles, equipment, and personnel
Steady green	Cleared for takeoff	Cleared to land	Cleared to cross; proceed; go
Flashing green	Cleared to taxi	Return for landing (to be followed by steady green at the proper time)	Not applicable
Steady red	Stop	Give way to other aircraft and continue circling	Stop
Flashing red	Taxi clear of landing area/runway in use	Airport unsafe—do not land	Clear the taxi/runway
Flashing white	Return to starting point on airport	Not applicable	Return to starting point on airport
Alternating red and green	General Warning Signal — Exercise Extreme Caution		

3-21 Reference. — ATCH 3-20.

3-22 RECEIVER INOPERATIVE

a. If pilots have reason to believe their receiver is inoperative, they should remain outside or above the airport traffic area until the direction and flow of traffic has been determined, then advise the tower of their type aircraft, position, altitude, intention to land and request to be controlled with light signals.

3-22a Example. —

Oxnard Tower, Skylane One Zero Three Golf Sierra over the airport at four thousand five hundred, receiver inoperative; I will be descending north of the field to enter left traffic Runway Seven, request light signals for landing.

b. When approximately 3 to 5 miles from the airport, pilots should advise the tower of their position and join the airport traffic pattern. From this point on, pilots should watch the tower for light signals. Thereafter, if a complete pattern is made, position downwind and/or turning base leg should be transmitted.

3-22b Examples. —

Skylane Three Golf Sierra is downwind north.

Skylane Three Golf Sierra is turning base. I see your green light and understand I am cleared to land.

3-22 Reference. — AIM 205.

3-23 RECEIVER ONLY

a. Pilots should remain outside or above the airport traffic area until the direction and flow has been determined, then join the airport traffic pattern.

b. Pilots should monitor the primary local control frequency as depicted on Sectional Charts for landing or traffic information, and look for a light signal which may be addressed to their aircraft.

3-23 Reference. — AIM 205.

3-24 RECEIVER-ONLY ACKNOWLEDGMENT

To obtain acknowledgment from an aircraft equipped with receiver only, the controller will request the aircraft to do the following:

a. Fixed-wing aircraft —

(1) Between sunrise and sunset —

(a) Move ailerons or rudders while on the ground.

(b) Rock wings while in flight.

(2) Between sunset and sunrise — flash navigation or landing lights.

b. Helicopters —

(1) Between sunrise and sunset —

(a) While hovering, either turn the helicopter toward the controlling facility and flash the landing light or rock the tip path plane.

(b) While in flight, either flash the landing light or rock the tip path plane.

(2) Between sunset and sunrise — Flash the landing light or the search light.

3-24 Reference. — ATCH 3-22.

3-25 TRANSMITTER AND RECEIVER INOPERATIVE

Pilots should remain outside or above the airport traffic area until the direction and flow of traffic has been determined, then join the airport traffic pattern and maintain visual contact with the tower to receive light signals.

3-25 Reference. — AIM 205.

3-26 DEPARTURES

If radio failure is experienced prior to leaving the parking areas, pilots should make every effort to have the equipment repaired. If unable to have the malfunction repaired, pilots should call the tower by telephone and request authorization to depart without two-way radio communications. If tower authorization is granted, the pilot will be given departure information and requested to monitor the tower frequency or watch for light signals, as appropriate.

3-26 Reference. — AIM 205.

3-27 WARNING SIGNAL

A general warning will be directed to aircraft or vehicle operators, as appropriate, when:*

a. Aircraft are converging and a collision hazard exists.

b. Mechanical trouble exists of which the pilot might not be aware.

c. Other hazardous conditions are present which call for intensified pilot or operator alertness. These conditions may include obstructions, soft field, ice on the runway, etc.

3-27 Note. — The warning signal is not a prohibitive signal and can be followed by any other light signal, as circumstances permit.

3-27 Reference. — ATCH 3-21.

3-28 and 3-29 RESERVED

Section 4. TRAFFIC INFORMATION AND AIRPORT ADVISORIES

3-30 GENERAL

When operating in accordance with the FAR's, it is the responsibility of the pilot to avoid collision with other aircraft. However, due to the limited space around terminal locations, traffic information given by ATC can aid pilots in avoiding collision between aircraft operating within control zones, airport traffic areas, terminal radar service areas, airport radar service areas, terminal control areas, and between transiting aircraft operating in proximity to terminal locations.*

3-30 Note. — Airport traffic control service is provided based only upon observed or known traffic and airport conditions.

3-30 Reference. — ATCH 3-1.

3-31 VEHICLES/EQUIPMENT/PERSONNEL ON ACTIVE RUNWAYS

Controllers must ensure that the runway to be used is clear of all known ground vehicles, equipment, and personnel before a departing aircraft starts takeoff or a landing aircraft crosses the runway threshold.

3-31 Reference. — ATCH 3-3.

3-32 VEHICLE/EQUIPMENT/PERSONNEL AND TRAFFIC DESCRIPTION

a. Vehicles, equipment, or personnel on or near the movement area will be described in a manner which will assist pilots in recognizing them.

3-32a Examples. —

Mower to left of Runway Two Seven.

Trucks crossing approach end of Runway Two Five.

Workman on Taxiway Bravo.

Aircraft to left of Runway One Eight.

b. Controllers will describe the relative position of traffic in an easy to understand manner, such as *"to your right,"* or *"ahead of you."*

3-32b Examples. —

Traffic, USAir Seven Thirty-seven on downwind leg to your left.

Twin Cessna inbound from outer marker on straight-in approach to Runway One Seven.

c. When using a certified tower radar display, controllers may issue traffic advisories using the standard phraseology described in paragraph 2-84.

3-32c Example. —

Twin Cessna Seven Two Mike, traffic two o'clock, three miles, type and altitude unknown.

3-32 Reference. — ATCH 3-5.

3-33 LOW LEVEL WIND SHEAR ALERT SYSTEM

a. LLWAS (low level wind shear alert system) detects the presence of a possible hazardous low-level wind shear by continuously comparing the winds measured by sensors installed around the periphery of an airport with the wind measured at the centerfield location. If the difference between the centerfield wind sensor and a peripheral wind sensor becomes excessive, a thunderstorm or thunderstorm gust front wind shear is probable. When this condition exists, the tower controller will provide arrival and departure aircraft with an advisory of the situation which includes the centerfield wind plus the remote site location and wind.

b. Since the sensors are not all associated with specific runways, descriptions of the remote sites will be based on an eight point compass system.

3-33b Example. —

East boundary wind ... Northeast boundary wind ...

3-33 Reference. — AIM 227.

3-34 LOW LEVEL WIND SHEAR ADVISORIES

When low level wind shear is reported by pilots or detected on a LLWAS, a statement will be included on the ATIS for 20 minutes following the last report or indication of wind shear.*

ATC Phraseology:

Low level wind shear advisories in effect.

At facilities without ATIS, ATC will ensure that wind shear information is broadcast to all arriving and departing aircraft for 20 minutes following the last report or indication of wind shear.

a. At locations equipped with LLWAS, the local controller will provide wind information as follows:

(1) If an alert is received, the centerfield wind and the displayed field boundary wind will be issued.

ATC Phraseology:

Wind shear alert. Centerfield wind (direction) **at** (velocity); (Location of sensor) **boundary wind** (direction) **at** (velocity).

3-34a(1) Example. —

Wind shear alert. Centerfield wind, two two zero at two seven. East boundary wind, zero five zero at seven.

(2) If multiple alerts are received, an advisory that there are wind shear alerts in two/several/all quadrants will be issued. After issuing the advisory, the controller will issue the centerfield wind followed by the field boundary wind most appropriate to the aircraft operation.

ATC Phraseology:

Wind shear alerts two/several/all quadrants. Centerfield wind (direction) **at** (velocity). (Location of sensor) **boundary wind** (direction) **at** (velocity).

3-34a(2) Example. —

Wind shear alerts two quadrants. Centerfield wind, one five zero at one zero. South boundary wind, two one zero at two five. North boundary wind zero three zero at four.

(3) If requested by the pilot, ATC will issue specific field boundary wind information even though the LLWAS may not be in alert status.

b. "Improved" LLWAS systems are designed to detect wind shear in the vicinity of the centerfield sensor as well as around the periphery. Locations equipped with "improved" LLWAS systems will issue centerfield wind variance when an alert is received from the centerfield area.

ATC Phraseology:

Wind shear alert. Centerfield wind (direction) **at** (velocity) **varying to** (direction) **at** (velocity).

3-34b Example. —

Wind shear alert. Centerfield wind, zero niner zero at one zero varying to one four zero at two five.

3-34 Note. — The LLWAS was designed to detect low level wind shear conditions around the periphery of an airport. It does not detect wind shear beyond that limitation.

3-34 Reference. — ATCH 3-8.

3-35 OBSERVED ABNORMALITIES

When requested by a pilot or when they deem it necessary, controllers will inform an aircraft of any observed abnormal aircraft condition.

ATC Phraseology:

(Item) **appear/s** (observed condition).

3-35 Examples. —

Landing gear appears down and in place.

Rear baggage door appears open.

3-35 Reference. — ATCH 3-10.

3-36 LANDING AREA CONDITION

If controllers observe or are informed of any condition which affects the safe use of a landing area they will:*

a. Relay the information to the aircraft manager concerned.

b. Copy verbatim any information received and record the name of the person submitting it.

c. Confirm information obtained from other than authorized airport or FAA personnel.*

d. If controllers are unable to contact the airport management or operator, they will issue a Notice to Airmen publicizing an unsafe condition and inform the management or operator as soon as practicable.*

3-36d Example. —

Disabled aircraft on Runway Two Seven Left.

e. Issue to aircraft only factual information, as reported by the airport management concerning the condition of the runway surface, describing the accumulation of precipitation.

3-36e Example. —

All runways covered by compacted snow six inches deep.

3-36 Note 1. — The airport management office is responsible for observing and reporting the condition of the landing area.

3-36 Note 2. — It is the responsibility of the agency operating the airport to provide the tower with current information regarding airport conditions.

3-36 Note 3. — A disabled aircraft on a runway, after occupants are clear, is normally handled by Flight Standards and airport management personnel in the same manner as any obstruction.

3-36c Note. — Airport managers are required to provide a list of airport employees who are authorized to issue information concerning conditions affecting the safe use of the airport.

3-36d Note. — Legally, only the airport management can close a runway.

3-36 Reference. — ATCH 3-30.

3-37 CLOSED/UNSAFE RUNWAY INFORMATION

If an aircraft requests to takeoff, land, or touch-and-go on a closed or unsafe runway, controllers will inform the pilot the runway is closed or unsafe, and

a. If the pilot persists in his request, the controller will quote him the appropriate parts of the Notice to Airmen applying to the runway and inform him that a clearance cannot be issued.

b. Then, if the pilot insists and in the controller's opinion the intended operation would not adversely affect other traffic, the controller will inform him that the operation will be at his own risk.

ATC Phraseology:

Runway (runway number) **closed/unsafe.**

If appropriate,

(Notice to Airmen information), **unable to issue departure/landing/touch-and-go clearance. Departure/Landing/Touch-and-go will be at your own risk.**

c. Where parallel runways are served by separate ILS/MLS systems and one of the runways is closed, the ILS/MLS associated with the closed runway may not be used for approaches unless not using the ILS/MLS would have an adverse impact on the operational efficiency of the airport.

3-37 Reference. — ATCH 3-31.

3-38 TIMELY AIRPORT INFORMATION

Airport condition information necessary for an aircraft's safe operation will be issued in time for it to be useful to the pilot. Included are the following, as appropriate:

a. Construction work on or immediately adjacent to the movement area.

b. Rough portions of the movement area.

c. Braking conditions caused by ice, snow, slush, or water.

d. Snowdrifts or piles of snow on or along the edges of the area and the extent of any plowed area.

e. Parked aircraft on the movement area.

f. Irregular operation of part or all of the airport lighting system.

g. Other pertinent airport conditions.

3-38 Reference. — ATCH 3-32.

3-39 BRAKING ACTION REPORTS

Quality of braking action, as received from pilots or the airport management, is furnished to all aircraft as follows:

a. The quality of braking action is described by using the terms *"good," "fair," "poor," "nil,"* or a combination of these terms. If the pilot or airport management reports braking action in other than the foregoing terms, ATC will ask him to categorize braking action in these terms.*

b. Type of aircraft or vehicle from which the report is received.

3-39a and b Examples. —

Braking action fair to poor, reported by a D-C Ten.

Braking action poor, reported by a Boeing Seven Twenty-seven.

c. If the braking action report affects only a portion of a runway, ATC will attempt to obtain enough information from the pilot or airport management to describe the braking action in terms easily understood by the pilot.*

3-39c Examples. —

Braking action poor first half of runway, reported by a Lockheed Ten Eleven.

Braking action poor beyond the intersection of Runway Two Seven, reported by a Boeing Seven Twenty-seven.

d. Runway friction measurement readings/values as received from airport management are furnished to aircraft. At locations where friction measuring devices, such as Mu-Meter, Saab Friction Tester (SFT), and Skiddometer are in use, information will be furnished to pilots on request. The name of the device is used followed by the number of each of three runway segments, a word describing the cause of the runway friction problem, and the time of the report.

3-39a Note. — The term "nil" is used to indicate bad or no braking action.

3-39c Note. — Descriptive terms, such as the first or the last half of the runway, will normally be used rather than landmark descriptions, such as opposite the fire station, south of a taxiway, etc. Landmarks extraneous to the landing runway can be difficult to distinguish during low visibility, at night, or any time a pilot is landing an aircraft.

3-39 Reference. — ATCH 3-33.

3-40 BRAKING ACTION ADVISORIES

a. When runway braking action reports are received from pilots or the airport management which include the terms "poor" or "nil," or whenever weather conditions are conducive to deteriorating or rapidly changing runway conditions, included on the ATIS broadcast is the statement *"BRAKING ACTION ADVISORIES ARE IN EFFECT."*

b. During the time Braking Action Advisories are in effect, the controller will take the following action:

(1) The latest braking action report is issued for the runway in use to each arriving and departing aircraft early enough to benefit the pilot. When possible, reports from heavy jet aircraft are included when the arriving or departing aircraft is a heavy jet.

(2) PIREP's of runway braking action will be solicited.

c. When runway friction measurement readings/values are received from airport management, included on the ATIS broadcast will be the statement *"RUNWAY FRICTION MEASUREMENT READINGS AVAILABLE ON REQUEST."* When a request is received, ATC will furnish the information as described in 3-39d.

3-40 Reference. — ATCH 3-34.

3-41 thru 3-49 RESERVED

Section 5. AIRPORT LIGHTING

3-50 EMERGENCY LIGHTING

Whenever controllers become aware that an emergency has or will occur, they will take action to provide for the operation of all appropriate airport lighting aids as required.

3-50 Reference. — ATCH 3-40.

3-51 RUNWAY END IDENTIFIER LIGHTS

When separate on-off controls are provided, REIL (runway end identifier lights) will be operated:

a. When the associated runway lights are lighted, the REIL will be turned off after:

(1) An arriving aircraft has landed.

(2) A departing aircraft has left the traffic pattern area.

(3) It is determined that the lights are of no further use to the pilot.

b. As required by facility directives to meet local conditions.

c. As requested by the pilot.

d. Intensity settings are in accordance with the values in the table except as described in paragraphs **b** and **c**.

3-51 Table. — REIL Intensity Setting — Three-Step System

	Visibility	
Settings	Day	Night
3	Less than 2 miles	Less than 1 mile
2	2 to 5 miles inclusive	1 to, but not including, 3 miles
1	When requested	3 miles or more

3-51 Reference. — ATCH 3-41.

3-52 VISUAL APPROACH SLOPE INDICATORS

VASI (visual approach slope indicator) systems with remote on-off switching will be operated when they serve the runway in use and where intensities are controlled in accordance with the Tables, except:*

a. As required by facility directives to meet local conditions.

b. As required by the pilot.

3-52 Table 1. — VASI Intensity Setting — Two-Step System

Step	Period/Condition
High	Day — Sunrise to sunset.
Low	Night — Sunset to sunrise.

3-52 Table 2. — VASI Intensity Setting — Three-Step System

Step	Period/Condition
High	Day — Sunrise to sunset.
Medium	Twilight — From sunset to 30 minutes after sunset and from 30 minutes before sunrise to sunrise, and during twilight in Alaska. Note —During a 1-year period, twilight may vary 26 to 43 minutes between 25 and 49N latitude.
Low	Night — From 30 minutes after sunset to 30 minutes before sunrise.

3-52 Note. — The basic FAA standard for VASI systems permits independent operation by means of photo-electric device. This system has no on-off control feature and is intended for continuous operation. Other VASI systems in use include those that are operated remotely from the control tower. These systems may consist of either a photo-electric intensity control with only an on-off switch, a two-step intensity system, or a three-step intensity system.

3-52 Reference. — ATCH 3-42.

3-53 APPROACH LIGHTS

The approach light system (ALS) will be operated:*

a. Between sunset and sunrise when one of the following conditions exists:

(1) They serve the landing runway.

(2) They serve a runway to which an approach is being made but aircraft will land on another runway.

b. Between sunrise and sunset when the ceiling is less than 1,000 feet or the prevailing visibility is 5 miles or less and approaches are being made to:

(1) A landing runway served by the lights.

(2) A runway served by the lights but aircraft are landing on another runway.

(3) The airport, but landing will be made on a runway served by the lights.

c. As required by the pilot.

d. As the controller deems necessary, if not contrary to pilot's request.

3-53 Note. — In the interest of energy conservation, the ALS may be turned off when not needed for aircraft operations.

3-53 Reference. — ATCH 3-43.

3-54 ALS INTENSITY SETTINGS

When operating ALS as prescribed in 3-53, intensity controls will be operated in accordance with the values in the Table except:*

a. When facility directives specify other settings to meet local atmospheric, topographic, and twilight conditions.

b. As requested by the pilot.

c. As the controller deems necessary, if not contrary to pilot's request.

3-54 Table. — ALS Intensity Setting

Step	Visibility — (Applicable to runway served by lights)	
	Day	Night
5	Less than 1 mile*	When requested
4	1 to, but not including, 3 miles	When requested
3	3 to, but not including, 5 miles	Less than 1 mile*
2	5 to, but not including, 7 miles	1 to 3 miles inclusive
1	When requested	Greater than 3 miles

*and/or 6,000 feet or less of the RVR on the runway served by the ALS and RVR.

3-54 Note. — Daylight Steps 2 and 3 provide recommended settings applicable to conditions in subparagraphs **b** and **c** at night, steps 4 or 5 will only be used when requested by a pilot.

3-54 Reference. — ATCH 3-44.

3-55 SEQUENCED FLASHING LIGHTS

Sequenced Flashing Lights (SFL) will be operated:*

a. When the visibility is less than 3 miles and instrument approaches are being made to the runway served by the associated ALS.

b. As requested by the pilot.

c. As the controller deems necessary, if not contrary to pilot's request.

3-55 Note. — SFL are a component of the ALS and cannot be operated when the ALS is off.

3-55 Reference. — ATCH 3-45.

3-56 MALSR/ODALS

MALSR/ODALS (medium approach light system with runway alignment indicator lights/omnidirectional approach lighting system) that have separate on-off and intensity setting controls will be operated in accordance with the following Tables except:

a. When facility directives specify other settings to meet local atmospheric, topographic, and twilight conditions.

b. As requested by the pilot.

c. As the controller deems necessary, if not contrary to pilot's request.

3-56 Table 1. — Two-Step MALSR/One-Step RAIL/Two-Step ODALS

Settings	Visibility	
	Day	Night
MALSR/ODALS ... High RAIL .... On	Less than 3 miles	Less than 3 miles*
MALSR/ODALS .... Low RAIL .... Off	When requested	3 miles or more

*At locations providing part-time control tower service, if duplicate controls are not provided in the associated FSS, the MALSR/ODALS will be set to low intensity during the hours of darkness when the tower is unmanned.

3-56 Table 2. — Three-Step MALSR/Three-Step RAIL/Three-Step ODALS

Settings	Visibility	
	Day	Night
3	Less than 2 miles	Less than 1 mile
2	2 to 5 miles inclusive	1 to, but not including, 3 miles*
1	When requested	3 miles or more

*At locations providing part-time control tower service, if duplicate controls are not provided in the FSS on the airport, the air-to-ground radio link will be activated during the hours of darkness when the tower is unmanned. If there is no radio air-to-ground control, the MALSR/ODALS will be set on intensity setting 2 during the hours of darkness when the tower is unmanned.

3-56 Reference. — ATCH 3-46.

3-57 ALSF-2/SSALR

a. ATC will operate the ALSF-2 (approach light system with sequenced flashing lights in ILS Cat II configuration) system as follows:

(1) When the prevailing visibility is ¾ mile or less, or the RVR is 4,000 feet or less:

(a) As requested by the pilot.

(b) As ATC deems necessary, if not contrary to pilot's request.

b. ATC will operate the SSALR (simplified short approach light system with runway alignment indicator lights) system when the conditions in **a** above are not a factor.

3-57 Reference. — ATCH 3-47.

3-58 RUNWAY EDGE LIGHTS

The runway edge light system/s serving the runway/s in use will be operated as follows:*

a. Between sunset and sunrise, the lights will be turned on:

(1) For departures - Before an aircraft taxis onto the runway and until it leaves the airport traffic area.

(2) For arrivals -

(a) IFR aircraft - Before the aircraft begins final approach, or

(b) VFR aircraft - Before the aircraft enters the airport traffic area, and

(c) Until the aircraft has taxied off the landing runway.

b. Between sunrise and sunset, the lights will be turned on as in (1) and (2) above when the surface visibility is less than 2 miles.

c. As required by facility directives to meet local conditions.

d. Different from **a, b,** or **c** above when:

(1) ATC considers it necessary, or

(2) Requested by a pilot and no other known aircraft will be adversely affected.*

e. ATC will not turn on the runway edge lights when a NOTAM closing the runway is in effect.

3-58 Note. — Application concerns use for takeoffs/landings/approaches and does not preclude turning lights on for use of unaffected portions of a runway for taxiing aircraft, surface vehicles, maintenance, repair, etc.

3-58d(2) Note. — Pilots may request lights to be turned on or off contrary to **a, b,** or **c** above. However, PART 135 operators are required to land/takeoff on lighted runways/heliport landing areas at night.

3-58 Reference. — ATCH 3-48.

3-59 HIGH INTENSITY RUNWAY, RUNWAY CENTERLINE, AND TOUCHDOWN ZONE LIGHTS

HIRL (high intensity runway lights) and associated RCLS (runway centerline light system) and TDZL (touchdown zone lights) will be operated in accordance with the Table, except:

a. Where a facility directive specifies other settings to meet local conditions.

b. As requested by the pilot.

c. As ATC deems necessary, if not contrary to pilot's request.

3-59 Table. — HIRL, RCLS, TDZL Intensity Setting

Step	Visibility	
	Day	Night
5	Less than 1 mile*	When requested
4	1 to, but not including, 2 miles*	Less than 1 mile*
3	2 to, but not including, 3 miles	1 to, but not including, 3 miles*
2	When requested	3 to 5 miles inclusive
1	When requested	More than 5 miles

*and/or appropriate RVR/RVV equivalent.

3-59 Reference. — ATCH 3-49.

3-60 HIRL ASSOCIATED WITH MALSR

HIRL, which control the associated MALSR, will be operated in accordance with the accompanying intensity setting Table, except:

a. As requested by the pilot.

b. As ATC deems necessary, if not contrary to pilot's request.

3-60 Table. — HIRL Associated With MALSR

Step	Visibility	
	Day	Night
5	Less than 1 mile	When requested
4	1 to, but not including, 2 miles	Less than 1 mile
3	2 to, but not including, 3 miles	1 to, but not including, 3 miles
2	When requested	3 to 5 miles inclusive
1	When requested	More than 5 miles

3-60 Reference. — ATCH 3-50.

3-61 MEDIUM INTENSITY RUNWAY LIGHTS

MIRL (medium intensity runway lights), or MIRL which control the associated MALSR, will be operated in accordance with the Table, except:

a. As requested by the pilot.

b. As ATC deems necessary, if not contrary to pilot's request.

3-61 Table. — MIRL Intensity Setting

Step	Visibility	
	Day	Night
3	Less than 2 miles	Less than 1 mile
2	2 to 3 miles	1 to 3 miles
1	When requested	More than 3 miles

3-61 Reference. — ATCH 3-52.

3-62 SIMULTANEOUS APPROACH AND RUNWAY EDGE LIGHT OPERATION

The runway edge lights will be turned on for the runway in use whenever the associated approach lights are on. If multiple runway light selection is not possible, ATC may leave the approach lights on and switch the runway lights to another runway to accommodate another aircraft.

3-62 Reference. — ATCH 3-53.

3-63 HIGH SPEED TURNOFF LIGHTS

High speed turnoff lights will be operated:

a. Whenever the associated runway lights are used for arriving aircraft. ATC will leave them on until the aircraft has either entered a taxiway or passed the last light.

b. As required by facility directives to meet local conditions.

c. As requested by the pilot.

3-63 Reference. — ATCH 3-54.

3-64 TAXIWAY LIGHTS

Taxiway lights serving the taxiways, or portions thereof, in use will be operated as follows:

a. Between sunset and sunrise - Before an aircraft taxis onto the taxiway (normally at the time taxi information is issued) and until it taxis off it.

b. At other times when ATC considers it necessary and as required by local instructions.

3-64 Reference. — ATCH 3-55.

3-65 OBSTRUCTION LIGHTS

If controls are provided, the lights will be turned on between sunset and sunrise.

3-65 Reference. — ATCH 3-56.

3-66 ROTATING BEACON

If controls are provided, the rotating beacon will be turned on:

a. Between sunset and sunrise.

b. Between sunrise and sunset when the reported ceiling or visibility is below basic VFR minima.

3-66 Reference. — ATCH 3-57.

3-67 thru 3-69 RESERVED

Section 6. TOWER RADAR

3-70 GENERAL

Many towers are equipped with a tower radar display. The radar uses are intended to enhance the effectiveness and efficiency of the tower. Tower radar displays are not intended to provide radar services or benefits to pilots except as they may accrue through a more efficient tower operation.

3-70 Reference. — AIM 221.

3-71 LOCATION DETERMINATION

Aircraft location determination is accomplished by radar identifying the VFR aircraft through any of the techniques available to a radar position. Once identified, the aircraft's position and spatial relationship to other aircraft can be quickly determined and standard instructions regarding VFR operation in the airport traffic area will be issued. Once initial radar identification of a VFR aircraft has been established and the appropriate instructions have been issued, radar monitoring may be discontinued. This is because the local controller's primary means of surveillance in VFR conditions is visually scanning the airport and local area.

3-71 Reference. — AIM 221.

3-72 TRAFFIC ADVISORIES

Radar traffic advisories may be provided to the extent that the local controller is able to monitor the radar display. Local control has primary control responsibilities to the aircraft operating on the runways, which will normally supersede radar monitoring duties.

3-72 Reference. — AIM 221.

3-73 SUGGESTED HEADINGS/DIRECTIONS

The local controller may provide pilots flying VFR with generalized instructions which will facilitate operations or issue suggested headings to establish radar identification. In both cases, the instructions are advisory aids and are not radar vectors. *PILOTS HAVE COMPLETE DISCRETION REGARDING ACCEPTANCE OF THE SUGGESTED HEADING OR DIRECTION AND HAVE SOLE RESPONSIBILITY FOR SEEING AND AVOIDING OTHER AIRCRAFT.*

3-73 Examples. —

Cessna Five Eight Whiskey, proceed southwestbound. Enter a right downwind, Runway Three Zero.

Cherokee Seven Two Mike, suggest heading two two zero for radar identification.

Cherokee Seven Two Mike unable to accept that heading due to weather.

3-73 Reference. — AIM 221.

3-74 LIMITATIONS

a. The above tower radar applications are intended to augment the standard functions of the local control position. There is no controller requirement to maintain constant radar identification and, in fact, such a requirement could compromise the local controllers' ability to visually scan the airport and local area to meet FAA responsibilities to the aircraft operating on the runways and within the airport traffic area. Normally, pilots will not be advised of being in "radar contact" since that continued status cannot be guaranteed and since the purpose of the radar identification is not to establish a link for the provision of radar services.

b. Some radar equipped towers are authorized to use tower radar displays to ensure separation between aircraft in specific situations, while still others may function as limited radar approach controls. The various radar uses are strictly a function of FAA operational need. The facilities may be indistinguishable to pilots since they are all referred to as tower and no publication lists the degree of radar use. Therefore, *WHEN IN COMMUNICATION WITH A TOWER CONTROLLER WHO MAY HAVE RADAR AVAILABLE, PILOTS SHOULD NOT ASSUME THAT CONSTANT RADAR MONITORING AND COMPLETE ATC RADAR SERVICES ARE BEING PROVIDED.*

3-74 Reference. — AIM 221.

3-75 thru 3-79 RESERVED

Section 7. AIRPORT SURFACE DETECTION PROCEDURES

3-80 EQUIPMENT USAGE

ASDE (airport surface detection equipment) is used to augment visual observation of aircraft and/or vehicular movements on runways and taxiways:

a. When visibility is less than the most distant point in the active movement area, and

b. When, in their judgment, its use will assist controllers in the performance of their duties at any time.

3-80 Reference. — ATCH 3-70.

3-81 INFORMATION USAGE

a. ASDE-derived information is used:

(1) To determine that the runway is clear of aircraft and vehicles prior to a landing or departure.

(2) To monitor compliance with control instructions by aircraft and vehicles on the taxiways and runways.

(3) To confirm pilot reported positions.

(4) To provide directional taxi information on pilot's request.

ATC Phraseology:

Turn (left/right) **on the taxiway/runway you are approaching.**

b. The controller will not provide specific navigational guidance (exact headings to be followed) unless an emergency exists or by mutual agreement with the pilot.*

3-81b Note. — It remains the pilot's responsibility to navigate visually via routes to the clearance limit specified by the controller and to avoid other parked or taxiing aircraft, vehicles, or persons in the movement area.

3-81 Reference. — ATCH 3-71.

3-82 thru 3-89 RESERVED

Section 8. RUNWAY SELECTION

3-90 RUNWAY IDENTIFICATION

Runways are identified by numbers which indicate the nearest 10-degree increment of the azimuth of the runway centerline. For example, where the magnetic azimuth is 183 degrees, the runway designation would be *one eight,* for a magnetic azimuth of 87 degrees, the runway designation would be *niner.* For a magnetic azimuth ending in the number 5, such as 185, the runway designation could be either *one eight* or *one niner.*

3-90 Reference. — AIM 226.

3-91 RUNWAY USE

a. When landing or taking off from an airport with an operating control tower, and for which a formal runway use program has been established by the FAA, each pilot of a turbine-powered airplane and each pilot of a large airplane, assigned a noise abatement runway by ATC, shall use that runway.*

b. At airports where no runway use program is established, ATC clearances may specify:*

(1) The runway most nearly aligned with the wind when it is 5 knots or more,

(2) The "calm wind" runway when wind is less than 5 knots, or

(3) Another runway if operationally advantageous.

3-91a Note. — At airports where a runway use program is established, ATC will assign runways deemed to have the least noise impact. In the interest of safety, if a runway different than that specified is preferred, the pilot is expected to advise ATC accordingly. ATC will honor such requests and advise pilots when the requested runway is noise sensitive. When use of a runway other than the one assigned is requested, pilot cooperation is encouraged to preclude disruption of traffic flows or creation of conflicting patterns.

3-91b Note. — It is not necessary for a controller to specifically inquire if the pilot will use a specific runway or to offer him a choice of runways. If a pilot prefers to use a different runway than that specified or the one most nearly aligned with the wind, he is expected to inform ATC accordingly.

3-91 References. — FAR 91.87; AIM 226.

3-92 STOL RUNWAYS

STOL (short takeoff and landing) runways are used as follows:

a. A designated STOL runway may be assigned only when requested by the pilot or as specified in a letter of agreement with an aircraft operator.

b. ATC will issue the measured STOL runway length if the pilot requests it.

3-92 Reference. — ATCH 3-61.

3-93 TAILWIND ADVISORY

When authorizing use of runways and a tailwind component exists, the controller will state both wind direction and velocity.*

3-93 Note. — The wind may be described as "calm" when appropriate.

3-93 Reference. — ATCH 3-62.

3-94 thru 3-99 RESERVED

Section 9. TAXI AND GROUND MOVEMENT PROCEDURES

3-100 GENERAL

a. Approval from ATC must be obtained prior to moving an aircraft or vehicle onto the movement area during the hours an airport traffic control tower is in operation.

b. ATC clearances or instructions pertaining to taxiing are predicated on known traffic and known physical airport conditions. Therefore, it is important that pilots clearly understand the clearance or instruction. Although an ATC clearance is issued for taxiing purposes, when operating in accordance with the FAR's, it is the responsibility of the pilot to avoid collision with other aircraft. Since "the pilot in command of an aircraft is directly responsible for, and is the final authority as to, the operation of that aircraft," the pilot should obtain clarification of any clearance or instruction which is not understood.

3-100 References. — FAR 91.3; AIM 241.

3-101 GROUND COMMUNICATIONS

a. Pilots of departing aircraft should communicate with the control tower on the appropriate ground control frequency to receive taxi information. Pilots should state the appropriate ATIS code on initial contact to ground control if clearance delivery was not contacted prior to taxi. ATC will provide current airport/departure information, as appropriate, when the ATIS is unavailable or omitted by the pilot. Pilots should include the following information on initial contact:*

(1) Full call sign.

(2) Location on the airport.

(3) ATIS code, if appropriate.

(4) Intention.

3-101a Example. —
Dubuque Ground, Tomahawk Two Three Four Seven Quebec at Crescent, taxi for takeoff.

b. Pilots should remain on ground control frequency during taxi and runup, then change to tower frequency when ready to request takeoff clearance, unless otherwise advised by the tower. Pilots of turbine-powered aircraft are considered ready for takeoff when they reach the end of the runway, unless they advise otherwise.

3-101a Note 1. — The majority of ground control frequencies are in the 121.6 - 121.9 MHz bandwidth. Ground control frequencies are provided to eliminate frequency congestion on the tower (local control) frequency and are limited to communications between the tower and aircraft on the ground and between the tower and utility vehicles on the airport and provide a clear VHF channel for arriving and departing aircraft. They are used for issuance of taxi information, clearances, and other necessary contacts between the tower and aircraft or other vehicles operated on the airport. Normally, only one ground control frequency is assigned at an airport; however, at locations where the traffic so warrants, a second ground control frequency may be assigned.

3-101a Note 2. — If initial contact with the tower facility is clearance delivery, it may be unnecessary to restate the ATIS code to ground control.

3-101 Reference. — AIM 235.

3-102 GROUND TRAFFIC MOVEMENT

Controllers will issue by radio or directional light signals specific instructions which approve or disapprove the movement of aircraft, vehicles, equipment, or personnel on the movement area.

a. Conditional instructions that are dependent upon the movement of an arrival aircraft on or approaching the runway or a departure aircraft established on a takeoff roll will not be issued. Controllers may not make statements such as, "Taxi into position and hold behind landing traffic," or "Taxi across Runway Three Six behind departing Jetstar." The above requirement does not preclude the controller issuing instructions to follow an aircraft observed to be operating on the movement area in accordance with an ATC clearance/instruction and in such a manner that the instructions to follow are not ambiguous.

b. Controllers will *NOT* use the word "cleared" in conjunction with authorization for aircraft to taxi. The prefix *"TAXI," "PROCEED,"* or *"HOLD"* will be used as appropriate.

3-102 Reference. — ATCH 3-80.

3-103 AIRPORT INFORMATION

a. ATC will provide current airport information, as appropriate, to departing aircraft. Airport/departure information contained in the ATIS broadcast may be omitted if the pilot states the appropriate ATIS code.

b. The controller will issue departure information by including the following:

(1) Taxi information, as necessary.

(2) Runway in use.

(3) Surface wind. Where appropriate, centerfield wind from the LLWAS display.

(4) Altimeter setting.

3-103b(1) thru (4) Example. —
Tomahawk Two Three Four Seven Quebec, Dubuque Ground, taxi to Runway Three Six. Wind three three zero at one zero. Altimeter three zero two zero.

(5) Time, when requested.

(6) The official ceiling and visibility will be used to a departing aircraft before takeoff as follows:

(a) To a VFR aircraft when weather is below VFR conditions.

(b) To an IFR aircraft when weather is below VFR conditions or highest takeoff minima, whichever is greater.*

(7) An advisory to *"check density altitude"* when appropriate.

(8) Braking action for the runway in use as received from pilots or the airport management when Braking Action Advisories are in effect.

3-103b(6)(b) Note. — Standard takeoff minimums are published in FAR 91.116(f). Takeoff minima other than standard are prescribed for specific airports/runways and published in a tabular form supplement to the NOS instrument approach procedures charts.

3-103 Reference. — ATCH 3-100.

3-104 TAXI INFORMATION

When ground movement information is required, controllers will issue the route for the aircraft to follow on the movement area in concise and easy to understand terms.

a. Controllers must determine the position of an aircraft before issuing taxi instructions.

b. Controllers need not issue taxi route information unless the pilot specifically requests it.

3-104b Example. —
Tomahawk Four Seven Quebec is unfamiliar with the airport, request progressive taxi instructions.

c. When authorizing an aircraft to taxi to any point other than an assigned takeoff runway, absence of holding instructions authorizes an aircraft to cross all taxiways and runways that intersect the taxi route. If it is the intent of the controller to hold the aircraft short of any given point along the taxi route, controllers will issue the route if necessary, then state the holding instructions.*

ATC Phraseology:
Hold position.
Hold for (reason).
Taxi/Continue taxiing/Proceed:
via (route),
or
on (runway number or taxiways, etc.),
or
to (location),
or
(direction),
or
across Runway (number),
or

via (route), **hold short of** (location),
or
follow (traffic)(restrictions as necessary),
or
behind (traffic).

3-104c Examples. —
Hold for landing traffic.

Taxi via Lima to the ramp.

Proceed northbound across Runway Two Seven via Juliet. Hold short of Runway Two Two.

Follow the Cessna ahead.

d. When authorizing an aircraft to taxi to an assigned takeoff runway and hold short instructions are not issued, controllers will specify the runway preceded by the phrase *"taxi to,"* and issue taxi instructions if necessary. This authorizes the aircraft to *"cross"* all runways/taxiways which the taxi route intersects except the assigned takeoff runway. This does *NOT* authorize the aircraft to *"enter"* or *"cross"* the assigned takeoff runway at any point.*

ATC Phraseology:
Taxi to Runway (number) **via** . . .

3-104d Examples. —
Taxi to Runway One Two.

Taxi to Runway Two Five Left via the inner to the outer at Golf.

e. When assigning a takeoff runway and *"hold short"* instructions are issued, controllers will specify the runway, issue taxi instructions if necessary, and then state the hold short instructions.

ATC Phraseology:
Runway (number),
taxi/proceed via (route if necessary),
hold:
short of (runway number),
or
short of (location),
or
on (taxi strip, runup pad, etc.),
and if necessary,
traffic (traffic information),
or
for (reason).

3-104e Example. —
Cessna Five Seven Echo, Runway Two Zero Left, taxi via Taxiway Delta. Hold short of Runway One Three.

Runway Two Zero Left. We will hold short of Runway One Three, Cessna Five Seven Echo.

f. Instructions to expedite a taxiing aircraft or a moving vehicle.

ATC Phraseology:

Taxi without delay (traffic if necessary).

Exit/Proceed/Cross (runway/taxiway) **without delay.**

3-104f Example. —
Cross Runway Two One without delay, traffic on a one mile final.

3-104c Note. — Movement of aircraft or vehicles on nonmovement areas is the responsibility of the pilot, aircraft operator, or airport management.

3-104c and d Note. — Good operating practice dictates that pilots acknowledge all runway crossing clearances and "hold short" instructions.

3-104 Reference. — ATCH 3-81.

3-105 HOLDING NEAR RUNWAYS

Aircraft should hold short of a runway as follows:

a. At established holding points marked by taxiway hold lines/signs.*

b. If no hold lines/signs are established, ATC will instruct aircraft where to hold short of a specific runway.

c. Traffic information will be issued by ATC as necessary.

3-105a Note. — When instructed by ATC *"HOLD SHORT OF (runway, ILS critical area, etc.),"* the pilot should stop so no part of the aircraft extends beyond the holding line.

3-105 Reference. — ATCH 3-83.

3-106 TAXIWAY MARKING

The taxiway centerline is marked with a continuous yellow line. The taxiway edge may be marked with two continuous yellow lines 6 inches apart. Taxiway HOLDING LINES consist of two continuous and two dashed lines, spaced 6 inches between lines, perpendicular to the taxiway centerline; more recently, HOLD LINES also consist of one or more signs at the edge of the taxiway, with white characters on a red sign face.

3-106 Reference. — AIM 60.

3-107 PRECISION APPROACH CRITICAL AREA

If an ILS/MLS critical area is marked and identifiable, aircraft and surface vehicle operations will be restricted, and ATC will provide information as follows when the ILS/MLS is being used for approach/landing guidance.*

a. ILS Obstacle Critical Area —

A rectangular obstacle critical area surrounds the approach end of each Category II and Category III ILS runway. When conditions are reported ceiling less than 200 feet and/or RVR 2,000 or less, ATC will not authorize vehicles/aircraft to be in the area when an aircraft conducting an approach/missed approach enters/is over the area.

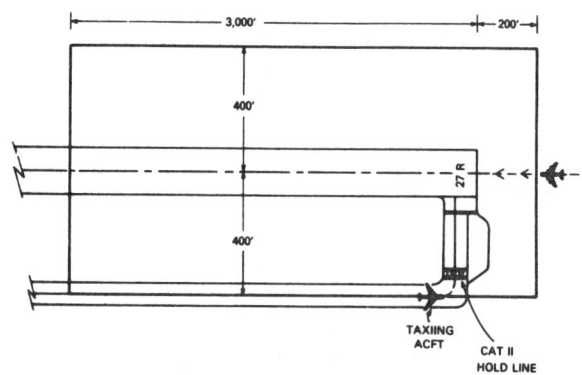

3-107a Illustration

b. Glide Slope Critical Area —

When conditions are less than reported ceiling 800 feet and/or visibility 2 miles, ATC will not authorize vehicles/aircraft to operate in the area when an arriving aircraft is inside the ILS OM or fix used in lieu of the OM unless that aircraft has reported the airport in sight and is circling/sidestepping to land on other than the ILS runway.*

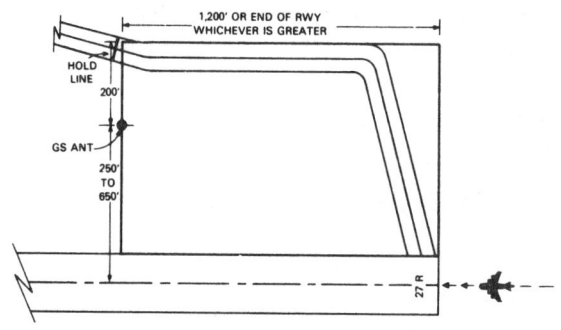

3-107b Illustration

c. Localizer Critical Area —

(1) When conditions are less than reported ceiling 800 feet and/or visibility 2 miles, ATC will not authorize vehicle or aircraft operations in or over the area when an arriving aircraft is between the ILS final approach fix and the airport, except:

(a) A preceding arriving aircraft on the same or another runway that passes over or through the area while landing or exiting the runway.

(b) A preceding departing aircraft or missed approach on the same or another runway that passes through or over the area.

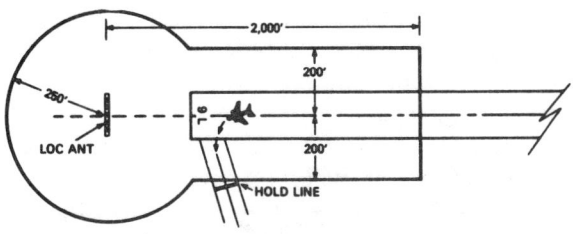

3-107c(1) Illustration*

(2) In addition to (1) above, when conditions are reported ceiling less than 200 feet and/or RVR 2,000 or less, ATC will not authorize vehicle or aircraft operations in or over the area when an arriving aircraft is inside the ILS MM.

d. Glideslope/Localizer Critical Area Advisories —

When conditions are such that vehicle/aircraft restrictions in/over the area are not required and an arriving aircraft advises the tower it will operate *"Coupled"* or *"Autoland"* or uses a similar phrase, the controller will promptly issue an advisory if a vehicle/aircraft will be in/over an area when the arriving aircraft is inside the ILS middle marker.

ATC Phraseology:

Localizer/Glideslope signal not protected.

3-107 Note 1. — Restrictions to the operation of aircraft and vehicles are required to assure the integrity of ILS/MLS course signals and to meet obstacle clearance needs. Airport operators are responsible for installing and maintaining appropriate signs and markings delineating taxi lanes, hold lines, and no parking areas associated with ILS/MLS critical areas.

3-107 Note 2. — For holding purposes, no point on the longitudinal axis of the aircraft is permitted past the hold line.

3-107b Note. — The glideslope critical area extends to the near edge of the runway that the ILS serves. It does not include the runway.

3-107c(1) Illustration Note. — The principal purpose of this graphic is to illustrate the parameters of operations within the critical area, not to define the actual limits of the area.

3-107 Reference. — ATCH 3-84.

3-108 GROUND OPERATIONS NEAR POSSIBLE WAKE TURBULENCE

ATC will avoid clearances which require:*

a. Heavy jet aircraft to use greater than normal taxiing power.

b. Small aircraft or helicopters to taxi in close proximity to taxiing or hover taxi helicopters.

3-108 Note. — The term wake turbulence as used by ATC includes vortices, thrust stream turbulence, jet blast, jet wash, propeller wash, and rotor wash both on the ground and in the air.

3-108 Reference. — ATCH 3-82.

3-109 TAXI DURING LOW VISIBILITY

a. Pilots and aircraft operators should be constantly aware that during certain low visibility conditions the movement of aircraft and vehicles on airports may not be visible to the tower controller. This may prevent visual confirmation of an aircraft's adherence to taxi instructions. Pilots should, therefore, exercise extreme vigilance and proceed cautiously under such conditions.

b. When vision difficulties are encountered pilots should immediately inform the controller. Pilots should proceed with extreme caution when taxiing toward the sun. Of vital importance is the need for pilots to notify the controller when difficulties are encountered or at the first indication of becoming disoriented.

3-109 Reference. — AIM 242.

3-110 thru 3-119 RESERVED

Section 10. AIRCRAFT SPACING

3-120 SEQUENCE/SPACING PROCEDURES

ATC will establish the sequence of arriving and departing aircraft by requiring them to adjust flight or ground operations as necessary to achieve proper spacing.*

ATC Phraseology:

Cleared for takeoff.

Cleared for immediate takeoff.

Cleared for immediate takeoff or hold short (traffic).

Cleared for immediate takeoff or taxi off the runway.

Extend downwind.

Make short approach.

Number (landing sequence number).

Follow (description and location of traffic) *or, if traffic is utilizing another runway,* **traffic is** (description and location) **landing Runway** (number of runway being used).

Circle the airport.

Make left/right three-sixty/two-seventy.

Go around.

Cleared to land.

Cleared for:

touch-and-go, *or*

stop-and-go, *or*

low approach.

Cleared for the option.

Option approved.

Unable option, make (specific type of approach/full stop landing),

Unable (type of option), **other options approved.**

3-120 Examples. —

Number two, follow the Learjet on a two mile final.

Cleared to land, Runway One Five Left. Traffic is a Bonanza landing One Five Right.

Unable option; make low approach.

Unable stop and go, other options approved.

3-120 Note. — For proper helicopter spacing, ATC may use speed adjustments rather than course changes.

3-120 Reference. — ATCH 3-90.

3-121 MANEUVERING TURNS

On occasion it may be necessary for a pilot to maneuver his aircraft to maintain spacing with the traffic he has been sequenced to follow. The controller can anticipate minor maneuvering such as shallow "S" turns. The controller cannot, however, anticipate a major maneuver such as a 360 degree turn. If a pilot makes a 360 degree turn after he has obtained a landing sequence, the result is usually a gap in the landing interval, and more importantly, it causes a chain reaction which may result in a conflict with following traffic and interruption of the sequence established by the tower or approach controller. Should a pilot decide he needs to make maneuvering turns to maintain spacing behind a preceding aircraft, he should always advise the controller if at all possible. Except when requested by the controller or in emergency situations, a 360 degree turn should never be executed in the traffic pattern or when receiving radar service without first advising the controller.

3-121 Reference. — AIM 224.

3-122 LOW APPROACH

a. A low approach (sometimes referred to as a low pass) is the go-around maneuver following approach. Instead of landing or making a touch-and-go, a pilot may wish to go around (low approach) in order to expedite a particular operation—a series of practice instrument approaches is an example of such an operation. Unless otherwise authorized by ATC, the low approach should be made straight ahead, with no turns or climb made until the pilot has made a thorough visual check for other aircraft in the area.

b. When operating within an airport traffic area, a pilot intending to make a low approach should contact the tower for approval. This request should be made prior to starting the final approach.

3-122 Reference. — AIM 232.

3-123 SHORT APPROACH

a. To achieve proper spacing, ATC may instruct an aircraft to *"make short approach."* The pilot is expected to alter his turn from downwind leg to base leg, in the traffic pattern, so as to make a short final approach.

b. A pilot may initiate a short approach. However, good operating practice dictates he inform the controller of such action. This will ensure ATC will be able to maintain proper sequencing and spacing of arriving and departing aircraft.

3-123 Reference.—ATCH & AIM Glossary.

3-124 THE OPTION

The "Option" procedure will permit an instructor, flight examiner, or pilot the option to make a touch-and-go, low approach, missed approach, stop-and-go, or full stop landing. This procedure can be very beneficial in a training situation in that neither the student pilot nor examinee would know what maneuver would be accomplished. The pilot should make his request for this procedure passing the final approach fix inbound on an instrument approach or reporting downwind for a VFR traffic pattern. The advantages of this procedure as a training aid are that it enables an instructor or examiner to obtain the reaction of a trainee or examinee under changing conditions, the pilot would not have to discontinue an approach in the middle of the procedure due to student error or pilot proficiency requirements, and finally, it allows more flexibility and economy in training programs. This procedure will only be used at those locations with an operational control tower and will be subject to ATC approval.

3-124 Reference. — AIM 245.

3-125 REQUEST FOR CLOSED TRAFFIC

Controllers may approve/disapprove pilot requests to remain in closed traffic for successive operations subject to local traffic conditions.*

ATC Phraseology:

Left/right (if required) **closed traffic approved. Report** (position if required), *or*

Unable closed traffic, (additional information as required).

3-125 Examples. —
Right closed traffic approved, report downwind.

Unable closed traffic due reduced visibility.

3-125 Note. — Segregated traffic patterns for helicopters to runways and other areas may be established by letter of agreement or other local operating procedures.

3-125 Reference. — ATCH 3-132.

3-126 AIRCRAFT CATEGORIES/CLASSES

a. For purposes of terminal operations, aircraft are categorized as follows:

(1) *Category I*—Light-weight, single-engine, personal-type propeller-driven aircraft. (Does not include higher performance, single-engine aircraft.)

(2) *Category II*—Light-weight, twin-engine, propeller-driven aircraft weighing 12,500 pounds or less, such as the Aero Commander, Beech Baron, Twin Cessna. (Does not include such aircraft as a Super King Air 300, Gulfstream I, or YS11.)

(3) *Category III*—All other aircraft such as the higher performance single-engine, large twin-engine, four-engine, and turbojet aircraft.

b. For the purposes of Wake Turbulence Separation Minima, ATC classifies aircraft as follows:

(1) *Heavy*—Aircraft capable of takeoff weights of 300,000 pounds or more, whether or not they are operating at this weight during a particular phase of flight.

(2) *Large*—Aircraft of more than 12,500 pounds, maximum certificated takeoff weight, up to 300,000 pounds.

(3) *Small*—Aircraft of 12,500 pounds or less maximum certificated takeoff weight.

3-126 References.—ATCH 3-105; ATCH & AIM Glossary.

3-127 SIMULTANEOUS SAME DIRECTION RUNWAY OPERATIONS

Simultaneous, same direction operations will be authorized on parallel runways, on parallel landing strips, or on a runway and a parallel landing strip only when the following conditions are met:

a. Operations are conducted in VFR conditions, unless visual separation is applied.

b. Two-way radio communication is maintained with the aircraft involved and pertinent traffic information is issued.

c. The distance between the runways or landing strips is in accordance with the minima in the Table (the greater minimum is used if two categories are involved).

3-127c Table. — Same Direction Distance Minima

Aircraft Category	Minimum distance (feet) between parallel	
	Runway centerlines	Edges of adjacent strips or runway and strip
Lightweight, single-engine, propeller-driven	300	200
Twin-engine, propeller-driven	500	400
All others	700	600

3-127 Reference. — ATCH 3-92.

3-128 SIMULTANEOUS OPPOSITE DIRECTION RUNWAY OPERATIONS

Simultaneous, opposite direction operations will be authorized on parallel runways, on parallel landing strips, or on a runway and a parallel landing strip only when the following conditions are met:

a. Operations are conducted in VFR conditions.

b. Two-way radio communication is maintained with the aircraft involved and pertinent traffic information is issued.

ATC Phraseology:

Traffic (description) landing/taking off/low approach, opposite direction on parallel runway/landing strip.

c. The distance between the runways or landing strips is in accordance with the minima in the Table.

3-128c Table. — Opposite Direction Distance Minima

	Minimum distance (feet) between parallel	
Time of Operation	Runway centerlines	Edges of adjacent strips or runway and strip
Between sunrise and sunset	1,400	1,400
Between sunset and sunrise	2,800	Not authorized

WAKE TURBULENCE APPLICATION

d. Category I or II aircraft will be separated behind a nonheavy Category III aircraft taking off or making a low-missed approach when ATC is utilizing opposite direction takeoffs on the same runway by *3 minutes*, unless a pilot has INITIATED a request to deviate from the *3-minute* interval. In the latter case, the controller will issue a wake turbulence advisory before clearing the aircraft for takeoff.*

e. ATC will separate aircraft behind a heavy jet departing or making a low/missed approach when utilizing opposite direction takeoffs or landing on the same or parallel runways separated by less than 2,500 feet — *3 minutes*.

f. The controller will inform an aircraft when it is necessary to hold in order to provide the required *3-minute* interval.

ATC Phraseology:

Hold for wake turbulence.

3-128d Note. — A request for takeoff does not initiate a waiver request; the request for takeoff must be accompanied by a request to deviate from the *3-minute* rule.

3-128 Reference. — ATCH 3-93.

3-129 RESERVED

Section 11. TAKEOFF

3-130 POSITION DETERMINATION

a. Controllers must determine the position of an aircraft before issuing a takeoff clearance.*

b. The local controller will consider that pilots of turbine-powered aircraft are ready for takeoff when they reach the runway or warm-up block unless advised otherwise.

3-130a Note. — The aircraft's position may be determined visually by the controller, by pilots, or through use of ASDE.

3-130 References. — ATCH 3-7, 3-108.

3-131 VFR DIRECTION OF FLIGHT

a. VFR aircraft departing a tower controlled airport should inform the tower of their proposed direction of flight if it differs from a standard departure.*

b. The following terms are used to describe traffic pattern departures:

(1) Straight-out departure.

(2) Left/Right crosswind departure.

(3) Left/Right downwind departure.

(4) Direction of flight referred to by one of the eight cardinal compass points, i.e., southwest departure, northbound departure, etc.

3-131a Note. — When prior communication with ATC has previously been established, i.e., ARSA clearance, this information may not be necessary.

3-131 Reference. — AIM 223.

3-132 AMENDED CLEARANCES

When a local controller delivers or amends an ATC clearance to an aircraft awaiting departure and that aircraft is holding short of a runway or is holding in position on a runway, an additional clearance will be issued to prevent the possibility of the aircraft inadvertently taxiing onto the runway and/or beginning takeoff roll. In such cases, one of the following ATC instructions will be appended as appropriate.

ATC Phraseology:

Hold short of runway, or

Hold in position.

3-132 Example. —

United Two Fifteen, change departure frequency to one two four point eight, maintain three thousand. Hold in position.

3-132 Reference. — ATCH 3-7.

3-133 TAKEOFF POSITION AND HOLD

a. A controller may authorize an aircraft to taxi into takeoff position and hold when takeoff clearance cannot be issued because of traffic. Traffic information may be issued to any aircraft so authorized. Controllers may omit traffic information when the traffic is another aircraft which has landed on or is taking off on the same runway and is clearly visible to the holding aircraft. Conditional phrases such as "behind landing traffic" or "after the departing aircraft" will not be used.

ATC Phraseology:

Taxi into position and hold.

If required, (traffic information).

b. When more than one runway is active, the controller will state the runway number, followed by the taxi into position clearance.

ATC Phraseology:

Runway (number), **taxi into position and hold.**

3-133b Example. —

Lear Two Five Golf, Runway Two Two, taxi into position and hold. Position and hold Runway Two Two, Lear Two Five Golf.

3-133 Reference. — ATCH 3-103.

3-134 ANTICIPATED TAKEOFF SEPARATION

Takeoff clearance need not be withheld until prescribed separation exists if there is a reasonable assurance it will exist when the aircraft starts takeoff roll.

3-134 Reference. — ATCH 3-104.

3-135 SAME RUNWAY TAKEOFF SEPARATION

A departing aircraft is separated from a preceding, departing, or arriving aircraft using the same runway by ensuring that it does not begin takeoff roll until:

a. The other aircraft has departed and crossed the runway end or turned to avert any conflict. If the controller can determine distances by reference to suitable landmarks, the other aircraft need only be airborne if the following minimum distance exists between aircraft:

(1) When only Category I aircraft are involved — *3,000 feet.*

(2) When a Category I aircraft is preceded by a Category II aircraft — *3,000 feet.*

(3) When either the succeeding or both are Category II aircraft — *4,500 feet.*

(4) When either is a Category III aircraft — *6,000 feet.*

(5) When the succeeding aircraft is a helicopter, visual separation may be applied in lieu of distance minima.

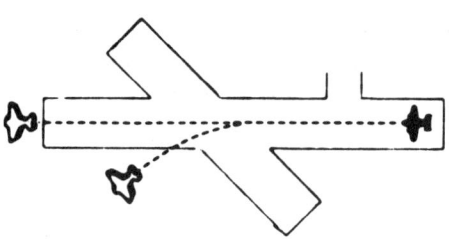

3-135a Illustration 1

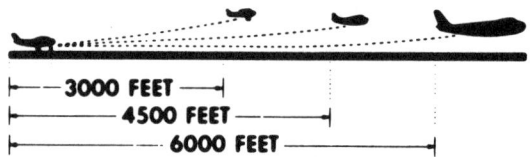

3-135a Illustration 2

b. A preceding landing aircraft has taxied off the runway.

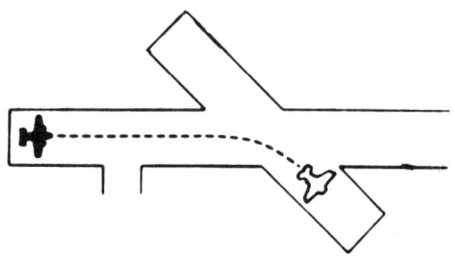

3-135b Illustration

WAKE TURBULENCE APPLICATION

c. Controllers will not issue clearances which imply or indicate approval of rolling takeoffs by heavy jet aircraft.

d. Controllers will not issue clearances to a small aircraft to taxi into position and hold on the same runway behind a departing heavy jet aircraft to apply the necessary intervals.

e. Radar separation minima may be applied in lieu of the 2-minute requirement in **f** below. When the radar separation minima is applied, controllers must ensure that the appropriate radar separation exists at or prior to the time the aircraft becomes airborne when taking off behind a heavy jet.*

f. IFR/VFR aircraft taking off behind a heavy jet departure are separated by *2 minutes*, when departing:*

(1) The same runway.

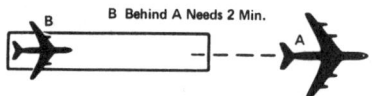

3-135f(1) Illustration

(2) A parallel runway separated by less than 2,500 feet.

g. Aircraft are separated from a heavy jet when operating on a runway with a displaced landing threshhold if projected flight paths will cross — *2 minutes* when:

(1) A departure follows a heavy jet arrival.

(2) An arrival follows a heavy jet departure.

h. The *2-minute* minimum may not be applied if the pilot of a departing IFR/VFR aircraft has initiated a request to deviate from the *2-minute* interval. In this case, the controller will issue a wake turbulence cautionary advisory before clearing the aircraft for takeoff.

i. ATC will separate a Category I or II aircraft behind a large aircraft taking off or making a low/missed approach when utilizing opposite direction takeoffs on the same runway by *3 minutes* unless a pilot has INITIATED a request to deviate from the *3-minute* interval. In the latter case, controllers will issue a wake turbulence advisory before clearing the aircraft for takeoff.*

j. ATC will separate aircraft behind a heavy jet departing or making a low/missed approach when utilizing opposite direction takeoffs or landings on the same or parallel runways separated by less than 2,500 feet — *3 minutes*.

k. Controllers will inform an aircraft when it is necessary to hold in order to provide the required *3-minute* interval.

ATC Phraseology:

Hold for wake turbulence.

3-135e Note. — Pilots may request additional separation, but should make this request before taxiing on the runway.

3-135f Note. — Takeoff clearance to the following aircraft will not be issued until *2 minutes* after the heavy jet begins takeoff roll.

3-135i Note. — A request for takeoff does not initiate a waiver request; the request for takeoff must be accompanied by a request to deviate from the *3-minute* rule.

3-135 Reference. — ATCH 3-106.

3-136 INTERSECTION TAKEOFFS

a. In order to enhance airport capacities, reduce taxiing distances, minimize departure delays, and provide for more efficient movement of air traffic, controllers may initiate intersection takeoffs as well as approve them when the pilot requests. Intersection takeoffs are handled as follows:*

(1) Controllers may initiate an intersection takeoff.

(2) Controllers may authorize an intersection takeoff if the pilot requests it.

(3) The measured distance from the intersection to the runway end will be issued to any pilot who requests it.

ATC Phraseology:

Runway (runway number) **intersection departure.**

If requested or required,

Runway (runway number) **intersection departure,** (remaining length) **feet available.**

3-136a Example. —
Runway Seven intersection departure, four thousand six hundred feet available.

b. An aircraft is expected to taxi to (but not onto) the end of the assigned runway unless prior approval for an intersection departure is received from ground control.

c. Pilots should state their position on the airport when calling the tower for takeoff from a runway intersection.

3-136c Examples. —
Duke Tower, Cessna Three Six One Two Seven intersection Ten Golf ready for takeoff.

Wright Tower, Cherokee One Six Zero Niner Tango at the intersection of Runways Seven and One Five ready for takeoff.

3-136a Note. — If for *ANY* reason a pilot prefers to use a different intersection or the full length of the runway, HE IS EXPECTED TO INFORM ATC ACCORDINGLY.

3-136 Reference. — AIM 230.

3-137 INTERSECTION TAKEOFF INTERVAL

WAKE TURBULENCE APPLICATION

a. Controllers will separate a small aircraft taking off from an intersection on the same runway (same or opposite direction takeoff) behind a preceding departing large aircraft by ensuring that it does not start takeoff roll until at least *3 minutes* after the large aircraft has taken off. Controllers will inform an aircraft when it is necessary to hold in order to provide the required *3-minute* interval.*

ATC Phraseology:

Hold for wake turbulence.

b. The *3-minute* interval is not required when:*

(1) A pilot has INITIATED a request to deviate from that interval, or*

(2) The intersection is 500 feet or less from the departure point of the preceding aircraft and both aircraft are taking off in the same direction.

(3) Successive touch-and-go and stop-and-go operations are conducted with a small aircraft following a large aircraft, provided the pilot of the small aircraft maintains visual separation/spacing behind the preceding large aircraft.

c. When applying the provisions of **b**, controllers will:*

(1) Issue a wake turbulence advisory before clearing the aircraft for takeoff.

(2) Not clear the intersection departure for an immediate takeoff.

(3) When applying (1) or (2) above, controllers will issue a clearance to permit the trailing aircraft to deviate from course enough to avoid the flight path of the preceding nonheavy Category III departure.

(4) Separation requirements in accordance with same runway separation must also apply.

d. Controllers will separate an aircraft taking off from an intersection on the same runway (same or opposite direction takeoff) and parallel runways separated by less than 2,500 feet, by ensuring that it does not start takeoff roll until at least *3 minutes* after a heavy jet has taken off.

3-137a Note. — Aircraft conducting touch-and-go and stop-and-go operations are considered to be departing from an intersection.

3-137b(1) Note. — A request for takeoff does not initiate a waiver request; the request for takeoff must be accompanied by a request to deviate from the *3-minute* interval.

3-137 Reference. — ATCH 3-107.

3-138 INTERSECTING RUNWAY SEPARATION

Controllers will separate departing aircraft from an aircraft using an intersecting runway, or nonintersecting runways when the flight paths intersect, by ensuring that the departure does not begin takeoff roll until one of the following exists:

a. The preceding aircraft has departed and passed the intersection, has crossed the departure runway, or is turning to avert any conflict.

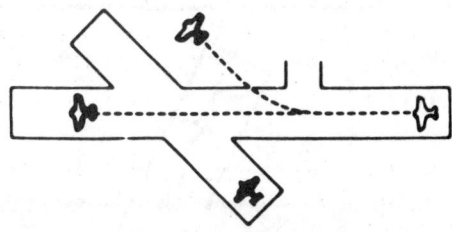

3-138a Illustration 1

WAKE TURBULENCE APPLICATION

c. IFR/VFR aircraft taking off behind a heavy jet departure are separated by *2 minutes,* when departing:*

(1) Crossing runways if projected flight paths will cross.

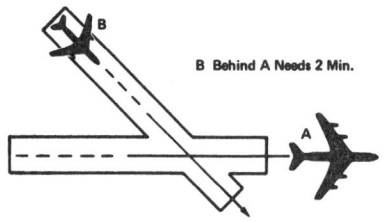

3-138c(1) Illustration

(2) A parallel runway separated by 2,500 feet or more if projected flight paths will cross.

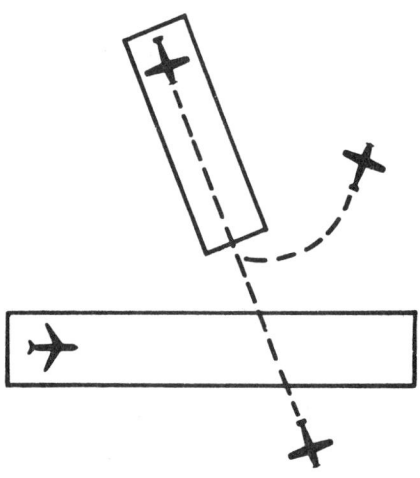

3-138a Illustration 2

b. A preceding arriving aircraft has taxied off the landing runway, completed the landing roll and will hold short of the intersection, passed the intersection, or has crossed over the departure runway.

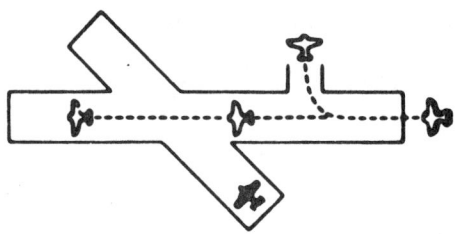

3-138b Illustration 1

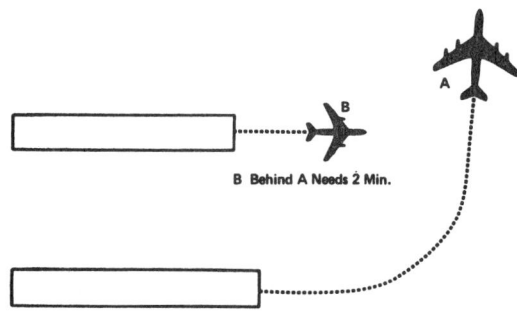

3-138c(2) Illustration

d. IFR/VFR aircraft departing behind a landing heavy jet on a crossing runway will be separated if the departure will fly through the airborne path of the arrival by *2 minutes.*

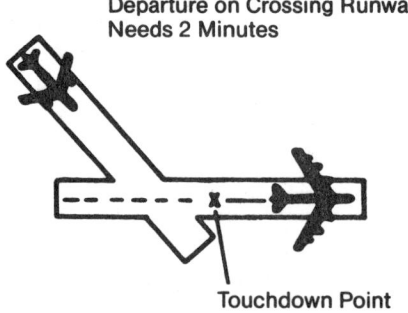

3-138d Illustration

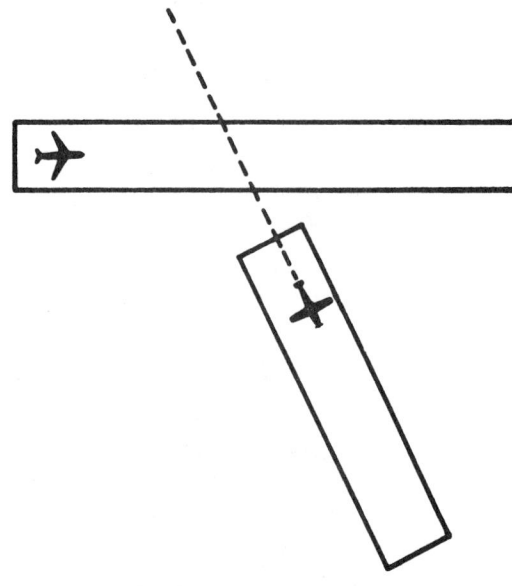

3-138b Illustration 2

e. The *2-minute* minimum need not be applied if the pilot of a departing IFR/VFR aircraft has initiated a request to deviate from the *2-minute* interval. In this case, controllers will issue a wake turbulence cautionary advisory before clearing the aircraft for takeoff.

3-138c Note. — Takeoff clearance to the following aircraft should not be issued by ATC until *2 minutes* after the heavy jet begins takeoff roll.

3-138 Reference. — ATCH 3-108.

3-139 TAKEOFF CLEARANCE PHRASEOLOGY

a. When only one runway is active, controllers may issue takeoff clearance without specifying the runway number.

ATC Phraseology:

Cleared for takeoff.

b. When more than one runway is active, the controller will first state the runway number followed by the takeoff clearance.

ATC Phraseology:

Runway (runway number), **cleared for takeoff.**

3-139b Example. —

United Ninety Heavy, change to Runway Three Five Right. You are cleared to land Runway Three Five Right, over.

Cleared to land Runway Three Five Right, United Ninety Heavy.

United Two-fifty, Runway Three Five Left, cleared for takeoff.

3-139 Reference. — ATCH 3-109.

3-140 CANCELLATION OF TAKEOFF CLEARANCE

Controllers will cancel a previously issued clearance for takeoff and inform the pilot of the reason if circumstances require.

ATC Phraseology:

Cancel takeoff clearance (reason).

3-140 Reference. — ATCH 3-110.

3-141 TAKEOFF ACTIONS

a. Pilots should not operate their transponder until ready for takeoff roll.

b. Pilots are encouraged to turn on their landing lights either *AFTER* takeoff clearance has been received (e.g., after being "in position") or upon reaching the runway, when beginning their takeoff roll.

c. Pilots should not change to departure control until advised to do so by the tower.

3-141 References. — AIM 246, 324.

3-142 DEPARTURE CONTROL INSTRUCTIONS

Departing IFR and VFR aircraft utilizing radar services will be informed, when about ½ mile beyond the runway end, to contact departure control provided further communication with the tower is not required.

ATC Phraseology:

Change to departure.

3-142 Reference. — ATCH 3-102.

3-143 thru 3-149 RESERVED

Section 12. LANDING

3-150 PATTERN TERMINOLOGY

a. The following terminology for the various components of a traffic pattern has been adopted as standard for use by ATC and pilots:

(1) *Upwind leg*—A flight path parallel to the landing runway in the direction of landing.

(2) *Crosswind leg*—A flight path at right angles to the landing runway off its takeoff end.

(3) *Downwind leg*—A flight path parallel to the landing runway in the opposite direction of landing.

(4) *Base leg*—A flight path at right angles to the landing runway off its approach end and extending from the downwind leg to the intersection of the extended runway centerline.

(5) *Final approach*—A flight path in the direction of landing along the extended runway centerline from the base leg to the runway.

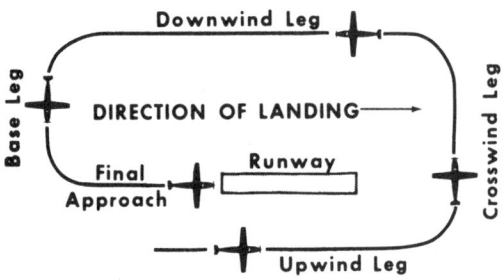

3-150a Illustration*

b. The following phraseology is used by ATC in giving traffic pattern instructions:

(1) *Left/Right traffic* — Pilots make a standard left/right traffic pattern entry, i.e., enter the traffic pattern on a 45° angle to the downwind leg.

(2) *Enter left/right base* — Pilots enter the traffic pattern from an extended left/right base leg.

(3) *Make straight-in* — Pilots enter the traffic pattern by intercepting the extended final approach course without executing any other portion of the traffic pattern.

3-150a Illustration Note. — This diagram is intended only to illustrate terminology used in identifying various components of a traffic patten. It should not be used as a reference or guide on how to enter a traffic pattern.

3-150 References. — AIM 221, 223, Glossary.

3-151 ARRIVAL INFORMATION

a. Initial call-up should be made by pilots about 15 miles from the airport unless terminal radar programs dictate otherwise.

3-151a Example. —

Key Tower, Grumman Six Zero One Two Mike is one five miles west, inbound for landing.

b. Current landing information will be provided, as appropriate, to arriving aircraft. Landing information contained in the ATIS broadcast may be omitted if the pilot states the appropriate ATIS code.

3-151b Example. —

Lafayette Tower, Cherokee One Six Seven Mike Alpha is one five miles south, inbound for landing, with UNIFORM.

c. Runway, wind, and altimeter may be omitted if a pilot uses the phrase "Have Numbers."*

3-151c Example. —

Whiteman Tower, Cessna Niner Three Three Two Hotel, Newhall Pass, with the numbers.

d. Controllers will issue landing information by including the following:

(1) Specific traffic pattern information (may be omitted if the aircraft is to circle the airport to the left).

ATC Phraseology:

Enter left/right base.

Straight-in.

Make straight-in.

Straight-in approved.

Right traffic.

Make right traffic.

Right traffic approved.

Continue.

(2) Runway in use.

(3) Surface wind.

(4) Altimeter setting.

(5) Any supplementary information.

(6) Clearance to land.

(7) Requests for additional position reports. Controllers use prominent geographical fixes which can be easily recognized from the air, preferably those depicted on sectional charts. This does not preclude the use of the legs of the traffic pattern as reporting point.*

(8) Ceiling and visibility, if either is below basic VFR minima.

(9) Braking action for the runway in use as received from the pilots or the airport management when Braking Action Advisories are in effect.

3-151d Examples. —

Grumman Six Zero One Two Mike, Key Tower, make right traffic Runway One Niner, wind one eight zero at one zero, altimeter two niner niner niner, report downwind west.

Cherokee One Six Seven Mike Alpha, Lafayette Tower, make right base Runway Five, report crossing the river.

Cessna Niner Three Three Two Hotel, Whiteman Tower, make straight-in Runway One Two. Use caution, numerous birds reported in the vicinity.

3-151c Note. — Pilot use of "Have Numbers" does not indicate receipt of the ATIS broadcast.

3-151d(7) Note. — At some locations, VFR checkpoints are depicted on Sectional Aeronautical and Terminal Area Charts. In selecting geographical fixes, depicted VFR checkpoints are preferred unless the pilot exhibits a familiarity with the local area.

3-151 Reference. — ATCH 3-120.

3-152 SAME RUNWAY LANDING SEPARATION

a. Controllers will separate an arriving aircraft from another aircraft using the same runway by ensuring that the arriving aircraft does not cross the landing threshold until one of the following conditions exists:

(1) The other aircraft has landed and taxied off the runway. Between sunrise and sunset, if the controller can determine distances by reference to suitable landmarks and the other aircraft has landed, it need not be clear of the runway if the following minimum distance from the landing threshold exists:

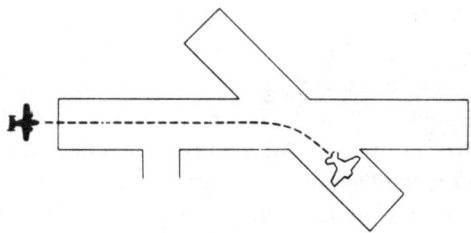

3-152a(1) Illustration

(a) When a Category I aircraft is landing behind a Category I or II — *3,000 feet.*

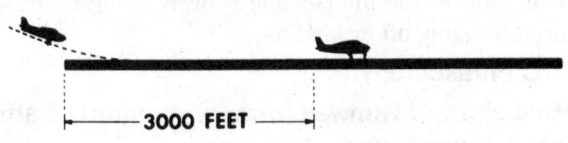

3-152a(1)(a) Illustration

(b) When a Category II aircraft is landing behind a Category I or II — *4,500 feet.*

3-152a(1)(b) Illustration

(2) The other aircraft has departed and crossed the runway end. If the controller can determine distances by reference to suitable landmarks and the other aircraft is airborne, it need not have crossed the runway end if the following minimum distance from the landing threshold exists:

(a) Category I aircraft landing behind Category I or II — *3,000 feet.*

(b) Category II aircraft landing behind Category I or II — *4,500 feet.*

(c) When either is a Category III aircraft — *6,000 feet.*

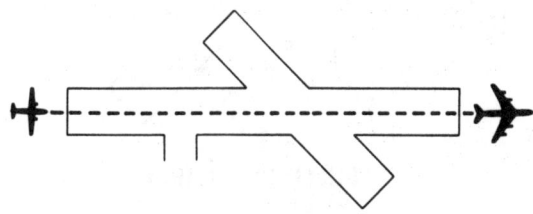

3-152a(2) Illustration 1

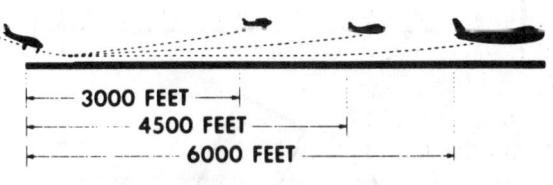

3-152a(2) Illustration 2

(3) When the succeeding aircraft is a helicopter, visual separation may be applied in lieu of distance minima.

WAKE TURBULENCE APPLICATION

b. Controllers will issue wake turbulence cautionary advisories and the position, altitude, if known, and direction of flight of the heavy jets to aircraft landing behind a departing/arriving heavy jet on the same or parallel runways separated by less than 2,500 feet.

3-152b Examples —

Cleared to land Runway Two Seven Left. Caution wake turbulence, heavy Boeing Seven Forty-seven departing Runway Two Seven Right.

Number two, follow the heavy Lockheed C-Five-A on a two-mile final. Caution wake turbulence.

3-152 Reference. — ATCH 3-122.

3-153 INTERSECTING RUNWAY SEPARATION

a. Controllers will separate an arriving aircraft using one runway from another aircraft using an intersecting runway or a nonintersecting runway when the flight paths intersect by ensuring that the arriving aircraft does not cross the landing threshold or flight path of the other aircraft until one of the following conditions exists:

(1) The preceding aircraft has departed and passed the intersection/flight path or is airborne and turning to avert any conflict.

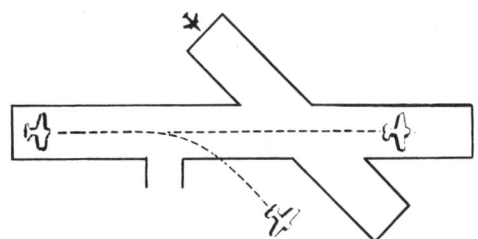

3-153a(1) Illustration 1

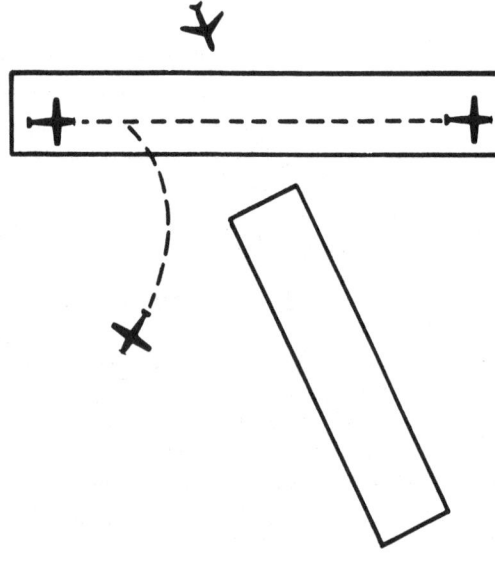

3-153a(1) Illustration 2

(2) A preceding arriving aircraft has taxied off the landing airway, completed landing roll and will hold short of the intersection/flight path, or has passed the intersection/flight path.

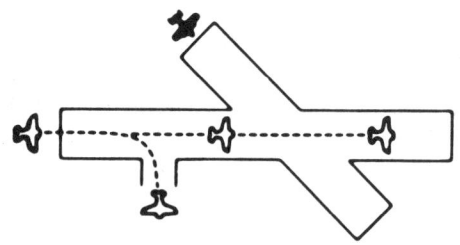

3-153a(2) Illustration 1

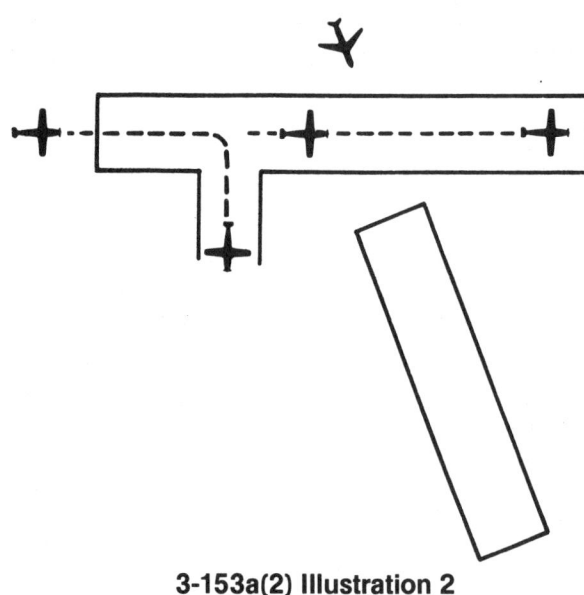

3-153a(2) Illustration 2

b. Where approved by the air traffic manager and in accordance with a facility directive, a controller may authorize an aircraft to takeoff from one runway and another aircraft to land simultaneously on an intersecting runway, or an aircraft to land on one runway and another aircraft to land simultaneously on an intersecting runway, as follows:*

(1) A simultaneous takeoff and landing operation may be conducted only in VFR conditions between sunrise and sunset.*

(2) The controller will instruct the landing aircraft to hold short of the intersecting runway being used by the aircraft taking off or landing.

ATC Phraseology:

Hold short of Runway (runway number), (traffic or other information).

(3) The controller will issue traffic information to both aircraft involved and MUST OBTAIN AN ACKNOWLEDGMENT from each.

3-153b(2) and (3) Example. —

Cincinnati Tower, Comair Thirty-two Thirty-one is on final for Runway One Eight.

Comair Thirty-two Thirty-one, Cincinnati Tower, cleared to land Runway One Eight. Hold short of Runway Two Seven Left, traffic landing Runway Two Seven Left.

Cleared to land Runway One Eight. Hold short of Runway Two Seven Left, Comair Thirty-two Thirty-one.

Delta Six Forty-eight, cleared to land Runway Two Seven Left, traffic landing Runway One Eight will hold short of Runway Two Seven Left.

Delta Six Forty-eight, roger.

(4) If requested by either aircraft, the controller will issue the measured distance from the landing threshold to the intersection.

3-153b(4) Example. —

Distance from the landing threshold of Runway One Eight to the intersection of Runway Two Four Left is six thousand forty-one feet.

(5) The conditions in (2), (3), and (4) will be met in sufficient time for the pilots to take other action if desired and no later than the time landing clearance is issued.

(6) Both runways must be dry with no reports that braking action is less than good.

(7) There is no tailwind for the landing aircraft restricted to hold short of the intersection.

(8) STOL aircraft operations are in accordance with a letter of agreement with the aircraft operator/pilot, or the pilot confirms that it is a STOL aircraft.

WAKE TURBULENCE APPLICATION

c. IFR/VFR aircraft landing behind a departing heavy jet on a crossing runway are separated if the arrival will fly through the airborne path of the departure by *2 minutes* or the appropriate radar separation minima.

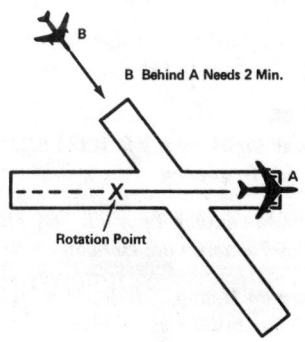

3-153c Illustration

d. Controllers will issue wake turbulence cautionary advisories and the position, altitude, if known, and direction of flight of the heavy jets to:

(1) IFR/VFR aircraft landing on crossing runways behind a departing heavy jet if the arrival flight path will cross the takeoff path behind the heavy jet and behind the heavy jet rotation point.

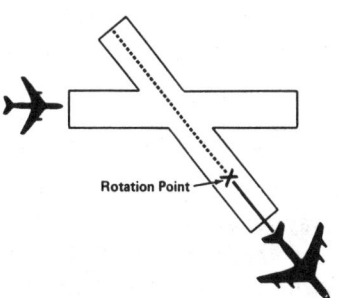

3-153d(1) Illustration

3-153d(1) Example. —

Cleared to land Runway Niner. Caution wake turbulence, heavy C-One Forty-one departing Runway One Five.

(2) VFR aircraft landing on a crossing runway behind an arriving heavy jet if the arrival flight path will cross.

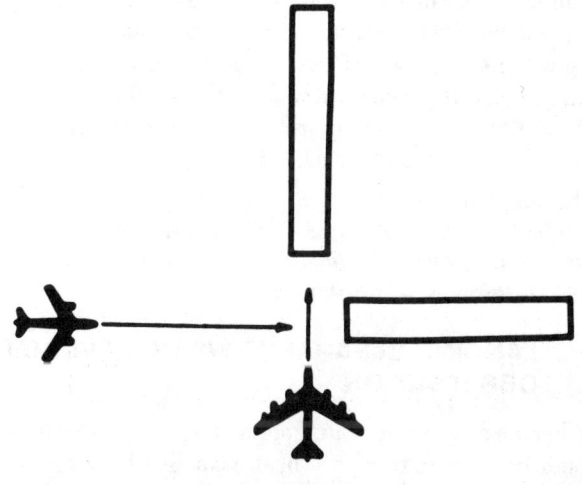

3-153d(2) Illustration

3-153d(2) Example. —

Cleared to land Runway Niner. Caution wake turbulence, heavy Boeing Seven Forty-seven landing Runway Three Six.

3-153b Note. — Application of these procedures does not relieve controllers from the responsibility of providing other appropriate separation.

3-153b(1) Note. — A simultaneous landing operation may be conducted during daytime or nighttime hours.

3-153 Reference. — ATCH 3-123.

3-154 PILOT RESPONSIBILITY—RUNWAY USE

The safety and operation of an aircraft remain the responsibility of the pilot. If for any reason (e.g., difficulty in discerning location of an intersection at night, inability to hold short of an intersection, wind factors, etc.) a pilot elects to use the full length of the runway, a different runway, or desires to obtain the distance from the landing threshold to the intersection, he is expected to promptly inform ATC accordingly.

3-154 Reference. — AIM 231.

3-155 LANDING CLEARANCE PHRASEOLOGY

Controllers will issue a landing clearance and restate the landing runway number whenever there is a possibility of a conflict with another aircraft which is using or planning to use another runway, or when an instrument approach is being conducted to a runway that is closed.

ATC Phraseology:

Cleared to land, *or*

Cleared to land, Runway (runway number).

3-155 Reference. — ATCH 3-126.

3-156 ANTICIPATED LANDING SEPARATION

Landing clearance to a succeeding aircraft in a landing sequence need not be withheld if the controller observes the positions of the aircraft and determines that prescribed runway separation will exist when the aircraft crosses the landing threshold. The controller will issue traffic information to the succeeding aircraft.

3-156 Example. —
Delta Forty-two, cleared to land. Traffic is a heavy Boeing Seven Sixty-seven, on a half mile final. Caution wake turbulence.

3-156 Reference. — ATCH 3-127.

3-157 LANDING CLEARANCE WITHOUT VISUAL OBSERVATION

When an arriving aircraft reports at a position where he should be seen but has not been visually observed, the controller will advise the aircraft as a part of the landing clearance that it is not in sight and restate the landing runway.*

ATC Phraseology:

Not in sight, cleared to land Runway (number).

3-157 Note. — Aircraft observed on the BRITE (tower) radar display *SATISFY* the visually observed requirement.

3-157 Reference. — ATCH 3-128.

3-158 WITHHOLDING LANDING CLEARANCE

Controllers will not withhold a landing clearance indefinitely even though it appears a violation of an FAR has been committed. The apparent violation might be the result of an emergency situation. In any event, controllers will assist the pilot to the extent possible.

3-158 Reference. — ATCH 3-129.

3-159 EXITING THE RUNWAY AFTER LANDING

a. After landing, unless otherwise instructed by the control tower, pilots should continue to taxi in the landing direction, proceed to the nearest suitable taxiway, and exit the runway without delay. Pilots should not turn on to another runway, or make a 180 degree turn to taxi back on an active runway, or change to ground control frequency while on the active runway without authorization from the tower.

b. An aircraft exiting the runway is not considered clear until all parts of the aircraft have crossed the holding line.

3-159 References. — AIM 60, 243.

3-160 RUNWAY EXITING INSTRUCTIONS

When appropriate, aircraft will be instructed where to turn off the runway after landing.*

ATC Phraseology:

Turn left/right (turning point), *or*

If able, turn left/right (turning point).

3-160 Examples. —
American Ten Heavy, turn right at the end.

Learjet Six One Golf, if able, turn left at the high speed.

3-160 Note. — It is not intended that runway exiting or taxi instructions normally be issued to airborne aircraft prior to landing.

3-160 Reference. — ATCH 3-130.

3-161 CHANGE TO GROUND

A pilot who has just landed should not change to ground control until he is directed to do so by the local controller.

3-161 Examples. —
Cessna Zero Four Eight, turn left at the high speed, taxi to the ramp. Remain this frequency.

Beech One Four November, turn left any intersection, contact ground point niner leaving the runway.

Clipper Four-eleven Heavy, if able, turn right at Kilo, contact ground one two one point seven five, exiting the runway.

3-161 Reference. — AIM 235.

3-162 thru 3-169 RESERVED

Section 13. HELICOPTER OPERATIONS

3-170 GENERAL

a. The following ATC procedures and phraseologies recognize the unique capabilities of helicopters and were developed to improve service to all users. Helicopter design characteristics and user needs often require operations from movement and nonmovement areas within the airport boundary. In order for ATC to properly apply these procedures, it is essential that pilots familiarize themselves with the local operations and make it known to controllers when additional instructions are necessary.

b. Insofar as possible, helicopter operations will be instructed to avoid the flow of fixed-wing aircraft to minimize overall delays; however, there will be many situations where faster/larger helicopters may be integrated with fixed-wing aircraft for the benefit of all concerned. Examples would include IFR flights, avoidance of noise sensitive areas, or use of runways/taxiways to minimize the hazardous effects of rotor downwash in congested areas.

c. Because helicopter pilots are intimately familiar with the effects of rotor downwash, they are best qualified to determine if a given operation can be conducted safely. Accordingly, the pilot has the final authority with respect to the specific airspeed/altitude combinations. ATC clearances are in no way intended to place the helicopter in a hazardous position. It is expected that pilots will advise ATC if a specific clearance will cause undue hazards to persons or property.

3-170 Reference. — AIM 238.

3-171 GROUND SERVICE

Controllers normally limit ATC ground service and instruction to *movement* areas; therefore, operations from *nonmovement* areas are conducted at pilot discretion and should be based on local policies, procedures, or letter of agreement. In order to maximize the flexibility of helicopter operations, it is necessary to rely heavily on sound pilot judgment. For example, hazards such as debris, obstructions, vehicles, or personnel must be recognized by the pilot, and action should be taken as necessary to avoid such hazards. Taxi, hover taxi, and air taxi operations are considered to be ground movements. Helicopters conducting such operations are expected to adhere to the same conditions, requirements, and practices as apply to other ground taxiing and ATC procedures.

3-171 Reference. — AIM 238.

3-172 TAXIING

a. The phraseology *"taxi"* is used when it is intended or expected that the helicopter will taxi on the airport surface, either via taxiways or other prescribed routes. *"Taxi"* is used primarily for helicopters equipped with wheels or in response to a pilot request. Preference should be given to this procedure whenever it is necessary to minimize effects of rotor downwash.

b. Pilots may request a *"hover taxi"* when a slow forward movement is desired, or when it may be appropriate to move very short distances. Pilots should avoid this procedure if rotor downwash is likely to cause damage to parked aircraft, or if blowing dust/snow could obscure visibility. If it is necessary to operate above 25 feet AGL when hover taxiing, the pilot should initiate a request to ATC.

c. *"Air taxi"* is the preferred method for helicopter ground movements on airports provided ground operations and conditions permit. Unless otherwise requested or instructed, pilots are expected to remain below 100 feet AGL. However, if a higher than normal airspeed or altitude is desired, the request should be made prior to lift-off. The pilot is solely responsible for selecting a safe airspeed for the altitude/operation being conducted. Use of *"air taxi"* enables the pilot to proceed at an optimum airspeed/altitude, minimize downwash effect, conserve fuel, and expedite movement from one point to another. Helicopters should avoid overflight of other aircraft, vehicles, and personnel during air taxi operations. Caution must be exercised concerning active runways and pilots must be certain that air taxi instructions are understood. Special precautions may be necessary at unfamiliar airports or airports with multiple/intersecting active runways.

3-172 Reference. — AIM 238.

3-173 TAKEOFF AND LANDING PROCEDURES— GENERAL

a. Helicopter operations may be conducted from a runway, taxiway, portion of a landing strip, or any clear area which could be used as a landing site such as the scene of an accident, a construction site, or the roof of a building. The terms used to describe designated areas from which helicopters operate are: movement area, landing/takeoff area, apron/ramp, heliport and helipad (see Pilot/Controller Glossary). These areas may be improved or unimproved and may be separate from or located on an airport/heliport. ATC will issue takeoff clearances from *movement* areas other than active runways, or in diverse directions from active runways, with additional instructions as necessary. Whenever possible, takeoff clearance will be issued in lieu of extended hover/air taxi operations.

b. Pilots should be alert to wind information as well as to wind indications in the vicinity of the helicopter. ATC should be advised of the intended method of departing. A pilot request to takeoff in a given direction indicates that the pilot is willing to accept the wind condition and controllers will honor the request if traffic permits. Departure points could be a significant distance from the control tower and it may be difficult or impossible for the controller to determine the helicopter's relative position to the wind.

c. If takeoff is requested from *nonmovement* areas, additional instructions will be issued as necessary. The pilot is responsible for operating in a safe manner and should exercise due caution.

d. Every effort will be made to permit helicopters to proceed direct and land as near as possible to their final destination on the airport. Traffic density, the need for detailed taxiing instructions, frequency congestion, or other factors may affect the extent to which service can be expedited. As with ground movement operations, a high degree of pilot/controller cooperation and communication is necessary to achieve safe and efficient operations.

3-173 Reference. — AIM 238.

3-174 HELICOPTER SURFACE OPERATIONS

a. When it is necessary for a wheeled helicopter to taxi on the surface, controllers will use the phraseology prescribed for aircraft taxi and vehicle operations.

b. When requested or necessary for a helicopter/VTOL aircraft to proceed at a slow speed above the surface, normally below 20 knots and in ground effect, controllers will use the following phraseology, supplemented as is appropriate.

ATC Phraseology:

Hover taxi (supplemented, as appropriate).

Caution (dust, blowing snow, loose debris, taxiing light aircraft, personnel, etc.).

c. When requested or necessary for a helicopter to proceed expeditiously from one point to another, normally below 100 feet AGL and at airspeeds above 20 knots, controllers will use the following phraseology, supplemented as is appropriate with the phraseology prescribed for aircraft taxi and vehicle operations.

ATC Phraseology:

Air taxi:

via (direct, as requested, or specified route) **to** (location, heliport, helipad, operating/movement area, active/inactive runway).

Avoid (aircraft/vehicles/personnel).

If required,

Remain at or below (altitude).

Caution (wake turbulence or other reasons above).

Land and contact tower, *or*

Hold for (reason — takeoff clearance, release, landing/taxiing aircraft, etc.).

WAKE TURBULENCE APPLICATION

d. ATC will avoid clearances which require small aircraft or helicopters to taxi in close proximity to taxiing or hover taxi.

3-174 Reference. — ATCH 3-140.

3-175 FREQUENCY CHANGES

Controllers will normally avoid issuing a radio frequency change to helicopters, known to be single-piloted, which are hovering, air taxiing, or flying near the ground. At times, it may be necessary for pilots to alert ATC regarding single pilot operations to minimize delay of essential ATC communications. Whever possible, ATC instructions will be relayed through the frequency being monitored until a frequency change can be accomplished. Pilots must promptly advise ATC if they are unable to comply with a frequency change. Also, ATC should be advised if the pilot must land to accomplish the frequency change, unless it is clear the landing, e.g., on a taxiway or in a helicopter operating area, will have no impact on other air traffic.

3-175 Reference. — AIM 235.

3-176 HELICOPTER TAKEOFF CLEARANCES

a. Controllers will issue takeoff clearance from movement areas other than active runways, or in diverse directions, as necessary. Whenever possible, controllers will issue takeoff clearance in lieu of extended hover taxi or air taxi operations.

ATC Phraseology:

Cleared for takeoff from (present position, taxiway, helipad, numbers). **Make right/left turn for** (direction, points of compass, heading, NAVAID radial) **departure/departure route** (number, name, or code).

Avoid (taxiing aircraft/vehicles/personnel), *or*

Remain (direction) **of** (active runways, parking areas, passenger terminals, etc.).

Caution (power lines, unlighted obstructions, trees, wake turbulence, etc.).

b. If takeoff is requested from nonmovement areas and, in the controller's judgment, the operation appears to be reasonable, the following phraseology will be used instead of the takeoff clearance in **a** above.

ATC Phraseology:

Proceed as requested, use caution (reason and additional instructions, as appropriate).

c. If takeoff is requested from an area not visible to the controller, an area not authorized for helicopter use, an unlighted, nonmovement area at night, or an area off the airport, and traffic is not a factor, the following phraseology will be used.

ATC Phraseology:

Departure from (requested location) **will be at your own risk** (reason and additional instructions, as necessary).

Traffic (as applicable), *or*

Traffic not a factor.

d. Unless requested by the pilot, controllers will *NOT* issue downwind takeoffs if the tailwind exceeds 5 knots.*

3-176d Note. — A pilot request to takeoff from a given point in a given direction constitutes such a request.

3-176 Reference. — ATCH 3-141.

3-177 HELICOPTER DEPARTURE SEPARATION

Controllers will separate a departing helicopter from other helicopters by ensuring that it does not take off until one of the following conditions exists:*

a. A preceding, departing helicopter has left the takeoff area.

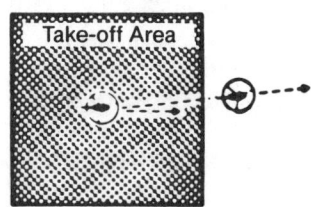

3-177a Illustration

b. A preceding, arriving helicopter has taxied off the landing area.

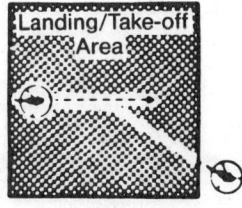

3-177b Illustration

3-177 Note. — Helicopters performing air taxiing operations within the boundary of the airport are considered to be taxiing aircraft.

3-177 Reference. — ATCH 3-142.

3-178 HELICOPTER ARRIVAL SEPARATION

Controllers will separate an arriving helicopter from other helicopters by ensuring that it does not land until one of the following conditions exists:

a. A preceding, arriving helicopter has come to a stop or taxied off the landing area.

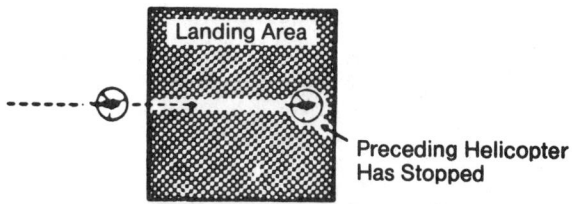

3-178a Illustration 1

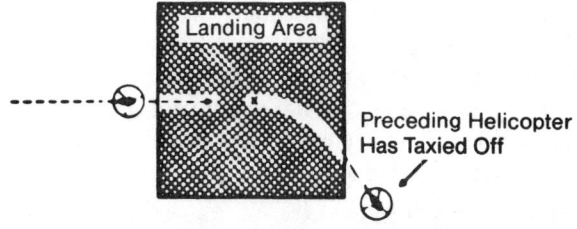

3-178a Illustration 2

b. A preceding, departing helicopter has left the landing area.

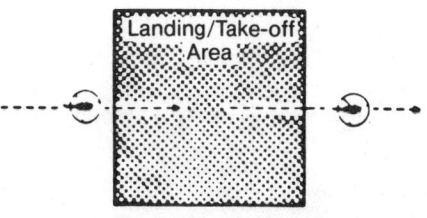

3-178b Illustration

3-178 Reference. — ATCH 3-143.

3-179 SIMULTANEOUS HELICOPTER LANDINGS OR TAKEOFFS

Controllers may authorize helicopters to conduct simultaneous landings or takeoffs if the distance between the landing or takeoff points is at least 200 feet and the courses to be flown do not conflict. Controllers will reference surface markings to determine the 200-foot minimum, or instruct a helicopter to remain at least 200 feet from another helicopter.

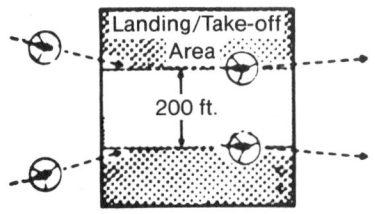

3-179 Illustration

3-179 Reference. — ATCH 3-144.

3-180 HELICOPTER LANDING CLEARANCES

a. Controllers may issue landing clearance for helicopters to movement areas other than active runways, or from diverse directions to points on active runways, with additional instructions, as necessary. Whenever possible, controllers will issue landing clearance in lieu of extended hover taxi or air taxi operations.

ATC Phraseology:

Make approach straight-in/circling left/right turn to (location, runway, taxiway, helipad, Maltese cross).

Arrival/Arrival route (number, name, or code).

Hold short of (active runway, extended runway centerline, other).

Remain (direction/distance; e.g. seven hundred feet **from** (runway, runway centerline, other helicopter/aircraft). **Caution** (power lines, unlighted obstructions, wake turbulence, etc.). **Cleared to land. Contact ground. Air taxi to ramp.**

b. If landing is requested to nonmovement areas and, in the controller's judgment, the operation appears to be reasonable, the following phraseology will be used instead of the landing clearance in **a** above.

ATC Phraseology:

Proceed as requested, use caution (reason and additional instructions, as appropriate).

c. If landing is requested to an area not visible to the controller, an area not authorized for helicopter use, an unlighted area at night, or an area off the airport, and traffic is not a factor, the following phraseology will be used.

ATC Phraseology:

Landing at (requested location) **will be at your own risk** (reason and additional instructions, as necessary).

Traffic (as applicable), *or*

Traffic not a factor.

d. Unless requested by the pilot, controllers will *NOT* issue downwind landings if the tailwind exceeds 5 knots.*

3-180d Note. — A pilot request to land at a given point from a given direction constitutes such a request.

3-180 Reference. — ATCH 3-145.

3-181 thru 3-189 RESERVED

Section 14. SEA LANE OPERATIONS

3-190 APPLICATION

Where Sea Lanes are established and controlled, the provisions of this section will be applied.

3-190 Reference. — ATCH 3-150.

3-191 DEPARTURE SEPARATION

Controllers will separate a departing aircraft from a preceding departing or arriving aircraft using the same sea lane by ensuring that it does not commence takeoff until:

a. The other aircraft has departed and crossed the end of the sea lane or turned to avert any conflict. If the controller can determine distances by reference to suitable landmarks, the other aircraft need only be airborne if the following minimum distance exists between aircraft:*

(1) When only Category I aircraft are involved - *1,500 feet.*

(2) When a Category I aircraft is preceded by a Category II aircraft - *3,000 feet.*

(3) When either the succeeding or both are Category II aircraft - *3,000 feet.*

(4) When either is a Category III aircraft - *6,000 feet.*

3-191a Illustration 1

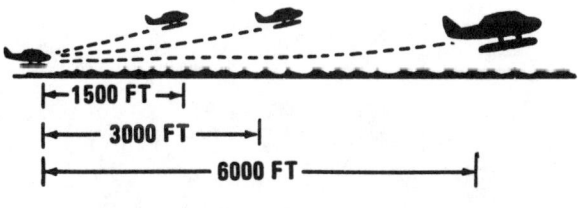

3-191a Illustration 2

b. A preceding landing aircraft has taxied out of the sea lane.

3-191a Note. — Due to the absence of braking capability, caution will be exercised by ATC when instructing a float plane to hold a position as the aircraft will continue to move because of prop generated thrust. Clearance to taxi into position and hold will, therefore, be followed by takeoff or other clearance as soon as practicable.

3-191 Reference. — ATCH 3-151.

3-192 ARRIVAL SEPARATION

Controllers will separate an arriving aircraft from another aircraft using the same sea lane by ensuring that the arriving aircraft does not cross the landing threshold until one of the following conditions exists:

a. The other aircraft has landed and taxied out of the sea lane. Between sunrise and sunset, if the controller can determine distances by reference to suitable landmarks and the other aircraft has landed, it need not be clear of the sea lane if the following minimum distance from the landing threshold exists:

(1) When a Category I aircraft is landing behind a Category I or II - *2,000 feet.*

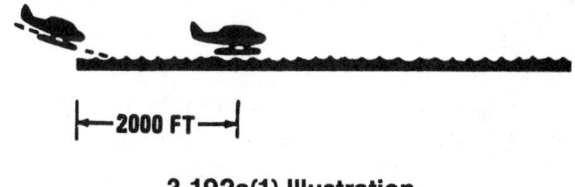

3-192a(1) Illustration

(2) When a Category II aircraft is landing behind a Category I or II - *2,500 feet.*

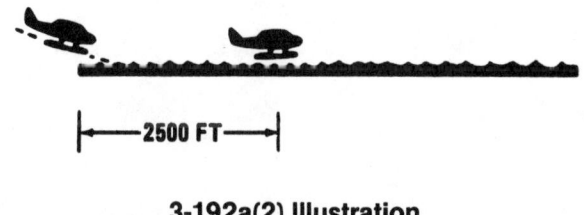

3-192a(2) Illustration

b. The other aircraft has departed and crossed the end of the sea lane or turned to avert any conflict. If the controller can determine distances by reference to suitable landmarks and other aircraft is airborne, it need not have crossed the end of the sea lane if the following minimum distance from the landing threshold exists:

(1) When only Category I aircraft are involved - *1,500 feet.*

(2) When either is a Category II aircraft - *3,000 feet.*

(3) When either is a Category III aircraft - *6,000 feet.*

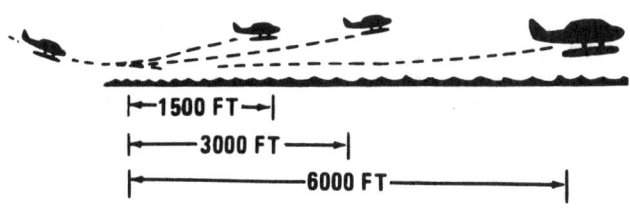

3-192b Illustration 2

3-192 Reference. — ATCH 3-152.

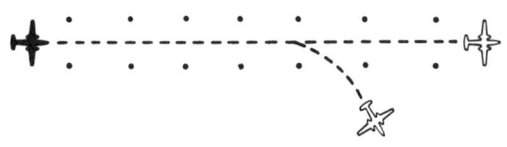

3-192b Illustration 1

BASIC IFR PROCEDURES

Chapter 4
TABLE OF CONTENTS

Section 1. IFR FLIGHT PLANNING

		Page
4-1	ATC Clearance and Flight Plan Required	4-1
4-2	Proposed Departure Time	4-1
4-3	Change In Proposed Departure Time	4-1
4-4	Type Suffixes	4-1
4-5	Airways/Jet Routes	4-1
4-6	Area Navigation	4-1
4-7	Long Range Navigation	4-2
4-8	Filing Tower En Route	4-2
4-9	Composite Flight Plan (VFR/IFR Flights)	4-3
4-10	IFR to VFR-On-Top	4-3
4-11	Cancelling Flight Plans	4-3
4-12—4-19	Reserved	4-4

Section 2. BASIC CLEARANCE ITEMS

4-20	Clearance Limit	4-5
4-21	Departure Procedure	4-5
4-22	Route of Flight	4-5
4-23	Altitude Data	4-5
4-24	Frequency Information	4-6
4-25	Beacon Code Assignment	4-6
4-26—4-29	Reserved	4-6

Section 3. CLEARANCE DELIVERY

4-30	Initial Call-Up	4-7
4-31	IFR Clearance Format	4-7
4-32	ATC Clearance Prefix	4-7
4-33	Clearance Recording and Readback	4-7
4-34	Pre-Taxi Clearance Procedures	4-7
4-35	Abbreviated Departure Clearance	4-8
4-36	Full Route Clearances	4-9
4-37	Route or Altitude Amendments	4-9
4-38—4-39	Reserved	4-9

Section 4. IFR RELEASE PROCEDURES

4-40	VFR Release of IFR Departure	4-10
4-41	IFR Departure Delay Sequencing	4-10
4-42	Departure Restrictions, Clearance Void Times, Hold for Release, and Release Times	4-10
4-43	Controlled Departure Time	4-11
4-44	Gate Holding Due to Departure Delays	4-11
4-45	Departure Delay Information	4-11
4-46—4-49	Reserved	4-11

BASIC IFR PROCEDURES

TABLE OF CONTENTS (Continued)

Section 5. DEPARTURE PROCEDURES

		Page
4-50	Departure Instructions	4-12
4-51	Standard Instrument Departures	4-12
4-52	SID Issuance	4-13
4-53	Obstacle Clearance	4-13
4-54 — 4-59	Reserved	4-13

Section 6. IFR ROUTES AND NAVAID LIMITS

4-60	Course To Be Flown	4-14
4-61	Positive Control Areas and Route Segments	4-14
4-62	Victor Airways	4-14
4-63	Jet Routes	4-14
4-64	Area Navigation Routes	4-14
4-65	Route Clearances	4-14
4-66	Route Transitions	4-15
4-67	Alternative Routes	4-15
4-68	Uncontrolled Airspace Routing	4-16
4-69	Direct Route Flights	4-16
4-70	Service Volume Limitations	4-16
4-71	Service Volume Exceptions	4-16
4-72	Crossing Altitude Limitations	4-16
4-73	Intersection and Fix Service Volume Limitations	4-17
4-74 — 4-79	Reserved	4-17

Section 7. ALTITUDE ASSIGNMENTS

4-80	Flight Direction Altitude Assignments	4-18
4-81	Random Altitude Assignment	4-18
4-82	Lowest Usable Flight Level	4-18
4-83	Adjusted Minimum Flight Level	4-18
4-84	Minimum En Route Altitudes	4-19
4-85	Altitude Assignments	4-19
4-86	Amended Altitude	4-20
4-87	Expected Altitude Changes	4-20
4-88	Normal Descents	4-20
4-89	At Pilot's Discretion	4-20
4-90	Profile Descents	4-21
4-91 — 4-99	Reserved	4-21

Section 8. AIRCRAFT HOLDING

4-100	Arrival Delay Procedures	4-22
4-101	Clearance Beyond Holding Fix	4-23
4-102	Arrival Delay Information	4-23
4-103	Holding Instruction Format	4-23
4-104	Holding Pattern Surveillance	4-23
4-105	Protected Airspace Deviation Advisories	4-23
4-106	Visual Holding Points	4-23
4-107	Holding at Unmonitored NAVAID's	4-24
4-108	ILS Protection/Critical Holding Areas	4-24
4-109	Reserved	4-24

TABLE OF CONTENTS (Continued)

Section 9. ARRIVAL

		Page
4-110	Standard Terminal Arrival Route	4-25
4-111	Arrival Clearance Information	4-25
4-112	Airport Condition Information	4-25
4-113	Airport Weather Information	4-25
4-114	Below Minimums Report By Pilot	4-25
4-115	Approach Information	4-26
4-116—4-119	Reserved	4-26

Section 10. APPROACH CLEARANCE PROCEDURES

4-120	Approach Clearances	4-27
4-121	Altitude Management	4-28
4-122	Special Instrument Approach Procedures	4-28
4-123	Approach Information for Unfamiliar Pilot	4-28
4-124	Relayed Approach Clearance	4-29
4-125	Approach Clearance Altitude	4-29
4-126	Procedure Turn	4-29
4-127	Limitations On Procedure Turns	4-29
4-128	Communications Release	4-29
4-129	Change to Advisory Frequency	4-29
4-130	Circling Approach Instructions	4-30
4-131	Circling Approach Exceptions	4-30
4-132	Side-Step Maneuver	4-30
4-133	Missed Approach	4-30
4-134—4-139	Reserved	4-30

Section 11. VISUAL APPROACHES

4-140	General	4-31
4-141	Visual Approach Clearance	4-31
4-142	Vectors for a Visual Approach	4-31
4-143	Visual Approach Clearance-Radar Separated Aircraft	4-32
4-144	Parallel/Multiple Runway Use	4-32
4-145	Charted Visual Flight Procedures - General	4-33
4-146	CVFP Procedures - ATC	4-33
4-147—4-149	Reserved	4-33

Section 12. CONTACT APPROACHES

4-150	General	4-34
4-151	Contact Approach Conditions	4-34
4-152—4-159	Reserved	4-34

Section 13. VFR CLEARANCES FOR IFR OPERATIONS

4-160	General	4-35
4-161	VFR-On-Top Clearance	4-35
4-162	Altitude for Direction of Flight	4-35
4-163	IFR to VFR-On-Top	4-36
4-164	VFR Climb or Descent	4-36
4-165	Maintain VFR Clearances	4-36
4-166—4-169	Reserved	4-36

TABLE OF CONTENTS (Continued)

Section 14. PRACTICE INSTRUMENT APPROACHES

		Page
4-170	General	4-37
4-171	Pilot Actions	4-37
4-172	Controller Actions	4-37
4-173	Nontower Airport Operations	4-38
4-174	Missed Approaches	4-38
4-175	Deviations	4-38
4-176	Vectoring	4-38
4-177	Communications With Tower	4-38
4-178	FSS Actions	4-38
4-179	Local Traffic	4-39

Chapter 4. BASIC IFR PROCEDURES

Section 1. IFR FLIGHT PLANNING

4-1 ATC CLEARANCE AND FLIGHT PLAN REQUIRED

A pilot may only operate an aircraft in controlled airspace under IFR if:

a. He has filed an IFR flight plan; and

b. He has received an appropriate ATC clearance.

4-1 Reference. — FAR 91.115.

4-2 PROPOSED DEPARTURE TIME

a. Pilots should file IFR flight plans at least 30 minutes prior to estimated time of departure to preclude possible delay in receiving a departure clearance from ATC.*

(1) The delay may be due to the amount of time spent processing flight plan data; or

(2) IFR weather conditions which exist or are forecast could delay entering the airspace at the destination airport.

b. Traffic saturation frequently prevents control personnel from accepting flight plans by radio. In such cases, the pilot is advised to contact the nearest FSS for the purpose of filing the flight plan.*

4-2a & b Note. — There are several methods of obtaining IFR clearances at nontower, nonFSS's, and outlying airports. The procedure may vary due to geographical features, weather conditions, and the complexity of the ATC system. To determine the most effective means of receiving an IFR clearance, pilots should ask the nearest FSS the most appropriate means of obtaining the IFR clearance.

4-2 Reference. — AIM 298.

4-3 CHANGE IN PROPOSED DEPARTURE TIME

To prevent computer saturation in the en route environment, parameters have been established to delete flight plans which have not been activated. Most centers have this parameter set so as to delete these flight plans a minimum of 1 hour after the proposed departure time. To ensure that a flight plan remains active, pilots whose actual departure time will be delayed 1 hour or more beyond their filed departure time, are requested to notify ATC of their revised departure time.

4-3 Reference. — AIM 302.

4-4 TYPE SUFFIXES

a. When filing an IFR flight plan for flight in an aircraft equipped with a radar beacon transponder, DME equipment, TACAN only equipment, or a combination of both, identify equipment capability as described in paragraph 2-23.

b. It is recommended that pilots file the maximum transponder or navigation capability of their aircraft in the equipment suffix. This will provide ATC with the necessary information to utilize all facets of navigational equipment and transponder capabilities available.

c. In the case of area navigation equipped aircraft, pilots should file the /C, /R, or /W capability of the aircraft even though an RNAV route or random RNAV route has not been requested. This will ensure ATC awareness of the pilot's ability to navigate point-to-point and may be utilized to expedite the flight.

4-4 References. — ATCH 2-57; AIM 298.

4-5 AIRWAYS/JET ROUTES

a. It is vitally important that the route of flight be accurately and completely described in the flight plan. To simplify definition of the proposed route, and to facilitate ATC, pilots are requested to file via airways or jet routes established for use at the altitude or flight level planned.

b. When filing an IFR plan, it is to the pilot's advantage to file a preferred route.*

c. ATC may issue a SID (standard instrument departure) or STAR (standard terminal arrival route) as appropriate.*

4-5b Note. — Preferred IFR routes are described and tabulated in the Airport/Facility Directory.

4-5c Note. — Pilots not desiring a SID or STAR should so indicate in the remarks section of the flight plan.

4-5 Reference. — AIM 298.

4-6 AREA NAVIGATION

Pilots of aircraft equipped with operational area navigation equipment may file for random RNAV (area navigation) routes throughout the National Airspace System, where radar monitoring by ATC is available, in accordance with the following procedures.

a. File airport to airport flight plans prior to departure.

b. File the appropriate RNAV equipment capability suffix in the flight plan.

c. Plan the random route portion of the flight plan to begin and end over appropriate arrival and departure transition fixes or appropriate navigation aids for the altitude stratum within which the flight will be conducted. The use of normal preferred departure and arrival routes (SID/STAR), where established, is recommended.

d. File route structure transitions to and from the random route portion of the flight.

e. Define the random route by waypoints. File route description waypoints by using degree-distance fixes based on navigational aids which are appropriate for the altitude stratum.

f. File a minimum of one route description waypoint for each ARTCC through whose area the random route will be flown. These waypoints must be located within 200 NM of the preceding center's boundary.

g. File an additional route description waypoint for each turnpoint in the route.

h. Plan additional route description waypoints as required to ensure accurate navigation via the filed route of flight. Navigation is the pilot's responsibility unless ATC assistance is requested.

i. Plan the route of flight so as to avoid Prohibited and Restricted Airspace by 3 NM unless permission has been obtained to operate in that airspace and the appropriate ATC facilities are advised.

4-6 Reference. — AIM 298.

4-7 LONG RANGE NAVIGATION

Pilots of aircraft equipped with latitude/longitude coordinate navigation capability, independent of VOR/TACAN references, may file for random RNAV routes at and above FL 390, within the conterminous United States, using the following procedures.

a. File airport to airport flight plans prior to departure.

b. File the appropriate RNAV capability certification suffix in the flight plan.

c. Plan the random route portion of the flight to begin and end over published departure/arrival transition fixes or appropriate navigation aids for airports without published transition procedures. The use of preferred departure and arrival routes, such as SID and STAR where established, is recommended.

d. Plan the route of flight so as to avoid prohibited and restricted airspace by 3 NM unless permission has been obtained to operate in that airspace and the appropriate ATC facility is advised.

e. Define the route of flight after the departure fix, including each intermediate fix (turnpoint) and the arrival fix for the destination airport in terms of latitude/longitude coordinates plotted to the nearest minute. The arrival fix must be identified by both the latitude/longitude coordinates and a fix identifier.

f. Record latitude/longitude coordinates by four figures describing latitude in degrees and minutes, followed by a solidus and five figures describing longitude in degrees and minutes.

g. File at FL 390 or above for the random degrees portion of the flight.

h. Fly all routes/route segments on Great Circle tracks.

i. Make an inflight request for random RNAV clearances or route amendments to an en route ATC facility.

4-7 Reference. — AIM 298.

4-8 FILING TOWER EN ROUTE

a. TEC (tower en route control) is an ATC program to provide a service to aircraft proceeding to and from metropolitan areas. It links designated approach control areas by a network of identified routes made of the existing airway structure of the National Airspace System. The program is entirely within the approach control airspace of multiple terminal facilities. Essentially, it is for relatively short flights. Participating pilots are encouraged to use TEC for flights of two hours duration or less. If longer flights are planned, extensive coordination may be required within the multiple complex, which could result in unanticipated delays.

b. There are no unique requirements upon pilots to use the TEC program. Normal flight plan filing procedures will ensure proper flight plan processing. Pilots should include the acronym "TEC" in the remarks section of the flight plan when requesting tower en route.*

c. Pilots requesting TEC are subject to the same delay factor at the destination airport as other aircraft in the ATC system. In addition, departure and en route delays may occur depending upon arrival facility workload. When a major metropolitan airport is incurring significant delays, pilots in the TEC program may want to consider an alternative airport experiencing no delay.

4-8b Note. — At certain locations tower en route clearances may be obtained directly from clearance delivery by using abbreviated IFR flight plan procedures.

4-8 Reference. — AIM 167.

4-9 COMPOSITE FLIGHT PLAN (VFR/IFR FLIGHTS)

a. Flight plans which specify VFR operation for one portion of a flight, and IFR for another portion, will be accepted by the FSS at the point of departure. If VFR flight is conducted for the first portion of the flight, the pilot should report his departure time to the FSS with which he filed his VFR/IFR flight plan; and, subsequently, close the VFR portion and request ATC clearance from the FSS nearest the point at which change from VFR to IFR is proposed. Regardless of the type facility the pilot is communicating with (FSS, center, or tower), it is the pilot's responsibility to request that facility to *"CLOSE MY VFR FLIGHT PLAN."* The pilot must remain in VFR weather conditions until operating in accordance with the IFR clearance.

b. When a flight plan indicates IFR for the first portion of flight and VFR for the latter portion, the pilot will normally be cleared to the point at which the change is proposed. Once the pilot has reported over the clearance limit and does not desire further IFR clearance, he should advise ATC to cancel the IFR portion of his flight plan. Then, he should contact the nearest FSS to activate the VFR portion of his flight plan. If the pilot desires to continue his IFR flight plan beyond the clearance limit, he should contact ATC at least 5 minutes prior to the clearance limit and request further IFR clearance. If the requested clearance is not received prior to reaching the clearance limit fix, the pilot will be expected to establish himself in a standard holding pattern on the radial or course to the fix unless a holding pattern for the clearance limit fix is depicted on a U.S. Government or commercially produced (meeting FAA requirements) Low or High Altitude En Route, Area or STAR Chart. In this case the pilot will hold according to the depicted pattern.

4-9 Reference. — AIM 297.

4-10 IFR TO VFR-ON-TOP

ATC may clear pilots to climb through clouds, smoke, haze, or other meteorological formations and then to *"maintain VFR-on-top."* Upon reaching VFR conditions, the pilot may cancel IFR. However, he may wish or be required to remain in contact with ATC for other services.

4-10 Reference. — ATCH 7-20.

4-11 CANCELLING FLIGHT PLANS

a. When a flight plan has been filed, the pilot in command, upon cancelling or completing the flight under the flight plan, shall notify the nearest FSS or ATC facility.

b. An IFR flight plan may be cancelled at any time the flight is operating in VFR conditions outside positive controlled airspace by the pilot stating *"CANCEL MY IFR FLIGHT PLAN"* to the controller. Immediately after cancelling an IFR flight plan, a pilot should take necessary action to change to the appropriate frequency, VFR radar beacon code, and VFR altitude or flight level.

c. ATC separation and information services will be discontinued, including radar services (where applicable). Consequently, if the cancelling flight desires VFR radar advisory service, the pilot must specifically request it.

4-11c Example. —

Cessna Two Three Delta, cancel my I-F-R flight plan. Request to remain with you for V-F-R advisories.

Cessna Two Three Delta, cancellation received, remain on your present code for V-F-R advisories.

d. Pilots must be aware that other procedures may be applicable to a flight that cancels an IFR flight plan within an area where a special program has been established such as a designated ARSA, TRSA, or TCA.

e. If a DVFR flight plan requirement exists, the pilot is responsible for filing this flight plan to replace the cancelled IFR flight plan. If a subsequent IFR operation becomes necessary, a new IFR flight plan must be filed and an ATC clearance obtained before operating in IFR conditions.

f. If operating on an IFR flight plan to an airport with a functioning control tower, the flight plan is automatically closed upon landing.

g. If operating on an IFR flight plan to an airport where there is no functioning control tower, the pilot must initiate cancellation of the IFR flight plan. This can be done after landing if there is a functioning FSS or other means of direct communications with ATC. In the event there is no FSS, and communications with ATC is not possible below a certain altitude, the pilot should, weather conditions permitting, cancel his IFR flight plan while still airborne and able to communicate with ATC by radio. This will not only save the time and expense of cancelling the flight plan by telephone but will quickly release the airspace for use by other aircraft.

4-11g Example. —

Delta Four Twenty-one, hold for release, I-F-R traffic inbound to the airport.

Baron Six Two Whiskey has the airport in sight. We would like to cancel I-F-R.

Baron Six Two Whiskey, cancellation received, radar service terminated, squawk one two zero zero, traffic will be a Delta Boeing Seven Thirty-seven departing Runway One Eight, change to advisory frequency approved.

Baron Six Two Whiskey, roger. We will be looking for the traffic.

Delta Four Twenty-one released. Report airborne this frequency. Traffic is a Beechcraft Baron five miles west of the airport, inbound for landing.

4-11 References. — FAR 91.83; AIM 304.

4-12 thru 4-19 RESERVED

Section 2. BASIC CLEARANCE ITEMS

4-20 CLEARANCE LIMIT

a. The clearance issued prior to departure will normally authorize flight to the airport of intended landing.

4-20a Example. —

. . . cleared to Detroit City Airport. . .

b. Under certain conditions, at some locations a short-range clearance procedure is utilized whereby a clearance is issued to a fix within or just outside of the terminal area and the pilot is advised of the frequency on which he will receive the long-range clearance direct from the center controller.

4-20 Reference. — AIM 262.

4-21 DEPARTURE PROCEDURE

Headings to fly and altitude restrictions may be issued to separate a departure from other air traffic in the terminal area. Where the volume of traffic warrants, standard instrument departure procedures (SID's) have been developed.

4-21 Examples. —

. . . After departure, fly runway heading . . .

. . . via the Savey Four Departure . . .

4-21 Reference. — AIM 262.

4-22 ROUTE OF FLIGHT

a. Clearances are normally issued for the route filed by the pilot. However, due to traffic conditions, it is frequently necessary for ATC to specify a route different from that requested by the pilot. In addition, flow patterns have been established in certain congested areas, or between congested areas, whereby traffic capacity is increased by routing all traffic on preferred routes. Information on these flow patterns is available in offices where preflight briefing is furnished or where flight plans are accepted.

4-22a Example. —

. . . as filed . . .

b. One or more of the following will be specified:

(1) Airway, route, course, heading, azimuth, arc, or vector.

(2) The routing a pilot can expect if any part of the route beyond a short range clearance limit differs from that filed.

ATC Phraseology:

Expect further clearance via (airways, routes, or fixes).

4-22b(1) Example. —

. . . via J-Forty-three, Salem . . .

4-22b(2) Example. —

. . . Expect further clearance via direct Falmouth . . .

4-22 References. — ATCH 4-21, AIM 262.

4-23 ALTITUDE DATA

a. The altitude or flight level instructions in an ATC clearance normally require that a pilot *"MAINTAIN"* the altitude or flight level at which the flight will operate when in controlled airspace.

b. ATC will assign one of the following, in the order of preference listed:

(1) The altitude filed by the pilot/company.

(2) An altitude within the highest route stratum filed and as near as possible to the altitude. Interim altitude assignments will not be used to satisfy this order of preference. They are covered in preference (3) below.

4-23b(2) Example. —

An aircraft has filed Flight Level 370. The nearest altitude within the filed route stratum that can be approved is Flight Level 330. The clearance will read:

Maintain flight level three three zero.

(3) ATC will assign an interim altitude within the highest route stratum filed or as near as possible to the highest route stratum filed, and:

(a) Controllers will inform the aircraft when to expect clearance to an altitude consistent with (1) or (2) above, unless instructions are contained in the specified SID.

(b) Controllers will comply with the provision of (1) or (2) above before the aircraft reaches the fix or prior to the time specified in the clearance.

ATC Phraseology:

Expect (the filed altitude or an altitude within the filed stratum as near as possible to the field altitude) **at** (time or fix).

4-23b(3)(b) Examples. —

An aircraft has filed Flight Level 350. Flight Level 230 is immediately available and Flight Level 350 will be available at the Appleton zero five zero radial 35 mile fix. The clearance will read:

Maintain flight level two three zero. Expect flight level three five zero at Appleton zero five zero radial three five mile fix.

An Aircraft has filed 9,000 feet. An interim altitude restriction is required because of facility procedures/requirements. The controller will assign the interim altitude and advise the aircraft as to what time/point he may expect his filed or final altitude. The clearance will read:

Maintain five thousand. Expect niner thousand, one zero minutes after departure.

4-23 References. — ATCH 4-21; AIM 262.

4-24 FREQUENCY INFORMATION

When a clearance is issued, the frequency to contact ATC after departure will be given. This frequency will either be departure control, approach control, or an en route center, depending on the airspace entered after departure.

4-24 Example. —
... departure frequency will be one two four point six ...

4-24 Reference. — ATCH 4-10.

4-25 BEACON CODE ASSIGNMENT

A discrete transponder beacon code will be issued to transponder-equipped aircraft entering a radar environment.

4-25 Example. —
... squawk five four seven six.

4-25 Reference. — ATCH 4-10.

4-26 thru 4-29 RESERVED

Section 3. CLEARANCE DELIVERY

4-30 INITIAL CALL-UP

Pilots should state the following information in the initial call-up to clearance delivery (or ground control, if appropriate) when no change has been made to the filed flight plan.

a. Aircraft call sign.

b. Location.

c. Type of operation (IFR).

d. Name of airport (or fix) filed to.

e. Current ATIS code (initial facility call-up only).

4-30 Example. —
Dulles Clearance Delivery, American Seventy-seven Heavy at Gate Delta Twenty-four, I-F-R Los Angeles, with information TANGO.

4-30 Reference. — AIM 322.

4-31 IFR CLEARANCE FORMAT

The following clearance items will be issued, as appropriate, in the order listed below:

a. Aircraft call sign.

b. Clearance limit.

c. Departure procedure or SID.

d. Route of flight.*

e. Altitude data in the order flown.

f. Holding instructions.

g. Any special information.

h. Frequency to contact ATC.

i. Transponder beacon (squawk) code.

4-31 Example. —
American Seventy-seven Heavy is cleared to the Los Angeles Airport via the Capital Three Departure, as filed. Maintain four thousand. Departure frequency will be one two five point zero five. Squawk seven two five three.

4-31d Note. — Includes PDR (preferential departure route)/PDAR (preferential departure arrival route)/PAR (preferential arrival route) when applied.

4-31 Reference. — ATCH 4-10.

4-32 ATC CLEARANCE PREFIX

a. A nonATC facility, i.e., Flight Service Station, will prefix a clearance, information, or a request for information which will be relayed to an aircraft by stating "A-T-C clears," "A-T-C advises," or "A-T-C requests."

4-32a Example. —
A-T-C clears Cherokee Four Seven Two Zero Golf...

b. The term "ATC" is omitted when a clearance, information, or a request for information is issued to an aircraft by direct ATC communications.

4-32 Reference. — ATCH 4-11.

4-33 CLEARANCE RECORDING AND READBACK

a. When conducting an IFR operation, pilots should make a written record of their clearance. The specified conditions which are part of the air traffic clearance may be somewhat different from those included in the flight plan. Additionally, ATC may find it necessary to *ADD* conditions, such as particular departure route.

b. Upon receiving and recording a clearance, the pilot should read back the items in the order received for verification.*

4-33b Example. —
American Seventy-seven Heavy is cleared to Los Angeles via the Capital Three Departure as filed. Maintain four thousand. Departure frequency will be one two five point zero five. Squawk seven two five three.

American Seventy-seven Heavy, readback correct.

4-33b Note 1. — It is the responsibility of the pilot to accept or refuse the clearance issued.

4-33b Note 2. — At certain terminal locations, due to frequency saturation, abbreviated readback procedures are used, i.e., beacon code and call sign only.

4-33 Reference. — AIM 265.

4-34 PRE-TAXI CLEARANCE PROCEDURES

a. Certain airports have established Pre-taxi Clearance programs whereby pilots of departing IFR aircraft may elect to receive their IFR clearances before they start taxiing for takeoff. The following provisions are included in such procedures:

(1) Pilot participation is not mandatory.

(2) Participating pilots call clearance delivery or ground control not more than 10 minutes before proposed taxi time.*

(3) IFR clearance (or delay information, if clearance cannot be obtained) is issued at the time of this initial call-up.

(4) When the IFR clearance is received on clearance delivery frequency, pilots call ground control when ready to taxi.

(5) Normally, pilots need not inform ground control that they have received IFR clearance on clearance delivery frequency. Certain locations may, however, require that the pilot inform ground control of a portion of his routing or that he has received his IFR clearance.

(6) If a pilot cannot establish contact on clearance delivery frequency or has not received his IFR clearance before he is ready to taxi, he should contact ground control and inform the controller accordingly.

b. Locations where these procedures are in effect are indicated in the Airport/Facility Directory.

4-34a(2) Note. — IFR clearances are generally available at the ATC facility 20-30 minutes prior to proposed departure time.

4-34 Reference. — AIM 320.

4-35 ABBREVIATED DEPARTURE CLEARANCE

a. ATC may issue an abbreviated departure clearance if its use reduces verbiage and the following conditions are met:

(1) The route of flight filed with ATC has not been changed by the pilot, company, operations officer, input operator, or in the stored flight plan program prior to departure.

(2) All ATC facilities concerned have sufficient route of flight information to exercise their control responsibilities.*

(3) When the flight will depart IFR, destination airport information is relayed between the facilities concerned prior to departure.*

(4) The assigned altitude is stated in the clearance.

b. The destination airport will be specified by ATC in the clearance.

c. When no changes are required in the filed route, the controller will state the phrase, *"Cleared to (destination) airport: (SID and SID transition, as appropriate); then, as filed."* If a SID is not assigned, the controller will follow with *"as filed."* Controllers will specify the assigned altitude; and, if required, add any additional instructions or information.

ATC Phraseology:

Cleared to (destination) **Airport**; and, as appropriate, (SID name and number) **Departure,** (transition name) **Transition; then, as filed.**

Maintain (altitude);

and, if required,

(additional instructions or information).

If a SID is not assigned,

Cleared to (destination) **Airport as filed.**

Maintain (altitude);

and, if required,

(additional instructions or information).

4-35c Examples. —

... cleared to Reynolds Airport, David Two R-NAV Departure, Kingham Transition, then, as filed. Maintain niner thousand. Expect flight level four one zero, one zero minutes after departure...

... cleared to Reynolds Airport as filed. Maintain niner thousand. Expect flight level four one zero, one zero minutes after departure...

d. When a filed route will require revisions, the controller responsible for initiating the clearance to the aircraft will either:

(1) Issue a full route clearance; or

(2) If it reduces verbiage, state the phrase, *"Cleared to (destination) airport, (SID and SID transition, as appropriate), then as filed, except...."* and specify the necessary revision; then, the assigned altitude; and, if required, add any additional instructions or information. If a SID is not assigned, the controller will state, *"Cleared to (destination) airport as filed, except...."* and specify the necessary revision, the assigned altitude; and, if required, ATC will add any additional instructions or information.

ATC Phraseology:

Cleared to (destination) **Airport;**

and, as appropriate,

(SID name and number) **Departure,** (transition name) **Transition; then, as filed, except change route to read** (amended route portion).

Maintain (altitude);

and, if required,

(additional instructions or information).

If a SID is not assigned,

Cleared to (destination) **Airport as filed, except change route to read** (amended route portion).

Maintain (altitude);

and, if required,

(additional instructions or information).

4-35d Examples. —

... cleared to Reynolds Airport, South Boston One Departure, then, as filed, except change route to read, South Boston, Victor Twenty, Greensboro. Maintain eight thousand, report leaving four thousand...

... cleared to Reynolds Airport as filed, except change route to read, South Boston, Victor Twenty, Greensboro. Maintain eight thousand...

e. In a non-radar environment ATC will specify one, two, or more fixes, as necessary, to identify the initial route of flight.

4-35e Example. —
The filed route of flight is from Hutchins V10 Emporia, thence V10N and V77 to St. Joseph. The clearance will read:

... cleared to Watson Airport as filed via Emporia, maintain seven thousand ...

f. ATC will not apply these procedures when a pilot requests a detailed clearance.

4-35a(2) Note. — The route of flight information to be provided may be covered in letters of agreement.

4-35a(3) Note. — Pilots are expected to furnish the facility concerned with destination airport information on initial radio call-up. This will provide the information necessary for detecting any destination airport differences on facility relay.

4-35 Reference. — ATCH 4-22.

4-36 FULL ROUTE CLEARANCES

a. A pilot may not wish to accept an abbreviated clearance if the route of flight filed with ATC has been changed by him or the company before departure. He is expected to inform the ATC facility on initial radio contact if he cannot accept the clearance. It is the responsibility of the company or operations officer to inform the pilot when they make a change.

b. If the flight plan has been changed, pilots should state so and request a full route clearance.

4-36b Example. —
Burbank Clearance, USAir Twenty-five Forty-one, Gate Four with HOTEL, request full route clearance to San Jose.

USAir Twenty-five Forty-one Burbank Clearance, roger. Cleared to the San Jose Airport via the Van Nuys Six Departure, Avenal Transition, J-Six, Robie. Maintain six thousand, expect flight level two eight zero five minutes after departure. Do not exceed two five zero knots until advised. Departure frequency will be one two four point six. Squawk one three zero three.

c. If it is necessary for ATC to modify a filed route of flight, the controller issuing the ATC clearance to the aircraft will issue a full route clearance.*

4-36c Note. — Changes such as those made to conform with traffic flows and preferred routings are only permitted to be made by the pilot (or his company) or the controller responsible for initiating the clearance to the aircraft.

4-36 References. — ATCH 4-22; AIM 322.

4-37 ROUTE OR ALTITUDE AMENDMENTS

a. ATC will amend route of flight in a previously issued clearance by one of the following:

(1) By stating which portion of the route is being amended and then state the amendment.

ATC Phraseology:

Change (portion of route) **to read** (amended route).

(2) By stating the amendment to the route and then stating that the rest of the route is unchanged.

ATC Phraseology:

(Amended route), **rest of route unchanged.**

(3) By issuing the entire route by stating the amendment.

4-37a Examples. —
Cessna 21A has been cleared to the Airville airport via V41 Delta VOR V174 Alpha VOR, direct Airville airport, maintain 9,000. Shortly before takeoff, the aircraft is rerouted via V41 Frank intersection, V71 Delta VOR, V174 Alpha VOR. The controller issues one of the following as an amended clearance:

Cessna Two One Alpha, change Victor Forty-one Delta to read Victor Forty-one Frank, Victor Seventy-one Delta, hold for release.

Cessna Two One Alpha, cleared via Victor Forty-one Frank, Victor Seventy-one Delta, rest of route unchanged, hold for release.

Cessna Two One Alpha, cleared via Victor Forty-one Frank, Victor Seventy-one Delta, Victor One-seventy-four Alpha, direct Airville airport, maintain niner thousand, hold for release.

b. When route or altitude in a previously issued clearance is amended, all applicable altitude restrictions will be restated.*

4-37b Example. —
A departing aircraft is cleared to cross Ollis intersection at or above 3,000; Gordonsville VOR at or above 12,000; maintain FL 200. Shortly before takeoff, the altitude to be maintained is changed to FL 240. Because altitude restrictions remain in effect, the controller issues amended clearance as follows:

Cross Ollis intersection at or above three thousand, cross Gordonsville at or above one two thousand. Maintain flight level two four zero, cleared for takeoff.

Shortly after departure, altitude restrictions are no longer applicable, the controller issues amended clearance as follows:

Climb and maintain flight level two four zero.

4-37b Note. — Restating previously issued altitude to "maintain" is an amended clearance. If altitude to "maintain" is changed or restated, whether prior to departure or while airborne, and previously issued altitude restrictions are omitted, altitude restrictions are cancelled, including SID altitude restrictions, if any.

4-37 Reference. — ATCH 4-14.

4-38 and 4-39 RESERVED

Section 4. IFR RELEASE PROCEDURES

4-40 VFR RELEASE OF IFR DEPARTURE

When an aircraft which has filed an IFR flight plan requests a VFR departure through a terminal facility, FSS, or air/ground communications station:

a. After obtaining, if necessary, approval from the facility/sector responsible for issuing the IFR clearance, the controller may authorize an IFR flight planned aircraft to depart VFR. Controllers will still inform the pilot of the proper frequency and if appropriate, where or when to contact the facility responsible for issuing the clearance.

ATC Phraseology:

VFR departure authorized. Contact (facility) **on** (frequency) **at** (location or time, if required) **for clearance.**

b. If the facility/sector responsible for issuing the clearance is unable to issue a clearance, the controller will inform the pilot and suggest that the delay be taken on the ground.

4-40b Example. —

Lear One Tango Charlie, Center advises they are unable to accept V-F-R handoffs due to sector saturation, say intentions.

4-40 Reference. — ATCH 4-27.

4-41 IFR DEPARTURE DELAY SEQUENCING

When aircraft elect to take delay on the ground before departure, ATC will issue departure clearances to them in the order in which the requests for clearance were originally made, if practicable.

4-41 Reference. — ATCH 4-24.

4-42 DEPARTURE RESTRICTIONS, CLEARANCE VOID TIMES, HOLD FOR RELEASE, AND RELEASE TIMES

ATC will assign departure restrictions, clearance void times, hold for release, or release times when necessary to separate departures from other traffic or to restrict or regulate the departure flow.

a. Clearance Void Times.

(1) When issuing clearance void times at airports not served by control towers, ATC will provide alternative instructions requiring the pilots to advise ATC of their intentions no later than 30 minutes after the clearance void time if not airborne.

(2) The facility delivering a clearance void time to a pilot will issue a time check.

ATC Phraseology:

Clearance void if not off by (clearance void time).

and, if required,

If not off by (clearance void time), **advise** (facility) **not later than** (time) **of intentions.**

Time check (time in hours, minutes, and the nearest quarter minute).

b. Hold For Release.

(1) *"Hold for release"* instructions will be used when necessary to inform a pilot or a controller that a departure clearance is not valid until additional instructions are received.

(2) When issuing *"hold for release"* instructions, ATC will include departure delay information.

ATC Phraseology:

(Aircraft identification) **cleared to** (destination) **Airport as filed, maintain** (altitude),

and, if required,

(additional instructions or information).

Hold for release, expect (time in hours and/or minutes) **departure delay.**

(3) When conditions allow, ATC will release the aircraft as soon as possible.

ATC Phraseology:

To a pilot at an airport not served by a control tower,

(aircraft identification) **released for departure.**

c. Release times.

(1) Release times will be issued to pilots when necessary to specify the earliest time an aircraft may depart.*

(2) The facility issuing a release time to a pilot will include a time check.

ATC Phraseology:

(Aircraft identification) **released for departure at** (time in hours and/or minutes),

and, if required,

If not off by (time), **advise** (facility) **not later than** (time) **of intentions.**

Time check (time in hours, minutes, and nearest quarter minute).

4-42c(1) Note. — A release time is a departure restriction issued to a pilot (either directly or through authorized relay) to separate a departing aircraft from other traffic.

4-42 Reference. — ATCH 4-23.

4-43 CONTROLLED DEPARTURE TIME

When controlled departure time (CDT) (flow control) procedures are in effect, the departure terminal will, to the extent possible, plan the ground movement of aircraft destined to the delay airport/airports so that the flight can depart as near as possible to its expected departure clearance time (EDCT). An aircraft may depart prior to its EDCT due to local traffic constraints; i.e., an aircraft with a later EDCT in the queue ahead of an aircraft with an earlier EDCT may be released in order to continue a good traffic flow. However, an aircraft normally will not be released earlier than 5 minutes prior to its EDCT.

4-43 Reference. — ATCH 4-23.

4-44 GATE-HOLDING DUE TO DEPARTURE DELAYS

Pilots should monitor the ground control or clearance delivery frequency for engine startup advisories or new proposed start time if the delay changes. The sequence for departure will be maintained in accordance with initial call-up unless modified by flow control restrictions.

4-44 Reference. — AIM 236.

4-45 DEPARTURE DELAY INFORMATION

a. When gate-hold procedures are in effect, the following departure delay information will be issued as appropriate:

ATC Phraseology:

Gate-hold procedures are in effect. All aircraft contact (position) **on** (frequency) **for engine start time.**

4-45a Example. —

Gate-hold procedures are in effect. All aircraft contact ground control on one two one point niner for engine start time.

b. Departing aircraft will be advised of the time at which the pilot can expect to receive his engine startup advisory.

ATC Phraseology:

Expect engine startup (time).

4-45b Example. —

T-W-A Fifteen Heavy, expect engine start time at one four three zero.

c. Departing aircraft will be advised when to start engines.

ATC Phraseology:

Start engines, advise when ready to taxi.

d. If the pilot requests to hold in a delay absorbing area, the request will be approved if space and traffic conditions permit.

e. Controllers will advise all aircraft on ground control/clearance delivery frequency upon termination of gate-hold procedures.

ATC Phraseology:

Gate-hold procedures no longer in effect.

4-45 Reference. — ATCH 3-101.

4-46 thru 4-49 RESERVED

Section 5. DEPARTURE PROCEDURES

4-50 DEPARTURE INSTRUCTIONS

a. ATC will specify direction of takeoff/turn or initial heading/azimuth to be flown after takeoff as follows:

(1) Locations with Airport Traffic Control Service — Departure procedures are specified as necessary.

(2) Locations without Airport Traffic Control Service, but within a Control Zone — Departure procedures are specified if necessary. ATC will obtain/solicit the pilot's concurrence concerning these items before issuing them in a clearance.*

ATC Phraseology:

Fly runway heading.

Depart (direction or runway).

Turn left/right.

(3) At all other airports — ATC will not specify direction of takeoff/turn after takeoff. If necessary for ATC to specify an initial heading/azimuth to be flown after takeoff, ATC will then issue the initial heading/azimuth so as to apply only within controlled airspace.

ATC Phraseology:

When entering controlled airspace (instruction), **fly heading** (degrees) **until reaching** (altitude, point or fix) **before proceeding on course.**

Fly a (degree) **bearing from** (fix) **until** (time), *or*

until reaching (fix or altitude)

and, if required,

before proceeding on course.

4-50a(3) Example. —

Dutchess Five Four One Two Mike, when entering controlled airspace, fly heading three zero zero until reaching two thousand four hundred before proceeding on course.

b. When IFR departure procedures are published for a location and pilot compliance is necessary to ensure separation, ATC will include the published departure procedure as part of the ATC clearance.*

c. Compatibility with a procedure issued may be verified by a controller asking the pilot if items obtained/solicited will allow him to comply with local traffic pattern, terrain, or obstruction avoidance.*

4-50c Examples. —

Verify right turn after departure will allow compliance with local traffic pattern.

Verify this clearance will allow compliance with terrain or obstruction avoidance.

4-50a(2) Note. — Direction of takeoff and turn after takeoff can be obtained/solicited directly from the pilot, or relayed by an FSS, dispatcher, etc., as obtained/solicited from the pilot.

4-50b Note. — IFR takeoff minimums and departure procedures are prescribed for specific airports/runways and published in a tabular form supplement to the NOS Instrument Approach Procedure Charts. These procedures are identified on Approach Landing Charts with a symbol ▼.

4-50c Note. — If a published IFR departure procedure is not included in an ATC clearance, compliance with such a procedure is the pilot's prerogative.

4-50 Reference. — ATCH 4-21.

4-51 STANDARD INSTRUMENT DEPARTURES

a. A SID (standard instrument departure) is a departure procedure, identified with a name and number, (e.g., Rosewood One Departure), which has been established at certain airports to simplify clearance delivery procedures.

b. Pilots of aircraft operating from locations where SID procedures are effective may expect ATC clearances containing a SID. Use of SID requires pilot possession of at least the textual description of the SID procedures. Controllers may omit the departure control frequency if a SID clearance is issued and the departure control frequency is published on the SID. If the pilot does not possess a charted SID or a preprinted SID description or, for any other reason, does not wish to use a SID, he is expected to advise ATC. Notification may be accomplished by filing "NO SID" in the remarks section of the filed flight plan.

c. SID procedures will be depicted in one of two basic forms.

(1) Pilot Navigation (Pilot NAV) SID's are established where the pilot is primarily responsible for navigation on the SID route. They are established for airports when terrain and safety related factors indicate the necessity for a pilot NAV SID. Some pilot NAV SID's may contain vector instructions which pilots are expected to comply with until instructions are received to resume normal navigation on the filed/assigned route or SID procedure.

(2) Vector SID's are established where ATC will provide radar navigational guidance to a filed/assigned route or to a fix depicted on the SID.

4-51 Reference. — AIM 325.

4-52 SID ISSUANCE

a. ATC will assign a SID (including transition, if necessary), a PDR, or the route filed by the pilot only when a SID is not established for the departure route to be flown or the pilot has indicated that he does not wish to use a SID.

ATC Phraseology:

(SID name and number) **Departure**.

(SID name and number) **Departure**, (transition name) **Transition**.

4-52a Examples. —

Stroudsburg One Departure.

Stroudsburg One Departure, Sparta Transition.

Stroudsburg One R-NAV Departure.

b. If it is necessary to assign a crossing altitude which differs from the SID altitude, the controller will repeat the changed altitude to the pilot for emphasis.

ATC Phraseology:

(SID name) **Departure, except** (revised altitude information). **I say again** (revised altitude information).

4-52b Examples. —

Stroudsburg One Departure, except cross Quaker at five thousand. I say again, cross Quaker at five thousand.

Astoria Two R-NAV Departure, except cross Astor waypoint at six thousand. I say again, cross Astor waypoint at six thousand.

c. Altitudes will be specified when they are not included in the SID.

ATC Phraseology:

(SID name) **Departure. Cross** (fix) **at** (altitude).

4-52c Examples. —

Stroudsburg One Departure. Cross Jersey intersection at four thousand. Cross Range intersection at six thousand.

Engle Two R-NAV Departure. Cross Pilim waypoint at or above five thousand. Cross Engle waypoint at or above seven thousand. Cross Gorge waypoint at niner thousand.

4-52 Reference. — ATCH 4-21.

4-53 OBSTACLE CLEARANCE

Each pilot, prior to departing an airport on an IFR flight, should consider the type of terrain and other obstacles on or in the vicinity of the departure airport and:

a. Determine whether a departure procedure and/or SID is available for obstacle avoidance.

b. Determine if obstacle avoidance can be maintained visually or that the departure procedure or SID should be followed.

c. Determine what action will be necessary and take such action that will assure a safe departure.*

4-53c Note 1. — The term *Radar Contact*, when used by the controller during departure, should not be interpreted as relieving pilots of their responsibility to maintain appropriate terrain and obstruction clearance. Terrain/obstruction clearance is not provided by ATC until the controller begins to provide navigational guidance, i.e., Radar Vectors.

4-53c Note 2. — Order 8260.19, Flight Procedures and Airspace, establishes guidelines for IFR departure turning procedures which assumes a climb to 400 feet above the airport elevation before a turn is commenced.

4-53 Reference. — AIM 325.

4-54 thru 4-59 RESERVED

Section 6. IFR ROUTES AND NAVAID LIMITS

4-60 COURSE TO BE FLOWN

An IFR aircraft must operate within controlled airspace unless otherwise authorized by ATC on:

a. A Federal airway, along the centerline of that airway.

b. Any other route, along the direct course between the navigational aids or fixes defining that route. However, this does not prohibit maneuvering the aircraft to pass well clear of other air traffic or the maneuvering of the aircraft, in VFR conditions, to clear the intended flight path both before and during climb or descent.

4-60 Reference. — FAR 91.123.

4-61 POSITIVE CONTROL AREAS AND ROUTE SEGMENTS

Except as authorized by ATC, no person may operate an aircraft within a positive control area or positive control route segment, designated in Part 71 of the FAR's, unless that aircraft is:

a. Operated under IFR at a specific flight level assigned by ATC;

b. Equipped with instruments and equipment required for IFR operations;

c. Flown by a pilot rated for instrument flight; and

d. Equipped, when in a positive control area, with:

(1) The applicable equipment specified in FAR 91.24; and

(2) A radio providing direct pilot controller communication on the frequency specified by ATC for the area concerned.

4-61 Reference. — FAR 91.97.

4-62 VICTOR AIRWAYS

a. The VOR Airway System consists of airways designated from 1,200 feet above the surface (or in some instances higher) up to, but not including, 18,000 feet MSL. These airways are depicted on En Route Low Altitude Charts.

b. With respect to position reporting, reporting points are designated for VOR Airway Systems. Flights using Victor Airways will report over these points unless advised otherwise by ATC, i.e., when advised *"Radar Contact."*

4-62 Reference. — AIM 343.

4-63 JET ROUTES

a. The Jet Route system consists of jet routes established from 18,000 feet MSL to FL 450 inclusive.

b. With respect to position reporting, reporting points are designated for Jet Route systems. Flights using Jet Routes will report over these points unless otherwise advised by ATC, i.e., when advised *"Radar Contact."*

4-63 Reference. — AIM 343.

4-64 AREA NAVIGATION ROUTES

a. RNAV (area navigation) is a method of navigation that permits aircraft operations on any desired course within the coverage of station referenced navigation signals, or within the limits of a self-contained system capability, or combination of these.

b. Fixed RNAV routes are permanent, published routes which can be flight planned for use by aircraft with RNAV capability. A previously established fixed RNAV route system has been terminated except for a few high altitude routes in Alaska.

c. Random RNAV routes are direct routes, based on area navigation capability, between waypoints defined in terms of latitude/longitude coordinates, degree-distance fixes, or offsets from established routes/airways at a specified distance and direction. Radar monitoring by ATC is required on all random RNAV routes.

4-64 Reference. — AIM 343.

4-65 ROUTE CLEARANCES

ATC will clear aircraft via airways, route structures, random RNAV routes, and NAVAID's established for the altitude stratum in which the operation is to be conducted by one or more of the following:*

a. Designated airways and routes.

ATC Phraseology:

Via:

Victor (airway number) (the word ROMEO when RNAV), *or*

J (route number) (the word ROMEO when RNAV), *or*

Substitute (airway or jet route) **from** (fix) **to** (fix).

Cross/Join Victor/ (airway number), (number of miles) **miles** (direction) **of** (fix).

b. Radials, courses, azimuths, or direct to or from NAVAID's.

ATC Phraseology:

Direct.

Via:

(name of NAVAID) (specified) **radial/course/azimuth** or (fix) **and** (fix), or

Radials of (airway or route) **and** (airway or route).

c. DME arcs of VORTAC, MLS, or TACAN aids.

d. Radials, courses, azimuths, and headings of departure or arrival routes.

e. SID's/STAR's.

f. Vectors.

g. Courses, azimuths, bearings, quadrants, or radials within a radius of NAVAID.

ATC Phraseology:

Cleared to fly (general direction from NAVAID) **of** (NAVAID name and type) **between** (specified) **courses to/bearings from/radials** (NAVAID name when a NDB) **within** (number of miles) **miles radius.**

or

Cleared to fly (specified) **quadrant of** (NAVAID name and type) **within** (number of miles) **mile radius.**

4-65g Examples. —

Cleared to fly east of Allentown VORTAC between the zero four five and the one three five radials within four zero mile radius.

Cleared to fly east of Crystal Lake radio beacon between the two two five and the three one five courses to Crystal Lake within three zero mile radius.

Cleared to fly northeast quadrant of Philipsburg VORTAC within four zero mile radius.

h. Fixes defined in terms of degree-distance from NAVAID's or offset from published or established routes/airways at a specified distance and direction for random (impromptu) RNAV Routes. ATC will provide radar monitoring at FL 450 and below.

ATC Phraseology:

Direct to the (facility) (radial) (distance) **fix.**

Offset (distance) **right/left of** (route).

4-65h Examples. —

Direct to the Appleton three one zero radial two five mile fix.

Offset eight miles right of Victor Six.

i. Waypoints defined in terms of latitude/longitude coordinates for random RNAV routes.

4-65 Note. — Airways, routes, and NAVAID's established for use at specified altitudes are shown on U.S. Government charts, except for certain NAVAID's/routes used by scheduled air carriers or authorized for specific uses in the control of IFR aircraft.

4-65 Reference. — ATCH 4-30.

4-66 ROUTE TRANSITIONS

To effect transition within or between routes, ATC will clear an aircraft by one or more of the following methods, based on VOR, VORTAC, or MLS NAVAID's (unless use of other NAVAID's is essential to aircraft operation or ATC efficiency):

a. Vectoring aircraft to or from radials, courses, or azimuths of the airway or route assigned.

b. Assigning a SID/STAR.

c. Clearing departing or arriving aircraft to climb or descend via radials, courses, or azimuths of the airway or jet route assigned.

d. Clearing departing or arriving aircraft directly to or between the NAVAID's forming the airway or route assigned.

e. Clearing aircraft to climb or descend via the airway or route on which flight will be conducted.

f. Clearing aircraft to climb or descend on specified radials, courses, or azimuths of NAVAID's.

g. Providing radar monitoring when transition to or from a designated or established RNAV route is made along random RNAV routes.

h. Clearing RNAV aircraft transitioning to or between designated or established RNAV routes direct to a named waypoint on the new route.

4-66 Reference. — ATCH 4-31.

4-67 ALTERNATIVE ROUTES

When any part of an airway or route is unusable because of NAVAID status, ATC will clear aircraft via one of the following alternative routes:

a. A route depicted on current U.S. Government charts/publications. Controllers will use the word "substitute" immediately preceding the alternative route in issuing the clearance.

b. A route defined by specifying NAVAID radials, courses, or azimuths.

c. A route defined as direct to or between NAVAID's.

d. Vectors.

4-67 Reference. — ATCH 4-33.

4-68 UNCONTROLLED AIRSPACE ROUTING

ATC will include routes through uncontrolled airspace only when requested by the pilot.*

4-68 Note. — Flight plans filed for random RNAV routes through uncontrolled airspace are considered a request by the pilot.

4-68 Reference. — ATCH 4-34.

4-69 DIRECT ROUTE FLIGHTS

All or any portions of the route which will not be flown on the radials or courses of established airways or routes, such as direct route flights, must be defined by indicating the radio fixes over which the flight will pass. Fixes selected to define the route shall be those over which the position of the aircraft can be accurately determined. Such fixes automatically become compulsory reporting points for the flight, unless advised otherwise by ATC, i.e., when advised *"Radar Contact."* Only those navigational aids established for use in a particular structure, i.e., in the low or high structures, may be used to define the en route phase of a direct flight within that altitude structure.

4-69 Reference. — AIM 298.

4-70 SERVICE VOLUME LIMITATIONS

a. The azimuth feature of a VOR and the azimuth and distance (DME) features of VORTAC and TACAN aids are assigned certain frequency protected areas of airspace which are intended for application to established airway and route use, and to provide guidance for planning flights outside of established airways or routes. These areas of airspace are expressed in terms of cylindrical service volumes of specified dimensions called "class limits" or "categories." An operational service volume has been established for each class in which adequate signal coverage and frequency protection can be assured.

b. When specifying a route other than an established airway or route, ATC may not exceed the limitations in the Table on any portion of the route which lies within controlled airspace.

4-70b Tables. —

VOR/VORTAC/TACAN NAVAID'S
Normal Usable Altitudes and Radius Distances

Class	Altitudes	Distance (miles)
T	12,000 and below	25
L	Below 18,000	40
H	Below 18,000	40
H	14,500–17,999	100
H	18,000–FL 450	130
H	Above FL 450	100

L/MF Radio Beacon (RBN)
Usable Radius Distances for All Altitudes

Class	Power (watts)	Distance (miles)
CL	Under 25	15
MH	Under 50	25
H	50–1,999	50
HH	2,000 or more	75

ILS
Usable Height and Distance*

Height above transmitter	Distance (miles) from transmitter
4,500	10 (for Glide Slope)
4,500	18 (for Localizer)

*Current flight check height/altitude limitations are used if different from the above minima.

MLS
Usable Height and Distance*

Height (feet) above transmitter	Distance (miles) from transmitter
20,000	20 (for glidepath)
20,000	20 (for azimuth)

*Current flight check height/altitude limitations are used if different from the above minima.

4-70 References. — ATCH 4-1; AIM 298.

4-71 SERVICE VOLUME EXCEPTIONS

Service volume limitations need not be applied when:

a. Routing is initiated by ATC and radar monitoring is provided.

b. Routing is requested by the pilot and radar flight following is provided for air traffic control purposes.

c. An aircraft requests to operate "VFR-on-top" on the route.

d. Operational necessity requires and approval has been obtained from the Frequency Management and Flight Inspection Offices to exceed them.

4-71 Reference. — ATCH 4-2.

4-72 CROSSING ALTITUDE LIMITATIONS

ATC will use an altitude consistent with the service volume limitations of the aid when clearing an aircraft to hold at or cross a fix.

4-72 Reference. — ATCH 4-3.

4-73 INTERSECTION AND FIX SERVICE VOLUME LIMITATIONS

a. ATC will request aircraft position reports only over fixes shown on charts used for the altitude being flown.*

b. Unpublished fixes may be used if the name of the NAVAID and, if appropriate, the radial/course/azimuth and frequency are given to the pilot. An unpublished fix is defined as one approved and planned for publication which is not yet depicted on the charts or one which is used in accord with the following:*

(1) Unpublished fixes are formed by the en route radial and either a DME distance from the same NAVAID or an intersecting radial from an off-route VOR/VORTAC. DME will be used in lieu of off-route radials, whenever possible.

(2) Except where known signal coverage restrictions exist, an unpublished fix may be used for ATC purposes if its location does not exceed NAVAID altitude and distance limitation, and when off-route radials are used, the angle of divergence meets the criteria prescribed below.

(3) ATC may not hold aircraft at unpublished fixes below the lowest assignable altitude dictated by terrain clearance for the appropriate holding pattern airspace area, regardless of the MEA for the route being flown.

(4) When the unpublished fix is located on an off-route radial and the radial providing course guidance, it will be used consistent with the following divergence angles.

(a) When holding operations are involved, with respect to (b) and (c) below, the angle of divergence will be at least 45 degrees.

(b) When both NAVAID's involved are located within 30 NM of the unpublished fix, the minimum divergence angle is 30 degrees.

(c) When the unpublished fix is located over 30 NM from the NAVAID generating the off-course radial, the minimum divergence angle will increase 1 degree per nautical mile up to 45 NM; e.g., 45 NM would require 45 degrees.

(d) When the unpublished fix is located beyond 45 NM from the NAVAID generating the off-course radial, the minimum divergence angle will increase ½ degree per nautical mile; e.g., 130 NM would require 88 degrees.

4-73a Note. — Waypoints filed in random RNAV routes automatically become compulsory reporting points for the flight unless otherwise advised by ATC.

4-73b Note. — Unpublished fixes should not negate the normal use of published intersections. Frequent routine use of an unpublished fix would justify establishing a fix.

4-73 Reference. — ATCH 4-5.

4-74 thru 4-79 RESERVED

Section 7. ALTITUDE ASSIGNMENTS

4-80 FLIGHT DIRECTION ALTITUDE ASSIGNMENTS

ATC will clear aircraft at altitudes according to the Table.

4-80 Table. — Altitude Assignment

Aircraft Operating	On course degrees magnetic	ATC will Assign	Examples
Below 3,000 feet above surface	Any course	Any altitude	
Below FL290	0 through 179	Odd cardinal altitudes or flight levels at intervals of 2,000 feet	3,000, 5,000, FL250, FL270
	180 through 359	Even cardinal altitudes or flight levels at intervals of 2,000 feet	4,000, 6,000 FL240, FL260
At or above FL290	0 through 179	Odd cardinal flight levels at intervals of 4,000 feet beginning with FL290	FL290, FL330, FL370
	180 through 359	Odd cardinal flight levels at intervals of 4,000 feet beginning with FL310	FL310, FL350, FL390
Within an ALTRV	Any course	Any altitude or flight level	
In transition to/from Oceanic airspace where composite separation is authorized	Any course	Any odd or even cardinal flight level including those above FL290	FL280, FL290, FL300, FL310, FL320, FL330, FL340

4-80 Reference. — ATCH 4-40.

4-81 RANDOM ALTITUDE ASSIGNMENT

When traffic, meteorological conditions, or aircraft operational limitations prevent assignment of altitudes prescribed in the preceding paragraph, ATC will assign any cardinal altitude or flight level below FL 290 or any odd cardinal flight level at or above FL 290 without regard to direction of flight as follows:

a. For traffic conditions, ATC will take this action only if one of the following conditions exists:

(1) Aircraft remain within a facility's area and prior approval is obtained from other affected positions or sectors, or the operations are covered in a Facility Directive.

(2) Aircraft will proceed beyond the facility's area and specific operations and procedures permitting random altitude assignment are covered in a letter of agreement between the appropriate facilities.

b. For meteorological conditions, ATC will take this action only if the controller obtains prior approval from other affected positions or sectors within his facility and, if necessary, from the adjacent facility concerned.

c. For aircraft operational limitations, ATC will take this action only if the pilot informs the controller that the available appropriate altitude exceeds the operational limitations of his aircraft and only after the controller obtains prior approval from other affected positions or sectors within his facility and, if necessary, from the adjacent facility concerned.

4-81 Reference. — ATCH 4-41.

4-82 LOWEST USABLE FLIGHT LEVEL

If a change in atmospheric pressure affects a usable flight level in a controller's area of jurisdiction, ATC will use the Table to determine the lowest usable flight level to clear aircraft at or above 18,000 feet MSL.

4-82 Table. — Lowest Usable FL

Altimeter Setting	Lowest Usable FL
29.92" or higher	180
29.91" to 28.92"	190
28.91" to 27.92"	200

4-82 Reference. — ATCH 4-42.

4-83 ADJUSTED MINIMUM FLIGHT LEVEL

When the prescribed minimum altitude for IFR operations is at or above 18,000 feet MSL, and the atmospheric pressure is less than 29.92", ATC will add the appropriate adjustment factor from the Table to the flight level equivalent of the minimum altitude in feet to determine the adjusted minimum flight level.

4-83 Table. — Minimum FL Adjustment

Altimeter Setting	Adjustment Factor
29.92" or higher	None
29.91" to 29.42"	500 feet
29.41" to 28.92"	1,000 feet
28.91" to 28.42"	1,500 feet
28.41" to 27.92"	2,000 feet

4-83 Reference. — ATCH 4-43.

4-84 MINIMUM EN ROUTE ALTITUDES

ATC will assign altitudes at or above the MEA (minimum en route altitude) for the route segment being flown, except as provided in **a** and **b** below. When a lower MEA for subsequent segments of the route is applicable, ATC will issue the lower MEA only after the aircraft is over or past the FIX/NAVAID beyond which the lower MEA applies unless a crossing restriction at or above the higher MEA is issued.

a. An aircraft may be cleared below the MEA, but not below the MOCA (minimum obstacle clearance altitude), for the route segment being flown if the altitude assigned is at least 300 feet above the floor of controlled airspace and the following conditions are met:

(1) Non-radar procedures are used only within 22 miles of a VOR, or VORTAC.

(2) Radar navigational guidance is provided until the aircraft is within at least 22 miles of the NAVAID, and lost communications instructions are issued.

b. An aircraft may be cleared to operate on jet routes below the MEA (but not below the prescribed minimum altitude for IFR operations) or above the maximum authorized altitude if, in either case, radar service is provided.*

c. Where a higher altitude is required because of a MEA, the aircraft will be cleared to begin climb to the higher MEA as follows:

(1) If no MCA (minimum crossing altitude) is specified, prior to or immediately after passing the fix where the higher MEA is designated.

(2) If a MCA is specified, prior to the fix so as to cross the fix at or above the MCA.

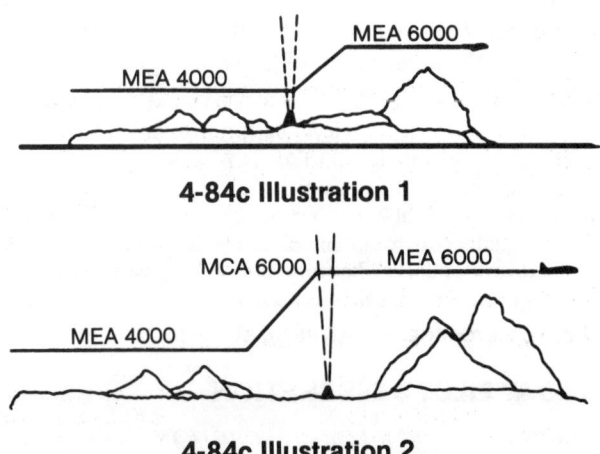

4-84c Illustration 1

4-84c Illustration 2

d. Where MEA's have not been established, ATC will clear an aircraft at or above the minimum altitude for IFR operations prescribed by FAR 91.119.

4-84b Note. — Minimum en route and maximum authorized altitudes for certain jet route segments have been established above the floor of the jet route structure due to limitations on navigational signal coverage.

4-84 Reference. — ATCH 4-44.

4-85 ALTITUDE ASSIGNMENTS

When controllers issue altitude information, included will be the following items, as appropriate:

a. Altitude to maintain.

ATC Phraseology:

Maintain (altitude).

b. Instructions to climb or descend, including restrictions, as required.

ATC Phraseology:

Climb/Descend and maintain (altitude).

If required,

After passing (fix), *or*

At (time).

Climb/Descend and maintain (altitude) **when established at least** (number of miles or minutes) **miles/minutes past** (fix) **on the** (NAVAID) (specified) **radial.**

Climb/Descend to reach (altitude) **at** (time or fix), *or* **a point** (number of miles) **miles** (direction) **of** (name of DME NAVAID).

c. Specified altitude over a specified fix.

ATC Phraseology:

Cross (fix) **at** (altitude).

Cross (fix) **at or above/below** (altitude).

d. Altitude assignments involving more than one altitude.

ATC Phraseology:

Maintain (altitude) **through** (altitude).

e. Altitude to cruise. When issuing cruise in conjunction with an airport clearance limit and an unpublished route will be used, ATC will issue an appropriate crossing altitude to ensure terrain clearance until the aircraft reaches a fix, point, or route where the altitude information is available to the pilot. When ATC is issuing a cruise clearance to an airport which does not have a published instrument approach, a cruise clearance without a crossing restriction may be issued.*

ATC Phraseology:

Cruise (altitude). **Maintain** (altitude) **until** (time), *or* **past** (fix), *or* (number of miles or minutes) **miles/minutes past** (fix).

Cross (fix, point) *or* **Intercept** (route) **at or above** (altitude), **cruise** (altitude).

4-85e Examples. —
Cruise six thousand.

Cross Jimbo at or above five thousand, cruise four thousand.

4-85e Note 1. — The term *CRUISE* may be used instead of *MAINTAIN* to assign a block of airspace, to a pilot, from the minimum IFR altitude up to and including the altitude specified in the cruise clearance. The pilot may level off at any intermediate altitude within this block of airspace. Climb/descent, within the block is to be made at the discretion of the pilot. However, once the pilot starts descent and reports leaving an altitude in the block, he may not return to that altitude without additional ATC clearance.

4-85e Note 2. — The crossing altitude must assure IFR obstruction clearance to the point where the aircraft is established on a segment of a published route or instrument approach procedure.

4-85e Note 3. — When an aircraft is issued a cruise clearance to an airport which does not have a published instrument approach procedure, it is not possible to satisfy the requirement for a crossing altitude that will ensure terrain clearance until the aircraft reaches a fix, point, or route where altitude information is available to the pilot. Under those conditions, a cruise clearance without a crossing restriction authorizes a pilot to determine the minimum IFR altitude as prescribed in FAR 91.119 and descend to it at pilot discretion if it is lower than the altitude specified in the cruise clearance.

4-85 References. — ATCH 4-45; AIM 262.

4-86 AMENDED ALTITUDE

When the route or altitude in a previously issued clearance is amended, the controller will restate applicable altitude restrictions. If altitude to maintain is changed or restated, whether prior to departure or while airborne, and previously issued altitude restrictions are omitted, those altitude restrictions are canceled, including SID altitude restrictions.

4-86 Examples. —

A departure flight receives a clearance to destination airport to maintain FL 290. The clearance incorporates a SID which has certain altitude crossing restrictions. Shortly after takeoff, the flight receives a new clearance changing the maintaining FL from 290 to 250. If the altitude restrictions are still applicable, the controller restates them.

A departing aircraft is cleared to cross Fluky intersection at or above 3,000 feet, Gordonville VOR at or above 12,000 feet, maintain FL 200. Shortly after departure, the altitude to be maintained is changed to FL 240. If the altitude restrictions are still applicable, the controller issues an amended clearance as follows:

Cross Fluky at or above three thousand, cross Gordonville at or above one two thousand, maintain flight level two four zero.

An arriving aircraft is cleared to his destination airport via V45 Delta VOR direct, he is cleared to cross Delta VOR at 10,000 feet and then, to maintain 6,000 feet. Prior to Delta VOR, the controller issues amended clearance as follows:*

Turn right, heading one eight zero vector to I-L-S Runway Three Six Approach, maintain six thousand.

4-86 Example Note. — Because the altitude restriction "cross Delta VOR at 10,000 feet" was omitted from the amended clearance, it is no longer in effect.

4-86 Reference. — AIM 270.

4-87 EXPECTED ALTITUDE CHANGES

If practicable, controllers will inform an aircraft when to expect climb or descent clearance or to request altitude change from another facility.

ATC Phraseology:

Expect climb/descent clearance in (number of miles or minutes) **miles/minutes,** *or*

at (fix). **Request altitude change from** (name of facility).

If required,

at (time, fix, or altitude).

4-87 Example. —

Cessna One Zero Five requesting lower.

Cessna One Zero Five, expect descent clearance in five miles.

4-87 Reference. — ATCH 4-46.

4-88 NORMAL DESCENTS

a. When ATC has NOT used the term *"AT PILOT'S DISCRETION"* nor imposed any climb or descent restrictions, pilots should initiate climb or descent promptly on acknowledgement of the clearance.

b. Pilots should descend or climb at an optimum rate consistent with the operating characteristics of the aircraft to 1,000 feet above or below the assigned altitude, and then attempt to descend or climb at a rate of 500 feet per minute until the assigned altitude is reached. If at any time the pilot is unable to climb or descend at a rate of at least 500 feet a minute, he should advise ATC.

c. If it is necessary to level off at an intermediate altitude during a normal climb or descent, pilots should advise ATC, except when leveling off at 10,000 feet MSL on descent or 3,000 feet above airport elevation (prior to entering an airport traffic area), when required for speed reduction.*

4-88c Note. — Leveling off at 10,000 feet MSL on descent, or 3,000 feet above airport elevation (prior to entering an airport traffic area), to comply with FAR 91.70 airspeed restrictions, is commonplace. Controllers anticipate this action and plan accordingly. Leveling off at any other time, on climb or descent, may seriously affect air traffic handling by ATC. Consequently, it is imperative that pilots make every effort to fulfill the above expected actions to aid ATC in safely handling and expediting traffic.

4-88 References. — FAR 91.70; AIM 270.

4-89 AT PILOT'S DISCRETION

a. The term *"AT PILOT'S DISCRETION"* included in the altitude information of an ATC clearance means that ATC has offered the pilot the option to start climb or descent when he wishes. He is authorized to conduct the climb or descent at any rate he wishes, and to temporarily level off at any intermediate altitude he may desire. However, once he has vacated an altitude, he may not return to that altitude.

b. If the altitude information of an ATC descent clearance includes a provision to cross a fix at or above or at or below, a specified altitude, the manner in which the descent is executed to comply with the crossing altitude is at the pilot's discretion. This authorization to descend at the pilot's discretion is only applicable to that portion of the flight to which the crossing altitude restriction applies, and the pilot is expected to comply with the crossing altitude as a provision of the clearance.

c. ATC will specify an altitude over a specified fix for that portion of a descent clearance where descent at the pilot's discretion is permissable. At any other time it is practicable, ATC will authorize climb/descend at pilot's discretion.*

ATC Phraseology:
Climb/Descend at pilot's discretion.

4-89c Example 1. —

United Four Seventeen, descend and maintain six thousand.

The pilot is expected to commence descent upon receipt of the clearance and to descend at the suggested rates specified in paragraph 4-88 until reaching the assigned altitude of 6,000 feet.

4-89c Example 2. —

United Four Seventeen, descend at pilot's discretion, maintain six thousand.

The pilot is authorized to conduct descent within the context of the term *"at pilot's discretion."*

4-89c Example 3. —

United Four Seventeen, cross Lakeview at or above flight level two zero zero, descend and maintain six thousand.

The pilot is authorized to conduct descent *"at pilot's discretion,"* until reaching Lakeview VOR. He must comply with the clearance provision to cross the Lakeview VOR at or above FL 200, and after passing Lakeview VOR, he is expected to descend at the rates specified in paragraph 4-88 until reaching the assigned altitude of 6,000 feet.

4-89c Example 4. —

United Four Seventeen, cross Lakeview at and maintain six thousand.

The pilot is authorized to conduct descent *"at pilot's discretion,"* but must comply with the clearance provision to cross Lakeview VOR at 6,000 feet.

4-89c Example 5. —

United Four Seventeen, descend now to flight level two seven zero, cross Lakeview at or below one zero thousand, descend and maintain six thousand.

The pilot is expected to promptly execute and complete descent to FL 270 upon receipt of the clearance. After reaching FL 270, he is authorized to descend *"at pilot's discretion"* until reaching Lakeview VOR. He must comply with the clearance provision to cross Lakeview VOR at or below 10,000 feet. After Lakeview VOR, he is expected to descend at the rates specified in paragraph 4-88 until reaching 6,000.

4-89c Note. — A descent clearance which specifies a crossing altitude authorizes descent at pilot's discretion for that portion of the flight to which the crossing altitude restriction applies. Any other time that authorization to descend at pilot's discretion is intended, it must be specifically stated by the controller.

4-89 References. — ATCH 4-45; AIM 270.

4-90 PROFILE DESCENTS

a. The enhancement of safety and reduction of noise is achieved in this program by minimizing low altitude maneuvering of arriving turbojet and turboprop aircraft weighing more than 12,500 pounds, and by permitting departure aircraft to climb to higher altitudes sooner, as arrivals are operating at higher altitudes at the points where their flight paths cross. The application of these procedures also reduces exposure time between controlled aircraft and uncontrolled aircraft at the lower altitudes in and around the terminal environment. Fuel conservation is accomplished by absorbing any necessary arrival delays for aircraft included in this program operating at the higher and more fuel efficient altitudes.

b. A fuel efficient descent is basically an uninterrupted descent (except where level flight is required for speed adjustment) from cruising altitude to the point when level flight is necessary for the pilot to stabilize his final approach. The procedure for a fuel efficient descent is based on an altitude loss which is most efficient for the majority of aircraft being served. This will generally result in a descent gradient window of 250-350 feet per nautical mile.

c. When crossing altitudes and speed restrictions are issued verbally or are depicted on a chart, ATC will expect the pilot to descend first to the crossing altitude and then reduce speed. Verbal clearances for descent will normally permit an uninterrupted descent in accordance with the procedure as described in paragraph **b** above. Acceptance of a charted fuel efficient descent (Runway Profile Descent) clearance requires the pilot to adhere to the altitudes, speeds, and headings depicted on the charts unless otherwise instructed by ATC. *PILOTS RECEIVING A CLEARANCE FOR A FUEL EFFICIENT DESCENT ARE EXPECTED TO ADVISE ATC IF THEY DO NOT HAVE RUNWAY PROFILE DESCENT CHARTS PUBLISHED FOR THAT AIRPORT OR ARE UNABLE TO COMPLY WITH THE CLEARANCE.*

4-90 Reference. — AIM 361.

4-91 thru 4-99 RESERVED

Section 8. AIRCRAFT HOLDING

4-100 ARRIVAL DELAY PROCEDURES

When it is necessary to clear an aircraft to a fix other than the destination airport, ATC will issue the following:

a. Clearance limit (if any part of the route beyond a clearance limit differs from the last routing cleared, ATC will issue the route the pilot can expect beyond the clearance limit).

ATC Phraseology:

Expect further clearance via (routing).

4-100a Example. —

Expect further clearance via direct Stillwater, Victor Two Twenty-six Snapy, direct.

b. Holding instructions.

(1) Holding instructions may be eliminated after the controller informs the pilot that no delay is expected.

(2) When the pattern is charted, the controller may omit all holding instructions except the charted holding direction and the statement *"as published."* The controller must issue complete holding instructions when the pilot requests them.*

ATC Phraseology:

Cleared to (fix), **hold** (direction), **as published,**
or
Cleared to (fix), **no delay expected.**

c. EFC. Controllers will not specify this item if no delay is expected.

(1) When additional holding is expected at any other fix in the facility's area, controllers will state the fix and the best estimate of the additional delay. When more than one fix is involved, the controller will state the total additional en route delay.*

ATC Phraseology:

Expect further clearance (time),
and, if required,
anticipate additional (time in minutes/hours) **minute/hour delay at** (fix),
or
anticipate additional (time in minutes/hours) **minute/hour en route delay.**

4-100c(1) Examples. —

Expect further clearance one niner two zero.

Expect further clearance one five one zero, anticipate additional three zero minute en route delay.

(2) When additional holding is expected in an approach control area, the controller will state the total additional terminal delay.

ATC Phraseology:

Expect further clearance (time),
and, if required,
anticipate additional (time in minutes/hours) **minute/hour terminal delay.**

(3) TERMINAL: When terminal delays exist or are expected, controllers will inform the appropriate center or approach control facility so that the information can be forwarded to arrival aircraft.

(4) When delay is expected, controllers will issue items 4-100**a, b,** and **c** at least 5 minutes before the aircraft is estimated to reach the clearance limit. If the traffic situation requires holding an aircraft that is less than 5 minutes from the holding fix, the controller will issue these items immediately.*

ATC Phraseology:

Delay indefinite (reason, if known), **expect further clearance** (time). (After determining the reason for the delay, controllers will advise the pilot as soon as possible.)

4-100c(4) Examples. —

Cleared to Drewe, hold west, as published, expect further clearance via direct Sidney, one three one five, anticipate additional two zero minute delay at Woody.

Cleared to Aston, hold west on Victor Two Twenty-five, seven mile legs, left turns, expect further clearance one niner two zero, anticipate additional one five minute terminal delay.

Cleared to Wayne, no delay expected.

Cleared to Wally, hold north, as published, delay indefinite, snow removal in progress, expect further clearance one one three zero.

4-100b(2) Note. — The most generally used holding patterns are depicted on U.S. Government or commercially produced low/high altitude en route, area, and STAR charts.

4-100c(1) Note. — Additional delay information may not be used by ATC to determine pilot action in the event of two-way communications failure. Pilots are expected to predicate their actions solely on the provisions of FAR 91.127.

4-100c(4) Note 1. — Pilots should start a speed reduction when 3 minutes or less from the holding fix. The additional 2 minutes contained in the 5-minute requirement are necessary to compensate for different pilot/controller ETA's at the holding fix, minor differences in clock times, and provision for sufficient planning and reaction times.

4-100c(4) Note 2. — When holding is necessary, the phrase *"delay indefinite"* will be used when an accurate estimate of the delay time and the reason for the delay cannot immediately be determined; i.e., disabled aircraft on the runway, terminal or center sector saturation, weather below landing minimums, etc. In any event, every attempt will be made to provide the pilot with the best possible estimate of his delay time and the reason for the delay.

4-100 Reference. — ATCH 4-50.

BASIC IFR PROCEDURES

4-101 CLEARANCE BEYOND HOLDING FIX

a. If no delay is expected, controllers will issue a clearance beyond the clearance limit as soon as possible and, whenever possible, at least 5 minutes before the aircraft reaches the fix.*

b. Included will be the following items when controllers issue a clearance beyond a clearance limit:

(1) Clearance limit or approach clearance.

(2) Route of flight. One of the following will be specified:

(a) Complete details of the route (airway, route, course, fix(es), azimuth course, heading, arc, or vector).

(b) The phrase *"via last routing cleared."* This phrase is used only when the most recently issued routing to the new clearance limit is valid and verbiage will be reduced.

ATC Phraseology:

Via last routing cleared.

(3) Assigned altitude if different from present altitude.

4-101a Note. — Except in the event of a two-way communications failure, when a clearance beyond a fix has not been received, pilots are expected to hold as depicted on U.S. Government or commercially produced (meeting FAA requirements) low/high altitude en route and area or STAR charts. If no holding pattern is charted and holding instructions have not been issued, pilots should ask ATC for holding instructions prior to reaching the fix. If a pilot is unable to obtain holding instructions prior to reaching a fix, he is expected to hold in a standard pattern on the course on which he approached the fix and request further clearance as soon as possible.

4-101 Reference. — ATCH 4-51.

4-102 ARRIVAL DELAY INFORMATION

When arrival delays reach or are anticipated to reach 30 minutes, ATC will take the following action:

a. EN ROUTE: Whenever possible, the delay information will be issued by the first center controller to communicate with the aircraft.

b. TERMINAL: Whenever possible, the delay information will be issued by the first terminal controller to communicate with the aircraft.

c. Unless a pilot requests delay information, the actions specified in 4-101b(1) and (2) above may be omitted when total delay information is available to pilots via ATIS.

ATC Phraseology:

(Airport) **arrival delays** (time in minutes/hours).

4-102 Reference. — ATCH 4-52.

4-103 HOLDING INSTRUCTION FORMAT

When issuing holding instructions, controllers will specify:

a. Direction of holding from the fix.

b. Holding fix.*

c. Radial, course, bearing, azimuth, airway, or route on which the aircraft is to hold.

d. Leg length in miles if DME or RNAV is to be used. Specify leg length in minutes if the pilot requests or controllers consider it necessary.

e. Direction of holding pattern turns only if left turns are to be made, the pilot requests, or controllers consider it necessary.

ATC Phraseology:

Hold (direction) **of** (fix) **on** (specified radial, course, bearing, azimuth, airway, route).

(Number of minutes/miles) **minute/mile leg.**

If direction of turn is specified,

Left/Right turns.

4-103e Example. —

United Five Fourteen, hold west of Chicago Heights on Victor Eight, one five mile legs, left turns.

4-103b Note. — The holding fix may be omitted if included at the beginning of the transmission as the clearance limit.

4-103 Reference. — ATCH 4-53.

4-104 HOLDING PATTERN SURVEILLANCE

Controllers will provide radar surveillance of outer fix holding pattern airspace areas, or any portions thereof, shown on their radar scope whenever aircraft are holding there. Controllers will attempt to detect any that stray outside the area. If they detect an aircraft straying outside the area, they will assist it to return to the assigned airspace.

4-104 Reference. — ATCH 5-9.

4-105 PROTECTED AIRSPACE DEVIATION ADVISORIES

Aircraft will be informed when they are observed in a position and on a track which will obviously cause the aircraft to deviate from its protected airspace area. If necessary, controllers will assist the aircraft to return to the assigned protected airspace.

4-105 Reference. — ATCH 5-10.

4-106 VISUAL HOLDING POINTS

Controllers may use as a holding fix a location which the pilot can determine by visual reference to the surface if he is familiar with it.

ATC Phraseology:

Hold at (location) **until** (time or other condition).

4-106 Reference. — ATCH 4-54.

4-107 HOLDING AT UNMONITORED NAVAID'S

Aircraft holding at a fan marker or an unmonitored NAVAID are separated from any other aircraft occupying the course which the holding aircraft will follow if it does not receive signals from the marker or NAVAID.

4-107 Reference. — ATCH 4-56.

4-108 ILS PROTECTION/CRITICAL HOLDING AREAS

When conditions are less than reported ceiling 800 feet and/or visibility 2 miles, ATC will not authorize aircraft to hold below 5,000 feet inbound toward the airport on or within 1 statute mile of the localizer between the ILS outer marker or the fix used in lieu of the outer marker and the airport.

4-108 Reference. — ATCH 4-57.

4-109 RESERVED

Section 9. ARRIVAL

4-110 STANDARD TERMINAL ARRIVAL ROUTE

a. A STAR (standard terminal arrival route) is an ATC coded IFR arrival route established for application to arriving IFR aircraft destined for certain airports. Its purpose is to simplify clearance delivery procedures.

b. Pilots of IFR civil aircraft destined to locations for which STAR's have been published may be issued a clearance containing a STAR whenever ATC deems it appropriate.

c. Use of STAR's requires pilot possession of at least the approved textual description. As with any ATC clearance or portion thereof, it is the responsibility of each pilot to accept or refuse an issued STAR. A pilot should notify ATC if he does not wish to use a STAR by placing "NO STAR" in the remarks section of the flight plan or by the less desirable method of verbally stating the same to ATC.

4-110 Reference. — AIM 360.

4-111 ARRIVAL CLEARANCE INFORMATION

ATC will clear an arriving aircraft to a clearance limit by specifying the following:

a. Name of fix or airport.

b. Route of flight including a STAR and STAR Transition, if appropriate. A STAR and STAR Transition may be assigned to any aircraft in lieu of other routes; e.g., airways or Preferential Arrival Routes, when the routings are the same. The clearance will include the name, the current number and the transition, if necessary, of the STAR to be flown.*

ATC Phraseology:

(STAR name and number) **Arrival.**

(STAR name and number) **Arrival,** (transition name) **Transition.**

4-111b Examples. —
Rosewood One Arrival.

Rosewood One Arrival, Delta Transition.

c. Assigned altitude if different from present altitude or when a STAR/STAR Transition is issued.

4-111c Example. —
Bayview Three R-NAV Arrival, Helen Transition, maintain flight level three three zero.

d. Holding instructions, EFC, and additional delay information as required.

e. Instructions regarding further communications as appropriate.

4-111b Note. — If a pilot does not wish to use a STAR issued in an ATC clearance or any other STAR published for that location, he is expected to advise ATC.

4-111 Reference. — ATCH 4-60.

4-112 AIRPORT CONDITION INFORMATION

a. EN ROUTE: Before issuing an approach clearance or en route descent, and subsequently as changes occur, controllers will inform an aircraft of any abnormal operation of approach and landing aids and of destination airport conditions that they know of which might restrict an approach or landing.

b. TERMINAL: On initial contact or as soon as possible thereafter, and subsequently as changes occur, controllers will inform an aircraft of any abnormal operation of approach and landing aids and of destination airport conditions that they know of which might restrict an approach or landing. This information may be omitted if it is contained in the ATIS broadcast and the pilot states the appropriate ATIS code.

4-112 Reference. — ATCH 4-70.

4-113 AIRPORT WEATHER INFORMATION

EN ROUTE

When an available official weather report indicates weather conditions are below a 1,000-foot ceiling or below the highest circling minimum, whichever is higher, or less than 3-miles visibility for the airport concerned, controllers will transmit the weather report and changes classified as special weather observations to an arriving aircraft prior to or as part of the approach clearance when:

a. It is transmitted directly to the pilot via center controller-to-pilot communications.

b. It is relayed through a communications station other than an air carrier company radio or through a non-approach control facility. Controllers may do this by telling the station or nonapproach control facility to use current weather.

4-113 Reference. — ATCH 4-66.

4-114 BELOW MINIMUMS REPORT BY PILOT

If an arriving aircraft reports weather conditions are below his landing minima, ATC will:*

a. Issue appropriate instructions to the aircraft to hold or proceed to another airport.

b. Adjust, as necessary, the position in the landing sequence of any other aircraft desiring to make approaches and issue approach clearance accordingly.

4-114 Note. — Determination that existing weather/visibility is adequate for approach/landing is the responsibility of the pilot/aircraft operator.

4-114 Reference. — ATCH 4-68.

4-115 APPROACH INFORMATION

TERMINAL

a. Controllers will provide current approach information to arriving aircraft on initial radio contact or as soon as possible thereafter. Approach information contained in the ATIS broadcast may be omitted if the pilot states the appropriate ATIS code; otherwise, controllers will issue approach information by including the following:

(1) Ceiling and visibility if the ceiling at the airport of intended landing is reported below 1,000 feet or below the highest circling minimum, whichever is greater, or the visibility is less than 3 miles.

(2) Surface wind.

(3) Altimeter setting for the airport of intended landing.

(4) Approach clearance or type approach to be expected if two or more approaches are published and the clearance limit does not indicate which will be used.

(5) Runway, if different from that to which the instrument approach is made.

ATC Phraseology:

Expect (type) **Approach.**

Expect visual approach.

b. Controllers will issue any known changes classified as special weather observations as soon as possible. Special weather observations need not be issued after they are included in the ATIS broadcast and the pilot states the appropriate ATIS code.

c. Controllers will advise pilots when the ILS/MLS on the runway in use is not operational if that ILS/MLS is on the same frequency as an operational ILS/MLS serving another runway.

4-115c Example. —

Expect visual approach Runway Two Five Right, Runway Two Five Right I-L-S not operational.

4-115 Reference. — ATCH 4-72.

4-116 thru 4-119 RESERVED

Section 10. APPROACH CLEARANCE PROCEDURES

4-120 APPROACH CLEARANCES

a. Controllers will clear aircraft for "standard" or "special" instrument approach procedures only. To require an aircraft to execute a particular instrument approach procedure, controllers will specify in the approach clearance the name of the approach as published on the approach chart. Where more than one procedure is published on a single chart and a specific procedure is to be flown, the approach clearance will be amended to specify execution of the specific approach to be flown. If only one instrument approach of a particular type is published, the approach need not be identified by the runway reference. An aircraft conducting an ILS/MLS approach when the glideslope/glidepath is reported out of service will be advised at the time an approach clearance is issued. Where adequate radar coverage exists, radar facilities may vector aircraft to the final approach course.*

ATC Phraseology:

Cleared for (type) **Approach.**

For a straight-in-approach — IFR,

Cleared for Straight-in (type) **Approach.**

To authorize a pilot to execute his choice of instrument approach, **Cleared for approach.**

Where more than one procedure is published on a single chart and a specific procedure is to be flown, **Cleared for** (specific procedure to be flown) **Approach.**

To authorize a pilot to execute an ILS/MLS approach when the glideslope/glidepath is out of service, **Cleared for** (type) **Approach, glideslope unusable.**

4-120a Examples. —

Cleared for V-O-R Approach.

Cleared for V-O-R Runway Three Six Approach.

Cleared for I-L-S Approach.

Cleared for Localizer Back Course Runway One Three Approach.

Cleared for R-NAV Runway Two Two Approach.

Cleared for Branch One R-NAV Arrival and R-NAV Runway One Three Approach.

Cleared for I-L-S Runway Three Six Approach, glideslope unusable.

Cleared for M-L-S Approach.

Cleared for M-L-S Runway Three Six Approach.

Cleared for M-L-S Runway Three Six Approach, glidepath unusable.

b. For aircraft operating on unpublished routes, controllers will issue the approach clearance only after the aircraft is:

(1) Established on a segment of a published route or instrument approach procedure, or

(2) Assigned an altitude to maintain until the aircraft is established on a segment of a published route or instrument approach procedure.*

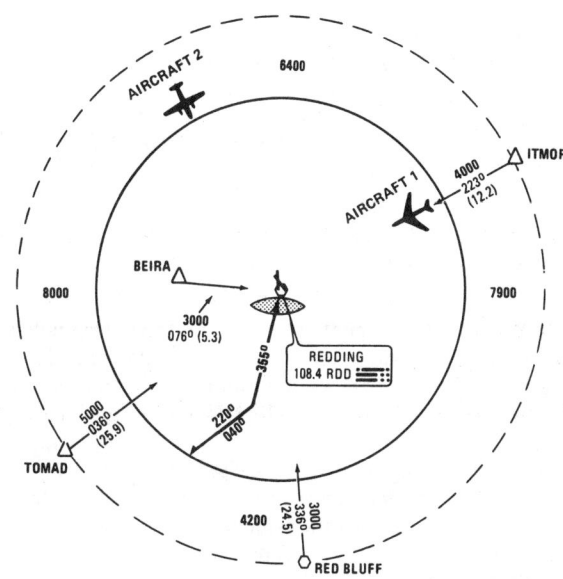

4-120b Illustration

4-120b(1) Example. —

Aircraft 1: The aircraft is established on a segment of a published route at 5,000 feet.

Cleared for V-O-R Runway Three Four Approach.

4-120b(2) Example. —

Aircraft 2: The aircraft is inbound to the VOR on an unpublished direct route at 7,000 feet. The minimum IFR altitude for IFR operations (FAR 91.119) along this flight path to the VOR is 5,000 feet.

Cross Redding at or above five thousand, cleared for V-O-R Runway Three Four Approach.

c. Except when applying radar procedures, timed, or visual approaches, controllers will clear an aircraft for an approach to an airport when the preceding aircraft has landed or cancelled its IFR flight plan.

4-120a Note 1. — Clearances authorizing instrument approaches are used on the basis that, if visual contact with the ground is made before the approach is completed, the entire approach procedure will be followed unless the pilot receives approval for a contact approach, is cleared for a visual approach, or cancels his IFR flight plan.

4-120a Note 2. — Approach clearances are issued based on known traffic. The receipt of an approach clearance does not relieve the pilot of his responsibility to comply with applicable FAR's and the notations on instrument approach charts which levy on the pilot the responsibility to comply with or act on an instruction; e.g., "Straight-in minima not authorized at night," "Procedure not authorized when glideslope/glidepath not used," "Use of procedure limited to aircraft authorized to use airport," or "Procedure not authorized at night."

4-120a Note 3. — The name of the approach, as published, is used to identify the approach even though a component of the approach aid, other than the localizer on an ILS or the azimuth on a MLS, is inoperative. Where more than one procedure is published on a single chart, the depicted runway or alphabetical suffixes apply to all procedures on that chart. For example, the Instrument Approach Procedures published on a chart as VOR/DME or ILS Rwy 6L would be stated as either *"VOR-DME Runway Six Left Approach,"* or *"ILS Runway Six Left Approach."*

4-120a Note 4. — FAR 91.116 requires a pilot to receive a clearance for a procedure turn when vectored to a final approach fix or position, conducting a timed approach, or when the procedure specifies "No PT."

4-120a Note 5. — An aircraft which has been cleared to a holding fix and prior to reaching that fix is issued a clearance for an approach, but not issued a revised routing; i.e., *"proceed direct to . . ."* may be expected to proceed via the last assigned route, a feeder route (if one is published on the approach chart), and then to commence the approach as published. If, by following the route of flight to the holding fix, the aircraft would overfly an IAF or the fix associated with the beginning of a feeder route to be used, the aircraft is expected to commence the approach using the published feeder route to the IAF or from the IAF as appropriate; i.e., the aircraft would not be expected to overfly and return to the IAF or feeder route.

4-120b(2) Note 1. — The altitude assigned must assure IFR obstruction clearance from the point at which the approach clearance is issued until established on a segment of a published route or instrument approach procedure.

4-120b(2) Note 2. — If the altitude assignment is VFR-on-top, it is conceivable that a pilot may elect to remain high until arrival over the final approach fix, which may require the pilot to circle to descend so as to cross the final approach fix at an altitude that would permit landing.

4-120 Reference. — ATCH 4-80.

4-121 ALTITUDE MANAGEMENT

When operating on an unpublished route or while being radar vectored, the pilot, when an approach clearance is received, shall, in addition to complying with the minimum altitudes for IFR operations, maintain his last assigned altitude unless a different altitude is assigned by ATC, or until the aircraft is established on a segment of a published route or IAP. After the aircraft is so established, published altitudes apply to descent within each succeeding route or approach segment unless a different altitude is assigned by ATC. Notwithstanding this pilot responsibility, for aircraft operating on unpublished routes or while being radar vectored, ATC will, except when conducting a radar approach, issue an IFR approach clearance only after the aircraft is established on a segment of a published route or IAP, or assigned an altitude to maintain until the aircraft is established on a segment of a published route or instrument approach procedure. For this purpose, the procedure turn of a published IAP shall not be considered a segment of that IAP until the aircraft reaches the initial fix or navigation facility upon which the procedure turn is predicated.

4-121 References. — FAR 91.116, 91.119; AIM 370.

4-122 SPECIAL INSTRUMENT APPROACH PROCEDURES

Pilots planning flights to locations served by special IAP's (Instrument Approach Procedures) should obtain advance approval from the owner of the procedure. Approval by the owner is necessary because special procedures are for the exclusive use of the single interest unless otherwise authorized by the owner. Additionally, some special approach procedures require certain crew qualifications training, or other special considerations in order to execute the approach. Also, some of these approach procedures are based on privately owned navigational aids. Owners of aids that are not for public use may elect to turn off the aid for whatever reason they may have; i.e., maintenance, conservation, etc. Air traffic controllers are not required to question pilots to determine if they have permission to use the procedure. Controllers presume a pilot has obtained approval and is aware of any details of the procedure if he files an IFR flight plan to that airport.

4-122 Reference. — AIM 370.

4-123 APPROACH INFORMATION FOR UNFAMILIAR PILOT

Controllers will specify the following in the approach clearance when the pilot says he is unfamiliar with the procedure:

a. Initial approach altitude.

b. Direction and distance from the holding fix within which procedure turn is to be completed.

c. Altitude at which the procedure turn is to be made.

d. Final approach course and altitude.

e. Missed approach procedures, if considered necessary.

ATC Phraseology:

Initial approach at (altitude), **procedure turn at** (altitude) (number) **minutes/miles** (direction), **final approach on** (name of NAVAID) (specified) **course/radial/azimuth at** (altitude).

4-123 Reference. — ATCH 4-89.

4-124 RELAYED APPROACH CLEARANCE

TERMINAL

When an approach clearance is relayed through a communication station other than an air carrier company radio, controllers will include the weather report, if required. Controllers may do this by telling the station to issue current weather.

4-124 Reference. — ATCH 4-82.

4-125 APPROACH CLEARANCE ALTITUDE

a. Controllers will specify in the approach clearance the altitude shown in the approach procedures when adherence to that altitude is required for separation.

b. When vertical separation will be provided from other aircraft by pilot adherence to the prescribed maximum, minimum, or mandatory altitudes, the controller may omit specifying the altitude in the approach clearance.

4-125 Reference. — ATCH 4-83.

4-126 PROCEDURE TURN

a. A procedure turn is the maneuver prescribed when it is necessary to reverse the aircraft direction to establish it inbound on an intermediate or final approach course. It is a required maneuver except when the symbol NoPT is shown, when RADAR VECTORING is provided, when a holding pattern is published in lieu of procedure turn, or when the procedure turn is not authorized. The altitude prescribed for the procedure turn is a *minimum* altitude until the aircraft is established on the inbound course. The maneuver must be completed within the distance specified in the profile view.

b. A procedure turn need not be established when an approach can be made from a properly aligned holding pattern. In such cases, the holding pattern is established over an intermediate fix or a final approach fix. The holding pattern maneuver is completed when the aircraft is established on the inbound course after executing the appropriate entry. If cleared for the approach prior to returning to the holding fix, and the aircraft is at the prescribed altitude, additional circuits of the holding pattern are not necessary nor expected by ATC. If the pilot elects to make additional circuits to lose excessive altitude or to become better established on course, it is his responsibility to so advise ATC when he receives his approach clearance.

c. A procedure turn is not required when an approach can be made directly from a specified intermediate fix to the final approach fix. In such cases, the term "NoPT" is used with the appropriate course and altitude to denote that the procedure turn is not required. If a procedure turn is desired, and when cleared to do so by ATC, descent below the procedure turn altitude should not be made until the aircraft is established on the inbound course, since some NoPT altitudes may be lower than the procedure turn altitudes.

4-126 Reference. — AIM 371.

4-127 LIMITATIONS ON PROCEDURE TURNS

a. In the case of a radar initial approach to a final approach fix or position, or a timed approach from a holding fix, or where the procedure specifies "NoPT," no pilot may make a procedure turn unless, when he receives his final approach clearance, he so advises ATC and a clearance is received.

b. When a teardrop procedure turn is depicted and a course reversal is required, this type turn must be executed.

c. When a holding pattern replaces the procedure turn, the standard entry and the holding pattern must be followed except when RADAR VECTORING is provided or when NoPT is shown on the approach course. As in the procedure turn, the descent from the minimum holding pattern altitude to the final approach fix altitude (when lower) may not commence until the aircraft is established on the inbound course.

d. The absence of the procedure turn barb in the Plan View (NOS charts) indicates that a procedure turn is not authorized for that procedure.

4-127 Reference. — AIM 371.

4-128 COMMUNICATIONS RELEASE

Aircraft operating on an IFR flight plan landing at an airport not being served by a tower will be advised to change to the airport advisory frequency when direct communications with ATC is no longer required. Towers and centers may not have nontower airport traffic and runway in use information. The instrument approach may not be aligned with the runway in use; therefore, if the information has not already been obtained, pilots should make an expeditious change to the airport advisory frequency when authorized.

4-128 Reference. — AIM 154.

4-129 CHANGE TO ADVISORY FREQUENCY

If an IFR aircraft intends to land at an airport not served by a tower or FSS, controllers will approve a change to the advisory service frequency when they no longer require direct communications.*

ATC Phraseology:

Change to advisory frequency approved.

4-129 Note 1. — Expeditious frequency change permits the aircraft to receive timely local airport traffic information in accordance with AC 90-42C.

4-129 Note 2. — When making an IFR approach to an airport not served by a tower or FSS, after the ATC controller advises *"CHANGE TO ADVISORY FREQUENCY APPROVED,"* pilots should broadcast their intentions, including the type of approach being executed, their position, and when over the final approach fix inbound (nonprecision approach) or when over the outer marker or fix used in lieu of the outer marker inbound (precision approach), on the appropriate frequency (UNICOM, etc.) and continue to monitor it for reports from other pilots.

4-129 References. — ATCH 4-87; AIM 363.

4-130 CIRCLING APPROACH INSTRUCTIONS

a. Circling approach instructions may only be given for aircraft landing at airports with operational control towers.

b. Included in the approach clearance instructions will be instructions to circle to the runway in use if landing will be made on a runway other than that aligned with the direction of instrument approach. When the direction of the circling maneuver in relation to the airport/runway is required, controllers will state the direction (eight cardinal compass points) and specify a left or right base/downwind leg as appropriate.*

ATC Phraseology:

Circle to Runway (runway number),

or

Circle (direction using eight cardinal compass points) **of the airport/runway for a left/right base/downwind to Runway** (runway number).

4-130b Example. —

Oxnard Tower, Citation Three Three Alpha Zulu is over the outer marker inbound.

Citation Three Three Alpha Zulu, Oxnard Tower, circle north of the airport for a left downwind Runway Seven, report turning off the localizer.

c. Controllers may not issue instructions, such as "extend downwind leg," which might cause an aircraft to exceed the circling approach area distance from the runways within which required circling approach obstacle clearance is assured.

4-130b Note. — Where Standard Instrument Approach Procedures authorize circling approaches, they provide a basic minimum of 300 feet of obstacle clearance at MDA within the circling area considered. The dimensions of these areas, expressed in distances from the runways, vary for the different approach categories of aircraft. In some cases a SIAP may otherwise restrict circling approach maneuvers.

4-130 Reference. — ATCH 4-85.

4-131 CIRCLING APPROACH EXCEPTIONS

The fact that a straight-in minimum is not published does not preclude the pilot from landing straight-in if he has the active runway in sight and has sufficient time to make a normal approach for landing. Under such conditions and when ATC has cleared him for landing on the runway, he is not expected to circle, even though only circling minimums are published. If he desires to circle he should advise ATC.*

4-131 Note. — When either the normal rate of descent (as defined in TERPS) or the runway alignment factor of 30 degrees is exceeded, a straight-in minimum is not published and a circling minimum applies.

4-131 Reference. — AIM 381.

4-132 SIDE-STEP MANEUVER

a. ATC may authorize an approach procedure which serves either one of parallel runways that are separated by 1,200 feet or less, followed by a straight-in landing on the adjacent runway.

b. Aircraft that will execute a side-step maneuver will be cleared for a specified approach and landing on the adjacent parallel runway. Pilots are expected to commence the side-step maneuver as soon as possible after the runway or runway environment is in sight.

4-132b Example. —

Cleared for I-L-S Runway Seven Left Approach. Side-step Runway Seven Right.

c. Landing minimums to the adjacent runway will be higher than the minimums to the primary runway, but will normally be lower than the published circling minimums.

4-132 Reference. — AIM 380.

4-133 MISSED APPROACH

a. Except in the case of a VFR aircraft practicing an instrument approach, an approach clearance automatically authorizes the aircraft to execute the missed approach procedure depicted for the instrument approach being flown. An alternate missed approach procedure may be assigned when necessary. Once an aircraft commences a missed approach, it may be radar vectored.*

b. At locations where ATC Radar Service is provided, the pilot should conform to radar vectors when provided by ATC in lieu of the published missed approach procedure.

c. When an approach has been missed, pilots should report to ATC and request clearance for specific action; i.e., to alternative airport, another approach, etc.

4-133a Note. — Alternate missed approach procedures require a detailed clearance when they are issued to the pilot.

4-133 References. — ATCH 4-88; AIM 342, 382.

4-134 thru 4-139 RESERVED

Section 11. VISUAL APPROACHES

4-140 GENERAL

a. Visual approaches are initiated by ATC to reduce pilot/controller workload and expedite traffic by shortening flight paths to the airport. It is the pilot's responsibility to advise ATC as soon as possible after initial contact if a visual approach is not desired.

b. Authorization to conduct a visual approach is an IFR authorization and does not alter IFR flight plan cancellation responsibility.

c. A visual approach is not an instrument approach procedure and has no missed approach segment. Pilots conducting visual approaches must be reasonably assured that in the event of a go-around VFR conditions can be maintained until further clearance is received from ATC.

4-140 Reference. — AIM 383.

4-141 VISUAL APPROACH CLEARANCE

Centers, approach control facilities, and towers may clear an aircraft for a visual approach if the following conditions exist:*

a. Potential conflicts with all other aircraft have been resolved.

b. Weather conditions at the airport of intended landing are reported VFR or, at airports without weather reporting service, the pilot has been informed that weather is not available and there is reasonable assurance that descent and flight to the airport can be made in VFR conditions.*

c. The pilot has reported sighting the airport.

d. The aircraft is number one in the approach sequence or has reported the preceding aircraft in sight and is instructed to follow it if the aircraft is landing on the same runway. When the preceding traffic is landing on another runway and visual separation is being applied, controllers will advise the aircraft of the traffic's intentions and instruct it to maintain visual separation.

4-141d Example. —

Cessna Five Six November has the airport and the Seven Sixty-seven in sight.

Cessna Five Six November, follow the American Heavy Seven Sixty-seven cleared for a visual approach to Runway One. Caution wake turbulence.

4-141 Note. — A visual approach is not an instrument approach procedure and, therefore, has no missed approach segment nor provision for a missed approach. Aircraft unable to complete a visual approach are expected to be handled as any go-around by being provided appropriate separation.

4-141b Note. — Prior to initiating visual approaches to airports without weather reporting, controllers are expected to consider weather conditions in the area using the sources available, including nearby observations and pilot reports. A pilot-initiated request for a visual approach indicates that descent and flight to the airport can be made in VFR conditions.

4-141 Reference. — ATCH 7-30.

4-142 VECTORS FOR A VISUAL APPROACH

a. Controllers may vector aircraft for a visual approach to the airport of intended landing if the following conditions are met:

(1) At airports with weather reporting service — The reported ceiling at the airport of intended landing is at least 500 feet above the MVA (minimum vectoring altitude)/MIA (minimum IFR altitude) and visibility is 3 miles or more, or

(2) At airports without weather reporting service — The pilot has been informed that weather is not available and there is reasonable assurance that descent and flight to the airport can be made in VFR conditions.*

(3) Separation is provided from any preceding IFR/ARSA/Stage III aircraft until visual separation is provided.

b. Vectors for simultaneous approaches at tower-controlled airports — Controllers may vector aircraft simultaneously for visual approaches while other aircraft are conducting other approaches to the same runway or another runway or airport if the conditions in **a** are met.

c. Controllers will continue radar monitoring and traffic information until the aircraft has landed or is instructed to contact the FSS, UNICOM, or airline company radio when the destination airport is not tower controlled, or upon pilot request.*

d. Radar service is automatically terminated without controllers advising the pilot, when the pilot is instructed to change to advisory frequency.

4-142a(2) Note. — Prior to initiating vectors for visual approaches to airports without weather reporting, controllers are expected to consider weather conditions in the area using the sources available, including nearby observations and pilot reports. A pilot-initiated request for a visual approach indicates that descent and flight to the airport can be made in VFR conditions.

4-142c Note 1. — The point at which an aircraft is instructed to contact the tower will vary depending on the runway in use, weather, etc. It is determined by prior coordination between the tower/center controller. Ordinarily, the changeover points are established far enough from the airport so that the tower controller can properly establish a landing sequence, normally prior to entering the airport traffic area.

4-142c Note 2. — When the destination is not a tower-controlled airport, the aircraft may be released to advisory frequency after potential conflicts with known traffic have been resolved.

4-142c Note 3. — Visual approaches and CVFP's (charted visual flight procedures) are not instrument approach procedures; therefore, they have no missed approach segments. An aircraft unable to complete a visual approach or a CVFP is expected to be handled as any go-around by being provided appropriate separation.

4-142 Reference. — ATCH 7-31.

4-143 VISUAL APPROACH CLEARANCE — RADAR SEPARATED AIRCRAFT

A radar-controlled aircraft may be cleared for a visual approach provided the following conditions are met:*

a. Traffic conflicts with other aircraft have been resolved, and

b. An aircraft not following another aircraft on approach reports the airport in sight, or

c. An aircraft reports sighting a preceding aircraft landing on the same runway and has been instructed to follow it, or

d. An aircraft reports the airport, but not the preceding aircraft in sight, provided radar separation is maintained or visual separation is provided.

4-143d Example. —

Delta Nine Sixty-four has the airport in sight.

Delta Nine Sixty-four, roger. Traffic is a Boeing Seven Thirty-seven on a two mile final for Runway Two Left. Cleared for visual approach Runway Two Left. Contact tower one one niner point seven, six D-M-E on final.

Cleared for visual approach Runway Two Left. Tower one one niner point seven, at six D-M-E, Delta Nine Sixty-four.

e. The aircraft is and can remain in VFR conditions.

f. Weather conditions at the airport are reported VFR; or at airports without weather reporting service, the pilot has been informed that weather is not available.

g. The tower is informed of the aircraft's position prior to communications transfer.

4-143 Note. — If an aircraft is being vectored for an instrument approach and subsequently reports the airport in sight, controllers may initiate a visual approach or pilots may request a visual approach. Under these conditions, the provisions of 4-142**a**(1) are not applicable, and a controller's only obligation as it relates to weather is to ensure compliance with 4-143**f** and to only authorize such operations when weather conditions are clearly not a prohibiting factor.

4-143 Reference. — ATCH 7-32.

4-144 PARALLEL/MULTIPLE RUNWAY USE

a. Parallel runways separated by less than 2,500 feet — Unless standard separation is provided by ATC, an aircraft must report sighting a preceding aircraft making an approach to the same or parallel runway, and all aircraft are informed that approaches are being conducted to the parallel runway.

4-144a Example. —

Expect visual approach Runway Two Four Right. Approaches in progress, Runway Two Four Left.

b. Parallel runways separated by at least 2,500 feet but less than 4,300 feet — Headings must be assigned which will permit aircraft to intercept the extended centerline of the runway at an angle not greater than 30 degrees unless standard separation is provided during the turn-on. Once the aircraft are established within 30 degrees of the final, these operations may be conducted simultaneously. All aircraft must be informed that approaches are being conducted to the parallel runway.*

4-144b Example. —

Citation Four Victor Alpha, expect visual approach Runway Two Zero Left. Approaches in progress, Runway Two Zero Right. Fly heading two three zero, vector for visual approach Runway Two Zero Left.

c. Intersecting/converging runways or parallel runways separated by 4,300 feet or more:*

(1) Visual approaches may be conducted simultaneously, provided standard separation is maintained until each aircraft has received and acknowledged for a visual approach clearance.

(2) Visual approaches may be conducted to one runway while instrument approaches are conducted simultaneously to the other, provided separation is maintained until the aircraft conducting the visual approach has received and acknowledged for a visual approach clearance.

(3) In either case, all aircraft must be informed that approaches are being conducted to the other runway.

4-144c Example. —

Cessna Five Six November has the airport in sight.

Cessna Five Six November, roger. Traffic is an American Heavy Seven Sixty-seven, twelve o'clock and four miles out of three thousand two hundred on final for Runway One Right. Report that traffic in sight.

Cessna Five Six November, traffic in sight.

Cessna Five Six November, roger. Maintain visual separation from that traffic. Cleared for visual approach Runway One Left. Caution wake turbulence.

Roger, we will maintain visual separation from that traffic. Cleared for visual approach Runway One Left, Cessna Five Six November.

4-144b Note. — The intent of the 30-degree intercept angle is to reduce the potential for overshoots of the final and to preclude side-by-side operations with one or both aircraft in a "belly-up" configuration during the turn-on. Aircraft performance, speed, and the number of degrees of turn to the final are factors to be considered by the controller when providing vectors to parallel runways.

4-144c Note. — Although simultaneous approaches may be conducted to intersecting runways when the conditions in 4-144**c** are met, staggered approaches may be necessary to meet intersecting runway separation requirements.

4-144 Reference. — ATCH 7-33.

4-145 CHARTED VISUAL FLIGHT PROCEDURES - GENERAL

a. CVFP's (charted visual flight procedures) are charted visual approaches established at locations with jet operations for noise abatement purposes. The approach charts depict prominent landmarks, courses, and recommended altitudes to specific runways.

b. These procedures will be used only in a radar environment at airports with an operating control tower.

c. Most approach charts will depict some NAVID information which is for supplemental navigational guidance only.

d. Unless indicating a TCA floor, all depicted altitudes are for noise abatement purposes and are recommended only. Pilots are not prohibited from flying other than recommended altitudes if operational requirements dictate.

e. When landmarks used for navigation are not visible at night, the approach will be annotated "procedure not authorized at night."

f. CVFP's usually begin within 15 flying miles from the airport.

g. Published weather minimums for CVFP's are based on minimum vectoring altitudes rather than the recommended altitudes depicted on charts.

h. CVFP's are not instrument approaches and do not have missed approach segments.

i. Pilots should advise ATC if at any point they are unable to continue an approach or lose sight of a preceding aircraft. Missed approaches will be handled as a go-around.

4-145 Reference. — AIM 384.

4-146 CVFP PROCEDURES — ATC

Charted visual flight procedures may be used if all the following conditions are met:*

a. The approach must be conducted in a radar environment.

b. There must be an operating control tower.

c. Reported weather meets the criteria in 4-142**a**(1) unless higher minimums are published for the particular CVFP.

d. The published name of the CVFP and the landing runway are specified in the clearance.

4-146d Example. —

United Five Thirty-six, cleared for Quiet Bridge Visual Runway Two Eight Right Approach.

e. An aircraft not following another aircraft on approach reports sighting a charted visual landmark, or

f. An aircraft reports sighting a preceding aircraft landing on the same runway and has been instructed to follow it, or

4-146f Example. —

Northwest Three Fifty-five, follow the United Heavy Boeing Seven Forty-seven. Cleared for Stadium Visual Runway Two Four Right Approach. Caution wake turbulence.

g. When using parallel or intersecting/converging runways, the criteria specified in 4-144 are applied.

4-146 Note. — Altitudes depicted on CVFP's are recommended altitudes only. They are not established for air traffic separation.

4-146 Reference. — ATCH 3-34.

4-147 thru 4-149 RESERVED

Section 12. CONTACT APPROACHES

4-150 GENERAL

A Contact Approach is an approach procedure that may be used by a pilot (with prior authorization from ATC) in lieu of conducting a standard or special IAP (instrument approach procedure) to an airport. It is not intended for use by a pilot on an IFR flight clearance to operate to an airport not having an authorized IAP. Nor is it intended for an aircraft to conduct an instrument approach to one airport and then, when "in the clear," to discontinue that approach and proceed to another airport. In the execution of a contact approach, the pilot assumes the responsibility for obstruction clearance. If radar service is being received, it will automatically terminate when the pilot is told to contact the tower.

4-150 Reference. — AIM 385.

4-151 CONTACT APPROACH CONDITIONS

ATC will clear an aircraft for a contact approach only if the following conditions are met:

a. The pilot has requested it.*

b. The reported ground visibility is at least 1 statute mile.

c. A standard or special instrument approach procedure has been published for the airport of intended landing.

d. Approved separation is applied between aircraft so cleared and other IFR or Special VFR aircraft. When applying vertical separation, ATC will not assign a fixed altitude, but clear the aircraft at or below an altitude which is at least 1,000 feet below any IFR traffic, but not below the minimum safe altitude prescribed in FAR 91.79.*

e. An alternative clearance is issued when weather conditions are such that a contact approach may be impracticable.

ATC Phraseology:

Cleared for contact approach,

and, if required,

at or below (altitude) (routing).

If not possible (alternative procedures) **and advise.**

4-151 Example. —

Cessna One Zero One, we have the airport in sight. Request contact approach.

Cessna One Zero One, cleared for contact approach, at or below two thousand five hundred, proceed straight-in Runway Three Zero. If not possible, maintain two thousand five hundred and advise.

4-151a Note. — When executing a contact approach, the pilot is responsible for maintaining the required flight visibility, cloud clearance, and terrain/obstruction clearance. Unless otherwise restricted, the pilot may find it necessary to descend, climb, and/or fly a circuitous route to the airport to maintain cloud clearance and/or terrain/obstruction clearance. It is not in any way intended that controllers will initiate or suggest a contact approach to a pilot.

4-151d Note. — FAR 91.79 specifies the minimum safe altitude to be flown (1) over congested areas, (2) other than congested areas, and (3) anywhere to provide for an emergency landing in the event of power failure and without undue hazard to persons or property on the surface.

4-151 Reference. — ATCH 7-35.

4-152 thru 4-159 RESERVED

Section 13. VFR CLEARANCES FOR IFR OPERATIONS

4-160 GENERAL

a. ATC authorization to *"MAINTAIN VFR-on-top/VFR CONDITIONS"* is not intended to restrict pilots to operate only *above* an obscuring meteorological formation (layer). Instead, it permits operation above, below, between layers, or in areas where there is no meteorological obscuration. It is imperative, however, that pilots understand that clearance to operate *"VFR-on-top/VFR CONDITIONS"* does not imply cancellation of the IFR flight plan.

b. Pilots operating VFR-ON-TOP/VFR CONDITIONS may receive traffic information, from ATC, on other pertinent IFR or VFR aircraft. However, aircraft operating in TCA's/ARSA's/TRSA's will be separated as required.*

c. ATC will not authorize VFR or VFR-ON-TOP operations in PCA's.

d. When operating in VFR conditions with an ATC authorization to *"MAINTAIN VFR-on-top/MAINTAIN VFR CONDITIONS,"* pilots on IFR flight plans must:

(1) Fly at the appropriate VFR altitude as prescribed in FAR 91.109.*

(2) Comply with the VFR visibility and distance from cloud criteria in FAR 91.105 (BASIC VFR WEATHER MINIMUMS).

(3) Comply with instrument flight rules that are applicable to this flight (i.e., *minimum IFR altitudes,* position reporting, radio communications, course to be flown, adherence to ATC clearance, etc.).

4-160b Note. — When operating in VFR weather conditions, it is the pilot's responsibility to be vigilant so as to see and avoid other aircraft.

4-160d(1) Note. — Pilots should advise ATC prior to any altitude change to ensure the exchange of accurate traffic information.

4-160 Reference. — AIM 266.

4-161 VFR-ON-TOP CLEARANCE

a. A pilot on an IFR flight plan operating in VFR weather conditions may request *"VFR-on-top"* in lieu of an assigned altitude. This permits a pilot to select an altitude or flight level of his choice (subject to any ATC restrictions.)*

b. ATC may clear an aircraft to maintain *"VFR-on-top"* if the pilot of an aircraft on an IFR flight plan requests the clearance.

ATC Phraseology:

Maintain VFR-on-top.

4-161b Example. —

Center, Twin Commanche Five Zero Papa is in V-F-R conditions, request V-F-R-on-top at niner thousand five hundred direct Baltimore.

Twin Commander Five Zero Papa, approved as requested. Maintain V-F-R-on-top. Advise of any altitude changes.

c. ATC may not clear an aircraft to maintain *"VFR-on-top"* between sunset and sunrise to separate holding aircraft from each other or from en route aircraft unless restrictions are applied to ensure the appropriate IFR vertical separation.

ATC Phraseology:

Maintain VFR-on-top at or above/below/between (altitudes).

4-161c Examples. —

Maintain V-F-R-on-top at or above one three thousand five hundred.

Maintain V-F-R-on-top at or below one two thousand five hundred.

Maintain V-F-R-on-top at or between six thousand five hundred and one zero thousand five hundred.

d. When in the controller's judgment, there is reason to believe that flight in VFR conditions may become impractical, the controller will issue an alternative clearance which will ensure separation from all other aircraft for which controllers have separation responsibility.

ATC Phraseology:

If unable (alternative procedure), **and advise.**

4-161a Note 1. — When an aircraft has been cleared to maintain *"VFR-on-top,"* the pilot is responsible to fly at an appropriate VFR altitude, comply with VFR visibility and distance from cloud criteria, and to be vigilant so as to see and avoid other aircraft.

4-161a Note 2. — Although standard IFR separation is not applied, controllers will continue to provide traffic advisories and safety alerts, and apply merging target procedures to aircraft operating VFR-on-top.

4-161 References. — ATCH 7-20; AIM 266.

4-162 ALTITUDE FOR DIRECTION OF FLIGHT

The controller will inform an aircraft maintaining *"VFR-on-top"* when a report indicates the pilot is not complying with FAR 91.109.*

ATC Phraseology:

VFR-on-top cruising levels for your direction of flight are:

More than 3,000 feet above the surface to FL 290:

Odd/Even altitudes/Flight levels plus five hundred feet.

Above FL 290:

Four thousand foot intervals beginning at flight level three zero zero/three two zero.

4-162 Note. — As required by FAR 91.109, the appropriate VFR altitudes for aircraft (not in a holding pattern of 2 minutes or less, or turning) operating *more than 3,000 feet above the surface to and including FL 290:*

Magnetic courses 0-179 — Odd cardinal altitudes plus 500 feet (e.g., 3,500, 5,500, FL 195, 275).

Magnetic courses 180-359 — Even cardinal altitudes plus 500 feet (e.g., 4,500, 8,500 FL 205, 285).

Above FL 290:

Magnetic courses 0-179 — 4,000 foot intervals beginning with FL 300 (e.g., 300, 340, 380).

Magnetic courses 180-359 — 4,000 foot intervals beginning with FL 320 (e.g., 320, 360, 400).

4-162 Reference. — ATCH 7-21.

4-163 IFR TO VFR-ON-TOP

ATC may clear an aircraft to climb through clouds, smoke, haze, or other meteorological formations and then to maintain *"VFR-on-top"* if the following conditions are met:

a. The pilot requests the clearance.

b. The controller informs the pilot of the reported height of the tops of the meteorological formation, or

c. The controller informs the pilot that no top reports are available.

d. When necessary, controllers ensure separation from all other traffic for which they have separation responsibility by issuing an alternative clearance.

e. When an aircraft is climbing to and reports reaching *"VFR-on-top,"* ATC will reclear the aircraft to maintain *"VFR-on-top."*

ATC Phraseology:

Climb to and report reaching VFR-on-top, *and* **tops reported** (altitude), *or* **no tops reports.**

If not on top at (altitude), **maintain** (altitude), **and advise.**

After reaching VFR-on-top,

Maintain VFR-on-top.

4-163 Examples. —

Climb to and report reaching V-F-R-on-top, tops reported four thousand two hundred.

Climb to and report reaching V-F-R-on-top, no tops reports. If not on top at four thousand, maintain four thousand and advise.

4-163 Reference. — ATCH 7-20.

4-164 VFR CLIMB OR DESCENT

If a pilot requests, controllers may clear an IFR aircraft to climb or descend VFR.

ATC Phraseology:

Climb/Descend VFR, *and, if required,*

between (altitude) **and** (altitude), *or*

above/below (altitude).

4-164 Example. —

Center, Cheyenne Three Tango Charlie requesting one five thousand as a final.

Cheyenne Three Tango Charlie, roger. Traffic twelve o'clock four miles same direction, level at one zero thousand. Maintain niner thousand. Higher when you are clear.

Cheyenne Three Tango Charlie, we are in V-F-R conditions, request V-F-R climb to one five thousand.

Cheyenne Three Tango Charlie, climb V-F-R between niner thousand and one one thousand. Leaving one one thousand, climb and maintain one five thousand.

4-164 Reference. — ATCH 7-2.

4-165 MAINTAIN VFR CLEARANCES

a. Controllers may clear aircraft to maintain *"VFR CONDITIONS."*

(1) In terminal areas the clearance will result in noise abatement benefits where part of the IFR departure route does not conform to an FAA-approved noise abatement route or altitude.

ATC Phraseology:

Maintain VFR conditions.

Maintain VFR conditions until (time or fix).

Maintain VFR conditions above/below (altitude).

b. When, in the controller's judgment, there is reason to believe that flight in VFR conditions may become impractical, ATC will issue an alternative clearance which will ensure separation from all other aircraft for which controllers have separation responsibility.

ATC Phraseology:

If unable, (alternative procedure), **and advise.**

4-165 Reference. — ATCH 7-2.

4-166 thru 4-169 RESERVED

Section 14. PRACTICE INSTRUMENT APPROACHES

4-170 GENERAL

Practice instrument approaches are considered to be instrument approaches made by either a VFR aircraft not on an IFR flight plan or an aircraft on an IFR flight plan. To achieve this and thereby enhance air safety, it is policy to provide for separation of such operations at locations where approach control facilities are located and, as resources permit, at certain other locations served by ARTCC's or parent approach control facilities. Pilot requests to practice instrument approaches may be approved by ATC subject to traffic and workload conditions. Pilots should anticipate that in some instances the controller may find it necessary to deny approval or withdraw previous approval when traffic conditions warrant. It must be clearly understood, however, that even though the controller may be providing separation, pilots on VFR flight plans are required to comply with basic visual flight rules. Application of ATC procedures or any action taken by the controller to avoid traffic conflicts does not relieve IFR and VFR pilots of their responsibility to see and avoid other traffic while operating in VFR conditions. In addition to the normal IFR separation minimums (which includes visual separation) during VFR conditions, 500 feet vertical separation may be applied between VFR aircraft and between a VFR aircraft and the IFR aircraft. Pilots not on IFR flight plans desiring practice instrument approaches should always state 'practice' when making requests to ATC. Controllers will instruct VFR aircraft requesting an instrument approach to *"maintain VFR."* This is to preclude misunderstandings between the pilot and controller as to the status of the aircraft. If a pilot wishes to proceed in accordance with instrument flight rules, he must specifically request and obtain an IFR clearance.

4-170 Reference. — AIM 244.

4-171 PILOT ACTIONS

Before practicing an instrument approach, pilots should inform the approach control facility or the tower of the type of practice approach they desire to make and how they intend to terminate it, i.e., full-stop landing, touch-and-go, or missed or low approach maneuver. This information may be furnished progressively when conducting a series of approaches. Pilots on an IFR flight plan, who have made a series of instrument approaches to full stop landings, should inform ATC when they make their final landing. The controller will control flights practicing instrument approaches so as to ensure that they do not disrupt the flow of arriving and departing itinerant IFR or VFR aircraft. The priority afforded itinerant aircraft over practice instrument approaches is not intended to be so rigidly applied that it causes grossly inefficient application of services. A minimum delay to itinerant traffic may be appropriate to allow an aircraft practicing an approach to complete that approach.

4-171 Reference. — AIM 244.

4-172 CONTROLLER ACTIONS

a. The Controller will provide approved separation between both VFR and IFR aircraft when authorization is granted to make practice approaches to airports where an approach control facility is located and to certain other airports served by approach control or an ARTCC. Controller responsibility for separation of VFR aircraft begins at the point where the approach clearance becomes effective, or when the aircraft enters ARSA/TCA/TRSA airspace, whichever comes first.

b. Controllers must ensure that neither VFR nor IFR practice approaches disrupt the flow of other arriving and departing IFR or VFR aircraft. Controllers may authorize, withdraw authorization, or refuse to authorize practice approaches as traffic conditions require. Normally, approaches in progress will not be terminated.*

c. Separation Procedures:

(1) IFR aircraft practicing instrument approaches will be afforded standard separation in accordance with ATC minima until:

(a) The aircraft lands and the flight is terminated, or

(b) The pilot cancels the flight plan.

(2) Where procedures require application of IFR separation to VFR aircraft practicing instrument approaches, standard separation will be provided. Controller responsibility for separation begins at the point where the approach clearance becomes effective. Except for heavy aircraft, *500 feet* vertical separation may be applied between VFR aircraft and between a VFR and an IFR aircraft.

(3) Where separation services are not provided to VFR aircraft practicing instrument approaches, the controller will:

(a) Instruct the pilot to maintain VFR.

(b) Advise the pilot that separation services are not provided.

(c) Provide traffic information or advise the pilot to contact the appropriate facility.

(4) If an altitude is assigned, including at-or-above/below altitudes, the altitude specified must meet MVA, minimum safe altitude, or minimum IFR altitude criteria.

(5) All VFR aircraft will be instructed to maintain VFR on initial contact or as soon as possible thereafter.*

4-172b Note. — The priority afforded other aircraft over practice instrument approaches is not intended to be so rigidly applied that it causes grossly inefficient application of services.

4-172c(5) Note. — This advisory is intended to remind the pilot that even though ATC is providing IFR-type instructions, the pilot is responsible for compliance with the applicable FAR's governing VFR flight.

4-172 References. — ATCH 4-90; AIM 244.

4-173 NONTOWER AIRPORT OPERATIONS

At airports without a tower, pilots wishing to make practice instrument approaches should notify the facility having control jurisdiction of the desired approach as indicated on the approach chart. All approach control facilities and ARTCC's are required to publish a Letter to Airmen depicting those airports where they provide standard separation to both VFR and IFR aircraft conducting practice instrument approaches.

4-173 Reference. — AIM 244.

4-174 MISSED APPROACHES

a. VFR aircraft practicing instrument approaches are not automatically authorized to execute the missed approach procedure. This authorization must be specifically requested by the pilot and approved by the controller. Separation will not be provided unless the missed approach has been approved by ATC.

TERMINAL

b. Before an aircraft which plans to execute a low approach or touch-and-go begins final descent, ATC will issue appropriate instructions to be followed upon completion of the approach. Climb-out instructions must include a specific heading and altitude except when the aircraft will maintain VFR and contact the tower.*

ATC Phraseology:

After completing low approach/touch-and-go; climb and maintain (altitude).

Turn (right or left) **heading** (degrees)/**fly runway heading,** or **maintain VFR, contact tower,** or (other instructions as appropriate).

4-174b Example. —
Cessna One Sierra Romeo, after completing low approach, turn left heading two six zero, climb and maintain three thousand. Contact Bayside Approach one two four point six when established on that heading.

4-174b Note. — This may be omitted after the first approach if instructions remain the same.

4-174 References. — ATCH 4-80; AIM 244.

4-175 DEVIATIONS

Except in an emergency, aircraft cleared to practice instrument approaches must not deviate from the approved procedure until cleared to do so by the controller.

4-175 Reference. — AIM 244.

4-176 VECTORING

At radar approach control locations when a full approach procedure (procedure turn, etc.,) cannot be approved, pilots should expect to be vectored to a final approach course for a practice instrument approach which is compatible with the general direction of traffic at that airport.

4-176 Reference. — AIM 244.

4-177 COMMUNICATIONS WITH TOWER

a. When granting approval for a practice instrument approach, the controller will usually ask the pilot to report to the tower prior to or over the final approach fix inbound (nonprecision approaches) or over the outer marker or fixer used in lieu of the outer marker inbound (precision approaches).

b. When authorization is granted to conduct practice instrument approaches to an airport with a tower, but where approved standard separation is not provided to aircraft conducting practice instrument approaches, the tower will approve the practice approach, instruct the aircraft to maintain VFR, and issue traffic information, as required.

4-177 Reference. — AIM 244.

4-178 FSS ACTIONS

When an aircraft notifies a FSS providing Airport Advisory Service to the airport concerned of the intent to conduct a practice instrument approach and whether or not separation is to be provided, the pilot will be instructed to contact the appropriate facility on a specified frequency prior to initiating the approach. At airports where separation is not provided, the FSS will acknowledge the message and issue known traffic information, but will neither approve nor disapprove the approach.

4-178 Reference. — AIM 244.

4-179 LOCAL TRAFFIC

Pilots conducting practice instrument approaches should be particularly alert for other aircraft operating in the local traffic pattern or in proximity to the airport.

4-179 Reference. — AIM 244.

BASIC RADAR PROCEDURES

Chapter 5
TABLE OF CONTENTS

Section 1. GENERAL

		Page
5-1	Limitations	5-1
5-2	Controller Limitations	5-1
5-3	Primary Radar	5-1
5-4	Secondary Surveillance Radar	5-1
5-5	Surveillance Radar Coverage	5-2
5-6	Radar Information Use	5-2
5-7—5-19	Reserved	5-2

Section 2. TRANSPONDER OPERATION

5-20	Transponder Operation - General	5-3
5-21	Transponder Emergency Operation	5-3
5-22	Transponder Operation Requirement	5-3
5-23	Transponder Code - VFR	5-3
5-24	Automatic Altitude Reporting	5-3
5-25	Mode C Transponder Requirements	5-3
5-26	ATC Authorized Deviations	5-4
5-27	Requests for In-Flight Deviations from Transponder/Mode C Requirements Between 10,000 Feet and 18,000 Feet	5-4
5-28	Failed Transponder In Positive Control Area	5-4
5-29	Code Assignment Criteria	5-5
5-30	Validation of Mode C Readout	5-5
5-31	Assigned Altitude Confirmation	5-5
5-32	Altitude Squawk Requests	5-5
5-33	Code Changes	5-6
5-34	Transponder Ident Feature	5-6
5-35	VFR Code Assignments	5-6
5-36	Broadband Code Assignment	5-6
5-37	Code 7600 Display	5-6
5-38	Emergency Code Assignment	5-6
5-39	Standby Or Low Sensitivity Transponder Operation	5-0
5-40	Inoperative/Malfunctioning Transponder	5-7
5-41	Inoperative/Malfunctioning Interrogator	5-7
5-42	Transponder Off Request	5-7
5-43—5-49	Reserved	5-7

Section 3. RADAR IDENTIFICATION AND SERVICE TERMINATION

5-50	Primary Identification Methods	5-8
5-51	Radar Contact Status	5-8
5-52	Radar Position Report	5-8
5-53	Position Reporting	5-8
5-54	Transponder Beacon Identification Methods	5-9
5-55	Questionable Identification	5-9
5-56	Radar Service Termination	5-9
5-57—5-59	Reserved	5-9

TABLE OF CONTENTS (Continued)

Section 4. SEPARATION

		Page
5-60	Radar Separation Application	5-10
5-61	Radar Separation Minima	5-10
5-62	Vertical Separation - Mode C	5-11
5-63	Vertical Separation Minima	5-11
5-64	Altitude Assignments	5-11
5-65—5-69	Reserved	5-11

Section 5. VECTORS

5-70	Vectoring Service	5-12
5-71	Minimum Vectoring Altitudes	5-12
5-72	Vectoring Methods	5-12
5-73	Initial Vector Advisory	5-13
5-74	Altitude Restrictions	5-13
5-75	Direct Routes	5-13
5-76	Area Navigation	5-13
5-77	Navigational Guidance	5-14
5-78	Vector Compliance	5-14
5-79	Communications Transfer	5-14
5-80—5-89	Reserved	5-14

Section 6. SPEED ADJUSTMENT

5-90	Application	5-15
5-91	Speed Adjustment Methods	5-15
5-92	Amended Clearances	5-16
5-93	Speed Adjustment Minima	5-16
5-94	Communications Transfer	5-16
5-95	Authorized Speed Adjustment	5-16
5-96	Cancellation of Speed Adjustment	5-16
5-97—5-99	Reserved	5-16

Section 7. DEPARTURES

5-100	Initial Departure Heading	5-17
5-101	Vectors Below Minimum Altitude	5-17
5-102	Successive or Simultaneous Radar Departures	5-17
5-103	Departure and Arrival Radar Separation	5-18
5-104	Departures and Arrivals on Parallel or Nonintersecting Diverging Runways	5-19
5-105—5-109	Reserved	5-20

Section 8. APPROACH PROCEDURES

5-110	General	5-21
5-111	Vectors to Final Approach Course	5-21
5-112	Final Approach Course Intercept Angles	5-21
5-113	Vectors Across Final Approach Course	5-22
5-114	Approach Instructions	5-22
5-115	Final Approach Deviations	5-24
5-116	Approach Separation Responsibility	5-24
5-117	Simultaneous ILS/MLS Approaches	5-24
5-118	Parallel ILS/MLS Approaches	5-25
5-119	Simultaneous Converging Instrument Approaches	5-26
5-120—5-129	Reserved	5-26

BASIC RADAR PROCEDURES

TABLE OF CONTENTS (Continued)

Section 9. RADAR APPROACHES

		Page
5-130	General	5-27
5-131	Radio Equipment Required	5-27
5-132	Surveillance Approach	5-27
5-133	No-Gyro Approach	5-27
5-134	Radar Approach Procedures	5-27
5-135	Radar Approach Information	5-27
5-136	No-Gyro Approach Procedures	5-28
5-137	Lost Communications Procedures	5-28
5-138	Radar Contact Lost	5-29
5-139	Approach Position Information	5-29
5-140	Altitude Information	5-29
5-141	Visual Reference Report	5-29
5-142	Descent Notification	5-29
5-143	Descent Instructions	5-29
5-144	Final Controller Changeover	5-30
5-145	Communications Check	5-30
5-146	Transmission Acknowledgment	5-30
5-147	Final Approach Guidance	5-30
5-148	Approach Guidance Termination	5-30
5-149	Missed Approach	5-31
5-150	After Low Approach and Touch-And-Go Departure Information	5-31
5-151	Radar Approach Tower Clearances	5-31
5-152	Final Approach Abnormalities	5-31

Chapter 5. BASIC RADAR PROCEDURES

Section 1. GENERAL

5-1 LIMITATIONS

a. It is very important for the aviation community to recognize the fact that there are limitations to radar service and that controllers may not always be able to issue traffic advisories concerning aircraft which are not under ATC control and cannot be seen on radar.

b. The characteristics of radio waves are such that they normally travel in a continuous straight line unless they are:

(1) "Bent" by abnormal atmospheric phenomena such as temperature inversions;

(2) Reflected or attenuated by dense objects such as heavy clouds, precipitation, ground obstacles, mountains, etc.; or

(3) Screened by high terrain features.

c. Relatively low altitude aircraft will not be seen if they are screened by mountains or are below the radar beam due to earth curvature. The only solution to screening is the installation of strategically placed multiple radars which has been done in some areas.

5-1 Reference. — AIM 30.

5-2 CONTROLLER LIMITATIONS

The controllers' ability to advise a pilot flying on instruments or in visual conditions of his proximity to another aircraft will be limited if the unknown aircraft is not observed on radar, if no flight plan information is available, or if the volume of traffic and workload prevent his issuing traffic information. The controller's first priority is given to establishing separation between aircraft flying under his control.

5-2 Reference. — AIM 30.

5-3 PRIMARY RADAR

Primary radar refers to the primary radar signal reflected back to the radar site from an aircraft. Primary targets displayed to the controller vary in size depending on the reflectability of the aircraft's structure and its size. Primary targets appear as "blips" and have no unique shape to distinguish one from another.

5-3 Reference. — ATCH & AIM Glossary.

5-4 SECONDARY SURVEILLANCE RADAR

a. Secondary surveillance radar consists of three main components:

(1) Interrogator. The Interrogator, a ground based radar beacon transmitter-receiver, scans with the primary radar and transmits discrete codes which repetitiously requests all transponders, on the codes being used, to reply. The replies received are then mixed with the primary returns and both may be displayed on the same radarscope.

(2) Transponder. This airborne radar beacon transmitter-responder automatically receives the signals from the interrogator and selectively replies with a specific pulse group (code) only to those interrogations being received on the mode to which it is set. These replies are independent of, and much stronger than a primary radar return.

(3) Radarscope. The radarscope used by the controller displays returns from both the primary and secondary radar systems. These returns, called targets, are what the controller refers to in the separation of traffic, issuance of safety alerts, and traffic advisories. Displayed along with most radar identified targets is an alphanumeric data block that may show the controller such information as aircraft identification, altitude, groundspeed, destination, runway assignment, etc.

b. Some of the advantages of secondary surveillance radar over primary radar are:

(1) Reinforcement of radar targets.

(2) Rapid target identification.

(3) Unique display of selected codes.

c. Automated radar systems use a facility based computer to make many of the functions of air traffic control automatic. Each computer uses secondary radar information to track certain targets and maintain continuous identity of a target. It can make the process of transferring control (handoff) of an aircraft from one sector to another automatic by eliminating or reducing verbal communication between sectors. The system can predict the paths of aircraft and automatically warn the controller of a potential conflict (conflict alert) or low altitude situation (minimum safe altitude warning/low altitude alert system). The advantage to this system is that it reduces both pilot/controller and controller/controller verbal communication by displaying both aircraft and control information on the radarscope.

d. At some locations within the ATC en route environment, secondary-radar-only (no primary radar) gap filler radar systems are used to give lower altitude radar coverage between two larger radar systems, each of which provides both primary and secondary radar coverage. In those geographical areas served by secondary-radar only, aircraft without transponders cannot be provided with radar service. Additionally, transponder equipped aircraft cannot be provided with radar advisories concerning primary targets and weather.

5-4 Reference. — AIM 31.

5-5 SURVEILLANCE RADAR COVERAGE

a. Surveillance radars are divided into two general categories: ASR (Airport Surveillance Radar) and ARSR (Air Route Surveillance Radar).

(1) ASR is designed to provide relatively short-range coverage in the general vicinity of an airport and to serve as an expeditious means of handling terminal area traffic through observation of precise aircraft locations on a radarscope. The ASR can also be used as an instrument approach aid.

(2) ARSR is a long-range radar system designed primarily to provide a display of aircraft locations over large areas.

b. Surveillance radars scan through 360 degrees of azimuth and present target information on a radar display located in a tower, approach control, or center. This information is used independently or in conjunction with other navigational aids in the control of air traffic.

5-5 Reference. — AIM 32.

5-6 RADAR INFORMATION USE

ATC will use radar information derived from primary and Mode 3/A/C secondary radar systems.

a. ATC will display and monitor both primary and secondary radar when available (see **b**), except that secondary radar may be used as the sole display source as follows:

(1) In PCA (positive control area).

(2) Outside PCA, or where mix of PCA/nonPCA exists, only when:

(a) Additional coverage is provided by secondary radar beyond that of the primary radar.

(b) The primary radar is temporarily unusable or out of service. Pilots will be advised when these conditions exist.*

ATC Phraseology:

Primary radar out of service. Traffic advisories available on transponder aircraft only.

b. TERMINAL: ATC will not use only secondary radar to conduct surveillance (ASR) final approaches unless an emergency exists and the pilot concurs.

5-6a(2)(b) Note. — This advisory may be omitted when provided on ATIS and pilots indicate having ATIS information.

5-6 Reference. — ATCH 5-3.

5-7 thru 5-19 RESERVED

Section 2. TRANSPONDER OPERATION

5-20 TRANSPONDER OPERATION—GENERAL

a. Pilots should be aware that proper application of transponder operating procedures will provide both VFR and IFR aircraft with a higher degree of safety. Transponders substantially increase the capability of radar to see an aircraft and the MODE C (automatic altitude reporting) feature enables the controller to build a 3-dimensional picture of the traffic environment in order to easily effect vertical separation and quickly determine where potential traffic conflicts may exist. Even VFR pilots who are not in contact with ATC will be afforded greater protection from IFR aircraft and VFR aircraft which are receiving traffic advisories. Nevertheless, pilots should never relax their visual scanning vigilance for other aircraft.

b. Transponders should be adjusted to the "on" or normal operating position as late as practicable prior to takeoff and to "off" or "standby" as soon as practicable after completing landing roll, unless the change to "standby" has been accomplished previously at the request of ATC.

c. If a pilot on an IFR flight cancels his IFR flight plan prior to reaching his destination, he should adjust his transponder according to VFR operations.

d. It should be noted by all users of the ATC transponders that the coverage they can expect is limited to "line of sight." Low altitude or aircraft antenna shielding by the aircraft itself may result in reduced range. Range can be improved by climbing to a higher altitude. It may be possible to minimize antenna shielding by locating the antenna where dead spots are only noticed during abnormal flight altitudes.

5-20 Reference. — AIM 170.

5-21 TRANSPONDER EMERGENCY OPERATION

a. When a *distress* or *urgency* condition is encountered, the pilot of an aircraft with a coded radar beacon transponder, who desires to alert a radar facility, should squawk MODE 3/A, Code 7700/Emergency and MODE C altitude reporting and then immediately establish communications with the facility.

b. Radar facilities are equipped so that Code 7700 normally triggers an alarm or special indicator at all control positions. Pilots should understand that they might not be within a radar coverage area. Therefore, they should continue squawking Code 7700 and establish radio communications as soon as possible.

5-21 Reference. — AIM 451.

5-22 TRANSPONDER OPERATION REQUIREMENT

While in controlled airspace or in the airspace as specified in paragraph 5-25, each person operating an aircraft equipped with an operable ATC transponder maintained in accordance with FAR 91.172 shall operate the transponder, including Mode C equipment if installed, and shall reply on the appropriate code or as assigned by ATC.

5-22 Reference. — FAR 91.24.

5-23 TRANSPONDER CODE — VFR

Pilots should adjust their transponder to reply on code 1200 regardless of altitude, unless otherwise instructed by an Air Traffic Control Facility.

5-23 Reference. — AIM 170.

5-24 AUTOMATIC ALTITUDE REPORTING

a. Many transponders are equipped with a MODE C automatic altitude reporting capability. This system converts aircraft altitude in 100 foot increments to coded digital information which is transmitted together with MODE C information to the interrogating radar facility. The manner in which transponder panels are designed differs, therefore, a pilot should be thoroughly familiar with the operation of his transponder so that ATC may realize its full capabilities.

b. The transponder must be adjusted to reply on the MODE 3/A code specified by ATC and, if equipped, to reply on MODE C with altitude reporting *capability activated,* unless deactivation is directed by ATC or unless the installed aircraft equipment has not been tested and calibrated as required by FAR 91.36. If deactivation is required by ATC, the altitude reporting feature of the transponder must be turned off. While an incorrect altimeter setting has no effect on the MODE C altitude information transmitted by a transponder (transponders are preset at 29.92), it would cause pilots to fly at an actual altitude different from their assigned altitude. When a controller indicates that an altitude readout is invalid, the pilot should initiate a check to verify that the aircraft altimeter is set correctly.*

5-24b Note. — Civil MODE A is identical to military MODE 3.

5-24 Reference. — AIM 170.

5-25 MODE C TRANSPONDER REQUIREMENTS

A pilot may operate an aircraft in the airspace described in this paragraph as long as that aircraft is equipped with an operating coded radar beacon transponder having either a Mode 3/A 4096 code capability, replying to Mode 3/A interrogations with the code specified by ATC, or a

Mode S capability, replying to Mode 3/A interrogations with the code specified by ATC and intermode and Mode S interrogations in accordance with the applicable provisions specified in TSO-C112, and that aircraft is equipped with automatic pressure altitude reporting equipment having a Mode C capability that automatically replies to Mode C interrogations by transmitting pressure altitude information in 100-foot increments. This requirement applies to:

a. *All aircraft.* In terminal control areas and positive control areas;

b. *All aircraft.* In all airspace within 30 nautical miles of a terminal control area primary airport, from the surface upward to 10,000 feet MSL;

c. Notwithstanding paragraph **b**, any aircraft which was not originally certificated with an engine-driven electrical system or which has not subsequently been certified with such a system installed, balloon, or glider may conduct operations in the airspace within 30 nautical miles of a terminal control area primary airport, provided such operations are conducted:

(1) Outside any terminal control area and positive control area; and

(2) Below the altitude of the terminal control area ceiling or 10,000 feet MSL, whichever is lower; and

d. *(Effective December 30, 1990) All aircraft:*

(1) In the airspace of an airport radar service area, and

(2) In all airspace above the ceiling and within the lateral boundaries of an airport radar service area upward to 10,000 feet MSL; and

e. *All aircraft* except any aircraft which was not originally certificated with an engine-driven electrical system or which has not subsequently been certified with such a system installed, balloon, or glider.

(1) In all airspace of the 48 contiguous states and the District of Columbia, at and above 10,000 feet MSL and below the floor of a positive control area, excluding the airspace at and below 2,500 feet AGL; and

(2) *(Effective December 30, 1990)* In the airspace from the surface to 10,000 feet MSL within a 10-nautical-mile radius of any airport listed in Appendix D of FAR 91, excluding the airspace below 1,200 feet AGL outside of the airport traffic area for that airport.

5-25 Reference. — FAR 91.24.

5-26 ATC AUTHORIZED DEVIATIONS

ATC may authorize deviations from paragraph 5-25:

a. Immediately, to allow an aircraft with an inoperative transponder to continue to the airport of ultimate destination, including any intermediate stops, or to proceed to a place where suitable repairs can be made, or both;

b. Immediately, for operations of aircraft with an operating transponder but without operating automatic pressure altitude reporting equipment having a Mode C capability; and

c. For operations of aircraft without a transponder, on a continuing basis, or for individual flights the request for a deviation must be submitted to the ATC facility having jurisdiction over the airspace concerned at least one hour before the proposed operation.

5-26 Reference. — FAR 91.24.

5-27 REQUESTS FOR IN-FLIGHT DEVIATIONS FROM TRANSPONDER/MODE C REQUIREMENTS BETWEEN 10,000 FEET AND 18,000 FEET

The following procedures apply to all aircraft except gliders operating in controlled conterminous U.S. airspace above 10,000 feet MSL and below 18,000 feet MSL, excluding airspace at and below 2,500 feet AGL.

a. ATC will not approve in-flight requests for authorization to deviate from FAR 91.24(b)(5) requirements originated by aircraft without transponder equipment installed except in an emergency.

b. ATC may approve or disapprove other in-flight deviation requests, or withdraw approval previously issued to such flights, solely on the basis of traffic conditions and other operational factors.

c. Controllers will adhere to the following sequence of action when an in-flight VFR deviation request is received from an aircraft with an inoperative transponder or Mode C, or is not Mode C equipped:

(1) Suggest that the aircraft conduct its flight in airspace unaffected by the FAR.

(2) Suggest that the aircraft file an IFR flight plan.

(3) Suggest that the aircraft provide a VFR route of flight and maintain radio contact with ATC.

d. ATC will not approve an in-flight deviation unless the aircraft has filed an IFR flight plan or a VFR route of flight is provided and radio contact with ATC is maintained.

e. ATC will approve or disapprove in-flight deviation requests within a reasonable period of time or advise when approval/disapproval can be expected.

5-27 Reference. — ATCH 5-41.

5-28 FAILED TRANSPONDER IN POSITIVE CONTROL AREA

ATC may disapprove a request or withdraw previously issued approval to operate in a positive control area with a failed transponder solely on the basis of traffic conditions or other operational factors.

5-28 Reference. — ATCH 5-36.

5-29 CODE ASSIGNMENT CRITERIA

Controllers will make code assignments to departing, en route, and arriving aircraft in accordance with the procedures specified in this section for the radar beacon code environment in which they are providing ATC service, unless otherwise specified in a directive or a letter of agreement. First preference will be given to the use of discrete beacon codes.

ATC Phraseology:

Squawk (code).

5-29 Example. —

Cessna Seven Tango Foxtrot, squawk zero three one two.

5-29 Reference. — ATCH 5-20.

5-30 VALIDATION OF MODE C READOUT

a. ATC must ensure that Mode C altitude readouts are valid after accepting a handoff from another facility if the pilot does not state his altitude on initial contact.*

ATC Phraseology:

Say altitude.

b. Pilots should report their exact altitude or flight level to the nearest hundred foot increment on initial contact to an ATC facility.*

5-30b Examples. —

Departure, Cessna One Four Four Zero Golf, out of ONE THOUSAND FOUR HUNDRED, climbing to eight thousand.

New York Center, USAir Thirty-five Ninety-five out of FLIGHT LEVEL TWO FOUR TWO, descending to flight level two zero zero.

c. ATC will consider an altitude readout valid when:

(1) It varies less than 300 feet from the pilot reported altitude, or

(2) Controllers receive a continuous readout from an aircraft on the airport and the readout varies by less than 300 feet from the field elevation, or

(3) Controllers have correlated the altitude information in their data block with the validated information in a data block generated in another facility (by verbally coordinating with the other controller) and their readout is exactly the same as the readout in the other data block.

d. When unable to validate the readout, controllers will not use the Mode C altitude information for separation.

e. Whenever controllers observe an invalid readout they will:

(1) Confirm that the pilot is using the correct altimeter setting and has accurately reported the altitude.

ATC Phraseology:

Verify altitude and altimeter setting.

(2) If the altimeter setting and the altitude are correct and the discrepancy still exists, controllers will instruct the pilot to turn off the altitude reporting part of his transponder and include the reason.

ATC Phraseology:

Stop altitude squawk, altitude differs by (number of feet) **feet.**

5-30a and b Note 1. — In the context of this paragraph, facility means a separate facility (interfacility), not another sector/position within a facility (intrafacility).

5-30a and b Note 2. — ATC will use valid MODE C readouts in the application of vertical separation (see Section 4, Separation, this chapter).

5-30 Reference. — ATCH 5-37.

5-31 ASSIGNED ALTITUDE CONFIRMATION

a. ATC will request a pilot to confirm assigned altitude on initial contact.

ATC Phraseology:

In level flight situations,

Verify at (altitude).

In climbing/descending situations,

Verify assigned altitude (altitude).

b. This is not required when:

(1) The pilot states his or her assigned altitude, or

(2) The controller assigns a new altitude to a climbing or a descending aircraft, or

(3) The Mode C readout is valid and indicates that the aircraft is established at the assigned altitude, or

(4) *TERMINAL:* The aircraft was transferred to the controller from another sector/position within his facility (intrafacility).

5-31b Examples. —

Departure, Cessna One Four Four Zero Golf, out of one thousand four hundred, climbing to EIGHT THOUSAND.

New York Center, USAir Thirty-five Ninety-five out of flight level two four two, descending to FLIGHT LEVEL TWO ZERO ZERO.

5-31 References. — ATCH 5-38, 5-39.

5-32 ALTITUDE SQUAWK REQUESTS

Controllers may inform a pilot when they want the automatic altitude reporting feature of the transponder turned on/off.

ATC Phraseology:

Squawk altitude, *or*

Stop altitude squawk.

5-32 Reference. — ATCH 5-40.

5-33 CODE CHANGES

a. When making routine code changes, pilots should avoid inadvertent selection of codes 7500, 7600, or 7700, thereby causing momentary false alarms at radar facilities. For example, when switching from code 2700 to 7200, switch first to 2200, then to 7200, NOT to 7700 and then 7200. This procedure applies to nondiscrete code 7500 and all discrete codes in the 7600 and 7700 series (i.e., 7600-7677, 7700-7777) which will trigger special indicators in radar facilities. Only nondiscrete code 7500 will be decoded as the hijack code.

b. Under no circumstances should a pilot of a civil aircraft operate the transponder on Code 7777. This code is reserved for military interceptor operations.

5-33 Reference. — AIM 170.

5-34 TRANSPONDER IDENT FEATURE

The transponder shall be operated only as specified by ATC. The pilot should activate the "IDENT" feature only upon request of the ATC controller.

5-34 Reference. — AIM 170.

5-35 VFR CODE ASSIGNMENTS

Controllers will instruct IFR aircraft which cancel an IFR flight plan and are not requesting radar advisory service and VFR aircraft for which radar advisory service is being terminated to squawk the VFR code.*

ATC Phraseology:

Squawk one two zero zero.

5-35 Example. —

Radar service terminated. Squawk one two zero zero, frequency change approved.

5-35 Note. — VFR aircraft which fly authorized SAR missions for the USAF or USCG may be advised to squawk 1277 in lieu of 1200 while en route to/from or within the designated search area.

5-35 Reference. — ATCH 5-29.

5-36 BROADBAND CODE ASSIGNMENT

When the narrowband system is no longer available/usable for ATC purposes, aircraft operating on computer assigned codes will be instructed to squawk the Beacon Code appropriate for the controller's area of responsibility.

ATC Phraseology:

All aircraft on this frequency squawk (appropriate code).

5-36 Reference. — ATCH 5-26.

5-37 CODE 7600 DISPLAY

When controllers observe a code 7600 (NORDO) display, they will apply the procedures required for aircraft communications failure.

5-37 Reference. — ATCH 5-28.

5-38 EMERGENCY CODE ASSIGNMENT

Controllers will assign codes to emergency traffic as follows:

a. Code 7700 when the pilot declares an emergency and the aircraft is not radar identified.

ATC Phraseology:

Squawk Mayday on seven seven zero zero.

b. After radio and radar contact have been established, controllers may request other than single-piloted helicopters and single-piloted turbojet aircraft to change from code 7700 to another code appropriate for their radar beacon code environment.*

ATC Phraseology:

Radar contact (position). **If feasible, squawk** (code).

5-38b Note. — The code change, based on pilot concurrence, the nature of the emergency, and current flight conditions will signify to other radar facilities that the aircraft in distress is identified and under ATC control.

5-38 Reference. — ATCH 5-27.

5-39 STANDBY OR LOW SENSITIVITY TRANSPONDER OPERATION

Controllers may instruct an aircraft operating on an assigned code to change transponder to "standby" or "low sensitivity" position:*

a. When approximately 15 miles from its destination and controllers no longer desire operation of the transponder.

b. When necessary to reduce clutter in a multi-target area, or to reduce "ring-around" or other phenomena, provided controllers instruct the aircraft to return to "normal sensitivity" position as soon as possible thereafter.

ATC Phraseology:

Squawk standby, *or*

Squawk low/normal.

5-39 Note. — National standards no longer require improved transponders to be equipped with the low sensitivity feature. Therefore, aircraft with late model transponders will be unable to respond to a request to "squawk low."

5-39 Reference. — ATCH 5-32.

5-40 INOPERATIVE/MALFUNCTIONING TRANSPONDER

a. Controllers will inform an aircraft with an operable transponder that the assigned beacon code is not being displayed.

ATC Phraseology:

(Identification) **reset transponder, squawk** (appropriate code).

b. Controllers will inform an aircraft when its transponder appears to be inoperative or malfunctioning.

ATC Phraseology:

(Identification) **your transponder appears inoperative/malfunctioning, reset, squawk** (appropriate code).

5-40 Reference. — ATCH 5-34.

5-41 INOPERATIVE/MALFUNCTIONING INTERROGATOR

Controllers will inform aircraft concerned when the ground interrogator appears to be inoperative or malfunctioning.

ATC Phraseology:

(Name of facility or control function) **beacon interrogator inoperative/malfunctioning.**

5-41 Reference. — ATCH 5-35.

5-42 TRANSPONDER OFF REQUEST

Controllers will inform a pilot when they want the aircraft transponder turned off.

ATC Phraseology:

Stop squawk.

5-42 Reference. — ATCH 5-42.

5-43 thru 5-49 RESERVED

Section 3. RADAR IDENTIFICATION AND SERVICE TERMINATION

5-50 PRIMARY IDENTIFICATION METHODS

Controllers will identify a primary or radar beacon target by using one of the following methods:

a. Observing a departing aircraft target within 1 mile of the takeoff runway end.

b. Observing a target whose position with respect to a fix (displayed on the video map, scribed on the map overlay, or displayed as a permanent echo) or a visual reporting point (whose range and azimuth from the radar antenna has been accurately determined and made available to the controller) corresponds with a direct position report received from an aircraft, and the observed track is consistent with the reported heading or route of flight. If a VORTAC is located within 6,000 feet of the radar antenna, the VORTAC may be used as a reference fix for radar identification without being displayed on the video map or map overlay.*

c. Observing a target make an identifying turn or turns of 30 degrees or more, provided the following conditions are met:*

(1) Except in the case of a lost aircraft, a pilot position report is received which assures controllers that the aircraft is within radar coverage and within the area being displayed.

(2) Only one aircraft is observed making these turns.

(3) For aircraft operating in accordance with an IFR clearance, controllers may either issue a heading away from an area, which will require an increased minimum IFR altitude, or have the aircraft climb to the highest minimum altitude in their area of jurisdiction before they issue a heading.

5-50b Note. — Visual reporting points used for radar identification are limited to those most used by pilots.

5-50c Note. — Use of identifying turns or headings which would cause the aircraft to follow normal IFR routes or known VFR flight paths might result in misidentification. When these circumstances cannot be avoided, additional methods of identification may be necessary.

5-50 Reference. — ATCH 5-51.

5-51 RADAR CONTACT STATUS

a. Controllers will inform an aircraft of radar contact when:

(1) Initial radar identification in the ATC system is established.

(2) Subsequent to loss of radar contact or terminating radar service, radar identification is re-established.

ATC Phraseology:

Radar contact (position, if required).

5-51a(2) Example. —

Cessna Two Three Four Bravo Romeo radar contact, one five miles north of Zanesville.

b. Controllers will inform an aircraft when radar contact is lost.

ATC Phraseology:

Radar contact lost (alternative instructions, when required).

5-51b Example. —

Lear Seven Charlie Lima, radar contact lost, report established on the localizer.

5-51 Reference. — ATCH 5-56.

5-52 RADAR POSITION REPORT

a. Position information need not be given to pilots when identification is established by:

(1) Position correlation, or

(2) When a departing aircraft is identified within 1 mile of the takeoff runway end.

b. Controllers will inform an aircraft of its position whenever radar identification is established by means of identifying turns or any of the beacon identification methods available.

5-52 Reference. — ATCH 5-55.

5-53 POSITION REPORTING

a. If necessary, controllers may request an aircraft to provide an ETA or report over a specific fix.*

b. When required, aircraft will be informed of their position with respect to a fix or airway.

ATC Phraseology:

Over/Passing (fix). (Number of miles) **miles from** (fix).

(Number of miles) **miles** (direction) **of** (fix, airway, or location).

Crossing/Joining/Departing (airway or route).

Intercepting/Crossing (name of NAVAID) (specified) **radial**.

5-53a Note. — After an IFR aircraft receives the statement *"radar contact"* from ATC, it discontinues reporting over compulsory reporting points. It resumes normal position reporting when ATC informs it *"radar contact lost"* or *"radar service terminated."*

5-53 Reference. — ATCH 5-12.

BASIC RADAR PROCEDURES

5-54 TRANSPONDER BEACON IDENTIFICATION METHODS

When using only Mode 3/A radar beacon to identify a target, ATC will use one of the following methods:

a. Request the aircraft to activate the "IDENT" feature of the transponder and then observe the identification display.

ATC Phraseology:

Ident.

Squawk (code) **and ident.**

5-54a Example. —

Squawk seven three two one and ident.

b. Request the aircraft to change to a specific discrete or nondiscrete code, as appropriate, and then observe the target or code display change.

c. Request the aircraft to change transponder to "standby." After controllers observe the target disappear for sufficient scans to assure that loss of target resulted from placing the transponder in "standby" position, they will request the aircraft to return transponder to normal operation and then observe the reappearance of the target.

ATC Phraseology:

Squawk standby,

then, **squawk** (code).

d. EN ROUTE: During narrowband operations, an aircraft may be considered identified when the full data block is automatically associated with the beacon target symbol of an aircraft that is squawking a discrete code assigned by the computer.*

ATC Phraseology:

Squawk (4-digit discrete code), *and if aircraft has Mode C automatic altitude reporting and the equipment has been deactivated* **and altitude.**

5-54d Note. — Pilots are informed to activate Mode C transponders with altitude reporting capability, unless deactivation is requested by ATC. *SQUAWK ALTITUDE* is included to provide applicable phraseology.

5-54 Reference. — ATCH 5-52.

5-55 QUESTIONABLE IDENTIFICATION

a. ATC will use more than one method of identification when proximity of targets, duplication of observed action, or any other circumstances cause doubt as to target identification.

b. If identification is questionable for any reason, ATC will take immediate action to re-identify the aircraft or terminate radar services.

5-55 Reference. — ATCH 5-54.

5-56 RADAR SERVICE TERMINATION

a. Aircraft will be informed when radar service is terminated.

ATC Phraseology:

Radar service terminated (non-radar routing, if required).

5-56a Example. —

Radar service terminated two zero miles west of Tuscaloosa, proceed direct Tuscaloosa and contact Birmingham Approach one two zero point one five.

b. Radar service is automatically terminated and the aircraft need not be advised of termination in the following cases:*

(1) An aircraft cancels its IFR flight plan, except within an ARSA, TCA, TRSA, or where Stage II service is provided.

(2) An aircraft conducting an instrument, visual, or contact approach has landed or has been instructed to change to advisory frequency.*

(3) TERMINAL: An arriving VFR aircraft receiving radar service to a tower controlled airport within an ARSA, TCA, TRSA, or where Stage II service is provided has landed, or to all other airports, is instructed to change to tower or advisory frequency.

(4) TERMINAL: An aircraft completes a radar approach.

5-56b Note. — Termination of radar monitoring when conducting simultaneous ILS/MLS approaches is described in Section 8, Approach Procedures, of this chapter.

5-56b(2) Note. — At tower controlled airports where radar coverage does not exist to within ½ mile of the runway, arriving aircraft will be informed when radar service is terminated.

5-56 Reference. — ATCH 5-13.

5-57 thru 5-59 RESERVED

Section 4. SEPARATION

5-60 RADAR SEPARATION APPLICATION

a. Radar separation may be applied between:

(1) Radar-identified aircraft.

(2) An aircraft taking off and another radar-identified aircraft when the aircraft taking off will be radar-identified within 1 mile of the runway end.

(3) A radar-identified aircraft and one not radar-identified when either is cleared to climb/descend through the altitude of the other provided:

(a) The performance of the radar system is adequate and, as a minimum, primary radar targets are being displayed on the display being used within the airspace within which radar separation is being applied, and

(b) Flight data on the aircraft not radar-identified indicate it is a type which can be expected to give adequate primary return in the area where separation is applied, and

(c) The airspace within which radar separation is applied is not less than the following number of miles from the edge of the radar display:

(i) When less than 40 miles from the antenna —
6 miles;

(ii) When 40 miles or more from the antenna —
10 miles;

(iii) Narrowband radio operations —
10 miles; and

(d) Radar separation is maintained between the radar-identified aircraft and all observed primary and secondary radar targets until non-radar separation is established from the aircraft not radar identified, and

(e) When the aircraft involved are on the same relative heading, the radar-identified aircraft is vectored a sufficient distance from the route of the aircraft not radar identified to assure the targets are not superimposed (on the radar display) prior to issuing the clearance to climb/descend.

b. Radar separation will be applied to all RNAV aircraft operating on a random (impromptu) route at or below FL 450.

5-60 Reference. — ATCH 5-70.

5-61 RADAR SEPARATION MINIMA

ATC will separate aircraft by the following minima:*

a. Broadband Radar System:

(1) When less than 40 miles from the antenna - *3 miles.*

(2) When 40 miles or more from the antenna - *5 miles.*

EN ROUTE

b. NAS Stage A/DARC (direct access radar channel):

(1) When less than 40 miles from the antenna:

(a) Below FL 180 - *3 miles,* except where facility directives specify *5 miles* separation.

(b) FL 180 to below FL 600 - *5 miles.*

(2) When 40 miles or more from the antenna — *5 miles.*

c. EARTS:

(1) When less than 40 miles from the antenna - *3 miles.*

(2) When 40 miles or more from the antenna - *5 miles.*

WAKE TURBULENCE APPLICATION

d. ATC will separate aircraft operating directly behind, or directly behind and less than 1,000 feet below, or following an aircraft conducting an instrument approach by:

(1) Heavy behind heavy - *4 miles.*

(2) Small/large behind heavy - *5 miles.*

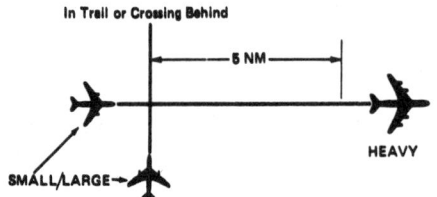

5-61d Illustration 1

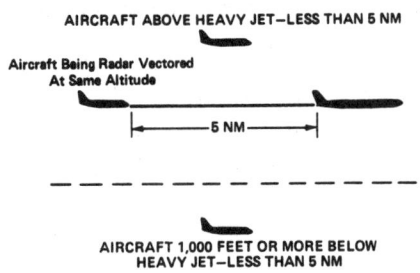

5-61d Illustration 2

e. TERMINAL: In addition to **d**, ATC will separate an aircraft landing behind another aircraft on the same runway, or one making a touch-and-go, stop-and-go, or low approach by ensuring the following minima will exist at the time the preceding aircraft is over the landing threshold:*

(1) Small behind large - *4 miles.*

(2) Small behind heavy - *6 miles.*

f. TERMINAL: Separation between aircraft may be reduced to 2.5 NM inside the final approach fix when:

(1) Facilities desiring implementation of this procedure have documented an operational need through the regional Air Traffic division to FAA headquarters;

(2) The leading aircraft's Weight Class is the same or less than the trailing aircraft;

(3) Heavy aircraft and the Boeing 757 are permitted to participate in the separation reduction as the trailing aircraft only;

(4) A runway occupancy time of 50 seconds or less is documented;

(5) BRITE/TCDD (tower radar) displays are operational and used for quick glance references;

(6) Turnoff points are visible from the control tower; and

(7) Runways are clear and dry.

5-61 Note. — Wake Turbulence procedures specify increased separation minima required for certain classes of aircraft because of the possible effects of wake turbulence.

5-61e Note. — Parallel runways less than 2,500 feet apart are considered as a single runway because of the possible effects of wake turbulence.

5-61 Reference. — ATCH 5-72.

5-62 VERTICAL SEPARATION — MODE C

ATC will use valid MODE C returns as the primary reference for maintaining vertical separation in a radar environment.

5-62 Reference. — ATCH 2-3.

5-63 VERTICAL SEPARATION MINIMA

ATC will separate aircraft by assigning different altitudes. The following minima will be used between altitudes:

a. Between VFR aircraft and between VFR and IFR aircraft in an ARSA, TCA, or TRSA—*500 feet.**

b. Between IFR aircraft, up to and including FL 290—*1,000 feet.*

c. Between IFR aircraft, above FL 290—*2,000 feet.*

5-63a Note. — 500 feet vertical separation will not be applied below a heavy jet.

5-63 References. — ATCH 5-81, 7-92, 7-102.

5-64 ALTITUDE ASSIGNMENTS

a. Normally, ATC will assign an altitude to an aircraft only after the aircraft previously at that altitude is observed on radar (valid MODE C) leaving that altitude. Pilot reported altitude will be used for aircraft with invalid MODE C readouts or for nonMODE C aircraft.*

b. As an exception to **a** above, ATC will assign an altitude to an aircraft only after an aircraft previously at that altitude achieves the required minimum separation from the vacated altitude when:

(1) Severe turbulence is reported.

(2) Aircraft are conducting military refueling.

(3) The aircraft previously at that altitude has been:

(a) Issued a clearance permitting climb/descent at pilot's discretion.

5-64b(3)(a) Example. —

An aircraft at 10,000 feet (valid Mode C) is issued a clearance *"descend at pilot's discretion maintain four thousand."* ATC may not assign 10,000 feet to another aircraft until the aircraft on the discretionary descent is observed on radar leaving 9,000 feet.

(b) Cleared to CRUISE (altitude), and the pilot reports leaving that altitude.

(4) Transitioning from minima of 1,000 feet to 2,000 feet vertical separation.

5-64a Note. — ATC will consider known aircraft performance characteristics, pilot furnished, and/or MODE C detected information which may indicate that a climb or descent will not be consistent with rates recommended in Para. 4-88.

5-64 References. — ATCH 5-80, 5-82.

5-65 thru 5-69 RESERVED

Section 5. VECTORS

5-70 VECTORING SERVICE

ATC will vector aircraft:

a. In controlled airspace for separation, safety, noise abatement, operational advantage, or when a pilot requests. Aircraft operating on an RNAV route will be allowed to remain on their own navigation to the extent possible.

b. In uncontrolled airspace only upon pilot request and as an additional service.

c. At or above MVA (minimum vectoring altitude) or the minimum IFR altitude except as authorized for missed approaches, radar approaches, departures, special VFR and VFR operations.*

d. In airspace for which controllers have control jurisdiction, unless otherwise coordinated.

e. So as to permit it to resume its own navigation within radar coverage.

f. Operating Special VFR only within control zones.

g. Operating VFR at those locations where a special program is established, or when a pilot requests, or controllers suggest and the pilot concurs.

5-70c Note. — VFR aircraft not at an altitude assigned by ATC may be vectored at any altitude. It is the responsibility of the pilot to comply with the applicable FAR's.

5-70 Reference. — ATCH 5-90.

5-71 MINIMUM VECTORING ALTITUDES

a. MVA's are established for use by ATC when radar ATC is exercised. MVA charts are prepared by air traffic facilities at locations where there are numerous different minimum IFR altitudes. Each MVA chart has sectors large enough to accommodate vectoring of aircraft within the sector at the MVA. Each sector boundary is at least 3 miles from the obstruction determining the MVA. To avoid a large sector with an excessively high MVA due to an isolated prominent obstruction, the obstruction may be enclosed in a buffer area whose boundaries are at least 3 miles from the obstruction. This is done to facilitate vectoring around the obstruction.

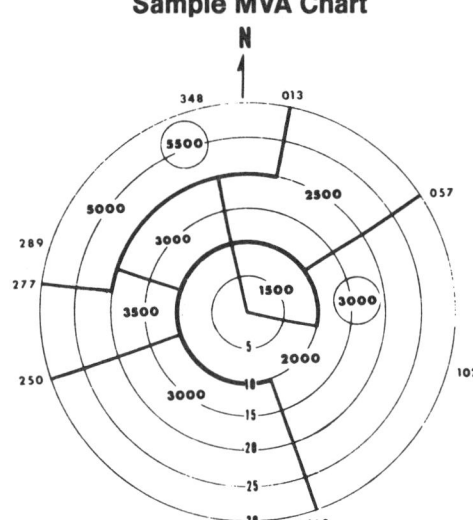

Sample MVA Chart

5-71a Illustration

b. The MVA in each sector provides 1,000 feet above the highest obstacle in nonmountainous areas and 2,000 feet above the highest obstacle in designated mountainous areas. Where lower MVA's are required in designated mountainous areas to achieve compatibility with terminal routes or to permit vectoring to an IAP, 1,000 feet of obstacle clearance may be authorized with the use of Airport Surveillance Radar (ASR). The MVA will provide at least 300 feet above the floor of controlled airspace.

c. Because of differences in the areas considered for MVA, and those applied to other minimum altitudes, and the ability to isolate specific obstacles, some MVA's may be lower than the non-radar MEA (minimum en route altitudes), MOCA (minimum obstruction clearance altitudes), or other minimum altitudes depicted on charts for a given location. While being radar vectored, IFR altitude assignments by ATC will be at or above MVA.

5-71 Reference. — AIM 364.

5-72 VECTORING METHODS

Controllers will vector aircraft by specifying:

a. Direction of turn, if appropriate, and magnetic heading to be flown, or

ATC Phraseology:

Fly present heading.

Turn left/right heading (degrees).

Fly heading (degrees).

Depart (fix) **heading** (degrees).

5-72a Examples. —

Turn left heading three four zero.

Fly heading zero two five until receiving Decatur.

United Two Twenty-four, depart Bradford heading zero five zero.
Depart Bradford heading zero five zero, United Two Twenty-four.

b. The number of degrees, in group form, to turn and the direction of turn, or

ATC Phraseology:

Turn (number of degrees) **degrees left/right.**

5-72b Example. —

Turn twenty degrees left, vector to Runway Two Zero Left . . .

c. For NO-GYRO procedures, the type of vector, direction of turn, and when to stop turn.

ATC Phraseology:

This will be a no-gyro vector, turn left/right. Then, **Stop turn.**

5-72 Reference. — ATCH 5-91.

5-73 INITIAL VECTOR ADVISORY

a. When initiating a vector, controllers will advise the pilot of the purpose.

ATC Phraseology:

(Vector),

vector for spacing.

for vector to final approach course,

or if the pilot does not have knowledge of the type of approach,

for vector to (approach name) **final approach course.**

for vector to (fix or airway).

for vector to intercept (name of NAVAID) (specified) **radial.**

5-73a Examples. —

Fly present heading for vector to I-L-S One Eight final approach course.

Turn left heading two seven zero for vector to intercept Nashville three five four radial.

b. If appropriate, controllers will advise the pilot what to expect when the vector is completed.*

ATC Phraseology:

Expect to resume (route, SID, STAR, etc.).

5-73b Note. — Controllers must ensure that the pilot is made aware if he is expected to resume a previously issued route/procedure.

5-73 Reference. — ATCH 5-91.

5-74 ALTITUDE RESTRICTIONS

Controllers will issue with the vector an altitude to maintain and all appropriate altitude restrictions when:

a. The vector will take the aircraft off an assigned procedure which contains altitude instructions, i.e., instrument approach, non-radar SID, etc.

b. The previously issued clearance included crossing restrictions.

5-74 Reference. — ATCH 5-51.

5-75 DIRECT ROUTES

a. Increasing use of self-contained airborne navigational systems which do not rely on the VOR/VORTAC/TACAN system has resulted in pilot requests for direct routes which exceed NAVAID service volume limits. These direct route requests will be approved only in a radar environment, with approval based on pilot responsibility for navigation on the authorized direct route. Radar flight following will be provided by ATC for ATC purposes.

b. At times, ATC will initiate a direct route in a radar environment which exceeds NAVAID service volume limits. In such cases ATC will provide radar monitoring and navigational assistance as necessary.

5-75b Example. —

Eagle Flight Five Fourteen, fly heading three six zero. When able, proceed direct South Bend.

5-75 Reference. — AIM 298.

5-76 AREA NAVIGATION

a. Random RNAV (area navigation) routes can only be approved in a radar environment. Factors that will be considered by ATC in approving random RNAV routes include the capability to provide radar monitoring and compatibility with traffic volume and flow. ATC will radar monitor each flight. However, navigation on the random RNAV route is the responsibility of the pilot.

b. To be certified for use in the National Airspace System, RNAV equipment must meet the specifications outlined in AC 90-45. The pilot is responsible for variations in equipment capability, and must advise ATC if a RNAV clearance can not be accepted as specified. The controller need only be concerned that the aircraft is RNAV equipped; if the flight plan equipment suffix denotes RNAV capability, the RNAV routing can be applied.

5-76 Reference. — AIM 298.

5-77 NAVIGATIONAL GUIDANCE

a. Radar navigational guidance will be provided until the aircraft is:

(1) Established within the airspace to be protected for the non-radar route to be flown, or

(2) On a heading that will, within a reasonable distance, intercept the non-radar route to be flown, and

(3) Informed of its position unless the aircraft is RNAV or DME equipped and being vectored toward a VORTAC or Waypoint and within the service volume of the NAVAID.

ATC Phraseology:

(Position with respect to course/fix along route), **resume own navigation,** or

Fly heading (degrees) **when able proceed direct** (name of fix), or

Resume (name-number SID/Transition/STAR/procedure).

5-77a Example. —

Baron Five Five Papa request direct Palmdale.

Baron Five Five Papa, roger. Cleared direct Palmdale.

Baron Five Five Papa, we need a vector from our present position.

Baron Five Five Papa, roger. Fly heading two five five, when able, proceed direct Palmdale.

Fly heading two five five. When able proceed direct Palmdale, Baron Five Five Papa.

b. Aircraft instructed to resume a procedure which contains restrictions (SID/STAR, etc.) will be issued/reissued all applicable restrictions or shall be advised to comply with those restrictions.

ATC Phraseology:

Resume (name-number SID/Transition/STAR), **comply with restrictions.**

c. Aircraft vectored off an RNAV route will be recleared to the next waypoint or as requested by the pilot.

d. Pilots will be informed when a vector will take the aircraft across a previously assigned non-radar route.

ATC Phraseology:

Expect vector across (NAVAID radial) (airway/route/course) **for** (purpose).

5-77d Example. —

Expect vector across localizer for spacing.

5-77 Reference. — ATCH 5-91.

5-78 VECTOR COMPLIANCE

a. When a heading is assigned or a turn is requested by ATC, pilots are expected to promptly initiate the turn, to complete the turn, and maintain the new heading unless issued additional instructions.

b. Assignment of radar headings and/or altitudes are based on the provision that a pilot operating in accordance with visual flight rules is expected to advise ATC if compliance with an assigned route, radar heading, or altitude will cause the pilot to violate such rules.

5-78b Example. —

Cessna Two Four Golf, turn right heading zero niner zero.

Cessna Two Four Golf unable to accept that heading due to clouds.

Cessna Two Four Golf, roger. Continue on present heading and advise when able to make right turn and maintain V-F-R. The airport is at two o'clock and one zero miles.

5-78 References. — FAR 91.90; AIM 270, 405.

5-79 COMMUNICATIONS TRANSFER

When making an interfacility frequency change such as from ARTCC to approach control, it is good operating practice to state the assigned heading or off-route clearance on initial radio contact.

5-79 Examples. —

Houston Center, Aerostar Five Four Two Five Papa, level at one five thousand heading zero niner zero assigned.

Indianapolis Center, USAir Nine Ninety-nine leaving flight level two seven zero descending to flight level two three zero, direct Boiler.

5-79 Reference. — AIM 405.

5-80 thru 5-89 RESERVED

Section 6. SPEED ADJUSTMENT

5-90 APPLICATION

a. Speed adjustments are kept to the minimum necessary to achieve or maintain required or desired spacing. Adjustments requiring alternate decreases and increases will be avoided. Pilots will be permitted to resume normal speed when previously specified adjustments are no longer needed.*

b. ATC will not assign speed adjustments to aircraft:

(1) At or above FL 290 without pilot consent.

(2) Executing a published high altitude instrument approach procedure.

(3) In a holding pattern.

(4) Inside the final approach fix on final or a point 5 miles from the runway, whichever is closer to the runway.

c. At the time approach clearance is issued, previously issued speed adjustments will be restated if required.*

d. Speed adjustments are expressed in terms of knots based on indicated airspeed (IAS) in 10-knot increments. At or above FL 240, speeds may be expressed in terms of mach numbers in 0.01 increments for turbojet aircraft with mach meters (i.e., mach 0.69, 0.70, 0.71, etc.)*

5-90a Note. — It is the pilot's responsibility and prerogative to refuse speed adjustment that he considers excessive or contrary to the aircraft's operating specifications.

5-90c Note. — Approach clearances supersede any prior speed adjustment assignments. Pilots are expected to make their own speed adjustments to complete the approach, unless the controller has issued a speed adjustment.

5-90d Note. — Pilots complying with speed adjustment instructions should maintain a speed within plus or minus 10 knots or 0.02 mach number of the specified speed.

5-90 Reference. — ATCH 5-100.

5-91 SPEED ADJUSTMENT METHODS

a. Controllers will instruct aircraft to:*

(1) Maintain present speed.

(2) Increase or reduce to a specified speed or by a specified number of knots.

(3) Avoid exceeding a specified speed.

ATC Phraseology:

Say airspeed.

Say mach number.

Maintain present speed.

Increase/Reduce speed: to (specified in knots), *or* **to mach** (mach number), *or* (number of knots) **knots. Do not exceed** (speed) **knots,** *or*

Mach (mach number).

5-91a Examples. —

Increase speed to mach point seven two.

Reduce speed to two five zero.

Reduce speed two zero knots.

Do not exceed mach point seven four.

(4) Reduce to a specified speed or amount less than the minimum speeds in 5-93, only if the pilot concurs.

ATC Phraseology:

If practical, reduce speed: to (specified speed in knots), *or* **to mach** (mach number), *or* (number of knots) **knots.**

b. Controllers will specify which action is expected first when combining speed reduction with a descent clearance.*

(1) Speed reductions prior to descent.

ATC Phraseology:

Reduce speed: to (specified speed), *or* (number of knots) **knots.**

Then, descend and maintain (altitude).

(2) Speed reduction following descent.

ATC Phraseology:

Descend and maintain (altitude).

Then, reduce speed: to (specified speed in knots), *or* **to mach** (mach number), *or* (number of knots) **knots.**

5-91b(1) and (2) Examples. —

United Four Seventeen, reduce speed to two one zero knots, then descend and maintain seven thousand.

King Air One Tango Mike, descend and maintain three thousand, then reduce speed to one eight zero knots, approach control request.

c. Controllers will specify combined speed/altitude fix crossing restrictions.

ATC Phraseology:

Cross (fix) **at and maintain** (altitude) **at** (specified speed) **knots.**

5-91c Example. —

Cross Robinsville at and maintain six thousand at two three zero knots.

5-91a Note. — A pilot operating at or above 10,000 feet MSL on an assigned speed adjustment greater than 250 knots is expected to comply with FAR 91.70(a) when cleared below 10,000 feet MSL without notifying ATC. Pilots are expected to comply with the other provisions of FAR 91.70 without notification unless otherwise authorized by ATC.

5-91b Note 1. — Simultaneous speed reduction and descent can be extremely difficult, particularly for turbojet aircraft. Specifying which action is to be accomplished first removes any doubt the pilot may have as to controller intent or priority.

5-91b Note 2. — When specifying descent prior to speed reduction, controllers will consider the maximum speed requirements specified in FAR 91.70. It may be necessary for the pilot to level off temporarily and reduce speed prior to descending below 10,000 feet MSL.

5-91 Reference. — ATCH 5-101.

5-92 AMENDED CLEARANCES

ATC will issue an amended clearance if a speed restriction is declined because it cannot be complied with concurrently with a previously issued altitude assigment.*

5-92 Example. —

An aircraft is cleared to cross Gordonsville VOR at 11,000. Shortly thereafter he is cleared to reduce his airspeed to 300 knots. The pilot informs the controller he is unable to comply with both clearances simultaneously. The controller issues an amended clearance as follows:

Cross Gordonsville at one one thousand. Then, reduce speed to three zero zero knots.

5-92 Note. — The phrase *"do the best you can"* or comparable phrases by ATC are not considered valid substitutes for an amended clearance with altitude or speed restrictions.

5-92 Reference. — ATCH 4-14.

5-93 SPEED ADJUSTMENT MINIMA

Unless a pilot concurs in the use of a lower speed, ATC will use the following minima:

a. To aircraft operating between FL 280 and 10,000 feet, a speed not less than 250 knots or the equivalent mach number.*

b. To arrival aircraft operating below 10,000 feet:

(1) Turbojet powered aircraft — A speed not less than 210 knots; except when the aircraft is within 20-flying miles of the runway threshold of the airport of intended landing, a speed not less than 170 knots.

(2) Reciprocating engine and turboprop aircraft — A speed not less than 200 knots; except when the aircraft is within 20-flying miles of the runway threshold of the airport of intended landing, a speed not less than 150 knots.

c. Departures:

(1) Turbojet powered aircraft — A speed not less than 230 knots.

(2) Reciprocating engine and turboprop aircraft — A speed not less than 150 knots.

d. Helicopters — A speed not less than 60 knots.

5-93a Note. — On a standard day the mach numbers equivalent to 250 knots CAS (subject to minor variations) are: FL 240 - 0.6; FL 250 - 0.61; FL 260 - 0.62; FL 270 - 0.64; FL 280 - 0.65; FL 290 - 0.66.

5-93 Reference. — ATCH 5-102.

5-94 COMMUNICATIONS TRANSFER

When in communications with the ARTCC or handoff from ARTCC to approach control, pilots should, as a good operating practice, state any ATC assigned speed restriction on initial radio contact.

5-94 Example. —

Wichita Approach, King Air One One Tango Mike level at three thousand with ZULU, restricted to one eight zero knots.

King Air One One Tango Mike, Wichita Approach, roger. Resume normal speed, expect vector for visual approach.

5-94 Reference. — AIM 272.

5-95 AUTHORIZED SPEED ADJUSTMENT

a. For operations in an airport traffic area, ATC is authorized to request or approve a speed greater than the maximum indicated airspeeds prescribed for operation within that airspace.

b. The Administrator may authorize an aircraft:

(1) In the airspace below 10,000 feet MSL to exceed an indicated airspeed of more than 250 knots (288 mph), or

(2) In the airspace underlying a TCA, or in a VFR corridor designated through a TCA, to exceed an indicated airspeed of more than 200 knots (230 mph).

5-95 References. — FAR 91.70; AIM 272.

5-96 CANCELLATION OF SPEED ADJUSTMENT

Controllers will advise aircraft when speed adjustment is no longer needed.

ATC Phraseology:

Resume normal speed.

5-96 Reference. — ATCH 5-104.

5-97 thru 5-99 RESERVED

Section 7. DEPARTURES

5-100 INITIAL DEPARTURE HEADING

a. Before departure, ATC will assign the initial heading to be flown if a departing aircraft is to be vectored immediately after takeoff.

ATC Phraseology:

Fly runway heading.

Turn left/right, heading (degrees).

b. Pilots operating in a radar environment are expected to associate departure headings with vectors to their planned route or flight. When given a vector taking his aircraft off a previously assigned non-radar route, the pilot will be advised briefly what the vector is to achieve. Thereafter, radar service will be provided until the aircraft has been reestablished "on-course" using an appropriate navigation aid and the pilot has been advised of his position or a handoff is made to another radar controller with further surveillance capabilities.

c. Order 8260.19, Flight Procedures and Airspace, establishes guidelines for IFR departure turning procedures which assumes a climb to 400 feet above the airport elevation before a turn is commenced.

5-100 References. — ATCH 5-111; AIM 324.

5-101 VECTORS BELOW MINIMUM ALTITUDE

Except in en route automated environments where more than *3-miles* separation minima is required, controllers may vector a departing IFR aircraft, or one executing a missed approach, within 40 miles of the antenna and before it reaches the minimum altitude for IFR operations, if separation from prominent obstructions shown on the radar scope is applied in accordance with the following:

a. If the flight path is 3 miles or more from the obstruction and the aircraft is climbing to an altitude at least 1,000 feet above the obstruction, controllers will vector the aircraft to maintain at least *3 miles* separation from the obstruction until the aircraft reports leaving an altitude above the obstruction.

b. If the flight path is less than 3 miles from the obstruction, and the aircraft is climbing to an altitude at least 1,000 feet above the obstruction, controllers will vector the aircraft to increase lateral separation from the obstruction until the *3-mile* minimum is achieved or until the aircraft reports leaving an altitude above the obstruction.

c. At those locations where diverse vector areas (DVA) have been established, terminal radar facilities may vector aircraft below the MVA/MIA within those areas and along those routes described in facility directives.

5-101 Reference. — ATCH 5-112.

5-102 SUCCESSIVE OR SIMULTANEOUS RADAR DEPARTURES

TERMINAL

Aircraft departing from the same airport/heliport or adjacent airports/heliports will be separated in accordance with the following minima, provided radar identification with the aircraft is established within 1 mile of the takeoff runway end/helipad and courses diverge by 15 degrees or more.*

a. Between aircraft departing the same runway/helipad or parallel runways/helicopter takeoff courses separated by less than 2,500 feet — *1 mile* if courses diverge immediately after departure.*

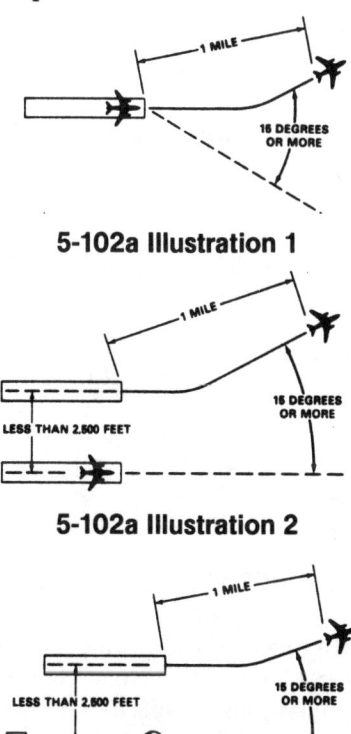

5-102a Illustration 1

5-102a Illustration 2

5-102a Illustration 3

b. Between aircraft departing from diverging runways:

(1) Nonintersecting runways - Simultaneous takeoffs will be authorized if runways diverge by 15 degrees or more.

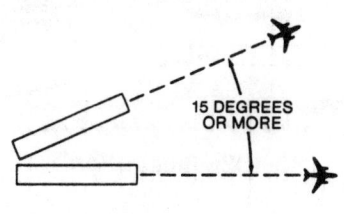

5-102b(1) Illustration

(2) Intersecting runways and/or helicopter takeoff courses which diverge by 15 degrees or more — ATC will authorize takeoff of a succeeding aircraft when the preceding aircraft has passed the point of runway and/or takeoff course intersection. The procedure in 3-138 will be applied, when applicable.*

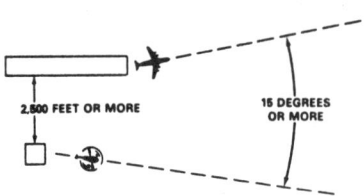

5-102c Illustration 2

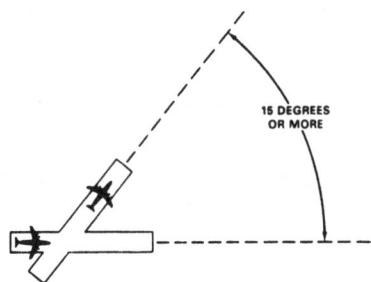

5-102b(2) Illustration 1

5-102 Note 1. — Order 8290.3, TERPS, the ILS missed approach criteria require a straight climb of 400 feet be specified where turns greater than 15 degrees are required.

5-102 Note 2. — ATC will consider known aircraft performance characteristics when applying initial separation to successive departing aircraft.

5-102 Note 3. — When one or both of the departure surfaces is a helipad, ATC will use the takeoff course of the helicopter as a reference, comparable to the centerline of a runway and the helipad center as the threshold.

5-102a Note. — This procedure does not apply when Category I or II aircraft are taking off from an intersection on the same runway behind a preceding departing heavy jet.

5-102b(2) Note. — This procedure does not apply when aircraft are departing behind a heavy jet.

5-102 Reference. — ATCH 5-113.

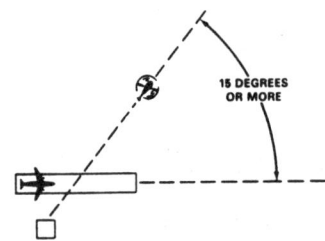

5-102b(2) Illustration 2

c. Between aircraft departing in the same direction from parallel runways/helicopter takeoff courses — ATC will authorize simultaneous takeoffs if the centerlines/takeoff courses are separated by at least 2,500 feet and courses diverge by 105 degrees or more immediately after departure.

5-103 DEPARTURE AND ARRIVAL RADAR SEPARATION

TERMINAL

Except as provided in 5-104, ATC will separate a departing aircraft from an arriving aircraft on final approach by a minimum of *2 miles* if separation will increase to a minimum of *3 miles* (*5 miles* when 40 miles or more from the antenna) within 1 minute after takeoff.*

5-103 Note 1. — This procedure permits a departing aircraft to be released so long as an arriving aircraft is no closer than 2 miles from the runway at the time. This separation is determined at the time the departing aircraft commences takeoff roll.

5-103 Note 2. — The effect of surface conditions will be considered, such as ice, snow, and other precipitation may have on known aircraft performance characteristics, and the influence these conditions may have on the pilot's ability to commence takeoff roll in a timely manner.

5-103 Reference. — ATCH 5-114.

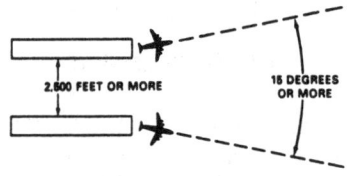

5-102c Illustration 1

5-104 DEPARTURES AND ARRIVALS ON PARALLEL OR NONINTERSECTING DIVERGING RUNWAYS

TERMINAL

Simultaneous operations between an aircraft departing on a runway and an aircraft on final approach to another parallel or nonintersecting diverging runway will be authorized if the departure course diverges immediately by at least 30 degrees from the missed approach course until separation is applied and provided one of the following conditions is met:*

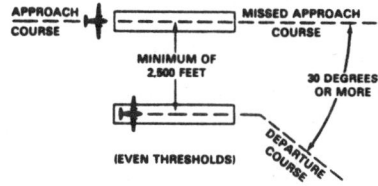

5-104 Illustration 1

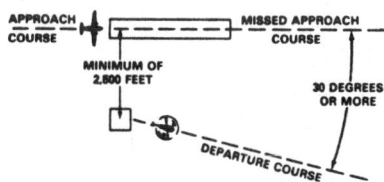

5-104 Illustration 2

a. When parallel runway thresholds are even, the runway centerlines are at least 2,500 feet apart.

b. When parallel runway thresholds are staggered and:

(1) The arriving aircraft is approaching the nearer runway - The centerlines are at least 1,000 feet apart and the landing thresholds are staggered at least 500 feet for each 100 feet less than 2,500 feet the centerlines are separated.*

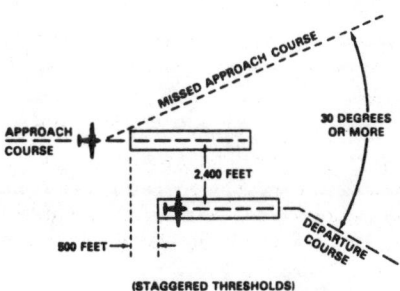

5-104b(1) Illustration 1

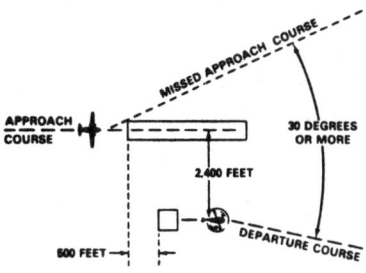

5-104b(1) Illustration 2

(2) The arriving aircraft is approaching the farther runway - The runway centerline separation exceeds 2,500 feet by at least 100 feet for each 500 feet the landing thresholds are staggered.

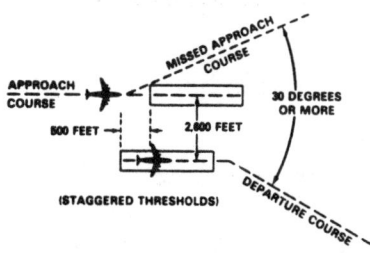

5-104b(2) Illustration

c. When nonintersecting runways diverge by 15 degrees or more and runway edges do not touch.

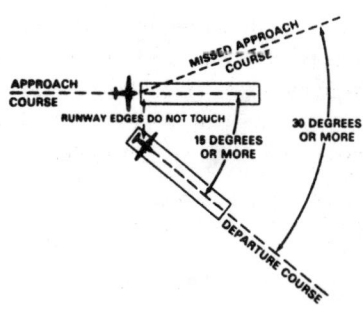

5-104c Illustration

5-104 Note. — When one or both of the takeoff/landing surfaces is a helipad, ATC will consider the helicopter takeoff course as the runway centerline and the helipad center as the threshold.

5-104b(1) Note. — In the event of a missed approach by a heavy jet, ATC will apply intersecting runway separation or ensure that the heavy jet does not overtake an aircraft departing from the adjacent parallel runway.

5-104 Reference. — ATCH 5-115.

5-105 thru 5-109 RESERVED

Section 8. APPROACH PROCEDURES

5-110 GENERAL

a. ATC may vector aircraft to the final approach course (ILS, MLS, VOR, ADF, etc.). Radar vectors and altitudes will be issued as required for spacing and separating aircraft. *THEREFORE, PILOTS MUST NOT DEVIATE FROM THE HEADINGS ISSUED BY APPROACH CONTROL.*

b. Aircraft will normally be informed when it is necessary to vector across the final approach course for spacing or other reasons. If approach course crossing is imminent and the pilot has not been informed that he will be vectored across the final approach course, he should query the controller. Pilots are not expected to turn inbound on the final approach course unless an approach clearance has been issued.

c. The approach clearance will normally be issued with the final vector for interception of the final approach course, and the vector will be such as to enable the pilot to establish his aircraft on the final approach course prior to reaching the final approach fix.

d. In the case of aircraft already inbound on the final approach course, approach clearance will be issued prior to the aircraft reaching the final approach fix. When established inbound on the final approach course, radar separation will be maintained and the pilot will be expected to complete the approach utilizing the approach aid designated in the clearance (ILS, MLS, VOR, radio beacons, etc.) as the primary means of navigation. Therefore, once established on the final approach course, pilots must not deviate from it unless a clearance to do so is received from ATC.

e. After passing the final approach fix on final approach, aircraft are expected to continue inbound on the final approach course and complete the approach or execute the missed approach procedure published for that airport or missed approach instructions issued by ATC.

f. Whether aircraft are vectored to the appropriate final approach course or provide their own navigation on published routes to it, radar service is automatically terminated when the landing is completed or when instructed to change to advisory frequency at uncontrolled airports, whichever occurs first.

5-110 Reference. — AIM 362.

5-111 VECTORS TO FINAL APPROACH COURSE

Except as provided by Radar Monitored Visual Approaches, ATC will vector arriving aircraft to intercept the final approach course:*

a. At least 2 miles outside the approach gate unless one of the following exists:*

(1) When the reported ceiling is at least 500 feet above the MVA/MIA and the visibility is at least 3 miles (report may be PIREP if no weather is reported for the airport), aircraft may be vectored to intercept the final approach course closer than 2 miles outside the approach gate, but no closer than the approach gate.

(2) If specifically requested by the pilot, aircraft may be vectored to intercept the final approach course inside the approach gate, but no closer than the final approach fix.

b. For a precision approach, at an altitude not above the glideslope/glidepath.

c. For a nonprecision approach, at an altitude which will allow descent in accordance with the published procedure.*

5-111 Note. — While being radar vectored, the pilot, when an approach clearance is received, shall in addition to complying with minimum altitudes for IFR operations (FAR 91.119), maintain the last altitude assigned to that pilot until the aircraft is established on a segment of a published route or instrument approach procedure unless a different altitude is assigned by ATC. After the aircraft is so established, published altitudes apply to descent within each suceeding route or approach segment unless a different altitude is assigned by ATC.

5-111 Note Example. —

Cessna Seven Two Lima, four miles from Bartey, turn left heading zero two zero, maintain three thousand until established on the localizer. Cleared for I-L-S Three Five Right Approach.

Left heading zero two zero, maintain three thousand until established, cleared for I-L-S Three Five Right Approach, Cessna Seven Two Lima.

5-111a Note. — An approach gate is an imaginary point used within ATC as a basis for vectoring aircraft to the final approach course. The gate will be established along the final course 1 mile from the outer marker (or the fix used in lieu of the outer marker) on the side away from the airport for precision approaches and 1 mile from the final approach fix on the side away from the airport for nonprecision approaches. In either case when measured along the final approach course, the gate will be no closer than 5 miles from the landing threshold.

5-111c Note. — A pilot request for an "evaluation approach," or a "coupled approach," or use of a similar term, indicates he desires the application of **a** and **b** above.

5-111 References. — FAR 91.116; ATCH 5-120; AIM Glossary.

5-112 FINAL APPROACH COURSE INTERCEPT ANGLES

Controllers will assign headings that will permit final approach course interception on a track that does not exceed the interception angles specified in the Table.*

5-112 Table. — Approach Course Interception Angle

Distance from interception point to approach gate	Maximum interception angle
Less than 2 miles	20 degrees
2 miles or more	30 degrees (45 degrees for helicopters)

5-112 Note. — The intent is to provide for a track-course intercept angle judged by the controller to be no greater than specified by this procedure.

5-112 Reference. — ATCH 5-121.

5-113 VECTORS ACROSS FINAL APPROACH COURSE

Controllers will inform the aircraft whenever a vector will take it across the final approach course and state the reason for such action.*

ATC Phraseology:

Expect vector across final approach course for (purpose).

5-113 Example. —

Expect vector across final approach course for spacing.

5-113 Note. — In the event a controller is unable to so inform the aircraft, the pilot is not expected to turn inbound on the final approach course unless approach clearance has been issued.

5-113 Reference. — ATCH 5-122.

5-114 APPROACH INSTRUCTIONS

Controllers must issue all of the following information to an aircraft before it reaches the approach gate:

a. *Position* relative to a fix on the final approach course. If none is portrayed on the radar display or if none is prescribed in the procedure, controllers will issue position information relative to the navigational aid which provides final approach guidance or relative to the airport.

b. *Heading* to intercept the final approach course, if required.

c. *Approach clearance,* except when conducting a radar approach. Controllers will issue approach clearance only after the aircraft is:

(1) Established on a segment of a published route or instrument approach procedure, or

(2) Assigned an altitude to maintain until the aircraft is established on a segment of a published route or instrument approach procedure.*

5-114c(1) Example. —

Aircraft 1 was vectored to the final approach course, but clearance was withheld. It is now at 4,000 feet and established on a segment of the instrument approach procedure.

Seven miles from X-ray. Cleared for I-L-S Runway Three Six Approach.

5-114c(2) Example 1. —

Aircraft 2 is being vectored to a published segment of the final approach course, 4 miles from Lima at 2,000 feet. The MVA for this area is 2,000 feet.

Four miles from Lima. Turn right heading three four zero. Maintain two thousand until established on the localizer. Cleared for I-L-S Runway Three Six Approach.

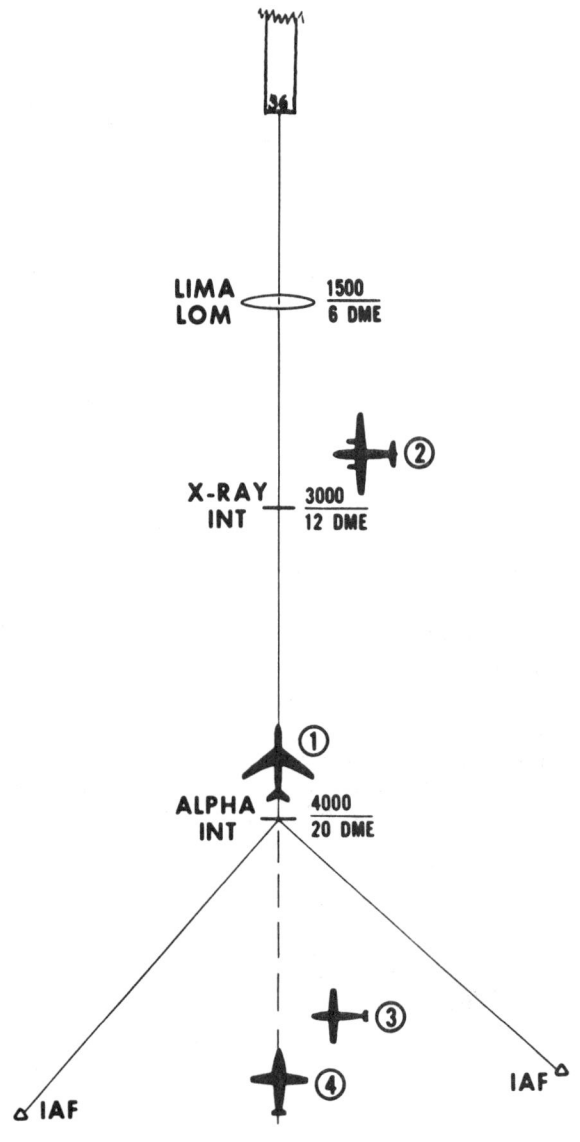

5-114c(2) Illustration 1 — ILS

5-114c(2) Example 2. —

Aircraft 3 is being vectored to intercept the final approach course beyond the approach segments, 5 miles from Alpha at 6,000 feet. The MVA for this area is 4,000 feet.

Eight miles from Alpha. Cross Alpha at or above four thousand. Cleared for I-L-S Runway Three Six Approach.

5-114c(2) Example 3. —

Aircraft 4 is established on the final approach course beyond the approach segments, 8 miles from Alpha at 6,000 feet. The MVA for this area is 4,000 feet.

Eight miles from Alpha. Cross Alpha at or above four thousand. Cleared for I-L-S Runway Three Six Approach.

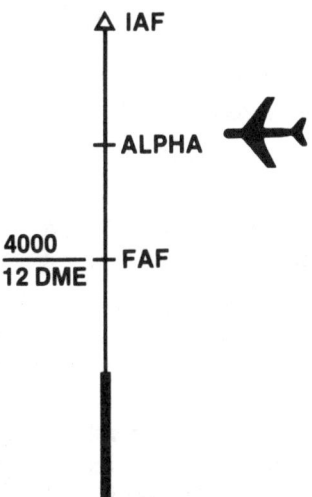

5-114c(2) Illustration 2 — Straight-in MLS

5-114c(2) Example 4.—

The aircraft is being vectored to a published segment of the MLS final approach course, 3 miles from Alpha at 4,000 feet. The MVA for this area is 4,000 feet.

Three miles from Alpha. Turn left heading two one zero. Maintain four thousand until established on the azimuth course. Cleared for M-L-S Runway One Eight Approach.

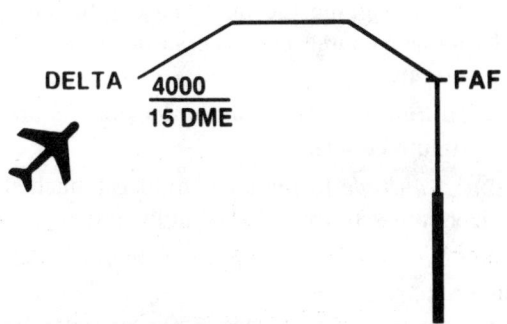

5-114c(2) Illustration 3 — Segmented MLS

5-114c(2) Example 5. —

The aircraft is en route to Delta Waypoint at 6,000 feet. The MVA for this area is 4,000 feet.

Cross Delta at or above four thousand. Cleared for M-L-S Runway One Eight Approach.

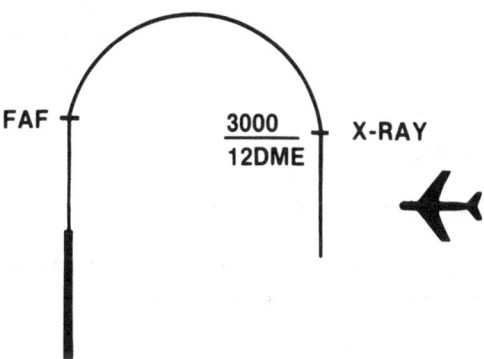

5-114c(2) Illustration 4 — Curved MLS

5-114c(2) Example 6. —

The aircraft is being vectored to an MLS curved approach, 3 miles from X-ray at 3,000 feet.

Three miles from X-ray. Turn right heading three three zero. Maintain three thousand until established on the azimuth course. Cleared for M-L-S Runway One Eight Approach.

d. *Frequency change instructions* by instructing the pilot to do one of the following:*

(1) Monitor local control frequency, reporting to the tower when over the approach fix.

(2) Contact the tower on local control frequency.

(3) Contact the final controller on the appropriate frequency if radar service will be provided on final on a different frequency.

(4) When radar is used to establish the final approach fix, controllers will inform the pilot that after being advised that he is over the fix he is to contact the tower on local frequency.*

5-114d(4) Example. —

Three miles from final approach fix. Turn left heading zero one zero. Maintain two thousand until established on the localizer. Cleared for I-L-S Runway Three Six Approach. I will advise when over the final approach fix.

Over final approach fix. Contact tower one one eight point one.

5-114c(2) Note 1. — The altitude assigned must assure IFR obstruction clearance from the point at which the approach clearance is issued until established on a segment of a published route or instrument approach procedure.

5-114c(2) Note 2. — If the altitude assignment is VFR-on-top, it is conceivable that the pilot may elect to remain high until arrival over the final approach fix, which may require the pilot to circle to descend so as to cross the final approach fix at an altitude that would permit landing.

5-114d Note. — The principal purpose of this procedure is to ensure that frequency changes are made prior to passing the final approach fix. However, at times it will be desirable for ATC to retain an aircraft on the approach control frequency to provide a single-frequency approach or other radar service. When this occurs, it will be necessary for ATC to relay tower clearances or instructions to preclude changing frequencies prior to landing or approach termination.

5-114d(4) Note. — ARSR may be used for establishment of initial approach and intermediate approach fixes only. ASR must be used to establish the final approach fix.

5-114 Reference. — ATCH 5-123.

5-115 FINAL APPROACH DEVIATIONS

If deviations from the final approach course are observed after initial course interception, ATC will apply the following:

a. Outside the approach gate: The procedures in accordance with 5-114**a** above or, if necessary, vector the aircraft for another approach.

b. Inside the approach gate: Make an advisory to the pilot of the aircraft's position and ask intentions.

ATC Phraseology:

(Ident) (distance) **miles from the airport,** (number) **mile right/left of the course, say intentions.**

5-115 Reference. — ATCH 5-121.

5-116 APPROACH SEPARATION RESPONSIBILITY

a. The radar controller performing the approach control function is responsible for separation of radar arrivals unless visual separation is provided by the tower, or a letter of agreement/facility directive authorizes otherwise. Radar final controllers ensure that established separation is maintained between aircraft under their control and other aircraft established on the same final approach course.*

b. When timed approaches are being conducted, the radar controller will maintain the radar separation specified in 7-64 until the aircraft is observed to have passed the final approach fix inbound and is within 5 miles of the runway on the final approach course or until visual separation can be provided by the tower.

5-116a Note. — The radar controller may be a controller in an ARTCC, a terminal facility, or a tower when authorized to perform the approach control function in a terminal area.

5-116 Reference. — ATCH 5-124.

5-117 SIMULTANEOUS ILS/MLS APPROACHES

TERMINAL

a. When parallel runways are at least 4,300 feet apart, ATC may authorize simultaneous ILS, MLS, or ILS and MLS approaches to parallel runways if:

(1) Straight-in landings will be made.

(2) ILS, MLS, radar, and appropriate frequencies are operating normally.

b. Prior to aircraft departing an outer fix, controllers will inform aircraft that simultaneous ILS/MLS approaches are in use. This information may be provided through the ATIS.

c. On the initial vector, controllers will inform the aircraft of the ILS/MLS runway number and the localizer frequency or the MLS channel.

ATC Phraseology:

ILS Runway (runway number)(left/right). **Localizer frequency is** (frequency).

MLS Runway (runway number) **left/right. MLS Channel is** (channel).

5-117c Example. —

American Five Twenty-two, depart Santa Monica heading zero seven zero. I-L-S Two Four Right Localizer frequency is one zero eight point five.

d. ATC will clear the aircraft to descend to the appropriate glideslope/glidepath intercept altitude soon enough to provide a period of level flight to dissipate excess speed. At least 1 mile of straight flight will be provided prior to final approach course intercept.*

e. Controllers will vector the aircraft to intercept the final approach course at an angle not greater than 30 degrees.

f. A minimum of 1,000 feet vertical or a minimum of *3 miles* radar separation will be provided between aircraft during turn-on to parallel localizer courses. The minimum *applicable* radar separation will be provided between aircraft on the same localizer course.*

g. When assigning the final heading to intercept the final approach course, controllers will issue the following to the aircraft:

(1) *Position* from a fix on the localizer course or the MLS azimuth course.

(2) An *altitude* to maintain until established on the localizer course or the MLS azimuth course.

(3) *Clearance* for the appropriate ILS/MLS runway number approach.

ATC Phraseology:

Position (number) **miles from** (fix).

Turn (left/right) **heading** (degrees).

Maintain (altitude) **until established on the localizer.**

Cleared for ILS Runway (number) (left/right) **approach.**

Position (number) **miles from** (fix).

Turn (left/right) **heading** (degrees).

Maintain (altitude) **until established on the final approach course.**

Cleared for MLS Runway (number)(left/right) **approach.**

h. ATC will monitor the local control frequency for any aircraft transmission. Separate monitor controllers, each with transmit/receive and override capability on the tower frequency, will ensure aircraft do not penetrate the depicted NTZ ("no transgression zone"). An NTZ at least 2,000 feet wide is established equidistant between runway centerlines extended and is depicted on the monitor display. ATC will monitor all simultaneous approaches regardless of weather and ensure separation between aircraft. Facility directives will delineate responsibility for providing minimum applicable longitudinal separation between aircraft on the same localizer course.*

(1) When an aircraft is observed overshooting the turn on or continuing on a track which will penetrate the NTZ, the monitor controller will instruct (on the tower frequency, possibly overriding the tower controller's transmission) the aircraft to return to the correct localizer immediately.

ATC Phraseology:

You have crossed the final approach course. Turn (left/right) **immediately and return to localizer/azimuth course,**

or

Turn (left/right) **and return to localizer/azimuth course.**

(2) When an aircraft is observed penetrating the NTZ, the controller will instruct aircraft on the adjacent final approach to alter course to avoid the deviating aircraft.

ATC Phraseology:

Turn (left/right) **heading** (degrees) **immediately, climb and maintain** (altitude).

(3) Pilots are not expected to acknowledge those transmissions unless specifically requested to do so.

(4) ATC will terminate radar monitoring when one of the following occurs:

(a) Visual separation is applied.

(b) The aircraft reports the approach lights or runway in sight.

(c) The aircraft is 1 mile or less from the runway threshold, if procedurally required and contained in facility directives.

(5) Controllers will not inform the aircraft when radar monitoring is terminated.

i. When simultaneous ILS, MLS, or ILS and MLS approaches are being conducted to parallel runways, consideration will be given to known factors that may in any way affect the safety of the instrument approach phase of flight, such as surface wind direction and velocity, wind shear alerts/reports, severe weather activity, etc. Controllers closely monitor weather activity that could impact the final approach course. Weather conditions in the vicinity of the final approach course may dictate a change of approach in use.

5-117d Note. — Not applicable to curved and segmented MLS approaches.

5-117f Note. — Aircraft established on a final approach course are separated from aircraft established on an adjacent parallel final approach course provided neither aircraft penetrates the depicted NTZ.

5-117h Note. — The primary responsibility for navigation on the localizer rests with the pilot. Therefore, control instructions and information are issued only to ensure separation between aircraft and that aircraft do not penetrate the NTZ.

5-117 Reference. — ATCH 5-126.

5-118 PARALLEL ILS/MLS APPROACHES

a. A parallel approach differs from a simultaneous approach in that the minimum distance between parallel runway centerlines is reduced; there is no requirement for radar monitoring or advisories; and a staggered separation of aircraft on the adjacent localizer course is required.

b. When conducting parallel ILS, MLS, or ILS and MLS approaches ATC will:

(1) Provide a minimum of 1,000 feet vertical or a minimum of 3 miles radar separation between aircraft during turn-on.

(2) Provide a minimum of *3 miles* radar separation between aircraft on the same localizer course and/or azimuth course.

(3) Provide a minimum of *2 miles* radar separation between successive aircraft on adjacent localizer/azimuth courses when the following conditions are met:

(a) Runway centerlines are at least 2,500 feet apart.

(b) This separation standard is applied only after aircraft are established on the parallel final approach courses.

(c) Straight-in landings will be made.

(d) Missed approach procedures do not conflict.

(e) Aircraft are informed that approaches to both runways are in use. This information may be provided through the ATIS.

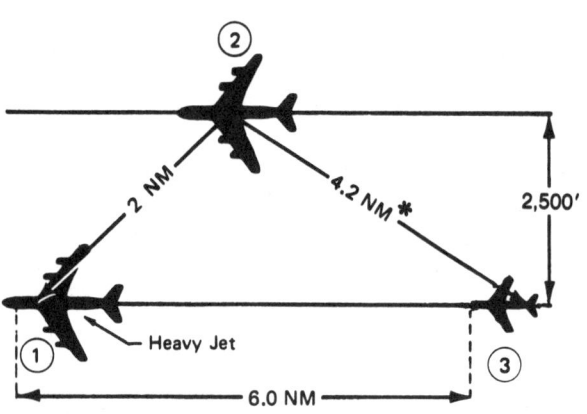

5-118b(3) Illustration 1

In this illustration, aircraft 2 is two miles from heavy aircraft 1. Aircraft 3 is a small aircraft and is six miles from aircraft 1. The resultant separation between aircraft 2 and 3 is 4.2 miles.

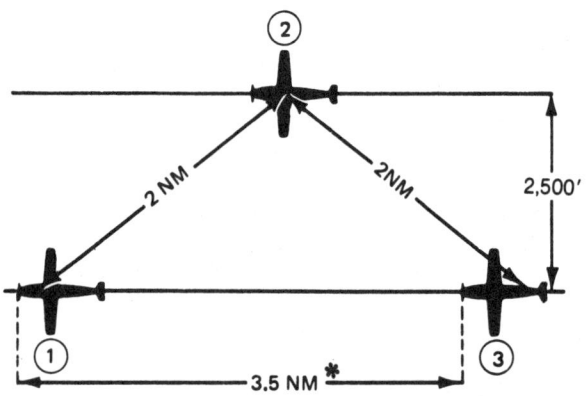

5-118b(3) Illustration 2

In this illustration, aircraft 2 is two miles from aircraft 1, and aircraft 3 is two miles from aircraft 2. The resultant separation between aircraft 1 and 3 is more than 3.5 miles.

c. Consideration may be given to known factors that may in any way affect the safety of the instrument approach phase of flight, such as surface wind direction and velocity, wind shear alerts/reports, severe weather activity, etc. Controllers closely monitor weather activity that could impact the final approach course. Weather conditions in the vicinity of the final approach course may dictate a change of approach in use.

5-118 References. — ATCH 5-125; AIM 376.

5-119 SIMULTANEOUS CONVERGING INSTRUMENT APPROACHES

a. ATC may conduct instrument approaches simultaneously to converging runways; i.e., runways having an included angle from 15 to 100 degrees, at airports where a program has been specifically approved to do so.

b. The basic concept requires that dedicated, separate standard instrument approach procedures be developed for each converging runway included. Missed approach points must be at least 3 miles apart and missed approach procedures ensure that missed approach protected airspace does not overlap.

c. Other requirements are: radar availability, nonintersecting final approach courses, precision (ILS/MLS) approach systems on each runway and, if runways intersect, controllers must be able to apply visual separation as well as intersecting runway separation criteria. Intersecting runways also require minimums of at least 700 and 2. Straight-in approaches and landings must be made.

d. Whenever simultaneous converging approaches are in progress, aircraft will be informed by the controller as soon as feasible after initial contact or via ATIS. Additionally, the radar controller will have direct communications capability with the tower controller where separation responsibility has not been delegated to the tower.

5-119 Reference. — AIM 377.

5-120 thru 5-129 RESERVED

Section 9. RADAR APPROACHES

5-130 GENERAL

A radar approach may be given to any aircraft upon request and may be offered to pilots of aircraft in distress, to expedite traffic, or assist in controller training. At times, a radar approach might not be approved unless there is an ATC operational requirement, or in an unusual or emergency situation. Acceptance of a radar approach by a pilot does not waive the prescribed weather minimums for the airport or for the particular aircraft operator concerned. The decision to make a radar approach when the reported weather is below the established minimums rests with the pilot.

5-130 Reference. — AIM 373.

5-131 RADIO EQUIPMENT REQUIRED

The only airborne radio equipment required for radar approaches is a functioning radio transmitter and receiver. The radar controller vectors the aircraft to align it with the runway centerline. The controller continues the vectors to keep the aircraft on course until the pilot can complete the approach and landing by visual reference to the surface.

5-131 Reference. — AIM 373.

5-132 SURVEILLANCE APPROACH

An ASR (surveillance approach) is one in which a controller provides navigational guidance in azimuth only. The pilot is furnished headings to fly to align his aircraft with the extended centerline of the landing runway. Since the radar information used for a surveillance approach is considerably less precise than that used for a precision approach, the accuracy of the approach will not be as great and higher minimums will apply. Guidance in elevation is not possible, but the pilot will be advised when to commence descent to the MDA (minimum descent altitude) or, if appropriate, to an intermediate step-down fix minimum crossing altitude and subsequently to the prescribed MDA. In addition, the pilot will be advised of the location of the MAP (missed approach point) prescribed for the procedure and his position each mile on final from the runway, airport, or heliport or MAP, as appropriate. If requested by the pilot, recommended altitudes will be issued at each mile, based on the descent gradient established for the procedure, down to the last mile that is at or above the MDA. Normally, navigational guidance will be provided until the aircraft reaches the MAP. Controllers will terminate guidance and instruct the pilot to execute a missed approach unless at the MAP the pilot has the runway, airport, or heliport in sight or, for a helicopter point-in-space approach, the prescribed visual reference with the surface is established. Also, if at any time during the approach the controller considers that safe guidance for the remainder of the approach can not be provided, he will terminate guidance and instruct the pilot to execute a missed approach. Similarly, guidance termination and missed approach will be effected upon pilot request and, for civil aircraft only, controllers may terminate guidance when the pilot reports the runway, airport/heliport, or visual surface route (point-in-space approach) in sight or otherwise indicates that continued guidance is not required. Radar service is automatically terminated at the completion of a radar approach.*

5-132 Note — The published MDA for straight-in approaches will be issued to the pilot before beginning descent. When a surveillance approach will terminate in a circle to land maneuver, the pilot must furnish the aircraft approach category to the controller. The controller will then provide the pilot with the appropriate MDA.

5-132 Reference. — AIM 373.

5-133 NO-GYRO APPROACH

A no-gyro approach is available to a pilot under radar control who experiences circumstances wherein his directional gyro or other stabilized compass is inoperative or inaccurate. When this occurs, he should advise ATC and request a no-gyro vector or approach. Pilots of aircraft not equipped with a directional gyro or other stabilized compass who desire radar handling may also request a no-gyro vector or approach. The pilot should make all turns at standard rate and should execute the turn immediately upon receipt of instructions.

5-133 Reference. — AIM 373.

5-134 RADAR APPROACH PROCEDURES

Radar approaches will be provided in accordance with standard or special instrument approach procedures.

5-134 Reference. — ATCH 5-130.

5-135 RADAR APPROACH INFORMATION

a. ATC will issue the following information to an aircraft that will conduct a radar approach. Current approach information contained in the ATIS broadcast may be omitted if the pilot states the appropriate ATIS broadcast code. All items listed below, except for (3), may be omitted after the first approach if repeated approaches are made and no change has occurred. Transmissions with aircraft in this phase of the approach should occur approximately every minute.

(1) Altimeter setting.

(2) Ceiling and visibility if ceiling at the airport of intended landing is reported below 1,000 feet or below the highest circling minimum, whichever is greater, or if the visibility is less than 3 miles.

(3) Any known changes classified as special weather observations. Special weather observations need not be issued after they are included in the ATIS broadcast and the pilot states the appropriate ATIS broadcast code.

(4) Pertinent information on known airport conditions if they are considered necessary to the safe operation of the aircraft concerned.

(5) Lost communication procedures as specified in 5-137.

b. Before starting final approach ATC will:*

(1) Inform the aircraft of the type of approach, runway, airport, heliport, or other point, as appropriate, to which the approach will be made. Controllers will specify the airport name when the approach is to a secondary airport.

ATC Phraseology:

This will be a surveillance approach to: Runway (runway number), *or* (airport name) **Airport, Runway** (runway number), *or* (airport name) **Airport/Heliport.**

(2) For surveillance approaches, specify the location of the MAP in relation to the runway/airport/heliport.

ATC Phraseology:

Missed approach point is (distance) **mile/s from Runway/Airport/Heliport,** *or, for a Point-In-Space Approach* **a missed approach point** (distance) **mile/s** (direction from landing area) **of** (airport name) **Airport/Heliport.**

5-135b(1) and (2) Example. —
Copter Two Two Zulu, this will be a surveillance approach to a missed approach point, three point five miles south of Creedon Heliport.

c. Controllers will inform an aircraft making an approach to an airport not served by a tower that no traffic or landing runway information is available for that airport.

ATC Phraseology:

No traffic or landing runway information available for the airport.

5-135b Note. — ASR approach procedures may be prescribed for specific runways, for an airport/heliport, and for helicopters only to a "point-in-space," i.e., a MAP from which a helicopter must be able to proceed to the landing area by visual reference to a prescribed surface route.

5-135 Reference. — ATCH 5-131.

5-136 NO-GYRO APPROACH PROCEDURES

When an aircraft will make a no-gyro surveillance approach controllers will:

a. Before issuing a vector, inform the aircraft of the type of approach.

ATC Phraseology:

This will be a no-gyro surveillance approach.

b. Instruct the aircraft when to start and stop turn.

ATC Phraseology:

Turn left/right. Stop turn.

c. After turn on to final approach has been made and prior to the aircraft reaching the approach gate, instruct the aircraft to make half-standard rate turns.

ATC Phraseology:

Make half-standard rate turns.

5-136 Reference. — ATCH 5-132.

5-137 LOST COMMUNICATIONS PROCEDURES

When weather reports indicate that an aircraft will likely encounter IFR weather conditions during the approach, controllers will take the following action as soon as possible after establishing radar identification and radio communications (may be omitted after the first approach when successive approaches are made and the instructions remain the same):*

a. If lost communications instructions will require the aircraft to fly on an unpublished route, the controller will issue an appropriate altitude to the pilot. If the lost communications instructions are the same for both pattern and final, the pattern/vector controller will issue both. Controllers will advise the pilot that if radio communications are lost for a specified time interval (not more than 1 minute) on vector to final approach, 15 seconds on a surveillance final approach, to:

(1) Attempt contact on a secondary or tower frequency.

(2) Proceed in accordance with visual flight rules, if possible.

(3) Proceed with an approved non-radar approach, or execute the specific lost communications procedure for the radar approach being used.

ATC Phraseology:

If no transmissions are received for (time interval) **in the pattern or fifteen seconds on final approach, attempt contact on** (frequency), **and**

if possibility exists,

Proceed VFR. If unable:

if approved,

Proceed with (non-radar approach), **maintain** (altitude) **until established on/over/fix/NAVAID/approach procedure,** *or* (alternative instructions).

b. If the final approach lost communications instructions are changed, differ from those for the pattern, or are not issued by the pattern controller, they will be issued by the final controller.

c. If the pilot states that he cannot accept a lost communications procedure due to weather conditions or other reasons, controllers will request the pilot's intention.*

5-137 Note. — Air traffic control facilities at U.S. Army and U.S. Air Force installations are not required to transmit lost communications instructions to military aircraft. All military facilities will issue specific lost communications instructions to civil aircraft when required.

5-137c Note. — The pilot is responsible for determining the adequacy of lost communications procedures with respect to aircraft performance, equipment capability, or reported weather.

5-137 Reference. — ATCH 5-133.

5-138 RADAR CONTACT LOST

If radar contact is lost during an approach and the aircraft has not started final approach, ATC will clear the aircraft to an appropriate NAVAID/fix for an instrument approach.

5-138 Reference. — ATCH 5-134.

5-139 APPROACH POSITION INFORMATION

Controllers will inform the aircraft of its position at least once before starting final approach.

ATC Phraseology:

(Number) **miles** (direction) **of airport,** *or*

Downwind/Base leg (number) **miles** (direction) **of airport.**

5-139 Reference. — ATCH 5-136.

5-140 ALTITUDE INFORMATION

Recommended altitudes will be provided on final approach if the pilot requests. If recommended altitudes are requested, ATC will inform the pilot that recommended altitudes which are at or above the published MDA will be given for each mile on final.

ATC Phraseology:

Recommended altitudes will be provided for each mile on final to minimum descent altitude/circling minimum descent altitude.

5-140 Reference. — ATCH 5-150.

5-141 VISUAL REFERENCE REPORT

Aircraft may be requested to report the runway, approach/runway lights, or airport in sight. Helicopters making a "point-in-space" approach may be requested to report when able to proceed to the landing area by visual reference to a prescribed surface route.

ATC Phraseology:

Report (runway, approach/runway lights, or airport) **in sight. Report when able to proceed visually to airport/heliport.**

5-141 Reference. — ATCH 5-151.

5-142 DESCENT NOTIFICATION

a. Controllers will issue advance notice of where descent will begin and issue the straight-in MDA prior to issuing final descent for the approaches.*

b. When it is determined that the surveillance approach will terminate in a circle-to-land maneuver, controllers will request the aircraft approach category from the pilot. After receiving the aircraft approach category, controllers will provide him with the applicable circling MDA prior to issuing final descent for the approach.*

ATC Phraseology:

Prepare to descend in (number) **mile/s.**

For straight-in approaches,

Published minimum descent altitude (altitude).

For circling approaches,

Request your aircraft approach category. (Upon receipt of aircraft approach category), **published circling minimum descent altitude** (altitude).

5-142a Note. — The point at which descent to the minimum descent altitude is authorized is the final approach fix unless an altitude limiting stepdown-fix is prescribed.

5-142b Note. — Pilots are normally expected to furnish the aircraft approach category to the controller when it is determined that the surveillance approach will terminate in a circle-to-land maneuver.

5-142 Reference. — ATCH 5-152.

5-143 DESCENT INSTRUCTIONS

When an aircraft reaches the descent point, ATC will issue one of the following, as appropriate:

a. Unless a descent restriction exists, controllers will advise the aircraft to descend to the MDA.

ATC Phraseology:

(Number) **miles from runway/airport/heliport. Descend to your minimum descent altitude.**

b. When a descent restriction exists, controllers will specify the prescribed restriction altitude. When the aircraft has passed the altitude limiting point, the controllers will advise the pilot to continue descent to MDA.

ATC Phraseology:

(Number) **miles from runway/airport/heliport. Descend and maintain** (restriction altitude). **Descend to your minimum descent altitude.**

5-143 Reference. — ATCH 5-153.

5-144 FINAL CONTROLLER CHANGEOVER

When instructing the aircraft to change frequency for final approach guidance, ATC will include the name of the facility.

ATC Phraseology:

Contact (name of facility) **final controller on** (frequency).

5-144 Reference. — ATCH 5-147.

5-145 COMMUNICATIONS CHECK

On initial contact with the final controller, the controller will ask the aircraft for a communications check.*

ATC Phraseology:

(Aircraft call sign), (name of facility) **final controller. How do you hear me?**

5-145 Note. — The controller may omit aircraft identification after initial callup when conducting the final portion of a radar approach.

5-145 Reference. — ATCH 5-138.

5-146 TRANSMISSION ACKNOWLEDGMENT

After contact has been established with the final controller and while on the final approach course, the controller will instruct the aircraft not to acknowledge further transmissions.

ATC Phraseology:

Do not acknowledge further transmissions.

5-146 Reference. — ATCH 5-139.

5-147 FINAL APPROACH GUIDANCE

a. Controllers will issue course guidance, inform the aircraft when it is on-course, and frequently inform the aircraft of any deviation from course. Transmissions with aircraft on surveillance final approach should occur approximately every 15 seconds.*

ATC Phraseology:

Heading (heading), **on-course,** or **slightly/well left/right of course.**

b. Controllers will issue trend information, as required, to indicate target position with respect to the extended runway centerline and to describe the target movement as appropriate corrections are issued. Trend information may be modified by the terms *RAPIDLY* and *SLOWLY,* as appropriate.

5-147b Examples. —

Going left of course.

Right of course and correcting.

c. Controllers will inform the aircraft of its distance from the runway, airport/heliport or MAP, as appropriate, each mile of final.

ATC Phraseology:

(Number) **mile/s from runway/airport/heliport** or **missed approach point.**

d. Recommended altitudes will be furnished, if requested, in accordance with 5-140, Altitude Information.

ATC Phraseology:

If requested, **altitude should be** (altitude).

5-147a Note. — Controllers will not key the radio transmitter continuously during radar approaches to preclude a lengthy communications block. The decision on how often transmitters are unkeyed is the controller's prerogative.

5-147 Reference. — ATCH 5-154.

5-148 APPROACH GUIDANCE TERMINATION

a. ATC will discontinue surveillance approach guidance when:

(1) Requested by the pilot.

(2) In the controller's opinion, continuation of a safe approach to the MAP is questionable.

(3) The aircraft is over the MAP.

b. Surveillance approach guidance may be discontinued when the pilot reports the runway or approach/runway lights in sight or, if a "point-in-space" approach, he reports able to proceed to the landing area by visual reference to a prescribed surface route.

c. When approach guidance is discontinued in accordance with **a** above and the aircraft has reported the runway or approach/runway lights in sight, the controller will advise the aircraft of its position and to proceed visually.

ATC Phraseology:

(Distance) **mile/s from runway/airport/heliport** or **over missed approach point.**

Proceed visually (additional instructions/clearance as required).

d. When approach guidance is discontinued in accordance with **a** above and the aircraft has not reported the runway or approach/runway lights in sight, the controller will advise the aircraft of its position and to execute a missed approach unless the runway or approach/runway lights are in sight or, if a "point-in-space" approach, unless able to proceed visually.*

ATC Phraseology:

(Distance) **mile/s from runway** or

Over missed approach point. If runway or

approach/runway lights not in sight, execute missed approach (missed approach instruction). (Additional instructions/clearance, as required.)

(Distance and direction) from airport/heliport/missed approach point.

If unable to proceed visually, execute missed approach. (Additional instructions/clearance, if required.)

5-148d Note. — Terminal Instrument Approach Procedures and Flight Inspection criteria require establishment of a MAP for each procedure, including the point to which satisfactory radar guidance can be provided.

5-148 Reference. — ATCH 5-155.

5-149 MISSED APPROACH

Before an aircraft starts final descent for a full stop landing and weather reports indicate that any portion of the final approach will be conducted in IFR conditions, ATC will issue a specific missed approach procedure approved for the radar approach being conducted.

ATC Phraseology:

Your missed approach procedure is (missed approach procedure).

5-149 Reference. — ATCH 5-141.

5-150 AFTER LOW APPROACH AND TOUCH-AND-GO DEPARTURE INFORMATION

Before an aircraft which plans to execute a low approach or touch-and-go begins final descent, ATC will issue appropriate departure instructions to be followed upon completion of the approach. Climb-out instructions must include a specific heading and altitude except when the aircraft will maintain VFR and contact the tower.*

ATC Phraseology:

After completing low approach/touch-and-go: climb and maintain (altitude). Turn (right or left) heading (degrees)/fly runway heading, or maintain VFR, contact tower, or (other instructions as appropriate).

5-150 Note. — This may be omitted after the first approach if instructions remain the same.

5-150 Reference. — ATCH 5-142.

5-151 RADAR APPROACH TOWER CLEARANCES

a. When an aircraft is on final approach to an airport served by a tower, ATC will obtain a clearance to land, touch-and-go, or make low approach and issue the clearance and the surface wind to the aircraft.

b. If the clearance is not obtained or is cancelled, ATC will inform the aircraft and issue alternative instructions.

ATC Phraseology:

Tower clearance cancelled/not received (alternative instructions).

5-151 Reference. — ATCH 5-143.

5-152 FINAL APPROACH ABNORMALITIES

ATC will instruct the aircraft, if runway environment is not in sight, to execute a missed approach if previously given; or climb to or maintain a specified altitude and fly a specified course whenever the completion of a safe approach is questionable because one or more of the following exists.

a. Safety limits are exceeded or radical target deviations are observed.

b. Position or identification of the aircraft is in doubt.

c. Radar contact is lost or a malfunctioning radar is suspected.*

d. Airport conditions or traffic preclude approach completion.

ATC Phraseology:

(Reason) if runway/approach lights/runway lights not in sight, execute missed approach/(alternative instructions).

and/or

Execute missed approach/(Alternative instructions). (Reason).

5-152 Examples. —

Radar contact lost.

Too far left for safe approach.

5-152c Note. — If the pilot requests, approval may be granted to proceed with the approach via ILS or other navigational aid/approach aid.

5-152 Reference. — ATCH 5-144.

TERMINAL AIRSPACE PROCEDURES

Chapter 6
TABLE OF CONTENTS

Section 1. TERMINAL AIRSPACE DESCRIPTIONS AND BASIC REGULATIONS

		Page
6-1	Airport Radar Service Area	6-1
6-2	ARSA Departures	6-1
6-3	ARSA Arrivals and Overflights	6-1
6-4	Satellite Airport Operations	6-1
6-5	ARSA Deviation	6-1
6-6	ARSA MODE C Requirement	6-1
6-7	Terminal Control Area	6-1
6-8	TCA Authorizations	6-1
6-9	TCA Communications and Navigation Equipment Requirements	6-2
6-10	TCA Transponder Requirement	6-2
6-11	Terminal Radar Service Area	6-2
6-12	Control Zones	6-2
6-13—6-19	Reserved	6-2

Section 2. TERMINAL RADAR PROGRAMS AND FLIGHT PROCEDURES

6-20	Terminal Radar Programs for VFR Aircraft	6-3
6-21	Pilot Responsibilities	6-3
6-22	Mandatory Participation	6-3
6-23	Basic Departure Procedures	6-3
6-24	Arrival Procedures	6-4
6-25	Change To Tower	6-5
6-26	Return To Approach Control	6-5
6-27	Service Provided When Tower Is Inoperative	6-5
6-28	Transiting Aircraft	6-5
6-29	Visual Holding of VFR Aircraft	6-5
6-30—6-39	Reserved	6-6

Section 3. AIRPORT RADAR SERVICE AREA PROCEDURES - ATC

6-40	Application	6-7
6-41	ARSA Services	6-7
6-42	Separation	6-7
6-43	Communications	6-7
6-44	Altitude Assignments	6-7
6-45	Separation Exceptions	6-7
6-46	Adjacent Airport Operations	6-7
6-47	Termination of Service	6-8
6-48—6-49	Reserved	6-8

TABLE OF CONTENTS (Continued)

Section 4. STAGE III PROCEDURES - ATC

		Page
6-50	Stage III Procedures	6-9
6-51	TCA Entry	6-9
6-52	TRSA Service Option	6-9
6-53	Issuance of EFC	6-9
6-54	Separation	6-9
6-55	Helicopter Traffic	6-9
6-56	Altitude Assignments	6-10
6-57	TCA/TRSA Exit Information	6-10
6-58—6-59	Reserved	6-10

Section 5. STAGE II PROCEDURES - ATC

6-60	General	6-11
6-61	Aircraft Sequencing	6-11
6-62—6-69	Reserved	6-11

Section 6. SPECIAL VFR

6-70	Special VFR Clearances	6-12
6-71	SVFR Authorization Conditions	6-12
6-72	IFR Aircraft Priority	6-12
6-73	SVFR Separation	6-13
6-74	SVFR Altitude Assignments	6-13
6-75	Local Special VFR	6-13
6-76	Climb to VFR Authorization	6-13
6-77	Ground Visibility Below One Mile	6-14
6-78	Flight Visibility Below One Mile	6-14
6-79	Special VFR Helicopter Separation	6-14
6-80	Local Helicopter SVFR Procedures	6-14

Chapter 6. TERMINAL AIRSPACE PROCEDURES

Section 1. TERMINAL AIRSPACE DESCRIPTIONS AND BASIC REGULATIONS

6-1 AIRPORT RADAR SERVICE AREA

a. An ARSA (Airport Radar Service Area) consists of controlled airspace within which all aircraft are subject to the operating rules and pilot and equipment requirements specified in FAR 91.88.

b. The basic standard ARSA design (with minor site specific variations) consists of two circles, both centered on the primary/ARSA airport.

(1) The *INNER CIRCLE* has a radius of 5 nautical miles and vertical dimensions which extend from the surface of the ARSA airport up to 4,000 feet above that airport.

(2) The *OUTER CIRCLE* has a radius of 10 nautical miles. The airspace between 5 and 10 nautical miles has a floor of 1,200 feet AGL and a ceiling of 4,000 feet above the airport elevation.

c. The *OUTER AREA,* in which pilot participation is voluntary, surrounds the ARSA. The outer area has a normal radius of 20 nautical miles (with some variations based on site specific requirements) and the vertical dimensions are dependent on the radar/radio coverage of the specific approach control.

d. In some locations, an ARSA may overlap the airport traffic area of a secondary airport. In order to allow that control tower to provide service to aircraft, portions of the overlapping ARSA may be procedurally excluded when the secondary airport tower is in operation.

6-1 References. — AIM 100, 101.

6-2 ARSA DEPARTURES

A pilot may operate an aircraft within an ARSA provided that two-way radio communications is maintained with ATC while in that area.

6-2 Reference. — FAR 91.88.

6-3 ARSA ARRIVALS AND OVERFLIGHTS

A pilot may operate an aircraft within an ARSA if two-way radio communications is established with ATC prior to entering the the ARSA and, thereafter, maintained with ATC while within that area.

6-3 Reference. — FAR 91.88.

6-4 SATELLITE AIRPORT OPERATIONS

a. A pilot may takeoff or land an aircraft at a satellite airport within an ARSA only in compliance with FAA arrival and departure traffic patterns.*

b. Aircraft departing a satellite airport must establish two-way radio communications as soon as practicable.

6-4a Note. — A satellite airport is any airport which lies within the *inner circle* of an ARSA.

6-4 Reference. — FAR 91.88.

6-5 ARSA DEVIATION

a. A pilot may deviate from any provision of FAR 91.88 under ATC authorization issued by the ATC facility having jurisdiction of the ARSA.

b. ATC may authorize a deviation on a continuing basis or for an individual flight, as appropriate.

6-5 Reference. — FAR 91.88.

6-6 ARSA MODE C REQUIREMENT

Effective December 30, 1990, all aircraft operating within an ARSA must be equipped with an operable transponder with MODE C.

6-6 Reference. — FAR 91.24.

6-7 TERMINAL CONTROL AREA

A TCA (Terminal Control Area) consists of controlled airspace extending upward from the surface or higher to specified altitudes, within which *ALL AIRCRAFT* are subject to the operating rules and pilot/equipment requirements specified in Part 91 of the FAR's. Each TCA location includes at least one primary airport around which the TCA is located. Descriptions of TCA's can be found in Part 71 of the FAR's.

6-7 Reference. — AIM 96.

6-8 TCA AUTHORIZATIONS

a. A pilot may operate an aircraft within a TCA only with an appropriate authorization from ATC prior to operation of that aircraft in that area.

b. Any person conducting pilot training at an airport within a TCA shall comply with any procedures established by ATC for such operations in the TCA.

6-8 Reference. — FAR 91.90.

6-9 TCA COMMUNICATIONS AND NAVIGATION EQUIPMENT REQUIREMENTS

a. All aircraft operating within a TCA must be equipped with an operable two-way radio capable of communications with ATC on appropriate frequencies for that TCA, unless otherwise authorized by ATC.

b. All aircraft operating within a TCA must be equipped with an operable VOR or TACAN receiver, unless otherwise authorized by ATC.

6-9 Reference. — FAR 91.90.

6-10 TCA TRANSPONDER REQUIREMENT

a. All aircraft operating in a TCA must be equipped with an operating transponder with MODE C (automatic altitude reporting capabilities) or a MODE S transponder.

b. All aircraft operating within 30 nautical miles of any designated TCA primary airport must be equipped with an operable MODE C transponder.

6-10 References. — FAR 91.90, 91.24.

6-11 TERMINAL RADAR SERVICE AREA

a. A TRSA (Terminal Radar Service Area) surrounds designated airports wherein ATC provides radar vectoring, sequencing, and separation for all IFR and participating VFR aircraft. Pilot participation in this program is urged but not mandatory.

b. There are no standard dimensions for a TRSA. The limits of a TRSA are site specific.

6-11 Reference. — AIM 100.

6-12 CONTROL ZONES

a. Control Zones are regulatory in nature and established as controlled airspace. They extend upward from the surface and terminate at the base of the Continental Control Area. Control Zones that do not underlie the Continental Control Area have no upper limit. A Control Zone is based on a primary airport, but may include one or more airports, and is normally a circular area within a radius of 5 statute miles around the primary airport, except that it may include extensions necessary to include instrument departure and arrival paths.

b. Two basic requirements for designating a Control Zone are communications and weather observation reporting.

(1) Communications capability with aircraft which normally operate within the Control Zone must exist down to the runway surface of the primary airport. Communications may be either direct from the ATC facility having jurisdiction over the Control Zone or by rapid relay through other communications facilities which are acceptable to that ATC facility.

(2) Federally certificated weather observers take hourly and special weather observations at the primary airport in the Control Zone during the time and dates a Control Zone is effective. The required weather observations must be forwarded expeditiously to the ATC facility having jurisdiction over the Control Zones.

6-12 Reference. — AIM 95.

6-13 thru 6-19 RESERVED

Section 2. TERMINAL RADAR PROGRAMS AND FLIGHT PROCEDURES

6-20 TERMINAL RADAR PROGRAMS FOR VFR AIRCRAFT

In addition to the use of radar for the control of IFR aircraft, all commissioned radar facilities provide traffic advisories and limited vectoring (on a workload permitting basis) to VFR aircraft. These services are categorized as follows:*

a. Stage II. Radar Advisories and Traffic Sequencing.

b. Stage III. Same as Stage II but includes ATC Separation between participating VFR aircraft and all IFR aircraft. Stage III service is provided within the airspace defined as a TCA (Terminal Control Area) or TRSA (Terminal Radar Service Area).

c. ARSA Service. Service includes standard IFR separation, IFR/VFR-traffic advisories and conflict resolution, and VFR/VFR-traffic advisories and, as appropriate, safety alerts.

6-20 Note 1. — When the Stage services were developed, two basic radar services (traffic advisories and limited vectoring) were identified as Stage I. This definition became, over the years, unnecessary. Therefore, the term Stage I has been eliminated.

6-20 Note 2. — Stage II, Stage III, and ARSA ATC services are outlined in detail in later sections of this chapter.

6-20 Reference. — AIM 165.

6-21 PILOT RESPONSIBILITIES

Terminal radar programs are not to be interpreted as relieving pilots of their responsibilities to see and avoid other traffic operating in basic VFR weather conditions, to adjust their operations and flight path as necessary to preclude serious wake encounters, to maintain appropriate terrain and obstruction clearance, or to remain in weather conditions equal to or better than the minimums required by FAR 91.105. Whenever compliance with an assigned route, heading, and/or altitude is likely to compromise pilot responsibility respecting terrain and obstruction clearance, vortex exposure, and weather minimums, approach control should be so advised and a revised clearance or instruction obtained.

6-21 Reference. — AIM 165.

6-22 MANDATORY PARTICIPATION

a. Pilot participation is mandatory within the airspace defined as an ARSA (Airport Radar Service Area) or a TCA (Terminal Control Area).

b. Pilot participation is urged but not mandatory in airspace defined as the *OUTER AREA* (associated with an ARSA) or TRSA (Terminal Radar Service Area).

6-22 Reference. — AIM 165.

6-23 BASIC DEPARTURE PROCEDURES

Pilots should use the following procedures to obtain authorization, clearance, or services as necessary at the departure airport.*

a. Monitor the ATIS for weather, runway, and airport information. The ATIS may include an advisory for aircraft to obtain a clearance prior to taxi.

6-23a Example. —

... All departures contact clearance delivery prior to taxi. VFR departures advise of initial heading and proposed altitude. Advise on initial contact you have information QUEBEC.

b. Contact ground control or clearance delivery, as appropriate, and provide the following:

(1) Full aircraft identification.

(2) Type aircraft, including appropriate equipment suffix.

(3) Initial heading or direction of flight.

(4) Proposed altitude.

(5) Any special information or request.

(6) ATIS code if appropriate.

6-23b Example. —

Daytona Clearance, Cessna Five Three Four Three Lima.

Cessna Five Three Four Three Lima, Daytona Clearance Delivery.

Cessna Four Three Lima is a Cessna One Seventy-two slant Uniform, request southbound departure heading one niner zero at four thousand five hundred. We have information QUEBEC.

Cessna Four Three Lima, roger. Stand by.

c. Ground control or clearance delivery may issue a departure frequency and transponder code and/or other information as necessary.

6-23c Example. —

Cessna Four Three Lima, Clearance.

Cessna Four Three Lima, go ahead.

Cessna Four Three Lima, departure frequency will be one one eight point eight five, squawk zero four two seven.

Cessna Four Three Lima, departure one one eight point eight five, squawk zero four two seven.

Cessna Four Three Lima, readback correct. Contact ground for taxi.

Cessna Four Three Lima, roger.

d. Shortly after takeoff, the tower may advise the aircraft to contact departure.

6-23d Example. —

Cessna Four Three Lima, contact departure.

Cessna Four Three Lima, good day.

e. On initial contact with departure control advise ATC of:

(1) Full aircraft identification.

(2) Altitude passing and altitude climbing to.

f. Departure control will establish identification and may assign headings, altitudes, traffic advisories, and/or other advisories as necessary.

6-23e and f Example. —

Daytona Departure, Cessna Five Three Four Three Lima leaving eight hundred climbing to four thousand five hundred.

Cessna Five Three Four Three Lima, Daytona Departure, radar contact, fly present heading, maintain two thousand five hundred. Traffic one o'clock, three miles, level three thousand, a Beech Bonanza. Report that traffic in sight.

Cessna Four Three Lima, present heading, maintain two thousand five hundred. Traffic in sight.

Cessna Four Three Lima, maintain visual separation from that traffic; climb to four thousand five hundred approved.

Climbing to four thousand five hundred, we will maintain visual separation from that traffic, Cessna Four Three Lima.

g. ATC will normally advise VFR aircraft when leaving the geographical limits of the terminal airspace. Radar services are not automatically terminated with this advisory unless specifically stated by the controller.

6-23g Examples. —

Cessna Four Three Lima, leaving the ARSA, radar service terminated, squawk one two zero zero, frequency change approved.

Cessna Four Three Lima, leaving the ARSA. Remain on your present code for further advisories southbound.

6-23 Note. — Local procedures may dictate the use/need of procedures not described in this paragraph. Local procedures may be covered in letters of agreement, facility directives, and/or take the form of a memorandum issued by the specific ATC facilities. These local procedures may be addressed to the local aviation community as necessary.

6-23 References. — ATCH 7-79; AIM 97, 165.

6-24 ARRIVAL PROCEDURES

a. Prior to contacting approach control, pilots should monitor the ATIS for the airport of intended landing for weather, runway information, and special arrival instructions for arriving aircraft.*

6-24a Examples. —

... All inbound V-F-R aircraft contact Approach Control for sequencing to the airport.

... V-F-R arrivals from the East, contact Approach Control one two five point five. V-F-R arrivals from the West, contact Approach Control one two four point seven. Advise on initial contact you have information LIMA.

b. Generally, ATC radar coverage extends well beyond the boundaries of designated terminal airspace. Therefore, pilots should contact approach control on the appropriate publicized frequency well prior to entering terminal airspace. Initial contact should be brief (facility name and aircraft identification) in order to allow time for the controller (who may be working another aircraft) to acknowledge the pilot on frequency. After initial contact, provide the following:

(1) Type aircraft, including appropriate equipment suffix.

(2) Location, referenced by distance and direction from a prominent geographical location, airport, or NAVAID.

(3) Altitude.

(4) Request and special information, if necessary.

(5) ATIS code for the airport of intended landing, if appropriate.

c. ATC may issue a transponder code. Once communication and/or radar identification is established, ATC may issue the following information as appropriate:

(1) Radar observed location in reference to a prominent geographical location, airport, or NAVAID.

(2) Navigation information which may include headings, geographical fixes, NAVAID's, etc.

(3) Altitude restrictions.

(4) Traffic pattern instructions (i.e., left/right base, straight-in).

(5) Runway assignment.

(6) Traffic advisories.

(7) Traffic information for sequencing to the airport.

(8) Wake turbulence advisories.

(9) Instructions to maintain visual separation.

(10) Time, location, and frequency to contact local control or advisory frequency.

6-24 b and c Example. —

Lakeville Approach, Twin Cessna Three One Zero Romeo.

Twin Cessna Three One Zero Romeo, Lakeville Approach.

Twin Cessna Three One Zero Romeo is a Cessna Three Ten slant Alpha over Lake Charles at six thousand five hundred V-F-R, landing Lakeville with BRAVO.

Twin Cessna One Zero Romeo, roger. Squawk zero three one two.

Twin Cessna One Zero Romeo, radar contact two five miles west of Lakeville. Proceed southeastbound to the power plant for left base entry Runway Three. Do not descend below three thousand until further advised.

Roger. At or above three thousand to the power plant for Runway Three, Twin Cessna One Zero Romeo.

Twin Cessna One Zero Romeo, traffic a Boeing Seven Twenty-seven on a four mile final just inside the power plant for Runway Three. Report that traffic in sight.

Twin Cessna One Zero Romeo, looking.

Twin Cessna One Zero Romeo has the Seven Twenty-seven in sight.

Twin Cessna One Zero Romeo, roger. Cancel the altitude restriction; follow the Boeing Seven Twenty-seven on final to Runway Three, caution wake turbulence. Contact tower one one niner point eight.

Roger, we will follow the Seven Twenty-seven for Runway Three, tower one one niner point eight, Twin Cessna One Zero Romeo.

6-24a Note. — Local procedures may dictate the use/need of procedures not described in this paragraph. Local procedures may be covered in letters of agreement, facility directives, and/or take the form of a memorandum issued by the specific ATC facilities. These local procedures may be addressed to the local aviation community as necessary.

6-24 References. — AIM 97, 165.

6-25 CHANGE TO TOWER

Approach control will instruct the pilot to contact the tower and inform the local controller of the aircraft's position. If, however, the local controller sights the aircraft before approach control takes the action specified above, the controller will instruct the aircraft to change to local control frequency if space is available in the landing sequence.*

6-25 Example. —

Lakeville Tower, Twin Cessna Three One Zero Romeo turning final over the power plant.

Twin Cessna Three One Zero Romeo, Lakeville Tower, follow the Boeing Seven Twenty-seven over the approach lights, cleared to land Runway Three. Caution wake turbulence, wind zero four zero at eight.

Cleared to land Runway Three, Cessna One Zero Romeo.

6-25 Note 1. — The point at which an aircraft is instructed to contact the tower is determined by prior coordination between the tower controller and the approach controller and will vary, depending on the runway in use, weather, etc. Ordinarily, the changeover occurs at least 5 miles from the runway. Changeover points must be far enough from the airport so that the tower controller can sequence the aircraft properly, but not at a distance that could derogate the provision of radar traffic information service.

6-25 Note 2. — When radar service is terminated prior to the tower frequency change, pilots should use full initial contact procedures when establishing communications with the tower.

6-25 Note 2 Example. —

Saratoga One Zero Golf, seven miles north of Metro, radar service terminated, squawk one two zero zero. Contact Metro Tower one one niner point three.

Roger, one two zero zero and Metro Tower one one niner point three, Saratoga One Zero Golf. Good day.

Metro Tower, Saratoga Two One One Zero Golf, six miles north with information ZULU.

Saratoga Two One One Zero Golf, Metro Tower. Make straight-in Runway One Eight. Report abeam the reservoir.

Saratoga One Zero Golf, roger.

6-25 Reference. — ATCH 7-77.

6-26 RETURN TO APPROACH CONTROL

When an aircraft, under tower control, abandons (i.e., go-around) the approach and coordination with approach control reveals no immediate space in the approach sequence, the tower will instruct the aircraft to change to approach control for sequencing.

6-26 Reference. — ATCH 7-78.

6-27 SERVICE PROVIDED WHEN TOWER IS INOPERATIVE

a. Approach control will provide the following services during hours when the tower is not in operation:

(1) Wind direction and velocity.

(2) Traffic information.

(3) Aircraft will be informed when radar service is terminated.

b. Approach control will not assign landing sequence.

6-27 Reference. — ATCH 7-80.

6-28 TRANSITING AIRCRAFT

a. Aircraft not landing or departing a primary or satellite airport may obtain ATC authorization to transit the area when traffic conditions permit and the TCA and transponder requirements of FAR 91.90 and FAR 91.24 are met as appropriate.

b. Transiting aircraft are encouraged, to the extent possible, to operate at altitudes above or below the designated terminal airspace or transit through established VFR corridors.*

6-28b Note. — Pilots operating in VFR corridors are urged to use frequency 122.75 MHz for the exchange of aircraft position information.

6-28 Reference. — AIM 97.

6-29 VISUAL HOLDING OF VFR AIRCRAFT

TERMINAL

When it becomes necessary for ATC to hold VFR aircraft, ATC will take the following actions:

a. Controllers will clear aircraft to hold at selected, prominent geographical fixes which can be easily recognized from the air, usually those depicted on sectional and VFR terminal area charts.

ATC Phraseology:

Hold at (location) **until** (time or other condition).

b. Traffic information will be issued to aircraft cleared to hold at the same fix.

Para. 6-30.

ATC Phraseology:
Traffic (description) **holding at** (fix, altitude if known),
or
Proceeding to (fix) **from** (direction or fix).

6-29 Reference. — ATCH 7-4.

6-30 thru 6-39 RESERVED

Section 3. AIRPORT RADAR SERVICE AREA PROCEDURES — ATC

6-40 APPLICATION

ATC will apply ARSA procedures within the designated Airport Radar Service Area and the associated outer area. The ARSA program is designed to keep ATC informed of all aircraft within the ARSA airspace, not to exclude operations. Two way radio communications are normally required for operations within an ARSA, but operations without radio communications can be conducted by letter of agreement, facility directive, or special arrangement with the ARSA controlling facility.

6-40 Reference. — ATCH 7-100.

6-41 ARSA SERVICES

a. ARSA services include the following:

(1) Sequencing of all aircraft to the primary airport.

(2) Standard IFR services to IFR aircraft.

(3) Separation, traffic advisories, and safety alerts between IFR and VFR aircraft.

(4) Mandatory traffic advisories and safety alerts between VFR aircraft.

b. ARSA services to all aircraft operating within the ARSA.

c. ARSA services to all participating aircraft in the outer area unless the pilot requests otherwise.

d. Aircraft will not normally be held. However, if holding is necessary, controllers will inform the pilot of the expected length of delay.

e. When a radar outage occurs, controllers will advise aircraft that ARSA services are not available and, if appropriate, when to contact the tower.

6-41 Reference. — ATCH 7-101.

6-42 SEPARATION

ATC will separate VFR aircraft from IFR aircraft by any one of the following:

a. Visual separation.

b. *500 feet* vertical separation; except when operating below heavy jets, ATC will apply the appropriate wake turbulence separation.

c. Conflict resolution when using broadband radar systems; except when operating behind heavy jets, ATC will apply the same. The application of conflict resolution at locations not using broadband radar will be individually approved by the Air Traffic Operations Service.

6-42 Reference. — ATCH 7-102.

6-43 COMMUNICATIONS

The ARSA program requires pilots to establish two-way radio communications before entering the ARSA. If the controller responds to a radio call with *"(a/c callsign) standby,"* radio communications have been established and the pilot can enter the ARSA. If workload or traffic conditions prevent immediate provision of ARSA services, the controller will inform the pilot to *"remain outside the ARSA"* until conditions permit the services to be provided.

ATC Phraseology:

(a/c callsign) **remain outside the ARSA and standby.**

6-43 Reference. — ATCH 7-103.

6-44 ALTITUDE ASSIGNMENTS

a. When necessary to assign altitudes to VFR aircraft, ATC will assign altitudes that meet the minimum vectoring altitude, minimum safe altitude, or minimum IFR altitude criteria.

b. When necessary for ATC to assign altitudes contrary to FAR 91.109, controllers will advise the aircraft to resume altitudes appropriate for the direction of flight when the altitude is no longer needed for separation, when leaving the outer area, or when terminating ARSA service.

ATC Phraseology:

Resume appropriate VFR altitudes.

6-44 Example. —

Grumman Three Seven Eight, traffic no longer a factor. Resume appropriate V-F-R altitudes.

Roger, Grumman Three Seven Eight. We will be climbing to five thousand five hundred.

6-44 Reference. — ATCH 7-104.

6-45 SEPARATION EXCEPTIONS

a. VFR helicopters need not be separated from IFR helicopters. Traffic information and safety alerts will be issued as appropriate.

b. Hot air balloons need not be separated from IFR aircraft. Traffic information and safety alerts will be issued as appropriate.

6-45 Reference. — ATCH 7-105.

6-46 ADJACENT AIRPORT OPERATIONS

a. Aircraft that will penetrate the ARSA after departing controlled airports within or adjacent to the ARSA will be provided the same services as those aircraft departing the primary airport. Procedures for handling this situation will be covered in a letter of agreement or a facility directive as appropriate.

b. Aircraft departing uncontrolled airports within the ARSA will be handled using procedures advertised in a letter to airmen.

6-46 Reference. — ATCH 7-106.

6-47 TERMINATION OF SERVICE

Unless aircraft are landing at secondary airports or have requested termination of service while in the outer area, ATC will provide services until the aircraft departs the associated outer area. ATC will terminate ARSA service to aircraft landing at other than the primary airport at a sufficient distance from the airport to allow the pilot to change to the appropriate frequency for traffic and airport information.

ATC Phraseology:

Change to advisory frequency approved,

or

Contact (facility identification).

6-47 Examples. —

Cherokee Five Niner X-ray, six miles north of Bradley, radar service terminated, squawk one two zero zero. Change to advisory frequency approved.

Cherokee Five Niner X-ray, roger. Squawk one two zero zero, good day.

Lifeguard Two Lima Foxtrot, five miles southeast of Van Nuys, radar service terminated, squawk one two zero zero, contact Van Nuys Tower.

6-47 Reference. — ATCH 7-107.

6-48 and 6-49 RESERVED

Section 4. STAGE III PROCEDURES - ATC

6-50 STAGE III PROCEDURES

In addition to the basic services described in this chapter and the Stage II services, ATC will apply Stage III procedures within the designated Terminal Control Area (TCA) or Terminal Radar Service Area (TRSA).

6-50 Reference. — ATCH 7-90.

6-51 TCA ENTRY

a. To the extent practical, ATC will clear large turbine engine-powered aircraft to/from the primary airport using altitudes and routes that avoid VFR corridors and airspace below the TCA floor where VFR aircraft are operating.

b. Workload and traffic conditions permitting, ATC will approve/deny requests from VFR aircraft to operate in TCA's.

6-51b Examples. —

Approved as requested. (Additional instructions, as necessary.)

Climb through T-C-A approved. Report leaving seven thousand.

Remain outside the T-C-A. (When necessary, reason and/or additional instructions.)

6-51 Reference. — ATCH 7-97.

6-52 TRSA SERVICE OPTION

Pilots are assumed to want Stage III services on initial contact with ATC. If a pilot does not wish Stage III service within a TRSA, the pilot should state *"negative Stage III"* or make a similar comment on initial contact with approach control or ground control as appropriate.

6-52 Reference. — AIM 165.

6-53 ISSUANCE OF EFC

When VFR aircraft are held either inside or outside the TCA/TRSA, ATC will inform the pilot when to expect further clearance (EFC).

6-53 Reference. — ATCH 7-91.

6-54 SEPARATION

Any of the following may be applied within a TCA/TRSA:*

a. Visual separation.

b. *500 feet* vertical separation between VFR aircraft and between a VFR and an IFR aircraft.*

c. Within 15 miles of the radar antenna, controllers will separate helicopters and Category I and II VFR aircraft from:*

(1) Other Category I or II VFR/IFR aircraft by a minimum of *1½ miles.*

(2) Category III VFR/IFR by *1½ miles* only when both aircraft are on parallel courses.

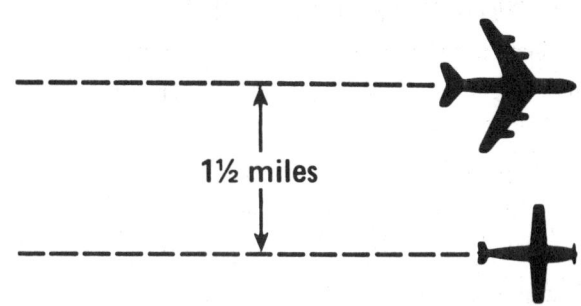

6-54c(2) Illustration 1

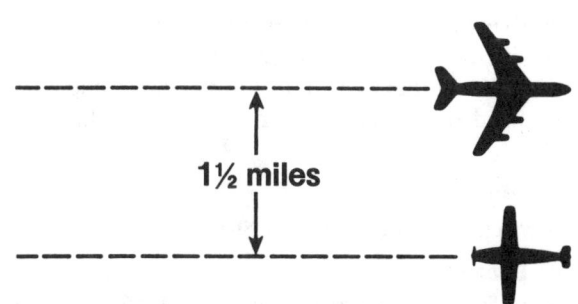

6-54c(2) Illustration 2

d. Within 1 mile of the runway end, *½ mile* lateral separation between a helicopter and a fixed-wing aircraft/IFR helicopter on a straight-in approach or a straight-out departure.*

6-54 Note 1. — Assignment of radar headings, routes, or altitudes is based on the provision that a pilot operating in accordance with VFR is expected to advise ATC if compliance will cause him to violate any FAR's.

6-54 Note 2. — Stage III separation and sequencing for VFR aircraft is dependent upon radar. When a radar outage occurs, efforts will be made to segregate VFR traffic from the IFR traffic flow.

6-54b Note. — *500 feet* vertical separation may not be applied below a heavy jet.

6-54c Note. — This procedure DOES NOT apply between IFR aircraft.

6-54d Note. — This procedure applies when either of the two aircraft being separated is within 1 mile of the runway end.

6-54 Reference. — ATCH 7-92.

6-55 HELICOPTER TRAFFIC

Helicopters need not be separated from other helicopters. Traffic information will be exchanged, as necessary.

6-55 Reference. — ATCH 7-93.

6-56 ALTITUDE ASSIGNMENTS

a. Pilots must maintain an altitude when assigned by ATC unless the altitude assignment is to maintain an altitude at or below a specified altitude.

b. When not assigned an altitude, the pilot should coordinate with ATC prior to any altitude change.

c. Altitude information contained in a clearance, instruction, or advisory to VFR aircraft must meet MVA, minimum safe altitude, or minimum IFR altitude criteria.

d. If required, ATC will issue altitude assignments consistent with the provisions of FAR 91.79, minimum safe altitudes.*

e. When necessary to assign an altitude for separation purposes to VFR aircraft contrary to FAR 91.109, controllers will advise the aircraft to resume altitudes appropriate for the direction of flight when the altitude assignment is no longer needed for separation or when leaving the TCA or TRSA.

ATC Phraseology:

Resume appropriate VFR altitudes.

6-56e Example. —

Centurion Seven Two Yankee, leaving the T-C-A to the east, resume appropriate V-F-R altitudes.
Centurion Seven Two Yankee, roger. I am climbing to one one thousand five hundred.

6-56d Note. — The minimum safe altitudes are (1) over congested areas, an altitude at least 1,000 feet above the highest obstacle, and (2) over other than congested areas, an altitude at least 500 feet above the surface.

6-56 Reference. — ATCH 7-94.

6-57 TCA/TRSA EXIT INFORMATION

a. ATC will provide separation until the aircraft leaves the TCA/TRSA.

b. Controllers will inform VFR participating aircraft when leaving the TCA/TRSA.

ATC Phraseology:

Leaving the (name) **TCA/TRSA,**

and, as appropriate,

resume own navigation,

stand by for traffic advisories,

radar service terminated,

squawk one two zero zero.

Other instructions as appropriate.

6-57b Example. —

Centurion Seven Two Yankee, leaving the T-C-A, resume own navigation, radar service terminated, squawk one two zero zero, frequency change approved.

Centurion Seven Two Yankee, roger. One two zero zero, good day.

6-57 Reference. — ATCH 7-96.

6-58 and 6-59 RESERVED

Section 5. STAGE II PROCEDURES - ATC

6-60 GENERAL

a. Stage II service has been implemented at certain terminal locations. (See locations listed in the Airport/Facility Directory.) The purpose of the service is to adjust the flow of arriving VFR and IFR aircraft into the traffic pattern in a safe and orderly manner and to provide radar traffic information to departing VFR aircraft. Pilot participation is urged but not mandatory.

b. Pilots of arriving VFR aircraft should initiate radio contact on the publicized frequency with approach control when approximately 25 miles from the airport at which Stage II services are being provided. On initial contact by VFR aircraft, approach control will assume that Stage II service is requested. ATC will provide vectors and traffic information as necessary for proper sequencing with other participating VFR and IFR traffic en route to the airport. Traffic information will be provided on a workload permitting basis. If an arriving aircraft does not want the service, the pilot should state *"negative Stage II"* or make a similar comment, on initial contact with approach control.

c. Standard radar separation will be provided between IFR aircraft until such time as the aircraft is sequenced and the pilot sees the traffic he is to follow. Standard radar separation between VFR or between VFR and IFR aircraft will not be provided.

6-60 Reference. — AIM 165.

6-61 AIRCRAFT SEQUENCING

a. After radar contact is established, VFR aircraft will be instructed to enter the traffic pattern at a specified point or be vectored to a position in the approach sequence and the controller will inform the pilot of the aircraft he is to follow. If the integrity of the approach sequence depends upon visual contact with a preceding aircraft, the controller will ensure that visual contact is established and that instructions to follow the aircraft are issued.

ATC Phraseology:

Follow (description) (position, if necessary).

6-61a Example. —

Twin Cessna One Zero Romeo, follow the Boeing Seven Twenty-seven on a three mile final, caution wake turbulence.

b. Controllers may direct a VFR aircraft to a point near the airport and instruct it to hold until it is positioned in the approach sequence for the runway in use; or, after coordination with the tower, controllers may vector it to another runway.

6-61 Reference. — ATCH 7-76.

6-62 thru 6-69 RESERVED

Section 6. SPECIAL VFR

6-70 SPECIAL VFR CLEARANCES

a. An ATC clearance must be obtained *prior* to operating within a control zone when the weather is less than that required for VFR flight. A VFR pilot may request and be given clearance to enter, leave, or operate within most control zones in Special VFR (SVFR) conditions, traffic permitting, and providing such flight will not delay IFR operations. All Special VFR flights must remain clear of clouds. The visibility requirements for Special VFR fixed-wing aircraft are:

(1) One mile flight visibility for operations within the control zone.

(2) One mile ground visibility if taking off or landing.

b. When a control tower is located within the control zone, requests for clearances should be to the tower. If no tower is located within the control zone, a clearance may be obtained from the nearest tower, FSS, or center.

c. It is not necessary to file a complete flight plan with the request for clearance, but the pilot should state his intentions in sufficient detail to permit ATC to fit his flight into the traffic flow. The clearance will not contain a specific altitude as the pilot must remain clear of clouds. The controller may require the pilot to fly at or below a certain altitude due to other traffic, but the altitude specified will permit flight at or above the minimum safe altitude. In addition, at radar locations, flights may be vectored if necessary for control purposes or on pilot request.*

d. Special VFR clearances are effective within control zones only. ATC does not provide separation after an aircraft leaves the control zone on a special VFR clearance.

e. Special VFR operations by fixed-wing aircraft are prohibited in some control zones due to the volume of IFR traffic. A list of these control zones is contained in FAR 93.113. They are also depicted on Sectional Aeronautical Charts.

f. ATC provides separation between special VFR flights and between these flights and other IFR flights.

g. Special VFR operations by fixed-wing aircraft are prohibited between sunset and sunrise unless the pilot is instrument rated and the aircraft is equipped for IFR flight.

6-70c Note. — The pilot is responsible for obstacle or terrain clearance (FAR 91.79).

6-70 Reference. — AIM 264.

6-71 SVFR AUTHORIZATION CONDITIONS

a. SVFR operations in weather conditions less than basic VFR minima are authorized:

(1) At any location not prohibited by FAR 93.113 or when an exemption to FAR 93.113 has been granted and an associated Letter of Agreement established.

(2) Only within control zones.

(3) Only when requested by the pilot.

(4) On the basis of weather conditions reported at the airport of intended landing/departure.

(5) When weather conditions are not reported at the airport of intended landing/departure and the pilot advises he is unable to maintain VFR and requests Special VFR.

ATC Phraseology:

Cleared to enter/out of/through Control Zone, *and, if required,* (direction) **of** (airport name) **Airport** (specified routing), *and* **maintain Special VFR conditions while in Control Zone;**

or, as applicable for operation under an exemption from FAR 93.113:

Cleared for (coded arrival or departure procedure) **arrival/departure** (additional instructions as required).

6-71a Example. —
Cleared for the Long Bridge Five Arrival. Maintain Special V-F-R at or below one thousand five hundred.

b. When the primary airport is reporting VFR, Special VFR operations may be authorized for aircraft transiting the control zone when the pilot advises that he is unable to maintain basic VFR.*

6-71b Note. — The basic requirements for issuance of a SVFR clearance in **a** apply with the obvious exception that weather conditions at the controlling airport are not required to be less than basic VFR minima.

6-71 Reference. — ATCH 7-40.

6-72 IFR AIRCRAFT PRIORITY

a. Fixed-wing (FW)/SVFR flights may be approved only if arriving and departing IFR aircraft are not delayed.*

6-72a Example 1. —
A FW/SVFR aircraft has been cleared to enter the control zone and subsequently an IFR aircraft is ready to depart or is in position to begin an approach. Less overall delay might accrue to the IFR aircraft if the FW/SVFR aircraft is allowed to proceed to the airport and land, rather than leave the control zone or be repositioned to provide IFR priority.

6-72a Example 2. —

A FW/SVFR aircraft is number one for takeoff and located in such a position that the number two aircraft, an IFR flight, cannot taxi past to gain access to the runway. Less overall delay might accrue to the IFR aircraft by releasing the FW/SVFR departure rather than by having the aircraft taxi down the runway to a turnoff point so the IFR aircraft could be released first.

b. When clearance cannot be granted for a FW/SVFR flight because of IFR traffic, the controller will inform the aircraft of the anticipated delay. EFC or expected departure time will not be issued.

ATC Phraseology:

Expect (number) **minutes delay** (additional instructions as necessary).

6-72a Note. — The priority afforded IFR aircraft over FW/SVFR aircraft is not intended to be so rigidly applied that it causes grossly inefficient use of airspace. If better overall efficiency will be gained thereby, the controller has the prerogative of allowing completion of the FW/SVFR operation already in progress when an IFR aircraft becomes a factor.

6-72 Reference. — ATCH 7-41.

6-73 SVFR SEPARATION

ATC will apply approved separation between:

a. Special VFR aircraft.

b. Special VFR aircraft and IFR aircraft.

c. Visual separation is the only separation standard which a nonapproach control tower may use to separate SVFR aircraft. This may be applied by a controller providing the separation or by a pilot seeing another aircraft and agreeing to maintain separation from it. Nonapproach control towers may be authorized to provide visual separation between aircraft within a control zone provided other separation is assured before and after the application of visual separation. Visual separation may be authorized between:

(1) An arriving and a departing aircraft when the tower has the arrival in sight.

(2) A departure and a departure when weather is at or above VFR minima.

(3) An arrival and an arrival provided the tower has both aircraft in sight and visual separation can be applied.

(4) Multiple SVFR operations which are conducted solely within the airport traffic pattern.

(5) Successive same direction SVFR departures which are departing the control zone provided the suceeding pilot sees the first departure and agrees to maintain separation from it.

6-73 References. — ATCH 7-10, 7-42.

6-74 SVFR ALTITUDE ASSIGNMENTS

ATC will not assign a fixed altitude when applying vertical separation, but clear the Special VFR aircraft at or below an altitude which is at least 500 feet below any conflicting IFR traffic but not below the minimum safe altitude prescribed in FAR 91.79.*

ATC Phraseology:

Maintain Special VFR conditions at or below (altitude).

6-74 Note 1. — Special VFR aircraft are not assigned fixed altitudes because of the clearance from clouds requirement.

6-74 Note 2. — The minimum safe altitudes are (1) over congested areas, an altitude at least 1,000 feet above the highest obstacle, and (2) over other than congested areas, an altitude at least 500 feet above the surface.

6-74 Reference. — ATCH 7-43.

6-75 LOCAL SPECIAL VFR

a. Local Special VFR operations will be authorized for a specified period (series of landings and takeoffs, etc.) upon request if the aircraft can be recalled when traffic or weather conditions require. Where warranted, letters of agreement may be consummated.

ATC Phraseology:

Local Special VFR operations in the immediate vicinity of (airport name) **airport are authorized until** (time).

Maintain Special VFR conditions.

b. Control facilities may also authorize an FSS to transmit SVFR clearances so that only one aircraft at a time operates in the control zone unless pilots agree that they will maintain visual separation with other aircraft operating in the control zone. Such authorization concerning visual separation by pilots shall be contained in a letter of agreement between the control facility and the FSS.

6-75 Reference. — ATCH 7-44.

6-76 CLIMB TO VFR AUTHORIZATION

Aircraft will be authorized to climb to VFR upon request if the only weather limitation is restricted visibility.

ATC Phraseology:

Climb to VFR within the control zone/within (a specified distance within Control Zone) **miles from** (airport name) **airport, maintain Special VFR conditions until reaching VFR.**

6-76 Reference. — ATCH 7-45.

6-77 GROUND VISIBILITY BELOW ONE MILE

When the ground visibility is officially reported at an airport at less than 1 mile, ATC will treat requests for Special VFR operations at that airport by other than helicopters as follows:*

a. By informing departing aircraft that ground visibility is less than 1 mile and that a clearance cannot be issued.

b. By informing arriving aircraft, operating outside of the control zone, that ground visibility is less than 1 mile and that, unless an emergency exists, a clearance cannot be issued.

c. By informing arriving aircraft, operating within the control zone, that ground visibility is less than 1 mile, and ask if the aircraft can depart the control zone with a flight visibility of at least 1 mile. If the reply is "affirmative," controllers will issue a clearance out of the control zone. If the reply is "negative," or an emergency exists, controllers will issue a clearance as soon as traffic conditions permit.

d. By authorizing scheduled air carrier aircraft in the United States to conduct operations if ground visibility is not less than ½ statute mile.*

e. By clearing an aircraft to fly through the control zone if he reports flight visibility is at least 1 statute mile.

6-77 Note. — FAR 91 does not prohibit helicopter Special VFR flights when visibility is less than 1 mile.

6-77d Note. — FAR 121 permits landing or takeoff by domestic scheduled air carriers where a local surface restriction to visibility is not less than ½ statute mile, provided all turns after takeoff or before landing and all flights beyond 1 statute mile from the airport boundary can be accomplished above or outside the area so restricted. The pilot is solely responsible for determining if the nature of the visibility restriction will permit compliance with the provisions of FAR 121.

6-77 Reference. — ATCH 7-46.

6-78 FLIGHT VISIBILITY BELOW ONE MILE

When weather conditions are not officially reported at an airport and the pilot advises the flight visibility is less than 1 statute mile, ATC will treat requests for Special VFR operations at that airport by other than helicopters as follows:*

a. By informing departing aircraft that a clearance cannot be issued.

b. By informing arriving aircraft operating outside of the control zone that a clearance cannot be issued unless an emergency exists.

c. By asking an arriving aircraft operating within a control zone if he can depart the control zone with a flight visibility of at least 1 statute mile. If the aircraft cannot depart the control zone accordingly, or an emergency exists, controllers will issue a clearance as soon as traffic conditions permit.

6-78 Note. — FAR 91 prescribes use of officially reported ground visibility at airports where it is provided, and landing or takeoff "flight visibility" where it is not, as the governing ground visibility for basic and Special VFR operations.

6-78 Reference. — ATCH 7-47.

6-79 SPECIAL VFR HELICOPTER SEPARATION

a. ATC will control a Special VFR helicopter by Special VFR procedures unless other procedures are contained in a letter of agreement.

TERMINAL

b. ATC will control a Special VFR helicopter by visual separation of Special VFR procedures unless local procedures are contained in a letter of agreement.*

6-79b Note. — Control of IFR helicopters is governed by nonradar or radar procedures and minima.

6-79 Reference. — ATCH 7-48.

6-80 LOCAL HELICOPTER SVFR PROCEDURES

TERMINAL

At locations where the volume or complexity of helicopter operations warrants, a letter of agreement will specify that Special VFR helicopters are required to maintain visual reference to the surface and the traffic patterns, routes, and reporting or holding fixes necessary to achieve separation, in accordance with the following minima:

a. Between Special VFR helicopters - *1 mile*. Controllers may, however, use *200 feet* if helicopters are departing simultaneously on diverging courses and the controller can determine this minimum by reference to the surface markings, or the controller instructs one to remain at least 200 feet from the other.

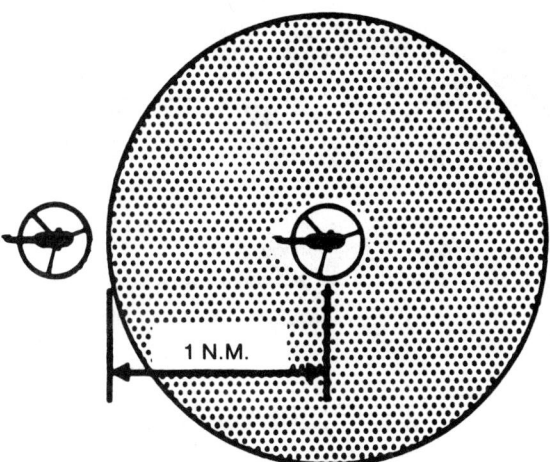

6-80a Illustration 1

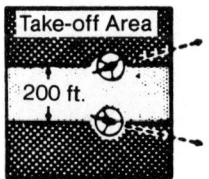

6-80a Illustration 2

b. Between an arriving Special VFR helicopter and an arriving IFR aircraft executing a straight-in approach:

(1) If the arriving IFR aircraft on a straight-in approach is less than 1 mile from the landing threshhold - ½ *mile*.

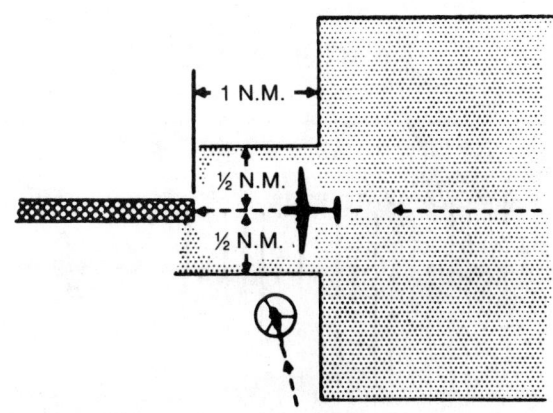

6-80b(1) Illustration

(2) If the arriving IFR aircraft on a straight-in approach is 1 mile or more from the landing threshhold - 1½ *miles*.

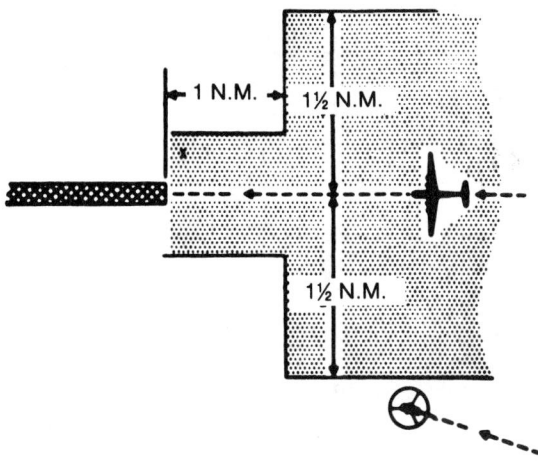

6-80b(2) Illustration

c. Between an arriving IFR aircraft executing a circling approach or a missed approach and an arriving Special VFR helicopter - 2 *miles*.

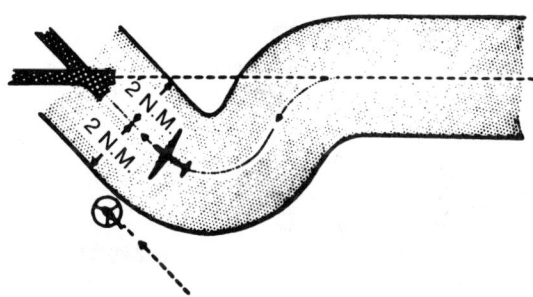

6-80c Illustration 1

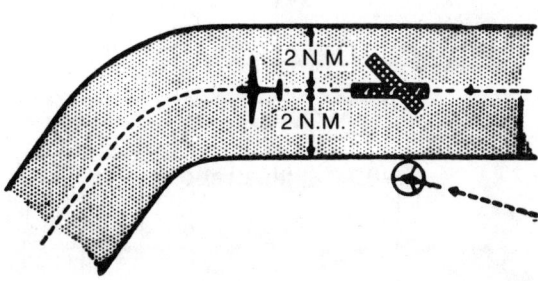

6-80c Illustration 2

d. Between a departing IFR aircraft and a Special VFR helicopter:

(1) If the departing aircraft is less than ½ mile beyond the runway end - *½ mile.*

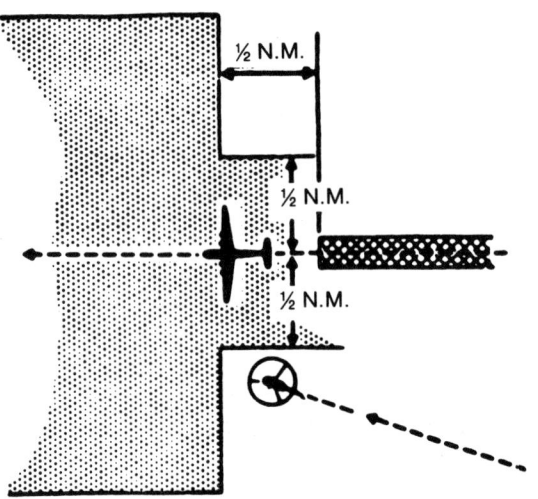

6-80d(1) Illustration

(2) If the departing aircraft is ½ mile or more beyond the runway end - *2 miles.*

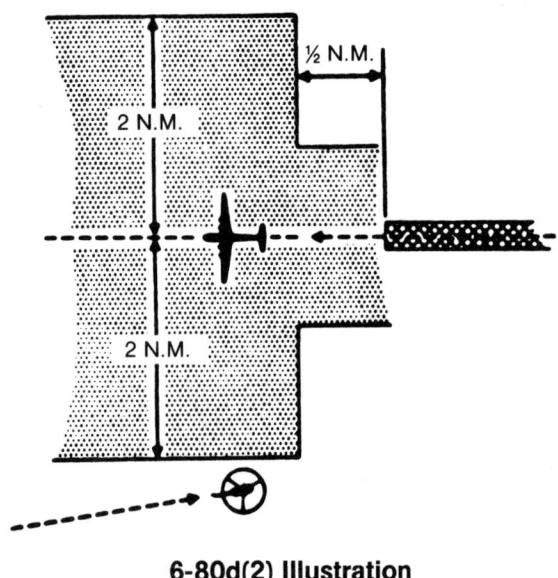

6-80d(2) Illustration

e. Between a departing Special VFR helicopter and a departing IFR aircraft - *½ mile,* if courses diverge by at least 45 degrees after takeoff.

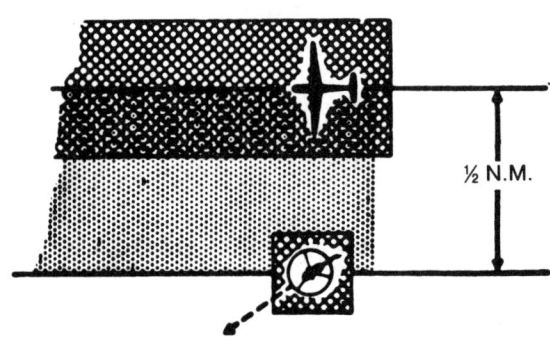

6-80e Illustration

f. Between an arriving IFR aircraft and a Special VFR helicopter - sufficient separation to assure that the helicopter takes off on a course which diverges by at least 45 degrees from the runway centerline before the arriving aircraft is 1 mile from the airport.

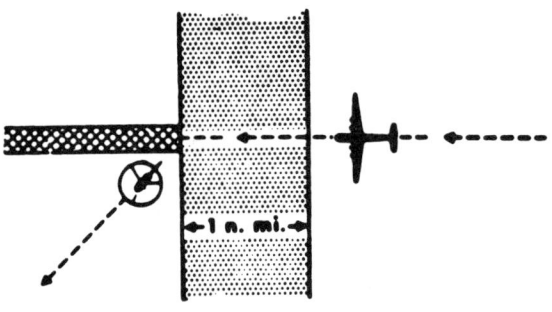

6-80f Illustration

6-80 Reference. — ATCH 7-49.

NON-RADAR PROCEDURES

Chapter 7
TABLE OF CONTENTS

Section 1. POSITION REPORTS

		Page
7-1	General	7-1
7-2	Position Indications	7-1
7-3	Position Reporting Points	7-1
7-4	Position Reporting Requirements	7-1
7-5	Position Report Format	7-1
7-6	Additional Reports	7-1
7-7	Altitude Verification - Non-Radar	7-2
7-8—7-9	Reserved	7-2

Section 2. INITIAL SEPARATION OF SUCCESSIVE DEPARTING AIRCRAFT

7-10	Minima On Diverging Courses	7-3
7-11	Separation Minima On Same Course	7-4
7-12—7-19	Reserved	7-4

Section 3. INITIAL SEPARATION OF DEPARTING AND ARRIVING AIRCRAFT

7-20	Separation Minima	7-5
7-21	Adjacent Airport Heavy Jet Separation	7-5
7-22—7-29	Reserved	7-6

Section 4. LONGITUDINAL SEPARATION

7-30	Requirements	7-7
7-31	Minima On Same, Converging, or Crossing Courses	7-7
7-32	Minima On Opposite Courses	7-9
7-33	Separation by Pilots	7-10
7-34	RNAV Aircraft Along VOR Airways/Routes	7-10
7-35—7-39	Reserved	7-10

Section 5. LATERAL SEPARATION

7-40	Separation Methods	7-11
7-41	Minima On Diverging Radials	7-11
7-42	DME Arc Minima	7-11
7-43	Minima Along Other Than Established Airways or Routes	7-12
7-44	RNAV Minima - Diverging/Slant Crossing Courses	7-13
7-45—7-49	Reserved	7-13

Section 6. VERTICAL SEPARATION

7-50	Altitude Reports	7-14
7-51	Vertical Separation Minima	7-14
7-52	Separation Exceptions	7-14
7-53	Separation by Pilots	7-14
7-54—7-59	Reserved	7-14

Section 7. TIMED APPROACHES

7-60	Required Conditions For Timed Approaches	7-15
7-61	Approach Sequence	7-15
7-62	Sequence Interruption	7-16
7-63	1-Minute Level Flight Restriction	7-16
7-64	Interval Minima	7-16
7-65	Time Check	7-16
7-66	Missed Approaches	7-16

Chapter 7. NON-RADAR PROCEDURES

Section 1. POSITION REPORTS

7-1 GENERAL

The safety and effectiveness of non-radar air traffic control depends to a large extent on accurate position reporting. In order to provide the proper separation and expedite aircraft movements, ATC must be able to make accurate estimates of the progress of every aircraft operating on an IFR flight plan.

7-1 Reference. — AIM 341.

7-2 POSITION INDICATIONS

a. When a position report is to be made passing a VOR radio facility, the time reported should be the time at which the first complete reversal of the "to/from" indicator is accomplished.

b. When a position report is made passing a facility by means of an ADF, the time reported should be the time at which the indicator makes a complete reversal.

c. When an aural or a light panel indication is used to determine the time passing a reporting point, the time should be noted when the signal is first received and again when it ceases. The mean of these two times should then be taken as the actual time over the fix.

d. If a position is given with respect to distance and direction from a reporting point, the distance and direction should be computed as accurately as possible.

e. Except for terminal area transition purposes, position reports or navigation with reference to aids not established for use in the structure in which flight is being conducted will not normally be required by ATC.

7-2 Reference. — AIM 341.

7-3 POSITION REPORTING POINTS

FAR's require pilots to maintain a listening watch on the appropriate frequency and, unless operating under the provisions of 7-4, to furnish position reports passing certain reporting points. Reporting points are indicated by symbols on en route charts. The designated compulsory reporting point symbol is a solid triangle and the "on request" reporting point symbol is the open triangle. Reports passing an "on request" reporting point are only necessary when requested by ATC.

7-3 Reference. — AIM 341.

7-4 POSITION REPORTING REQUIREMENTS

a. A position report is required by all flights regardless of altitude, including those operating in accordance with an ATC clearance specifying *"VFR-ON-TOP,"* over each designated compulsory reporting point or over each reporting point used in the flight plan to define the route of flight.

b. When informed by ATC *"RADAR CONTACT," pilots should discontinue position reports over designated reporting points.* Pilots should resume position reporting when ATC advises *"RADAR CONTACT LOST"* or *"RADAR SERVICE TERMINATED."*

7-4 Reference. — AIM 341.

7-5 POSITION REPORT FORMAT

Position reports should include the following items:

a. Identification,

b. Position,

c. Time,

d. Altitude or flight level (include actual altitude or flight level when operating on a clearance specifying *"VFR-ON-TOP"*),

e. Type of flight plan (not required in IFR position reports made directly to ARTCC's or approach control),

f. ETA and name of next reporting point,

g. The name only of the next succeeding reporting point along the route of flight, and

h. Pertinent remarks.

7-5 Reference. — AIM 341.

7-6 ADDITIONAL REPORTS

The following reports should be made to ATC or FSS facilities without a specific ATC request:

a. A corrected estimate at anytime it becomes apparent that an estimate as previously submitted is in error in excess of 3 minutes.

b. When vacating any previously assigned altitude or flight level for a newly assigned altitude or flight level.

c. When an altitude change will be made if operating on a clearance specifying VFR ON TOP.

d. When *unable* to climb/descend at a rate of at least 500 feet per minute.

e. Change in the average true airspeed (at cruising altitude) when it varies by 5 percent or 10 knots (whichever is greater) from that filed in the flight plan.

f. The time and altitude or flight level upon reaching a holding fix or point to which cleared.

g. When leaving any assigned holding fix or point.

h. When leaving final approach fix inbound on final approach (nonprecision approach) or when leaving the outer marker or fix used in lieu of the outer marker inbound on final approach (precision approach).

7-6 Reference. — AIM 342.

7-7 ALTITUDE VERIFICATION — NON-RADAR

Controllers will request a pilot to verify altitude on initial contact and when position reports are received, *UNLESS:*

a. The pilot states his altitude at the time, or

b. The controller has assigned a new altitude to a climbing or descending aircraft, or

c. TERMINAL: The aircraft was intrafacility transferred.

ATC Phraseology:

In level flight situations **Verify at** (altitude).

In climbing/descending situations **Verify assigned altitude** (altitude).

7-7 Note. — For the purpose of this paragraph, *initial contact* means a pilot's first radio contact with each sector/position.

7-7 Reference. — ATCH 4-47.

7-8 and 7-9 RESERVED

Section 2. INITIAL SEPARATION OF SUCCESSIVE DEPARTING AIRCRAFT

7-10 MINIMA ON DIVERGING COURSES

ATC will separate aircraft that will fly courses diverging by 45 degrees or more after departing the same or adjacent airports by use of one of the following minima:*

a. When aircraft will fly diverging courses:

(1) Immediately after takeoff - *1 minute* until courses diverge.

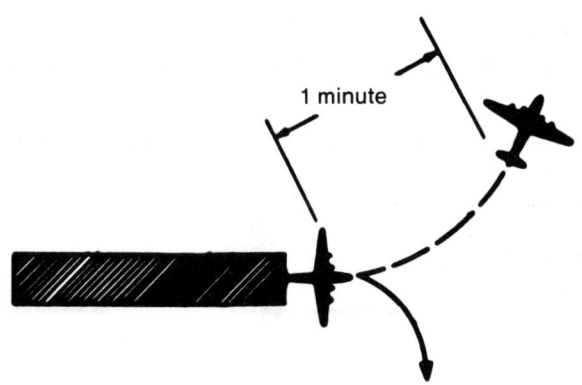

7-10a(1) Illustration

(2) Within 5 minutes after takeoff - *2 minutes* until courses diverge.

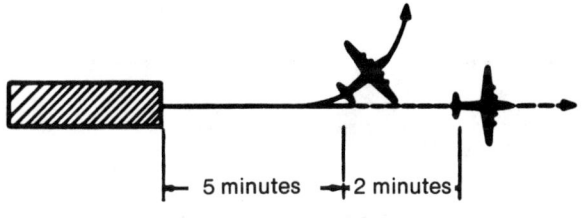

7-10a(2) Illustration

(3) Within 13 miles DME after takeoff - *3 miles* until courses diverge.

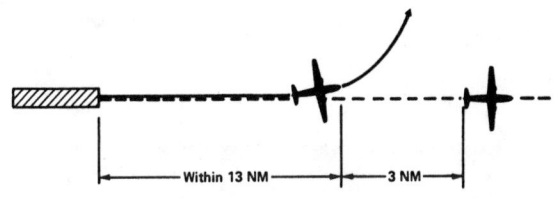

7-10a(3) Illustration

b. TERMINAL: Between aircraft departing in the same direction from different runways whose centerlines are parallel and separated by at least 3,500 feet. Simultaneous takeoffs will be authorized when the aircraft will fly diverging courses immediately after takeoff.

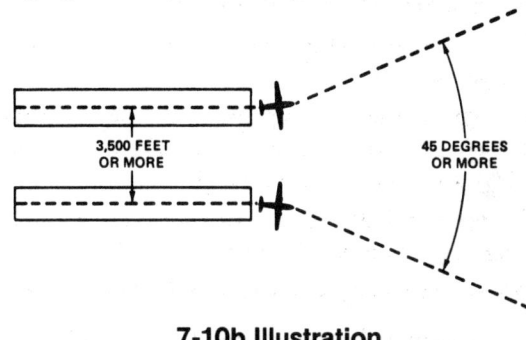

7-10b Illustration

c. TERMINAL: Between aircraft that will fly diverging courses immediately after takeoff from diverging runways:

(1) Nonintersecting runways - Simultaneous takeoffs will be authorized when either of the following conditions exists:

(a) The runways diverge by 30 degrees or more.

(b) The distance between runway centerlines at and beyond the points where takeoffs begin is at least:

(i) 2,000 feet and the runways diverge by 15 to 19 degrees, inclusive.

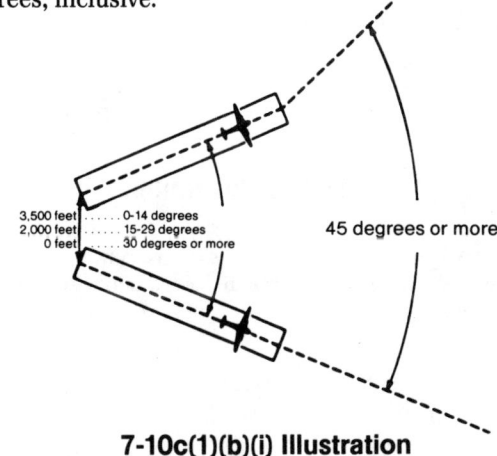

7-10c(1)(b)(i) Illustration

(ii) 3,500 feet and the runways diverge by less than 15 degrees.

(2) Intersecting runways - Takeoff of a succeeding aircraft will be authorized when the preceding aircraft has passed the point of runway intersection, and

(a) The runways diverge by 30 degrees or more.

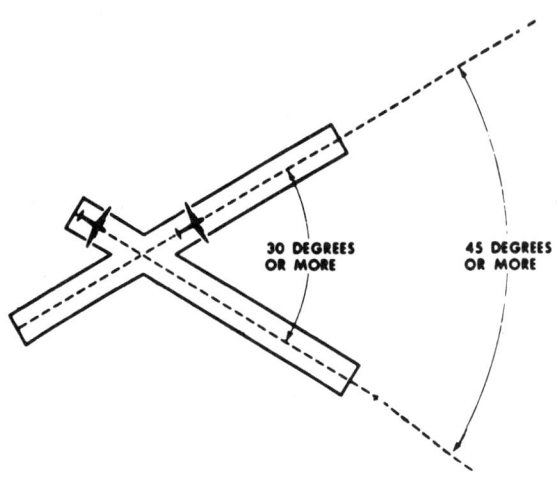

7-10c(2)(a) Illustration

(b) The runways diverge by 15 to 29 degrees inclusive and the preceding aircraft has commenced a turn.

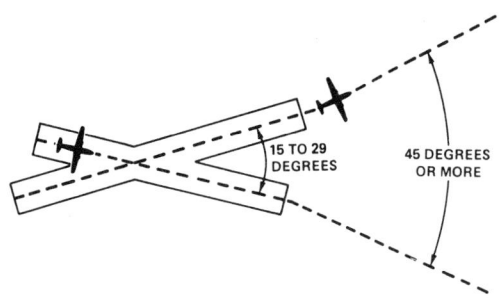

7-10c(2)(b) Illustration

7-10 Note 1. — ATC will consider known aircraft performance characteristics when applying initial separation to successive departing aircraft.

7-10 Note 2. — When one or both of the departure surfaces is a helipad, ATC will use the takeoff course of the helicopter as a reference, comparable to the centerline of a runway and the helipad center as the threshold.

7-10 Reference. — ATCH 6-10.

7-11 SEPARATION MINIMA ON SAME COURSE

ATC will separate aircraft that will fly the same course when the following aircraft will climb through the altitude assigned to the leading aircraft by using a minimum of *3 minutes* until the following aircraft passes through the assigned altitude of the leading aircraft; or *5 miles* if both aircraft are using DME.

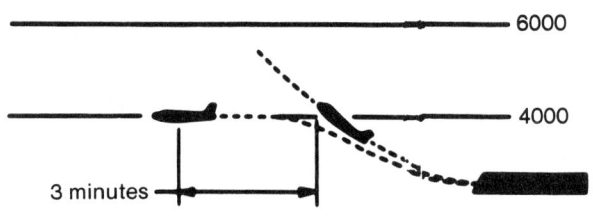

7-11 Illustration 1

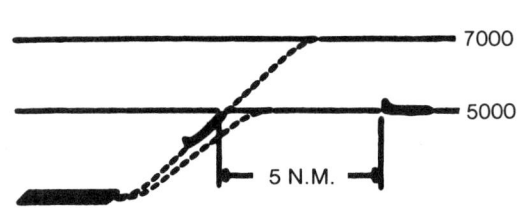

7-11 Illustration 2

7-11 Reference. — ATCH 6-11.

7-12 thru 7-19 RESERVED

Section 3. INITIAL SEPARATION OF DEPARTING AND ARRIVING AIRCRAFT

7-20 SEPARATION MINIMA

ATC will separate a departing aircraft from an arriving aircraft making an instrument approach to the same airport by using one of the following minima until vertical or lateral separation is achieved:

a. TERMINAL: When takeoff direction differs by at least 45 degrees from the reciprocal of the final approach course - The departing aircraft takes off before the arriving aircraft leaves a fix inbound not less than *4 miles* from the airport.

b. TERMINAL: When takeoff direction is other than in **a** - The departing aircraft takes off so that it is established on a course diverging by at least 45 degrees from the reciprocal of the final approach course before the arriving aircraft leaves a fix inbound not less than *4 miles* from the airport.

c. TERMINAL: When the absence of appropriate fix precludes the application of **a** or **b**, and at airports where approach control service is not provided - The separation in **d** or **e** will be applied.

d. When takeoff direction differs by at least 45 degrees from the reciprocal of the final approach course - The departing aircraft takes off *3 minutes* before the arriving aircraft is estimated at the airport.

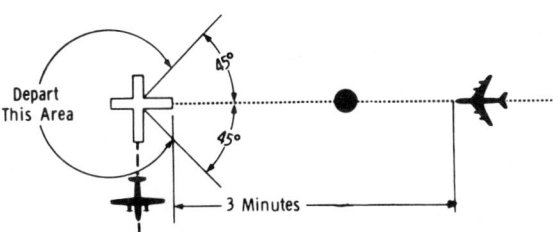

7-20d Illustration

e. When takeoff direction is other than in **d** - The departing aircraft takes off so that it is established on a course diverging by at least 45 degrees from the reciprocal of the final approach course *5 minutes* before the arriving aircraft is estimated at the airport or before it starts procedure turn.

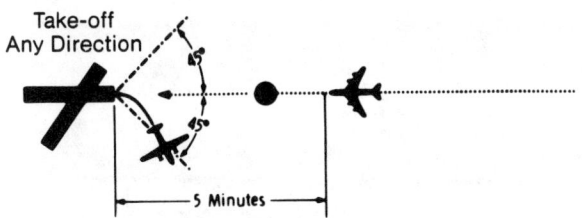

7-20e Illustration 1

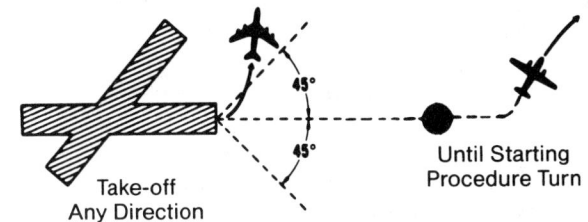

7-20e Illustration 2

7-20 Reference. — ATCH 6-20.

7-21 ADJACENT AIRPORT HEAVY JET SEPARATION

WAKE TURBULENCE APPLICATION

a. The ATC facility providing service to heavy jets and having control jurisdiction at adjacent airports will separate arriving or departing IFR aircraft on a course that will cross behind the flight path of a heavy jet by *2 minutes*.

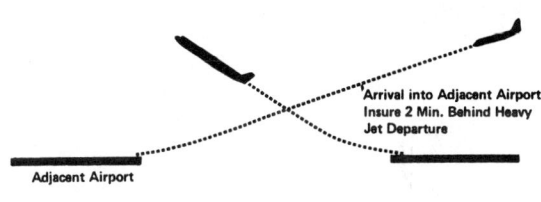

7-21a Illustration 1

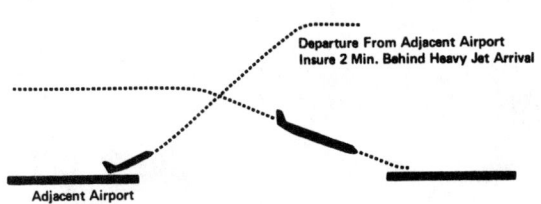

7-21a Illustration 2

TERMINAL

WAKE TURBULENCE APPLICATION

b. ATC will separate IFR aircraft landing behind an arriving heavy jet by *2 minutes* when arriving on:

(1) The same runway (*3 minutes* will be used for a small aircraft behind a heavy jet).

(2) A parallel runway separated by less than 2,500 feet.

(3) A crossing runway if projected flight paths will cross.

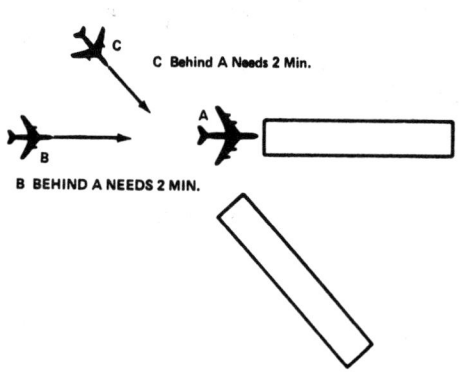

7-21b(1) and (3) Illustration

7-21 Reference. — ATCH 6-2.

7-22 thru 7-29 RESERVED

Section 4. LONGITUDINAL SEPARATION

7-30 REQUIREMENTS

ATC will separate aircraft longitudinally by requiring them to do one of the following, as appropriate:

a. Depart at a specified time.

b. Arrive at a fix at a specified time.

ATC Phraseology:

Cross (fix) **at or before** (time).

Cross (fix) **at or later than** (time).

c. Hold at a fix until a specified time.

d. Change altitude at a specified time or fix.

7-30 Reference. — ATCH 6-30.

7-31 MINIMA ON SAME, CONVERGING, OR CROSSING COURSES

ATC will separate aircraft on the same, converging, or crossing courses by an interval expressed in time or distance, using the following minima:

a. When the leading aircraft maintains a speed of at least 44 knots faster than the following aircraft - *5 miles* between aircraft using DME and/or RNAV; or *3 minutes* between other aircraft if, in either case, one of the following conditions is met:

(1) A departing aircraft follows a preceding aircraft which has taken off from the same or adjacent airport.

(2) A departing aircraft follows a preceding en route aircraft which has reported over a fix serving the departure airport.

(3) An en route aircraft follows a preceding en route aircraft which has reported over the same fix.

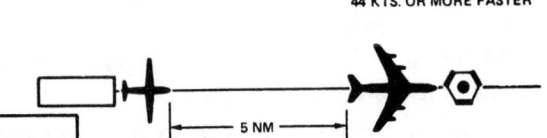

7-31a Illustration 1

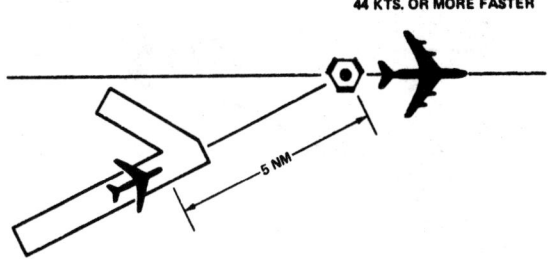

7-31a Illustration 2

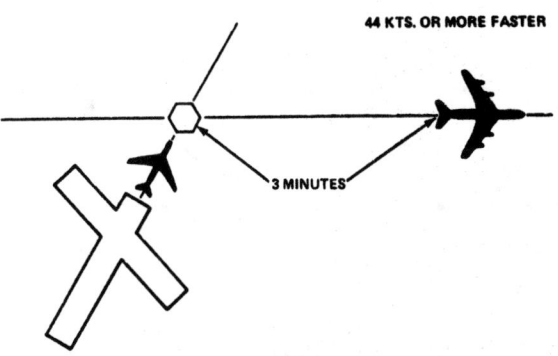

7-31a Illustration 3

b. When the leading aircraft maintains a speed at least 22 knots faster than the following aircraft - *10 miles* between aircraft using DME and/or RNAV; or *5 minutes* between other aircraft if, in either case, one of the following conditions exists:

(1) A departing aircraft follows a preceding aircraft which has taken off from the same or an adjacent airport.

(2) A departing aircraft follows a preceding en route aircraft which has reported over a fix serving the departure airport.

(3) An en route aircraft follows a preceding en route aircraft which has reported over the same fix.

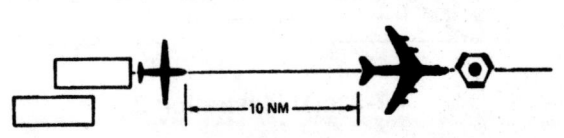

7-31b Illustration 1

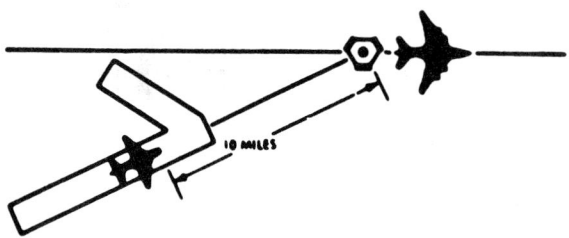

7-31b Illustration 2

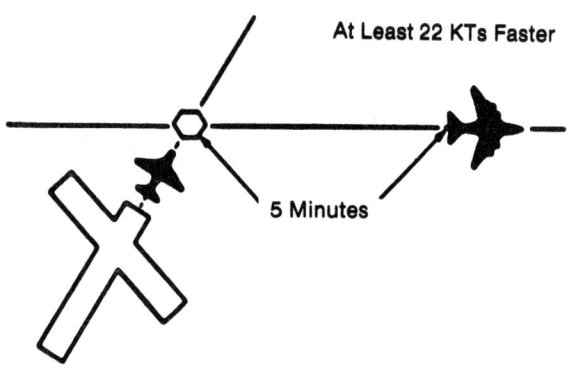

7-31b Illustration 3

c. When an aircraft is climbing or descending through the altitude of another aircraft:

(1) Between aircraft using DME - *10 miles*, if the descending aircraft is leading or the climbing aircraft is following.

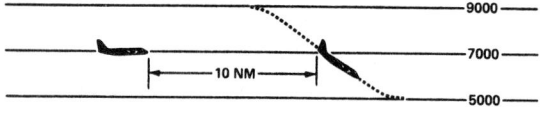

7-31c(1) Illustration 1

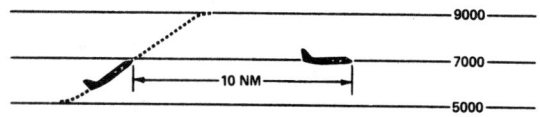

7-31c(1) Illustration 2

(2) Between other aircraft - *5 minutes*, if all of the following conditions are met:

(a) The descending aircraft is leading or climbing aircraft is following.

(b) The aircraft were separated by not more than 4,000 feet when the altitude change started.

(c) The change is started within 10 minutes after a following aircraft reports over a fix reported over by the leading aircraft or has acknowledged a clearance specifying the time to cross the same fix.

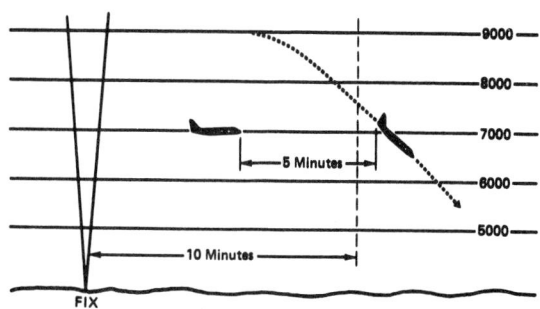

7-31c(2) Illustration 1

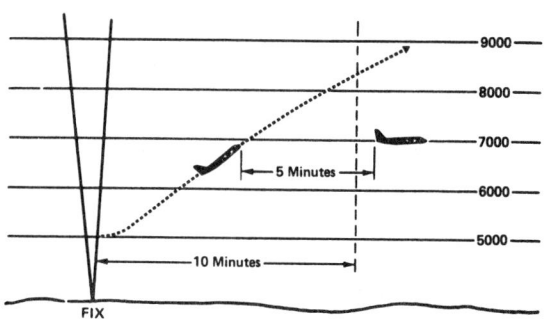

7-31c(2) Illustration 2

(3) Between RNAV aircraft that are operating along an RNAV route that is eight miles or less in width - *10 miles* provided the following conditions are met:

(a) The descending aircraft is leading or the climbing aircraft is following.

(b) The aircraft were separated by not more than 4,000 feet when the altitude change started.

d. When the conditions of **a**, **b**, or **c** above cannot be met - *20 miles* between aircraft using DME and/or RNAV; or *10 minutes* between other aircraft.

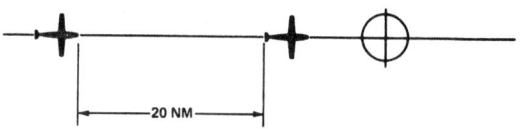

7-31d Illustration 1

NON-RADAR PROCEDURES

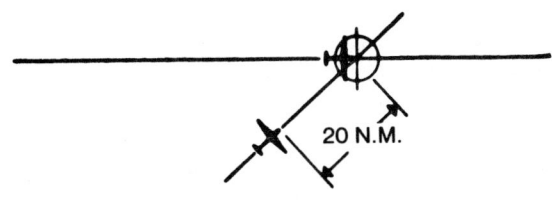

7-31d Illustration 2

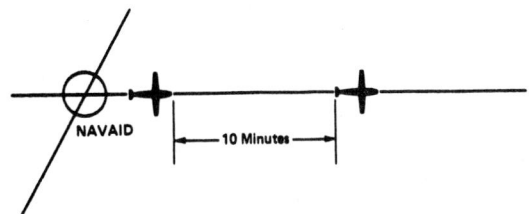

7-31d Illustration 3

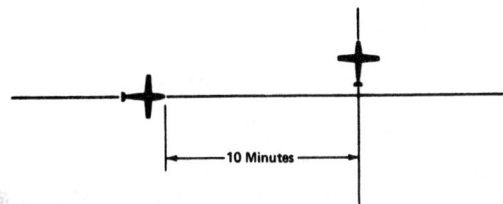

7-31d Illustration 4

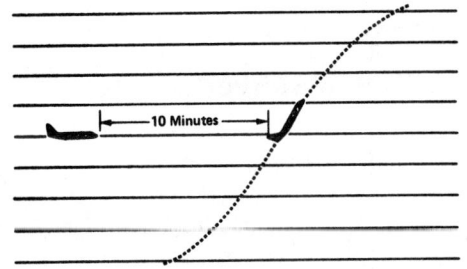

7-31d Illustration 5

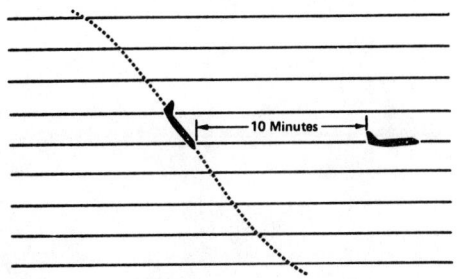

7-31d Illustration 6

e. Between aircraft, when one aircraft is using DME and the other is not - *30 miles* if both the following conditions are met:

(1) The aircraft using DME derives distance information by reference to the same NAVAID over which the aircraft not using DME has reported.

(2) The aircraft not using DME is within 15 minutes of the NAVAID.

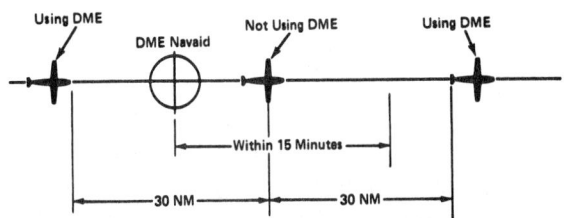

7-31e Illustration 1

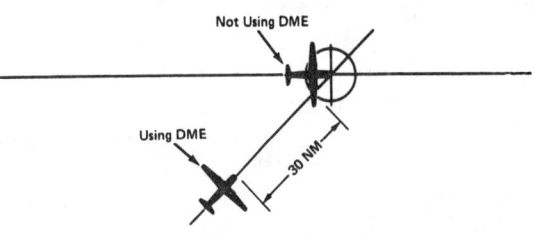

7-31e Illustration 2

f. Between aircraft when one aircraft is using RNAV and the other is using neither DME nor RNAV - *30 miles*.

7-31 Reference. — ATCH 6-31.

7-32 MINIMA ON OPPOSITE COURSES

ATC will separate aircraft traveling opposite courses by assigning different altitudes consistent with the approved vertical separation from *10 minutes* before, until *10 minutes* after, they are estimated to pass. Vertical separation may be discontinued after one of the following conditions is met:*

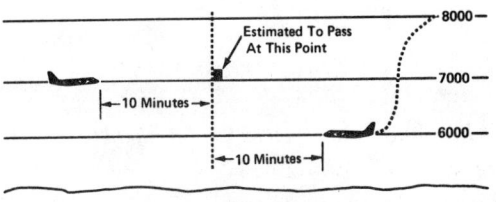

7-32 Illustration

a. Both aircraft have reported passing NAVAID's or DME fixes indicating they have passed each other.*

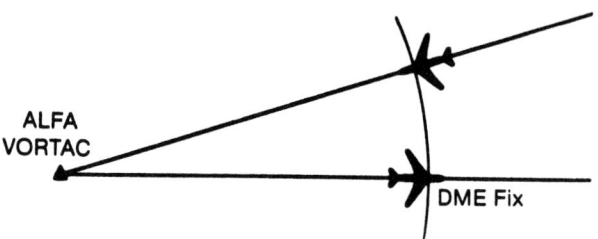

7-32a Illustration

b. Both aircraft have reported passing the same intersection and they are at least *3 minutes* apart.

c. Two RNAV aircraft have reported passing the same position and are at least *8 miles* apart if operating along a route that is *8 miles* or less in width; or *18 miles* apart if operating along an expanded route; except that *30 miles* will be applied if operating along that portion of any route segment defined by a navigation station requiring extended usable distance limitations beyond 130 miles.

d. An aircraft utilizing RNAV and an aircraft utilizing VOR have reported passing the same position and the RNAV aircraft is at least *4 miles* beyond the reported position when operating along a route that is *8 miles* or less in width; *9 miles* beyond the point when operating along an expanded route; except that *15 miles* will be applied if operating along that portion of any route segment defined by a navigation station requiring extended usable distance limitation beyond 130 miles; or *3 minutes* apart, whichever is greater.

7-32 Note. — RNAV route segments that have been expanded in the proximity to reference facilities for slant range effect are not to be considered "expanded" for purposes of applying separation criteria in this paragraph.

7-32a Note. — It is not intended to limit application of this procedure only to aircraft operating in opposite directions along the same airway or radial. This procedure may also be applied to aircraft established on diverging airways or radials of the same NAVAID.

7-32 Reference. — ATCH 6-32.

7-33 SEPARATION BY PILOTS

When pilots of aircraft on the same course in direct radio communication with each other concur, ATC may authorize the following aircraft to maintain longitudinal separation of *10 minutes;* or *20 miles* if they are using DME.

ATC Phraseology:

Maintain at least one zero minutes/two zero miles separation from (identification).

7-33 Reference. — ATCH 6-33.

7-34 RNAV AIRCRAFT ALONG VOR AIRWAYS/ROUTES

Controllers may advise the pilot to use DME distances when applying DME separation to an RNAV aircraft operating along VOR airways/routes.

ATC Phraseology:

Use DME distances.

7-34 Reference. — ATCH 6-34.

7-35 thru 7-39 RESERVED

Section 5. LATERAL SEPARATION

7-40 SEPARATION METHODS

ATC will separate aircraft laterally by one of the following methods:

a. Clearing aircraft on different airways or routes whose widths or protected airspace do not overlap.*

b. Clearing aircraft below 18,000 to proceed to and report over or hold at different geographical locations determined visually or by reference to NAVAID's.

c. Clearing aircraft to hold over different fixes whose holding pattern airspace areas do not overlap each other or other airspace to be protected.

d. Clearing departing aircraft to fly specified headings which diverge by at least 45 degrees.

7-40a Note. — Airspace protected for airways is based on airway widths described in FAR 71.5 and airspace protected for routes will be consistent with those widths. Airspace to be protected for RNAV routes, including SID's and STAR's, is defined in FAA Order 7110.18.

7-40 Reference. — ATCH 6-40.

7-41 MINIMA ON DIVERGING RADIALS

a. Separation is considered to exist between aircraft established on radials of the same NAVAID that diverge by at least 15 degrees when either aircraft is clear of the airspace to be protected for the other aircraft.*

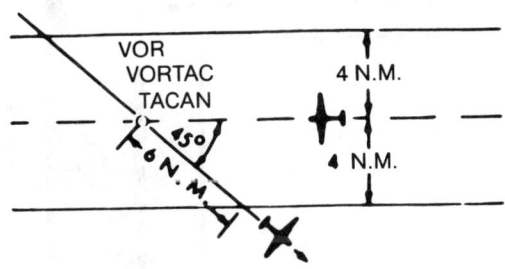

7-41a Illustration

b. The Tables are used to determine the distance required for various divergence angles to clear the airspace to be protected. For divergence that falls between two values, ATC will use the lesser divergence value to obtain the distance.*

7-41b Table 1. — Non-DME Divergence-Distance Minima*

Divergence (degrees)	Distance (NM)
15	16
20	12
25	10
30	8
35	7
45	6
55	5
90	4

7-41b Table 2. — Divergence-Distance Minima*

Divergence (degrees)	Distance (NM)	
	Below FL 180	FL 180 through FL 450
15	17	18
20	13	15
25	11	13
30	9	11
35	8	11
45	7	11
55	6	11
90	5	11

7-41a Note. — The procedure may be applied to converging as well as diverging aircraft. For example, the aircraft depicted 6 miles from the NAVAID in Illustration 7-41a would require vertical separation until reaching the 6-mile point. Reversing direction, the same aircraft would require vertical separation before passing the 6-mile point.

7-41b Note. — For altitudes of 3,000 feet or less above the elevation of the NAVAID, DME slant-range error is neglible and the values in 7-41b, Table 1, may be used.

7-41b Table 1 Note. — This table is for non-DME application only.

7-41b Table 2 Note. — This table is for DME application and compensates for DME slant-range error.

7-41 Reference. — ATCH 6-41.

7-42 DME ARC MINIMA

ATC will apply lateral DME separation by requiring aircraft using DME to fly an arc about a NAVAID at a specified distance using the following minima:

a. Between different arcs about a NAVAID, regardless of direction of flight:

(1) At 35 miles or less from the NAVAID - *10 miles*.

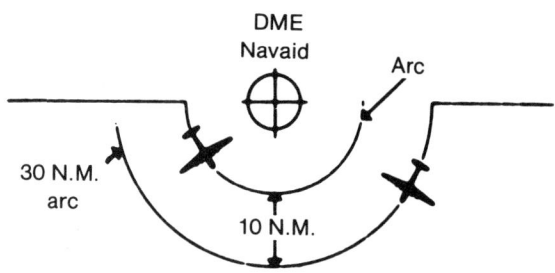

7-42a(1) Illustration

(2) More than 35 miles from the NAVAID - *20 miles*.

b. Between an arc about a NAVAID and other airspace to be protected:*

(1) At 35 miles or less from the NAVAID - *5 miles*.

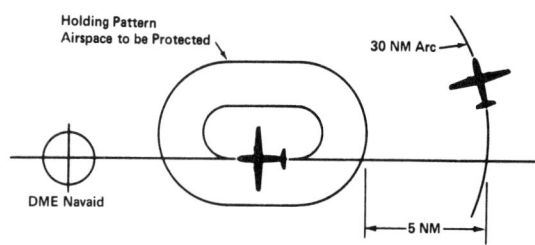

7-42b(1) Illustration

(2) More than 35 miles from the NAVAID - *10 miles*.

ATC Phraseology:

Via (number of miles) **miles arc** (direction) **of** (name of DME NAVAID).

7-42b Note. — The other airspace to be protected may be a MOA, a holding pattern, airway or route, ATCAA, warning area, restricted area, prohibited area, etc.

7-42 Reference. — ATCH 6-42.

7-43 MINIMA ALONG OTHER THAN ESTABLISHED AIRWAYS OR ROUTES

Airspace is protected along other than established airways or routes as follows:

a. Direct courses and course changes of 15 degrees or less:

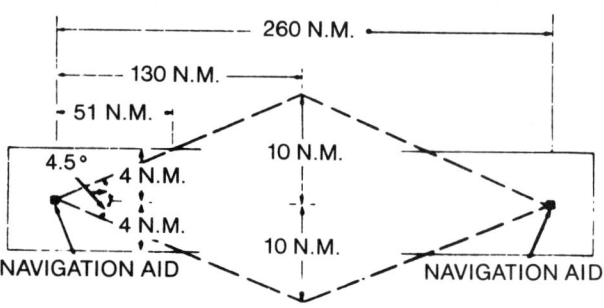

7-43a Illustration

(1) Via NAVAID's or radials FL 600 and below - *4 miles* on each side of the route to a point 51 miles from the NAVAID, then increasing in width on a 4½ degree angle to a width of *10 miles* on each side of the route at a distance of 130 miles from the NAVAID.

(2) Via degree-distance fixes for RNAV flights above FL 450 - *10 miles* on each side of the route.*

b. When course change is 16 degrees through 90 degrees, the airspace is protected on the overflown side, beginning at the point where the course changes, as follows:

(1) Below FL 180 - same as **a**(1) or (2).

(2) FL 180 to FL 230, inclusive - *14 miles*.

(3) Above FL 230 to FL 600, inclusive - *17 miles*.

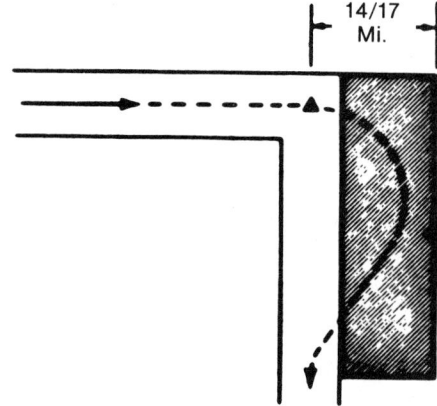

7-43b Illustration

c. When the course change is 91 degrees through 180 degrees, the airspace is protected on the overflown side, beginning at the point where the course changes, as follows:

(1) Below FL 180 - same as **a**(1) or (2).

(2) FL 180 to FL 230, inclusive - *28 miles*.

(3) Above FL 230 to FL 600, inclusive - *34 miles*.

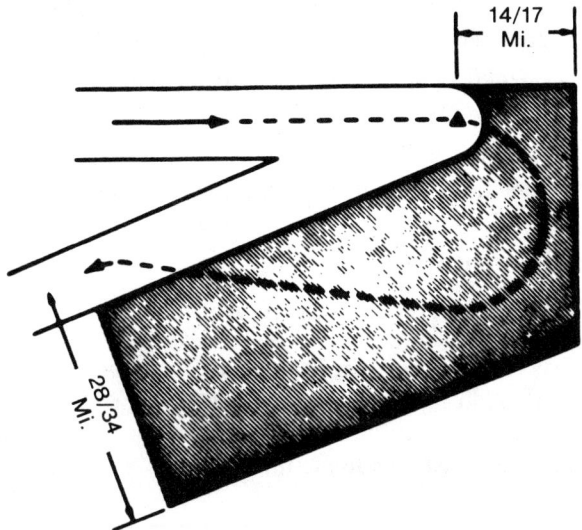

7-43c Illustration

d. After the course changes specified in **b** or **c** have been completed and the aircraft is back on course, the appropriate minima in **a** may be used.

7-43a(2) Note. — Degree-distance RNAV flight (random routes) at FL 450 and below are provided radar separation.

7-43 Reference. — ATCH 6-43.

7-44 RNAV MINIMA — DIVERGING/CROSSING COURSES

Lateral separation is considered to exist when an RNAV aircraft is beyond the point where the lateral protected airspace of that aircraft has ceased to overlap the lateral protected airspace of another by at least:

a. When operating along a route that is 8 miles or less in width - *4 miles*.

b. When operating along an expanded route - *9 miles*, except that *15 miles* will be applied along that portion of any route segment requiring extended usable distance limitation beyond 130 miles of the reference facility.

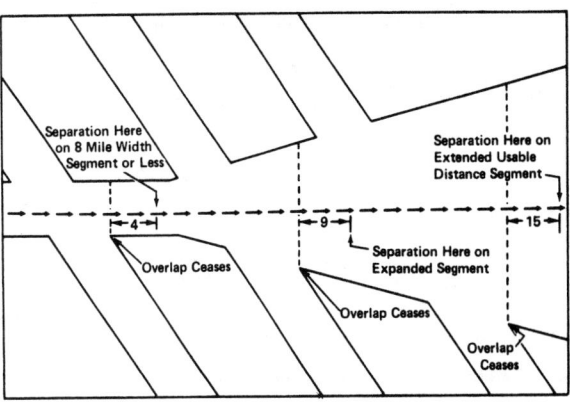

7-44 Illustration 1

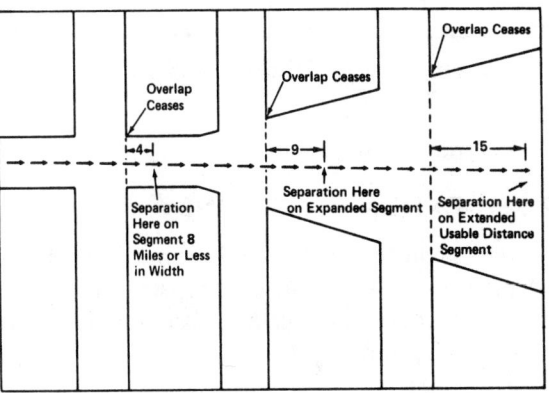

7-44 Illustration 2

7-44 Reference. — ATCH 6-44.

7-45 thru 7-49 RESERVED

Section 6. VERTICAL SEPARATION

7-50 ALTITUDE REPORTS

ATC will assign an altitude to an aircraft only after the aircraft previously at that altitude has reported leaving that altitude.*

ATC Phraseology:

Report leaving/reaching (altitude).

Report leaving odd/even altitudes/flight levels.

Say altitude.

7-50 Note.—Controllers will consider known aircraft performance characteristics or pilot furnished information which indicate that climb/descent will not be consistent with the rates recommended in paragraph 4-88.

7-50 Reference. — ATCH 6-50.

7-51 VERTICAL SEPARATION MINIMA

ATC will separate IFR aircraft by assigning different altitudes using the following minima between altitudes:

   a. Up to and including FL 290 - *1,000 feet.*

   b. Above FL 290 - *2,000 feet.*

7-51 Reference. — ATCH 6-51.

7-52 SEPARATION EXCEPTIONS

ATC will assign an altitude to an aircraft only after the aircraft previously at that altitude has reported at or passing through another altitude separated from the first by the appropriate minimum when:

   a. Severe turbulence is reported.

   b. Aircraft are conducting military aerial refueling.

   c. The aircraft previously at the altitude has been:

      (1) Issued a clearance permitting climb/descent at pilot's discretion.

      (2) Cleared to CRUISE (altitude).

   d. Transitioning from minima of 1,000 feet to 2,000 feet vertical separation.

7-52 Reference. — ATCH 6-52.

7-53 SEPARATION BY PILOTS

When pilots of aircraft in direct radio communication with each other during climb and descent concur, ATC may authorize the lower aircraft, if climbing, or the upper aircraft, if descending, to maintain vertical separation.

ATC Phraseology:

Maintain at least one/two thousand feet above/below (identification).

7-53 Reference. — ATCH 6-53.

7-54 thru 7-59 RESERVED

Section 7. TIMED APPROACHES

7-60 REQUIRED CONDITIONS FOR TIMED APPROACHES

Timed approaches using either non-radar procedures or radar vectors to the final approach course may be used at airports served by a tower if the following conditions are met:*

a. Direct pilot/controller communication is maintained until the pilot is instructed to contact the tower.

b. If more than one missed approach procedure is available, none require course reversal.

c. If only one missed approach procedure is available, the following conditions are met:

(1) Course reversal is not required.

(2) Reported ceiling and visibility are equal to or greater than the highest prescribed circling minimums for the instrument approach procedure in use.*

7-60 Note. — These procedures require NAVAID's and standard/special instrument approach procedures or adequate radar coverage which permit an aircraft to:

a. Hold at a fix located on the approach course or to be radar vectored to the final approach course for a straight-in approach in accordance with the interval minima specified in 7-64.

b. Proceed in the direction of the airport along the approach course crossing the holding/approach fix at a specified altitude, if required.

c. Continue descent for an approach to destination airport.

7-60c(2) Note. — Determination of whether or not an existing ceiling meets minima is accomplished by comparing MDA (MSL) with ceiling (AGL) plus the airport elevation.

7-60 Reference. — ATCH 6-60.

7-61 APPROACH SEQUENCE

When an aircraft passes the final approach fix inbound (nonprecision approach) or the outer marker or the fix used in lieu of the outer marker inbound (precision approach), ATC will issue clearances for a succeeding time approach in accordance with the following:

a. ATC will clear the succeeding aircraft for approach, to descend to the altitude vacated by the preceding aircraft, and to leave the final approach fix inbound (nonprecision approach) or the outer marker or the fix used in lieu of the outer marker inbound (precision approach) at a specified time; or when using radar to sequence and position aircraft on the final approach course, vector aircraft to cross the final approach fix/outer marker or the fix used in lieu of the outer marker in compliance with 7-64.

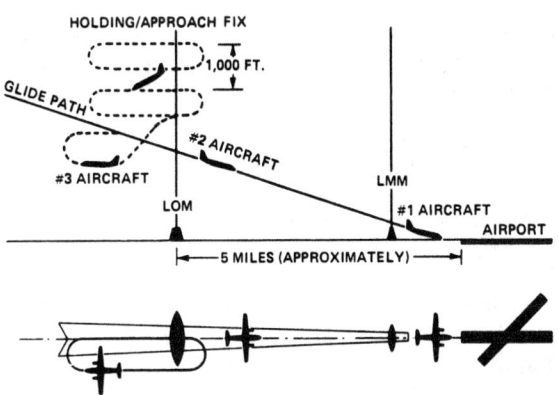

7-61a Illustration

This illustration depicts the application of timed approach procedures using an ILS and applying longitudinal separation only. Using an interval of 2 minutes between successive approaches, the #1 and #2 aircraft have already passed the outer locator (LOM) on final approach, and the #3 aircraft has been cleared for approach and to depart the LOM minutes after the #2 aircraft reported leaving the LOM inbound on final approach. After aircraft in the approach sequence depart the holding/approach fix (LOM) inbound, vertical separation is no longer provided and longitudinal separation is utilized.

b. If an alternative missed approach is not available and weather conditions are less than required by 7-60c(2), ATC will clear the succeeding aircraft for an approach when the preceding aircraft has landed or canceled its IFR flight plan.

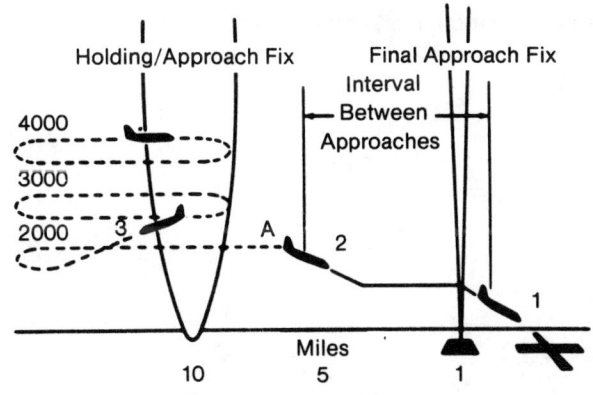

7-61b Illustration

This illustration depicts the application of timed approach procedures using a holding/approach fix on a bearing of an NDB and applying a combination of longitudinal and vertical separation.

The #3 aircraft has been instructed to descend to 2,000 after the #2 aircraft has reported departing the holding/approach fix inbound and leaving 2,000 at Point A. The #2 aircraft has departed the holding/approach fix inbound at the designated time, maintaining 2,000 until cleared for approach at Point A. The #1 aircraft has been sighted, enabling the controller to issue approach clearance to the #2 aircraft at Point A.

c. ATC will change the aircraft to the tower before it reaches the final approach fix.

7-61 Reference. — ATCH 6-61.

7-62 SEQUENCE INTERRUPTION

ATC may interrupt the established timed approach sequence if necessary to allow an aircraft to execute a different type of approach.

7-62 Reference. — ATCH 6-62.

7-63 1-MINUTE LEVEL FLIGHT RESTRICTION

If the weather report indicates an aircraft will be in IFR conditions over the final approach fix (nonprecision approach) or the outer marker or fix used in lieu of the outer marker (precision approach) when 7-61b is applied, ATC will clear the second aircraft for an approach early enough to allow at least 1 minute of level flight before crossing the final approach fix/outer marker or the fix used in lieu of the outer marker.

7-63 Reference. — ATCH 6-63.

7-64 INTERVAL MINIMA

ATC will use a *2-minute* or *5-mile* radar interval (except for a small aircraft behind a heavy aircraft - a *3-minute* or *6-mile* radar interval) as the minimum between successive approaches and increase the interval, as necessary, taking into account the:*

a. Relative speeds of aircraft concerned.

b. Existing weather conditions.

c. Distance between approach fix and airport.

d. Type of approach being made.

7-64 Note. — Increased separation is required for small aircraft behind heavy aircraft because of the possible effects of wake turbulence.

7-64 Reference. — ATCH 6-64.

7-65 TIME CHECK

Controllers will issue a time check to an aircraft before specifying a time to leave the approach fix inbound unless the aircraft is vectored to the final approach course.

7-65 Reference. — ATCH 6-65.

7-66 MISSED APPROACHES

a. If weather conditions are such that an aircraft will likely miss an approach, ATC will issue an alternative missed approach procedure to the next aircraft.

b. If an aircraft misses an approach, ATC will allow the next aircraft to continue approach if it has been assigned an alternative missed approach procedure. ATC will retain radar control or hold any remaining aircraft at assigned altitudes until traffic conditions permit issuance of approach clearances.

c. When 7-61b is applied and the first aircraft misses approach, ATC will retain radar control or clear the second aircraft to maintain the last assigned altitude (minimum holding altitude) and return to the holding/approach fix to hold until traffic conditions permit issuance of approach clearances.

7-66 Reference. — ATCH 6-66.

SPECIAL FLIGHTS

Chapter 8
TABLE OF CONTENTS

Section 1. SPECIAL USE AND ATC ASSIGNED AIRSPACE

		Page
8-1	Restricted Areas	8-1
8-2	Military Operations Areas	8-1
8-3	Application	8-1
8-4	Aircraft - Airspace Separation	8-1
8-5	VFR-On-Top Routes	8-2
8-6	Special Use Airspace Avoidance	8-2
8-7	Temporary Flight Restrictions	8-2
8-8	Emergency Air Traffic Rules	8-3
8-9	Reserved	8-3

Section 2. FUEL DUMPING

8-10	Fuel Dumping Advisories	8-4
8-11	Information Requirements	8-4
8-12	Fuel Dump Routing	8-4
8-13	Altitude Assignments	8-4
8-14	Separation Minima	8-4
8-15—8-19	Reserved	8-4

Section 3. UNMANNED BALLOONS

8-20	General	8-5
8-21	Application	8-5
8-22	Derelict Balloons	8-5
8-23—8-29	Reserved	8-6

Section 4. PARACHUTE JUMPING

8-30	Parachute Jump Altitude Advisory	8-7
8-31	Jump Coordination	8-7
8-32	Jump Authorization	8-7
8-33	Control Zone Jumps	8-7
8-34	Other Controlled Airspace Jumps	8-7

Chapter 8. SPECIAL FLIGHTS

Section 1. SPECIAL USE AND ATC ASSIGNED AIRSPACE

8-1 RESTRICTED AREAS

ATC facilities apply the following procedures when aircraft are operating on an IFR clearance (including those cleared by ATC to maintain *"VFR-on-top"*) via a route which lies within joint-use airspace.*

a. If the restricted area is not active and has been released to the controlling agency (FAA), the ATC facility will allow the aircraft to operate in the restricted airspace without issuing specific clearance for it to do so.

b. If the restricted area is active and has not been released to the controlling agency (FAA), the ATC facility will issue a clearance which will ensure the aircraft avoids the restricted airspace unless it is on an approved altitude reservation mission or has obtained its own permission to operate in the airspace and so informs the controlling facility.

8-1 Note 1. — The above apply only to joint-use restricted airspace and not to prohibited and nonjoint-use airspace. For the latter categories, the ATC facility will issue a clearance so the aircraft will avoid the restricted airspace unless it is on an approved altitude reservation mission or has obtained its own permission to operate in the airspace and so informs the controlling facility.

8-1 Note 2. — Restricted Areas contain airspace identified by an area on the surface of the earth within which the flight of the aircraft, while not wholly prohibited, is subject to restrictions. Activities within these areas must be confined because of their nature or limitations imposed upon aircraft operations that are not part of those activities or both. Restricted areas denote the existence of unusual, often invisible, hazards to aircraft such as artillery firing, aerial gunnery, or guided missiles. Penetration of Restricted Areas without authorization from the using or controlling agency may be extremely hazardous to the aircraft and its occupants. Restricted Areas are published in the Federal Register and constitute FAR 73.

8-1 Reference. — AIM 112.

8-2 MILITARY OPERATIONS AREAS

MOA's (military operations areas) consist of airspace of defined vertical and lateral limits established for the purpose of separating certain military training activities from IFR traffic. Whenever a MOA is being used, nonparticipating IFR traffic may be cleared through a MOA if IFR separation can be provided by ATC. Otherwise, ATC will reroute or restrict nonparticipating IFR traffic.

8-2 Reference. — AIM 114.

8-3 APPLICATION

ATC will apply the procedures in this section to aircraft operating in proximity to special use or ATCAA (ATC assigned airspace) unless the airspace is designated an Alert Area/Controlled Firing Area or one of the following conditions exists:*

a. The pilot informs ATC that permission has been obtained from the using agency to operate in the airspace.

b. The using agency informs ATC they have given permission for the aircraft to operate in the airspace.*

c. The Restricted/Warning Area, MOA, or ATCAA has been released to the controlling agency.

d. The aircraft is on an approved ALTRV, unless the airspace area in question is an ATCAA.

8-3 Note. — These procedures are not applicable to Alert Areas or Controlled Firing Areas. See Glossary (Special Use Airspace).

8-3b Note. — Using agency permission may be relayed to the pilot.

8-3 Reference. — ATCH 8-50.

8-4 AIRCRAFT — AIRSPACE SEPARATION

Nonparticipating aircraft will be separated from the upper/lower limits of active special use airspace and ATCAA by the following minima:

a. Prohibited/Restricted/Warning Area, MOA or ATCAA - ATC will assign an altitude consistent with 8-3, 8-4, and 8-5, which is at least 500 feet (above FL 290 -1,000 feet) above/below the upper/lower limit, unless 8-4b below applies.

b. Some Prohibited/Restricted Areas are established for security reasons or to contain hazardous activities not involving aircraft operations. Nonparticipating aircraft may be assigned any appropriate altitude above or below these Prohibited/Restricted Areas, provided the areas have been identified by facility management.

c. Prohibited Area - ATC will clear aircraft on airways or routes whose widths or protected airspace do not overlap the peripheral boundary.

d. Restricted/Warning Area/MOA/ATCAA - ATC will clear in accordance with 8-4c above, unless clearance of nonparticipating aircraft in/through the area is provided for in a letter of agreement.

e. Prohibited/Restricted/Warning Area, MOA or ATCAA - *3 miles* (En Route Stage A/DARC, FL 600 and above - *6 miles*), unless clearances of nonparticipating aircraft in/through/adjacent to the area is provided for in a letter of agreement/facility directive.

f. Exception. Some Prohibited/Restricted Areas are established for security reasons or to contain hazardous activities not involving aircraft operations. The above minima for these Prohibited/Restricted Areas is not required if the areas have been identified by facility management. When separation minima are not required, ATC will vector aircraft to avoid the airspace.

8-4 Reference. — ATCH 8-51.

8-5 VFR-ON-TOP ROUTES

If the aircraft's route, track, or altitude may cause it to enter an active Prohibited/Restricted/Warning Area, MOA, or ATCAA controllers will:

a. Inform the pilot to conduct flight *"VFR-ON-TOP"* at least 500 feet (FL 290 and above - 1,000 feet) above the upper limit or below the lower limit of the airspace (subject to 7-20); or

ATC Phraseology:

Maintain VFR-on-top at least 500 feet (FL 290 and above - 1,000 feet) **above/below** (upper/lower limit of airspace) **across** (name or number of airspace) **between** (fix) **and** (fix);

and, if the airspace is an ATCAA,

(name of ATCAA) **is ATC assigned airspace.**

b. Clear the aircraft via a routing which provides approved separation from the airspace.

c. Exception. Some Prohibited/Restricted Areas are established for security reasons or to contain hazardous activities not involving aircraft operations. The addition of 500 (or 1,000) feet to the upper/lower limit of these Prohibited/Restricted Areas is not required if the areas have been identified by facility management.

8-5 Reference. — ATCH 8-52.

8-6 SPECIAL USE AIRSPACE AVOIDANCE

The following action will be taken if a nonparticipating aircraft's route or track will cause it to enter special use or ATC assigned airspace and 8-3**a, b, c,** or **d** above do not apply:*

a. For Prohibited/Restricted/Warning Areas - ATC will clear nonparticipating aircraft via routing which will provide approved separation from the airspace, unless clearance of nonparticipating aircraft in/through the area is provided for in a memorandum/letter of agreement.*

b. For MOA's and ATCAA's —

(1) ATC will clear nonparticipating aircraft in/through a MOA/ATCAA provided prior coordination has been accomplished as covered in a letter of agreement between the controlling and using (scheduling) agencies and approved separation will be applied between MOA/ATCAA operations and nonparticipating aircraft.

(2) If unable to clear nonparticipating aircraft in/through a MOA/ATCAA in accordance with 8-6b(1) above, ATC will clear aircraft via routing which will provide approved separation from the MOA/ATCAA airspace.

8-6 Note. — Nonparticipating aircraft refers to those aircraft for which controllers have separation responsibility and which have not been authorized by the using agency to operate in/through the special use airspace or ATCAA in question.

8-6a Note. — The FAA has no jurisdictional authority over the use of prohibited or nonjoint use restricted/warning airspace; therefore, clearance cannot be issued for flight therein.

8-6 Reference. — ATCH 8-53.

8-7 TEMPORARY FLIGHT RESTRICTIONS

ATC may authorize operations in a temporary flight restrictions area under its own authority only when flight restrictions are established under FAR 91.91(c) and (d) and only when such operations are conducted under IFR (instrument flight rules). The appropriate ARTCC/air traffic control tower manager, will, however, ensure that such authorized flights do not hamper activities or interfere with the event for which restrictions were implemented. However, ATC will not authorize local IFR flights into the temporary flight restrictions area.

8-7 Reference. — AIM 123.

8-8 EMERGENCY AIR TRAFFIC RULES

a. Whenever the Administrator determines that an emergency condition exists, or will exist, relating to the FAA's ability to operate the air traffic control system and during which normal flight operations cannot be conducted consistent with the required levels of safety and efficiency—

(1) The Administrator issues an immediately effective Air Traffic rule or regulation in response to that emergency condition, and

(2) The Administrator, or the Director, Air Traffic Service, may utilize the NOTAM (Notice to Airmen) system to provide notification of the issuance of the rule or regulation.

b. When this type of NOTAM has been issued, no person may operate an aircraft, or other device governed by the regulation concerned, within the designated airspace, except in accordance with the authorizations, terms, and conditions prescribed in the regulation covered by the NOTAM.

8-8 Reference. — FAR 91.100.

8-9 RESERVED

Section 2. FUEL DUMPING

8-10 FUEL DUMPING ADVISORIES

a. Should it become necessary to dump fuel, the pilot should immediately advise ATC.

b. Facilities concerned will broadcast an advisory on appropriate radio frequencies at 3-minute intervals until the dumping stops.

ATC Phraseology:

Attention all aircraft. Fuel dumping in progress over (location) **at** (altitude) **by** (type aircraft), (flight direction).

c. Upon receipt of such a broadcast, pilots of aircraft affected, which are not on IFR flight plans or special VFR clearances, should clear the area specified in the advisory. Aircraft on IFR flight plans or special VFR clearances will be provided specific separation by ATC.

d. ATC will broadcast a terminating advisory when the fuel dumping operation is completed.

ATC Phraseology:

Attention all aircraft. Fuel dumping by (type aircraft) **terminated.**

8-10 References. — ATCH 8-64; AIM 464.

8-11 INFORMATION REQUIREMENTS

When information is received that an aircraft plans to dump fuel, ATC will determine the route and altitude it will fly and the weather conditions in which the operation will be conducted.

8-11 Reference. — ATCH 8-60.

8-12 FUEL DUMP ROUTING

Except when it is dumping fuel for emergency reasons, an aircraft in either VFR or IFR conditions may be requested to fly a different route.

8-12 Reference. — ATCH 8-61.

8-13 ALTITUDE ASSIGNMENTS

If an aircraft is dumping fuel in IFR conditions, ATC will assign an altitude at least 2,000 feet above the highest obstacle within 5 miles of the route or pattern being flown.

8-13 Reference. — ATCH 8-62.

8-14 SEPARATION MINIMA

ATC will separate known aircraft from the aircraft dumping fuel as follows:

a. IFR aircraft, by one of the following:

(1) *1,000 feet (2,000 feet* above FL 290) above it.

(2) *2,000 feet* below it.

(3) *5 miles* radar.

(4) *5 miles* laterally.

b. VFR radar-identified aircraft by *5 miles* and in accordance with radar vectoring.

8-14 Reference. — ATCH 8-53.

8-15 thru 8-19 RESERVED

Section 3. UNMANNED BALLOONS

8-20 GENERAL

The majority of unmanned free balloons currently being operated have, extending below them, either a suspension device to which the payload or instrument package is attached, or a trailing wire antenna, or both. In many instances these balloon subsystems may be invisible to the pilot until his aircraft is close to the balloon, thereby creating a potentially dangerous situation. Therefore, good judgment on the part of the pilot dictates that aircraft should remain well clear of all unmanned free balloons and flight below them should be avoided at all times.

8-20 Reference. — ATCH 8-80.

8-21 APPLICATION

Controllers will apply the following procedures, as appropriate, when unmanned free balloons are within airspace for which they have control jurisdiction:*

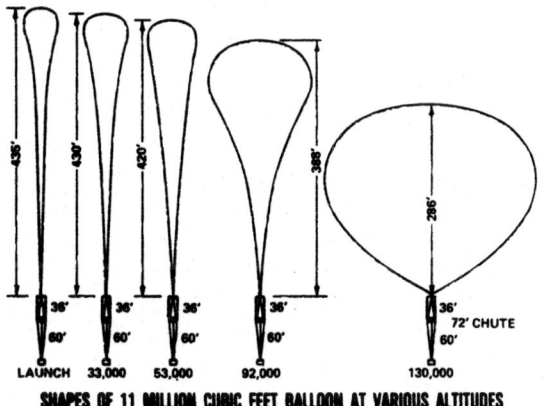

8-21 Illustration

a. ATC will radar flight follow balloons to the extent that equipment capabilities permit. If radar flight following is not possible, tracking may be attempted by communication with the "chase plane," telephone contact with the operator, pilot, or ground observation reports.*

b. With pilot concurrence, ATC will provide separation between aircraft and balloons when they are satisfied that the balloon information is sufficiently reliable to provide the service. Controllers may not attempt to separate aircraft from the balloon by using vertical separation unless they have accurate balloon altitude information.

c. Traffic advisories will be provided to all affected aircraft during initial contact specifying the balloon's known or estimated position, direction of movement, and altitude as "unknown" or "reported," as appropriate.*

ATC Phraseology:

Unmanned free balloon over (name of location), *or*

Estimated over (name of location), **moving** (direction of movement).

Last reported altitude at (altitude as reported by the operator or determined from pilot report), *or*

Altitude unknown.

8-21 Note. — These procedures apply to unmanned free balloons that carry payloads as described in FAR 101.1(a)(4). Payloads may weigh several hundred pounds and the physical shape of the balloons change at various altitudes/flight levels. Balloon and payload ascend at an average rate of 400 feet a minute. Over the descent area, the payload is normally released from the balloon and descends by parachute at a minimum rate of 1,000 feet a minute. The balloon is normally deflated automatically when the payload is released. The operator is required to advise ATC one hour in advance of descent in accordance with FAR 101.39.

8-21a Note. — Some operators have equipped their balloons with transponder beacons in addition to a radar reflection device or material required by FAR 101.35. But at cruise altitude, the balloon's communications equipment and transponder, if so equipped, are operated intermittently to conserve battery energy.

8-21c Note. — Unless ATC requires otherwise, operators of unmanned free balloons are required to monitor the course of the balloon and record its position at least every two hours. Except as required in FAR 101.39(h), balloon position reports are not forwarded by the operator unless requested by the ATC.

8-21 Reference. — ATCH 8-80.

8-22 DERELICT BALLOONS

Balloons become derelict when a moored balloon slips its mooring and becomes a hazard to air navigation or when an unmanned free balloon flight cannot be terminated as planned. When this occurs:

a. In the case of a moored balloon which has slipped its moorings, ATC will issue traffic advisories.

b. In the case of an unmanned free balloon, ATC will flight follow the balloon and, to the extent possible, provide aircraft under its control separation from the balloon.

c. If radar contact with the balloon is lost, ATC will broadcast an advisory to all aircraft operating in the airspace affected by the derelict balloon at 10-minute intervals, continuing until the derelict balloon is no longer a factor.

ATC Phraseology:
Advisory to all aircraft.
Derelict balloon:
reported in the vicinity of (location), *or*
estimated in vicinity of (location), *or*
reported over (location), *or*
radar reported over (location).
Last reported altitude at (altitude as reported by operator or pilot report), *or*
Altitude unknown.

8-22 Reference. — ATCH 8-81.

8-23 thru 8-29 RESERVED

Section 4. PARACHUTE JUMPING

8-30 PARACHUTE JUMP ALTITUDE ADVISORY

Pilots of aircraft engaged in parachute jump operations are reminded that all reported altitudes must be with reference to mean sea level, or flight level, as appropriate, to enable ATC to provide meaningful traffic information.*

8-30 Note. — Procedures relating to parachute jump areas are contained in FAR-105. Tabulations of parachute jump areas in the U.S. are contained in the Airport/Facility Directory.

8-30 Reference. — AIM 135.

8-31 JUMP COORDINATION

ATC will coordinate any pertinent information prior to and at the end of each parachute jump or series of jumps which begin or end in its area of jurisdiction with other affected ATC facilities/sectors.*

8-31 Note. — FAR 105.25 prescribes the information required from each person requesting authorization or submitting notification for nonemergency parachute jumping activity.

8-31 Reference. — ATCH 8-90.

8-32 JUMP AUTHORIZATION

EN ROUTE

a. ATC will authorize parachute jumping only within airspace designated for the jumping activity.

b. ATC will separate aircraft, other than those participating in the jump operation, from the airspace authorized for the jumping activity.

c. ATC will impose, as necessary, any conditions and restrictions which in the controller's judgment would promote the safety of the operation.

8-32 Reference. — ATCH 8-91.

8-33 CONTROL ZONE JUMPS

TERMINAL

ATC will handle requests to conduct jump operations in or into a Control Zone in which there is a functioning control tower operated by the United States as follows:

a. By authorizing parachute jumping with respect to known or observed traffic.

b. By issuing advisory information to the jump aircraft and to nonparticipating aircraft as necessary for the safe conduct of the jump operation.

8-33 Reference. — ATCH 8-92.

8-34 OTHER CONTROLLED AIRSPACE JUMPS

ATC will handle notifications to conduct jump operations in other controlled airspace as follows:

a. By issuing a traffic advisory to the jump aircraft before the jump. Aircraft type, altitude, and direction of flight of all known traffic which will transit the airspace within which the jump will be conducted will be included.*

b. By issuing advisories to all known aircraft which will transit the airspace within which the jump operations will be conducted. Advisories will consist of the location, time, duration, and altitude from which the jump will be made.

c. When time or numbers of aircraft make individual transmissions impractical, advisories to nonparticipating aircraft may be broadcast on appropriate control frequencies, or when available, the ATIS broadcast.

d. When requested by the pilot and to the extent possible, ATC will assist nonparticipating aircraft to avoid the airspace within which the jump will be conducted.

8-34a Note. — FAR 105.14 prescribes that, except when otherwise authorized by ATC, parachute jumping is not allowed in or into controlled airspace unless radio communications have been established between the aircraft and the nearest FAA ATC facility or FSS at least 5 minutes before the jumping activity is to begin for the purpose of receiving information from the aircraft about known air traffic in the vicinity of the jump aircraft.

8-34 Reference. — ATCH 8-93.

Chapter 9
TABLE OF CONTENTS

Section 1. GENERAL

		Page
9-1	Pilot Responsibility and Emergency Responsibility	9-1
9-2	Emergency Actions	9-1
9-3	Emergency Assistance	9-1
9-4	Emergency Determination	9-2
9-5	Emergency Information Requested/Required by ATC	9-2
9-6	Emergency Frequencies	9-2
9-7	Altitude Change for Improved Reception	9-2
9-8	Frequency Changes	9-2
9-9	In-Flight Monitoring of Emergency Frequencies	9-3
9-10	Aircraft Orientation Methods	9-3
9-11	Emergency Airport Recommendation	9-3
9-12	Guidance to Emergency Airport	9-3
9-13	Airport Ground Emergency	9-3
9-14	National Airspace Security Plan	9-3
9-15—9-19	Reserved	9-4

Section 2. HIJACKINGS AND BOMB THREATS

9-20	Special Emergency (Air Piracy)	9-5
9-21	Code 7500 Display	9-5
9-22	Aircraft Bomb Emergencies	9-5
9-23	Explosive Detection K-9 Teams	9-6
9-24—9-29	Reserved	9-6

Section 3. EMERGENCY RADAR ASSISTANCE

9-30	VFR Aircraft In Weather Difficulty	9-7
9-31	Radar Assistance to VFR Aircraft in Weather Difficulty	9-7
9-32	Radar Assistance Techniques	9-7
9-33	Emergency Obstruction Video Map	9-7
9-34	Pilot Responsibility	9-7
9-35	Controller Discretion	9-8
9-36—9-39	Reserved	9-8

TABLE OF CONTENTS (Continued)

Section 4. IFR COMMUNICATIONS FAILURE

		Page
9-40	General	9-9
9-41	VFR Conditions	9-9
9-42	IFR Conditions	9-9
9-43	Pilot Responsibility	9-9
9-44	ATC Actions	9-9
9-45	Transponder Operation During Two-Way Communications Failure	9-10
9-46	Reestablishing Radio Contact	9-10
9-47	ARTCC Radio Frequency Outage	9-10
9-48	Overdue Aircraft	9-10
9-49	Traffic Restrictions	9-11
9-50	Airport Lighting Requirements	9-11
9-51	Traffic Resumption	9-11
9-52—9-59	Reserved	9-11

Section 5. DIRECTION FINDING SERVICE

9-60	Actions Required	9-12
9-61	Direction Finding Instrument Approach Procedure	9-12
9-62	DF Fixing by Net	9-12
9-63	DF Fixing by One Facility	9-12
9-64	Action After Position Determination	9-12
9-65	VFR DF Service	9-12
9-66	Emergency DF Approach Procedures	9-13

Chapter 9. EMERGENCIES

Section 1. GENERAL

9-1 PILOT RESPONSIBILITY AND EMERGENCY RESPONSIBILITY

a. The pilot in command of an aircraft is directly responsible for and is the final authority as to the operation of that aircraft. In an emergency requiring immediate action, the pilot in command has the authority to deviate from any rule in the FAR, Subpart A, General, and Subpart B, Flight Rules, to the extent required to meet that emergency.

b. If the emergency authority of FAR 91.3(b) is used to deviate from the provisions of an ATC clearance, the pilot in command shall, upon the request of the administrator, send a written report of that deviation to the administrator.

c. Unless deviation is necessary under the emergency authority of FAR 91.3, pilots of IFR flights experiencing two-way radio communications failure are expected to adhere to the procedures prescribed under FAR 91.127 "IFR operations, two-way radio communications failure."

9-1 References. — FAR 91.3, 91.127; AIM 440.

9-2 EMERGENCY ACTIONS

a. An emergency can be either a *Distress* or *Urgency* condition, as defined in the "Pilot/Controller Glossary."

b. A pilot who encounters a *Distress* condition should declare an emergency by beginning the initial communication with the word *"Mayday,"* preferably repeated three times. For an *Urgency* condition, the word *"Pan-Pan"* should be used in the same manner.*

c. If the words *"Mayday"* or *"Pan-Pan"* are not used and the controller is in doubt that a situation constitutes an emergency or potential emergency, it will be handled as though it were an emergency.

d. Because of the infinite variety of possible emergency situations, specific procedures cannot be prescribed. However, when controllers believe an emergency exists or is imminent, they will select and pursue a course of action which appears to be most appropriate under the circumstances and which most nearly conforms to the instructions in the *Air Traffic Control Handbook*.

9-2b Note. — Pilots who become apprehensive for their safety for *any* reason should *request assistance immediately.* Ready and willing help is available in the form of radio, radar, direction finding stations, and other aircraft. Delay has caused accidents and cost lives. *SAFETY IS NOT A LUXURY! TAKE ACTION!*

9-2 References. — ATCH 9-1; AIM 441.

9-3 EMERGENCY ASSISTANCE

ATC will provide maximum assistance to aircraft in distress. They will enlist the services of available radar facilities and DF facilities operated by the FAA, the military services, and the Federal Communications Commission, as well as their emergency services and facilities, when the pilot requests or when ATC deems necessary.*

9-3 Note 1. — The National SAR Plan assigns search and rescue responsibilities as follows:

a. To the military agencies - Conducting physical search and rescue operations.

b. To the FAA -

(1) Providing emergency service to aircraft in distress.

(2) Assuring that SAR procedures will be initiated if an aircraft becomes overdue or unreported. This is accomplished through the ATC system for IFR aircraft and the flight plan system for VFR aircraft.

(3) Attempting to locate overdue or unreported aircraft by INREQ and ALNOT communications search.

(4) Making all possible facilities available for use by the searching agencies.

9-3 Note 2. — FSS's serve as the central points for collecting and disseminating information on an overdue or missing aircraft which is not on an IFR flight plan.

9-3 Note 3. — Centers serve as the central points for collecting information, for coordinating with SAR, and for conducting a communications search by distributing any necessary ALNOT's concerning:

a. Overdue or missing IFR aircraft.

b. IFR aircraft in an emergency situation occurring in their respective areas.

c. Aircraft on a combination VFR/IFR or an airfield IFR flight plan and 30 minutes have passed since the pilot requested IFR clearance and neither communication nor radar contact can be established with it. For SAR purposes, these aircraft are treated the same as IFR aircraft.

d. Overdue or missing aircraft which have been authorized to operate in accordance with Special VFR clearance.

9-3 Note 4. — The ARTCC serves as the central point for collecting information and coordinating with the RCC on ELT signals.

9-3 Reference. — ATCH 9-3.

9-4 EMERGENCY DETERMINATION

ATC will consider that an aircraft emergency exists when:

a. An emergency is declared by either:

(1) The pilot.

(2) ATC facility personnel.*

(3) Officials responsible for the operation of the aircraft.

b. Reports indicate that the aircraft has made a forced landing, is about to do so, or its operating efficiency is so impaired that a forced landing will be necessary.

c. Reports indicate the crew has abandoned the aircraft or is about to do so.

d. An emergency radar beacon response is received.

e. Intercept or escort aircraft services are required.

f. The need for ground rescue appears likely.

g. An Emergency Locator Transmitter (ELT) signal is heard or reported.

9-4a(2) Note. — An example of an emergency which may be declared by ATC personnel is simultaneous unexpected loss of radar contact and radio communications with an aircraft.

9-4 Reference. — ATCH 9-15.

9-5 EMERGENCY INFORMATION REQUESTED/REQUIRED BY ATC

a. Controllers will start assistance as soon as enough information has been obtained upon which to act. Information requirements will vary, depending on the existing situation. Minimum required information for in-flight emergencies is:

(1) Aircraft identification and type.

(2) Nature of the emergency.

(3) Pilot's desires.

b. After initiating action, controllers will obtain the following items or any other pertinent information from the pilot or aircraft operator, as necessary:

(1) Aircraft altitude.

(2) Fuel remaining in time.

(3) Pilot reported weather.

(4) Pilot capability for IFR flight.

(5) Time and place of last known position.

(6) Heading since last known position.

(7) Airspeed.

(8) Navigation equipment capability.

(9) NAVAID signals received.

(10) Visible landmarks.

(11) Aircraft color.

(12) Number of people on board.

(13) Point of departure and destination.

(14) Emergency equipment on board.

9-5 Reference. — ATCH 9-10.

9-6 EMERGENCY FREQUENCIES

Although the frequency in use or other frequencies assigned by ATC are preferable, the following emergency frequencies may be used for distress or urgency communications, if necessary or desirable:

a. 121.5 MHz and 243.0 MHz - Both have a range generally limited to line of sight. 121.5 MHz is guarded by direction finding stations and some military and civil aircraft. 243.0 MHz is guarded by military aircraft. Both 121.5 MHz and 243.0 MHz are guarded by military towers, most civil towers, FSS's, and ATC radar facilities. Normally ARTCC emergency frequency capability does not extend to radar coverage limits. If an ARTCC does not respond when called on 121.5 MHz or 243.0 MHz, pilots should call the nearest tower or FSS.

b. 2182 kHz - The range of this frequency is generally less than 300 miles for the average aircraft installation. It can be used to request assistance from stations in the maritime service. 2182 kHz is guarded by major radio stations serving Coast Guard Rescue Coordination Centers, and Coast Guard units along the sea coasts of the U.S. and shores of the Great Lakes. The call "Coast Guard" will alert all Coast Guard Radio Stations within range. 2182 kHz is also guarded by most coastal commercial radio stations and some maritime vessels.

9-6 Reference. — AIM 460.

9-7 ALTITUDE CHANGE FOR IMPROVED RECEPTION

When ATC considers it necessary and if weather and circumstances permit, controllers will recommend that the aircraft maintain or increase altitude to improve communications, radar, or DF reception.

9-7 Reference. — ATCH 9-13.

9-8 FREQUENCY CHANGES

Although 121.5 MHz and 243.0 MHz are emergency frequencies, ATC considers it best to keep the aircraft on the initial contact frequency. Frequency changes will only be issued when there is a valid reason.

9-8 Reference. — ATCH 9-11.

9-9 IN-FLIGHT MONITORING OF EMERGENCY FREQUENCIES

Pilots are encouraged to monitor 121.5 MHz and/or 243.0 MHz while in-flight to assist in identifying possible emergency ELT transmissions. On receiving a signal, pilots should report the following information to the nearest ATC facility:

a. Position at the time the signal was first heard.

b. Position at the time the signal was last heard.

c. Position at maximum signal strength.

d. Flight altitudes and frequency on which the emergency signal was heard - 121.5 MHz or 243.0 MHz. If possible, positions should be given relative to a navigation aid. If the aircraft has homing equipment, the pilot should provide the bearing to the emergency signal with each reported position.

9-9 Reference. — AIM 454.

9-10 AIRCRAFT ORIENTATION METHODS

Aircraft will be oriented by the means most appropriate to the circumstances. Recognized methods include:

a. Radar.

b. DF.

c. NAVAID's.

d. Pilotage.

e. Sighting by other aircraft.

9-10 Reference. — ATCH 9-12.

9-11 EMERGENCY AIRPORT RECOMMENDATION

ATC will consider the following factors when recommending an emergency airport:

a. Remaining fuel in relation to airport distances.

b. Weather conditions.

c. Airport conditions.

d. NAVAID status.

e. Aircraft type.

f. Pilot's qualifications.

g. Vectoring or homing capability to the emergency airport.

9-11 Reference. — ATCH 9-29.

9-12 GUIDANCE TO EMERGENCY AIRPORT

When necessary, ATC will use any of the following for guidance to the airport:

a. Radar.

b. DF.

c. Following another aircraft.

d. NAVAID's.

e. Pilotage by landmarks.

f. Compass headings.

9-12 Reference. — ATCH 9-30.

9-13 AIRPORT GROUND EMERGENCY

TERMINAL

When an emergency occurs on the airport proper, ATC will control other air and ground traffic to avoid conflicts in the area where the emergency is being handled. This also applies when routes within the airport proper are required for movement of local emergency equipment going to or from an emergency which occurs outside the airport proper.*

9-13 Note. — Aircraft operated in proximity to accident or other emergency or disaster locations may cause hindrances to airborne and surface rescue or relief operations. Congestion, distraction, or other effects such as wake turbulence from nearby airplanes and helicopters could prevent or delay proper execution of these operations.

9-13 Reference. — ATCH 9-6.

9-14 NATIONAL AIRSPACE SECURITY PLAN

a. During defense emergency or air defense emergency conditions, additional special security instructions may be issued in accordance with the SCATANA (Security Control of Air Traffic and Air Navigation Aids) plan.

b. Under the provisions of the SCATANA plan, the military will direct the action to be taken—in regard to landing, grounding, diversion, or dispersal of aircraft, and the control of air navigation aids in the defense of the U.S. during emergency conditions.

c. At the time a portion of all of SCATANA is implemented, ATC facilities will broadcast appropriate instructions received from the military over available ATC frequencies. Depending on instructions received from the military, VFR flights may be directed to land at the nearest airport, and IFR flights will be expected to proceed as directed by ATC.

d. Pilots on the ground may be required to file a flight plan and obtain an approval (through the FAA) prior to conducting flight operations.

e. In view of the above, pilots should guard an ATC or FSS frequency at all times while conducting flight operations.

9-14 Reference. — AIM 430.

9-15 thru 9-19 RESERVED

Section 2. HIJACKINGS AND BOMB THREATS

9-20 SPECIAL EMERGENCY (AIR PIRACY)

a. A special emergency is a condition of air piracy, or other hostile act by a person(s) aboard an aircraft, which threatens the safety of the aircraft or its passengers.

b. The pilot of an aircraft reporting a special emergency condition should:

(1) If circumstances permit, apply *distress or urgency* communication procedures. Include the details of the special emergency.

(2) If circumstances do not permit the use of prescribed *distress or urgency* procedures, transmit on the frequency in use at the time as many as possible of the following elements spoken distinctly and in the following order:

(a) Facility identification (time and circumstances permitting).

(b) The identification of the aircraft and present position.

(c) The nature of the special emergency condition and pilot intentions (circumstances permitting).

(d) If unable to provide this information, use code words and/or transponder as follows: state *"TRANSPONDER SEVEN FIVE ZERO ZERO."* Meaning: *"I am being hijacked/forced to a new destination;"* and/or use Transponder Setting MODE 3/A, Code 7500.*

c. If it is possible to do so without jeopardizing the safety of the flight, the pilot of a hijacked passenger aircraft, after departing from the cleared routing over which the aircraft was operating, should attempt one or more of the following procedures, insofar as circumstances may permit:

(1) Maintain a true airspeed of no more than 400 knots, and preferably an altitude of between 10,000 and 25,000 feet.

(2) Fly a course toward the destination which the hijacker has announced.

d. If these procedures result in either radio contact or air intercept, the pilot should attempt to comply with any instructions received which may direct him to an appropriate landing field.

9-20b(2)(d) Note. — Code 7500 will never be assigned by ATC without prior notification from the pilot that his aircraft is being subjected to unlawful interference. The pilot should refuse the assigment of Code 7500 in any other situation and inform the controller accordingly. Code 7500 will trigger the special emergency indicator in all radar ATC facilities.

9-20 Reference. — AIM 463.

9-21 CODE 7500 DISPLAY

When controllers observe a Mode 3/A Code 7500, they will do the following:*

a. ATC will acknowledge and confirm receipt of Code 7500 by asking the pilot to verify it. If the aircraft is not being subjected to unlawful interference, the pilot should respond to the query by broadcasting in the clear that he is not being subjected to unlawful interference. If the reply is in the affirmative or if no reply is received, the controller will not question the pilot further but be responsive to the aircraft requests.*

ATC Phraseology:

(Call-sign) (name of facility), **verify squawking seven five zero zero.**

b. ATC will flight follow aircraft and use normal handsoff procedures without requiring transmissions or responses by aircraft unless communications have been established by the aircraft.

c. If aircraft are dispatched to escort the hijacked aircraft, ATC will provide all possible assistance to the escort aircraft to aid in placing them in a position behind the hijacked aircraft.

d. To the extent possible, ATC will afford the same control service to the aircraft operating VFR observed on the hijack code.

9-21 Note 1. — Military facilities will notify the appropriate FAA ARTCC, or the host nation agency responsible for en route control, of any indication that an aircraft is being hijacked. They will also provide full cooperation with the civil agencies in the control of such aircraft.

9-21 Note 2. — EN ROUTE: During narrowband radar operations, Code 7500 causes HIJK to blink in the data block.

9-21 Note 3. — Only nondiscrete Code 7500 will be decoded as the hijack code.

9-21a Note. — Code 7500 is only assigned upon notification from the pilot that his aircraft is being subjected to unlawful interference. Therefore, pilots have been requested to refuse the assignment of Code 7500 in any other situation and to inform the controller accordingly.

9-21 Reference. — ATCH 9-22.

9-22 AIRCRAFT BOMB EMERGENCIES

a. When a threat is targeted against a specific aircraft and controllers are in contact with the suspect aircraft, they will take the following actions as appropriate:

(1) Advise the pilot of the threat.

(2) Inform the pilot that technical assistance can be obtained from an FAA Aviation Explosive Expert.

(3) Ask the pilot if he desires to climb or descend to an altitude that would equalize or reduce the outside air pressure/existing cabin air pressure differential. ATC will issue or relay an appropriate clearance considering MEA, MOCA, MRA, and weather.

(4) Handle the aircraft as an emergency and/or provide the most expeditious handling possible with respect to the safety of other aircraft, ground facilities, and personnel.*

(5) Issue or relay clearances to a new destination if requested.

(6) When a pilot requests technical assistance or if it is apparent that a pilot may need such assistance, controllers may not suggest what actions the pilot should take concerning a bomb, but will obtain the following information:

(a) Type, series, and model of the aircraft.

(b) Precise location/description of the bomb device if known.

(c) Other details which may be pertinent.*

b. When a bomb threat involves an aircraft on the ground and ATC is in contact with the suspect aircraft, they will take the following actions, in addition to those discussed in the preceding paragraph, which may be appropriate:

(1) If the aircraft is at an airport where tower control or FSS advisory service is not available, or if the pilot ignores the threat at any airport, ATC will recommend that takeoff be delayed until the pilot or aircraft operator establishes that a bomb is not aboard in accordance with FAR, Part 121. If the pilot insists on taking off and in ATC's opinion the operation will not adversely affect other traffic, controllers will issue or relay an ATC clearance.

(2) ATC will advise the aircraft to remain as far away from other aircraft and facilities as possible, to clear the runway, if appropriate, and to taxi to an isolated or designated search area. When it is impractical or if the pilot takes an alternative action (e.g., parking and off-loading immediately), ATC will advise other aircraft to remain clear of the suspect aircraft by at least 100 yards, if able.*

c. When a pilot reports the discovery of a bomb or suspected bomb on an aircraft which is airborne or on the ground, ATC will determine the pilot's intentions and comply with his requests insofar as possible. All the actions discussed in the preceding paragraphs will be taken which may be appropriate under the existing circumstance.

d. Because the handling of aircraft when a hijacker has or is suspected of having a bomb requires special considerations, ATC will apply hijacking procedures and offer assistance to the pilot according to the preceding paragraphs, if needed.

9-22a(4) Note. — Emergency handling is discretionary and will be based on the situation. With certain types of threats, plans may call for a low-key action or response.

9-22a(6)(c) Note. — The following details may be of significance if known, but it is not intended that the pilot should disturb a suspected bomb/bomb container to ascertain the information: the altitude or time set for the bomb to explode, type of detonating action (barometric, time, anti-handling, remote radio transmitter), power source (battery, electrical, mechanical), type of initiator (blasting cap, flash bulb, chemical), and the type of explosive/incendiary charge (dynamite, black powder, chemical).

9-22b(2) Note. — Passenger deplaning may be of paramount importance and must be considered before the aircraft is parked or moved away from service areas. The decision to use ramp facilities rests with the pilot, aircraft operator, or airport manager.

9-22 Reference. — ATCH 9-27.

9-23 EXPLOSIVE DETECTION K-9 TEAMS

ATC will take the following actions should controllers receive an aircraft request for the location of the nearest explosive detection K-9 team.

a. When controllers receive the nearest location of the explosive detection K-9 team, they will relay the information to the pilot.

b. If the aircraft wishes to divert to the airport location provided by ATC, controllers will obtain an estimated arrival time from the pilot.

9-23 Reference. — ATCH 9-28.

9-24 thru 9-29 RESERVED

Section 3. EMERGENCY RADAR ASSISTANCE

9-30 VFR AIRCRAFT IN WEATHER DIFFICULTY

If a VFR aircraft requests assistance when it encounters or is about to encounter IFR weather conditions, ATC will request the aircraft to contact the appropriate facility and inform that facility of the situation. If the aircraft is unable to communicate with the control facility, information and clearances will be relayed.

9-30 Reference. — ATCH 9-23.

9-31 RADAR ASSISTANCE TO VFR AIRCRAFT IN WEATHER DIFFICULTY

a. If a VFR aircraft requests radar assistance when it encounters or is about to encounter IFR weather conditions, ATC will ask the pilot if he is qualified for and capable of conducting IFR flight.

b. If the pilot states he is qualified for and capable of IFR flight, ATC will request him to file an IFR flight plan and then issue clearance to destination airport, as appropriate.

c. If the pilot states he is not qualified for or not capable of conducting IFR flight, or if he refuses to file an IFR flight plan, ATC will take whichever of the following actions is appropriate:

(1) ATC will inform the pilot of airports where VFR conditions are reported, provide other pertinent weather information, and ask if he will elect to conduct VFR flight to such an airport.

(2) If the action in (1) is not feasible or the pilot declines to conduct VFR flight to another airport, ATC will provide radar assistance if the pilot:

(a) Declares an emergency.

(b) Refuses to declare an emergency and controllers have determined the exact nature of the radar services the pilot desires.

(3) If the aircraft has already encountered IFR conditions, ATC will inform the pilot of the minimum safe altitude. If the aircraft is below the minimum safe altitude and sufficiently accurate position information has been received or radar identification is established, ATC will furnish a heading or radial on which to climb to reach the minimum safe altitude.

9-31 Reference. — ATCH 9-24.

9-32 RADAR ASSISTANCE TECHNIQUES

The following techniques are used to the extent possible when controllers provide radar assistance to a pilot not qualified to operate in IFR conditions:*

a. Radio frequency changes are avoided except when necessary to provide a clear communications channel.

b. Turns will be made while the aircraft is in VFR conditions so it will be in a position to fly a straight course while in IFR conditions.

c. Pilots will be asked to lower gear and slow aircraft to approach speed while in VFR conditions.

d. Requiring a climb or descent while in a turn if in IFR conditions will be avoided.

e. Abrupt maneuvers will be avoided.

f. Aircraft will be vectored to VFR conditions.

9-32 Note. — In many cases, the controller will be unable to determine if flight into instrument conditions will result from his instructions. To avoid possible hazards resulting from being vectored into IFR conditions, pilots should keep the controller advised of the weather conditions in which they are operating and along the course ahead.

9-32 References. — ATCH 9-25; AIM 164.

9-33 EMERGENCY OBSTRUCTION VIDEO MAP

a. The EOVM (Emergency Obstruction Video Map) is intended to facilitate advisory service to an aircraft in an emergency situation wherein an appropriate terrain/obstacle clearance minimum altitude cannot be maintained. It will only be used and the service provided under the following conditions:*

(1) The pilot has declared an emergency.

(2) The controller has determined that an emergency condition exists or is imminent because of the pilot's inability to maintain an appropriate terrain/obstacle clearance minimum altitude.

b. When providing emergency vectoring service, the controller will advise the pilot that any headings issued are emergency advisories intended only to direct the aircraft toward and over an area of lower terrain/obstacle elevation.

9-33a Note. — Appropriate terrain/obstacle clearance minimum altitudes may be defined as Minimum IFR Altitude (MIA), Minimum En Route Altitude (MEA), Minimum Obstruction Clearance Altitude (MOCA), or Minimum Vectoring Altitude (MVA).

9-33 Reference. — ATCH 9-31.

9-34 PILOT RESPONSIBILITY

Pilots should clearly understand that authorization to proceed in accordance with such radar navigational assistance does not constitute authorization for the pilot to violate FAR's. In effect, assistance provided is on the basis that navigational guidance information issued is advisory in nature and the responsibility of flying the aircraft safely, remains with the pilot.

9-34 Reference. — AIM 164.

9-35 CONTROLLER DISCRETION

Radar navigation assistance (vectors) and other radar derived information may be provided in response to pilot requests. Many factors, such as limitations of radar, volume of traffic, communications frequency, congestion, and controller workload could prevent the controller from providing it. The controller has complete discretion for determining if he is able to provide the service in a particular case. His decision not to provide the service in a particular case is not subject to question.

9-35 Reference. — AIM 164.

9-36 thru 9-39 RESERVED

Section 4. IFR COMMUNICATIONS FAILURE

9-40 GENERAL

Unless otherwise authorized by ATC, a pilot who has two-way radio communications failure when operating under IFR shall comply with the rules of FAR 91.127, described in part herein.

9-40 Reference. — FAR 91.127.

9-41 VFR CONDITIONS

If radio failure occurs in VFR conditions, or if VFR conditions are encountered after the failure, each pilot shall continue the flight under VFR and land as soon as practicable.

9-41 Reference. — FAR 91.127.

9-42 IFR CONDITIONS

If radio failure occurs in IFR conditions, each pilot shall continue the flight according to the following:

a. *Route.*

(1) By the route assigned in the last ATC clearance received;

(2) If being radar vectored, by the direct route from the point of radio failure to the fix, route, or airway specified in the vector clearance;

(3) In the absence of an assigned route, by the route that ATC has advised may be expected in a further clearance; or

(4) In the absence of an assigned route or a route that ATC has advised may be expected in a further clearance, by the route filed in the flight plan.

b. *Altitude.* At the highest of the following altitudes or flight levels for the route segment being flown:

(1) The altitude or flight level assigned in the last ATC clearance received;

(2) The minimum altitude (converted, if appropriate, to minimum flight level as prescribed in FAR 91.81(c)) for IFR operations; or

(3) The altitude or flight level ATC has advised may be expected in a further clearance.

c. *Leaving the clearance limit.*

(1) When the clearance limit is a fix from which an approach begins, commence descent or descent and approach as close as possible to the expect further clearance time if one has been received, or if one has not been received, as close as possible to the estimated time of arrival as calculated from the filed or amended (with ATC) estimated time en route.

(2) If the clearance limit is not a fix from which an approach begins, leave the clearance limit at the expect further clearance time if one has been received, or if none has been received, upon arrival over the clearance limit, and proceed to a fix from which an approach begins and commence descent and approach as close as possible to the estimated time of arrival as calculated from the filed or amended (with ATC) estimated time en route.

9-42 Reference. — FAR 91.127.

9-43 PILOT RESPONSIBILITY

a. It is virtually impossible to provide regulations and procedures applicable to all possible situations associated with two-way radio communications failure. During two-way radio communications failure, when confronted by a situation not covered in the regulation, pilots are expected to exercise good judgment in whatever action they elect to take. Should the situation so dictate, they should not be reluctant to use the emergency authority contained in FAR 91.3(b).

b. Whether two-way communications failure constitutes an emergency depends on the circumstances, and in any event, it is a determination made by the pilot. FAR 91.3(b) authorizes a pilot to deviate from any rule in Part 91, Subparts A and B, to the extent required to meet an emergency.

c. In the event of two-way radio communications failure, ATC service will be provided on the basis that the pilot is operating in accordance with FAR 91.127. A pilot experiencing two-way communications failure should (unless emergency authority is exercised) comply with FAR 91.127.

9-43 Reference. — AIM 470.

9-44 ATC ACTIONS

The following actions will be taken, as appropriate, if two-way radio communications is lost with an aircraft:*

a. ATC will broadcast clearances through any available means of communications, including the voice feature of NAVAID's.*

b. ATC will attempt to reestablish communications by having the aircraft use its transponder or make turns to acknowledge clearances and answer questions. ATC may request any of the following in using the transponder:

(1) By requesting the aircraft to reply Mode 3/A *"IDENT."*

(2) By requesting the aircraft to reply on Code 7600 or, if already on Code 7600, the appropriate stratum code.

(3) By requesting the aircraft to change to *"stand-by"* for sufficient time for ATC to be sure that the lack of a target is the result of the requested action.

ATC Phraseology:

Reply not received, if you hear me (appropriate instructions). (Action) **observed, will continue radar control.**

c. ATC will broadcast a clearance for the aircraft to proceed to its filed alternate airport at the MEA if the aircraft operator concurs.

9-44 Note. — When an IFR aircraft experiences two-way radio communications failure, air traffic control is based on anticipated pilot actions.

9-44a Note. — 'Any available means' includes the use of FSS and ARINC.

9-44 Reference. — ATCH 9-43.

9-45 TRANSPONDER OPERATION DURING TWO-WAY COMMUNICATIONS FAILURE

a. If a pilot of an aircraft with a coded radar beacon transponder experiences a loss of two-way radio capability, he should:

(1) Adjust his transponder to reply on Mode 3/A, Code 7700 for a period of 1 minute.

(2) Then change to Code 7600 and remain on 7600 for a period of 15 minutes or the remainder of the flight, whichever comes first.

(3) Repeat steps (1) and (2) as practicable.

b. The pilot should understand that he may or may not be in an area of radar coverage.

9-45 Reference. — AIM 471.

9-46 REESTABLISHING RADIO CONTACT

a. In addition to monitoring the NAVAID voice feature, the pilot should attempt to reestablish communications by attempting contact:

(1) On the previously assigned frequency, or

(2) With an FSS or ARINC.*

b. If communications are established with an FSS or ARINC, the pilot should advise that radio communications on the previously assigned frequency have been lost giving the aircraft's position, altitude, and last assigned frequency, and then request further clearance from the controlling facility. The preceding does not preclude the use of 121.5 MHz. There is no priority on which action should be attempted first. If the capability exists, do all at the same time.

9-46a(2) Note. — Aeronautical Radio/Incorporated (ARINC) is a commercial communications corporation which designs, constructs, operates, leases, or otherwise engages in radio activities serving the aviation community. ARINC has the capability of relaying information to/from ATC facilities throughout the country.

9-46 Reference. — AIM 472.

9-47 ARTCC RADIO FREQUENCY OUTAGE

ARTCC's normally have at least one back up radio receiver and transmitter system for each frequency which can usually be placed into service quickly with little or no disruption of ATC service. Occasionally, technical problems may cause a delay but switchover seldom takes more than 60 seconds. When it appears that the outage will not be quickly remedied, the ARTCC will usually request a nearby aircraft, if there is one, to switch to the affected frequency to broadcast communications instructions. It is important, therefore, that the pilot wait at least 1 minute before deciding that the ARTCC has actually experienced a radio frequency failure. When such an outage does occur, the pilot should, if workload and equipment capability permit, maintain a listening watch on the affected frequency while attempting to comply with the following recommended procedures:

a. If two-way communications cannot be established with the ARTCC after changing frequencies, a pilot should attempt to recontact the previous controller for the assignment of an alternative frequency or other instructions.

b. When an ARTCC radio frequency failure occurs after two-way communications have been established, the pilot should attempt to reestablish contact with the center on any other known ARTCC frequency, preferably that of the next responsible sector when practicable, and ask for instructions.*

c. If communications cannot be reestablished by either method, the pilot is expected to request communications instructions from the FSS appropriate to the route of flight.

9-47b Note. — The exchange of information between an aircraft and an ARTCC through an FSS is quicker than relay via company radio because the FSS has direct interphone lines to the responsible ARTCC sector. Accordingly, when circumstances dictate a choice between the two, during an ARTCC frequency outage, relay via FSS radio is recommended.

9-47 Reference. — AIM 340.

9-48 OVERDUE AIRCRAFT

An aircraft is considered to be overdue when neither communications nor radar contact can be established with it and 30 minutes have passed since:

a. Its ETA over a specified or compulsory reporting point or at a clearance limit.

b. Its clearance void time.

9-48 Reference. — ATCH 9-14.

9-49 TRAFFIC RESTRICTIONS

Unless radar separation is used, when an aircraft is unreported or overdue, the facility responsible will restrict or suspend other IFR traffic for 30 minutes after whichever of the following times is applicable:

a. The time at which approach clearance was delivered to the pilot.

b. The EFC time delivered to the pilot.

c. The arrival time over the NAVAID serving the destination airport.

d. The current estimate, either the control facility's or the pilot's, whichever is later, at:

(1) The appropriate en route NAVAID or fix, and

(2) The NAVAID serving the destination airport.

e. The clearance void/release time.

9-49 Reference. — ATCH 9-40.

9-50 AIRPORT LIGHTING REQUIREMENTS

a. EN ROUTE: At nontower or nonFSS locations, ATC will request the airport management to light all runway lights, approach lights, and all other required airport lighting systems for at least 30 minutes before the ETA of the unreported aircraft, until the aircraft has been located or for 30 minutes after its fuel supply is estimated to be exhausted.

b. TERMINAL: Runway lights, approach lights, and all other required airport lighting systems will be operated for at least 30 minutes before the ETA of the unreported aircraft, until the aircraft has been located or for 30 minutes after its fuel supply is estimated to be exhausted.

9-50 Reference. — ATCH 9-41.

9-51 TRAFFIC RESUMPTION

After the 30-minute traffic suspension period has expired, ATC will resume normal air traffic control if the operators or pilots of other aircraft concur. This concurrence must be maintained for a period of 30 minutes after the suspension period has expired.

9-51 Reference. — ATCH 9-42.

9-52 thru 9-59 RESERVED

Section 5. DIRECTION FINDING SERVICE

9-60 ACTIONS REQUIRED

When providing DF (direction finding) services to an aircraft in emergency status ATC will:

a. Determine if aircraft is in VFR or IFR weather conditions, fuel remaining, altitude, and heading.

b. If the aircraft is operating in IFR weather conditions, inform the pilot of the minimum safe altitude.

c. Determine if aircraft is on a flight plan. If the aircraft is not on an IFR flight plan and is in VFR weather conditions, ATC will advise the pilot to remain VFR.

9-60 Reference. — ATCH 9-50.

9-61 DIRECTION FINDING INSTRUMENT APPROACH PROCEDURE

a. DF equipment has long been used to locate lost aircraft and to guide aircraft to areas of good weather or to airports. Now at most DF equipped airports, DF instrument approaches may be given to aircraft in a *distress* or *urgency* condition.

b. Experience has shown that most emergencies requiring DF assistance involve pilots with little flight experience. With this in mind, DF approach procedures provide maximum flight stability in the approach by using small turns, and wings-level descents. The DF specialist will give the pilot headings to fly and tell the pilot when to begin descent.

c. DF instrument approach procedures are for emergency use only and will not be used in IFR weather conditions unless the pilot has declared a *distress* or *urgency* condition.

d. To become familiar with the procedures and other benefits of DF, pilots are urged to request practice DF guidance and approaches in VFR weather conditions. DF specialists welcome the practice and will honor such requests, workload permitting.

9-61 Reference. — AIM 452.

9-62 DF FIXING BY NET

When a DF Net is in operation, controllers will determine aircraft position as follows:

a. TERMINAL: Tell the aircraft to transmit for 10 seconds.

b. TERMINAL: Plot bearings obtained from two or more stations, and inform the aircraft of its position.

9-62 Reference. — ATCH 9-51.

9-63 DF FIXING BY ONE FACILITY

One DF facility can determine an aircraft's position by:*

a. Plotting bearings from a reported VOR radial and an observed DF bearing.

b. Time method, ATC will:

(1) Determine the aircraft's heading and DF bearing.

(2) Tell the aircraft to turn left or right, whichever requires the lesser amount of turn, to a heading perpendicular to the DF bearing.

(3) After turn is completed, tell the aircraft to transmit (normal 10 seconds).

(4) One minute later, request another transmission, determine bearing and turn aircraft toward DF site.

c. Distance method, ATC will:

Use the procedures specified in steps (1) through (4) in **b** above, and request aircraft's true airspeed.

9-63 Note. — One-station DF fixing is based on zero winds.

9-63 Reference. — ATCH 9-52.

9-64 ACTION AFTER POSITION DETERMINATION

EN ROUTE

When the position of the aircraft has been determined, ATC will inform the pilot and provide any requested information, such as direction and distance to the nearest airport. If aircraft is operating in IFR weather conditions, ATC will clear the aircraft to an area where one of the following conditions exists:

a. VFR weather conditions are reported.

b. The aircraft can continue flight using NAVAID's or radar guidance.

c. Transition to an approach aid can be made and an instrument approach executed.

9-64 Reference. — ATCH 9-55.

9-65 VFR DF SERVICE

TERMINAL

a. ATC will provide DF service to VFR aircraft when either of the following conditions exists:

(1) The pilot requests the service.

(2) The controller suggests the service and the pilot concurs.

b. After determining an aircraft's bearing, ATC will

provide DF service by specifying direction of turn and magnetic heading to be flown after completion of turn.

    c. The following information will be issued to the aircraft:

      (1) Altimeter setting.

      (2) Pertinent information on known field conditions and the latest weather information at the destination airport.

    d. ATC will request the aircraft's heading and altitude.

ATC Phraseology:

What is your heading and altitude?

    e. While receiving the reply, ATC will determine the bearing; then, inform the aircraft of the following:

      (1) Direction of turn.

      (2) Heading, spoken in three digits.

      (3) Nature of service.

      (4) Necessity to remain VFR.

      (5) Microphone technique.

      (6) Request for report when airport is in sight.

ATC Phraseology:

Turn left/right heading (degrees) **for DF guidance to** (name of airport, fix, or location). **Maintain VFR at all times. When a request for transmission is received, press your microphone button for the specified number of seconds,**

and, if appropriate,

Report (name) **airport in sight.**

    f. ATC will request the aircraft to transmit for specified periods, as required. The frequency of these requests will vary depending on such factors as wind, frequency congestion, and distance, but may be made at least once each minute until aircraft reports airport in sight or service is terminated.

ATC Phraseology:

Transmit (number - normally 10) **seconds. Turn left/right, heading** (degrees),

or

Continue heading, (degrees).

    g. ATC will inform aircraft when DF service is terminated.*

ATC Phraseology:

DF service terminated.

9-65g Note. — Service may be terminated when airport is in sight, the desired fix or location reached, practice steers or approaches are discontinued, etc.

9-65 Reference. — ATCH 9-53.

9-66 EMERGENCY DF APPROACH PROCEDURES

TERMINAL

    a. Under emergency conditions where a standard instrument approach cannot be executed, ATC will provide DF guidance and instrument approach service as follows:

      (1) By obtaining and relaying ATC clearances, including radio failure procedures.

      (2) By issuing destination airport weather.

      (3) By providing guidance as specified in 9-65e, except without the VFR requirement. To avoid large turns over the DF site, aircraft may be guided to pass over the DF site established on the course that it will maintain on the outbound leg of the approach.

ATC Phraseology:

Turn left/right heading (degrees) **for DF guidance and approach to the** (name) **airport. Maintain** (altitude specified by ATC). **When a request for transmission is received, press your microphone button for the specified number of seconds. Report airport in sight. If no transmissions are received for** (time interval) **proceed VFR. If unable, proceed** (routing, fix, and altitude as specified by ATC). **Contact** (facility) **on** (frequency).

    b. ATC will inform the pilot when he is over the DF site, advise him to perform landing check, and provide guidance for outbound track.

ATC Phraseology:

Over DF site, perform landing check, continue heading (degrees),

or

Turn left/right, heading (degrees).

    c. ATC will provide DF approach guidance in accordance with approved procedures.*

      (1) Triangle Approach Pattern.

        (a) Time the outbound leg and issue descent information. Normally, the outbound track will be maintained for 3 minutes, but this may be adjusted, depending on airspeed and nature of the emergency.

ATC Phraseology:

On outbound leg. Descend and maintain (altitude specified).

        (b) When outbound leg is completed, ATC will issue turn instructions so that the aircraft's course is perpendicular to the final approach course and issue further descent information. If so specified, missed approach procedures will be issued.

ATC Phraseology:

On base leg. In case of missed approach, climb to (altitude) **on course** (degrees) **within** (number) **miles.**

(c) At least two turns will be made onto final approach.

(d) When aircraft is on final approach, ATC will advise it to start descent and provide minimum descent altitude and field elevation information.

ATC Phraseology:

On final approach, begin descent. Minimum descent altitude (number of feet). **Field elevation** (number of feet).

(2) Teardrop Approach Pattern.

(a) ATC will provide guidance to establish the aircraft on the outbound course. ATC will issue descent information, if appropriate.

(b) ATC will issue direction of turn and inbound heading information. ATC will issue missed approach procedures as specified.

(c) When procedure turn is complete, ATC will provide directional guidance and issue descent information.

9-66c Note. — Depending on the terrain factor, it may be necessary for ATC to include climb instructions in radio failure procedures.

9-66 Reference. — ATCH 9-54.

APPENDIX
PILOT/CONTROLLER GLOSSARY

This Glossary was compiled to promote a common understanding of the terms used in the Air Traffic Control system. It includes those terms which are intended for pilot/controller communications. Those terms most frequently used in pilot/controller communications are printed in **bold italics**. The definitions are primarily defined in an operational sense applicable to both users and operators of the National Airspace System. Use of the Glossary will preclude any misunderstandings concerning the system's design, function, and purpose.

Because of the international nature of flying, terms used in the *Lexicon*, published by the International Civil Aviation Organization (ICAO), are included when they differ from FAA definitions. These terms are *italicized*. For the reader's convenience, there are also cross references to related terms in other parts of the Glossary and to other documents, such as the Federal Aviation Regulations (FAR's) and the Airman's Information Manual (AIM).

This Glossary will be revised, as necessary, to maintain a common understanding of the system.

ABBREVIATED IFR FLIGHT PLANS — An authorization by ATC requiring pilots to submit only that information needed for the purpose of ATC. It includes only a small portion of the usual IFR flight plan information. In certain instances, this may be only aircraft identification, location, and pilot request. Other information may be requested if needed by ATC for separation/control purposes. It is frequently used by aircraft which are airborne and desire an instrument approach or by aircraft which are on the ground and desire a climb to VFR-on-top. (See VFR-ON-TOP) (Refer to AIM)

ABEAM — An aircraft is "abeam" a fix, point, or object when that fix, point, or object is approximately 90 degrees to the right or left of the aircraft track. Abeam indicates a general position rather than a precise point.

ABORT — To terminate a preplanned aircraft maneuver; e.g., an aborted takeoff.

ACKNOWLEDGE — Let me know that you have received my message.

ICAO—ACKNOWLEDGE — Let me know that you have received and understood this message.

ACROBATIC FLIGHT — An intentional maneuver involving an abrupt change in an aircraft's attitude, an abnormal attitude, or abnormal acceleration not necessary for normal flight. (Refer to FAR Part 91)

ICAO—ACROBATIC FLIGHT — Manoeuvres intentionally performed by an aircraft involving an abrupt change in its attitude, an abnormal attitude, or an abnormal variation in speed.

ADDITIONAL SERVICES — Advisory information provided by ATC which includes but is not limited to the following:

1. Traffic advisories.
2. Vectors, when requested by the pilot, to assist aircraft receiving traffic advisories to avoid observed traffic.
3. Altitude deviation information of 300 feet or more from an assigned altitude as observed on a verified (reading correctly) automatic altitude readout (Mode C).
4. Advisories that traffic is no longer a factor.
5. Weather and chaff information.
6. Weather assistance.
7. Bird activity information.
8. Holding pattern surveillance.

Additional services are provided to the extent possible contingent only upon the controller's capability to fit them into the performance of higher priority duties and on the basis of limitations of the radar, volume of traffic, frequency congestion, and controller workload. The controller has complete discretion for determining if he is able to provide or continue to provide a service in a particular case. The controller's reason not to provide or continue to provide a service in a particular case is not subject to question by the pilot and need not be

A-1

made known to him. (See Traffic Advisories) (Refer to AIM)

ADMINISTRATOR — The Federal Aviation Administrator or any person to whom he has delegated his authority in the matter concerned.

ADVISE INTENTIONS — Tell me what you plan to do.

ADVISORY — Advice and information provided to assist pilots in the safe conduct of flight and aircraft movement. (See Advisory Service)

ADVISORY FREQUENCY — The appropriate frequency to be used for Airport Advisory Service. (See Airport Advisory Service and UNICOM) (Refer to Advisory Circular No. 90-42 and AIM)

ADVISORY SERVICE — Advice and information provided by a facility to assist pilots in the safe conduct of flight and aircraft movement. (See Airport Advisory Service, Traffic Advisories, Safety Alerts, Additional Services, Radar Advisory, En Route Flight Advisory Service) (Refer to AIM)

AERIAL REFUELING/IN-FLIGHT REFUELING — A procedure used by the military to transfer fuel from one aircraft to another during flight. (Refer to VFR/IFR Wall Planning Charts).

AERODROME — A defined area on land or water (including any buildings, installations and equipment) intended to be used either wholly or in part for the arrival, departure, and movement of aircraft.

AERONAUTICAL BEACON — A visual NAVAID displaying flashes of white and/or colored light to indicate the location of an airport, a heliport, a landmark, a certain point of a Federal airway in mountainous terrain, or an obstruction. (See Airport Rotating Beacon) (Refer to AIM)

AERONAUTICAL CHART — A map used in air navigation containing all or part of the following: Topographic features, hazards and obstructions, navigation aids, navigation routes, designated airspace, and airports. Commonly used aeronautical charts are:

1. Sectional Charts (1:500,000) — Designed for visual navigation of slow or medium speed aircraft. Topographic information on these charts features the portrayal of relief and a judicious selection of visual check points for VFR flight. Aeronautical information includes visual and radio aids to navigation, airports, controlled airspace, restricted areas, obstructions, and related data.

2. VFR Terminal Area Charts (1:250,000) — Depict Terminal Control Area (TCA) airspace which provides for the control or segregation of all the aircraft within the TCA. The chart depicts topographic information and aeronautical information which includes visual and radio aids to navigation, airports, controlled airspace, restricted areas, obstructions, and related data.

3. World Aeronautical Charts (WAC) (1:1,000,000) — Provide a standard series of aeronautical charts covering land areas of the world at a size and scale convenient for navigation by moderate speed aircraft. Topographic information includes cities and towns, principal roads, railroads, distinctive landmarks, drainage, and relief. Aeronautical information includes visual and radio aids to navigation, airports, airways, restricted areas, obstructions, and other pertinent data.

4. En Route Low Altitude Charts — Provide aeronautical information for en route instrument navigation (IFR) in the low altitude stratum. Information includes the portrayal of airways, limits of controlled airspace, position identification and frequencies of radio aids, selected airports, minimum en route and minimum obstruction clearance altitudes, airway distances, reporting points, restricted areas, and related data. Area charts, which are a part of this series, furnish terminal data at a larger scale in congested areas.

5. En Route High Altitude Charts — Provide aeronautical information for en route instrument navigation (IFR) in the high altitude stratum. Information includes the portrayal of jet routes, identification and frequencies of radio aids, selected airports, distances, time zones, special use airspace, and related information.

6. Instrument Approach Procedures (IAP) Charts — Portray the aeronautical data which is required to execute an instrument approach to an airport. These charts depict the procedures, including all related data, and the airport diagram. Each procedure is designated for use with a specific type of electronic navigation system including NDB, TACAN, VOR, ILS/MLS, and RNAV. These charts are identified by the type of navigational aid(s) which provide final approach guidance.

7. Standard Instrument Departure (SID) Charts — Designed to expedite clearance delivery and to facilitate transition between takeoff and en route operations. Each SID procedure is presented as a separate chart and may serve a single airport or more than one airport in a given geographical location.

8. Standard Terminal Arrival (STAR) Charts — Designed to expedite air traffic control arrival procedures and to facilitate transition between en route and instrument approach operations. Each STAR procedure is presented as a separate chart and may serve a single airport or more than one airport in a given geographical location.

9. Airport Taxi Charts — Designed to expedite the efficient and safe flow of ground traffic at an airport. These charts are identified by the official airport name; e.g., Washington National Airport.

ICAO—AERONAUTICAL CHART — A representation of a portion of the earth, its culture and relief, specifically designated to meet the requirements of air navigation.

AFFIRMATIVE — Yes.

AIR CARRIER DISTRICT OFFICE/ACDO — An FAA field office serving an assigned geographical area, staffed with Flight Standards personnel serving the aviation industry and the general public on matters related to the certification and operation of scheduled air carriers and other large aircraft operations.

AIRCRAFT — Device/s that are used or intended to be used for flight in the air, and when used in air traffic control terminology, may include the flight crew.

ICAO—AIRCRAFT — Any machine that can derive support in the atmosphere from the reactions of the air other than the reactions of the air against the earth's surface.

AIRCRAFT APPROACH CATEGORY — A grouping of aircraft based on a speed of 1.3 times the stall speed in the landing configuration at maximum gross landing weight. An aircraft shall fit in only one category. If it is necessary to maneuver at speeds in excess of the upper limit of a speed range for a category, the minimums for the next higher category should be used. For example, an aircraft which falls in Category A, but is circling to land at a speed in excess of 91 knots, should use the approach Category B minimums when circling to land. The categories are as follows:

1. Category A—Speed less than 91 knots.
2. Category B—Speed 91 knots or more but less than 121 knots.
3. Category C—Speed 121 knots or more but less than 141 knots.
4. Category D—Speed 141 knots or more but less than 166 knots.
5. Category E—Speed 166 knots or more.

(Refer to FAR Parts 1 and 97)

AIRCRAFT CLASSES — For the purposes of Wake Turbulence Separation Minima, ATC classifies aircraft as Heavy, Large, and Small as follows:

1. Heavy—Aircraft capable of takeoff weights of 300,000 pounds or more whether or not they are operating at this weight during a particular phase of flight.
2. Large—Aircraft of more than 12,500 pounds, maximum certificated takeoff weight, up to 300,000 pounds.
3. Small—Aircraft of 12,500 pounds or less maximum certificated takeoff weight. (Refer to AIM)

AIR DEFENSE EMERGENCY — A military emergency condition declared by a designated authority. This condition exists when an attack upon the continental U.S., Alaska, Canada, or U.S. installations in Greenland by hostile aircraft or missiles is considered probable, is imminent, or is taking place. (Refer to AIM)

AIR DEFENSE IDENTIFICATION ZONE/ADIZ — The area of airspace over land or water, extending upward from the surface, within which the ready identification, the location, and the control of aircraft are required in the interest of national security.

1. Domestic Air Defense Identification Zone—An ADIZ within the United States along an international boundary of the United States.
2. Coastal Air Defense Identification Zone—An ADIZ over the coastal waters of the United States.
3. Distant Early Warning Identification Zone (DEWIZ)—An ADIZ over the coastal waters of the State of Alaska.

ADIZ locations and operating and flight plan requirements for civil aircraft operations are specified in FAR Part 99. (Refer to AIM)

AIRMAN'S INFORMATION MANUAL/AIM — A primary FAA publication whose purpose is to instruct airmen about operating in the National Airspace System of the U.S. It provides basic flight information, ATC Procedures and general instructional information concerning health, medical facts, factors affecting flight safety, accident and hazard reporting, and types of aeronautical charts and their use.

ICAO—AERONAUTICAL INFORMATION PUBLICATION — A publication issued by or with the authority of a State and containing aeronautical information of a lasting character essential to air navigation.

***AIRMET*/WA/AIRMAN'S METEOROLOGICAL INFORMATION** — In-flight weather advisories issued only to amend the area forecast concerning weather phenomena which are of operational interest to all aircraft and potentially hazardous to aircraft having limited capability because of lack of equipment, instrumentation, or pilot qualifications. AIRMET's concern weather of less severity than that covered by SIGMET's or Convective SIGMET's. AIRMET's cover moderate icing, moderate turbulence, sustained winds of 30 knots or more at the surface, widespread areas of ceilings less than 1,000 feet and/or visibility less than 3 miles, and extensive mountain obscurement. (See AWW, SIGMET, Convective SIGMET, and CWA) (Refer to AIM)

AIR NAVIGATION FACILITY — Any facility used in, available for use in, or designed for use in, aid of air navigation, including landing areas, lights, any apparatus or equipment for disseminating weather information, for signaling, for radio-directional finding, or for radio or other electrical communication, and any other structure or mechanism having a similar purpose for guiding or controlling flight in the air or the landing and take-off of aircraft. (See Navigational Aid)

AIRPORT — An area on land or water that is used or intended to be used for the landing and takeoff of aircraft and includes its buildings and facilities, if any.

AIRPORT ADVISORY AREA — The area within ten miles of an airport without a control tower or where the tower is not in operation, and on which a Flight Service Station is located. (See Airport Advisory Service) (Refer to AIM)

AIRPORT ADVISORY SERVICE/AAS — A service provided by flight service stations or the military at airports not serviced by an operating control tower. This service consists of providing information to arriving and departing aircraft concerning wind direction and speed, favored runway, altimeter setting, pertinent known traffic, pertinent known field conditions, airport taxi routes and traffic patterns, and authorized instrument approach procedures. This information is advisory in nature and does not constitute an ATC clearance. (See Airport Advisory Area)

AIRPORT ELEVATION/FIELD ELEVATION — The highest point of an airport's usable runways measured in feet from mean sea level. (See Touchdown Zone Elevation)

ICAO—AERODROME ELEVATION — The elevation of the highest point of the landing area.

AIRPORT/FACILITY DIRECTORY — A publication designed primarily as a pilot's operational manual containing all airports, seaplane bases, and heliports open to the public including communications data, navigational facilities, and certain special notices and procedures. This publication is issued in seven volumes according to geographical area.

AIRPORT INFORMATION DESK/AID — An airport unmanned facility designed for pilot self-service briefing, flight planning, and filing of flight plans. (Refer to AIM)

AIRPORT LIGHTING — Various lighting aids that may be installed on an airport. Types of airport lighting include:

1. Approach Light System/ALS—An airport lighting facility which provides visual guidance to landing aircraft by radiating light beams in a directional pattern by which the pilot aligns the aircraft with the extended centerline of the runway on his final approach for landing. Condenser-Discharge Sequential Flashing Lights/Sequenced Flashing Lights may be installed in conjunction with the ALS at some airports. Types of Approach Light Systems are:

    a. ALSF-1—Approach Light System with Sequenced Flashing Lights in ILS Cat-I configuration.
    b. ALSF-2—Approach Light System with Sequenced Flashing Lights in ILS Cat-II configuration. The ALSF-2 may operate as an SSALR when weather conditions permit.
    c. SSALF—Simplified Short Approach Light System with Sequenced Flashing Lights.
    d. SSALR—Simplified Short Approach Light System with Runway Alignment Indicator Lights.
    e. MALSF—Medium Intensity Approach Light System with Sequenced Flashing Lights.
    f. MALSR—Medium Intensity Approach Light System with Runway Alignment Indicator Lights.
    g. LDIN—Sequenced Flashing Lead-in Lights.
    h. RAIL—Runway Alignment Indicator Lights (Sequenced Flashing Lights which are installed only in combination with other light systems).
    i. ODALS—Omnidirectional Approach Lighting System consists of seven omnidirectional flashing lights located in the approach area of a nonprecision runway. Five lights are located on the runway centerline extended with the first light located 300 feet from the threshold and extending at equal intervals up to 1,500 feet from the threshold. The other two lights are located, one on each side of the runway threshold, at a lateral distance of 40 feet from the runway edge, or 75 feet from the runway edge when installed on a runway equipped with a VASI. (Refer to Order 6850.2A)

2. Runway Lights/Runway Edge Lights—Lights having a prescribed angle of emission used to define the lateral limits of a runway. Runway lights are uniformly spaced at intervals of approximately 200 feet, and the intensity may be controlled or preset.

3. Touchdown Zone Lighting—Two rows of tranverse light bars located symmetrically about the runway centerline normally at 100 foot intervals. The basic system extends 3,000 feet along the runway.

4. Runway Centerline Lighting—Flush centerline lights spaced at 50-foot intervals beginning 75 feet from the landing threshold and extending to within 75 feet of the opposite end of the runway.

5. Threshold Lights—Fixed green lights arranged symmetrically left and right of the runway centerline, identifying the runway threshold.

6. Runway End Identifier Lights/REIL—Two synchronized flashing lights, one on each side of the runway threshold, which provide rapid and positive identification of the approach end of a particular runway.

7. Visual Approach Slope Indicator/VASI—An airport lighting facility providing vertical visual approach slope guidance to aircraft during approach to landing by radiating a directional pattern of high intensity red and white focused light beams which indicate to the pilot that he is "on path" if he sees red/white, "above path" if white/white, and

"below path" if red/red. Some airports serving large aircraft have three-bar VASIs which provide two visual glide paths to the same runway.

8. Boundary Lights—Lights defining the perimeter of an airport or landing area. (Refer to AIM)

AIRPORT MARKING AIDS — Markings used on runway and taxiway surfaces to identify a specific runway, a runway threshold, a centerline, a hold line, etc. A runway should be marked in accordance with its present usage such as:

1. Visual.

2. Nonprecision instrument.

3. Precision instrument. (Refer to AIM)

AIRPORT RADAR SERVICE AREA/ARSA — (See Controlled Airspace)

AIRPORT ROTATING BEACON — A visual NAVAID operated at many airports. At civil airports, alternating white and green flashes indicate the location of the airport. At military airports, the beacons flash alternately white and green, but are differentiated from civil beacons by dualpeaked (two quick) white flashes between the green flashes. (See Special VFR Operations, Instrument Flight Rules) (Refer to AIM, Rotating Beacons)

ICAO—AERODROME BEACON .— Aeronautical beacon used to indicate the location of an aerodrome from the air.

AIRPORT SURFACE DETECTION EQUIPMENT/ASDE — Radar equipment specifically designed to detect all principal features on the surface of an airport, including aircraft and vehicular traffic, and to present the entire image on a radar indicator console in the control tower. Used to augment visual observation by tower personnel of aircraft and/or vehicular movements on runways and taxiways.

AIRPORT SURVEILLANCE RADAR/ASR — Approach control radar used to detect and display an aircraft's position in the terminal area. ASR provides range and azimuth information but does not provide elevation data. Coverage of the ASR can extend up to 60 miles.

AIRPORT TRAFFIC AREA — Unless otherwise specifically designated in FAR Part 93, that airspace within a horizontal radius of 5 statute miles from the geographical center of any airport at which a control tower is operating, extending from the surface up to, but not including, an altitude of 3,000 feet above the elevation of an airport. Unless otherwise authorized or required by ATC, no person may operate an aircraft within an airport traffic area except for the purpose of landing at or taking off from an airport within that area. ATC authorizations may be given as individual approval of specific operations or may be contained in written agreements between airport users and the tower concerned. (Refer to FAR, Parts 1 and 91).

AIRPORT TRAFFIC CONTROL SERVICE — A service provided by a control tower for aircraft operating on the movement area and in the vicinity of an airport. (See Movement Area, Tower)

ICAO-AERODROME CONTROL SERVICE — Air traffic control service for aerodrome traffic.

AIR ROUTE SURVEILLANCE RADAR/ARSR — Air route traffic control center (ARTCC) radar used primarily to detect and display an aircraft's position while en route between terminal areas. The ARSR enables controllers to provide radar air traffic control service when aircraft are within the ARSR coverage. In some instances, ARSR may enable an ARTCC to provide terminal radar services similar to but usually more limited than those provided by a radar approach control.

AIR ROUTE TRAFFIC CONTROL CENTER/ARTCC — A facility established to provide air traffic control service to aircraft operating on IFR flight plans within controlled airspace and principally during the en route phase of flight. When equipment capabilities and controller workload permit, certain advisory/assistance services may be provided to VFR aircraft. (See NAS Stage A, En Route Air Traffic Control Service) (Refer to AIM)

AIRSPEED — The speed of an aircraft relative to its surrounding air mass. The unqualified term "airspeed" means one of the following:

1. Indicated Airspeed—The speed shown on the aircraft airspeed indicator. This is the speed used in pilot/controller communications under the general term "airspeed." (Refer to FAR Part 1)

2. True Airspeed—The airspeed of an aircraft relative to undisturbed air. Used primarily in flight planning and en route portion of flight. When used in pilot/controller communications, it is referred to as "true airspeed" and not shortened to "airspeed."

AIRSTART — The starting of an aircraft engine while the aircraft is airborne, preceded by engine shutdown during training flights or by actual engine failure.

AIR TAXI — Used to describe a helicopter/VTOL aircraft movement conducted above the surface but normally not above 100 feet AGL. The aircraft may proceed either via hover taxi or flight at speeds more than 20 knots. The pilot is solely responsible for selecting a safe airspeed/altitude for the operation being conducted. (See Hover Taxi) (Refer to AIM)

AIR TRAFFIC — Aircraft operating in the air or on an airport surface, exclusive of loading ramps and parking areas.

ICAO—AIR TRAFFIC — All aircraft in flight or operating on the manoeuvring area of an aerodrome.

AIR TRAFFIC CLEARANCE/ATC CLEARANCE — An authorization by air traffic control, for the purpose of preventing collision between known aircraft, for

A-5

an aircraft to proceed under specified traffic conditions within controlled airspace. (See ATC Instructions)

ICAO—AIR TRAFFIC CONTROL CLEARANCE — Authorization for an aircraft to proceed under conditions specified by an air traffic control unit.

Note 1. — For conveniece, the term *air traffic control clearance* is frequently abbreviated to *clearance* when used in appropriate contexts.

Note 2. — The abbreviated term *clearance* may be prefixed by the words *taxi, takeoff, departure, en route, approach* or *landing* to indicate the particular portion of flight to which the air traffic control clearance relates.

AIR TRAFFIC CONTROL/ATC — A service operated by appropriate authority to promote the safe, orderly and expeditious flow of air traffic.

ICAO—AIR TRAFFIC CONTROL SERVICE — A service provided for the purpose of:

1) Preventing collisions:

   a) Between aircraft; and
   b) On the maneuvering area between aircraft and obstructions; and

2) Expediting and maintaining an orderly flow of air traffic.

AIR TRAFFIC CONTROL COMMAND CENTER/ ATCCC — An Air Traffic Operations Service facility consisting of four operational units.

1. Central Flow Control Function/CFCF—Responsible for coordination and approval of all major intercenter flow control restrictions on a system basis in order to obtain maximum utilization of the airspace. (See Quota Flow Control)

2. Central Altitude Reservation Function/CARF—Responsible for coordinating, planning, and approving special user requirements under the Altitude Reservation (ALTRV) concept. (See Altitude Reservation)

3. Airport Reservation Office/ARO—Responsible for approving IFR flights at designated high density traffic airports (John F. Kennedy, LaGuardia, O'Hare, and Washington National) during specified hours. (Refer to FAR Part 93 and Airport/Facility Directory)

4. ATC Contingency Command Post—A facility which enables the FAA to manage the ATC system when significant portions of the system's capabilities have been lost or are threatened.

AIR TRAFFIC CONTROL SERVICE — (See Air Traffic Control)

AIR TRAFFIC CONTROL SPECIALIST/CONTROLLER — A person authorized to provide air traffic control service. (See Air Traffic Control, Flight Service Station)

ICAO—CONTROLLER — A person authorized to provide air traffic control services.

AIRWAY BEACON — Used to mark airway segments in remote mountain areas. The light flashes Morse Code to identify the beacon site. (Refer to AIM)

AIRWAY/FEDERAL AIRWAY — A control area or portion thereof established in the form of a corridor, the centerline of which is defined by radio navigational aids. (Refer to FAR Part 71, AIM)

ICAO—AIRWAY — A control area or portion thereof established in the form of corridor equipped with radio navigational aids.

ALERT AREA — (See Special Use Airspace)

ALERT NOTICE/ALNOT — A request originated by a flight service station (FSS) or an air route traffic control center (ARTCC) for an extensive communication search for overdue, unreported, or missing aircraft.

ALPHANUMERIC DISPLAY/DATA BLOCK — Letters and numerals used to show identification, altitude, beacon code, and other information concerning a target on a radar display. (See Automated Radar Terminal Systems, NAS Stage A)

ALTERNATE AIRPORT — An airport at which an aircraft may land if a landing at the intended airport becomes inadvisable.

ICAO—ALTERNATE AERODROME — An aerodrome specified in the flight plan to which a flight may proceed when it becomes inadvisable to land at the aerodrome of intended landing.

Note. — An alternate aerdrome may be the aerodrome of departure.

ALTIMETER SETTING — The barometric pressure reading used to adjust a pressure altimeter for variations in existing atmospheric pressure or to the standard altimeter setting (29.92). (Refer to FAR Part 91, AIM)

ALTITUDE — The height of a level, point, or object measured in feet Above Ground Level (AGL) or from Mean Sea Level (MSL). (See Flight Level)

1. MSL Altitude—Altitude expressed in feet measured from mean sea level.

2. AGL Altitude—Altitude expressed in feet measured above ground level.

3. Indicated Altitude—The altitude as shown by an altimeter. On a pressure or barometric altimeter it is altitude as shown uncorrected for instrument error and uncompensated for variation from standard atmospheric conditions.

ICAO—ALTITUDE — The vertical distance of a level, a point or an object considered as a point, measured from mean sea level (MSL).

ALTITUDE READOUT/AUTOMATIC ALTITUDE REPORT — An aircraft's altitude, transmitted via the

Mode C transponder feature, that is visually displayed in 100-foot increments on a radar scope having readout capability. (See Automated Radar Terminal Systems, NAS Stage A, Alphanumeric Display) (Refer to AIM)

ALTITUDE RESERVATION/ALTRV — Airspace utilization under prescribed conditions normally employed for the mass movement of aircraft or other special user requirements which cannot otherwise be accomplished. ALTRVs are approved by the appropriate FAA facility. (See Air Traffic Control Command Center)

ALTITUDE RESTRICTION — An altitude or altitudes, stated in the order flown, which are to be maintained until reaching a specific point or time. Altitude restrictions may be issued by ATC due to traffic, terrain, or other airspace considerations.

ALTITUDE RESTRICTIONS ARE CANCELED — Adherence to previously imposed altitude restrictions is no longer required during a climb or descent.

APPROACH CLEARANCE — Authorization by ATC for a pilot to conduct an instrument approach. The type of instrument approach for which a clearance and other pertinent information is provided in the approach clearance when required. (See Instrument Approach Procedure, Cleared for Approach) (Refer to AIM and FAR Part 91)

APPROACH CONTROL FACILITY — A terminal ATC facility that provides approach control service in a terminal area. (See Approach Control Service, Radar Approach Control Facility.

APPROACH CONTROL SERVICE — Air traffic control service provided by an approach control facility for arriving and departing VFR/IFR aircraft and, on occasion, en route aircraft. At some airports not served by an approach control facility, the ARTCC provides limited approach control service. (Refer to AIM)

ICAO—APPROACH CONTROL SERVICE — Air traffic control service for arriving or departing controlled flights.

APPROACH GATE — An imaginary point used within ATC as a basis for vectoring aircraft to the final approach course. The gate will be established along the final approach course 1 mile from the outer marker (or the fix used in lieu of the outer marker) on the side away from the airport for precision approaches and 1 mile from the final approach fix on the side away from the airport for nonprecision approaches. In either case when measured along the final approach course, the gate will be no closer than 5 miles from the landing threshold.

APPROACH LIGHT SYSTEM — (See Airport Lighting)

APPROACH SEQUENCE — The order in which aircraft are positioned while on approach or awaiting approach clearance. (See Landing Sequence)

ICAO—APPROACH SEQUENCE — The order in which two or more aircraft are cleared to approach to land at the aerodrome.

APPROACH SPEED — The recommended speed contained in aircraft manuals used by pilots when making an approach to landing. This speed will vary for different segments of an approach as well as for aircraft weight and configuration.

APRON/RAMP — A defined area on an airport or heliport intended to accommodate aircraft for purposes of loading or unloading passengers or cargo, refueling, parking, or maintenance. With regard to seaplanes, a ramp is used for access to the apron from the water.

ICAO—APRON — A defined area, on a land aerodrome, intended to accommodate aircraft for purposes of loading or unloading passengers, mail or cargo, refuelling, parking or maintenance.

ARC — The track over the ground of an aircraft flying at a constant distance from a navigational aid by reference to distance measuring equipment (DME).

AREA NAVIGATION/RNAV — A method of navigation that permits aircraft operation on any desired course within the coverage of station-referenced navigation signals or within the limits of a self-contained system capability. Random area navigation routes are direct routes, based on area navigation capability, between waypoints defined in terms of latitude/longitude coordinates, degree/distance fixes, or offsets from published or established routes/airways at a specified distance and direction. The major types of equipment are:

1. VORTAC referenced or Course Line Computer (CLC) systems, which account for the greatest number of RNAV units in use. To function, the CLC must be within the service range of a VORTAC.

2. OMEGA/VLF, although two separate systems, can be considered as one operationally. A long-range navigation system based upon Very Low Frequency radio signals transmitted from a total of 17 stations worldwide.

3. Inertial (INS) systems, which are totally self-contained and require no information from external references. They provide aircraft position and navigation information in response to signals resulting from inertial effects on components within the system.

4. MLS Area Navigation (MLS/RNAV), which provides area navigation with reference to an MLS ground facility.

5. LORAN-C is a long-range radio navigation system that uses ground waves transmitted at low frequency to provide user position information at ranges of up to 600 to 1,200 nautical miles at both en route and approach altitudes. The useable signal coverage areas are determined by the signal-to-noise ratio, the envelope-to-cycle difference, and

the geometric relationship between the positions of the user and the transmitting stations.

ICAO—AREA NAVIGATION/RNAV — A method of navigation which permits aircraft operation on any desired flight path within the coverage of station-referenced navigation aids or within the limits of the capability of self-contained aids, or a combination of these.

ARMY AVIATION FLIGHT INFORMATION BULLETIN/USAFIB — A bulletin that provides air operation data covering Army, National Guard, and Army Reserve aviation activities.

ARRESTING SYSTEM — A safety device consisting of two major components, namely, engaging or catching devices and energy absorption devices for the purpose of arresting both tailhook and/or nontailhook-equipped aircraft. It is used to prevent aircraft from overrunning runways when the aircraft cannot be stopped after landing or during aborted takeoff. Arresting systems have various names; e.g., arresting gear, hook device, wire barrier cable. (See Abort) (Refer to AIM)

ARRIVAL TIME — The time an aircraft touches down on arrival.

ARTCC — (See Air Route Traffic Control Center)

ASR APPROACH — (See Surveillance Approach)

ATC ADVISES — Used to prefix a message of non-control information when it is relayed to an aircraft by other than an air traffic controller. (See Advisory)

ATC ASSIGNED AIRSPACE/ATCAA — Airspace of defined vertical/lateral limits, assigned by ATC, for the purpose of providing air traffic segregation between the specified activities being conducted within the assigned airspace and other IFR air traffic. (See Special Use Airspace)

ATC CLEARANCE — (See Air Traffic Clearance)

ATC CLEARS — Used to prefix an ATC clearance when it is relayed to an aircraft by other than an air traffic controller.

ATC INSTRUCTIONS — Directives issued by air traffic control for the purpose of requiring a pilot to take specific actions; e.g., "Turn left heading two five zero," "Go around," "Clear the runway." (Refer to FAR Part 91)

ATCRBS — (See Radar)

ATC REQUESTS — Used to prefix an ATC request when it is relayed to an aircraft by other than an air traffic controller.

AUTOLAND APPROACH —An autoland approach is a precision instrument approach to touchdown and, in some cases, through the landing rollout. An autoland approach is performed by the aircraft autopilot which is receiving position information and/or steering commands from onboard navigation equipment (See Coupled Approach).

Note. — Autoland and coupled approaches are flown in VFR and IFR. It is common for carriers to require their crews to fly coupled approaches and autoland approaches (if certified) when the weather conditions are less than approximately 4,000 RVR.

AUTOMATED RADAR TERMINAL SYSTEMS/ ARTS — The generic term for the ultimate in functional capability afforded by several automation systems. Each differs in functional capabilities and equipment. ARTS plus a suffix roman numeral denotes a specific system. A following letter indicates a major modification to that system. In general, an ARTS displays for the terminal controller aircraft identification, flight plan data, other flight associated information; e.g., altitude, speed, and aircraft position symbols in conjunction with his radar presentation. Normal radar co-exists with the alphanumeric display. In addition to enhancing visualization of the air traffic situation, ARTS facilitate intra/inter-facility transfer and coordination of flight information. These capabilities are enabled by specially designed computers and subsystems tailored to the radar and communications equipments and operational requirements of each automated facility. Modular design permits adoption of improvements in computer software and electronic technologies as they become available while retaining the characteristics unique to each system.

1. ARTS II—A programmable nontracking, computer-aided display subsystem capable of modular expansion. ARTS II systems provide a level of automated air traffic control capability at terminals having low to medium activity. Flight identification and altitude may be associated with the display of secondary radar targets. The system has the capability of communicating with ARTCC's and other ATRS II, IIA, III, and IIIA facilities.

2. ARTS IIA—A programmable radar-tracking computer subsystem capable of modular expansion. The ARTS IIA detects, tracks, and predicts secondary radar targets. The targets are displayed by means of computer- generated symbols, ground speed, and flight plan data. Although it does not track primary radar targets, they are displayed coincident with the secondary radar as well as the symbols and alphanumerics. The system has the capability of communicating with ARTCC's and other ARTS II, IIA, III, and IIIA facilities.

3. ARTS III—The Beacon Tracking Level (BTL) of the modular programmable automated radar terminal system in use at medium to high activity terminals. ARTS III detects, tracks, and predicts secondary radar-derived aircraft targets. These are displayed by means of computer-generated symbols and alphanumeric characters depicting flight identification, aircraft altitude, ground speed, and flight plan data. Although it does not track primary targets, they are displayed coincident with the secondary radar as well as the symbols and alphanu-

merics. The system has the capability of communicating with ARTCC's and other ARTS III facilities.

4. ARTS IIIA—The Radar Tracking and Beacon Tracking Level (RT&BTL) of the modular, programmable automated radar terminal system. ARTS IIIA detects, tracks, and predicts primary as well as secondary radar-derived aircraft targets. This more sophisticated computer-driven system upgrades the existing ARTS III system by providing improved tracking, continuous data recording, and fail-soft capabilities.

AUTOMATIC ALTITUDE REPORTING — That function of a transponder which responds to Mode C interrogations by transmitting the aircraft's altitude in 100-foot increments.

AUTOMATIC CARRIER LANDING SYSTEM/ACLS — U.S. Navy final approach equipment consisting of precision tracking radar coupled to a computer data link to provide continuous information to the aircraft, monitoring capability to the pilot, and a backup approach system.

AUTOMATIC DIRECTION FINDER/ADF — An aircraft radio navigation system which senses and indicates the direction to a L/MF nondirectional radio beacon (NDB) ground transmitter. Direction is indicated to the pilot as a magnetic bearing or as a relative bearing to the longitudinal axis of the aircraft depending on the type of indicator installed in the aircraft. In certain applications, such as military, ADF operations may be based on airborne and ground transmitters in the VHF/UHF frequency spectrum. (See Bearing, Nondirectional Beacon)

AUTOMATIC TERMINAL INFORMATION SERVICE/ATIS — The continuous broadcast of recorded noncontrol information in selected terminal areas. Its purpose is to improve controller effectiveness and to relieve frequency congestion by automating the repetitive transmission of essential but routine information; e.g., "Los Angeles information Alfa. One three zero zero Coordinated Universal Time. Weather, measured ceiling two thousand overcast, visibility three, haze, smoke, temperature seven one, dew point five seven, wind two five zero at five, altimeter two niner niner six. I-L-S Runway Two Five Left approach in use, Runway Two Five Right closed, advise you have Alfa." (Refer to AIM)

ICAO—AUTOMATIC TERMINAL INFORMATION SERVICE — The provision of current, routine information to arriving and departing aircraft by means of continuous and repetitive broadcasts throughout the day or a specified portion of the day.

AUTOROTATION — A rotorcraft flight condition in which the lifting rotor is driven entirely by action of the air when the rotorcraft is in motion.

1. Autorotative Landing/Touchdown Autorotation—Used by a pilot to indicate that he will be landing without applying power to the rotor.

2. Low Level Autorotation—Commences at an altitude well below the traffic pattern, usually below 100 feet AGL and is used primarily for tactical military training.

3. 180 degrees Autorotation—Initiated from a downwind heading and is commenced well inside the normal traffic pattern. "Go around" may not be possible during the latter part of this maneuver.

AVIATION WEATHER SERVICE — A service provided by the National Weather Service (NWS) and FAA which collects and disseminates pertinent weather information for pilots, aircraft operators, and ATC. Available aviation weather reports and forecasts are displayed at each NWS office and FAA FSS. (See En Route Flight Advisory Service, Transcribed Weather Broadcast, Weather Advisory, Pilots Automatic Telephone Weather Answering Service) (Refer to AIM)

AZIMUTH, MLS — A magnetic bearing extending from an MLS navigation facility. Note: azimuth bearings are described as magnetic and are referred to as "azimuth" in radio telephone communications.

BASE LEG — (See Traffic Pattern)

BEACON — (See Radar, Nondirectional Beacon, Marker Beacon, Airport Rotating Beacon, Aeronautical Beacon, Airway Beacon))

BEARING — The horizontal direction to or from any point, usually measured clockwise from true north, magnetic north, or some other reference point through 360 degrees. (See Nondirectional Beacon)

BELOW MINIMUMS — Weather conditions below the minimums prescribed by regulation for the particular action involved; e.g., landing minimums, takeoff minimums.

BLAST FENCE — A barrier that is used to divert or dissipate jet or propeller blast.

BLIND SPEED — The rate of departure or closing of a target relative to the radar antenna at which cancellation of the primary radar target by moving target indicator (MTI) circuits in the radar equipment causes a reduction or complete loss of signal.

ICAO—BLIND VELOCITY — The radial velocity of a moving target such that the target is not seen on primary radars fitted with certain forms of fixed echo suppression.

BLIND SPOT/BLIND ZONE — An area from which radio transmissions and/or radar echoes cannot be received. The term is also used to describe portions of the airport not visible from the control tower.

BOUNDARY LIGHTS — (See Airport Lighting)

BRAKING ACTION (GOOD, FAIR, POOR, OR NIL) — A report of conditions on the airport movement area providing a pilot with a degree/quality of braking that he might expect. Braking action is reported in terms of good, fair, poor, or nil. (See Runway Condition Reading)

BRAKING ACTION ADVISORIES — When tower controllers have received runway braking action reports which include the terms "poor" or "nil," or whenever weather conditions are conducive to deteriorating or rapidly changing runway braking conditions, the tower will include on the ATIS broadcast the statement, "BRAKING ACTION ADVISORIES ARE IN EFFECT." During the time Braking Action Advisories are in effect, ATC will issue the latest braking action report for the runway in use to each arriving and departing aircraft. Pilots should be prepared for deteriorating braking conditions and should request current runway condition information if not volunteered by controllers. Pilots should also be prepared to provide a descriptive runway condition report to controllers after landing.

BROADCAST — Transmission of information for which an acknowledgement is not expected.

ICAO—BROADCAST — A transmission of information relating to air navigation that is not addressed to a specific station or stations.

CALL UP — Initial voice contact between a facility and an aircraft, using the identification of the unit being called and the unit initiating the call. (Refer to AIM)

CARDINAL ALTITUDES OR FLIGHT LEVELS — "Odd" or "Even" thousand-foot altitudes or flight levels; e.g., 5,000, 6,000, 7,000, FL 250, FL 260, FL 270. (See Altitude, Flight Levels)

CEILING — The heights above the earth's surface of the lowest layer of clouds or obscuring phenomena that is reported as "broken," "overcast," or "obscuration," and not classified as "thin" or "partial".

ICAO—CEILING — The height above the ground or water of the base of the lowest layer of cloud below 6 000 metres (20 000 feet) covering more than half the sky.

DELAY INDEFINITE (REASON IF KNOWN) EXPECT FURTHER CLEARANCE (TIME) — Used by ATC to inform a pilot when an accurate estimate of the delay time and the reason for the delay cannot immediately be determined; e.g., a disabled aircraft on the runway, terminal or center area saturation, weather below landing minimums, etc. (See Expect Further Clearance)

CENTER — (See Air Route Traffic Control Center)

CENTER'S AREA — The specified airspace within which an air route traffic control center (ARTCC) provides air traffic control and advisory service. (See Air Route Traffic Control Center) (Refer to AIM)

CENTER WEATHER ADVISORY/CWA — An unscheduled weather advisory issued by Center Weather Service Unit meteorologists for ATC use to alert pilots of existing or anticipated adverse weather conditions within the next 2 hours. A CWA may modify or redefine a SIGMET. (See AWW, SIGMET, Convective SIGMET, and AIRMET) (Refer to AIM)

CHAFF — Thin, narrow metallic reflectors of various lengths and frequency responses, used to reflect radar energy. These reflectors when dropped from aircraft and allowed to drift downward result in large targets on the radar display.

CHARTED VFR FLYWAYS — Charted VFR Flyways are flight paths recommended for use to bypass areas heavily traversed by large turbine-powered aircraft. Pilot compliance with recommended flyways and associated altitudes is strictly voluntary. VFR Flyway Planning charts are published on the back of existing VFR Terminal Area charts.

CHARTED VISUAL FLIGHT PROCEDURE (CVFP) APPROACH — An approach wherein a radar-controlled aircraft on an IFR flight plan, operating in VFR conditions and having an ATC authorization, may proceed to the airport of intended landing via visual landmarks and altitudes depicted on a charted visual flight procedure.

CHASE/CHASE AIRCRAFT — An aircraft flown in proximity to another aircraft normally to observe its performance during training or testing.

CIRCLE-TO-LAND MANEUVER/CIRCLING MANEUVER — A maneuver initiated by the pilot to align the aircraft with a runway for landing when a straight-in landing from an instrument approach is not possible or is not desirable. This maneuver is made only after ATC authorization has been obtained and the pilot has established required visual reference to the airport (See Circle to Runway, Landing Minimums) (Refer to AIM)

CIRCLE TO RUNWAY (RUNWAY NUMBERED) — Used by ATC to inform the pilot that he must circle to land because the runway in use is other than the runway aligned with the instrument approach procedure. When the direction of the circling maneuver in relation to the airport/runway is required, the controller will state the direction (eight cardinal compass points) and specify a left or right downwind or base leg as appropriate; e.g., "Cleared VOR Runway Three Six Approach circle to Runway Two Two," or "Circle northwest of the airport for a right downwind to Runway Two Two." (See Circle-to-Land Maneuver, Landing Minimums) (Refer to AIM)

CIRCLING APPROACH — (See Circle-to-Land Maneuver)

CIRCLING MINIMA — (See Landing Minimums)

CLEAR-AIR TURBULENCE/CAT — Turbulence encountered in air where no clouds are present. This term is commonly applied to high-level turbulence associated with wind shear. CAT is often encountered in the vicinity of the jet stream. (See Wind Shear, Jet Stream)

CLEARANCE — (See Air Traffic Clearance)

CLEARANCE LIMIT — The fix, point, or location to which an aircraft is cleared when issued an air traffic clearance.

ICAO—CLEARANCE LIMIT — The point of which an aircraft is granted an air traffic control clearance.

CLEARANCE VOID IF NOT OFF BY (TIME) — Used by ATC to advise an aircraft that the departure clearance is automatically cancelled if takeoff is not made prior to a specified time. The pilot must obtain a new clearance or cancel his IFR flight plan if not off by the specified time.

ICAO—CLEARANCE VOID TIME — A time specified by an air traffic control unit at which a clearance ceases to be valid unless the aircraft concerned has already taken action to comply therewith.

CLEARED AS FILED — Means the aircraft is cleared to proceed in accordance with the route of flight filed in the flight plan. This clearance does not include the altitude, SID, or SID Transition. (See Request Full Route Clearance) (Refer to AIM)

CLEARED FOR (Type Of) APPROACH — ATC authorization for an aircraft to execute a specific instrument approach procedure to an airport; e.g., "Cleared for ILS Runway Three Six Approach." (See Instrument Approach Procedure, Approach Clearance) (Refer to AIM, FAR Part 91)

CLEARED FOR APPROACH — ATC authorization for an aircraft to execute any standard or special instrument approach procedure for that airport. Normally, an aircraft will be cleared for a specific instrument approach procedure. (See Instrument Approach Procedure, Cleared for (Type of) Approach) (Refer to AIM, FAR Part 91)

CLEARED FOR TAKEOFF — ATC authorization for an aircraft to depart. It is predicated on known traffic and known physical airport conditions.

CLEARED FOR THE OPTION — ATC authorization for an aircraft to make a touch-and-go, low approach, missed approach, stop and go, or full stop landing at the discretion of the pilot. It is normally used in training so that an instructor can evaluate a student's performance under changing situations. (See Option Approach) (Refer to AIM)

CLEARED THROUGH — ATC authorization for an aircraft to make intermediate stops at specified airports without refiling a flight plan while en route to the clearance limit.

CLEARED TO LAND — ATC authorization for an aircraft to land. It is predicated on known traffic and known physical airport conditions.

CLEARWAY — An area beyond the takeoff runway under the control of airport authorities within which terrain or fixed obstacles may not extend above specified limits. These areas may be required for certain turbine-powered operations and the size and upward slope of the clearway will differ depending on when the aircraft was certificated. (Refer to FAR Part 1)

CLIMBOUT — That portion of flight operation between takeoff and the initial cruising altitude.

CLIMB TO VFR — ATC authorization for an aircraft to climb to VFR conditions within a control zone when the only weather limitation is restricted visibility. The aircraft must remain clear of clouds while climbing to VFR. (See Special VFR) (Refer to AIM)

CLOSED RUNWAY — A runway that is unusable for aircraft operations. Only the airport management/military operations office can close a runway.

CLOSED TRAFFIC — Successive operations involving takeoffs and landings or low approaches where the aircraft does not exit the traffic pattern.

CLUTTER — In radar operations, clutter refers to the reception and visual display of radar returns caused by precipitation, chaff, terrain, numerous aircraft targets, or other phenomena. Such returns may limit or preclude ATC from providing services based on radar. (See Ground Clutter, Chaff, Precipitation, Target)

ICAO—Radar Clutter — The visual indication on a radar display of unwanted signals.

COASTAL FIX — A navigation aid or intersection where an aircraft transitions between the domestic route structure and the oceanic route structure.

CODES/TRANSPONDER CODES — The number assigned to a particular multiple pulse reply signal transmitted by a transponder. (See Discrete Code)

COMBINED CENTER-RAPCON/CERAP — An air traffic facility which combines the functions of an ARTCC and a radar approach control facility. (See Air Route Traffic Control Center/ARTCC, Radar Approach Control Facility)

COMMON ROUTE/COMMON PORTION — That segment of a North American Route between the inland navigation facility and the coastal fix.

COMMON TRAFFIC ADVISORY FREQUENCY/ CTAF — A frequency designed for the purpose of carrying out airport advisory practices while operating to or from an uncontrolled airport. The CTAF may be a UNICOM, Multicom, FSS, or tower frequency and is identified in appropriate aeronautical publications. (Refer to AC—90-42E)

COMPASS LOCATOR — A low power, low or medium frequency (L/MF) radio beacon installed at the site of the outer or middle marker of an instrument landing system (ILS). It can be used for navigation at distances of approximately 15 miles or as authorized in the approach procedure.

1. Outer Compass Locator/LOM—A compass locator installed at the site of the outer marker of an instrument landing system. (See Outer Marker)

2. **Middle Compass Locator/LMM**—A compass locator installed at the site of the middle marker of an instrument landing system. (See Middle Marker)

ICAO—LOCATOR — An LM/MF NDB used as an aid to final approach.

Note. — A locator usually has an average radius of rated coverage of between 18.5 and 46.3 km (10 and 25 NM).

COMPASS ROSE — A circle, graduated in degrees, printed on some charts or marked on the ground at an airport. It is used as a reference to either true or magnetic direction.

COMPOSITE FLIGHT PLAN — A flight plan which specifies VFR operation for one portion of flight and IFR for another portion. It is used primarily in military operations. (Refer to AIM)

COMPOSITE ROUTE SYSTEM — An organized oceanic route structure, incorporating reduced lateral spacing between routes, in which composite separation is authorized.

COMPOSITE SEPARATION — A method of separating aircraft in a composite route system where, by management of route and altitude assignments, a combination of half the lateral minimum specified for the area concerned and half the vertical minimum is applied.

COMPULSORY REPORTING POINTS — Reporting points which must be reported to ATC. They are designated on aeronautical charts by solid triangles or filed in a flight plan as fixes selected to define direct routes. These points are geographical locations which are defined by navigation aids/fixes. Pilots should discontinue position reporting over compulsory reporting points when informed by ATC that their aircraft is in "radar contact."

CONFLICT ALERT — A function of certain air traffic control automated systems designed to alert radar controllers to existing or pending situations recognized by the program parameters that require his immediate attention/action.

CONFLICT RESOLUTION — The resolution of potential conflicts between IFR aircraft and VFR aircraft that are radar identified and in communication with ATC by ensuring that radar targets do not touch. Pertinent traffic advisories shall be issued when this procedure is applied. Note: This separation procedure will not be provided utilizing fully digitized radar systems. (See Controlled Airspace: Airport Radar Service Area/ARSA; Outer Area)

CONSOLAN — A low frequency, long-distance NAVAID used principally for transoceanic navigations.

CONTACT —

1. Establish communication with (followed by the name of the facility and, if appropriate, the frequency to be used).

2. A flight condition wherein the pilot ascertains the attitude of his aircraft and navigates by visual reference to the surface. (See Contact Approach, Radar Contact)

CONTACT APPROACH — An approach wherein an aircraft on an IFR flight plan, having an air traffic control authorization, operating clear of clouds with at least 1 mile flight visibility and a reasonable expectation of continuing to the destination airport in those conditions, may deviate from the instrument approach procedure and proceed to the destination airport by visual reference to the surface. This approach will only be authorized when requested by the pilot and the reported ground visibility at the destination airport is at least 1 statute mile. (Refer to AIM)

CONTERMINOUS U.S. — The 48 adjoining States and the District of Columbia.

CONTINENTAL CONTROL AREA — (See Controlled Airspace)

CONTINENTAL UNITED STATES — The 49 States located on the continent of North America and the District of Columbia.

CONTROL AREA — (See Controlled Airspace)

CONTROLLED AIRSPACE — Airspace designated as a control zone, airport radar service area, terminal control area, transition area, control area, continental control area, and positive control area within which some or all aircraft may be subject to air traffic control. (Refer to AIM, FAR Part 71)

ICAO—CONTROLLED AIRSPACE — Airspace of defined dimensions within which air traffic control service is provided to controlled flights.

Types of U.S. Controlled Airspace:

1. **Control Zone**—Controlled airspace which extends upward from the surface of the earth and terminates at the base of the continental control area. Control zones that do not underlie the continental control area have no upper limit. A control zone may include one or more airports and is normally a circular area with a radius of 5 statute miles and any extensions necessary to include instrument approach and departure paths.

ICAO—Control Zone—A controlled airspace extending upwards from the surface of the earth to a specified upper limit.

2. **Airport Radar Service Area/ARSA**—Regulatory airspace surrounding designated airports wherein ATC provides radar vectoring and sequencing on a full-time basis for all IFR and VFR aircraft. The service provided in an ARSA is called ARSA service which includes: IFR/IFR—standard IFR separation; IFR/VFR—traffic advisories and conflict resolution; and VFR/VFR—traffic advisories and, as appropriate, safety alerts. The AIM contains an explanation of ARSA. The ARSA's are depicted on VFR aeronautical charts. (See Conflict

Resolution, Outer Area) (Refer to AIM, Airport/Facility Directory, FAR Part 91)

3. Terminal Control Area/TCA—Controlled airspace extending upward from the surface or higher to specified altitudes, within which all aircraft are subject to operating rules and pilot and equipment requirements specified in FAR Part 91. TCA's are depicted on Sectional, World Aeronautical, En Route Low Altitude, DOD FLIP, and TCA charts. (Refer to FAR Part 91, AIM)

ICAO—Terminal Control Area—A control area normally established at the confluence of ATS routes in the vicinity of one or more major aerodromes.

4. Transition Area—Controlled airspace extending upward from 700 feet or more above the surface of the earth when designated in conjunction with an airport for which an approved instrument approach procedure has been prescribed; or from 1,200 feet or more above the surface of the earth when designated in conjunction with airway route structures or segments. Unless otherwise specified, transition areas terminate at the base of the overlying controlled airspace. Transition areas are designed to contain IFR operations in controlled airspace during portions of the terminal operation and while transiting between the terminal and en route environment.

5. Control Area—Airspace designated as Colored Federal airways, VOR Federal airways, control areas associated with jet routes outside the continental control area (FAR 71.161), additional control areas (FAR 71.163), control area extensions (FAR 71.165), and area low routes. Control areas do not include the continental control area, but unless otherwise designated, they do include the airspace between a segment of a main VOR Federal airway and its associated alternate segments with the vertical extent of the area corresponding to the vertical extent of the related segment of the main airway. The vertical extent of the various categories of airspace contained in control areas is defined in FAR Part 71.

ICAO—Control Area—A controlled airspace extending upward from a specified limit above the earth.

6. Continental Control Area—The airspace of the 48 contiguous States, the District of Columbia and Alaska, excluding the Alaska peninsula west of Long. 160° 00' 00"W, at and above 14,500 feet MSL, but does not include:
    a. The airspace less than 1,500 feet above the surface of the earth; or
    b. Prohibited and restricted areas, other than the restricted areas listed in FAR Part 71.

7. Positive Control Area/PCA—Airspace designated in FAR, Part 71 within which there is positive control of aircraft. Flight in PCA is normally conducted under instrument flight rules. PCA is designated throughout most of the conterminous United States and its vertical extent is from 18,000 feet MSL to and including flight level 600. In Alaska PCA does not include the airspace less than 1,500 feet above the surface of the earth nor the airspace over the Alaska Peninsula west of longitude 160 degrees West. Rules for operating in PCA are found in FARs 91.97 and 91.24.

CONTROLLED DEPARTURE TIME (CDT) PROGRAMS — These programs are the flow control process whereby aircraft are held on the ground at the departure airport when delays are projected to occur in either the en route system or the terminal of intended landing. The purpose of these programs is to reduce congestion in the air traffic system or to limit the duration of airborne holding in the arrival center or terminal area. A CDT is a specific departure slot shown on the flight plan as an expected departure clearance time (EDCT).

CONTROLLER — (See Air Traffic Control Specialist)

CONTROL SECTOR — An airspace area of defined horizontal and vertical dimensions for which a controller or group of controllers has air traffic control responsibility, normally within an air route traffic control center or an approach control facility. Sectors are established based on predominant traffic flows, altitude strata, and controller workload. Pilot-communications during operations within a sector are normally maintained on discrete frequencies assigned to the sector. (See Discrete Frequency)

CONTROL SLASH — A radar beacon slash representing the actual position of the associated aircraft. Normally, the control slash is the one closest to the interrogating radar beacon site. When ARTCC radar is operating in narrowband (digitized) mode, the control slash is converted to a target symbol.

CONTROL ZONE — (See Controlled Airspace)

CONVECTIVE SIGMET /WST/CONVECTIVE SIGNIFICANT METEOROLOGICAL INFORMATION — A weather advisory concerning convective weather significant to the safety of all aircraft. Convective SIGMET's are issued for tornadoes, lines of thunderstorms, embedded thunderstorms of any intensity level, areas of thunderstorms greater than or equal to VIP level 4 with an areal coverage of 4/10 (40%) or more, and hail 3/4 inch or greater. (See AWW, SIGMET, CWA, and AIRMET) (Refer to AIM)

COORDINATES — The intersection of lines of reference, usually expressed in degrees/minutes/seconds of latitude and longitude, used to determine position or location.

COORDINATION FIX — The fix in relation to which facilities will handoff, transfer control of an aircraft, or coordinate flight progress data. For terminal facilities, it may also serve as a clearance for arriving aircraft.

PILOT/CONTROLLER GLOSSARY

CORRECTION — An error has been made in the transmission and the correct version follows.

COUPLED APPROACH — A coupled approach is an instrument approach performed by the aircraft autopilot which is receiving position information and/or steering commands from onboard navigation equipment. In general, coupled nonprecision approaches must be discontinued and flown manually at altitudes lower than 50 feet below the minimum descent altitude, and coupled precision approaches must be flown manually below 50 feet ALG (See Autoland Approach).

Note. — Coupled and autoland approaches are flown in VFR and IFR. It is common for carriers to require their crews to fly coupled approaches and autoland approaches (if certified) when the weather conditions are less than approximately 4,000 RVR.

COURSE —

1. The intended direction of flight in the horizontal plane measured in degrees from north.

2. The ILS localizer signal pattern usually specified as the front course or the back course.

3. The intended track along a straight, curved, or segmented MLS path.

(See Bearing, Radial, Instrument Landing System, Microwave Landing System)

CRITICAL ENGINE — The engine which, upon failure, would most adversely affect the performance or handling qualities of an aircraft.

CROSS (FIX) AT (ALTITUDE) — Used by ATC when a specific altitude restriction at a specified fix is required.

CROSS (FIX) AT OR ABOVE (ALTITUDE) — Used by ATC when an altitude restriction at a specified fix is required. It does not prohibit the aircraft from crossing the fix at a higher altitude than specified; however, the higher altitude may not be one that will violate a succeeding altitude restriction or altitude assignment. (See Altitude Assignment, Altitude Restriction.) (Refer to AIM)

CROSS (FIX) AT OR BELOW (ALTITUDE) — Used by ATC when a maximum crossing altitude at a specific fix is required. It does not prohibit the aircraft from crossing the fix at a lower altitude; however, it must be at or above the minimum IFR altitude. (See Minimum IFR Altitude, Altitude Restriction) (Refer to FAR Part 91)

CROSSWIND —

1. When used concerning the traffic pattern, the word means "crosswind leg." (See Traffic Pattern)

2. When used concerning wind conditions, the word means a wind not parallel to the runway or the path of an aircraft. (See Crosswind Component)

CROSSWIND COMPONENT — The wind component measured in knots at 90 degrees to the longitudinal axis of the runway.

CRUISE — Used in an ATC clearance to authorize a pilot to conduct flight at any altitude from the minimum IFR altitude up to and including the altitude specified in the clearance. The pilot may level off at any intermediate altitude within this block of airspace. Climb/descent within the block is to be made at the discretion of the pilot. However, once the pilot starts descent and verbally reports leaving an altitude in the block, he may not return to that altitude without additional ATC clearance. Further, it is approval for the pilot to proceed to and make an approach at destination airport and can be used in conjunction with:

1. An airport clearance limit at locations with a standard/special instrument approach procedure. The FAR's require that if an instrument letdown to an airport is necessary, the pilot shall make the letdown in accordance with a standard/special instrument approach procedure for that airport, or

2. An airport clearance limit at locations that are within/below/outside controlled airspace and without a standard/special instrument approach procedure. Such a clearance is NOT AUTHORIZATION for the pilot to descend under IFR conditions below the applicable minimum IFR altitude nor does it imply that ATC is exercising control over aircraft in uncontrolled airspace; however, it provides a means for the aircraft to proceed to destination airport, descend, and land in accordance with applicable FAR's governing VFR flight operations. Also, this provides search and rescue protection until such time as the IFR flight plan is closed. (See Instrument Approach Procedure)

CRUISING ALTITUDE/LEVEL — An altitude or flight level maintained during en route level flight. This is a constant altitude and should not be confused with a cruise clearance. (See Altitude)

ICAO—CRUISING LEVEL — A level maintained during a significant portion of a flight.

DECISION HEIGHT/DH — With respect to the operation of aircraft, means the height at which a decision must be made during an ILS, MLS, or PAR instrument approach to either continue the approach or to execute a missed approach.

ICAO—DECISION ALTITUDE/HEIGHT (DA/DH) — A specified altitude or height (A/H) in the precision approach at which a missed approach must be initiated if the required visual reference to continue the approach has not been established.

Note 1. — Decision altitude (DA) is referenced to mean sea level (MSL) and decision height (DH) is referenced to the threshold elevation.

Note 2. — The required visual reference means that section of the visual aids or of the approach area which should have been in view for sufficient time for the pilot to have made an assessment of the aircraft position and rate of change of position, in relation to the desired flight path.

DECODER — The device used to decipher signals received from ATCRBS transponders to effect their display as select codes. (See Codes, Radar)

DEFENSE VISUAL FLIGHT RULES/DVFR — Rules applicable to flights within an ADIZ conducted under the visual flight rules in FAR, Part 91. (See Air Defense Identification Zone) (Refer to FAR, Part 99)

DEPARTURE CONTROL — A function of an approach control facility providing air traffic control service for departing IFR and, under certain conditions, VFR aircraft. (See Approach Control) (Refer to AIM)

DEPARTURE TIME — The time an aircraft becomes airborne.

DEVIATIONS —

1. A departure from a current clearance, such as an off course maneuver to avoid weather or turbulence.
2. Where specifically authorized in the FAR's and requested by the pilot, ATC may permit pilots to deviate from certain regulations. (Refer to AIM)

DF APPROACH PROCEDURE — Used under emergency conditions where another instrument approach procedure cannot be executed. DF guidance for an instrument approach is given by ATC facilities with DF capability. (See DF Guidance, Direction Finder) (Refer to AIM)

DF FIX — The geographical location of an aircraft obtained by one or more direction finders. (See Direction Finder)

DF GUIDANCE/DF STEER — Headings provided to aircraft by facilities equipped with direction finding equipment. These headings, if followed, will lead the aircraft to a predetermined point such as the DF station or an airport. DF guidance is given to aircraft in distress or to other aircraft which request the service. Practice DF guidance is provided when workload permits. (See Direction Finder, DF Fix) (Refer to AIM)

DIRECT — Straight line flight between two navigational aids, fixes, points, or any combination thereof. When used by pilots in describing off-airway routes, points defining direct route segments become compulsory reporting points unless the aircraft is under radar contact.

DIRECT ALTITUDE AND IDENTITY READOUT/ DAIR — The DAIR System is a modification to the AN/TPX-42 Interrogator System. The Navy has two adaptations of the DAIR System — Carrier Air Traffic Control Direct Altitude and Identification Readout System for Aircraft Carriers and Radar Air Traffic Control Facility Direct Altitude and Identity Readout System for land-based terminal operations. The DAIR detects, tracks, and predicts secondary radar aircraft targets. Targets are displayed by means of computer-generated symbols and alphanumeric characters depicting flight identification, altitude, ground speed, and flight plan data. The DAIR System is capable of interfacing with ARTCC's.

DIRECTION FINDER/DF/UDF/VDF/UVDF — A radio receiver equipped with a directional sensing antenna used to take bearings on a radio transmitter. Specialized radio direction finders are used in aircraft as air navigation aids. Others are ground-based, primarily to obtain a "fix" on a pilot requesting orientation assistance or to locate downed aircraft. A location "fix" is established by the intersection of two or more bearing lines plotted on a navigational chart using either two separately located Direction Finders to obtain a fix on an aircraft or by a pilot plotting the bearing indications of his DF on two separately located ground-based transmitters, both of which can be identified on his chart. UDF's receive signals in the ultra high frequency radio broadcast band; VDF's in the very high frequency band; and UVDF's in both bands. ATC provides DF service at those air traffic control towers and flight service stations listed in the Airport/Facility Directory and the DOD FLIP IFR En Route Supplement. (See DF Guidance, DF Fix)

DISCRETE CODE/DISCRETE BEACON CODE — As used in the Air Traffic Control Radar Beacon System (ATCRBS), any one of the 4096 selectable Mode 3/A aircraft transponder codes except those ending in zero zero; e.g., discrete codes: 0010, 1201, 2317, 7777; non-discrete codes: 0100, 1200, 7700. Non-discrete codes are normally reserved for radar facilities that are not equipped with discrete decoding capability and for other purposes such as emergencies (7700), VFR aircraft (1200), etc. (See Radar) (Refer to AIM)

DISCRETE FREQUENCY — A separate radio frequency for use in direct pilot-controller communications in air traffic control which reduces frequency congestion by controlling the number of aircraft operating on a particular frequency at one time. Discrete frequencies are normally designated for each control sector in en route/terminal ATC facilities. Discrete frequencies are listed in the Airport/Facility Directory and the DOD FLIP IFR En Route Supplement. (See Control Sector)

DISPLACED THRESHOLD — A threshold that is located at a point on the runway other than the designated beginning of the runway. (See Threshold) (Refer to AIM)

DISTANCE MEASURING EQUIPMENT/DME — Equipment (airborne and ground) used to measure, in nautical miles, the slant range distance of an aircraft from the DME navigational aid. (See TACAN, VORTAC, Microwave Landing System)

DISTRESS — A condition of being threatened by serious and/or imminent danger and of requiring immediate assistance.

DIVERSE VECTOR AREA/DVA — In a radar environment, that area in which a prescribed departure route is not required as the only suitable route to avoid obstacles. The area in which random radar vectors below the MVA/MIA, established in accordance with the TERPS criteria for diverse departures obstacles and terrain avoidance, may be issued to departing aircraft.

DME FIX — A geographical position determined by reference to a navigational aid which provides distance and azimuth information. It is defined by a specific distance in nautical miles and a radial, azimuth, or course (i.e., localizer) in degrees magnetic from that aid. (See Distance Measuring Equipment/DME, Fix, Microwave Landing System)

DME SEPARATION — Spacing of aircraft in terms of distances (nautical miles) determined by reference to distance measuring equipment (DME). (See Distance Measuring Equipment)

DOD FLIP — Department of Defense Flight Information Publications used for flight planning, en route, and terminal operations. FLIP is produced by the Defense Mapping Agency for world-wide use. United States Government Flight Information Publications (en route charts and instrument approach procedure charts) are incorporated in DOD FLIP for use in the National Airspace System (NAS).

DOWNWIND LEG — (See Traffic Pattern)

DRAG CHUTE — A parachute device installed on certain aircraft which is deployed on landing roll to assist in deceleration of the aircraft.

EMERGENCY — A *distress* or an *urgency* condition.

EMERGENCY LOCATOR TRANSMITTER/ELT — A radio transmitter attached to the aircraft structure which operates from its own power source on 121.5 MHz and 243.0 MHz. It aids in locating downed aircraft by radiating a downward sweeping audio tone, 2-4 times per second. It is designed to function without human action after an accident. (Refer to FAR, Part 91, AIM)

EMERGENCY SAFE ALTITUDE — (See Minimum Safe Altitude)

E-MSAW — (See En Route Minimum Safe Altitude Warning)

EN ROUTE AIR TRAFFIC CONTROL SERVICES — Air traffic control service provided aircraft on IFR flight plans, generally by centers, when these aircraft are operating between departure and destination terminal areas. When equipment, capabilities, and controller workload permit, certain advisory/assistance services may be provided to VFR aircraft. (See NAS Stage A, Air Route Traffic Control Center) (Refer to AIM)

EN ROUTE AUTOMATED RADAR TRACKING SYSTEM/EARTS — An automated radar and radar beacon tracking system. Its functional capabilities and design are essentially the same as the terminal ARTS IIIA system except for the EARTS capability of employing both short-range (ASR) and long-range (ARSR) radars, use of full digital radar displays, and fail-safe design. (See Automated Radar Terminal Systems/ARTS)

EN ROUTE CHARTS — (See Aeronautical Charts)

EN ROUTE DESCENT — Descent from the en route cruising altitude which takes place along the route of flight.

EN ROUTE FLIGHT ADVISORY SERVICE/FLIGHT WATCH — A service specifically designed to provide, upon pilot request, timely weather information pertinent to his type of flight, intended route of flight, and altitude. The FSS's providing this service are listed in the Airport/Facility Directory. (Refer to AIM)

EN ROUTE MINIMUM SAFE ALTITUDE WARNING/E-MSAW — A function of the NAS Stage A en route computer that aids the controller by alerting him when a tracked aircraft is below or predicted by the computer to go below a predetermined minimum IFR altitude (MIA).

ICAO—ESTIMATED ELAPSED TIME — The estimated time required to proceed from one significant point to another. (See Total Estimated Elapsed Time)

ICAO—ESTIMATED OFF-BLOCK TIME — The estimated time at which the aircraft will commence movement associated with departure.

EXECUTE MISSED APPROACH — Instructions issued to a pilot making an instrument approach which means continue inbound to the missed approach point and execute the missed approach procedure as described on the Instrument Approach Procedure Chart or as previously assigned by ATC. The pilot may climb immediately to the altitude specified in the missed approach procedure upon making a missed approach. No turns should be initiated prior to reaching the missed approach point. When conducting an ASR or PAR approach, execute the assigned missed approach procedure immediately upon receiving instructions to "execute missed approach." (Refer to AIM)

EXPECT (ALTITUDE) AT (TIME) or (FIX) — Used under certain conditions to provide a pilot with an altitude to be used in the event of two-way communications failure. It also provides altitude information to assist the pilot in planning. (Refer to AIM)

EXPECTED DEPARTURE CLEARANCE TIME/EDCT — The runway release time assigned to an aircraft in a controlled departure time program and shown on the flight progress strip as an EDCT.

EXPECT FURTHER CLEARANCE (TIME)/EFC — The time a pilot can expect to receive clearance beyond a clearance limit.

EXPECT FURTHER CLEARANCE VIA (AIRWAYS, ROUTES OR FIXES) — Used to inform a pilot of the routing he can expect if any part of the route beyond a short range clearance limit differs from that filed.

EXPEDITE — Used by ATC when prompt compliance is required to avoid the development of an imminent situation.

FAST FILE — A system whereby a pilot files a flight plan via telephone that is tape recorded and then transcribed for transmission to the appropriate air traffic facility. Locations having a fast file capability are contained in the Airport/Facility Directory. (Refer to AIM)

FEATHERED PROPELLER — A propeller whose blades have been rotated so that the leading and trailing edges are nearly parallel with the aircraft flight path to stop or minimize drag and engine rotation. Normally used to indicate shutdown of a reciprocating or turboprop engine due to malfunction.

FEEDER FIX — The fix depicted on Instrument Approach Procedure Charts which establishes the starting point of the feeder route.

FEEDER ROUTE — A route depicted on instrument approach procedure charts to designate routes for aircraft to proceed from the en route structure to the initial approach fix (IAF). (See Instrument Approach Procedure)

FERRY FLIGHT — A flight for the purpose of:

1. Returning an aircraft to base.
2. Delivering an aircraft from one location to another.
3. Moving an aircraft to and from a maintenance base.

Ferry flights, under certain conditions, may be conducted under terms of a special flight permit.

FILED — Normally used in conjunction with flight plans, meaning a flight plan has been submitted to ATC.

FILED EN ROUTE DELAY — Any of the following preplanned delays at points/areas along the route of flight which require special flight plan filing and handling techniques.

1. Terminal Area Delay—A delay within a terminal area for touch-and-go, low approach, or other terminal area activity.
2. Special Use Airspace Delay—A delay within a Military Operating Area, Restricted Area, Warning Area, or ATC Assigned Airspace.
3. Aerial Refueling Delay—A delay within an Aerial Refueling Track or Anchor.

FINAL — Commonly used to mean that an aircraft is on the final approach course or is aligned with a landing area. (See Final Approach Course, Final Approach—IFR, Traffic Pattern, Segments of an Instrument Approach Procedure)

FINAL APPROACH COURSE — A published MLS course, a straight line extension of a localizer, a final approach radial/bearing, or a runway centerline all without regard to distance. (See Final Approach-IFR, Traffic Pattern)

FINAL APPROACH FIX/FAF — The fix from which the final approach (IFR) to an airport is executed and which identifies the beginning of the final approach segment. It is designated on Government charts by the Maltese Cross symbol for nonprecision approaches and the lightning bolt symbol for precision approaches; or when ATC directs a lower-than-published Glideslope/path Intercept Altitude, it is the resultant actual point of the glideslope/path intercept. (See Final Approach Point, Glideslope/path Intercept Altitude, Segments of an Instrument Approach Procedure)

FINAL APPROACH-IFR — The flight path of an aircraft which is inbound to an airport on a final instrument approach course, beginning at the final approach fix or point and extending to the airport or the point where a circle-to-land maneuver or a missed approach is executed. (See Segments of an Instrument Approach Procedure, Final Approach Fix, Final Approach Course, Final Approach Point)

ICAO—FINAL APPROACH — That part of an instrument approach procedure which commences at the specified final approach fix or point, or where such a fix or point is not specified,

a) At the end of the last procedure turn, base turn or inbound turn of a racetrack procedure, if specified; or

b) At the point of interception of the last track specified in the approach procedure; and ends at a point in the vicinity of an aerodrome from which:

 1) A landing can be made; or
 2) A missed approach procedure is initiated.

FINAL APPROACH POINT/FAP — The point, applicable only to a nonprecision approach with no depicted FAF (such as an on-airport VOR), where the aircraft is established inbound on the final approach course from the procedure turn and where the final approach descent may be commenced. The FAP serves as the FAF and identifies the beginning of the final approach segment. (See Final Approach Fix, Segments of an Instrument Approach Procedure)

FINAL APPROACH SEGMENT — (See Segments of an Instrument Approach Procedure)

FINAL APPROACH-VFR — (See Traffic Pattern)

FINAL CONTROLLER — The controller providing information and final approach guidance during PAR and ASR approaches utilizing radar equipment. (See Radar Approach)

FIX — A geographical position determined by visual reference to the surface, by reference to one or more radio NAVAIDs, by celestial plotting, or by another navigational device.

FLAG/FLAG ALARM — A warning device incorporated in certain airborne navigation and flight instruments indicating that:

1. Instruments are inoperative or otherwise not operating satisfactorily, or

2. Signal strength or quality of the received signal falls below acceptable values.

FLAMEOUT — Unintended loss of combustion in turbine engines resulting in the loss of engine power.

FLIGHT CHECK — A call-sign prefix used by FAA aircraft engaged in flight inspection/certification of navigational aids and flight procedures. The word "recorded" may be added as a suffix; e.g., "Flight Check 320 recorded" to indicate that an automated flight inspection is in progress in terminal areas. (See Flight Inspection/Flight Check) (Refer to AIM).

FLIGHT INFORMATION REGION/FIR — An airspace of defined dimensions within which Flight Information Service and Alerting Service are provided.

1. Flight Information Service—A service provided for the purpose of giving advice and information useful for the safe and efficient conduct of flights.

2. Alerting Service—A service provided to notify appropriate organizations regarding aircraft in need of search and rescue aid and to assist such organizations as required.

FLIGHT INSPECTION/FLIGHT CHECK — Inflight investigation and evaluation of a navigational aid to determine whether it meets established tolerances. (See Navigational Aid)

FLIGHT LEVEL — A level of constant atmospheric pressure related to a reference datum of 29.92 inches of mercury. Each is stated in three digits that represent hundreds of feet. For example, flight level 250 represents a barometric altimeter indication of 25,000 feet; flight level 255, an indication of 25,500 feet.

ICAO—FLIGHT LEVEL — A surface of constant atmospheric pressure which is related to a specific pressure datum, 1013.2 hPa (1013.2 mb), and is separated from other such surfaces by specific pressure intervals.

Note 1. — A pressure type altimeter calibrated in accordance with the standard atmosphere:

a) When set to a QNH altimeter setting, will indicate altitude;

b) When set to a QFE altimeter setting, will indicate height above the QFE reference datum; and

c) When set to a pressure of 1013.2 hPa (1013.2 mb), may be used to indicate flight levels.

Note 2. — The terms *height* and *altitude*, used in *Note 1* above, indicate altimetric rather than geometric heights and altitudes.

FLIGHT LINE — A term used to describe the precise movement of a civil photogrammetric aircraft along a predetermined course(s) at a predetermined altitude during the actual photographic run.

FLIGHT PATH — A line, course, or track along which an aircraft is flying or intended to be flown. (See Track, Course)

FLIGHT PLAN — Specified information relating to the intended flight of an aircraft that is filed orally or in writing with an FSS or an ATC facility. (See Fast File, Filed) (Refer to AIM)

FLIGHT RECORDER — A general term applied to any instrument or device that records information about the performance of an aircraft in flight or about conditions encountered in flight. Flight recorders may make records of airspeed, outside air temperature, vertical acceleration, engine RPM, manifold pressure, and other pertinent variables for a given flight.

ICAO—FLIGHT RECORDER — Any type of recorder installed in the aircraft for the purpose of complementing accident/incident investigation.

Note. — See Annex 6, Part I, for specifications relating to flight recorders.

FLIGHT SERVICE STATION/FSS — Air traffic facilities which provide pilot briefing, en route communications and VFR search and rescue services, assist lost aircraft and aircraft in emergency situations, relay ATC clearances, originate Notices to Airmen, broadcast aviation weather and NAS information, receive and process IFR flight plans, and monitor NAVAID's. In addition, at selected locations, FSS's provide Enroute Flight Advisory Service (Flight Watch), take weather observations, issue airport advisories, and advise Customs and Immigration of transborder flights. (Refer to AIM)

FLIGHT STANDARDS DISTRICT OFFICE/FSDO — An FAA field office serving an assigned geographical area and staffed with Flight Standards personnel who serve the aviation industry and the general public on matters relating to the certification and operation of air carrier and general aviation aircraft. Activities include general surveillance of operational safety, certification of airmen and aircraft, accident prevention, investigation, enforcement, etc.

FLIGHT TEST — A flight for the purpose of:

1. Investigating the operation/flight characteristics of an aircraft or aircraft component.

2. Evaluating an applicant for a pilot certificate or rating.

FLIGHT VISIBILITY — (See Visibility)

FLIGHT WATCH — A shortened term for use in air-ground contacts to identify the flight service station providing En Route Flight Advisory Service; e.g., "Oakland Flight Watch." (See En Route Flight Advisory Service)

FLIP — (See DOD FLIP)

FLOW CONTROL — Measures designed to adjust the flow of traffic into a given airspace, along a given route, or bound for a given aerodrome (airport) so as to ensure the most effective utilization of the airspace. (See Quota Flow Control) (Refer to Airport/Facility Directory

FLY HEADING (DEGREES) — Informs the pilot of the heading he should fly. The pilot may have to turn to, or continue on, a specific compass direction in order to comply with the instructions. The pilot is expected to turn in the shorter direction to the heading unless otherwise instructed by ATC.

FORMATION FLIGHT — More than one aircraft which, by prior arrangement between the pilots, operate as a single aircraft with regard to navigation and position reporting. Separation between aircraft within the formation is the responsibility of the flight leader and the pilots of the other aircraft in the flight. This includes transition periods when aircraft within the formation are maneuvering to attain separation from each other to effect individual control and during join-up and breakaway.

1. A standard formation is one in which a proximity of no more than 1 mile laterally or longitudinally and within 100 feet vertically from the flight leader is maintained by each wingman.

2. Nonstandard formations are those operating under any of the following conditions:

   a. When the flight leader has requested and ATC has approved other than standard formation dimensions.

   b. When operating within an authorized altitude reservation (ALTRV) or under the provisions of a letter of agreement.

   c. When the operations are conducted in airspace specifically designed for a special activity. (See Altitude Reservation) (Refer to FAR Part 91)

FSS — (See Flight Service Station)

FUEL DUMPING — Airborne release of usable fuel. This does not include the dropping of fuel tanks. (See Jettisoning of External Stores)

FUEL SIPHONING/FUEL VENTING — Unintentional release of fuel caused by overflow, puncture, loose cap, etc.

GATE HOLD PROCEDURES — Procedures at selected airports to hold aircraft at the gate or other ground location whenever departure delays exceed or are anticipated to exceed 15 minutes. The sequence for departure will be maintained in accordance with initial call-up unless modified by flow control restrictions. Pilots should monitor the ground control/clearance delivery frequency for engine startup advisories or new proposed start time if the delay changes. (See Flow Control)

GENERAL AVIATION — That portion of civil aviation which encompasses all facets of aviation except air carriers holding a certificate of public convenience and necessity from the Civil Aeronautics Board and large aircraft commercial operators.

ICAO—GENERAL AVIATION — All civil aviation operations other than scheduled air services and non-scheduled air transport operations for remuneration or hire.

GENERAL AVIATION DISTRICT OFFICE/GADO — An FAA field office serving a designated geographical area and staffed with Flight Standards personnel who have the responsibility for serving the aviation industry and the general public on all matters relating to the certification and operation of general aviation aircraft.

GLIDESLOPE/GLIDEPATH — Provides vertical guidance for aircraft during approach and landing. The glideslope/glidepath is based on the following:

1. Electronic components emitting signals which provide vertical guidance by reference to airborne instruments during instrument approaches such as ILS/MLS, or

2. Visual ground aids, such as VASI, which provide vertical guidance for a VFR approach or for the visual portion of an instrument approach and landing.

3. PAR. Used by ATC to inform an aircraft making a PAR approach of its vertical position (elevation) relative to the descent profile.

ICAO—GLIDEPATH — A descent profile determined for vertical guidance during a final approach.

GLIDESLOPE/GLIDEPATH INTERCEPT ALTITUDE — The minimum altitude to intercept the glideslope/path on a precision approach. The intersection of the published intercept altitude with the glideslope/path, designated on Government charts by the lightning bolt symbol, is the precision FAF; however, when ATC directs a lower altitude, the resultant lower intercept position is then the FAF. (See Final Approach Fix, Segments of an Instrument Approach Procedure)

GO AHEAD — Proceed with your message. Not to be used for any other purpose.

GO AROUND — Instructions for a pilot to abandon his approach to landing. Additional instructions may follow. Unless otherwise advised by ATC, a VFR aircraft or an aircraft conducting visual approach should overfly the runway while climbing to traffic pattern altitude and enter the traffic pattern via the crosswind leg. A pilot on an IFR flight plan making an instrument approach should execute the published missed approach procedure or proceed as instructed by ATC; e.g., "Go around" (additional instructions if required). (See Low Approach, Missed Approach)

GROUND CLUTTER — A pattern produced on the radar scope by ground returns which may degrade other radar returns in the affected area. The effect of ground clutter is minimized by the use of moving target indicator (MTI) circuits in the radar equipment resulting in a radar presentation which displays only targets which are in motion. (See Clutter)

GROUND CONTROLLED APPROACH/GCA — A radar approach system operated from the ground by air traffic control personnel transmitting instructions to the pilot by radio. The approach may be conducted with surveillance radar (ASR) only or with both surveillance and precision approach radar (PAR). Usage of the term "GCA" by pilots is discouraged except when referring to a GCA facility. Pilots should specifically request a "PAR" approach when a precision radar approach is desired or request an "ASR" or "surveillance" approach when a nonprecision radar approach is desired. (See Radar Approach)

GROUND DELAY — The amount of delay attributed to ATC, encountered prior to departure, usually associated with a CDT program.

GROUND SPEED — The speed of an aircraft relative to the surface of the earth.

GROUND VISIBILITY — (See Visibility)

HANDOFF — An action taken to transfer the radar identification of an aircraft from one controller to another if the aircraft will enter the receiving controller's airspace and radio communications with the aircraft will be transferred.

HAVE NUMBERS — Used by pilots to inform ATC that they have received runway, wind, and altimeter information only.

HAZARDOUS INFLIGHT WEATHER ADVISORY SERVICE/HIWAS — A program for broadcasting hazardous weather information (AWW's, SIGMET's, Convective SIGMET's, CWA's, AIRMET's, and Urgent PIREP's) on a continuous basis over selected VOR's. (Refer to AIM)

HEAVY (AIRCRAFT) — (See Aircraft Classes)

HEIGHT ABOVE AIRPORT/HAA — The height of the Minimum Descent Altitude above the published airport elevation. This is published in conjunction with circling minimums. (See Minimum Descent Altitude)

HEIGHT ABOVE LANDING/HAL — The height above a designated helicopter landing area used for helicopter instrument approach procedures. (Refer to FAR Part 97)

HEIGHT ABOVE TOUCHDOWN/HAT — The height of the Decision Height or Minimum Descent Altitude above the highest runway elevation in the touchdown zone (first 3,000 feet of the runway). HAT is published on instrument approach charts in conjunction with all straight-in minimums. (See Decision Height, Minimum Descent Altitude)

HELICOPTER/COPTER — Rotorcraft that, for its horizontal motion, depends principally on its engine-driven rotors.

ICAO—HELICOPTER — A heavier-than-air aircraft supported in flight chiefly by the reactions of the air on one or more power-driven rotors on substantially vertical axes.

HELIPAD — A small, designated area, usually with a prepared surface, on a heliport, airport, landing/takeoff area, apron/ramp, or movement area used for takeoff, landing, or parking of helicopters.

HELIPORT — An area of land, water, or structure used or intended to be used for the landing and takeoff of helicopters and includes its buildings and facilities if any.

HERTZ/HZ — The standard radio equivalent of frequency in cycles per second of an electromagnetic wave. Kilohertz (kHz) is a frequency of one thousand cycles per second. Megahertz (MHz) is a frequency of one million cycles per second.

HIGH FREQUENCY/HF — The frequency band between 3 and 30 MHz. (See High Frequency Communications)

HIGH FREQUENCY COMMUNICATIONS/HF COMMUNICATIONS — High radio frequencies (HF) between 3 and 30 MHz used for air-to-ground voice communication in overseas operations.

HIGH SPEED TAXIWAY/EXIT/TURNOFF — A long radius taxiway designed and provided with lighting or marking to define the path of aircraft, traveling at high speed (up to 60 knots), from the runway center to a point on the center of a taxiway. Also referred to as long radius exit or turn-off taxiway. The high speed taxiway is designed to expedite aircraft turning off the runway after landing, thus reducing runway occupancy time.

HOLD/HOLDING PROCEDURE — A predetermined maneuver which keeps aircraft within a specified airspace while awaiting further clearance from air traffic control. Also used during ground operations to keep aircraft within a specified area or at a specified point while awaiting further clearance from air traffic control. (See Holding Fix) (Refer to AIM)

HOLDING FIX — A specified fix identifiable to a pilot by NAVAID's or visual reference to the ground used as a reference point in establishing and maintaining the position of an aircraft while holding. (See Fix, Hold, Visual Holding) (Refer to AIM)

HOLD FOR RELEASE — Used by ATC to delay an aircraft for traffic management reasons; i.e., weather, traffic volume, etc. Hold for release instructions (including departure delay information) are used to inform a pilot or a controller (either directly or through an authorized relay) that a departure clearance is not valid until a release time or additional instructions have been received.

ICAO—HOLDING POINT — A specified location, identified by visual or other means, in the vicinity of which the position of an aircraft in flight is maintained in accordance with air traffic control clearances.

HOMING — Flight toward a NAVAID, without correcting for wind, by adjusting the aircraft heading to maintain a relative bearing of zero degrees. (See Bearing)

ICAO—HOMING — The procedure of using the direction-finding equipment of one radio station with the emission of another radio station, where at least one of the stations is mobile, and whereby the mobile station proceeds continuously towards the other station.

HOVER CHECK — Used to describe when a helicopter/VTOL aircraft requires a stabilized hover to conduct a performance/power check prior to hover taxi, air taxi, or takeoff. Altitude of the hover will vary based on the purpose of the check.

HOVER TAXI — Used to describe a helicopter/VTOL aircraft movement conducted above the surface and in ground effect at airspeeds less than approximately 20 knots. The actual height may vary, and some helicopters may require hover taxi above 25 feet AGL to reduce ground effect turbulence or provide clearance for cargo slingloads. (See Air Taxi, Hover Check) (Refer to AIM)

HOW DO YOU HEAR ME? — A question relating to the quality of the transmission or to determine how well the transmission is being received.

IDENT — A request for a pilot to activate the aircraft transponder identification feature. This will help the controller to confirm an aircraft identity or to identify an aircraft. (Refer to AIM)

IDENT FEATURE — The special feature in the Air Traffic Control Radar Beacon System (ATCRBS) equipment. It is used to immediately distinguish one displayed beacon target from other beacon targets. (See Ident)

IF FEASIBLE, REDUCE SPEED TO (SPEED) — (See Speed Adjustment)

IF NO TRANSMISSION RECEIVED FOR (TIME) — Used by ATC in radar approaches to prefix procedures which should be followed by the pilot in event of lost communications. (See Lost Communications)

IFR AIRCRAFT/IFR FLIGHT — An aircraft conducting flight in accordance with instrument flight rules.

IFR CONDITIONS — Weather conditions below the minimum for flight under visual flight rules. (See Instrument Meteorological Conditions)

IFR DEPARTURE PROCEDURE — (See IFR Takeoff Minimums and Departure Procedures) (Refer to AIM)

IFR MILITARY TRAINING ROUTES (IR) — Routes used by the Department of Defense and associated Reserve and Air Guard units for the purpose of conducting low-altitude navigation and tactical training in both IFR and VFR weather conditions below 10,000 feet MSL at airspeeds in excess of 250 knots IAS.

IFR TAKEOFF MINIMUMS AND DEPARTURE PROCEDURES — FAR, Part 91, prescribes standard takeoff rules for certain civil users. At some airports, obstructions or other factors require the establishment of nonstandard takeoff minimums, departure procedures, or both to assist pilots in avoiding obstacles during climb to the minimum en route altitude. Those airports are listed in NOS/DOD Instrument Approach Charts (IAP's) under a section entitled "IFR Takeoff Minimums and Departure Procedures." The NOS/DOD IAP chart legend illustrates the symbol used to alert the pilot to nonstandard takeoff minimums and departure procedures. When departing IFR from such airports or from any airports where there are no departure procedures, SID's, or ATC facilities available, pilots should advise ATC of any departure limitations. Controllers may query a pilot to determine acceptable departure directions, turns, or headings after takeoff. Pilots should be familiar with the departure procedures and must assure that their aircraft can meet or exceed any specified climb gradients.

ILS CATEGORIES —

1. ILS Category I—An ILS approach procedure which provides for approach to a height above touchdown of not less than 200 feet and with runway visual range of not less than 1,800 feet.

2. ILS Category II—An ILS approach procedure which provides for approach to a height above touchdown of not less than 100 feet and with runway visual range of not less than 1,200 feet.

3. ILS Category III.

    a. IIIA—An ILS approach procedure which provides for approach without a decision height minimum and with runway visual range of not less than 700 feet.

    b. IIIB—An ILS approach procedure which provides for approach without a decision height minimum and with runway visual range of not less than 150 feet.

    c. IIIC—An ILS approach procedure which provides for approach without a decision height minimum and without runway visual range minimum.

IMMEDIATELY — Used by ATC when such action compliance is required to avoid an imminent situation.

INCREASE SPEED TO (SPEED) — (See Speed Adjustment)

INFORMATION REQUEST/INREQ — A request originated by an FSS for information concerning an overdue VFR aircraft.

INITIAL APPROACH FIX/IAF — The fixes depicted on instrument approach procedure charts that identify the beginning of the initial approach segment(s). (See Fix, Segments of an Instrument Approach Procedure)

INITIAL APPROACH SEGMENT — (See Segments of an Instrument Approach Procedure)

INNER MARKER/IM/INNER MARKER BEACON — A marker beacon used with an ILS (CAT II) precision approach located between the middle marker and the end of the ILS runway, transmitting a radiation pattern keyed at six dots per second and indicating to the pilot, both aurally and visually, that he is at the designated decision height (DH), normally 100 feet above the touchdown zone elevation, on the ILS CAT II approach. It also marks progress during a CAT III approach. (See Instrument Landing System) (Refer to AIM)

INSTRUMENT APPROACH PROCEDURE/IAP/INSTRUMENT APPROACH — A series of predetermined maneuvers for the orderly transfer of an aircraft under instrument flight conditions from the beginning of the initial approach to a landing or to a point from which a landing may be made visually. It is prescribed and approved for a specific airport by competent authority. (See Segments of an Instrument Approach Procedure) (Refer to FAR, Part 91, AIM)

1. U. S. civil standard instrument approach procedures are approved by the FAA as prescribed under FAR, Part 97 and are available for public use.

2. U.S. military standard instrument approach procedures are approved and published by the Department of Defense.

3. Special instrument approach procedures are approved by the FAA for individual operators but are not published in FAR, Part 97 for public use.

ICAO—INSTRUMENT APPROACH PROCEDURE — A series of predetermined manoeuvres by reference to flight instruments with specified protection from obstacles from the intial approach fix, or where applicable, from the beginning of a defined arrival route to a point from which a landing can be completed and thereafter, if a landing is not completed, to a position at which holding or en route obstacle clearance criteria apply.

INSTRUMENT FLIGHT RULES/IFR — Rules governing the procedures for conducting instrument flight. Also a term used by pilots and controllers to indicate type of flight plan. (See Visual Flight Rules, Instrument Meteorological Conditions, Visual Meteorological Conditions) (Refer to AIM)

ICAO—INSTRUMENT FLIGHT RULES — A set of rules governing the conduct of flight under instrument meteorological conditions.

INSTRUMENT LANDING SYSTEM/ILS — A precision instrument approach system which normally consists of the following electronic components and visual aids:

1. Localizer. (See Localizer)

2. Glideslope. (See Glideslope)

3. Outer Marker. (See Outer Marker)

4. Middle Marker. (See Middle Marker)

5. Approach Lights. (See Airport Lighting)

(Refer to FAR Part 91, AIM)

INSTRUMENT METEOROLOGICAL CONDITIONS/IMC — Meteorological conditions expressed in terms of visibility, distance from cloud, and ceiling less than the minima specified for visual meteorological conditions. (See Visual Meteorological Conditions, Instrument Flight Rules, Visual Flight Rules)

INSTRUMENT RUNWAY — A runway equipped with electronic and visual navigation aids for which a precision or nonprecision approach procedure having straight-in landing minimums has been approved.

ICAO—INSTRUMENT RUNWAY — One of the following types of runways intended for the operation of aircraft using instrument approach procedures:

a) Non-precision Approach Runway. An instrument runway served by visual aids and a nonvisual aid providing at least directional guidance adequate for a straight-in approach.

b) Precision Approach Runway, Category I. An instrument runway served by ILS and visual aids intended for operations down to 60 m (200 feet) decision height and down to an RVR of the order of 800 m.

c) Precision Approach Runway, Category II. An instrument runway served by ILS and visual aids intended for operations down to 30 m (100 feet) decision height and down to an RVR of the order of 400 m.

d) Precision Approach Runway, Category III. An instrument runway served by ILS to and along the surface of the runway and:

A — Intended for operations down to an RVR of the order of 200 m (no decision height being applicable) using visual aids during the final phase of landing;

B — Intended for operations down to an RVR of the order of 50 m (no decision height being applicable) using visual aids for taxiing;

C — Intended for operations without reliance on visual reference for landing or taxiing.

Note 1. — See Annex 10, Volume I, Part I Chapter 3, for related ILS specifications.

Note 2. — Visual aids need not necessarily be matched to the scale of non-visual aids provided. The criterion for the selection of visual aids is the conditions in which operations are intended to be conducted.

INTERMEDIATE APPROACH SEGMENT — (See Segments of an Instrument Approach Procedure)

INTERMEDIATE FIX/IF — The fix that identifies the beginning of the intermediate approach segment of an instrument approach procedure. The fix is not normally identified on the instrument approach chart as an intermediate fix (IF). (See Segments of an Instrument Approach Procedure)

INTERNATIONAL AIRPORT — Relating to international flight, it means:

1. An airport of entry which has been designated by the Secretary of Treasury or Commissioner of Customs as an international airport for customs service.

2. A landing rights airport at which specific permission to land must be obtained from customs authorities in advance of contemplated use.

3. Airports designated under the Convention on International Civil Aviation as an airport for use by international commercial air transport and/or international general aviation. (Refer to Airport/Facility Directory and IFIM).

ICAO—INTERNATIONAL AIRPORT — Any airport designated by the Contracting State in whose territory it is situated as an airport of entry and departure for international air traffic, where the formalities incident to customs, immigration, public health, animal and plant quarantine and similar procedures are carried out.

INTERNATIONAL CIVIL AVIATION ORGANIZATION/ICAO — A specialized agency of the United Nations whose objective is to develop the principles and techniques of international air navigation and to foster planning and development of international civil air transport.

INTERNATIONAL FLIGHT INFORMATION MANUAL/IFIM — A publication designed primarily as a pilot's preflight planning guide for flights into foreign airspace and for flights returning to the U.S. from foreign locations.

INTERROGATOR — The ground-based surveillance radar beacon transmitter-receiver, which normally scans in synchronism with a primary radar, transmitting discrete radio signals which repetitiously request all transponders on the mode being used to reply. The replies received are mixed with the primary radar returns and displayed on the same plan position indicator (radar scope). Also, applied to the airborne element of the TACAN/DME system. (See Transponder) (Refer to AIM)

INTERSECTING RUNWAYS — Two or more runways which cross or meet within their lengths. (See Intersection)

INTERSECTION —

1. A point defined by any combination of courses, radials, or bearings of two or more navigational aids.

2. Used to describe the point where two runways, a runway and a taxiway, or two taxiways cross or meet.

INTERSECTION DEPARTURE/INTERSECTION TAKEOFF — A takeoff or proposed takeoff on a runway from an intersection. (See Intersection)

I SAY AGAIN — The message will be repeated.

JAMMING — Electronic or mechanical interference which may disrupt the display of aircraft on radar or the transmission/reception of radio communications/navigation.

JET BLAST — Jet engine exhaust (thrust stream turbulence). (See Wake Turbulence)

JET ROUTE — A route designed to serve aircraft operations from 18,000 feet MSL up to and including flight level 450. The routes are referred to as ''J'' routes with numbering to identify the designated route; e.g., J105. (See Route) (Refer to FAR Part 71)

JET STREAM — A migrating stream of high-speed winds present at high altitudes.

JETTISONING OF EXTERNAL STORES — Airborne release of external stores; e.g., tiptanks, ordnance. (See Fuel Dumping) (Refer to FAR Part 91)

JOINT USE RESTRICTED AREA — (See Restricted Area)

KNOWN TRAFFIC — With respect to ATC clearances, means aircraft whose altitude, position, and intentions are known to ATC.

LANDING/TAKEOFF AREA — Any locality either on land, water, or structures, including airports/heliports and intermediate landing fields, which is used, or intended to be used, for the landing and takeoff of aircraft whether or not facilities are provided for the shelter, servicing, or for receiving or discharging passengers or cargo.

ICAO—LANDING AREA — That part of a movement area intended for the landing or takeoff of aircraft.

LANDING DIRECTION INDICATOR — A device which visually indicates the direction in which landings and takeoffs should be made. (See Tetrahedron) (Refer to AIM)

LANDING MINIMUMS/IFR LANDING MINIMUMS — The minimum visibility prescribed for landing a civil aircraft while using an instrument approach procedure. The minimum applies with other limitations set forth in FAR Part 91 with respect to the Minimum Descent Altitude (MDA) or Decision Height (DH) prescribed in the instrument approach procedures as follows:

1. Straight-in landing minimums—A statement of MDA and visibility, or DH and visibility, required for a straight-in landing on a specified runway, or

2. Circling minimums—A statement of MDA and visibility required for the circle-to-land maneuver.

Descent below the established MDA or DH is not authorized during an approach unless the aircraft is in a position from which a normal approach to the runway of intended landing can be made and adequate visual reference to required visual cues is maintained. (See Straight-in Landing, Circle-to-Land Maneuver, Decision Height, Minimum Descent Altitude, Visibility, Instrument Approach Procedure) (Refer to FAR Part 91)

LANDING ROLL — The distance from the point of touchdown to the point where the aircraft can be brought to a stop or exit the runway.

LANDING SEQUENCE — The order in which aircraft are positioned for landing. (See Approach Sequence)

LAST ASSIGNED ALTITUDE — The last altitude/flight level assigned by ATC and acknowledged by the pilot. (See Maintain) (Refer to FAR Part 91)

LATERAL SEPARATION — The lateral spacing of aircraft at the same altitude by requiring operation on different routes or in different geographical locations. (See Separation)

LIGHTED AIRPORT — An airport where runway and obstruction lighting is available. (See Airport Lighting) (Refer to AIM)

LIGHT GUN — A handheld directional light signaling device which emits a brilliant narrow beam of white, green, or red light as selected by the tower controller. The color and type of light transmitted can be used to approve or disapprove anticipated pilot actions where radio communication is not available. The light gun is used for controlling traffic operating in the vicinity of the airport and on the airport movement area. (Refer to AIM)

LOCALIZER — The component of an ILS which provides course guidance to the runway. (See Instrument Landing System) (Refer to AIM)

ICAO—LOCALIZER COURSE (ILS) — The locus of points, in any given horizontal plane, at which the DDM (difference in depth of modulation) is zero.

LOCALIZER TYPE DIRECTIONAL AID/LDA — A NAVAID used for nonprecision instrument approaches with utility and accuracy comparable to a localizer but which is not a part of a complete ILS and is not aligned with the runway. (Refer to AIM)

LOCALIZER USABLE DISTANCE — The maximum distance from the localizer transmitter at a specified altitude, as verified by flight inspection, at which reliable course information is continuously received. (Refer to AIM)

LOCAL TRAFFIC — Aircraft operating in the traffic pattern or within sight of the tower, or aircraft known to be departing or arriving from flight in local practice areas, or aircraft executing practice instrument approaches at the airport. (See Traffic Pattern)

LONGITUDINAL SEPARATION — The longitudinal spacing of aircraft at the same altitude by a minimum distance expressed in units of time or miles. (See Separation) (Refer to AIM)

LORAN/LONG RANGE NAVIGATION — An electronic navigational system by which hyperbolic lines of position are determined by measuring the difference in the time of reception of synchronized pulse signals from two fixed transmitters. Loran A operates in the 1750-1950 kHz frequency band. Loran C and D operate in the 100-110 kHz frequency band. (Refer to AIM)

LOST COMMUNICATIONS/TWO-WAY RADIO COMMUNICATIONS FAILURE — Loss of the ability to communicate by radio. Aircraft are sometimes referred to as NORDO (No Radio). Standard pilot procedures are specified in FAR Part 91. Radar controllers issue procedures for pilots to follow in the event of lost communications during a radar approach when weather reports indicate that an aircraft will likely encounter IFR weather conditions during the approach. (Refer to FAR Part 91, AIM)

LOW ALTITUDE AIRWAY STRUCTURE/FEDERAL AIRWAYS — The network of airways serving aircraft operations up to but not including 18,000 feet MSL. (See Airway) (Refer to AIM)

LOW ALTITUDE ALERT, CHECK YOUR ALTITUDE IMMEDIATELY — (See Safety Alert)

LOW ALTITUDE ALERT SYSTEM/LAAS — An automated function of the TPX-42 that alerts the controller when a Mode C transponder-equipped aircraft on an IFR flight plan is below a predetermined minimum safe altitude. If requested by the pilot, LAAS monitoring is also available to VFR Mode C transponder-equipped aircraft.

LOW APPROACH — An approach over an airport or runway following an instrument approach or a VFR approach including the go-around maneuver where the pilot intentionally does not make contact with the runway. (Refer to AIM)

LOW FREQUENCY/LF — The frequency band between 30 and 300 kHz. (Refer to AIM)

MACH NUMBER — The ratio of true airspeed to the speed of sound; e.g., MACH .82, MACH 1.6. (See Airspeed)

MAINTAIN —

1. Concerning altitude/flight level, the term means to remain at the altitude/flight level specified. The phrase "climb and" or "descend and" normally precedes "maintain" and the altitude assignment; e.g., "descend and maintain 5,000."

2. Concerning other ATC instructions, the term is used in its literal sense; e.g., maintain VFR.

MAKE SHORT APPROACH — Used by ATC to inform a pilot to alter his traffic pattern so as to make a short final approach. (See Traffic Pattern)

MANDATORY ALTITUDE — An altitude depicted on an instrument Approach Procedure Chart requiring the aircraft to maintain altitude at the depicted value.

MARKER BEACON — An electronic navigation facility transmitting a 75 MHz vertical fan or boneshaped radiation pattern. Marker beacons are identified by their modulation frequency and keying code, and when received by compatible airborne equipment, indicate to the pilot, both aurally and visually, that he is passing over the facility. (See Outer Marker, Middle Marker, Inner Marker) (Refer to AIM)

MAXIMUM AUTHORIZED ALTITUDE/MAA — A published altitude representing the maximum usable altitude or flight level for an airspace structure or route segment. It is the highest altitude on a Federal airway, jet route, area navigation low or high route, or other direct route for which an MEA is designated in FAR Part 95 at which adequate reception of navigation aid signals is assured.

MAYDAY — The international radiotelephony distress signal. When repeated three times, it indicates imminent and grave danger and that immediate assistance is requested. (See Pan-Pan) (Refer to AIM)

METEOROLOGICAL IMPACT STATEMENT/MIS — An unscheduled planning forecast describing conditions expected to begin within 4 to 12 hours which may impact the flow of air traffic in a specific center's (ARTCC) area.

METERING — A method of time-regulating arrival traffic flow into a terminal area so as not to exceed a predetermined terminal acceptance rate.

METERING FIX — A fix along an established route from over which aircraft will be metered prior to entering terminal airspace. Normally, this fix should be established at a distance from the airport which will facilitate a profile descent 10,000 feet above airport elevation (AAE) or above.

MIA — (See Minimum IFR Altitudes)

MICROWAVE LANDING SYSTEM/MLS — A precision instrument approach system operating in the microwave spectrum which normally consists of the following components:

1. Azimuth Station.
2. Elevation Station.
3. Precision Distance Measuring Equipment. (See MLS Categories)

MIDDLE COMPASS LOCATOR — (See Compass Locator)

MIDDLE MARKER/MM — A marker beacon that defines a point along the glide slope of an ILS normally located at or near the point of decision height (ILS Category I). It is keyed to transmit alternate dots and dashes, with the alternate dots and dashes keyed at the rate of 95 dot/dash combinations per minute on a 1300 Hz tone, which is received aurally and visually by compatible airborne equipment. (See Marker Beacon, Instrument Landing System) (Refer to AIM)

MID RVR — (See Visibility)

MILITARY AUTHORITY ASSUMES RESPONSIBILITY FOR SEPARATION OF AIRCRAFT/MARSA — A condition whereby the military services involved assume responsibility for separation between participating military aircraft in the ATC system. It is used only for required IFR operations which are specified in letters of agreement or other appropriate FAA or military documents.

MILITARY OPERATIONS AREA/MOA — (See Special Use Airspace)

MILITARY TRAINING ROUTES/MTR — Airspace of defined vertical and lateral dimensions established for the conduct of military flight training at airspeeds in excess of 250 knots IAS. (See IFR (IR) and VFR (VR) Military Training Routes)

MINIMUM CROSSING ALTITUDE/MCA — The lowest altitude at certain fixes at which an aircraft must cross when proceeding in the direction of a higher minimum en route IFR altitude (MEA). (See Minimum En Route IFR Altitude)

MINIMUM DESCENT ALTITUDE/MDA — The lowest altitude, expressed in feet above mean sea level, to which descent is authorized on final approach or during circle-to-land maneuvering in execution of a standard instrument approach procedure where no electronic glide slope is provided. (See Nonprecision Approach Procedure)

MINIMUM EN ROUTE IFR ALTITUDE/MEA — The lowest published altitude between radio fixes which assures acceptable navigational signal coverage and meets obstacle clearance requirements between those fixes. The MEA prescribed for a Federal airway or segment thereof, area navigation low or high route, or other direct route applies to the entire width of the airway, segment, or route between the radio fixes defining the airway, segment, or route. (Refer to FAR Parts 91 and 95; AIM)

MINIMUM FUEL — Indicates that an aircraft's fuel supply has reached a state where, upon reaching the destination, it can accept little or no delay. This is not an emergency situation but merely indicates an emergency situation is possible should any undue delay occur. (Refer to AIM)

MINIMUM HOLDING ALTITUDE/MHA — The lowest altitude prescribed for a holding pattern which assures navigational signal coverage, communications, and meets obstacle clearance requirements.

MINIMUM IFR ALTITUDES/MIA — Minimum altitudes for IFR operations as prescribed in FAR Part 91. These altitudes are published on aeronautical charts and prescribed in FAR Part 95 for airways and routes, and in FAR Part 97 for standard instrument approach procedures. If no applicable minimum altitude is prescribed in FAR Parts 95 or 97, the following minimum IFR altitude applies:

1. In designated mountainous areas, 2,000 feet above the highest obstacle within a horizontal distance of 5 statute miles from the course to be flown; or

2. Other than mountainous areas, 1,000 feet above the highest obstacle within a horizontal distance of 5 statute miles from the course to be flown; or

3. As otherwise authorized by the Administrator or assigned by ATC. (See Minimum En Route IFR Altitude, Minimum Obstruction Clearance Altitude, Minimum Crossing Altitude, Minimum Safe Altitude, Minimum Vectoring Altitude) (Refer to FAR Part 91)

MINIMUM OBSTRUCTION CLEARANCE ALTITUDE/MOCA — The lowest published altitude in effect between radio fixes on VOR airways, off-airway routes, or route segments which meets obstacle clearance requirements for the entire route segment and which assures acceptable navigational signal coverage only within 25 statute (22 nautical) miles of a VOR. (Refer to FAR Part 91 and 95)

MINIMUM RECEPTION ALTITUDE/MRA — The lowest altitude at which an intersection can be determined. (Refer to FAR Part 95)

MINIMUM SAFE ALTITUDE/MSA —

1. The minimum altitude specified in FAR Part 91 for various aircraft operations.

2. Altitudes depicted on approach charts which provide at least 1,000 feet of obstacle clearance for emergency use within a specified distance from the navigation facility upon which a procedure is predicated. These altitudes will be identified as Minimum Sector Altitudes or Emergency Safe Altitudes and are established as follows:

    a. Minimum Sector Altitudes—Altitudes depicted on approach charts which provide at least 1,000 feet of obstacle clearance within a 25-mile radius of the navigation facility upon which the procedure is predicated. Sectors depicted on approach charts must be at least 90 degrees in scope. These altitudes are for emergency use only and do not necessarily assure acceptable navigational signal coverage.

ICAO—Minimum Sector Altitude—The lowest altitude which may be used under emergency conditions which will provide a minimum clearance of 300 m (1 000 feet) above all obstacles located in an area contained within a sector of a circle of 46 km (25 NM) radius centered on a radio aid to navigation.

    b. Emergency Safe Altitudes—Altitudes depicted on approach charts which provide at least 1,000 feet of obstacle clearance in nonmountainous areas and 2,000 feet of obstacle clearance in designated mountainous areas within a 100-mile radius of the navigation facility upon which the procedure is predicated and normally used only in military procedures. These altitudes are identified on published procedures as "Emergency Safe Altitudes."

MINIMUM SAFE ALTITUDE WARNING/MSAW — A function of the ARTS III computer that aids the controller by alerting him when a tracked Mode C-equipped aircraft is below or is predicted by the computer to go below a predetermined minimum safe altitude. (Refer to AIM)

MINIMUMS/MINIMA— Weather condition requirements established for a particular operation or type of operation; e.g., IFR takeoff or landing, alternate airport for IFR flight plans, VFR flight, etc. (See Landing Minimums, IFR Takeoff Minimums, VFR Conditions, IFR Conditions) (Refer to FAR Part 91, AIM)

MINIMUM VECTORING ALTITUDE/MVA — The lowest MSL altitude at which an IFR aircraft will be vectored by a radar controller, except as otherwise authorized for radar approaches, departures, and missed approaches. The altitude meets IFR obstacle clearance criteria. It may be lower than the published MEA along an airway or J-route segment. It may be utilized for radar vectoring only upon the controller's determination that an adequate radar return is being received from the aircraft being controlled. Charts depicting minimum vectoring altitudes are normally available only to the controllers and not to pilots. (Refer to AIM)

MISSED APPROACH —

1. A maneuver conducted by a pilot when an instrument approach cannot be completed to a landing. The route of flight and altitude are shown on instrument approach procedure charts. A pilot executing a missed approach prior to the Missed Approach Point (MAP) must continue along the final approach to the MAP. The pilot may climb immediately to the altitude specified in the missed approach procedure.

2. A term used by the pilot to inform ATC that he is executing the missed approach.

3. At locations where ATC radar service is provided, the pilot should conform to radar vectors when provided by ATC in lieu of the published missed approach procedure. (See Missed Approach Point) (Refer to AIM)

ICAO—MISSED APPROACH PROCEDURE — The procedure to be followed if the approach cannot be continued.

MISSED APPROACH POINT/MAP — A point prescribed in each instrument approach procedure at which a missed approach procedure shall be executed if the required visual reference does not exist. (See Missed Approach, Segments of an Instrument Approach Procedure)

MISSED APPROACH SEGMENT — (See Segments of an Instrument Approach Procedure)

MLS — (See Microwave Landing System)

MLS CATEGORIES —

1. MLS Category I—An MLS approach procedure which provides for an approach to a height above touchdown of not less than 200 feet and a runway visual range of not less than 1,800 feet.

2. MLS Category II—Undefined until data gathering/analysis completion.

3. MLS Category III—Undefined until data gathering/analysis completion.

MODE — The letter or number assigned to a specific pulse spacing of radio signals transmitted or received by ground interrogator or airborne transponder components of the Air Traffic Control Radar Beacon System (ATCRBS). Mode A (military Mode 3) and Mode C (altitude reporting) are used in air traffic control. (See Transponder, Interrogator, Radar) (Refer to AIM)

ICAO—MODE (SSR MODE) — The letter or number assigned to a specific pulse spacing of the interrogation signals transmitted by an interrogator. There are 4 modes, A, B, C and D specified in Annex 10, corresponding to four different interrogation pulse spacings.

MOVEMENT AREA — The runways, taxiways, and other areas of an airport/heliport which are utilized for taxiing/hover taxiing, air taxiing, takeoff, and landing of aircraft, exclusive of loading ramps and parking areas. At those airports/heliports with a tower, specific approval for entry onto the movement area must be obtained from ATC.

ICAO—MOVEMENT AREA — That part of an aerodrome to be used for the takeoff, landing and taxiing of aircraft, consisting of the manoeuvring area and the apron(s).

MOVING TARGET INDICATOR/MTI — An electronic device which will permit radar scope presentation only from targets which are in motion. A partial remedy for ground clutter.

MSAW — (See Minimum Safe Altitude Warning)

MULTICOM — A mobile service not open to public correspondence used to provide communications essential to conduct the activities being performed by or directed from private aircraft (FAR 87.277).

NAS STAGE A — The en route ATC system's radar, computers and computer programs, controller plan view displays (PVDs/Radar Scopes), input/output devices, and the related communications equipment which are integrated to form the heart of the automated IFR air traffic control system. This equipment performs Flight Data Processing (FDP) and Radar Data Processing (RDP). It interfaces with automated terminal systems and is used in the control of en route IFR aircraft. (Refer to AIM)

NATIONAL AIRSPACE SYSTEM/NAS — The common network of U.S. airspace; air navigation facilities, equipment and services, airports or landing areas; aeronautical charts, information and services; rules, regulations and procedures, technical information, and manpower and material. Included are system components shared jointly with the military.

NATIONAL BEACON CODE ALLOCATION PLAN AIRSPACE/NBCAP AIRSPACE — Airspace over United States territory located within the North American continent between Canada and Mexico, including adjacent territorial waters outward to about boundaries of oceanic control areas (CTA)/Flight Information Regions (FIR). (See Flight Information Region)

NATIONAL FLIGHT DATA CENTER/NFDC — A facility in Washington D.C., established by FAA to operate a central aeronautical information service for the collection, validation, and dissemination of aeronautical data in support of the activities of government, industry, and the aviation community. The information is published in the National Flight Data Digest. (See National Flight Data Digest)

NATIONAL FLIGHT DATA DIGEST/NFDD — A daily (except weekends and Federal holidays) publication of flight information appropriate to aeronautical charts, aeronautical publications, Notices to Airmen, or other media serving the purpose of providing operational flight data essential to safe and efficient aircraft operations.

NATIONAL SEARCH AND RESCUE PLAN — An interagency agreement which provides for the effective utilization of all available facilities in all types of search and rescue missions.

NAVAID CLASSES — VOR, VORTAC, and TACAN aids are classed according to their operational use. The three classes of NAVAID's are:

T—Terminal.

L—Low altitude.

H—High altitude.

The normal service range for T, L, and H class aids is found in the AIM. Certain operational requirements make it necessary to use some of these aids at greater service ranges than specified. Extended range is made possible through flight inspection determinations. Some aids also have lesser service range due to location, terrain, frequency protection, etc. Restrictions to service range are listed in Airport/Facility Directory.

NAVIGABLE AIRSPACE — Airspace at and above the minimum flight altitudes prescribed in the FAR's including airspace needed for safe takeoff and landing. (Refer to FAR Part 91)

NAVIGATIONAL AID/NAVAID — Any visual or electronic device airborne or on the surface which provides point-to-point guidance information or position data to aircraft in flight. (See Air Navigation Facility)

NDB — (See Nondirectional Beacon)

NEGATIVE — "No," or "permission not granted," or "that is not correct."

PILOT/CONTROLLER GLOSSARY

NEGATIVE CONTACT — Used by pilots to inform ATC that:

1. Previously issued traffic is not in sight. It may be followed by the pilot's request for the controller to provide assistance in avoiding the traffic.

2. They were unable to contact ATC on a particular frequency.

NIGHT — The time between the end of evening civil twilight and the beginning of morning civil twilight, as published in the American Air Almanac, converted to local time.

ICAO—NIGHT — The hours between the end of evening civil twilight and the beginning of morning civil twilight or such other period between sunset and sunrise as may be specified by the appropriate authority.

Note. — Civil twilight ends in the evening when the centre of the sun's disk is 6 degrees below the horizon and begins in the morning when the centre of the sun's disk is 6 degrees below the horizon.

NO GYRO APPROACH/VECTOR — A radar approach/vector provided in case of a malfunctioning gyro-compass or directional gyro. Instead of providing the pilot with headings to be flown, the controller observes the radar track and issues control instructions "turn right/left" or "stop turn" as appropriate. (Refer to AIM)

NONAPPROACH CONTROL TOWER — Authorizes aircraft to land or takeoff at the airport controlled by the tower or to transit the airport traffic area. The primary function of a nonapproach control tower is the sequencing of aircraft in the traffic pattern and on the landing area. Nonapproach control towers also separate aircraft operating under instrument flight rules clearances from approach controls and centers. They provide ground control services to aircraft, vehicles, personnel, and equipment on the airport movement area.

NONCOMPOSITE SEPARATION — Separation in accordance with minima other than the composite separation minimum specified for the area concerned.

NONDIRECTIONAL BEACON/RADIO BEACON/NDB — An L/MF or UHF radio beacon transmitting nondirectional signals whereby the pilot of an aircraft equipped with direction finding equipment can determine his bearing to or from the radio beacon and "home" on or track to or from the station. When the radio beacon is installed in conjunction with the Instrument Landing System marker, it is normally called a Compass Locator. (See Compass Locator, Automatic Direction Finder)

NONPRECISION APPROACH PROCEDURE/NONPRECISION APPROACH — A standard instrument approach procedure in which no electronic glide slope is provided; e.g., VOR, TACAN, NDB, LOC, ASR, LDA, or SDF approaches.

NONRADAR — Precedes other terms and generally means without the use of radar, such as:

1. Nonradar Approach—Used to describe instrument approaches for which course guidance on final approach is not provided by ground-based precision or surveillance radar. Radar vectors to the final approach course may or may not be provided by ATC. Examples of nonradar approaches are VOR, NDB, TACAN, and ILS/MLS approaches. (See Final Approach—IFR, Final Approach Course, Radar Approach, Instrument Approach Procedure)

2. Nonradar Approach Control—An ATC facility providing approach control service without the use of radar. (See Approach Control, Approach Control Service)

3. Nonradar Arrival—An aircraft arriving at an airport without radar service or at an airport served by a radar facility and radar contact has not been established or has been terminated due to a lack of radar service to the airport. (See Radar Arrival, Radar Service)

4. Nonradar Route—A flight path or route over which the pilot is performing his own navigation. The pilot may be receiving radar separation, radar monitoring, or other ATC services while on a nonradar route. (See Radar Route)

5. Nonradar Separation—The spacing of aircraft in accordance with established minima without the use of radar; e.g., vertical, lateral, or longitudinal separation. (See Radar Separation)

ICAO—Nonradar Separation—The separation used when aircraft position information is derived from sources other than radar.

NORDO — (See Lost Communications)

NORTH AMERICAN ROUTE — A numerically coded route preplanned over existing airway and route systems to and from specific coastal fixes serving the North Atlantic. North American Routes consist of the following:

1. Common Route/Portion—That segment of a North American Route between the inland navigation facility and the coastal fix.

2. Non-Common Route/Portion—That segment of a North American Route between the inland navigation facility and a designated North American terminal.

3. Inland Navigation Facility—A navigation aid on a North American Route at which the common route and/or the non-common route begins or ends.

4. Coastal Fix—A navigation aid or intersection where an aircraft transitions between the domestic route structure and the oceanic route structure.

NOTICES TO AIRMEN PUBLICATION — A publication designed primarily as a pilot's operational manual containing current NOTAM information consid-

A-28

ered essential to the safety of flight as well as supplemental data to other aeronautical publications. (See Notice to Airmen/NOTAM)

NOTICE TO AIRMEN/NOTAM — A notice containing information (not known sufficiently in advance to publicize by other means) concerning the establishment, condition, or change in any component (facility, service, or procedure of, or hazard in the National Airspace System) the timely knowledge of which is essential to personnel concerned with flight operations.

1. NOTAM(D)—A NOTAM given (in addition to local dissemination) distant dissemination beyond the area of responsibility of the Flight Service Station. These NOTAM's will be stored and available until canceled.

2. NOTAM(L)—A NOTAM given local dissemination by voice and other means, such as teleautograph and telephone, to satisfy local user requirements.

3. FDC NOTAM—A NOTAM regulatory in nature, transmitted by USNOF and given system wide dissemination.

ICAO—NOTAM — A notice containing information concerning the establishment, condition or change in any aeronautical facility, service, procedure or hazard, the timely knowledge of which is essential to personnel concerned with flight operations.

Class I Distribution. Distribution by means of telecommunication.

Class II Distribution. Distribution by means other than telecommunications.

NUMEROUS TARGETS VICINITY (LOCATION) — A traffic advisory issued by ATC to advise pilots that targets on the radar scope are too numerous to issue individually. (See Traffic Advisories)

OBSTACLE — An existing object, object of natural growth, or terrain at a fixed geographical location or which may be expected at a fixed location within a prescribed area with reference to which vertical clearance is or must be provided during flight operation.

OBSTRUCTION — Any object/obstacle exceeding the obstruction standards specified by FAR Part 77, Subpart C.

OBSTRUCTION LIGHT — A light or one of a group of lights, usually red or white, frequently mounted on a surface structure or natural terrain to warn pilots of the presence of an obstruction.

OFF-ROUTE VECTOR — A vector by ATC which takes an aircraft off a previously assigned route. Altitudes assigned by ATC during such vectors provide required obstacle clearance.

OFFSET PARALLEL RUNWAYS — Staggered runways having centerlines which are parallel.

ON COURSE —

1. Used to indicate that an aircraft is established on the route centerline.

2. Used by ATC to advise a pilot making a radar approach that his aircraft is lined up on the final approach course. (See On-Course Indication)

ON-COURSE INDICATION — An indication on an instrument, which provides the pilot a visual means of determining that the aircraft is located on the centerline of a given navigational track, or an indication on a radar scope that an aircraft is on a given track.

OPTION APPROACH — An approach requested and conducted by a pilot which will result in either a touch-and-go, missed approach, low approach, stop-and-go, or full stop landing. (See Cleared for the Option) (Refer to AIM)

ORGANIZED TRACK SYSTEM — A moveable system of oceanic tracks that traverses the North Atlantic between Europe and North America the physical position of which is determined twice daily taking the best advantage of the winds aloft.

OUT — The conversation is ended and no response is expected.

OUTER AREA (associated with ARSA) — Nonregulatory airspace surrounding designated ARSA airports wherein ATC provides radar vectoring and sequencing on a full-time basis for all IFR and participating VFR aircraft. The service provided in the outer area is called ARSA service which includes: IFR/IFR—standard IFR separation; IFR/VFR—traffic advisories and conflict resolution; and VFR/VFR—traffic advisories and, as appropriate, safety alerts. The normal radius will be 20 nautical miles with some variations based on site-specific requirements. The outer area extends outward from the primary ARSA airport and extends from the lower limits of radar/radio coverage up to the ceiling of the approach control's delegated airspace excluding the ARSA and other airspace as appropriate. (See Controlled Airspace—Airport Radar Service Area / ARSA, Conflict Resolution)

OUTER COMPASS LOCATOR — (See Compass Locator)

OUTER FIX — A general term used within ATC to describe fixes in the terminal area, other than the final approach fix. Aircraft are normally cleared to these fixes by an Air Route Traffic Control Center or an Approach Control Facility. Aircraft are normally cleared from these fixes to the final approach fix or final approach course.

OUTER MARKER/OM — A marker beacon at or near the glide slope intercept altitude of an ILS approach. It is keyed to transmit two dashes per second on a 400 Hz tone, which is received aurally and visually by compatible airborne equipment. The OM is normally located four to seven miles from the runway threshold on the extended centerline of the runway.

(See Marker Beacon, Instrument Landing System) (Refer to AIM)

OVER — My transmission is ended; I expect a response.

OVERHEAD APPROACH/360 OVERHEAD — A series of predetermined maneuvers prescribed for VFR arrival of military aircraft (often in formation) for entry into the VFR traffic pattern and to proceed to a landing. The pattern usually specifies the following:

1. The radio contact required of the pilot.
2. The speed to be maintained.
3. An initial approach 3 to 5 miles in length.
4. An elliptical pattern consisting of two 180 degree turns.
5. A break point at which the first 180 degree turn is started.
6. The direction of turns.
7. Altitude (at least 500 feet above the conventional pattern).
8. A "Roll-out" on final approach not less than 1/4 mile from the landing threshold and not less than 300 feet above the ground.

PAN-PAN — The international radio-telephony urgency signal. When repeated three times, indicates uncertainty or alert followed by the nature of the urgency. (See MAYDAY) (Refer to AIM)

PARALLEL ILS/MLS APPROACHES — Approaches to parallel runways by IFR aircraft which, when established inbound toward the airport on the adjacent final approach courses, are radar-separated by at least 2 miles. (See Final Approach Course, Simultaneous ILS/MLS Approaches).

PARALLEL OFFSET ROUTE — A parallel track to the left or right of the designated or established airway/route. Normally associated with Area Navigation (RNAV) operations. (See Area Navigation)

PARALLEL RUNWAYS — Two or more runways at the same airport whose centerlines are parallel. In addition to runway number, parallel runways are designated as L (left) and R (right) or, if three parallel runways exist, L (left), C (center), and R (right).

PERMANENT ECHO — Radar signals reflected from fixed objects on the earth's surface; e.g., buildings, towers, terrain. Permanent echoes are distinguished from "ground clutter" by being definable locations rather than large areas. Under certain conditions they may be used to check radar alignment.

PHOTO RECONNAISSANCE (PR) — Military activity that requires locating individual photo targets and navigating to the targets at a preplanned angle and altitude. The activity normally requires a lateral route width of 16NM and altitude range of 1,500 feet to 10,000 feet AGL.

PILOT BRIEFING/PRE-FLIGHT PILOT BRIEFING — A service provided by the FSS to assist pilots in flight planning. Briefing items may include weather information, NOTAMS, military activities, flow control information, and other items as requested. (Refer to AIM)

PILOT IN COMMAND — The pilot responsible for the operation and safety of an aircraft during flight time. (Refer to FAR Part 91)

PILOTS AUTOMATIC TELEPHONE WEATHER ANSWERING SERVICE/PATWAS — A continuous telephone recording containing current and forecast weather information for pilots. (See Flight Service Station) (Refer to AIM)

PILOT'S DISCRETION — When used in conjunction with altitude assignments, means that ATC has offered the pilot the option of starting climb or descent whenever he wishes and conducting the climb or descent at any rate he wishes. He may temporarily level off at any intermediate altitude. However, once he has vacated an altitude, he may not return to that altitude.

PILOT WEATHER REPORT/PIREP — A report of meteorological phenomena encountered by aircraft in flight. (Refer to AIM)

POSITION REPORT/PROGRESS REPORT — A report over a known location as transmitted by an aircraft to ATC. (Refer to AIM)

POSITION SYMBOL — A computer-generated indication shown on a radar display to indicate the mode of tracking.

POSITIVE CONTROL — The separation of all air traffic within designated airspace by air traffic control. (See Positive Control Area)

POSITIVE CONTROL AREA/PCA — (See Controlled Airspace)

PRACTICE INSTRUMENT APPROACH — An instrument approach procedure conducted by a VFR or an IFR aircraft for the purpose of pilot training or proficiency demonstrations.

PRECIPITATION — Any or all forms of water particles (rain, sleet, hail, or snow) that fall from the atmosphere and reach the surface.

PRECISION APPROACH PROCEDURE/PRECISION APPROACH — A standard instrument approach procedure in which an electronic glideslope/glidepath is provided; e.g., ILS/MLS and PAR. (See Instrument Landing System, Microwave Landing System, Precision Approach Radar)

PRECISION APPROACH RADAR/PAR — Radar equipment in some ATC facilities operated by the FAA and/or the military services at joint-use civil/military locations and separate military installations to detect and display azimuth, elevation, and range of aircraft on the final approach course to a runway. This equipment may be used to monitor certain nonradar approaches, but is primarily used to conduct a precision instrument approach (PAR) wherein the controller issues guidance instructions to the pilot based on the aircraft's position in relation to the final approach course (azimuth), the glidepath (elevation), and the distance (range) from the touchdown point on the runway as displayed on the radar scope. (See Glidepath, PAR) (Refer to AIM)

The abbreviation "PAR" is also used to denote preferential arrival routes in ARTCC computers. (See Preferential Routes)

ICAO—PRECISION APPROACH RADAR (PAR) — Primary radar equipment used to determine the position of an aircraft during final approach, in terms of lateral and vertical deviations relative to a nominal approach path, and in range relative to touchdown.

> *Note.* — Precision approach radars are designed to enable pilots of aircraft to be given guidance by radiocommunication during the final stages of the appraoch to land.

PREFERENTIAL ROUTES — Preferential routes (PDR's, PAR's, and PDAR's) are adapted in ARTCC computers to accomplish inter/intrafacility controller coordination and to assure that flight data is posted at the proper control positions. Locations having a need for these specific inbound and outbound routes normally publish such routes in local facility bulletins, and their use by pilots minimizes flight plan route amendments. When the workload or traffic situation permits, controllers normally provide radar vectors or assign requested routes to minimize circuitous routing. Preferential routes are usually confined to one ARTCC's area and are referred to by the following names or acronyms:

1. Preferential Departure Route/PDR—A specific departure route from an airport or terminal area to an en route point where there is no further need for flow control. It may be included in a Standard Instrument Departure (SID) or a Preferred IFR Route.

2. Preferential Arrival Route/PAR—A specific arrival route from an appropriate en route point to an airport or terminal area. It may be included in a Standard Terminal Arrival (STAR) or a Preferred IFR Route. The abbreviation "PAR" is used primarily within the ARTCC and should not be confused with the abbreviation for Precision Approach Radar.

3. Preferential Departure and Arrival Route/PDAR—A route between two terminals which are within or immediately adjacent to one ARTCC's area. PDAR's are not synonomous with Preferred IFR Routes but may be listed as such as they do accomplish essentially the same purpose. (See Preferred IFR Routes, NAS Stage A)

PREFERRED IFR ROUTES — Routes established between busier airports to increase system efficiency and capacity. They normally extend through one or more ARTCC areas and are designed to achieve balanced traffic flows among high density terminals. IFR clearances are issued on the basis of these routes except when severe weather avoidance procedures or other factors dictate otherwise. Preferred IFR Routes are listed in the Airport/Facility Directory. If a flight is planned to or from an area having such routes but the departure or arrival point is not listed in the Airport/Facility Directory, pilots may use that part of a Preferred IFR Route which is appropriate for the departure or arrival point that is listed. Preferred IFR Routes are correlated with SID's and STAR's and may be defined by airways, jet routes, direct routes between NAVAID's, Waypoints, NAVAID radials/DME, or any combinations thereof. (See Standard Instrument Departure, Standard Terminal Arrival, Preferential Routes, Center's Area) (Refer to Airport/Facility Directory and Notices to Airmen Publication)

PREVAILING VISIBILITY — (See Visibility)

PROCEDURE TURN INBOUND — That point of a procedure turn maneuver where course reversal has been completed and an aircraft is established inbound on the intermediate approach segment or final approach course. A report of "procedure turn inbound" is normally used by ATC as a position report for separation purposes. (See Final Approach Course, Procedure Turn, Segments of an Instrument Approach Procedure)

PROCEDURE TURN/PT — The maneuver prescribed when it is necessary to reverse direction to establish an aircraft on the intermediate approach segment or final approach course. The outbound course, direction of turn, distance within which the turn must be completed, and minimum altitude are specified in the procedure. However, unless otherwise restricted, the point at which the turn may be commenced and the type and rate of turn are left to the discretion of the pilot.

ICAO—PROCEDURE TURN — A manoeuvre in which a turn is made away from a designated track followed by a turn in the opposite direction to permit the aircraft to intercept and proceed along the reciprocal of the designated track.

> *Note 1.* — Procedure turns are designated "left" or "right" according to the direction of the initial turn.

> *Note 2.* — Procedure turns may be designated as being made either in level flight or while descending, according to the circumstances of each individual appraoch procedure.

PROFILE DESCENT — An uninterrupted descent (except where level flight is required for speed adjustment; e.g., 250 knots at 10,000 feet MSL) from cruising altitude/level to interception of a glide slope or to a minimum altitude specified for the initial or intermediate approach segment of a nonprecision instrument approach. The profile descent normally terminates at the approach gate or where the glide slope or other appropriate minimum altitude is intercepted.

PROGRAMMABLE INDICATOR DATA PROCESSOR/PIDP — The PIDP is a modification to the AN/TPX-42 interrogator system currently installed in fixed RAPCON's. The PIDP detects, tracks, and predicts secondary radar aircraft targets. These are displayed by means of computer-generated symbols and alphanumeric characters depicting flight identification, aircraft altitude, ground speed, and flight plan data. Although primary radar targets are not tracked, they are displayed coincident with the secondary radar targets as well as with the other symbols and alphanumerics. The system has the capability of interfacing with ARTCC's.

PROHIBITED AREA — (See Special Use Airspace).

ICAO—PROHIBITED AREA — An airspace of defined dimensions, above the land areas or territorial waters of a State, within which the flight of aircraft is prohibited.

PROPOSED BOUNDARY CROSSING TIME/PBCT — Each center has a PBCT parameter for each internal airport. Proposed internal flight plans are transmitted to the adjacent center if the flight time along the proposed route from the departure airport to the center boundary is less than or equal to the value of PBCT or if airport adaptation specifies transmission regardless of PBCT.

PUBLISHED ROUTE — A route for which an IFR altitude has been established and published; e.g., Federal Airways, Jet Routes, Area Navigation Routes, Specified Direct Routes.

QUADRANT — A quarter part of a circle, centered on a NAVAID, oriented clockwise from magnetic north as follows: NE quadrant 000-089, SE quadrant 090-179, SW quadrant 180-269, NW quadrant 270-359.

QUICK LOOK — A feature of NAS Stage A and ARTS which provides the controller the capability to display full data blocks of tracked aircraft from other control positions.

QUOTA FLOW CONTROL/QFLOW — A flow control procedure by which the Central Flow Control Function (CFCF) restricts traffic to the ARTC Center area having an impacted airport, thereby avoiding sector/area saturation. (See Air Traffic Control Systems Command Center) (Refer to Airport/Facility Directory)

RADAR/RADIO DETECTION AND RANGING — A device which, by measuring the time interval between transmission and reception of radio pulses and correlating the angular orientation of the radiated antenna beam or beams in azimuth and/or elevation, provides information on range, azimuth, and/or elevation of objects in the path of the transmitted pulses.

ICAO—RADAR — A radio detection device which provides information on range, azimuth and/or elevation of objects.

1. Primary Radar—A radar system in which a minute portion of a radio pulse transmitted from a site is reflected by an object and then received back at that site for processing and display at an air traffic control facility.

ICAO—Primary Radar—A radar system which uses reflected radio signals.

2. Secondary Radar/Radar Beacon/ATCRBS—A radar system in which the object to be detected is fitted with cooperative equipment in the form of a radio receiver/transmitter (transponder). Radar pulses transmitted from the searching transmitter/receiver (interrogator) site are received in the cooperative equipment and used to trigger a distinctive transmission from the transponder. This reply transmission, rather than a reflected signal, is then received back at the transmitter/receiver site for processing and display at an air traffic control facility. (See Transponder, Interrogator) (Refer to AIM)

ICAO—Secondary Radar—A radar system wherein a radio signal transmitted from a radar station initiates the transmission of a radio signal from another station.

RADAR ADVISORY — The provision of advice and information based on radar observations. (See Advisory Service)

RADAR APPROACH — An instrument approach procedure which utilizes Precision Approach Radar (PAR) or Airport Surveillance Radar (ASR). (See PAR Approach, Surveillance Approach, Airport Surveillance Radar, Precision Approach Radar, Instrument Approach Procedure) (Refer to AIM)

ICAO—RADAR APPROACH — An approach, executed by an aircraft, under the direction of a radar controller.

RADAR APPROACH CONTROL FACILITY — A terminal ATC facility that uses radar and nonradar capabilities to provide approach control services to aircraft arriving, departing, or transiting airspace controlled by the facility (see Approach Control Service). Provides radar ATC services to aircraft operating in the vicinity of one or more civil and/ or military airports in a terminal area. The facility may provide services of a ground controlled approach (GCA); i.e., ASR and PAR approaches. A radar approach control facility may be operated by FAA, USAF, US Army, USN, USMC, or jointly by FAA and a military service. Specific facility nomenclatures are used for administrative purposes only and are related to the physical location of the facility and the operating service generally as follows:

Army Radar Approach Control/ARAC (Army).

Radar Air Traffic Control Facility/ RATCF (Navy/FAA).

Radar Approach Control/RAPCON (Air Force/FAA).

Terminal Radar Approach Control/TRACON (FAA).

Tower/Airport Traffic Control Tower/ATCT (FAA). (Only those towers delegated approach control authority.)

RADAR ARRIVAL — An aircraft arriving at an airport served by a radar facility and in radar contact with the facility. (See Nonradar Arrival)

RADAR BEACON — (See Radar)

RADAR CONTACT —

1. Used by ATC to inform an aircraft that it is identified on the radar display and radar flight following will be provided until radar identification is terminated. Radar service may also be provided within the limits of necessity and capability. When a pilot is informed of "radar contact," he automatically discontinues reporting over compulsory reporting points. (See Radar Flight Following, Radar Contact Lost, Radar Service, Radar Service Terminated). (Refer to AIM)

2. The term used to inform the controller that the aircraft is identified and approval is granted for the aircraft to enter the receiving controllers airspace.

ICAO—RADAR CONTACT — The situation which exists when the radar blip or radar position symbol of a particular aircraft is seen and identified on a radar display.

RADAR CONTACT LOST — Used by ATC to inform a pilot that radar identification of his aircraft has been lost. The loss may be attributed to several things including the aircraft's merging with weather or ground clutter, the aircraft's flying below radar line of sight, the aircraft's entering an area of poor radar return, or a failure of the aircraft transponder or the ground radar equipment. (See Clutter, Radar Contact)

RADAR ENVIRONMENT — An area in which radar service may be provided. (See Radar Contact, Radar Service, Additional Services, Traffic Advisories)

RADAR FLIGHT FOLLOWING — The observation of the progress of radar identified aircraft, whose primary navigation is being provided by the pilot, wherein the controller retains and correlates the aircraft identity with the appropriate target or target symbol displayed on the radar scope. (See Radar Contact, Radar Service) (Refer to AIM)

RADAR IDENTIFICATION — The process of ascertaining that an observed radar target is the radar return from a particular aircraft. (See Radar Contact, Radar Service)

ICAO—RADAR IDENTIFICATION — The process of correlating a particular radar blip or radar position symbol with a specific aircraft.

RADAR IDENTIFIED AIRCRAFT — An aircraft, the position of which has been correlated with an observed target or symbol on the radar display. (See Radar Contract, Radar Contact Lost)

RADAR MONITORING — (See Radar Service)

RADAR NAVIGATIONAL GUIDANCE — (See Radar Service)

RADAR POINT OUT/POINT OUT — Used between controllers to indicate radar handoff action where the initiating controller plans to retain communications with an aircraft penetrating the other controller's airspace and additional coordination is required.

RADAR REQUIRED — A term displayed on charts and approach plates and included in FDC Notams to alert pilots that segments of either an instrument approach procedure or a route are not navigable because of either the absence or unusability of a NAVAID. The pilot can expect to be provided radar navigational guidance while transiting segments labeled with this term. (See Radar Route and Radar Service)

RADAR ROUTE — A flight path or route over which an aircraft is vectored. Navigational guidance and altitude assignments are provided by ATC. (See Flight Path, Route)

RADAR SEPARATION — (See Radar Service)

RADAR SERVICE — A term which encompasses one or more of the following services based on the use of radar which can be provided by a controller to a pilot of a radar identified aircraft.

ICAO—RADAR SERVICE — Term used to indicate a service provided directly by means of radar.

1. Radar Monitoring—The radar flight-following of aircraft, whose primary navigation is being performed by the pilot, to observe and note deviations from its authorized flight path, airway, or route. When being applied specifically to radar monitoring of instrument approaches; i.e., with precision approach radar (PAR) or radar monitoring of simultaneous ILS/MLS approaches, it includes advice and instructions whenever an aircraft nears or exceeds the prescribed PAR safety limit or simultaneous ILS/MLS no transgression zone. (See Additional Services, Traffic Advisories)

ICAO—Radar Monitoring—The use of radar for the purpose of providing aircraft with information and advice relative to significant deviations from nominal flight path.

2. Radar Navigational Guidance—Vectoring aircraft to provide course guidance.

3. Radar Separation—Radar spacing of aircraft in accordance with established minima.

ICAO—Radar Separation—The separation used when aircraft position information is derived from radar sources.

RADAR SERVICE TERMINATED — Used by ATC to inform a pilot that he will no longer be provided any of the services that could be received while in radar contact. Radar service is automatically terminated, and the pilot is not advised in the following cases:

1. An aircraft cancels its IFR flight plan, except within a TCA, TRSA, ARSA, or where Stage II service is provided.

PILOT/CONTROLLER GLOSSARY

2. An aircraft conducting an instrument, visual, or contact approach has landed or has been instructed to change to advisory frequency.

3. An arriving VFR aircraft, receiving radar service to a tower-controlled airport within a TCA, TRSA, ARSA, or where Stage II service is provided, has landed; or to all other airports, is instructed to change to tower or advisory frequency.

4. An aircraft completes a radar approach.

RADAR SURVEILLANCE — The radar observation of a given geographical area for the purpose of performing some radar function.

RADAR TRAFFIC ADVISORIES — Advisories issued to alert pilots to known or observed radar traffic which may affect the intended route of flight of their aircraft. (See Traffic Advisories)

RADAR TRAFFIC INFORMATION SERVICE — (See Traffic Advisories)

RADAR WEATHER ECHO INTENSITY LEVELS — Existing radar systems cannot detect turbulence. However, there is a direct correlation between the degree of turbulence and other weather features associated with thunderstorms and the radar weather echo intensity. The National Weather Service has categorized six levels of radar weather echo intensity. The levels are sometimes expressed during communications as "VIP LEVEL" 1 through 6 (derived from the component of the weather radar that produces the information—Video Integrator and Processor). The following list gives the weather features likely to be associated with these levels during thunderstorm weather situations:

1. Level 1 (WEAK) and Level 2 (MODERATE). Light to moderate turbulence is possible with lightning.

2. Level 3 (STRONG). Severe turbulence possible, lightning.

3. Level 4 (VERY STRONG). Severe turbulence likely, lightning.

4. Level 5 (INTENSE). Severe turbulence, lightning, organized wind gusts, hail likely.

5. Level 6 (EXTREME). Severe turbulence, large hail, lightning, extensive wind gusts, and turbulence.

RADIAL — A magnetic bearing extending from a VOR/VORTAC/TACAN navigation facility.

RADIO —

1. A device used for communication.

2. Used to refer to a flight service station; e.g., "Seattle Radio" is used to call Seattle FSS.

RADIO ALTIMETER/RADAR ALTIMETER — Aircraft equipment which makes use of the reflection of radio waves from the ground to determine the height of the aircraft above the surface.

RADIO BEACON — (See Nondirectional Beacon)

RADIO MAGNETIC INDICATOR/RMI — An aircraft navigational instrument coupled with a gyro compass or similar compass that indicates the direction of a selected NAVAID and indicates bearing with respect to the heading of the aircraft.

RAMP — (See Apron)

READ BACK — Repeat my message back to me.

RECEIVING CONTROLLER/FACILITY — A controller/facility receiving control of an aircraft from another controller/facility.

REDUCE SPEED TO (SPEED) — (See Speed Adjustment)

RELEASE TIME — A departure time restriction issued to a pilot by ATC (either directly or through an authorized relay) when necessary to separate a departing aircraft from other traffic.

ICAO—RELEASE TIME — Time prior to which an aircraft should be given further clearance or prior to which it should not proceed in case of radio failure.

REMOTE COMMUNICATIONS AIR/GROUND FACILITY/RCAG — An unmanned VHF/UHF transmitter/receiver facility which is used to expand ARTCC air/ground communications coverage and to facilitate direct contact between pilots and controllers. RCAG facilities are sometimes not equipped with emergency frequencies 121.5 MHz and 243.0 MHz. (Refer to AIM)

REMOTE COMMUNICATIONS OUTLET/RCO AND REMOTE TRANSMITTER/RECEIVER/RTR — An unmanned communications facility remotely controlled by air traffic personnel. RCO's serve FSS's. RTR's serve terminal ATC facilities. An RCO or RTR may be UHF or VHF and will extend the communication range of the air traffic facility. There are several classes of RCO's and RTR's. The class is determined by the number of transmitters or receivers. Classes A through G are used primarily for air/ground purposes. RCO and RTR class O facilities are nonprotected outlets subject to undetected and prolonged outages. RCO (O's) and RTR (O's) were established for the express purpose of providing ground-to-ground communications between air traffic control specialists and pilots located at a satellite airport for delivering en route clearances, issuing departure authorizations, and acknowledging instrument flight rules cancellations or departure/landing times. As a secondary function, they may be used for advisory purposes whenever the aircraft is below the coverage of the primary air/ground frequency.

REMOTE TRANSMITTER/RECEIVER/RTR — (See Remote Communications Outlet)

REPORT — Used to instruct pilots to advise ATC of specified information; e.g., "Report passing Hamilton VOR."

REPORTING POINT — A geographical location in relation to which the position of an aircraft is reported. (See Compulsory Reporting Point) (Refer to AIM)

ICAO—REPORTING POINT — A specified geographical location in relation to which the position of an aircraft can be reported.

REQUEST FULL ROUTE CLEARANCE/FRC — Used by pilots to request that the entire route of flight be read verbatim in an ATC clearance. Such request should be made to preclude receiving an ATC clearance based on the original filed flight plan when a filed IFR flight plan has been revised by the pilot, company, or operations prior to departure.

RESCUE COORDINATION CENTER/RCC — A search and rescue (SAR) facility equipped and manned to coordinate and control SAR operations in an area designated by the SAR plan. The U.S. Coast Guard and the U.S. Air Force have responsibility for the operation of RCC's.

ICAO—RESCUE CO-ORDINATION CENTRE — A unit responsible for promoting efficient organization of search and rescue service and for co-ordinating the conduct of search and rescue operations within a search and rescue region.

RESTRICTED AREA — (See Special Use Airspace).

ICAO—RESTRICTED AREA — An airspace of defined dimensions, above the land areas or territorial waters of a State, within which the flight of aircraft is restricted in accordance with certain specified conditions.

RESUME OWN NAVIGATION — Used by ATC to advise a pilot to resume his own navigational responsibility. It is issued after completion of a radar vector or when radar contact is lost while the aircraft is being radar vectored. (See Radar Contact Lost, Radar Service Terminated)

RNAV — (See Area Navigation)

RNAV APPROACH — An instrument approach procedure which relies on aircraft area navigation equipment for navigational guidance. (See Instrument Approach Procedure, Area Navigation)

ROAD RECONNAISSANCE (RC) — Military activity requiring navigation along roads, railroads, and rivers. Reconnaissance route/route segments are seldom along a straight line and normally require a lateral route width of 10NM to 30NM and an altitude range of 500 feet to 10,000 feet AGL.

ROGER — I have received all of your last transmission. It should not be used to answer a question requiring a yes or a no answer. (See Affirmative, Negative)

ROLLOUT RVR — (See Visibility)

ROUTE — A defined path, consisting of one or more courses in a horizontal plane, which aircraft traverse over the surface of the earth. (See Airway, Jet Route, Published Route, Unpublished Route)

ROUTE SEGMENT — As used in Air Traffic Control, a part of a route that can be defined by two navigational fixes, two NAVAID's, or a fix and a NAVAID. (See Fix, Route)

ICAO—ROUTE SEGMENT — A portion of a route to be flown, as defined by two consecutive significant points specified in a flight plan.

RUNWAY — A defined rectangular area on a land airport prepared for the landing and takeoff run of aircraft along its length. Runways are normally numbered in relation to their magnetic direction rounded off to the nearest 10 degrees; e.g., Runway 01, Runway 25. (See Parallel Runways)

ICAO—RUNWAY — A defined rectangular area on a land aerodrome prepared for the landing and takeoff of aircraft.

RUNWAY CENTERLINE LIGHTING — (See Airport Lighting)

RUNWAY CONDITION READING/RCR — Numerical decelerometer readings relayed by air traffic controllers at USAF and certain civil bases for use by the pilot in determining runway braking action. These readings are routinely relayed only to USAF and Air National Guard Aircraft. (See Braking Action)

RUNWAY END IDENTIFIER LIGHTS — (See Airport Lighting)

RUNWAY GRADIENT — The average slope, measured in percent, between two ends or points on a runway. Runway gradient is depicted on Government aerodrome sketches when total runway gradient exceeds 0.3%.

RUNWAY HEADING — The magnetic direction indicated by the runway number. When cleared to "fly/maintain runway heading," pilots are expected to comply with the ATC clearance by flying the heading indicated by the runway number without applying any drift correction; e.g., Runway 4, 040° magnetic heading; Runway 20, 200° magnetic heading.

RUNWAY IN USE/ACTIVE RUNWAY/DUTY RUNWAY — Any runway or runways currently being used for takeoff or landing. When multiple runways are used, they are all considered active runways.

RUNWAY LIGHTS — (See Airport Lighting)

RUNWAY MARKINGS — (See Airport Marking Aids.)

RUNWAY PROFILE DESCENT — An instrument flight rules (IFR) air traffic control arrival procedure to a runway published for pilot use in graphic and/or textual form and may be associated with a STAR. Runway Profile Descents provide routing and may depict crossing altitudes, speed restrictions, and headings to be flown from the en route structure to the point where the pilot will receive clearance for and execute an instrument approach procedure. A Runway Profile Descent may apply to more than one runway if so stated on the chart. (Refer to AIM)

RUNWAY USE PROGRAM — A noise abatement runway selection plan designed to enhance noise abatement efforts with regard to airport communities for arriving and departing aircraft. These plans are developed into runway use programs and apply to all turbojet aircraft 12,500 pounds or heavier; turbojet aircraft less than 12,500 pounds are included only if the airport proprietor determines that the aircraft creates a noise problem. Runway use programs are coordinated with FAA offices, and safety criteria used in these programs are developed by the Office of Flight Operations. Runway use programs are administered by the Air Traffic Service as "Formal" or "Informal" programs.

1. Formal Runway Use Program—An approved noise abatement program which is defined and acknowledged in a Letter of Understanding between Flight Operations, Air Traffic Service, the airport proprietor, and the users. Once established, participation in the program is mandatory for aircraft operators and pilots as provided for in FAR 91.87.

2. Informal Runway Use Program—An approved noise abatement program which does not require a Letter of Understanding, and participation in the program is voluntary for aircraft operators/pilots.

RUNWAY VISIBILITY VALUE — (See Visibility)

RUNWAY VISUAL RANGE — (See Visibility)

SAFETY ALERT — A safety alert issued by ATC to aircraft under their control if ATC is aware the aircraft is at an altitude which, in the controller's judgment, places the aircraft in unsafe proximity to terrain, obstructions, or other aircraft. The controller may discontinue the issuance of further alerts if the pilot advises he is taking action to correct the situation or has the other aircraft in sight.

1. Terrain/Obstruction Alert—A safety alert issued by ATC to aircraft under their control if ATC is aware the aircraft is at an altitude which, in the controller's judgment, places the aircraft in unsafe proximity to terrain/obstructions; e.g., "Low Altitude Alert, check your altitude immediately."

2. Aircraft Conflict Alert—A safety alert issued by ATC to aircraft under their control if ATC is aware of an aircraft that is not under their control at an altitude which, in the controller's judgment, places both aircraft in unsafe proximity to each other. With the alert, ATC will offer the pilot an alternate course of action when feasible; e.g., "Traffic Alert, advise you turn right heading zero niner zero or climb to eight thousand immediately."

The issuance of a safety alert is contingent upon the capability of the controller to have an awareness of an unsafe condition. The course of action provided will be predicated on other traffic under ATC control. Once the alert is issued, it is solely the pilot's prerogative to determine what course of action, if any, he will take.

SAIL BACK — A maneuver during high wind conditions (usually with power off) where float plane movement is controlled by water rudders/opening and closing cabin doors.

SAY AGAIN — Used to request a repeat of the last transmission. Usually specifies transmission or portion thereof not understood or received; e.g., "Say again all after ABRAM VOR."

SAY ALTITUDE — Used by ATC to ascertain an aircraft's specific altitude/flight level. When the aircraft is climbing or descending, the pilot should state the indicated altitude rounded to the nearest 100 feet.

SAY HEADING — Used by ATC to request an aircraft heading. The pilot should state the actual heading of the aircraft.

SEA LANE — A designated portion of water outlined by visual surface markers for and intended to be used by aircraft designed to operate on water.

SEARCH AND RESCUE FACILITY — A facility responsible for maintaining and operating a search and rescue (SAR) service to render aid to persons and property in distress. It is any SAR unit, station, NET, or other operational activity which can be usefully employed during an SAR Mission; e.g., a Civil Air Patrol Wing, or a Coast Guard Station. (See Search and Rescue)

SEARCH AND RESCUE/SAR — A service which seeks missing aircraft and assists those found to be in need of assistance. It is a cooperative effort using the facilities and services of available Federal, state and local agencies. The U.S. Coast Guard is responsible for coordination of search and rescue for the Maritime Region, and the U.S. Air Force is responsible for search and rescue for the Inland Region. Information pertinent to search and rescue should be passed through any air traffic facility or be transmitted directly to the Rescue Coordination Center by telephone. (See Flight Service Station, Rescue Coordination Center) (Refer to AIM)

SEE AND AVOID — A visual procedure wherein pilots of aircraft flying in visual meteorological conditions (VMC), regardless of type of flight plan, are charged with the responsibility to observe the presence of other aircraft and to maneuver their aircraft as required to avoid the other aircraft. Right-of-way rules are contained in FAR, Part 91. (See Instrument Flight Rules, Visual Flight Rules, Visual Meteorological Conditions, Instrument Meteorological Conditions)

SEGMENTED CIRCLE — A system of visual indicators designed to provide traffic pattern information at airports without operating control towers. (Refer to AIM)

SEGMENTS OF AN INSTRUMENT APPROACH PROCEDURE — An instrument approach procedure may have as many as four separate segments depending on how the approach procedure is structured.

1. Initial Approach—The segment between the initial approach fix and the intermediate fix or the point where the aircraft is established on the intermediate course or final approach course.

ICAO—Initial Approach Segment—That segment of an instrument approach procedure between the initial approach fix and the intermediate approach fix or, where applicable, the final approach fix or point.

2. Intermediate Approach—The segment between the intermediate fix or point and the final approach fix.

ICAO—Intermediate Approach Segment—That segment of an instrument approach procedure between either the intermediate approach fix and the final approach fix or point, or between the end of a reversal, race track or dead reckoning track procedure and the final approach fix or point, as appropriate.

3. Final Approach—The segment between the final approach fix or point and the runway, airport, or missed approach point.

ICAO—Final Approach Segment—That segment of an instrument approach procedure in which alignment and descent for landing are accomplished.

4. Missed Approach—The segment between the missed approach point or the point of arrival at decision height and the missed approach fix at the prescribed altitude. (Refer to FAR, Part 97)

ICAO—Missed Approach Procedure—The procedure to be followed if the approach cannot be continued.

SEPARATION — In air traffic control, the spacing of aircraft to achieve their safe and orderly movement in flight and while landing and taking off. (See Separation Minima)

ICAO—SEPARATION — Spacing between aircraft, levels or tracks.

SEPARATION MINIMA — The minimum longitudinal, lateral, or vertical distances by which aircraft are spaced through the application of air traffic control procedures. (See Separation)

SEVERE WEATHER AVOIDANCE PLAN/SWAP — An approved plan to minimize the affect of severe weather on traffic flows in impacted terminal and/or ARTCC areas. SWAP is normally implemented to provide the least disruption to the ATC system when flight through portions of airspace is difficult or impossible due to severe weather.

SEVERE WEATHER FORECAST ALERTS/AWW — Preliminary messages issued in order to alert users that a Severe Weather Watch Bulletin (WW) is being issued. These messages define areas of possible severe thunderstorms or tornado activity. The messages are unscheduled and issued as required by the National Severe Storm Forecast Center at Kansas City, Missouri. (See SIGMET, Convective SIGMET, CWA, and AIRMET)

SHORT RANGE CLEARANCE — A clearance issued to a departing IFR flight which authorizes IFR flight to a specific fix short of the destination while air traffic control facilities are coordinating and obtaining the complete clearance.

SHORT TAKEOFF AND LANDING AIRCRAFT/ STOL AIRCRAFT — An aircraft which, at some weight within its approved operating weight, is capable of operating from a STOL runway in compliance with the applicable STOL characteristics, airworthiness, operations, noise, and pollution standards. (See Vertical Takeoff and Landing Aircraft)

SIDESTEP MANEUVER — A visual maneuver accomplished by a pilot at the completion of an instrument approach to permit a straight-in landing on a parallel runway not more than 1,200 feet to either side of the runway to which the instrument approach was conducted. (Refer to AIM)

SIGMET/WS/**SIGNIFICANT METEOROLOGICAL INFORMATION** — A weather advisory issued concerning weather significant to the safety of all aircraft. SIGMET advisories cover severe and extreme turbulence, severe icing, and widespread dust or sandstorms that reduce visibility to less than 3 miles. (See AWW, Convective SIGMET, CWA, and AIRMET) (Refer to AIM)

ICAO—SIGMET INFORMATION — Information issued by a meteorological watch office concerning the occurrence or expected occurrence of specified en-route weather phenomena which may affect the safety of aircraft operations.

SIMPLIFIED DIRECTIONAL FACILITY/SDF — A NAVAID used for nonprecision instrument approaches. The final approach course is similar to that of an ILS localizer except that the SDF course may be offset from the runway, generally not more than 3 degrees, and the course may be wider than the localizer, resulting in a lower degree of accuracy. (Refer to AIM)

SIMULATED FLAMEOUT/SFO — A practice approach by a jet aircraft (normally military) at idle thrust to a runway. The approach may start at a relatively high altitude over a runway (high key) and may continue on a relatively high and wide downwind leg with a high rate of descent and a continuous turn to final. It terminates in a landing or low approach. The purpose of this approach is to simulate a flameout. (See Flameout)

SIMULTANEOUS ILS/MLS APPROACHES — An approach system permitting simultaneous ILS/MLS approaches to airports having parallel runways separated by at least 4,300 feet between centerlines. Integral parts of a total system are ILS/MLS, radar, communications, ATC procedures, and appropriate airborne equipment. (See Parallel Runways) (Refer to AIM)

SINGLE DIRECTION ROUTES — Preferred IFR Routes which are sometimes depicted on high altitude en route charts and which are normally flown in one direction only. (See Preferred IFR Route) (Refer to Airport/Facility Directory)

SINGLE FREQUENCY APPROACH/SFA — A service provided under a letter of agreement to military single-piloted turbojet aircraft which permits use of a single UHF frequency during approach for landing. Pilots will not normally be required to change frequency from the beginning of the approach to touchdown except that pilots conducting an en route descent are required to change frequency when control is transferred from the air route traffic control center to the terminal facility. The abbreviation "SFA" in the DOD FLIP IFR Supplement under "Communications" indicates this service is available at an aerodrome.

SINGLE-PILOTED AIRCRAFT — A military turbojet aircraft possessing one set of flight controls, tandem cockpits, or two sets of flight controls but operated by one pilot is considered single-piloted by ATC when determining the appropriate air traffic service to be applied. (See Single Frequency Approach)

SLASH — A radar beacon reply displayed as an elongated target.

SLOW TAXI — To taxi a float plane at low power or low RPM.

SPEAK SLOWER — Used in verbal communications as a request to reduce speech rate.

SPECIAL EMERGENCY — A condition of air piracy or other hostile act by a person(s) aboard an aircraft which threatens the safety of the aircraft or its passengers.

SPECIAL INSTRUMENT APPROACH PROCEDURE — (See Instrument Approach Procedure)

SPECIAL USE AIRSPACE — Airspace of defined dimensions identified by an area on the surface of the earth wherein activities must be confined because of their nature and/or wherein limitations may be imposed upon aircraft operations that are not a part of those activities. Types of special use airspace are:

1. Alert Area—Airspace which may contain a high volume of pilot training activities or an unusual type of aerial activity, neither of which is hazardous to aircraft. Alert Areas are depicted on aeronautical charts for the information of nonparticipating pilots. All activities within an Alert Area are conducted in accordance with Federal Aviation Regulations, and pilots of participating aircraft as well as pilots transiting the area are equally responsible for collision avoidance.

2. Controlled Firing Area—Airspace wherein activities are conducted under conditions so controlled as to eliminate hazards to nonparticipating aircraft and to ensure the safety of persons and property on the ground.

3. Military Operations Area (MOA)—An MOA is an airspace assignment of defined vertical and lateral dimensions established outside positive control areas to separate/segregate certain military activities from IFR traffic and to identify for VFR traffic where these activities are conducted. (Refer to AIM).

4. Prohibited Area—Designated airspace within which the flight of aircraft is prohibited. (Refer to En Route Charts, AIM).

5. Restricted Area—Airspace designated under FAR, Part 73, within which the flight of aircraft, while not wholly prohibited, is subject to restriction. Most restricted areas are designated joint use and IFR/VFR operations in the area may be authorized by the controlling ATC facility when it is not being utilized by the using agency. Restricted areas are depicted on en route charts. Where joint use is authorized, the name of the ATC controlling facility is also shown. (Refer to FAR, Part 73 and AIM)

6. Warning Area—Airspace which may contain hazards to nonparticipating aircraft in international airspace.

SPECIAL VFR CONDITIONS — Weather conditions in a control zone which are less than basic VFR and in which some aircraft are permitted flight under Visual Flight Rules. (See Special VFR Operations) (Refer to FAR, Part 91)

SPECIAL VFR OPERATIONS — Aircraft operating in accordance with clearances within control zones in weather conditions less than the basic VFR weather minima. Such operations must be requested by the pilot and approved by ATC. (See Special VFR Conditions)

ICAO—SPECIAL VFR FLIGHT — A controlled VFR flight authorized by air traffic control to operate within a control zone under meteorological conditions below the visual meteorological conditions.

SPEED — (See Airspeed, Groundspeed)

SPEED ADJUSTMENT — An ATC procedure used to request pilots to adjust aircraft speed to a specific value for the purpose of providing desired spacing. Pilots are expected to maintain a speed of plus or minus 10 knots or 0.02 mach number of the specified speed.

Examples of speed adjustments are:

1. "Increase/reduce speed to mach point (number)."

2. "Increase/reduce speed to (speed in knots)" or "Increase/reduce speed (number of knots) knots."

SPEED BRAKES/DIVE BRAKES — Moveable aerodynamic devices on aircraft that reduce airspeed during descent and landing.

SQUAWK (Mode, Code, Function) — Activate specific modes/codes/functions on the aircraft transponder; e.g., "Squawk three/alpha, two one zero five, low." (See Transponder)

STAGE I/II/III SERVICE — (See Terminal Radar Program)

STANDARD INSTRUMENT APPROACH PROCEDURE/SIAP — (See Instrument Approach Procedure)

STANDARD INSTRUMENT DEPARTURE/SID — A preplanned instrument flight rule (IFR) air traffic control departure procedure printed for pilot use in graphic and/or textual form. SID's provide transition from the terminal to the appropriate en route structure. (See IFR Takeoff Minima and Departure Procedures) (Refer to AIM)

STANDARD RATE TURN — A turn of three degrees per second.

STANDARD TERMINAL ARRIVAL/STAR — A preplanned instrument flight rule (IFR) air traffic control arrival procedure published for pilot use in graphic and/or textual form. STAR's provide transition from the en route structure to an outer fix or an instrument approach fix/arrival waypoint in the terminal area.

STAND BY — Means the controller or pilot must pause for a few seconds, usually to attend to other duties of a higher priority. Also means to wait as in "stand by for clearance." If a delay is lengthy, the caller should reestablish contact.

STATIONARY RESERVATIONS — Altitude reservations which encompass activities in a fixed area. Stationary reservations may include activities, such as special tests of weapons systems or equipment, certain U.S. Navy carrier, fleet, and anti-submarine operations, rocket, missile and drone operations, and certain aerial refueling or similar operations.

STEPDOWN FIX — A fix permitting additional descent within a segment of an instrument approach procedure by identifying a point at which a controlling obstacle has been safely overflown.

STEP TAXI — To taxi a float plane at full power or high RPM.

STEP TURN — A maneuver used to put a float plane in a planing configuration prior to entering an active sea lane for takeoff. The STEP TURN maneuver should only be used upon pilot request.

STEREO ROUTE — A routinely used route of flight established by users and ARTCC's identified by a coded name; e.g., ALPHA 2. These routes minimize flight plan handling and communications.

STOP ALTITUDE SQUAWK — Used by ATC to inform an aircraft to turn-off the automatic altitude reporting feature of its transponder. It is issued when the verbally reported altitude varies 300 feet or more from the automatic altitude report. (See Altitude Readout, Transponder)

STOP AND GO — A procedure wherein an aircraft will land, make a complete stop on the runway, and then commence a takeoff from that point. (See Low Approach, Option Approach)

STOPOVER FLIGHT PLAN — A flight plan format which permits in a single submission the filing of a sequence of flight plans through interim full-stop destinations to a final destination.

STOP SQUAWK (Mode or Code) — Used by ATC to tell the pilot to turn specified functions of the aircraft transponder off. (See Stop Altitude Squawk, Transponder)

STOP STREAM/BURST/BUZZER — Used by ATC to request a pilot to suspend electronic countermeasure activity. (See Jamming)

STOPWAY — An area beyond the takeoff runway designated by the airport authorities as able to support an airplane during an aborted takeoff. (Refer to FAR, Part 1)

STRAIGHT-IN APPROACH—IFR — An instrument approach wherein final approach is begun without first having executed a procedure turn, not necessarily completed with a straight-in landing or made to straight-in landing minimums. (See Straight-in Landing, Landing Minimums, Straight-in Approach-VFR)

STRAIGHT-IN APPROACH—VFR — Entry into the traffic pattern by interception of the extended runway centerline (final approach course) without executing any other portion of the traffic pattern. (See Traffic Pattern)

STRAIGHT-IN LANDING — A landing made on a runway aligned within 30° of the final approach course following completion of an instrument approach. (See Straight-in Approach-IFR)

STRAIGHT-IN LANDING MINIMUMS/ STRAIGHT-IN MINIMUMS — (See Landing Minimums)

SUBSTITUTE ROUTE — A route assigned to pilots when any part of an airway or route is unusable because of NAVAID status. These routes consist of:

1. Substitute routes which are shown on U.S. Government charts.

2. Routes defined by ATC as specific NAVAID radials or courses.

3. Routes defined by ATC as direct to or between NAVAID's.

SUNSET AND SUNRISE — The mean solar times of sunset and sunrise as published in the Nautical Almanac, converted to local standard time for the locality concerned. Within Alaska, the end of evening civil twilight and the beginning of morning civil twilight, as defined for each locality.

SUPER HIGH FREQUENCY/SHF —The frequency band between 3 and 30 gigahertz (gHz). The elevation and azimuth stations of the microwave landing system operate from 5031MHz to 5091MHz in this spectrum.

PILOT/CONTROLLER GLOSSARY

SURVEILLANCE APPROACH — An instrument approach wherein the air traffic controller issues instructions, for pilot compliance, based on aircraft position in relation to the final approach course (azimuth), and the distance (range) from the end of the runway as displayed on the controller's radar scope. The controller will provide recommended altitudes on final approach if requested by the pilot. (See PAR Approach) (Refer to AIM)

SYSTEM STRATEGIC NAVIGATION/SN — Military activity accomplished by navigating along a preplanned route using internal aircraft systems to maintain a desired track. This activity normally requires a lateral route width of 10NM and altitude range of 1,000 feet to 6,000 feet AGL with some route segments that permit terrain following.

TACAN-ONLY AIRCRAFT — An aircraft, normally military, possessing TACAN with DME but no VOR navigational system capability. Clearances must specify TACAN or VORTAC fixes and approaches.

TACTICAL AIR NAVIGATION/TACAN — An ultra-high frequency electronic rho-theta air navigation aid which provides suitably equipped aircraft a continuous indication of bearing and distance to the TACAN station. (See VORTAC) (Refer to AIM)

TARGET — The indication shown on a radar display resulting from a primary radar return or a radar beacon reply. (See Radar, Target Symbol)

ICAO—TARGET — In radar:

1. Generally, any discrete object which reflects or retransmits energy back to the radar equipment.

2. Specifically, an object of radar search or surveillance.

TARGET SYMBOL — A computer-generated indication shown on a radar display resulting from a primary radar return or a radar beacon reply.

TAXI — The movement of an airplane under its own power on the surface of an airport (FAR Part 135.100-Note). Also, it describes the surface movement of helicopters equipped with wheels. (See Air Taxi, Hover Taxi) (Refer to AIM)

TAXI INTO POSITION AND HOLD — Used by ATC to inform a pilot to taxi onto the departure runway in takeoff position and hold. It is not authorization for takeoff. It is used when takeoff clearance cannot immediately be issued because of traffic or other reasons. (See Hold, Cleared for Takeoff)

TAXI PATTERNS — Patterns established to illustrate the desired flow of ground traffic for the different runways or airport areas available for use.

TELEPHONE INFORMATION BRIEFING SERVICE (TIBS) — A continuous telephone recording of meteorological and/or aeronautical information. (refer to AIM)

TERMINAL AREA — A general term used to describe airspace in which approach control service or airport traffic control service is provided.

TERMINAL AREA FACILITY — A facility providing air traffic control service for arriving and departing IFR, VFR, Special VFR, and on occasion en route aircraft. (See Approach Control, Tower)

TERMINAL CONTROL AREA — (See Controlled Airspace)

TERMINAL RADAR PROGRAM — A national program instituted to extend the terminal radar services provided IFR aircraft to VFR aircraft. Pilot participation in the program is urged but is not mandatory. The program is divided into two parts and referred to as Stage II and Stage III. The Stage service provided at a particular location is contained in the Airport/Facility Directory.

1. Stage I originally comprised two basic radar services (traffic advisories and limited vectoring to VFR aircraft). These services are provided by all commissioned terminal radar facilities, but the term "Stage I" has been deleted from use.

2. Stage II/Radar Advisory and Sequencing for VFR Aircraft—Provides, in addition to the basic radar services, vectoring and sequencing on a full-time basis to arriving VFR aircraft. The purpose is to adjust the flow of arriving IFR and VFR aircraft into the traffic pattern in a safe and orderly manner and to provide traffic advisories to departing VFR aircraft.

3. Stage III/Radar Sequencing and Separation Service for VFR Aircraft—Provides, in addition to the basic radar services and Stage II, separation between all participating VFR aircraft. The purpose is to provide separation between all participating VFR aircraft and all IFR aircraft operating within the airspace defined as a Terminal Radar Service Area (TRSA) or Terminal Control Area (TCA). (See Controlled Airspace, Terminal Radar Service Area) (Refer to AIM, Airport/Facility Directory)

TERMINAL RADAR SERVICE AREA/TRSA — Airspace surrounding designated airports wherein ATC provides radar vectoring, sequencing, and separation on a full-time basis for all IFR and participating VFR aircraft. Service provided in a TRSA is called Stage III Service. The AIM contains an explanation of TRSA. TRSA's are depicted on VFR aeronautical charts. Pilot participation is urged but is not mandatory. (See Terminal Radar Program) (Refer to AIM, Airport/Facility Directory)

TERRAIN FOLLOWING/TF — The flight of a military aircraft maintaining a constant AGL altitude above the terrain or the highest obstruction. The altitude of the aircraft will constantly change with the varying terrain and/or obstruction.

TETRAHEDRON — A device normally located on uncontrolled airports and used as a landing direction indicator. The small end of a tetrahedron points in the direction of landing. At controlled airports, the tetrahedron, if installed, should be disregarded because tower instructions supersede the indicator. (See Segmented Circle) (Refer to AIM)

THAT IS CORRECT — The understanding you have is right.

THRESHOLD — The beginning of that portion of the runway usable for landing. (See Airport Lighting, Displaced Threshold)

THRESHOLD CROSSING HEIGHT/TCH — The theoretical height above the runway threshold at which the aircraft's glideslope antenna would be if the aircraft maintains the trajectory established by the mean ILS glideslope or MLS glidepath. (See Glide Slope, Threshold)

THRESHOLD LIGHTS — (See Airport Lighting)

TIME GROUP — Four digits representing the hour and minutes from the 24-hour clock. Time groups without time zone indicators are understood to be UTC (Coordinated Universal Time); e.g., "0205." The term "Zulu" is used when ATC procedures require a reference to UTC. A time zone designator is used to indicate local time; e.g., "0205M." The end and the beginning of the day are shown by "2400" and "0000," respectively.

TORCHING — The burning of fuel at the end of an exhaust pipe or stack of a reciprocating aircraft engine, the result of an excessive richness in the fuel air mixture.

ICAO—TOTAL ESTIMATED ELAPSED TIME — For IFR flights, the estimated time required from take-off to arrive over that designated point, defined by reference to navigation aids, from which it is intended that an instrument approach procedure will be commenced, or, if no navigation aid is associated with the destination aerodrome, to arrive over the destination aerodrome. For VFR flights, the estimated time required from takeoff to arrive over the destination aerodrome. (See Estimated Elapsed Time)

TOUCH-AND-GO/TOUCH-AND-GO LANDING — An operation by an aircraft that lands and departs on a runway without stopping or exiting the runway.

TOUCHDOWN —

1. The point at which an aircraft first makes contact with the landing surface.

2. Concerning a precision radar approach (PAR), it is the point where the glide path intercepts the landing surface.

ICAO—TOUCHDOWN — The point where the nominal glide path intercepts the runway.

> *Note.* — *Touchdown as defined above is only a datum and is not necessarily the actual point at which the aircraft will touch the runway.*

TOUCHDOWN RVR — (See Visibility)

TOUCHDOWN ZONE — The first 3,000 feet of the runway beginning at the threshold. The area is used for determination of Touchdown Zone Elevation in the development of straight-in landing minimums for instrument approaches.

ICAO—TOUCHDOWN ZONE — The portion of a runway, beyond the threshold, where it is intended landing aircraft first contact the runway.

TOUCHDOWN ZONE ELEVATION/TDZE — The highest elevation in the first 3,000 feet of the landing surface. TDZE is indicated on the instrument approach procedure chart when straight-in landing minimums are authorized. (See Touchdown Zone)

TOUCHDOWN ZONE LIGHTING — (See Airport Lighting)

TOWER/AIRPORT TRAFFIC CONTROL TOWER/ATCT — A terminal facility that uses air/ground communications, visual signaling, and other devices to provide ATC services to aircraft operating in the vicinity of an airport or on the movement area. Authorizes aircraft to land or takeoff at the airport controlled by the tower or to transit the airport traffic area regardless of flight plan or weather conditions (IFR or VFR). A tower may also provide approach control services (radar or nonradar). (See Airport Traffic Area, Airport Traffic Control Service, Approach Control/Approach Control Facility, Approach Control Service, Movement Area, Tower En Route Control Service/Tower to Tower) (Refer to AIM)

ICAO—AERODROME CONTROL TOWER — A unit established to provide air traffc control service to aerodrome traffic.

TOWER EN ROUTE CONTROL SERVICE/TOWER TO TOWER — The control of IFR en route traffic within delegated airspace between two or more adjacent approach control facilities. This service is designed to expedite traffic and reduce control and pilot communication requirements.

TPX-42 — A numeric beacon decoder equipment/system. It is designed to be added to terminal radar systems for beacon decoding. It provides rapid target identification, reinforcement of the primary radar target, and altitude information from Mode C. (See Automated Radar Terminal Systems, Transponder)

TRACK — The actual flight path of an aircraft over the surface of the earth. (See Course, Route, Flight Path)

ICAO—TRACK — The projection on the earth's surface of the path of an aircraft, the direction of which path at any point is usually expressed in degrees from North (True, Magnetic, or Grid).

TRAFFIC —

1. A term used by a controller to transfer radar identification of an aircraft to another controller for the purpose of coordinating separation action. Traffic is normally issued (a) in response to a handoff or

point out, (b) in anticipation of a handoff or point out, or (c) in conjunction with a request for control of an aircraft.

2. A term used by ATC to refer to one or more aircraft.

TRAFFIC ADVISORIES — Advisories issued to alert pilots to other known or observed air traffic which may be in such proximity to the position or intended route of flight of their aircraft to warrant their attention. Such advisories may be based on:

1. Visual observation.

2. Observation of radar identified and nonidentified aircraft targets on an ATC radar display, or

3. Verbal reports from pilots or other facilities.

The word "traffic" followed by additional information, if known, is used to provide such advisories; e.g., "Traffic, 2 o'clock, one zero miles, southbound, eight thousand."

Traffic advisory service will be provided to the extent possible depending on higher priority duties of the controller or other limitations; e.g., radar limitations, volume of traffic, frequency congestion, or controller workload. Radar/nonradar traffic advisories do not relieve the pilot of his responsibility to see and avoid other aircraft. Pilots are cautioned that there are many times when the controller is not able to give traffic advisories concerning all traffic in the aircraft's proximity; in other words, when a pilot requests or is receiving traffic advisories, he should not assume that all traffic will be issued. (Refer to AIM, Radar Traffic Information Service)

(Identification), TRAFFIC ALERT. ADVISE YOU TURN LEFT/RIGHT (specific heading if appropriate), AND/OR CLIMB/DESCEND (specific altitude if appropriate) IMMEDIATELY. (See Safety Alert)

TRAFFIC ALERT AND COLLISION AVOIDANCE SYSTEM/TCAS — An airborne collision avoidance system based on radar beacon signals which operates independent of ground-based equipment. TCAS-I generates traffic advisories only. TCAS-II generates traffic advisories, and resolution (collision avoidance) advisories in the vertical plane.

TRAFFIC INFORMATION — (See Traffic Advisories)

TRAFFIC IN SIGHT — Used by pilots to inform a controller that previously issued traffic is in sight. (See Negative Contact, Traffic Advisories)

TRAFFIC NO LONGER A FACTOR — Indicates that the traffic described in a previously issued traffic advisory is no longer a factor.

TRAFFIC PATTERN — The traffic flow that is prescribed for aircraft landing at, taxiing on, or taking off from an airport. The components of a typical traffic pattern are upwind leg, crosswind leg, downwind leg, base leg, and final approach.

1. Upwind Leg—A flight path parallel to the landing runway in the direction of landing.

2. Crosswind Leg—A flight path at right angles to the landing runway off its upwind end.

3. Downwind Leg—A flight path parallel to the landing runway in the direction opposite to landing. The downwind leg normally extends between the crosswind leg and the base leg.

4. Base Leg—A flight path at right angles to the landing runway off its approach end. The base leg normally extends from the downwind leg to the intersection of the extended runway centerline.

5. Final Approach—A flight path in the direction of landing along the extended runway centerline. The final approach normally extends from the base leg to the runway. An aircraft making a straight-in approach VFR is also considered to be on final approach.

(See Straight-In Approach--VFR, Taxi Patterns) (Refer to AIM, FAR Part 91)

ICAO—AERODROME TRAFFIC CIRCUIT — The specified path to be flown by aircraft operating in the vicinity of an aerodrome.

TRANSCRIBED WEATHER BROADCAST/TWEB — A continuous recording of meteorological and aeronautical information that is broadcast on L/MF and VOR facilities for pilots. (Refer to AIM)

TRANSFER OF CONTROL — That action whereby the responsibility for the separation of an aircraft is transferred from one controller to another.

ICAO—TRANSFER OF CONTROL — Transfer of responsibility for providing air traffic control service.

TRANSFERRING CONTROLLER/FACILITY — A controller/facility transferring control of an aircraft to another controller/facility.

ICAO—TRANSFERRING UNIT/CONTROLLER — Air traffic control unit/air traffic controller in the process of transferring the responsibility for providing air traffic control service to an aircraft to the next air traffic control unit/air traffic controller along the route of flight.

Note. — See definition of *accepting unit/controller.*

TRANSITION —

1. The general term that describes the change from one phase of flight or flight condition to another; e.g., transition from en route flight to the approach or transition from instrument flight to visual flight.

2. A published procedure (SID Transition) used to connect the basic SID to one of several en route airways/jet routes, or a published procedure (STAR Transition) used to connect one of several en route

airways/jet routes to the basic STAR. (Refer to SID/STAR Charts)

TRANSITION AREA — (See Controlled Airspace)

TRANSMISSOMETER — An apparatus used to determine visibility by measuring the transmission of light through the atmosphere. It is the measurement source for determining runway visual range (RVR) and runway visibility value (RVV). (See Visibility)

TRANSMITTING IN THE BLIND/BLIND TRANSMISSION — A transmission from one station to other stations in circumstances where two-way communication cannot be established, but where it is believed that the called stations may be able to receive the transmission.

TRANSPONDER — The airborne radar beacon receiver/transmitter portion of the Air Traffic Control Radar Beacon System (ATCRBS) which automatically receives radio signals from interrogators on the ground, and selectively replies with a specific reply pulse or pulse group only to those interrogations being received on the mode to which it is set to respond. (See Interrogator) (Refer to AIM)

ICAO—TRANSPONDER — A receiver/transmitter which will generate a reply signal upon proper interrogation; the interrogation and reply being on different frequencies.

TURBOJET AIRCRAFT — An aircraft having a jet engine in which the energy of the jet operates a turbine which in turn operates the air compressor.

TURBOPROP AIRCRAFT — An aircraft having a jet engine in which the energy of the jet operates a turbine which drives the propeller.

T-VOR/TERMINAL-VERY HIGH FREQUENCY OMNIDIRECTIONAL RANGE STATION — A very high frequency terminal omnirange station located on or near an airport and used as an approach aid. (See Navigational Aid, VOR)

TWO WAY RADIO COMMUNICATIONS FAILURE — (See Lost Communications)

ULTRAHIGH FREQUENCY/UHF — The frequency band between 300 and 3,000 MHz. The bank of radio frequencies used for military air/ground voice communications. In some instances this may go as low as 225 MHz and still be referred to as UHF.

ULTRALIGHT VEHICLE — An aeronautical vehicle operated for sport or recreational purposes which does not require FAA registration, an airworthiness certificate, nor pilot certification. They are primarily single occupant vehicles, although some two-place vehicles are authorized for training purposes. Operation of an ultralight vehicle in certain airspace requires authorization from ATC. (See FAR 103)

UNABLE — Indicates inability to comply with a specific instruction, request, or clearance.

UNCONTROLLED AIRSPACE — Uncontrolled airspace is that portion of the airspace that has not been designated as continental control area, control area, control zone, terminal control area, or transition area and within which ATC has neither the authority nor the responsibility for exercising control over air traffic. (See Controlled Airspace)

UNDER THE HOOD — Indicates that the pilot is using a hood to restrict visibility outside the cockpit while simulating instrument flight. An appropriately rated pilot is required in the other control seat while this operation is being conducted. (Refer to FAR, Part 91)

UNICOM — A nongovernment communication facility which may provide airport information at certain airports. Locations and frequencies of UNICOMs are shown on aeronautical charts and publications. (Refer to AIM, Airport/Facility Directory)

UNPUBLISHED ROUTE — A route for which no minimum altitude is published or charted for pilot use. It may include a direct route between NAVAIDS, a radial, a radar vector, or a final approach course beyond the segments of an instrument approach procedure. (See Published Route, Route)

UPWIND LEG — (See Traffic Pattern)

URGENCY — A condition of being concerned about safety and of requiring timely but not immediate assistance; a potential *distress* condition.

ICAO—URGENCY — A condition concerning the safety of an aircraft or other vehicle, or of person on board or in sight, but which does not require immediate assistance.

VECTOR — A heading issued to an aircraft to provide navigational guidance by radar.

ICAO—RADAR VECTORING — Provision of navigational guidance to aircraft in the form of specific headings, based on the use of radar.

VERIFY — Request confirmation of information; e.g., "verify assigned altitude."

VERIFY SPECIFIC DIRECTION OF TAKEOFF (OR TURNS AFTER TAKEOFF) — Used by ATC to ascertain an aircraft's direction of takeoff and/or direction of turn after takeoff. It is normally used for IFR departures from an airport not having a control tower. When direct communication with the pilot is not possible, the request and information may be relayed through an FSS, dispatcher, or by other means. (See IFR Takeoff Minimums and Departure Procedures)

VERTICAL SEPARATION — Separation established by assignment of different altitudes or flight levels. (See Separation)

ICAO—VERTICAL SEPARATION — Separation between aircraft expressed in units of vertical distance.

VERTICAL TAKEOFF AND LANDING AIRCRAFT/VTOL AIRCRAFT — Aircraft capable of vertical climbs and/or descents and of using very short runways or small areas for takeoff and landings. These aircraft include, but are not limited to, helicopters. (See Short Takeoff and Landing Aircraft)

VERY HIGH FREQUENCY/VHF — The frequency band between 30 and 300 MHz. Portions of this band, 108 to 118 MHz, are used for certain NAVAIDS; 118 to 136 MHz are used for civil air/ground voice communications. Other frequencies in this band are used for purposes not related to air traffic control.

VERY LOW FREQUENCY/VLF — The frequency band between 3 and 30 kHz.

VFR AIRCRAFT/VFR FLIGHT — An aircraft conducting flight in accordance with visual flight rules. (See Visual Flight Rules)

VFR CONDITIONS — Weather conditions equal to or better than the minimum for flight under visual flight rules. The term may be used as an ATC clearance/instruction only when:

1. An IFR aircraft requests a climb/descent in VFR conditions.

2. The clearance will result in noise abatement benefits where part of the IFR departure route does not conform to an FAA approved noise abatement route or altitude.

3. A pilot has requested a practice instrument approach and is not on an IFR flight plan.

All pilots receiving this authorization must comply with the VFR visibility and distance from cloud criteria in FAR Part 91. Use of the term does not relieve controllers of their responsibility to separate aircraft in TCAs/TRSAs as required by FAA Handbook 7110.65. When used as an ATC clearance/instruction, the term may be abbreviated "VFR;" e.g., "MAINTAIN VFR," "CLIMB/DESCEND VFR," etc.

VFR-ON-TOP — ATC authorization for an IFR aircraft to operate in VFR conditions at any appropriate VFR altitude (as specified in FAR and as restricted by ATC). A pilot receiving this authorization must comply with the VFR visibility, distance from cloud criteria, and the minimum IFR altitudes specified in FAR Part 91. The use of this term does not relieve controllers of their responsibility to separate aircraft in TCA's/TRSA's as required by FAA Handbook 7110.65.

VFR MILITARY TRAINING ROUTES/VR — Routes used by the Department of Defense and associated Reserve and Air Guard units for the purpose of conducting low-altitude navigation and tactical training under VFR below 10,000 feet MSL at airspeeds in excess of 250 knots IAS.

VFR NOT RECOMMENDED — An advisory provided by a flight service station to a pilot during a preflight or inflight weather briefing that flight under visual flight rules is not recommended. To be given when the current and/or forecast weather conditions are at or below VFR minimums. It does not abrogate the pilot's authority to make his own decision.

VIDEO MAP — An electronically displayed map on the radar display that may depict data such as airports, heliports, runway centerline extensions, hospital emergency landing areas, NAVAID's and fixes, reporting points, airway/route centerlines, boundaries, handoff points, special use tracks, obstructions, prominent geographic features, map alignment indicators, range accuracy marks, minimum vectoring altitudes.

VISIBILITY — The ability, as determined by atmospheric conditions and expressed in units of distance, to see and identify prominent unlighted objects by day and prominent lighted objects by night. Visbility is reported as statute miles, hundreds of feet or meters. (Refer to FAR Part 91, AIM)

ICAO—VISIBILITY — The ability, as determined by atmospheric conditions and expressed in units of distance, to see and identify prominent unlighted objects by day and prominent lighted objects by night.

1. Flight Visibility—The average forward horizontal distance, from the cockpit of an aircraft in flight, at which prominent unlighted objects may be seen and identified by day and prominent lighted objects may be seen and identified by night.

ICAO—Flight Visibility—The visibility forward from the cockpit of an aircraft in flight.

2. Ground Visibility—Prevailing horizontal visibility near the earth's surface as reported by the United States National Weather Service or an accredited observer.

ICAO—Ground Visibility—The visibility at an aerodrome as reported by an accredited observer.

3. Prevailing Visibility—The greatest horizontal visibility equaled or exceeded throughout at least half the horizon circle which need not necessarily be continuous.

4. Runway Visibility Value/RVV—The visibility determined for a particular runway by a transmissometer. A meter provides a continuous indication of the visibility (reported in miles or fractions of miles) for the runway. RVV is used in lieu of prevailing visibility in determining minimums for a particular runway.

5. Runway Visual Range/RVR—An instrumentally derived value, based on standard calibrations, that represents the horizontal distance a pilot will see down the runway from the approach end. It is based on the sighting of either high intensity runway lights or on the visual contrast of other targets whichever yields the greater visual range. RVR, in contrast to prevailing or runway visibility, is based on what a pilot in a moving aircraft should see looking down the runway. RVR is horizontal visual range, not slant visual range. It is based on the measurement of a transmissometer

made near the touchdown point of the instrument runway and is reported in hundreds of feet. RVR is used in lieu of RVV and/or prevailing visibility in determining minimums for a particular runway.

    a. Touchdown RVR—The RVR visibility readout values obtained from RVR equipment serving the runway touchdown zone.

    b. Mid-RVR—The RVR readout values obtained from RVR equipment located midfield of the runway.

    c. Rollout RVR—The RVR readout values obtained from RVR equipment located nearest the rollout end of the runway.

ICAO—Runway Visual Range (RVR)—The range over which the pilot of an aircraft on the centre line of a runway can see the runway surface markings or the lights delineating the runway or identifying its centre line.

VISUAL APPROACH — An approach wherein an aircraft on an IFR flight plan, operating in VFR conditions under the control of an air traffic control facility and having an air traffic control authorization, may proceed to the airport of destination in VFR conditions.

ICAO—VISUAL APPROACH — An approach by an IFR flight when either part or all of an instrument approach procedure is not completed and the approach is executed in visual reference to terrain.

VISUAL APPROACH SLOPE INDICATOR — (See Airport Lighting)

VISUAL DESCENT POINT/VDP — A defined point on the final approach course of a nonprecision straight-in approach procedure from which normal descent from the MDA to the runway touchdown point may be commenced, provided the approach threshold of that runway, or approach lights, or other markings identifiable with the approach end of that runway are clearly visible to the pilot.

VISUAL FLIGHT RULES/VFR — Rules that govern the procedures for conducting flight under visual conditions. The term "VFR" is also used in the United States to indicate weather conditions that are equal to or greater than minimum VFR requirements. In addition, it is used by pilots and controllers to indicate type of flight plan. (See Instrument Flight Rules, Instrument Meteorological Conditions, Visual Meteorological Conditions) (Refer to FAR, Part 91 and AIM)

VISUAL HOLDING — The holding of aircraft at selected, prominent geographical fixes which can be easily recognized from the air. (See Hold, Holding Fixes)

VISUAL METEOROLOGICAL CONDITIONS/ VMC — Meteorological conditions expressed in terms of visibility, distance from cloud, and ceiling equal to or better than specified minima. (See Instrument Flight Rules, Instrument Meteorological Conditions, Visual Flight Rules)

VISUAL SEPARATION — A means employed by ATC to separate aircraft in terminal areas. There are two ways to effect this separation:

1. The tower controller sees the aircraft involved and issues instructions, as necessary, to ensure that the aircraft avoid each other.

2. A pilot sees the other aircraft involved and upon instructions from the controller provides his own separation by maneuvering his aircraft as necessary to avoid it. This may involve following another aircraft or keeping it in sight until it is no longer a factor. (See See and Avoid) (Refer to FAR, Part 91)

VORTAC/VHF OMNIDIRECTIONAL RANGE/ TACTICAL AIR NAVIGATION — A navigation aid providing VOR azimuth, TACAN azimuth, and TACAN distance measuring equipment (DME) at one site. (See Distance Measuring Equipment, Navigational Aid TACAN, VOR) (Refer to AIM)

VORTICES/WING TIP VORTICES — Circular patterns of air created by the movement of an airfoil through the air when generating lift. As an airfoil moves through the atmosphere in sustained flight, an area of area of low pressure is created above it. The air flowing from the high pressure area to the low pressure area around and about the tips of the airfoil tends to roll up into two rapidly rotating vortices, cylindrical in shape. These vortices are the most predominant parts of aircraft wake turbulence and their rotational force is dependent upon the wing loading, gross weight, and speed of the generating aircraft. The vortices from medium to heavy aircraft can be of extremely high velocity and hazardous to smaller aircraft. (See Aircraft Classes Wake Turbulence) (Refer to AIM)

VOR/VERY HIGH FREQUENCY OMNIDIRECTIONAL RANGE STATION — A ground-based electronic navigation aid transmitting very high frequency navigation signals, 360 degrees in azimuth, oriented from magnetic north. Used as the basis for navigation in the National Airspace System. The VOR periodically identifies itself by Morse Code and may have an additional voice identification feature. Voice features may be used by ATC or FSS for transmitting instructions/information to pilots. (See Navigational Aid) (Refer to AIM)

VOT/VOR TEST SIGNAL — A ground facility which emits a test signal to check VOR receiver accuracy. Some VOT's are available to the user while airborne, and others are limited to ground use only. (Refer to FAR, Part 91, AIM, Airport/Facility Directory)

WAKE TURBULENCE — Phenomena resulting from the passage of an aircraft through the atmosphere. The term includes vortices, thrust stream turbulence, jet blast, jet wash, propeller wash, and rotor wash both on the ground and in the air. (See Aircraft Classes, Jet Blast, Vortices) (Refer to AIM)

WARNING AREA — (See Special Use Airspace)

PILOT/CONTROLLER GLOSSARY

WAYPOINT — A predetermined geographical position used for route/instrument approach definition, or progress reporting purposes, that is defined relative to a VORTAC station or in terms of latitude/longitude coordinates.

WEATHER ADVISORY/INFLIGHT WEATHER ADVISORY — (See SIGMET, AIRMET)

WEATHER ADVISORY/WS/WST/WA/CWA — In aviation weather forecast practice, an expression of hazardous weather conditions not predicted in the area forecast, as they affect the operation of air traffic and as prepared by the NWS.

WHEN ABLE — When used in conjunction with ATC instructions, gives the pilot the latitude to delay compliance until a condition or event has been reconciled. Unlike "pilot discretion," when instructions are prefaced "when able," the pilot is expected to seek the first opportunity to comply. Once a maneuver has been initiated, the pilot is expected to continue until the specifications of the instructions have been met. "When able," should not be used when expeditious compliance is required.

WILCO — I have received your message, understand it, and will comply with it.

WIND SHEAR — A change in wind speed and/or wind direction in a short distance resulting in a tearing or shearing effect. It can exist in a horizontal or vertical direction and occasionally in both.

WORDS TWICE —

1. As a request: "Communication is difficult. Please say every phrase twice."

2. As information: "Since communications are difficult, every phrase in this message will be spoken twice."

INDEX

(References are to Paragraph Numbers)

A

ABBREVIATED CALL SIGNS
   Normal Use **2-41**
   Precautions In Use of **2-21**
ABBREVIATED DEPARTURE CLEARANCE **4-35**
Abbreviated IFR Flight Plans (Glossary)
ABBREVIATIONS **1-11**
ACDO *see* Air Carrier District Office (Glossary)
ACKNOWLEDGMENT OF
   ATC Instructions **2-43**
   ATIS **3-4**
   Frequency Changes **2-46**
   Immediate Action Clearances **2-44**
   Radar Approach Instructions **5-146**
ADDITIONAL SERVICES **2-67**
Additional Services (Glossary)
Administrator (FAA) (Glossary)
ADVANCE APPROACH INFORMATION (IFR) **4-115**
ADVERSE FLIGHT CONDITION INFORMATION **2-100**
ADVISORIES
   Check Density Altitude **3-2, 3-103**
   Derelict Balloons **8-22**
   Ground Traffic **3-32**
   Safety Alert **2-88**
   Traffic - Radar **2-84**
   Unmanned Balloon **2-108, 8-21**
   Unmanned Balloons **8-21**
   Wake Turbulence **2-80**
Advisory (Glossary)
ADVISORY CIRCULAR CHECKLIST **1-2**
Advisory Frequency (Glossary)
ADVISORY FREQUENCY, CHANGE TO
   ARSA Operations **6-47**
   IFR Approach **4-129**
Advisory Service (Glossary)
AIR AMBULANCE IDENTIFICATION **2-25**
AIR CARRIER IDENTIFICATION/CALL SIGNS **2-20**
Air Carrier District Office (Glossary)
AIR PIRACY **9-20**
AIR ROUTE TRAFFIC CONTROL CENTER **2-4**
Air Taxi (Glossary)
AIR TAXI IDENTIFICATION **2-20**
Air Traffic (Glossary)
Air Traffic Clearance (Glossary)
AIR TRAFFIC CLEARANCE - GENERAL **2-61**
Air Traffic Control (Glossary)
Air Traffic Control Command Center (Glossary)
Air Traffic Control Specialist (Glossary)
AIR TRAFFIC PRIORITY **2-68**
Aircraft (Glossary)

AIRCRAFT CATEGORIES FOR TERMINAL OPERATIONS **3-126**
AIRCRAFT CLASSES BY WEIGHT **3-126**
AIRCRAFT IDENTIFICATION **2-20** thru **2-28**
AIRCRAFT PRIORITY SPECIAL VFR **2-68, 6-72**
AIRPORT CONDITION INFORMATION FOR IFR
   ARRIVALS **4-112**
AIRPORT EMERGENCY LIGHTING **3-50**
AIRPORT INFORMATION FOR DEPARTING AIRCRAFT **3-103**
AIRPORT LIGHTING **3-50** thru **3-66**
AIRPORT RADAR SERVICE AREA *see* ARSA
AIRPORT TRAFFIC AREA TRANSIT AUTHORIZATION **3-13, 3-14**
AIRPORT TRAFFIC PATTERN - VFR **3-131**
Airway (Glossary)
AIRWAYS
   Description **2-30**
   IFR Filing **4-5**
   Jet Routes **4-63**
   Victor **4-62**
ALERT - SAFETY **2-88**
Alert Notice (Glossary)
ALNOT *see* Alert Notice
ALPHANUMERIC DISPLAY **5-4**
Alphanumeric Display (Glossary)
ALTERNATIVE ROUTES (IFR) **4-67**
ALTIMETER SETTINGS **2-140**
Altimeter Setting (Glossary)
Altitude (Glossary)
ALTITUDE ADVISORY - PARACHUTE JUMPING **8-30**
ALTITUDE AMENDMENT (IFR) **4-37, 4-86**
ALTITUDE CHANGES (IFR) **4-87**
ALTITUDE FOR DIRECTION OF FLIGHT (IFR) **4-80**
ALTITUDE INFORMATION - RADAR APPROACH **5-140**
ALTITUDE MANAGEMENT DURING IFR APPROACH
   General **4-121, 4-125**
   Vectors **5-114**
Altitude Readout (Glossary)
ALTITUDE READOUT VALIDATION **5-30**
Altitude Readout (Glossary)
ALTITUDE REPORTS **5-64, 7-50**
Altitude Reservation (Glossary)
ALTITUDE RESTRICTIONS WHILE BEING VECTORED **5-74**
Altitude Restriction (Glossary)
ALTITUDE SQUAWK REQUESTS **5-54**
ALTITUDE VERIFICATION **5-30, 7-7**
ALTRV *see* Altitude Reservation (Glossary)
AMENDED CLEARANCE **2-64**
AMENDED CLEARANCES PRIOR TO TAKEOFF **3-132**
APPROACH CLEARANCE **4-120**

INDEX

(References are to Paragraph Numbers)

Approach Clearance (Glossary)
APPROACH CONTROL FACILITY **2-2**
Approach Control Service (Glossary)
Approach Gate (Glossary)
APPROACH GATE - VECTORS TO **5-111**
APPROACH INFORMATION (IFR) **4-115**
APPROACH INSTRUCTION FORMAT - RADAR **5-111, 5-114**
APPROACH LIGHTS **3-53**
APPROACH PROCEDURES (IFR/RADAR) **5-110 thru 5-119**
APPROACH SEQUENCE
   Airport Traffic Pattern **3-120**
   Timed Approaches **7-61**
Approach Sequence (Glossary)
Approach Speed (Glossary)
AREA NAVIGATION
   Flight Planning **4-6**
   Route Assignment **4-64**
Area Navigation (Glossary)
ARRIVAL DELAY PROCEDURES/HOLDING **4-100, 4-102**
ARRIVAL INFORMATION - TERMINAL **3-1, 3-151**
ARRIVAL DELAY INFORMATION **4-102**
ARRIVAL PROCEDURES (VFR)
   Airport Traffic Patterns **3-151**
   ATIS Monitoring **3-4**
   VFR Terminal Radar Programs **6-24**
Arrival Time (Glossary)
ARSA
   Adjacent Airport Operations **6-46**
   Altitude Assignments **6-44**
   Arrivals and Overflights **6-3**
   Communications Procedure **6-43**
   Departures **6-2**
   Description **6-1**
   Deviations **6-5**
   Mode C Requirement **6-6**
   Procedures ATC **6-40**
   Satellite Airport Operations **6-4**
   Separation Exceptions **6-45**
   Separation Standards **6-42**
   Services **6-41**
ARSA *see* Controlled Airspace (Glossary)
ARSA *see* Outer Area (Glossary)
ARTCC RADIO FREQUENCY OUTAGE **9-47**
ARTS *see* Automated Radar Terminal Systems (Glossary)
ASSIGNED ALTITUDE, CONFIRMATION OF **5-31**
ASSISTANCE DURING AN EMERGENCY **9-3**
ATC Assigned Airspace (Glossary)
ATC CLEARANCES - GENERAL
   Air Traffic Priority **2-68**
   Airport Traffic Areas **3-10 thru 3-15**
   Amendments **2-64**
   Compliance with **2-62**
   Helicopter Takeoff **3-176**
   Landing **3-155**
   Landing Priority **2-69**
   Pilot Responsibility **2-63**
   Special VFR **6-70**
   Takeoff **3-139**

ATC CLEARANCES - IFR
   Abbreviated Departure Clearance **4-35**
   Altitude Amendments **4-37**
   Approach Clearances **4-120**
   Contact Approach **4-151**
   IFR Flight Plan Required **4-1**
   Prefix **4-32**
   Pre-Taxi **4-34**
   Relayed Approach Clearance **4-124**
   Route Amendments **4-37**
   Route Clearance **4-65**
   Visual Approach **4-141**
   Visual Approach - Radar Separated Aircraft **4-143**
ATC Clearance *see* Air Traffic Clearance (Glossary)
ATC CLEARANCE ITEMS (IFR)
   Altitude Data **4-23**
   Beacon Code Assignment **4-25**
   Clearance Limit **4-20**
   Departure Procedure **4-21**
   Frequency Information **4-24**
   Route of Flight **4-22**
ATC FACILITY IDENTIFICATION **2-12**
ATC Instructions (Glossary)
ATC INSTRUCTIONS - COMPLIANCE WITH **2-62**
ATC LIGHT GUN SIGNALS **3-21**
ATC RADAR WEATHER DISPLAY **2-128**
ATC SERVICE ADDITIONAL SERVICES **2-67**
ATC SERVICE PROCEDURES **2-60**
ATIS **3-1 thru 3-4**
AUTHORIZED FREQUENCY USE **2-50**
AUTHORIZED SPEEDS **5-95**
Autoland Approach (Glossary)
AUTOMATED RADAR SYSTEM DESCRIPTION **5-4**
Automated Radar Terminal Systems (Glossary)
Automatic Altitude Report *see* Altitude Readout (Glossary)
AUTOMATIC ALTITUDE REPORTING **5-62, 5-64**
Automatic Altitude Reporting (Glossary)
AUTOMATIC TERMINAL INFORMATION SERVICE **3-1 thru 3-4**
AVIATION SAFETY REPORT PROGRAM **2-110**
Aviation Weather Service (Glossary)
AVIONICS MALFUNCTION REPORTS **2-103, 2-104**
AWW *see* Severe Weather Forecast Alerts (Glossary)
Azimuth (Glossary)

B

Base Leg *see* Traffic Pattern (Glossary)
Below Minimums (Glossary)
BELOW IFR MINIMUMS REPORT TO ATC **4-114**
BOMB EMERGENCIES
   In-Flight **9-22**
   K-9 Explosive Detection Teams **9-23**
   Threat **9-22**
BRAKING ACTION ADVISORIES **3-40**
Braking Action Advisories (Glossary)
BRAKING ACTION REPORTS **3-39**
Broadcast (Glossary)

INDEX

(References are to Paragraph Numbers)

C

CALL SIGNS - AIRCRAFT/AIR CARRIER **2-20**
CALM WIND DESCRIPTION **2-131**
CANCELLATION OF SPEED RESTRICTION **5-96**
CANCELLING IFR FLIGHT PLAN **2-163, 4-11**
Ceiling (Glossary)
CENTER **2-4**
CENTER FREQUENCY OUTAGE **9-47**
CENTER WEATHER ADVISORY **2-120**
Center Weather Advisory (Glossary)
Center's Area (Glossary)
Chaff (Glossary)
CHAFF DEVIATION **2-130**
CHANGE OF ATIS CODE **3-3**
CHARTED VISUAL APPROACH PROCEDURES **4-145, 4-146**
Charted Visual Flight Procedure (Glossary)
Circle-To-Land Maneuver (Glossary)
CIRCLING APPROACH INSTRUCTIONS **4-130**
CIRCLING APPROACH WITH STRAIGHT-IN LANDING **4-131**
Circling Maneuver *see* Circle-To-Land Maneuver (Glossary)
CLEAR AIR TURBULENCE (CAT) REPORTS **2-126**
Clear-Air Turbulence (Glossary)
CLEARANCE BEYOND HOLDING FIX **4-101**
CLEARANCE DELIVERY FORMAT (IFR) **4-31**
CLEARANCE LIMIT **4-20**
Clearance Limit (Glossary)
CLEARANCE READBACK **2-43, 4-33**
CLEARANCE VOID TIME **4-42**
Closed Runway (Glossary)
CLOSED RUNWAY INFORMATION **3-37**
Closed Traffic (Glossary)
CLOSED TRAFFIC, REQUESTS FOR **3-125**
CLOSING VFR FLIGHT PLAN **2-164**
Coastal Fix (Glossary)
CODE 7500 DISPLAY **9-21**
Codes (Glossary)
Common Traffic Advisory Frequency (Glossary)
COMMUNICATIONS WITH CONTROL TOWERS **3-13**
COMPLIANCE WITH ATC CLEARANCES **2-62**
COMPOSITE FLIGHT PLAN **4-9**
Composite Flight Plan (Glossary)
Composite Route System (Glossary)
Composite Separation (Glossary)
COMPULSORY REPORTING POINTS **7-3**
Compulsory Report Points (Glossary)
CONFLICT ALERT **2-88**
Conflict Alert (Glossary)
Conflict Resolution (Glossary)
Contact Approach (Glossary)
CONTACT APPROACHES **4-150, 4-151**
Control Area *see* Controlled Airspace (Glossary)
Control Sector (Glossary)
CONTROL TOWERS
    Description **2-1, 2-2, 2-12**
    Service Provided **3-30**
    Timely Airport Information **3-38**
Control Zone *see* Controlled Airspace (Glossary)
CONTROL ZONES
    Description **6-12**

CONTROL ZONES (Cont.)
    Special VFR **6-70** thru **6-80**
Controlled Airspace (Glossary)
CONTROLLED DEPARTURE TIME **4-43**
Controlled Departure Time (Glossary)
CONTROLLER DISCRETION IN RADAR ASSISTANCE **9-35**
Controller *see* Air Traffic Control Specialist (Glossary)
Convective Sigmet (Glossary)
Convective Significant Meteorological Information *see* Convective Sigmet (Glossary)
Coupled Approach (Glossary)
Course (Glossary)
Crosswind (Glossary)
Crosswind Leg *see* Traffic Pattern (Glossary)
Cruise (Glossary)
CRUISE CLEARANCE **4-85**
Cruising Altitude (Glossary)
CTAF *see* Common Traffic Advisory Frequency (Glossary)

D

Data Block *see* Alphanumeric Display (Glossary)
Decision Height (Glossary)
DEPARTURE CONTROL **2-3**
DEPARTURE DELAY (IFR)
    Information **4-45**
    Sequencing **4-41**
DEPARTURE INSTRUCTIONS (IFR) **4-50**
DEPARTURE OBSTACLE CLEARANCE (IFR) **4-53**
DEPARTURE PROCEDURE
    Airport Traffic Pattern-VFR **3-131**
    ATIS Monitoring **3-4**
    IFR **4-20, 4-21**
    VFR Terminal Radar Programs **6-23**
DEPARTURE RESTRICTIONS IFR **4-42**
Departure Time (Glossary)
DERELICT BALLOONS **8-22**
DESCENTS
    At Pilot's Discretion **4-89, 5-64, 7-52**
    Normal **4-88**
    Profile **4-90**
DESCRIPTION OF AIRCRAFT TYPES FOR COMMUNICATIONS **2-22**
DEVIATIONS - FROM WEATHER **2-130**
DEVIATIONS ON FINAL APPROACH **5-115, 5-152**
DF Guidance (Glossary)
DF STEER **9-65, 9-66**
DH *see* Decision Height (Glossary)
DIRECT ROUTE (IFR) **4-69**
DIRECT ROUTE - RADAR ENVIRONMENT **5-75**
Direction Finder (Glossary)
DIRECTION OF FLIGHT - ALTITUDE (IFR) **4-80**
DISCRETE CODE **5-29**
Discrete Code (Glossary)
Discrete Frequency (Glossary)
DISCRETIONARY DESCENT
    Altitude Assignment **4-85**
    Mode C Indications, During **5-64**
    Procedures **4-89**
DIVERSE VECTOR AREA **5-101**

INDEX

(References are to Paragraph Numbers)

Diverse Vector Area (Glossary)
DME Fix (Glossary)
Downwind Leg *see* Traffic Pattern (Glossary)

E

EMERGENCY
   Air Piracy **9-20**
   Air Traffic Rules **8-8**
   Airport **9-13**
   Airport Lighting Requirements **9-50**
   Airport Recommendation **9-11**
   Altitude Change for Improved Radio Reception **9-7**
   Assistance **9-3**
   Authority - Pilot **9-1**
   Declaration **9-2**
   Defense Emergency Conditions **9-14**
   Definitions **9-2**
   Determination **9-4**
   Frequencies **9-6**
   Frequencies In-Flight Monitoring **9-9**
   Guidance to Emergency Airport **9-12**
   Information Requested by ATC **9-5**
   Information Required by ATC **9-5**
   Obstruction Video Map **9-33**
   Orientation Methods **9-10**
   Radar Assistance **9-31, 9-32**
   Radar Assistance Controller Discretion **9-35**
   Radar Assistance - Pilot Responsibility **9-34**
   Responsibilities - Pilot **9-1**
Emergency (Glossary)
En Route Automated Radar Tracking System (Glossary)
En Route Flight Advisory Service (Glossary)
En Route Minimum Safe Altitude Warning (Glossary)
EQUIPMENT MALFUNCTION REPORTS **2-103, 2-104**
EXPECT FURTHER CLEARANCE TIME
   ARSA **6-41**
   IFR Arrival **4-100**
   Stage III **6-53**
EXPECTED DEPARTURE CLEARANCE TIME **4-43**
Expected Departure Clearance Time (Glossary)
EXPEDITIOUS INSTRUCTIONS **2-65**

F

FAILED TRANSPONDER IN POSITIVE CONTROL AIRSPACE **5-28**
Federal Airway *see* Airway (Glossary)
Federal Airways *see* Low Altitude Airway Structure (Glossary)
FINAL **3-150**
Final (Glossary)
Final Approach Course (Glossary)
FINAL APPROACH DEVIATIONS **5-115**
Final Approach Fix (Glossary)
FINAL APPROACH GUIDANCE - RADAR APPROACHES **5-147, 5-148**
Final Approach *see* Traffic Pattern (Glossary)
Final Approach (IFR) (Glossary)
Final Controller (Glossary)
FINAL CONTROLLER, CHANGE TO **5-144**
Flight Check (Glossary)

Flight Check *see* Flight Inspection (Glossary)
FLIGHT CONDITIONS, REPORT OF **2-122**
FLIGHT FOLLOWING *see* Radar Flight Following (Glossary)
FLIGHT INSPECTION AIRCRAFT IDENTIFICATION **2-28**
Flight Inspection (Glossary)
Flight Level (Glossary)
FLIGHT LEVEL - MINIMUM USABLE **4-83**
Flight Path (Glossary)
FLIGHT PLAN
   Cancelling IFR **2-163**
   Closing VFR **2-164**
   Composite **2-162**
   Information **2-160**
Flight Plan (Glossary)
FLIGHT SERVICE STATIONS **2-5**
Flight Standards District Office (Glossary)
Flight Visibility *see* Visibility (Glossary)
Flight Watch (Glossary)
Flight Watch *see* En Route Flight Advisory Service (Glossary)
FLOW CONTROL **4-43**
Flow Control (Glossary)
FOREIGN REGISTRY IDENTIFICATION **2-20**
FREQUENCIES - EMERGENCY **9-6**
FREQUENCY CHANGE
   After Acknowledgment of **2-46**
   After Compliance with **2-47**
   After Landing **3-161**
   During an Emergency **9-8**
   Helicopter Pilots **3-175**
   Instructions IFR Approach **4-128, 4-129, 5-114**
   Temporary **2-48**
   To Departure **3-141, 3-142**
   To Final Controller **5-144**
FSDO *see* Flight Standards District Office (Glossary)
Fuel Dumping (Glossary)
FUEL DUMPING ADVISORIES **8-10**
FULL ROUTE CLEARANCES **4-36**
Full Route Clearance *see* Request Full Route Clearance (Glossary)

G

GADO *see* General Aviation District Office (Glossary)
GATE-HOLD PROCEDURES **4-44**
Gate-Hold Procedures (Glossary)
General Aviation District Office (Glossary)
GLIDE SLOPE CRITICAL AREA **3-107**
Glidepath *see* Glideslope (Glossary)
Glideslope (Glossary)
Glideslope/Glidepath Intercept Altitude (Glossary)
GROUND CONTROL
   Change to After Landing **3-161**
   Communications **3-101**
   Taxi Information **3-104**
Ground Delay (Glossary)
GROUND OPERATIONS NEAR WAKE TURBULENCE **3-108**
Ground Visibility *see* Visibility (Glossary)

H

HANDOFF
   Frequency Change **2-45**

INDEX

(References are to Paragraph Numbers)

HANDOFF (Cont.)
    Speed Adjustment From Other Facility **5-94**
    Vector From Another Facility **5-79**
Handoff (Glossary)
HAZARDOUS IN-FLIGHT WEATHER ADVISORY SERVICE **2-121**
HEAVY AIRCRAFT DESCRIPTION **2-20**
HELICOPTER
    Operations **3-170, 3-174**
    Separation - Special VFR **6-79, 6-80**
    Stage III Service **6-55**
    Taxiing **3-172, 3-174**
Helipad (Glossary)
Heliport (Glossary)
High Speed Taxiway (Glossary)
HIJACKINGS **9-20**
HIWAS **2-121**
HOLD FOR RELEASE **4-42**
HOLDING (IFR) VISUAL **4-106**
HOLD (GROUND)
    At ILS Critical Areas **3-107**
    Near Runways **3-105**
    On the Runway **3-133**
HOLDING (IFR)
    At Unmonitored NAVAIDS **4-107**
    Delay Information **4-100**
    Instruction Format **4-103**
    Pattern Surveillance - Radar **4-104**
    Pattern Deviation Advisories **4-105**
HOLDING OF VFR AIRCRAFT **6-29**
Holding Procedure *see* Hold (Glossary)
Hover Taxi (Glossary)

I

ICAO *see* International Civil Aviation Organization (Glossary)
ICING REPORTS **2-124**
IDENT FEATURE **5-34**
Ident Feature (Glossary)
IDENT REQUEST **5-54**
IFR Conditions (Glossary)
IFR FLIGHT PLANS - GENERAL **2-161**
IFR Landing Minimums *see* Landing Minimums
IFR ROUTE TRANSITIONS **4-66**
IFR ROUTING THROUGH UNCONTROLLED AIRSPACE **4-68**
IFR Takeoff Minimums and Departure Procedures (Glossary)
IFR TO VFR-ON-TOP **4-10, 4-160**
ILS APPROACHES
    Parallel ILS **5-118**
    Simultaneous ILS **5-117**
ILS HOLD LINES **3-107**
IN-FLIGHT MONITORING OF EMERGENCY FREQUENCIES **9-9**
In-Flight Refueling *see* Aerial Refueling (Glossary)
Inertial (INS) Systems *see* Area Navigation (Glossary)
INITIAL COMMUNICATIONS FORMAT **2-40**
INITIAL HEADING - RADAR (IFR) **5-100**
INOPERATIVE TRANSPONDER **5-40**
Instrument Flight Rules (Glossary)

Instrument Meteorological Conditions (Glossary)
Instrument Runway (Glossary)
INSTRUMENT RUNWAY, ATIS ADVISORY **3-2**
INTERCHANGE AIRCRAFT DESCRIPTION **2-26**
International Civil Aviation Organization (Glossary)
INTERROGATOR **5-4**
Interrogator (Glossary)
INTERROGATOR INOPERATIVE OR MALFUNCTIONING **5-41**
INTERSECTION TAKEOFFS **3-136, 3-137**

J

JET ROUTES **4-5, 4-63**

K

Known Traffic (Glossary)

L

LAAS **2-88**, *see* Low Altitude Alert System (Glossary)
Landing Area (Glossary)
LANDING AREA CONDITION **3-36**
LANDING CLEARANCE PHRASEOLOGY **3-155**
LANDING CLEARANCE WITHOUT VISUAL OBSERVATION **3-157**
LANDING INSTRUCTIONS **3-151**
Landing Minimums (Glossary)
LANDING PRIORITY **2-69**
Landing Roll (Glossary)
LANDING SEPARATION **3-152 thru 3-156**
LANDING SEQUENCING PROCEDURES **3-120**
LANDING TO HOLD SHORT OF ANOTHER RUNWAY **3-153, 3-154**
LATERAL SEPARATION **7-40 thru 7-44**
Lateral Separation (Glossary)
Level *see* Cruising Altitude (Glossary)
LIFEGUARD FLIGHTS **2-25, 2-68**
Light Gun (Glossary)
LIMITATIONS OF RADAR SERVICE **5-1**
LOCAL SPECIAL VFR **6-75**
Localizer (Glossary)
LOCALIZER CRITICAL AREA **3-107**
LONG RANGE NAVIGATION FLIGHT PLANNING **4-7**
Long Range Navigation *see* LORAN (Glossary)
LONGITUDINAL SEPARATION **7-30 thru 7-34**
Longitudinal Separation (Glossary)
LORAN (Glossary)
LORAN-C *see* Area Navigation (Glossary)
LOSS OF COMMUNICATIONS
    IFR **9-42**
    Reestablishing Radio Contact **9-46**
    Transponder Operation **9-45**
    VFR **3-20**
Lost Communications (Glossary)
Low Altitude Airway Structure (Glossary)
LOW ALTITUDE ALERT SYSTEM **2-88**
Low Altitude Alert System (Glossary)
LOW APPROACH **3-122**

INDEX

(References are to Paragraph Numbers)

Low Approach (Glossary)
LOW LEVEL WIND SHEAR
   Alert Advisories **3-34**
   Alert System **3-33**
   Report Of **2-125**
LOWEST USABLE FLIGHT LEVEL **4-82**

M

MAINTAIN VFR CLEARANCES **4-165**
MALFUNCTIONING TRANSPONDER **5-40**
Mandatory Altitude (Glossary)
Marker Beacon (Glossary)
MERGING TARGET PROCEDURES **2-89**
Microwave Landing System (Glossary)
Military Authority Assumes Responsibility For Separation of Aircraft (Glossary)
MILITARY OPERATIONS AREAS **8-2**
MINIMUM CROSSING ALTITUDE **4-84**
Minimum Descent Altitude (Glossary)
Minimum En Route IFR Altitude (Glossary)
MINIMUM EN ROUTE ALTITUDES **4-84**
Minimum Fuel (Glossary)
MINIMUM FUEL ADVISORY **2-105**
Minimum Safe Altitude (Glossary)
MINIMUM SAFE ALTITUDE WARNING **2-88**
Minimum Safe Altitude Warning (Glossary)
MINIMUM VECTORING ALTITUDES **5-71**
Minimum Vectoring Altitudes (Glossary)
Minimums (Glossary)
MISSED APPROACH
   From Practice Approach **4-174**
   From Radar Approach **5-149**
   From Timed Approach **6-66**
   IFR - General **4-133**
   Instructions - Radar Approach **5-150**
MLS APPROACH, VECTORS TO **5-114**
MLS *see* Area Navigation (Glossary)
MLS *see* Azimuth (Glossary)
MLS *see* Microwave Landing System (Glossary)
MODE C
   Automatic Altitude Reporting **5-24**
   Approved Deviations **5-26, 5-27**
   ARSA Requirement **6-6**
   Requirements **5-25**
   Validation of Readout **5-30**
MONITOR CONTROLLERS (NTZ) **5-117**
Movement Area (Glossary)
MSA *see* Minimum Safe Altitude (Glossary)

N

NAS *see* National Airspace System (Glossary)
NAS Stage A (Glossary)
NASA REPORT **2-110**
NATIONAL AIRSPACE SECURITY PLAN **9-14**
National Airspace System (Glossary)
National Flight Data Center (Glossary)
National Search and Rescue Plan (Glossary)
NAVAID Classes (Glossary)
NAVAID MALFUNCTIONS **2-101, 2-102**
NAVAID SERVICE VOLUME LIMITS **4-70**
NAVAID TERMS **2-31**
NAVIGATIONAL GUIDANCE - RADAR **5-77**
NEAR MID-AIR COLLISION REPORT **2-109**
NO-GYRO APPROACH **5-133**
NO RADIO PROCEDURES
   Airport Traffic Area **3-20**
   IFR **9-40** thru **9-51**
NO TRANSGRESSION ZONE **5-117**
NONAPPROACH CONTROL TOWER **2-1**
Non-Radar (Glossary)
NON-RADAR POSITION REPORTS **7-1**
NORMAL DESCENT **4-88**
Notice to Airmen/NOTAM (Glossary)
Numbers *see* Have Numbers (Glossary)
NUMBERS USAGE **2-11**

O

OBSTRUCTION ALERT **2-88**
OBSTRUCTION LIGHTS **3-65**
OFF-ROUTE VECTOR **5-77**
   Off-Route Vector (Glossary)
OMEGA *see* Area Navigation (Glossary)
OPERATING IN PROXIMITY TO SPECIAL USE OR ATCAA AIRSPACE **8-3**
OPERATION RAINCHECK **2-6**
OPPOSITE DIRECTION RUNWAY OPERATIONS **3-128**
OPTION APPROACH **3-124**
Option Approach (Glossary)
Outer Area (Glossary)
Outer Fix (Glossary)
Outer Marker (Glossary)
OWN NAVIGATION **5-77**
OWN NAVIGATION *see* Resume Own Navigation (Glossary)

P

PARACHUTE JUMP AUTHORIZATION **8-32, 8-34**
PARALLEL ILS/MLS APPROACHES **5-118**
PARALLEL RUNWAY OPERATIONS
   General **3-127, 3-128**
   Visual Approaches To **4-144**
Parallel Runways (Glossary)
PCA *see* Controlled Airspace (Glossary)
PHONETIC ALPHABET **2-10**
Pilot in Command (Glossary)
PILOT IN COMMAND AUTHORITY **2-63**
PILOT REPORT INFORMATION **2-122**
PILOT REPORTS
   Airframe Icing **2-124**

INDEX

(References are to Paragraph Numbers)

PILOT REPORTS (Cont.)
   Clear Air Turbulence **2-126**
   Turbulence **2-123**
   Wind Shear **2-125**
PILOT RESPONSIBILITY RADAR ASSISTANCE **9-34**
Pilot's Discretion (Glossary)
Position Report (Glossary)
POSITION REPORT FORMAT (IFR) **7-5**
POSITION REPORTING REQUIREMENTS (IFR) **7-4**
POSITIVE CONTROL AREA **4-61**
Positive Control Area *see* Controlled Airspace (Glossary)
PRACTICE INSTRUMENT APPROACHES **4-170** thru **4-179**
Practice Instrument Approach (Glossary)
PRE-TAXI CLEARANCE PROCEDURES **4-34**
Preferential Routes (Glossary)
Preferred IFR Routes (Glossary)
Prevailing Visibility *see* Visibility (Glossary)
PRIMARY RADAR **5-3**
PRIMARY RADAR UNUSABLE **5-6**
PROCEDURE TURN **4-120**, **4-126**, **4-127**
Procedure Turn (Glossary)
PROFILE DESCENT **4-90**
Profile Descent (Glossary)
Profile Descent *see* Runway Profile Descent (Glossary)
PROGRESSIVE TAXI INSTRUCTIONS **3-104**
PROPOSED DEPARTURE TIME **4-2**, **4-3**

R

Radar (Glossary)
RADAR APPROACH **5-130**
Radar Approach (Glossary)
RADAR APPROACH CONTROL **2-2**
Radar Arrival (Glossary)
RADAR CONTACT STATUS **5-51**
RADAR DEPARTURES (IFR) **5-102**
Radar Environment (Glossary)
Radar Flight Following (Glossary)
RADAR IDENTIFICATION **5-50**, **5-54**
Radar Identification (Glossary)
RADAR INFORMATION USE **5-6**
RADAR LIMITATIONS **5-1**
RADAR POSITION REPORT **5-52**
Radar Route (Glossary)
RADAR SEPARATION
   Application **5-60**
   Approach Separation Responsibility **5-116**
   ARSA **6-42**
   Departure From Arrival **5-103**
   Minima **5-61**
   Reduced Separation **5-61**
   Stage III **6-54**
RADAR SERVICE
   Additional Service Priority **2-67**
   For VFR Aircraft in Difficulty **2-127**
   Termination **5-56**
Radar Service (Glossary)

Radar Surveillance (Glossary)
Radar Traffic Advisories (Glossary)
RADAR WEATHER DISPLAY **2-128**
Radar Weather Levels (Glossary)
RADARSCOPE **5-4**
Radial (Glossary)
Radio (Glossary)
RADIO COMMUNICATION INFORMATION CALL-UP FORMAT **2-40**
Radio Detection and Ranging *see* Radar (Glossary)
RADIO EQUIPMENT MALFUNCTION REPORTS **2-103**, **2-104**
RANDOM ALTITUDE ASSIGNMENT **4-81**
RAPCON **2-2**
READBACK OF IFR CLEARANCE **4-33**
READBACKS **2-43**
RELEASE PROCEDURES (IFR) **4-42**
Release Time (Glossary)
RELEASE TIMES **4-42**
REPORT OF DEVIATION IN AN EMERGENCY **9-1**
REPORTING ALTITUDE **5-64**, **7-50**
REPORTS
   Aircraft Equipment Malfunction **2-103**
   Altitude, Non-Radar **7-50**
   Below Minimum Report by Pilot **4-114**
   Bird and Other Wildlife Hazards **2-106**, **2-107**
   Emergency Information **9-5**
   Minimum Fuel Advisory **2-105**
   Missed Approach **4-133**
   NAVAID Malfunction **2-102**
   NAVAID Performance **2-101**
   PIREP Information **2-122**
   Reporting Requirements (IFR) **7-4**
   Safety of Flight Information **2-100**
   Unmanned Balloons **2-108**
Request Full Route Clearance (Glossary)
RESTRICTED AREA AUTHORIZATION **8-1**
Resume Own Navigation (Glossary)
RNAV *see* Area Navigation (Glossary)
RNAV ROUTE - FLIGHT PLAN (IFR) **4-6**
ROTATING BEACON OPERATION, AIRPORT **3-66**
ROUTE AMENDMENTS **4-37**
Runway (Glossary)
RUNWAY LIGHTS, OPERATION OF
   Centerline Lights **3-59**
   Edge Lights **3-58**
   End Identifier Lights **3-51**
RUNWAY EXITING **3-159**, **3-160**
Runway Heading (Glossary)
RUNWAY IDENTIFICATION **2-11**, **3-190**
RUNWAY IN USE **3-91**
Runway in Use (Glossary)
RUNWAY OPERATIONS
   Simultaneous Opposite Direction **3-128**
   Simultaneous Same Direction **3-127**
RUNWAY PROFILE DESCENT **4-90**
Runway Profile Descent (Glossary)

INDEX

(References are to Paragraph Numbers)

RUNWAY USE PROGRAM **3-91**
Runway Use Program (Glossary)
RUNWAY VISIBILITY REPORTING **2-150**
Runway Visibility Value/RVV *see* Visibility (Glossary)
Runway Visual Range/RVR *see* Visibility (Glossary)
RVR/RVV REPORTING TERMINOLOGY **2-152**

S

SAFETY ALERT **2-88**
Safety Alert (Glossary)
SAR *see* Search and Rescue (Glossary)
SCATANA PLAN **9-14**
SEA LANE OPERATIONS **3-190**
SEARCH AND RESCUE (SAR) AIRCRAFT PRIORITY **2-68**
Search and Rescue (Glossary)
Search and Rescue Facility (Glossary)
SECONDARY SURVEILLANCE RADAR **5-4, 5-5**
See and Avoid (Glossary)
SEPARATION
    Aircraft Landing **3-152** thru **3-156, 7-10, 7-11, 7-20, 7-21**
    Aircraft Taking Off **3-134** thru **3-138, 7-20, 7-21**
    Lateral **7-40**
    Longitudinal **7-30**
    Radar **5-60**
    Special VFR **6-73**
    Vertical - Exceptions Non-Radar **7-52**
    Vertical - Non-Radar **7-51**
    Vertical - Radar **5-62, 5-63**
    Visual **2-87**
SEQUENCED FLASHING LIGHTS **3-55**
SERVICE VOLUME LIMITATIONS **4-70, 4-73**
Severe Weather Avoidance Plan (Glossary)
Severe Weather Forecast Alerts (Glossary)
SHORT APPROACH **3-123**
Short Range Clearance (Glossary)
SID **4-51, 4-52**
SIDE-STEP MANEUVER **4-132**
Sidestep Maneuver (Glossary)
SIGMET **2-120**
Sigmet (Glossary)
Significant Meteorological Information *see* Sigmet (Glossary)
SIMULTANEOUS CONVERGING INSTRUMENT APPROACHES **5-119**
SIMULTANEOUS HELICOPTER LANDINGS AND TAKEOFFS **3-179**
SIMULTANEOUS ILS/MLS APPROACHES **5-117**
SIMULTANEOUS RADAR DEPARTURES **5-102**
SPECIAL EMERGENCY **9-20**
SPECIAL INSTRUMENT APPROACH CLEARANCES **4-120, 4-122**
Special Use Airspace (Glossary)
SPECIAL USE AIRSPACE AVOIDANCE **8-6**
SPECIAL VFR
    Authorization **6-71**
    Climb To VFR **6-76**
    Helicopter Separation **6-79**
    IFR Aircraft Priority **6-72**

Special VFR Conditions (Glossary)
Special VFR Operations (Glossary)
Speed Adjustment (Glossary)
SPEED ADJUSTMENT APPLICATION **5-90**
SPEED ADJUSTMENTS - AIRPORT TRAFFIC AREAS **3-15**
STAGE II
    Aircraft Sequencing **6-61**
    General **6-60**
STAGE III
    Altitude Assignments **6-56**
    Helicopter Traffic **6-55**
    Procedures **6-50**
    Separation **6-54**
STANDARD INSTRUMENT DEPARTURES (SID) **4-51**
Standard Terminal Arrival (Glossary)
STANDARD TERMINAL ARRIVAL CLEARANCE INFORMATION **4-111**
STANDARD TERMINAL ARRIVAL ROUTE (STAR) **4-110**
STOL RUNWAYS **3-92**
Stop and Go (Glossary)
Straight-In Approach (IFR) (Glossary)
STRAIGHT-IN APPROACH (VFR) **3-150**
Straight-In Approach (VFR) (Glossary)
STUDENT PILOT RADIO IDENTIFICATION **2-24**
Substitute Route (Glossary)
SUCCESSIVE RADAR DEPARTURES **5-102**
SUGGESTED HEADINGS/DIRECTIONS **3-73**
SURVEILLANCE APPROACH **5-132**
Surveillance Approach (Glossary)
SURVEILLANCE RADAR **5-5**

T

TAILWIND ADVISORY **3-93**
TAKEOFF - USE OF AIRCRAFT LIGHTS **3-141**
TAKEOFF AND LANDING PROCEDURES - HELICOPTERS **3-173**
Takeoff Area *see* Landing Area (Glossary)
TAKEOFF CLEARANCE
    Cancellation **3-140**
    Helicopters **3-173, 3-176**
    Phraseology **3-139**
TAKEOFF POSITION AND HOLD **3-133**
TAKEOFF SEPARATION
    Anticipated **3-134**
    Clearances **3-139**
    Helicopter **3-177**
    Intersecting Runways **3-138**
    Same Runway **3-135**
Target Symbol (Glossary)
Taxi (Glossary)
TAXI INFORMATION FROM GROUND CONTROL **3-104**
TAXI PROCEDURES - GENERAL **3-100**
TAXIWAY LIGHTS **3-64**
TAXIWAY MARKING **3-106**
TCA
    Authorizations **6-8**
    Description **6-7**
    Entry **6-51**
    Equipment Requirements **6-9**

INDEX

(References are to Paragraph Numbers)

TCA (Cont.)
    Exit Information **6-57**
    Transponder Requirement **6-10**
TCA *see* Controlled Airspace (Glossary)
TEMPORARY FLIGHT RESTRICTIONS **8-7**
TEMPORARY FREQUENCY CHANGES **2-48**
Terminal Area (Glossary)
Terminal Control Area *see* Controlled Airspace (Glossary)
TERMINAL DELAY INFORMATION (IFR) **4-100**
TERMINAL RADAR APPROACH CONTROL **2-2**
TERMINAL RADAR PROGRAMS
    For VFR Aircraft **6-20, 6-21**
    Mandatory Participation **6-22**
    Pilot Responsibilities **6-21**
Terminal Radar Program (Glossary)
Terminal Radar Service Area (Glossary)
TERMINATION OF ARSA SERVICE **6-47**
TERMINATION OF RADAR SERVICE **5-56**
THE OPTION **3-124**
THREE-MINUTE RULE
    Intersection Takeoffs **3-137**
    Opposite Direction Operations **3-128**
TIME CHECK **2-11**
TIME CHECK DURING TIMED APPROACH **7-65**
TIMED APPROACHES **7-60**
TOUCHDOWN ZONE LIGHTS **3-59**
TOWER CLEARANCES BY APPROACH CONTROL **5-151**
Tower En Route Control (Glossary)
TOWER EN ROUTE CONTROL (TEC) **4-8**
TOWER FREQUENCY OVERRIDE **5-117**
TOWER RADAR **3-70 THRU 3-74**
Tower to Tower *see* Tower En Route Control (Glossary)
Track (Glossary)
TRACON **2-2**
TRAFFIC ADVISORIES
    Acknowledgment Of **2-85**
    Controller Limitations **5-2**
    General **2-67, 2-84, 2-90**
    Limitations **5-1**
    Safety Alert **2-88**
    Termination Of **2-90**
    Tower Radar **3-72**
    Visual Separation **2-87**
    Wind Effect **2-86**
Traffic Advisories (Glossary)
TRAFFIC PATTERN
    Instructions **3-151**
    Terminology **3-150**
Traffic Pattern (Glossary)
Transfer of Control (Glossary)
Transition Area *see* Controlled Airspace (Glossary)
TRANSPONDER **5-4**
Transponder (Glossary)
TRANSPONDER, USE OF ON TAKEOFF **3-141**
TRANSPONDER CODE
    Assignment **5-29**

TRANSPONDER CODE (Cont.)
    Changes **5-33**
    Emergency Code Assignment **5-38**
    Hijacking **9-20, 9-21**
    No Radio **5-37**
    VFR **5-23**
Transponder Codes *see* Codes (Glossary)
TRANSPONDER OPERATION
    General **5-20**
    Off Request **5-42**
    Standby or Low Sensitivity **5-39**
    Requirement **5-22**
TRSA
    Description **6-11**
    Exit Information **6-57**
    Service Option **6-52**
TURBULENCE REPORTS **2-123**
TWO-MINUTE RULE - SAME RUNWAY OPERATIONS **3-135**
Two-Way Radio Communications Failure *see* Lost Communications (Glossary)
TYPE SUFFIXES **2-23, 4-4**

U

UNSAFE RUNWAY INFORMATION **3-37**
Upwind Leg *see* Traffic Pattern (Glossary)
USE OF THE WORD 'MAYDAY' **9-2**

V

VECTOR
    Across Final Approach Course **5-113**
    Altitude Restrictions **5-74**
    Below Minimum Altitude **5-101**
    Compliance With **5-78**
    Direct **5-75**
    Final Approach Course Intercept Angles **5-112**
    For a Visual Approach **4-142**
    For Practice Approach **4-176**
    In Lieu of Published Missed Approach Procedure **4-133**
    Initial Vector Advisory **5-73**
    Inside Approach Gate **5-111**
    Methods **5-72**
    Minimum Vectoring Altitudes **5-71**
    RNAV Navigation **5-76**
    To Final Approach Course **5-111**
Vector (Glossary)
VERTICAL SEPARATION
    Altitude Assignments **5-64**
    Minima **5-63**
    Mode C, Use Of **5-62**
    Non-Radar **7-51**
Vertical Separation (Glossary)
VFR AIRCRAFT TRANSITING TERMINAL AIRSPACE **6-28**
VFR ARRIVAL PROCEDURES - TERMINAL RADAR PROGRAMS **6-24**
VFR AUTHORIZATION FOR IFR OPERATIONS **4-160**

INDEX

(References are to Paragraph Numbers)

VFR CLIMB **4-164**
VFR CODE ASSIGNMENTS **5-35**
VFR CONDITION CLEARANCES **4-165**
VFR Conditions (Glossary)
VFR DEPARTURE PROCEDURES - TERMINAL RADAR PROGRAMS **6-23**
VFR DESCENT **4-164**
VFR DIRECTION OF DEPARTURE - ADVISORY **3-131**
VFR IN CONGESTED AREAS **2-83**
VFR RELEASE OF IFR DEPARTURE **4-40**
VFR *see* Visual Flight Rules (Glossary)
VFR-ON-TOP **4-160**, **4-161**
VFR-On-Top (Glossary)
VICTOR AIRWAYS **2-30**, **4-62**
Video Map (Glossary)
Visibility (Glossary)
VISIBILITY REPORTS **2-132**
VISITS TO AIR TRAFFIC FACILITIES **2-6**
VISUAL APPROACH
   Advisory **4-115**
   Charted **4-145**
   Clearance **4-141**, **4-143**
   Parallel/Multiple Runways **4-144**
   Vectors For **4-142**
   Wake Turbulence Responsibility **2-87**
Visual Approach (Glossary)
Visual Flight Rules (Glossary)
VISUAL HOLDING OF VFR AIRCRAFT **6-29**
Visual Meteorological Conditions (VMC) (Glossary)

VISUAL SEPARATION **2-87**
Visual Separation (Glossary)
VLF *see* Area Navigation (Glossary)
VOR (Glossary)
VORTAC *see* Area Navigation (Glossary)

W

WAKE TURBULENCE
   Cautionary Advisories **2-80**
   On the Ground **3-108**
   Pilot Responsibility **2-82**
   Procedures (ATC) **2-81**
Wake Turbulence (Glossary)
WEATHER ADVISORIES **2-120** thru **2-133**
Weather Advisory (Glossary)
WEATHER AVOIDANCE ASSISTANCE **2-129**
WEATHER DEVIATION **2-130**
WEATHER REPORTS
   General Weather Information **2-133**
   Prevailing Visibility **2-132**
WIND DESCRIPTION **2-11**
WIND SHEAR ALERT **3-34**
WIND SHEAR DETECTION **3-33**
WIND SHEAR REPORTS **2-125**
Wind Shear (Glossary)
WS/WST/WA *see* Weather Advisory (Glossary)

Z

ZULU TIME **2-11**

NOTES

NOTES